GRAMMARS OF RESURRECTION

*Best Book of the Year Award for 2010
from the College Theology Society*

*First Place Award for Best Book in Theology for 2010
from the Catholic Press Association*

GRAMMARS OF RESURRECTION

A CHRISTIAN THEOLOGY OF PRESENCE AND ABSENCE

Brian D. Robinette

A *Herder & Herder* Book
The Crossroad Publishing Company
New York

The Crossroad Publishing Company
www.CrossroadPublishing.com.

© 2009 by Brian D. Robinette.

All rights reserved. No part of this book may be reproduced, stored in a retrieval system, or transmitted, in any form or by any means, electronic, mechanical, photocopying, recording, or otherwise, without the written permission of The Crossroad Publishing Company.

In continuation of our 200-year tradition of independent publishing, The Crossroad Publishing Company proudly offers a variety of books with strong, original voices and diverse perspectives. The viewpoints expressed in our books are not necessarily those of The Crossroad Publishing Company, any of its imprints, or of its employees. No claims are made or responsibility assumed for any health or other benefit.

Printed in the United States of America.

The text of this book is set in 10.5/13 Sabon. The display face is Poppl Laudatio.

Library of Congress Cataloging-in-Publication Data
Robinette, Brian DuWayne.
    Grammars of resurrection : a Christian theology of presence and absence / Brian D. Robinette.
    p. cm.
    "A Herder & Herder book."
    Includes bibliographical references and indexes.
    ISBN 978-0-8245-2563-7 (alk. paper)
    1. Jesus Christ – Resurrection. I. Title.
BT482.R63 2009
232'.5 – dc22
                                             2009043961

ISBN 978-0-8245-2370-1 (epub)

*This book is dedicated with love
to my wife and sons,
Krista Dawn Robinette,
Trevor Andrew Robinette,
and
Austin Keith Robinette*

Contents

Acknowledgments   ix

PART ONE

Introduction   3
   A Generative Opening   3
   The Resurrection and Christian Grammar   6
   Resurrecting Resurrection: Problems and Prospects   12
   Gift, Hospitality, and the Body   21
   The Ecclesial Presupposition for Resurrection Belief   25

1. CONDITIONS OF THE POSSIBILITY   31
   The Historical *Aporia*   31
   The Eschatological Imperative   34
   Three Approaches to the Resurrection   42
   History *in Excess*   64

2. THE IM-POSSIBLE GIFT   67
   The Resurrection as "Saturated Phenomenon"   76

3. BODIES *IN ABSENTIA*   116
   The Scandal of the Empty Tomb   116
   A Claim upon the World   121
   Bodily Resurrection and Late Antiquity   125
   The Body as "Thing" and Modernity's "Disengaged Self"   130
   The Absent Body   134
   The Othered Self   148

4. I WILL BE MY BODY   150
   A Profounder Materialism   150
   The Corporeality of Grace   159
   I Will Be My Body   177

PART TWO

Introduction: Grammars of Resurrection — 181
On Avoiding Grammatical Absolutism in Christian Theology — 182
The Resurrection Proclaimed — 188

5. SUFFERING, *MEMORIA*, AND VINDICATION: RETRIEVING THE APOCALYPTIC IMAGINATION — 195
Retrieving the Apocalyptic Imagination — 195
Time, *Memoria*, and Justice — 211

6. TRANSFIGURING THE VICTIM — 227
A View from the Victims — 228
Transfiguring the Victim — 245

7. *MIMESIS*, SCAPEGOATING, AND THE CRUCIFIED — 250
The Bible and Violence — 250
Desire, *Mimesis*, and Scapegoat Violence — 259
Unveiling Scapegoat Violence — 271

8. THE GIFT OF THE FORGIVING VICTIM — 291
Resurrection as Reconciliation — 291
Christus Victor Revisited — 309

9. THE GRAMMAR OF FULFILLMENT AND CHRISTOLOGY — 319
"I Am the Resurrection and the Life":
  Manifestation and Presence in the Fourth Gospel — 321
Resurrection and Christology — 334

10. ORIGINAL PEACE, DIVINIZATION, AND BEAUTY OF FORM — 352
Original Peace: Creation in Retrospect — 352
Transcendence, Form, and Beauty — 364
The Eternal Significance of Jesus' Humanity:
  The Heart of Christian Spirituality — 372
The Beauty and Comfort of the Resurrection — 377

Notes — 383

Scripture Index — 433

General Index — 439

Acknowledgments

If it is true, as I maintain throughout this work, that the body is the primordial bond between the self and the Other, and that therefore no genuinely *human* fulfillment is possible that ultimately forsakes that bond — the "resurrection of the body" means nothing, if not this — then it is no less true to say that the body of this text, now come to fruition in publication, was made possible and enriched by many bonds over the course of its composition and final production. I wish to acknowledge some of the most important of those here.

First, to those who provided scholarly support to me at various stages of composition, either by reading portions of the manuscript and offering incisive feedback, or by engaging me in extensive, personal conversation in ways that helped shape its "heteroglossia." From my doctoral studies days at the University of Notre Dame, where several of the book's thematic lines first germinated, I must especially thank Larry Cunningham, Cathy Hilkert, Matt Ashley, and Cyril O'Regan. Each continues to provide extraordinary mentorship for me in my ongoing formation as a theologian. From Saint Louis University, the institutional context of the book's composition, I would like to thank Mike McClymond, Dan Finucane, Jay Hammond, and Josh Benson for their generosity, encouragement and frequently brilliant insights. Michael Pahls, as dear a friend to me as any friend could be, was a uniquely close interlocutor over the course of the writing process — and long before that. Thank you, Michael, for the gift of friendship.

Others from the SLU community who helped make this work possible include: Maureen Walsh, Mike Corte, and Russell Brewer, three remarkable graduate assistants who worked very closely with me, and whose diligence greatly improved the manuscript; Fr. Wayne Hellmann, my department chair, who helped provide departmental and institutional support for seeing the project through; the Office of the Provost for granting a semester's leave at a pivotal moment of creation; and, no less crucially, the many undergraduate and graduate students with whom I have been blessed to share in the enterprise of theological discovery.

I wish to thank The Crossroad Publishing Company for its initiatives in supporting a new generation of Catholic theologians. John Jones, my editor, not only provided expert editorial direction, but extended hospitality and profound intellectual sensitivity to the theological and stylistic sensibilities that appear in the present work. I especially cherish the many hours of conversations poured over music, poetry, and the spiritual life. My sincere gratitude also extends to Margaret Hammerot, who skillfully copyedited the manuscript and suggested many improvements. Her encouragement in my continuing work has provided me a wonderfully unexpected and deep source of inspiration.

Lastly, and most of all, I wish to thank my wife, Krista, and our two beautiful sons, Trevor and Austin. So much of the manuscript breathes the atmosphere of the home we share, and not simply because a significant portion of it was written in close proximity. It is because of you, Krista, Trevor, and Austin, that I have learned all the more richly and concretely what it means to say that we are othered-from-within, and thus what it means to live into the hope of a resurrection that shall redeem and eternally fulfill the many relationships we cultivate throughout our lives. It is to you that this book is lovingly dedicated.

PART ONE

Introduction

"He has been raised; he is not here." — Mark 16:6

"Do not hold on to me, because I have not yet ascended to the Father." — John 20:17

And he has gone from our sight that we should "return to our heart" (Isa. 46:8) and find him there. He went away and behold, here he is. — St. Augustine, *The Confessions*[1]

A GENERATIVE OPENING

Mary Magdalene's was a triple loss.

The first, and most grievous, at the foot of the cross. With soldiers drawing lots for Jesus' tunic behind them, the three Marys — the mother of Jesus, the wife of Clopas, and the Magdalene — huddled together to witness the brutal lynching of a son, a friend, a teacher, and with him their messianic hopes for their people.

The second, and most vexing, bent over looking into an empty tomb. But not entirely empty: for two angelic heralds, awash in white, sat at the head and foot of where Jesus once lay to ask the reason for her weeping. Having gone to the tomb on the first day of the week — early, while it was still dark, we are told — Mary encountered a shocking absence. At once she ran to tell Simon Peter and the Beloved Disciple: "They have taken the Lord out of the tomb, and we do not know where they have laid him" (John 20:2). Back at the tomb, Mary expresses her loss twice more, once to the querying angels ("They have taken away my Lord, and I do not know where they have laid him," v. 13), and finally to the mysterious gardener ("Sir, if you have carried him away, tell me where you have laid him, and I will take him away," v. 15). This loss upon loss would not even allow for that most meager of comforts — the knowledge of a loved one's victimized body interred and in final repose.

The third, and most enduring of the losses, upon recognizing the risen Lord. Initially supposing him to be a gardener, Mary asks the risen

Jesus to indicate the whereabouts of the crucified body. Oddly, she does not recognize him, not even as he stands directly in front of her! The darkness of the early morning cannot account for this most bizarre of mis-identifications. Something else prevents her from recognizing what she most desires. Indeed, she knows not what to desire, or how to desire it. An epistemic gap, a gulf in imagination, a constrained horizon will not permit her to perceive what is manifestly before her. Mary's reaction does not suggest even the faintest hope for a living encounter with the one she had previously called "Rabbouni," much less that she would momentarily be the first to bear witness to the dawning of the new age. Indeed, had he not called her by name — "Mary!" — she never would have recognized him. Only in *being recognized* was she capable of perceiving truly. Only in *being named* was she able to call out, "Rabbouni!" (v. 16). Only in receiving a gracious call from a humanly untraversable space — death — was she able to awaken to the effective promise of new, eschatological life. But why should this be considered a loss?

Reaching out to grab him, to hold him, to cling to the Jesus she had once known and loved, Mary finds her immediate desires denied. "Jesus said to her, 'Do not hold on to me, because I have not yet ascended to the Father'" (v. 17). At the precise moment of recognition, this moment which would instantly ease, if not entirely erase, the pain and bewilderment of the previous two losses, Jesus withdraws from the reach of familiarity. Though fully "present" to her in his transfigured corporeality, the risen Christ appears in the mode of "absence," in a way that at once communicates his identity and person while overwhelming her wildest expectations and capacities for comprehension. This strangeness of one so familiar was not the result of a disfigured given, however: there was nothing deficient or deceptive in the self-manifestation of the crucified-and-risen One. Rather, the mis-identification sprang from an *eschatological excess,* a surplus of phenomenality that could not (and cannot) be fully absorbed or grasped, an unanticipated and ever surprising Gift that continues to lure its recipients towards a self-transcending hospitality.

Above all, this "appearance" through "dis-appearance" served as an invitation: an invitation to a new way of perceiving, to a new way of relating; an invitation to accede to a new dispensation, one that can only come from the loss of a graspable body. For in withdrawal the crucified-and-risen One instructs her: "But go to my brothers and say to them, 'I am ascending to my Father and your Father, to my God and your God'" (v. 17). The withdrawal is a generative spacing and a summons: it throws open the possibility for the materialization of an ecclesial body — the "body of Christ" — wherein the crucified-and-risen One may be richly, diversely, and inexhaustibly encountered. So far from being a gesture of callous indifference, the withdrawal of the risen One from Mary's reach is a gracious opening. By it he imparts distance — that "letting be" which alone establishes the possibility for genuine communion. "Loving," writes Jean-Luc Marion, "requires an exteriority that is not provisional but effective, an exteriority that remains for long enough that one may cross it seriously. Loving requires distance and the crossing of distance. Loving requires more than a feigned distance, or one that is not truly dug out or truly crossed. In the drama of love, actions must be accomplished effectively over distance — distributing, going, coming, returning."[2]

So much distributing, so much going, so much coming, so much returning: the empty tomb and appearance narratives in the gospels are full of crossings, spacings, gatherings, veerings, and sendings. In just this one vignette we discover a remarkably complex overlapping of movements: Mary's early arrival results in her "being sent" in apostolic mission, with her expectations thwarted and desires dramatically transformed; her discovery of a shocking loss becomes an unspeakable gain, her mournful isolation now ameliorated as she is redirected to an ecclesial gathering — and all because of Jesus' return in the mode of a gracious withdrawal, where through his "absence" he may now become "present" to the reconciled community that bodies him forth in history as the "body of Christ."

The whole of the Easter event must be imagined according to the dynamic relations unfurled (and unfurling) in this loving distance. What spreads out in its wake is nothing less than the whole range of Christian experience, practice, and understanding: the ecclesial body that forms as two or more are gathered in his name (Matt. 18:20); the textual bodies and sacramental signs that commemorate and analogize the presence-absence of the risen One in our ongoing history; the prophetic and politically charged memory of dead, forgotten, and victimized bodies; acts of reconciliation precisely where victims and victimizers remain locked in spirals of violence; and the hope for the absolute fulfillment (or "divinization") of creation in all its particularity, which Christians call "eternal life." It is the resurrection of Jesus from the dead that constitutes the basic grammar for authentic Christian discourse and praxis.

THE RESURRECTION AND CHRISTIAN GRAMMAR

The Centrality of the Resurrection

In his magisterial study, *The Great Code: The Bible and Literature*, Northrop Frye observes that at the level of *myth* — and by this he means "story," not falsehood — the only event that really takes place in the Old Testament is the exodus. Everything else presupposes and prisms it. This is true even of the creation stories. Although preceding the story of the exodus in the Bible's narrative sequence, the Genesis accounts were composed well after the historical exodus and reflect the meaning the Hebrew people had long associated with it. The biblical account of "the beginning" represents an act of *memoria* that flows through the experience of their deliverance from Egyptian imperial power. It represents a backward glance through a particular aperture whose filtering characteristics were molded by the narrative retelling and ritual enactment of their liberation. The *mythos* of the exodus not only extends backwards, or protologically, in the biblical narrative, even to time immemorial; it projects forward, or eschatologically, as it establishes the narrative framework through which all subsequent events in Israel's history are related and interpreted. From the possession of the land to the emergence and demise of the united kingdom; from the Babylonian exile to the period of the second temple; from the persecutions of the mid-second century to the hoped-for restoration under Roman rule in the first century: the history of Israel is narrated as a sequence of antitypes *(mythoi)* to the primary type *(mythos)* that gives them narrative and metaphorical coherence. The exodus story is Israel's "primal narrative," to borrow a phrase from Walter Brueggemann.[3] It is a founding narrative that identifies the ultimate character of Israel's God and God's people. It is primal in the sense in that it forms the grammar for Israel's testimony. "Exodus grammar," writes Brueggemann, "saturates the imagination of Israel." The recital of the exodus, whether in fuller narrative or simple declarative utterances, is "paradigmatic of Israel's testimony about Yahweh." Its memory forms "the entire field of grammar" for scripture.[4]

What the exodus is to the Old Testament, the resurrection of Jesus is to the New. As Frye puts it, "the resurrection of Christ, around which the New Testament revolves, must be, from the New Testament's point of view, the antitype of the Exodus. The life of Christ as presented in the Gospels becomes less puzzling when we realize that it is being presented in this form."[5] In the "strange new world" of the New Testament, the resurrection of Jesus does not appear as just one event among others.

Although it occurs *in medias res,* appearing as a climactic moment within a sequence of events, the resurrection, like the exodus, is that event which gives all of the events in the New Testament their intelligibility and permanent point of reference. It is the reason why there is a New Testament at all. The new and final exodus — the "new covenant" and the "new creation" — Jesus' resurrection from the dead reveals the ultimate goal of salvation history. Even where the resurrection is not the explicit thematic focus in the New Testament, it is present at a subtending level. More than a discrete assertion in the Christian creed, the resurrection "pervades Christian speech" as such. As Pheme Perkins declares, "one might even go so far as to say that it is the condition for the emergence of Christian speech itself."[6]

Easter is axial in the New Testament universe. As is evident in its characteristic genres, including its commission narratives, kerygmatic formulae, apocalypses, hymns, and paranetic materials, the imagination of the New Testament is ordered around the claim, "He has been raised; he is not here" (Mark 16:6). It reveals what might be aptly called a "resurrection hermeneutic." Written from the perspective of the Easter experience, the gospels retrospectively confer meaning upon its various elements and vignettes by relating them within a narrative whole, blending form and content into a kerygmatic *gestalt*. The gospels invite the reader to inhabit a narrative space so as to be reformed in imagination and desire. "Written so that you may believe" (John 20:31), they extend to the reader an invitation that, whether it elicits a "yes" or "no," is radically self-involving. Its proclamation demands much more than an intellectual consideration. It is a summons to participate in a particular form of life, to become a "new creation" in Christ. In this way we may describe the resurrection of Jesus as the "grammar" of the New Testament: it establishes the framework and ambiance for all Christian discourse and imagination. It forms both the *what* of Christian faith (its thematic content) and its *how* (the condition of its possibility). As Paul the Apostle put it in 1 Cor. 15, if Christ has not been raised we are still in our sins (content) and our faith is vain (how).

The Ambiguity of the Resurrection in Christian Theology

Paradoxically, because the resurrection is so central in the New Testament it can elude explicit identification and clear-cut meaning. Again, Perkins: "The foundational character of resurrection speech has led to an awkward inability to explore the boundaries of resurrection as a category in Christian theology."[7] Part of this ambiguity derives from the very nature of the Easter event itself. It is an eschatological event, indeed, the eschatological event *par excellence*. Though it has a historical character, it is not reducible to our history. The resurrection is a "trans-historical" reality. It occurs within our common history and produces a history of effects, yet it is more-than-historical. It cannot be plotted within a historical continuum without remainder. It is the absolute future *of* history made present *within* history. This remarkable tension between past, present, and future characterizes all Christian discourse at its most basic level. We speak of salvation as having already occurred in Christ, and yet we await the ultimate fulfillment of salvation in a future that comes gratuitously from God. Part of the unique challenge of learning to speak of the resurrection is learning to speak in terms of this "already" and "not-yet." This requires simultaneous acts of saying and un-saying: "He has been raised; he is not here."

But there is another kind of ambiguity we must identify. It is the ambiguity that derives from the resurrection's role as both grammar and theme. The resurrection of Jesus is, of course, *a* theme in the New Testament — and by no means the only one. Several other themes can lay claim to centrality, including the Kingdom of God, the cross, the story of the church and its mission, creation, ethics, etc. Even if we agree with C. F. Evans that Christianity is a "religion of resurrection," this must be understood in a way that does not ignore or conflate other thematic foci.[8] And yet, because the resurrection of Jesus from the dead exercises a grammatical role in Christian discourse; because it provides the background horizon that allows various themes and concerns to come into focus in a meaningful way, it can be challenging to give an account of resurrection belief in a discrete manner. In the same way speakers of a language adhere to grammatical rules, speaking *from* or *through* rules that are learned slowly through practice and made explicit in language only from time to time, and even then using grammar to do so — grammar is the receding horizon of its own thematization — so too do Christians implicitly affirm the resurrection even when speaking of other matters pertaining to Christian reality. The resurrection can recede into the background to a foreground object of focus, even if that object becomes a focus only because the resurrection brings it into view.

To illustrate, we may refer again to the exodus. As the primary *mythos* of the Old Testament, the exodus story provides thematic content while establishing the hermeneutical field within which various *mythoi* come into perspective. Even when the focus is protological, as with the creation stories, the exodus is present at the level of grammar to provide structure and implicit meaning. The creation accounts in the Old Testament, despite all they share with the cosmogonies of Mesopotamian origin, gain their peculiar significance from Israel's primal testimony to YHWH's deliverance. The primordial chaos of the seas represents "the watery, threatening chaos in the arena of creation and as the escape route of the Exodus. In both usages," states Brueggemann, "the God of Israel is confessed to be in ready control, able to administer the waters."[9] As with protology, so too with eschatology. The memory of the exodus provided the Israelites with a future-oriented hope, especially in times of national distress. Projected into the future, God's act of deliverance from the Egyptians functioned archetypally for articulating the anticipation that God would do the same in the time of exile. As we shall see later in this study, this "exodus memory" provided Israel the grounds for an apocalyptic imagination during times of widespread persecution and cultural assimilation by external imperial power. It is within this context that the metaphorical language of "resurrection," spoken to refer to Israel's corporate deliverance from oppression (read: "exodus"), becomes metonymic to speak of God's ultimate vindication of God's people in terms of the "resurrection of the dead."

We see a similar dynamic in the New Testament. The evolution of the New Testament's soteriology and christology evidences a process of reflection in which the experience and proclamation of the risen Christ established for Christians a context for understanding, quite retrospectively, the meaning of Jesus' life and death. In soteriological matters, the only reason why Jesus' death could be thought of as in any way salvific, rather than the colossal failure of a would-be messiah, was the radically new perceptual field imparted to his earliest followers by the Easter event. As Walter Künneth rightly states: "The cross is, to be sure, the presupposition for the resurrection of Jesus, but it is the latter that gives the cross its meaning. It is only the Easter interpretation of the cross that lifts the end of Jesus beyond the chances and dubieties of history and makes it a saving event. Theological reflection on the cross of Jesus is essentially rooted in the resurrection."[10]

Now, as is evident in the history of Western Christian theology especially, the cross, rather than the resurrection, would eventually come to dominate how Christians thematized salvation. This did not occur all at once, or with such comprehensiveness that the resurrection was wholly abandoned as a source for soteriological reflection. And yet, it is abundantly clear that especially since Anselm of Canterbury in the eleventh century, who emphasized the juridical themes of the Latin patristic tradition (particularly as developed by Tertullian and Cyprian) and reinterpreted them in the context of his own feudal culture, Western theology became dominated by a sacrificial atonement theory centered on the cross. "Generally speaking," complains Gerald O'Collins, "both Catholic and Protestant theologians have proved loyal successors to St. Anselm...who managed to discuss the redemption...while completely ignoring Christ's resurrection....Looking back on much Western theology we might parody Paul and cry out: 'Resurrection is swallowed up in crucifixion. O Resurrection, where is thy victory? O Resurrection, where is thy sting'?"[11] Although the church has never formulated a single, universally binding doctrinal definition of salvation in a way comparable to, say, the christological definitions of the fourth and fifth centuries, the sacrificial atonement theory provided by Anslem exerted so much influence on subsequent Western theology that it would become the de facto official view. The consequence here is that whereas the resurrection was front and center in the soteriologies of the first, second, and third centuries, it eventually receded into the background to other foci. Although the resurrection is what gives Jesus' death its meaning, as Künneth observes above, it would eventually become subordinate to sacrificial atonement theories that essentially isolate the cross as the precision instrument through which God offers us reconciliation. A broad survey of the atonement in Scholastic, Reformed, and post-Tridentine theology makes it difficult to determine how the resurrection is materially involved in God's offer of salvation. Once redemption is secured by an act of reparation through the cross, Easter is made to seem a kind of aftereffect, significant primarily in terms of the private destiny of Jesus, or, as Karl Rahner puts it, "honoured at best as a confirmation of the fact that our interpretation of Good Friday is correct."[12]

Christologically speaking, a similar process occurs as the resurrection takes an increasingly diminished role relative to the incarnation for articulating Jesus' identity. As will be explained more thoroughly later, the experience of the risen Christ in the paschal community is both historically and logically prior to the development of incarnational theology. In tracing the historical course of the christological process, we discover a shift of emphasis from resurrection to incarnation to express the identity and full ontological reality of this man from Nazareth. Whereas first generation christology (pre-50 C.E.) highlighted Jesus' resurrection as the moment of his investment of lordship over creation — the climactic point at which he "becomes" or is appointed "Son of God" — subsequent generations of christology reveal a backward projection of this Son of God language. Although we should avoid thinking of this too simplistically, generally speaking, the ongoing reflection on the nature of Jesus results in a retroactive movement of resurrection theology so that his identity as Son of God, first fully manifested in his post-mortem appearances to the disciples, is associated with decisive moments further and further back in his life-story — his death, his transfiguration, his baptism, his conception, and finally, as we find most explicitly in the Logos poem of John, to a timeless origin antecedent to creation itself. This process is entirely logical. When properly thought through, the resurrection of Jesus from the dead demands that we reflect upon the relationship between Jesus' *function* and *person*. As we do, we will find that God's work of salvation is intimately connected with Jesus' very "being." By raising him from the dead for the definitive salvation of humanity, the Proclaimer (Jesus) and Proclaimed (the Kingdom of God) become so conjoined that Christians cannot adequately articulate the meaning of one without the other. The resurrection provides the catalyst for the christological process which leads to the affirmation of Jesus' whole body-person as God's very *self*-expression in history. "For us and for our salvation, he came down from heaven" resounds the fourth-century Nicene-Constantinopolitan Creed in churches around the world even now, echoing the patristic axiom formulated early on by Irenaeus of Lyons that "He became human that we might become divine." That the divine could "become" in any way, or that the man from Nazareth was somehow "God," transgresses so many conventional presuppositions about the nature of reality — in ancient or modern contexts, it hardly matters — that it took considerable time to sort through its implications and learn to speak consistently and appropriately of its mystery. This, in effect, is the tale of the christological controversies and councils of the fourth and fifth centuries.

We cannot fail to observe, however, that although this process was crucially important for creedal Christianity, the resurrection of Jesus became increasingly recessive to incarnation language. If we recall that the formation of conciliar christology was greatly facilitated by a Greek metaphysics inclined to speak of absolute origins, the *arche* — Greek thought is instinctively protological, not eschatological — it is not difficult to see how the debate with Arianism naturally diverted attention away from the resurrection as that defining moment when Jesus "becomes" Son of God. He was *always* the Son, ontologically speaking, and his divinity is not subject to enhancement or diminishment. His divine and eternal origin, more than his eschatological future, reveals his identity. And so, as the narrative discourse closely related to Jesus' concretely lived existence shifted into a more metaphysical discourse in Christian theology, Easter as a dramatic moment of identity-manifestation increasingly became absorbed by an incarnation language more summarily expressive of the Christ event in its total ontological reality.

RESURRECTING RESURRECTION: PROBLEMS AND PROSPECTS

Salvation in Stereo

The present work represents an effort to retrieve the resurrection of Jesus as a central site for thinking theologically. I have already spoken of soteriological and christological matters. Regarding the former, we will examine the drama and dynamics of human salvation under three related aspects that together flow from the Easter event: justice, forgiveness, and divinization. This is the primary objective of Part Two. It is my contention that the eventual marginalization of the resurrection from soteriological reflection, especially in the Latin West, where sacrificial atonement theories have long dominated, has led to truncated, and in certain important respects distorted, views of salvation. Among the most problematic distortion is the implication of God in the violence that led to Jesus' death. When the cross is isolated from the broader narrative sweep of the Christ event, there is frequently a failure to understand the resurrection as anything more than a kind of ratification or postlude, when in fact it is God's dramatic in-breaking into and unmasking of the cyclical violence that led to Jesus' lynching. Indeed, often enough sacrificial atonement theories imply or explicitly affirm God's complicity in the violence so graphically displayed on the cross, quite as though God were underwriting the very human disease that the gospels in fact would name, demystify, and abolish — the production of victims. Only if we see the meaning of the cross in light of Jesus' resurrection from the dead, which is nothing if not the vindication of a victim from unjust death, will we grasp that God is a God *of* victims; that, in point of fact, God has become *our* victim in order to liberate us from producing and becoming victims (justice), to offer us pardon for our continued and frequently unconscious production of victims (forgiveness), and to draw us into active participation in the inner life of God through the imitation of the crucified-and-risen victim, who is the image of the invisible God (divinization).

It should be observed here that the retrieval of the resurrection deepens our understanding of the cross while also drawing us into further reflection upon Jesus' life-ministry. The resurrection is precisely an act of *memoria,* God's transformative memory. Resurrection purifies and redeems memory. As with the story of the travelers to Emmaus, the presence of the risen stranger facilitates an act of recollection in which the disciples are capable of remembering Jesus' life from a fundamentally new perspective. They remember what he said and what he did, but they now do so in the light of a transformative experience, brought to consciousness in the breaking of the bread, that purges and deepens memory. It is imperative that any systematic consideration of the resurrection as a soteriological event traces this process of critical *memoria* by envisioning Jesus' life-ministry in its light. Only a superficial and deeply misguided understanding of the resurrection can lend itself to the temptation to characterize salvation in ahistorical terms. To relegate the resurrection to some abstract eschatological future that bears little to no relation to concrete human history, or to associate Easter with a *theologia gloriae* of such height that is loses all meaningful connection with the grit and grief of human existence as actually lived: these are the kinds of caricatures of resurrection faith that must be corrected in view of its actual meaning. So far from leading to the neglect or diminishment of Jesus' life-ministry, or the problems of suffering, injustice, and mutual victimization that so frequently dominate human existence — problems that Jesus himself aggressively set out to address with his message and ministry of the *basilea* — the resurrection in fact puts them squarely in view. The resurrection is God's eschatological "amen" upon the concrete life of Jesus of Nazareth, a vindication and reversal which is also, and for that very reason, a fulfillment. Even if resurrection faith is not simply reducible to the faith inspired by Jesus' historical ministry — it serves much more than a redundancy element, as I hope to make clear — it is nevertheless continuous and coherent with that ministry. In short, then, the resurrection as a *topos* for thinking about salvation must include within it a comprehensive understanding of Jesus' life, his death, and their inner relationship. It triangulates them. It allows us to hear them more "stereoscopically," to understand them with greater depth and meaning.

On Keeping Christology Critical

As stated, while Jesus' resurrection remains the condition of the possibility of Christian speech, it can become so thematically recessive to other foci that it loses its unique power and significance as a christological and soteriological event. When this occurs, not only will this negatively impact our competence in speaking of the resurrection; it will negatively impact the very foci to which it has become subordinate.

As Christian theologians in the third to the fifth centuries found it increasingly urgent to clarify the Son's *eternal* relationship to the Father, the resurrection, despite its historical and logical priority in the process of christological discovery, would take on a decidedly recessive role to the incarnation, especially as the theological discourse in emergent orthodoxy was oppositionally shaped by an Arian theology not at all uncomfortable with attributing creaturely "becoming" to the Son. In the wake of the christological debates, as Christ's metaphysical identity became a foreground concern, the eschatological drama of the resurrection would soon assume a subsidiary position in assessing Jesus' identity. In fact, the resurrection would be confined increasingly to the role of confirming the truth of the incarnation rather than functioning as a departure for christology in its own right.

To illustrate how the dramatic character of Easter can become interpretively overdetermined by the incarnation, we may briefly examine a passage from Athanasius's *De Incarnatione Verbi Dei*:

> Even on the cross He did not hide Himself from sight; rather, He made all creation witness to the presence of its Maker. Then, having once let it be seen that it was truly dead, He did not allow that temple of His body to linger long, but forthwith on the third day raised it up, impassible and incorruptible, the pledge and token of His victory.
>
> It was, of course, within His power thus to have raised His body and displayed it as alive directly after death. But the all-wise Saviour did not do this, lest some should deny that it had really or completely died. Besides this, had the interval between His death and resurrection been but two days, the glory of His incorruption might not have appeared. He waited one whole day to show that His body was really dead, and then on the third day showed it incorruptible to all... and it was evident to all that it was from no natural weakness that the body which the Word indwelt had died, but in order that in it by the Saviour's power death might be done away.[13]

Whereas the New Testament speaks almost exclusively of Jesus as the passive recipient of the Father's act — the passive construction "is raised" is by far the most common — Athanasius insists that Jesus has the power to "raise himself" from the dead. Jesus "lets it be seen" that he is dead in order to show that indeed he was dead (though it seems difficult to understand how a truly dead person could do anything otherwise); and, apparently dead, yet somehow the agent of the ensuing action, he "waits" just a little while, not letting his body linger long: this, "not from a natural weakness," but in order to show his power over death. An elementary analysis of this passage leads to the awkward conclusion that a dead man is in complete control. The doctrine of eternal pre-existence and incarnation utterly dominates the action, giving this christology such height that, notwithstanding its clear assertion of the *communicatio idiomatum,* death loses its abyssal character.

The resurrection, which is narrated in the New Testament as God's dramatic counter-action to death, sin, and evil, appears quite like a foregone conclusion, almost a matter of course. The memory of the "eschatological shock" of Easter has become muted as the temporal interval of its irruption gets concentrated, nearly collapsed, into a timeless present.

Should we be committed to bringing the resurrection back into thematic focus and reassert its proper relation with other christological foci, this will not require us to assert that Jesus only "becomes" Son of God at his resurrection, which would amount to a variety of adoptionism. We can continue to affirm that the resurrection possesses a "retroactive force," so that, as Wolfhart Pannenberg argues, it is possible to know *"from the perspective of the resurrection* that Jesus was previously one with God."[14] But this confirmatory role of the resurrection cannot remain its primary significance. If theology is to account for the unique power of Jesus' resurrection from the dead, it will need to better speak its language, which in the first place requires that we gain a deeper appreciation for its *event-character*. We must attempt to behold something of its dramatic and interruptive dynamism, the way it gives itself to imagination and speech in its *eschatological excess*. We must be willing to purge ourselves progressively of the ways we tend to domesticate the Easter event, either through an overly dominant incarnational theology that flattens out its counter-factual character, or a theology of the cross that trumps its soteriological impact. It is a matter of better following the story (the *oikonomia*) so as to allow the reversal structure of the resurrection to appear with greater force and determinative meaning. As we do, we shall be in a far better position to maintain a creative tension between the "already" and "not yet" character of salvation and Christ's role in it.

In the conclusion of his major study on the incarnation in the New Testament, James D. G. Dunn observes that the emphasis on the resurrection in New Testament christology is crucial to keep in focus in order to prevent distortions from developing in Christian theology and practice.

> The danger is that a lack of proper balance between incarnation and resurrection in christology will result in an unbalanced gospel and an unbalanced doctrine of the church, often signaled by a too casual use of the phrase, "An incarnational theology requires or implies that...."
>
> For example, an overemphasis on the incarnation as God's taking humanity into the Godhead will readily produce a gospel which

proclaims to man that he has already been redeemed, is already a Christian, whether he knows it or not, whether he likes it or not — a kind of gnostic gospel which consists in calling men to the self-realization that their humanity has already been divinized in the incarnation, that they are already in Christ in God.[15]

Without other, countervailing influences from the "not yet" pole of the eschatological spectrum, the "already" realized eschatology that often attends strongly incarnational theologies is susceptible to legitimizing (or being co-opted by) the present order of things. To the extent that we keep the event-character of Jesus' resurrection more squarely in view — and thus the counterfactual nature of God's incursion into every historical and ideological totality — we will better grasp that salvation is something we anticipate and "work towards" (in the Pauline sense) through vigilance, criticism, hope, and tireless praxis.

> But where the resurrection is recognized to have christological significance, as a becoming in *Christ's* own relation with God, the gospel has to include much more of Jesus' own call for conversion, much more of the "not yet" in Paul's concept of salvation, much more of the call to commitment to life "according to the Spirit" and against life "according to the flesh" — where the slogan is not so much "Become what you are," but "Become what you are becoming...." [W]hen the resurrection of Christ is recognized as marking a not yet in Jesus' own becoming, the church will be seen not so much as representing the world but rather as representing the forces that seek to change the world.[16]

The Scandal of the Resurrection

If I have attempted thus far to show reasons for the underdevelopment of the resurrection as a christological and soteriological theme in theology, it may be objected that in fact quite a bit has written on the subject in recent years. This is quite true, if in need of considerable qualification. To begin with, Walter Kasper echoes the point already made, but adds another:

> In traditional theology, hermeneutical discussion of the Resurrection testimonies [in scripture] was greatly neglected. It was, in general, regarded as sufficient simply to quote the testimony of faith. Since it was never questioned fundamentally, it was never the subject of fundamental reflection, as was the case with the problem of the Incarnation. Hence the doctrine of the Resurrection was

ousted from the central fundamental position accorded it in the New Testament. In contrast with the Incarnation and the Passion, the Resurrection never played a formative part in Christology; it served more or less as a miraculous affirmation of faith in the Godhead of Christ and the redeeming power of the sacrifice on the cross. This situation only altered fundamentally with the advent of modern critical theology.[17]

There are two important clarifications that must be made to this otherwise correct assessment. The first is that the resurrection did, in fact, play a formative role in pre-Nicene theology. Perhaps no issue preoccupied the apologists of the second and third centuries more than the claim of bodily resurrection. As we shall see in Part One, the claim that Christians made for the body in the order of salvation provoked considerable scandal in a Greco-Roman cultural context that possessed few, if any, intellectual resources for imagining, much less enthusiastically celebrating, the body's participation in eschatological life. It is for this reason that theologians like Irenaeus, Tertullian, and Origen spent considerable time defending and illuminating this highly sensitive claim. This is important to reflect upon since many mistakenly suppose that the affirmation of bodily resurrection presents unique problems to modern people. It turns out that the scandal of the empty tomb was no less scandalous in antiquity than it is today. This requires us to give proper attention to this scandal, to ask questions centered on why the empty tomb provokes so much intellectual and even aesthetic offense. Why is it that this absence traumatizes imagination and speech? Is there something discernable in our cultural practices and intellectual traditions that inspires the rather spontaneous objection to the body's constitutive and permanent role in the formation of personal identity? Is there something in our experience as body-persons that leads us to theorize our experience in more or less dualistic terms? May it be, then, that in addition to its profound importance for christology and soteriology, the affirmation "He has been raised; he is not here" is just as significant for anthropology? If the second- and third-century debates over bodily resurrection show us anything it is that questions of christology, soteriology, eschatology, and anthropology are intimately bound together.

The second clarification is that while it is certainly true that the advent of modern criticism brings the resurrection into renewed focus, the kind of focus given to it largely remains preoccupied — one might even say obsessed — with questions of historical veracity. Rather than exploring the world of meaning that the resurrection proposes for imaginative inhabitation, especially what such inhabitation might entail regarding the formation of attitudinal and behavioral patterns, the resurrection of Jesus is typically treated according to the rather narrow concerns of traditional fundamental theology. Even a cursory glance at the many recent works on the resurrection reveals a fixation over the historical reliability of the New Testament witness, or whether things like bodily resurrections can be commended to belief in a post-Copernican world. Rather than exploring the rich *content* of resurrection faith, discussion and analysis usually remain riveted to the *ground* of belief, i.e., what justifies intellectual assent. Granted that the ground and content of Christian faith are intimately connected — indeed, I shall argue for their inseparability — we may wonder whether works committed to determining the historical genesis of resurrection belief, even those trenchantly defensive of traditional truth-claims, have helped us very much to appreciate and understand its meaning and practical significance once embraced.

This relegation of the resurrection to the ground of faith is one of the negative legacies of its slow displacement from christology and soteriology in Christian theology. The dominance of the incarnation since the conciliar definitions, and the hegemony of sacrificial atonement theories since the early medieval period, must be seen as contributing significantly to the configuration of standard treatises in scholastic theology in which Christ's "person" and "work" were essentially associated with the incarnation and cross respectively. The resurrection was left to a discussion of revelation, miracles, or general eschatology. As Christian theology sought to contend with the Enlightenment's suspicion of revelation and miracles, the resurrection became thematically controlled by apologetic defenses of Christian faith, i.e., as the great miracle which justifies belief. Itself supported by a series of proofs (especially the empty tomb and appearance narratives, which were treated as straightforward historical accounts), the resurrection became *the* proof of Jesus' divinity and the saving efficacy of his death. Francis Schüssler Fiorenza summarizes the trend in this way:

> One of the distinctive characteristics of [traditional] fundamental theology was its independence as a theological discipline seeking to provide a complete foundation for the Christian religion.... The central section [in many of these fundamental theologies] defended not only the possibility of revelation but also the de facto reality of revelation. Within this central section the resurrection of Jesus was indeed the linchpin, for the demonstration of the truth of Jesus' resurrection would amount not only to a proof of the truth and

reality of Christian revelation. Since the resurrection of Jesus was the ultimate example of divine intervention in history, the proof of its truth amounted to the proof of Christian revelation.[18]

It is difficult to say that much has changed. Although greater consideration to the role of hermeneutics in interpreting the resurrection narratives has brought with it more attention to its meaning for the Christian theology of salvation history, one cannot help but notice that its discussion in biblical, historical, and systematic studies remains as focused as ever on veracity. Questions like "what *really* happened on Easter day?" or "can bodies be 'risen' from the dead?" or "why are the textual data in the New Testament so contradictory?" or "could a video camera have recorded the so-called 'appearances' to the disciples?" are so dominant in the ever-bourgeoning number of books on the resurrection that questions of meaning and practical significance are too infrequently explored with the thoroughness they deserve.

There are pastoral implications to this discussion, of course. Although to date no real hard data have been collected to indicate how Christian faith communities appropriate resurrection belief,[19] in Paul Avis's view belief in Jesus' bodily resurrection from the dead has become problematic for many contemporary Christians:

> Pastoral experience suggests that there are many who can make the central affirmation of Christianity — "God was in Christ reconciling the world to himself" (2 Corinthians 5:19) — but who find the miraculous accompaniments of this saving presence of God in Jesus not only utterly incredible but also totally meaningless. They have a faith, but it does not include the virginal conception, the physical resurrection, and nature miracles of Jesus, the Ascension and the second coming.[20]

Such sentiments may or may not reflect those of the larger Christian public, and no doubt convictions vary from tradition to tradition, even person to person within traditions. Still, Avis asks out of pastoral concern whether it is necessary for Christians to believe in the bodily resurrection of Jesus. It seems not, if only because the disciples, before Jesus' death and any assertion of his post-mortem appearances, were able to have faith in him by being his committed followers during his lifetime.[21] He concedes that historically "Easter faith is the living heart of Christian faith," but then hastily adds that "Christian theism has shown itself almost infinitely flexible" such that it permits "a version of the Christian faith...in which the outcome of the death [is] not seen as any different from that of other human beings."²² What Avis seems to have in mind here is an incorporeal participation in beatific reality, an ascent of the "soul" into eternal life immediately upon death. Oddly, Avis considers that in this interpretation "the fact of the Incarnation, rather than any particular interpretation of the Resurrection, would be the touchstone of Christian faith and Christian theology, and what is believed about the Resurrection would be brought into line with what many already believe about the virginal conception," which is, it would seem, legendary and largely inconsequential.²³

Leaving aside the claim that Christian faith has proven "almost infinitely flexible," as though we might include or excise this or that aspect according to prevailing cultural sensibilities, it is strange that the incarnation should be thought of as its touchstone when not only the disciples knew nothing of such a doctrine during Jesus' lifetime — the exact point he makes about the resurrection — but the incarnation itself is considered in various quarters to be a hopeless piece of mythology.²⁴ Aside from the fact that it is the resurrection which is logically and chronologically prior to the doctrine of the incarnation, this view of the incarnation means, ultimately, that what has been incarnated is "sloughed off" at Jesus' death — an oddly cropped off interpretation of the incarnation. (Modifying the patristic axiom, can we not assert, "What has been assumed cannot be severed?") It is not at all clear — indeed, it is manifestly inaccurate to claim — that the resurrection is peripheral to what it means to say that through Christ God reconciles the world. At least when one reads the New Testament, any notion of "reconciliation" without "resurrection" is tantamount to affirming "salvation" without "exodus" in the Old. The fact that such could be proposed by a well-meaning and respected theologian (Avis is hardly alone on this score) is just one example of what can occur when Jesus' resurrection from the dead becomes a kind of epilogue in christology and soteriology rather than acknowledged as its grammar *and* thematic focus: it becomes dispensable, at least negotiable; an outer husk that may be shucked for accessing an inner essence; a vestige of a pre-modern anthropology; a symbol to be tossed on a heap of broken images. How surprising it would be to those first Christians who encountered the risen Christ, and who proclaimed God's victory over sin and death, to learn that, after all, this "event" did not so much enter our world with an eschatological bang but was interpreted away with only a whimper.

We can readily acknowledge that the belief in Jesus' bodily resurrection from the dead remains one of the most challenging aspects of Christian faith for many people today. No wonder, then, that much of the recent theological literature on the subject focuses on whether and in what way we can say it occurred. We should recall that it was challenging for the early church as well. Such things don't exactly occur everyday. As we shall see throughout this book, Jesus' resurrection from the dead is *sui generis:* an event like none other; the irruption of the ultimate within history; an eschatological event whose relationship to history is one of structural ambiguity, an ambiguity that does not indicate weakness but eschatological *excess*. This is not to suggest that the resurrection is dialectically opposed to history, as if its radically exceptional character meant that it bears no real relation to history. Easter is the *fulfillment* of our history, its inmost promise. It is that act *already* realized in our history which reveals history's ultimate *future*. Though it occurs *within* the story, *in medias res,* it proleptically inaugurates its climax while revealing its original purpose.

If the challenging nature of the resurrection is one of the chief reasons for the ongoing need for its defense, since whatever the cultural-historical milieu of its proclamation it presses credulity to its utmost limits (not least for the disciples!), we cannot remain satisfied with the hegemony apologetics currently exercises over it in contemporary theology. Even if "new and shocking discoveries" about the resurrection seem to appear daily from scholars who propose to liberate us from the misconceptions of previous generations and to give us a surer (read: "scientific") basis for Christian faith — assuming it is faith they still promote — Christian theology cannot assume that rummaging through the textual and historical problems associated with the New Testament writings, while elaborating reasons for their credibility for people in the modern world, satisfies the demands for its fuller theological treatment. It may not even be the starting point.

GIFT, HOSPITALITY, AND THE BODY

Observers of post-modern trends in philosophy and theology will readily recognize the currency of the above terms. Discussions of "gift" and "hospitality" have emerged from the continental scene in philosophy, particularly from French phenomenology and post-structuralism, while the studies of "the body" have emerged from a variety of fields, including phenomenology, epistemology, social theory, cultural anthropology, and gender studies. Without presuming to synthesize the wildly diverse trajectories found in post-modern discussions of "gift," "hospitality," and "the body," the present study of Jesus' resurrection from the dead is inspired by the fresh perspectives that some of these trajectories provide.

At the outset, I must state quite clearly that the present study is not an effort to provide an apologetic defense of Jesus' resurrection from the dead, not at least in the sense that *apologia* has taken since its modern configuration. There are so many works that attempt some such defense that another offering here would be redundant. This is not to refuse the responsibility to give an answer to those who ask the reasons for the hope Christians have (1 Pet. 3:15). But such an *apologia* cannot rely upon external and putatively self-evident criteria.

The present work presumes the "non-foundational" character of knowledge. By this I do not mean that there is no reliable knowledge; that no tests exist for validating knowledge or providing warrants for belief; that people cannot converse across cultural-linguistic horizons to arrive at shared knowledge and consensus. Neither do I mean that all knowledge is constructed only for the purpose of exercising power over others, though we can readily admit that this frequently happens. Even if we agree that knowledge is in fact "constructed" out of cultural-linguistic milieus, from vast networks of social practices that often operate at a tacit level in human culture, this will not mean that the Christian claim "Jesus is risen" has no referential value, that such a statement does not *refer* to an actual state of affairs independent of those who believe and assert it. When Christians affirm that God has raised Jesus from the dead, they are making a claim about *Jesus*. Something happened to Jesus of Nazareth who was crucified under Pontius Pilate. This "something" is the reason for belief. "If Christ has not been raised, your faith is vain; you are still in your sins." Something has therefore happened in and for our *world*. The resurrection of Jesus is an ontological reality. It concerns a *body*, and the body, from a Christian point of view, is not the impermanent shell for an immortal soul; it is just the way personhood is enacted in the world. "Body" and "world" are inextricably bound, so that what we say of the eschatological future of one inevitably pertains to the other. As Karl Rahner powerfully puts it: "The resurrection of Christ is essentially... the event in which God irrevocably adopts the creature as his own reality, [and] likewise the event in which God so divinizes and transfigures the creature that this glorification is accomplished as the total acceptance of this divine assumption by the freedom of the creature itself."[25] We will miss the meaning of the resurrection, and fatally so, if we do not account for this "objective" reality.

This does not mean, however, that we will be able to provide objective reasons for believing in the resurrection, if by "objective" we mean "grounds" other than what the resurrection itself provides. The resurrection of Jesus from the dead is *sui generis:* an event unlike all others, an eschatological irruption in our world that cannot be directly perceived or anticipated, but only known indirectly and in mediation. Though it stands as the ultimate fulfillment *of* history, it is not itself reducible *to* history. No image, no narrative, no analogy measures up to its immeasurable givenness. It "saturates" all perspectives. Hence, no historical or transcendental argumentation stands in a symmetrical relationship to it. Belief in Jesus' resurrection from the dead cannot be secured by an external ground; *it is the condition of its own possibility,* and so in some sense is "groundless." From a Christian point of view, it is the ground that grounds *our* "foundations." Approaching the resurrection will therefore be more like *being approached.* (The regular usage of the passive voice in this work may be seen as a stylistic liability, but it is quite necessary given our subject matter.) It will be much more like heeding a word that comes to us gratuitously, as Gift. Responding to it is subsequent to its givenness. The resurrection cannot therefore fit within our a priori horizons of intelligibility, or what *we* assume in advance to constitute "history," but will instead call us to and lead us through a process of conversion to reveal what "history" really *is,* what it *can be,* what it *will be.* The attitude called for here is one of *hospitality:* of becoming radically receptive to the Other *qua* Other. Such hospitality is demanding, and in at least two ways.

First, the hospitality required to receive the Gift of resurrection calls us to undergo a process of purgation, to progressively "let go" of the intellectual and affective obstacles that prevent us from responding to God's gratuitous and loving word of resurrection with a "yes." Some of these obstacles we have set up for ourselves through habits of thought. We say that such a thing is historically impossible. Bodies don't rise from the dead. People don't walk out of tombs. Something like this cannot possibly be believed. Perhaps the objection is wrapped up in aesthetic terms, so that the idea of a body "being raised" from the dead strikes us with the aesthetic offensiveness it did Celsus in the second century, who described Easter as a "mere hope of worms." As I shall argue in Part One, the resistance to bodily resurrection in both the ancient and modern world is the result, not so much of a principled objection, but a sense of revulsion at an almost visceral level that I *am* my body. (The mind-body or soul-body duality that pervades much Western culture is no more pointedly contested than by the Christian affirmation of bodily resurrection.) Some of the resistance to the words of resurrection also stems from perspectives and practices that are mired in human conflict. Belief that victims are raised from the dead, or that victimizers are offered the gift of salvation from the crucified-and-risen One, may be resisted as a result of our unwillingness to desire it. If the resurrection narratives show us anything, however, it is that our *desires* are frequently distorted and in need of the transformation that can only take place once we respond to the Gift of the crucified-and-risen One who comes to us, first with an offer of *shalom* and forgiveness (a forgiveness we didn't know we needed), and with a call to conversion through the admission of our guilt (a guilt we didn't know we were implicated in).

Second, hospitality to the resurrection is demanding insofar as it calls us to a way of life that may very well be remarkably different from the one we are currently living. It will call us to engage in practices of justice and reconciliation that may put us at odds with much of the world's conception of power. Though it may seem odd at first blush, only because we have done much to anesthetize its original vitality, the belief in Jesus' resurrection from the dead is an explosive idea with wide-ranging political import. Because it concerns bodies, and since human bodies are woven into the warp and woof of social, cultural, and political bodies, the eschatological future of "the body" explicitly means the transformation of the *humanum* in all its dimensions. Christians cannot, without fundamentally misunderstanding their faith, disassociate the "historical" from the "eternal," the "political" from the "eschatological," the "public" from the "private." When properly understood, and when viewed within the historic-dramatic context of its revelation, belief in Jesus' resurrection issues a commission to live a life that involves potential danger since it involves bringing justice and reconciliation wherever personal and structural violence is found in the world. Among other meanings, the resurrection is the divine vindication and legitimation of a man who was brutally tortured and publicly crucified by religious and political powers, and not by accident, but of the sort of "necessity" we can ascribe to history simply by observing the way it happens again and again when such powers are provoked — mechanically and without remorse.

It should be obvious here that subscribing to a "non-foundational" approach does not deny the publicness of theology. Claiming that Jesus' resurrection cannot be externally grounded by historical or transcendental argumentation is not fideism. It is not a retreat from accountability to, or dialogue with, the Other, either by insulating itself in a private language-game that assumes it has nothing to do with other language-games, or by defining itself in an over-and-against relationship out of rivalry. Neither do I intend to suggest that all forms of contemporary apologetics are without any merit. (Though it is not clear to me how such projects provide much more than an initial brush stroke for understanding the frequently counter-intuitive character of Christian reality.

Apologetics tends to exploit continuities between belief systems rather than giving honest appraisals of discontinuities.) The non-foundational starting point does insist, however, that we appreciate the way knowledge emerges in social-cultural contexts that give it characteristic shape. We are *embodied* human beings. All knowledge is therefore situated, social, and mediated by culture. We come to *know* in and through social practices and traditions, so that what we call "knowledge" courses through complex webs of social and cultural relations, often at a tacit level. Since all knowledge is thus "embedded," there is no neutral or absolute point of view from which we may survey all things to adjudicate competing truth-claims. We are still given the task to make qualitative distinctions between positions, i.e., judgments. But we must be prepared to acknowledge that we do so *from* a position.

THE ECCLESIAL PRESUPPOSITION FOR RESURRECTION BELIEF

Christianity begins with a disappearance. To be sure, the New Testament witnesses to an "appearance." Jesus "appears" *(ophthe)* to his disciples. He makes himself known. Or, as one formulation puts it, God raised him from the dead and "let him be seen" by his earliest followers (Acts 10:40), who immediately preceding this encounter, found themselves in various postures of despair: mourning, panic, guilt, bewilderment, etc. But the appearances of Jesus also imply a dis-appearance, namely the withdrawal of a body. In Mark, the women approach the tomb of the crucified Jesus only to be startled. Expecting to see and anoint a body, what they witnessed instead was a shocking absence. The tomb was empty. Forthwith they were informed by a herald: "He is risen; he is not here." They were then given instructions to go to Galilee to tell the disciples what they saw, which was literally no-thing. There, among the disciples *in community*, they would encounter the risen Jesus who has gone before them.

Again and again we find in the resurrection narratives the paradox of seeing and not-seeing, of "presence" and "absence." But always the encounters with the risen Jesus occur within, or immediately lead to, community. Being-with-the-Other is the time and place for being-with-the-crucified-and-risen-One. The risen Christ's "presence" in the community occurs in the midst of his "absence," for he is no longer an object of perception in the normal sense, but now encountered in the mediation of community, sacrament, and apostolic mission. This "absence" is not negative whatsoever. It is his withdrawal in resurrection and ascension that opens up the "space" for the paschal community to emerge, where he is "present" in a qualitatively new way.

If all this sounds strange, it is only the strangeness of the resurrection narratives themselves. Always in the encounter with the risen Christ is he acknowledged in the midst of *alterity*, as a stranger, in the mode of transcendence, and thus in the mode of "absence." But again, this "absence" is not a result of a weakness in the given. It is the result of an *excess*. In the same way unadjusted eyes see darkness when flooded with light, the perceptual absence in the resurrection narratives is the correlate to the eschatological surplus of Jesus' risen presence, which cannot be objectified or reduced to a single horizon of perception. This paradoxical relationship is the ultimate key for understanding the resurrection narratives in their extant form. While some may argue that the ambiguity in the New Testament witness renders it suspect — the incongruities within and between the narratives, we are told, lead to serious questions about their reliability — the exact opposite is the case. Precisely in and through the paradoxes, tensions, and ambiguities of the resurrection narratives will we find their uniquely disclosive power. They are "eschatological signs" of *the eschatological event par excellence*. The narratives share in the eschatological character of Jesus' resurrection itself. The complex relationship of familiarity and strangeness, presence and absence in the narratives make them textual analogies (or "traces") of the Easter event. Our task is therefore not one of searching for a historical substrate "behind" the texts, to somehow submit them to our standards of what constitutes a properly "historical" event. Our task is to "read off" these texts *as they give themselves* to us, as they *body-forth* meaning. We must be willing to allow the texts to *show themselves* in their givenness, and thus we must approach them phenomenologically, with a hermeneutics of hospitality to the Gift.

Where is the time and place for our encounter with these narratives? Where shall we pick up and read? Where is the site for listening to and appropriating their testimony? Obviously their textuality enables us to read them anywhere. One need not be in a Christian community to read them. But if we read them in the way they were meant to be read; if we read them analogously to the way the earliest Christians came to affirm Jesus' resurrection, we will read them in community, in an ecclesial context where resurrection belief is shared, celebrated, propagated, and practiced by members who have acquired distinctive skills. Learning to speak of the resurrection is quite like learning a language: it is something that must be acquired through practice. It involves becoming immersed in a *habitus* — a world, a cultural-historical setting, a community of shared beliefs and practices. In the New Testament, coming to affirm the resurrection of Jesus, and living out the implications entailed in this belief, takes place in (or leads to) community. This *habitus* of which we speak is the church, the "body of Christ." It is only within this body that the statement "Jesus is risen" can really gain meaning. Though it is *referential* by pointing to a reality "out there," signifying that something has really and truly happened to Jesus of Nazareth, its referential aspect will only become *meaningful* to us to the extent it is lived-into. The church is the generative space for this happening. This is more or less what I mean by subscribing to a non-foundational approach: the belief in Jesus' resurrection gives birth to a worldview in which we are invited to inhabit with others in community. Whatever analogies we may draw from our experience to help us initially approach it, the affirmation that "Jesus is risen" entails much more than a proposition that might be placed along side other propositions. Spoken with relative competency, it entails an interpretive framework that gives distinctive shape to how we understand the world. It constitutes the primary *mythos* by which we live, the *grammar* by which we speak.

Coming to affirm Jesus' resurrection from the dead is possible only because of apostolic testimony. Again, Acts 10:40: "[B]ut God raised him on the third day and allowed him to appear, not to all the people but to us who were chosen by God as witnesses, and who ate and drank with him after he rose from the dead." Although, as I shall argue later, we can legitimately speak of encounters with the risen Christ that are analogous to those of the apostles, we must acknowledge the uniqueness and non-repeatability of those original encounters. All Christian faith is dependent upon and mediated by apostolic witness. Resurrection faith comes to us in relation, from a community, animated by the Holy Spirit, that extends organically throughout history as the "body of Christ." Though we are conditioned by much in our culture to seek gnostic immediacy, resurrection faith is an embodied faith, one of "mediated-immediacy." Along with Louis-Marie Chauvet, we may call this the "corporeality of the faith," the "arch-sacramentality of the faith," or thinking about God "according to corporeality." By this he means the mediated nature of all experience and knowledge, including that of God, Christ, and Spirit.

> [T]here is no faith unless somewhere inscribed, inscribed in a body — a body from a specific culture, a body with a concrete history, a body of desire.... One becomes a Christian only by entering an institution and in letting this institution stamp its "trademark,"

its "character," on one's body. The faith thus appears to us as "sacramental" in its constitutions, and not simply by derivation. Our existence is Christian insofar as it is always-already structured by sacramentality, better still, as it is always-already inscribed in the order of the sacramental. It is thus impossible to conceive of the faith outside of the body.[26]

It is just this lesson that the resurrection narratives give us, argues Chauvet. The resurrection and ascension of Jesus' body from the dead is a withdrawal, a gracious departure that opens up a "space" or *habitus* for his followers to continue making present in community, through proclamation, sacrament, and praxis, his eschatological presence in the world.[27] Though the risen Christ is not subsumed into the community — for he remains its "head" and "lord" — the ecclesial community bodies-forth the reality of Christ in the world in a sacramental and historically effective way. Not always perfectly, we must hasten to add. In fact, the church constantly stands under the judgment of the risen Christ who can never be co-opted by any program or ideology. Still, the community of the church remains the time and place for allowing one's desires to be transformed by the crucified-and-risen One. However much we may come to learn about Jesus' resurrection through our study of the narrative testimonies, and whatever we may say in this present work about the reality and ongoing significance of the Easter event, such remains derivative, but hopefully supportive, of the living and breathing "body of Christ" that is his church.

"Hence the way is Christ, but equally the Church," writes John Milbank. "And both are 'real' as the cultural happening of 'meaning'; 'liberal versus conservative' debates about the historicity of the resurrection etc. will have no place in a postmodern theology."[28] This comment succinctly captures what I might call a "learned indifference" to some of the scholarly debates that keep studies of the resurrection caught within a kind of intellectual spasm. This is not to say that works of historical and literary criticism will be of no interest to us. Neither do I forswear the responsibility theologians share for providing an *apologia* for the faith, although I can deny that the mode of this *apologia* must labor long over the debates concerning its contested historicity. This work *presupposes* the reality of the resurrection. It is a work of confessional theology, not a work of foundational theology. It is my conviction, however, that speaking of the resurrection from the position of belief, by attempting to illuminate something of its truth, goodness, and beauty *as given* — rather than adducing external supports for establishing its credibility according to prevailing intellectual sensibilities — is actually a more effective *apologia* than other approaches. Perhaps I can put it this way: the task undertaken here is one of *showing*, of extending an invitation to the reader to explore a world of meaning, thinking, speaking, and living. It is my hope that something of the goodness, truth, and beauty of the resurrection, which is compelling in its self-presentation, and which is more adequately encountered in the living ecclesial communities to which it has given rise, may be reflected in the present work, which is nothing if not an act of testimony and contemplation.

Chapter One

CONDITIONS OF THE POSSIBILITY

THE HISTORICAL *APORIA*

Contemporary studies of Jesus' resurrection typically linger around a single question, as if answering it from a historical point of view exhausts the task of engaging it: "What *really* happened on Easter morning?" Whether asked by those who would attempt an alternative explanation for Easter belief, and thus the rise of Christianity itself, or by those who would attempt a defense of its historicity and credibility against its "cultured despisers," studies of the resurrection continue to be dominated, as they have since the eighteenth century, by historical criticism and apologetics.

It is not just that Jesus' resurrection raises all sorts of challenging questions about what is metaphysically possible, what constitutes a historical event, what could possibly be the nature of a risen body, and the like. It is also that the complexities and incongruities of the resurrection narratives endlessly supply historians, exegetes, and theologians alike those historical, textual, and conceptual problems that have become standard features of resurrection studies. It is well known, for example, that the diverse thematic emphases and chronological orderings of the events in the gospels resist complete harmonization. Inconsistencies in detail related to time, place, visual phenomena, witnesses, reactions of witness, and exchange of dialogue remain basically insoluble. No doubt the casual reader of the gospels will experience some confusion as to the actual status of the risen Jesus. Sometimes he is portrayed in a most earthly fashion, suddenly appearing in the midst of the disciples, eating with them, breaking bread, expositing scripture, delivering discourses, and presenting his wounds to incredulous fingers. At other times a most unearthly Jesus is flanked by blazing white angels, an elusive and nimble presence capable of walking through walls and closed doors, later ascending into heaven out of view.

In what is widely regarded as one of the oldest strands of resurrection kerygma in the New Testament, Paul "hands on" a tradition "of first importance" to the Corinthians that he himself received: "that Christ died for our sins in accordance with the scriptures; that he was buried; that he was raised on the third day in accordance with the scriptures" (1 Cor. 15:3–4). What at first blush seems straightforward quickly becomes complicated, not only because Paul's subsequent list of witnesses differs from other such lists in the New Testament, but the analogies and metaphors he uses to explicate the tradition, especially that of the "spiritual body" (*soma pneumatikon*), present the reader with what many regard as some of the most complex and semantically turbulent of his writings, so much so that scholars still take wildly diverse stances on his meaning. The centrality of the resurrection in the New Testament is beyond question, as is the broad coherence of its proclamation; but taken as a canonically bound whole, the diversity of its presentation proves difficult, if not impossible, to master. There appears a marked contrast, observes C. F. Evans, between the centrality of the resurrection in the New Testament and the "almost fortuitous character" of the narratives, metaphors, and kerygmatic traditions that support it. "Whatever the Easter event was," Evans speculates, "it must be supposed to be of such a kind as to be responsible for the production of these traditions as its deposit at whatever remove."[1] And with this statement — one that expresses as much theological intrigue as it does exegetical exasperation — we find our point of departure.

In what follows, I do not attempt to straighten out all the historical and exegetical problems associated with the resurrection, as this is the chief preoccupation of many works written on the subject in the past several decades. This is not to say that I am uninterested in historical criticism as one (though necessarily limited) methodological aid. The results of historical criticism will at various times be taken up as helpful for arriving at a deeper appreciation of the New Testament witness. Neither is my interest here to justify resurrection belief and language by demonstrating that the reality of Jesus' resurrection fulfills the existential question and transcendental desire of the subject, which is what anthropological starting points typically hope to achieve. These approaches have some merit (as do other "correlational" strategies in theology) and will be invoked occasionally throughout the rest of our study, though primarily for purposes of thematic explication, not apologetics. Our interest here is quite different: we seek to discharge the air, to "prepare a way" for an im-possible event, to initiate an act of intellectual purgation so that we may allow the echoes and traces of Jesus' resurrection to be heard and felt in their eschatological givenness, above all in their narrative presentations. Ours is a fundamental theology in reverse,

Conditions of the Possibility

an unapologetic theology. I adopt this phrase from William Placher, who writes:

> When the Christian story is told most persuasively, then the sweep of that epic gives our own part in it far greater meaning, not less, in a way that becomes most clear not through some argumentative analysis but precisely in the power of the narrative in which the general movement and the character of individual episodes illuminate each other. Christian faith sorts out the world by seeing a pattern in things. One does not "prove" such a way of looking at the world, if "proof" means a series of syllogisms from universally accepted premises. Yet Christians want to claim that these really *are* the patterns of reality.[2]

The point here is that while Christians believe their story is true, its truth cannot be guaranteed by external criteria but only discovered within the narrative itself, which becomes the framework for interpreting the rest of reality. For Placher, this does not lead to a kind of collective solipsism or vicious circularity. It does not lead to an indifferent or exclusivist attitude toward other narratives and truth-claims. It is convinced that conversation in our pluralistic context will become fruitful only once we acknowledge and speak out of the particularities of narratives and worldviews rather than assuming they can be adjudicated from a position of "nowhere," a neutral and universally valid standpoint that acts as the ultimate "foundation." Such an ideal is one of the hallmark "myths" of modernity. And so, rather than elaborating arguments (historical or transcendental) to arrive at the resurrection as our endpoint, we unclasp the hands of our reflexive need for "foundations" and become open to that which gives itself to thought and language by way of the Gift, as that which saturates and potentially transforms our pre-established horizons of expectation and intelligibility.

Let me introduce this endeavor with the following questions: What sort of event could Jesus' resurrection from the dead possibly be, if indeed it is an "event" in any ordinary sense? Is there something about its peculiar irruption that generates of necessity the very kind of turbulent forces in thought and language to which I have alluded? What is it about the resurrection that might make the historical, textual, and conceptual ambiguities found in the New Testament an unavoidable outcome? Might it be that the ambiguities of the resurrection narratives are uniquely disclosive as textual traces of an event whose eschatological character necessarily exceeds and overwhelms the capacity of representation, thereby reflecting something of the dynamism and historical ambiguity of the resurrection itself? Rather than submitting the apparent textual problems to the Procrustean bed of an explanatory framework, which is what so much historical criticism is wont to do, whether of a skeptical or apologetic stripe, might we attempt to "read off" their emergent complexity as signifying a "presence" whose unique manner of self-giving is also, and for that very reason, an "absence"?

"But where scholarship returns again and again to an historical aporia," writes Rowan Williams, "the theologian may be pardoned for taking this as matter for reflection."[3] Noting that scholarship constantly founders on the paradoxical shoals of Jesus' resurrection, which as both historical *and* trans-historical produces a history of effects, but is never itself only one historical event among others, Williams suggests that the remarkable diversity in historical critical approaches to the resurrection itself reflects, willy-nilly, the inability to master the sovereign presence of the crucified and risen One. Not surprisingly, perhaps, the indeterminacy in scholarship mirrors the indeterminacy of the resurrection narratives themselves. "The central image of the gospel narratives is not any one apparition but the image of an absence, an image of the failure of images, which is also an absence that confirms the reality of a creative liberty, an agency not sealed and closed, but still obstinately engaged with a material environment and an historical process."[4]

With this historical *aporia* as our focus, we will adopt a phenomenological style of reflection, particularly in the next chapter, so as to become hospitable to the peculiar givenness of Jesus' resurrection from the dead in our history. This will involve a strategy quite different from those ardently determined to submit the narratives and metaphors to an explanatory framework, usually with a firm set of presuppositions (an implied metaphysics) about what constitutes a proper and meaningful event in advance. The "condition of the possibility" for thinking and speaking of the disturbing presence/absence of Jesus' resurrection comes, rather paradoxically, through the progressive dismantling of those very conditions.

THE ESCHATOLOGICAL IMPERATIVE

Nearly every modern treatment of Jesus' resurrection begins with discussion of the difficulty the "modern mind" has believing in it. We would be mistaken to suppose however that the conceptual difficulties in its consideration are unique to modern people. They abounded for the early church as well. Apologetic features pepper the New Testament, evidencing doubt, misunderstanding, and outright denial at the very inception of

Christian faith. In the "longer ending" of Mark, Mary Magdalene tells the disciples of Jesus' appearance to her, but "they would not believe" (Mark 16:11). Matthew assures his reader strict orders were given to secure the tomb with guards, "otherwise his disciples may go and steal him away, and tell the people, 'He has been raised from the dead' " (Matt. 27:64). Such insistence in Matthew, not evident in the earlier Marcan account, indicates that some early critics of Christian faith would make the precise claim that the disciples stole Jesus' body from the grave.[5] Paul's readers either had difficulty believing in the resurrection (1 Cor. 15:12-19), or at least properly understanding its nature and implications (1 Cor. 15:35-58; 2 Tim. 2:18). That John's story of the "doubting Thomas" has reached the level of cliché only further confirms the point (John 20:24-29). If all of this is true of the early church, how much more so in subsequent centuries of Christian doctrine and practice? How much more so today, two millennia removed?

A well-known quote from Rudolf Bultmann will do as well as any to outline the contemporary challenge:

> Man's knowledge and mastery of the world have advanced to such an extent through science and technology that it is no longer possible for anyone seriously to hold the New Testament view of the world — in fact, there is no one who does. What meaning, for instance, can we attach to such phrases in the creed as "descended into hell" or "ascended into heaven?" We no longer believe in the three-storied universe which the creeds take for granted. The only honest way of reciting the creeds is to strip the mythological framework from the truth they enshrine — that is, assuming that they contain any truth at all, which is just the question that theology has to ask. No one who is old enough to think for himself supposes that God lives in a local heaven. There is no longer any heaven in the traditional sense of the word. The same applies to hell in the sense of a mythical underworld beneath our feet. And if this is so, the story of Christ's descent into hell and of his Ascension into heaven is done with. We can no longer look for the return of the Son of Man on the clouds of heaven or hope that the faithful will meet him in the air (1 Thess. 4:15ff.).[6]

The greatest challenge to the Christian affirmation of Jesus' resurrection, argues Bultmann, is that we no longer inhabit the symbolic cosmology presupposed by the New Testament. The crudely spatial imagery which may at one time have provided a meaningful framework for understanding is incoherent in a post-Copernican view of the world.

This shift in cosmology does not necessarily require the simple rejection of the Christian kerygma, though it will require sophisticated interpretive strategies ("demythologization") to distill from the New Testament what is existentially meaningful and abiding. The language of resurrection, whatever sort of "event" it intends to describe, cannot refer to a "historical" event in any modern sense. Imagining that it does leads to the unseemly conclusion of a resuscitated corpse, which raises the specter of mythology outright. Bultmann is willing to grant that something "happens" in the resurrection, as it were, though it is unclear how it takes on any sort of event-character in itself, independent of the subjectivity of the Christian who proclaims the saving import of the cross. And indeed, that is the extent of its signification and meaning: "faith in the resurrection is really the same thing as faith in the saving efficacy of the cross, faith in the cross as the cross of Christ."[7] The resurrection, one might say, is not eventful in itself but the ongoing *proclamation* of God's forgiveness of humanity in Jesus' self-sacrifice. Karl Barth once summarized Bultmann's position as asserting Jesus is "risen into the kerygma," to which Bultmann replied: "I accept this formula. It is completely correct, given only that it is correctly understood. It presupposes that the kerygma itself is an eschatological event; and it means that Jesus is truly present in the kerygma.... To believe in Christ present in the kerygma is the essence of the Easter faith."[8] In what amounts to the conflation of signified and signifier (the kerygma *is* the event), Bultmann avoids altogether, he thinks, the historical *aporia* of the resurrection, which he rather presumptuously states "is not of interest to Christian belief."[9] Having thus extracted the resurrection entirely from the category of history — again, because he seems incapable of imagining how any reference to history avoids the implication of mere resuscitation — Bultmann insists on its existential meaningfulness. It affords us "an opportunity of understanding ourselves," it "opens up for men the possibility of authentic life."[10]

It is well known that Bultmannn's adoption of existential language is indebted to Martin Heidegger. But it is at least as reflective of the Kantian "turn to the subject," particularly in its embrace of Kant's critique of knowledge. Kant's critique of metaphysics continues to haunt contemporary considerations of the resurrection, especially those taking up the question of its historicity and intelligibility.[11] Concerned to outline the proper limits of human knowledge — "the conditions of its possibility" — Kant argues that we are not the passive recipients of objective knowledge from a meta-empirical reality, a noumenal realm "out there." The sort of cosmocentric and objectivist character of classical metaphysics is no longer tenable. Rather, the human subject, conditioned as it is by the categorical (spatio-temporal) realm within which it exists, actively constructs the data of experience into objects of knowledge. To humanly know is not to know the thing-in-itself, but to know according to the strictures of the knower. All knowledge is necessarily restricted by the transcendental conditions of common experience, e.g., space and time, unity, cause and effect, etc. The intellect actively constructs knowledge in and through these categories, giving conceptual shape to sensual experience. Like a key made to fit a specific keyhole, all knowledge conforms to the power and makeup of the knowing subject.

The job of philosophy is to think through these transcendental conditions and set knowledge upon a secure and rational ("scientific") ground. Doing so requires a systematic and radical critique, one that must reign in the boundaries of knowledge far more tightly than allowed by traditional metaphysics, which has long been willing to freely speculate about things-in-themselves, including such meta-empirical realities as "God," "heaven," and the "soul." Because rational knowledge may only rightly be concerned with empirical realities, the terrain traditionally occupied by metaphysics and theology must be considered largely beyond the proper limits of reason. It may be that the human intellect seeks to unify experience into more and more comprehensive frameworks of understanding, thus reaching out to an unconditioned and utterly simple ground for all experience and knowing; still, that ground, which we might call "God," cannot itself be a proper object of knowledge since all knowing is conditioned by the categories of experience (phenomenality) while "God," by definition, is not. Kant may in fact believe that his critique of traditional metaphysics leaves room for faith, but it is clear that he sets up an almost insuperable dichotomy between the phenomenal (experience, history, empirical knowledge) and the noumenal (God, the soul, revelation).

The broader significance of Kant's thought for our purposes will become evident as we begin asking probing questions about the "conditions of the possibility": whether in establishing such conditions in advance we have not also preempted the perceptual and intellectual hospitality alone capable of receiving an im-possible Gift — one that, rather than simply conforming to the power of the knower, exceeds and transforms it. For now our interest is to further examine the basic problematic set up by Kant as reflected in Bultmann's hermeneutic. By arguing that demythologization is necessary to reinterpret a Christian faith first emerging from a cosmological context that could, without intellectual difficulty or embarrassment, describe Jesus' post-mortem existence in spatial terms ("resurrection" and "ascension"), Bultmann fully accepts the Kantian critique of knowledge. Declaring Jesus' resurrection as historically irrelevant, since otherwise we would project spatio-temporality onto a meta-empirical screen, he rules out the possibility of the resurrection bearing an event-character in itself, just as he seeks to salvage its relevance for the Christian in existential terms. "Mythology is the use of imagery to express the other worldly in terms of this world and the divine in terms of human life, the *other side* in terms of *this side*."[12] Myth renders objective and concrete what is invisible and existential. Bultmann's epistemological-metaphysical border between "history" and "myth" is isomorphic with Kant's border between the phenomenal and noumenal.

Perhaps more than any other affirmation in the New Testament, Jesus' bodily resurrection from the dead blatantly transgresses this boundary. Not surprisingly, Kant declares in his *Religion Within the Limits of Reason Alone* that the resurrection and ascension "cannot be used in the interest of religion within the limits of reason alone without doing violence to their historical valuation." Reason takes no interest "in dragging along, through eternity, a body," nor "can it render conceivable that this calcareous earth, of which the body is composed, should be in heaven."[13] Kant can, however, affirm the immortality of the soul as a summons to the moral life, even though one ought to do the good, not for the extrinsic reasons of punishment or reward, but for the good itself.[14] Bultmann too assures us that "an historical fact which involves a resurrection from the dead is utterly inconceivable!"[15] The empty tomb and appearance narratives are unquestionably later mythological interpretations of a more primordial experience which, while having an event-character within the subjectivity of the earliest disciples who proclaimed it, is necessarily beyond all historical valuation. The value of the narratives is not to be found in their descriptive adequacy but their expressive capacity. "The real Easter faith is faith in the word of preaching which brings illumination. If the event of Easter Day is in any sense an historical event additional to the event of the cross, it is nothing else than the rise of faith in the risen Lord, since it was this faith which led to the apostolic preaching. The resurrection itself is not an event of past history."[16]

By removing the question of history from consideration — for as Kant puts it, we cannot reasonably appropriate the narratives without doing violence to them — we have apparently solved, or at least avoided, the historical *aporia*. Demoted from their quasi-objective character, the resurrection narratives now become expressive of interior states and moral imperatives. Bultmann's approach therefore stands in continuity with the "experiential-expressivist" hermeneutics associated with Romanticism, especially Schleiermacher, which opposed the "cognitive-propositional" approaches of traditional apologetics. On this view, resurrection language does not refer to an event "out there," but expresses a faith experience "in here." Taken too literally, resurrection language blurs the boundary of the "this worldly" and the "other worldly." But disentangling it from history through techniques of demythologization allows us to rehabilitate the symbol of resurrection as the "coming to faith" of the disciples after Jesus' death. Again, the signifier and signified are conflated. Jesus is "risen into the kerygma."

What seems like an attractive solution may result in its own kind of violence, however: a hermeneutical violence whereby the content and meaning of resurrection language is significantly altered, even disfigured, when extracted entirely from all considerations of history. It may be true that we cannot easily apply, if at all, many of our preconceived notions of history to the resurrection narratives without doing violence to them (Kant is absolutely correct on this point); but we would be seriously mistaken to imagine that resurrection language is made obsolete, or lacks all significance as a historical event, with the shift to modern cosmology. We may also ask whether a hermeneutical method that rejects the resurrection narratives out of hand as bearing no historical value is governed by an implicit metaphysics that lacks the sort of necessary hospitality for attending to something radically new in our history. A truly hospitable hermeneutics might instead ask whether the operative pre-understanding of "history" that dogmatically excludes in advance an event like Jesus' resurrection from the dead is itself subject to question and possible revision.

Quite paradoxically, Bultmann's existentialist reading of eschatology only leaves the positivist's view of history as a closed system of causes and effects perfectly intact. As he concludes his *History and Eschatology*, Bultmann rhapsodizes: "Always in your present lies the meaning in history, and you cannot see it as a spectator, but only in your responsible decisions. In every moment slumbers the possibility of being the eschatological moment. You must awaken it."[17] As Jürgen Moltmann observes, this interpretation of eschatology in terms of the "eternal moment" of decision may appear to possess a certain value, but it lacks any real sense of temporality and futurity, any sense of the God *of* history. The transposition of eschatology into the eternal present, whether of a mystical or an existentialist kind, effectively makes individualistic and subjective what is social and concrete.

Christian eschatology teaches hope not only for the soul — the word used for existence in earlier times — but also for the body; not only for the individual but also for the community; not only for the church but also for Israel; not only for human beings but also for the cosmos. This supra-individual horizon of hope can then only be called mythological if one has no concern for the conditions over which this horizon spans its bow. The resignation which confines people to their own selves can hardly be called Christian.[18]

To approach history from the point of view of eschatology may indeed rest upon a prior theological commitment. But this is the unavoidable starting point for a Christianity that affirms Jesus' resurrection with the significance the New Testament accords it. The proclamation that "Jesus is risen from the dead" is not simply a naïve way of saying something else. Its specific meaning cannot be recuperated by translating it into an existentialist hermeneutics that determines history an unfit category for its appropriation. The resurrection has *everything* to do with history; but it does so in an utterly unique way. Oscar Cullmann puts it well:

> It belongs to the very stuff of the New Testament that it thinks in temporal categories, and this is because the belief that in Christ the resurrection is achieved as the starting-point of all Christian living and thinking. When one starts from this principle, then the chronological tension between "already fulfilled" and "not yet consummated" constitutes the *essence* of the Christian faith.... Accordingly, the fact that there is a resurrection body — Christ's body — defines the first Christians' whole interpretation of time.[19]

To the extent that we take the New Testament claim of Jesus' resurrection seriously we must attempt to speak in a way that accounts for, rather than avoids, this chronological tension — what I have called the historical *aporia* of Easter faith. Accordingly, Jesus' resurrection is not just one event among other events *in* history. It is not simply reducible to history. If it were, then we would not be talking about "resurrection," but "resuscitation." But neither is the resurrection a-historical or a-temporal, something like the instant translation of Jesus' incorporeal identity into eternity, beyond all time and space. *Resurrection means that the total personal reality of Jesus of Nazareth is transformed into the fullness of eschatological life. Eschatology is not the negation of space-time, but its fullness, its confluence and transfiguration.* The specification of the "body," which as Cullmann points out defined the early Christian view of time in terms of "already" and "not-yet," means something much more than the inert, physical "thing" that the instrumentalist and mechanistic anthropologies of our day presuppose. Resurrection language precisely means that something happened to the whole body-person of Jesus of Nazareth, that the concretely lived history of this man, which can only be thought of in terms of narrative identity (not metaphysical essence), has been eschatologically validated, transformed, and fulfilled. Hence, the resurrection is not "a-historical" but "more-than-historical," where the "more-than" is inclusive of but not reducible to history. Though a challenging undertaking, resurrection language requires those who wish to speak of it with relative competence to constantly balance affirmative and negative statements. The resurrection is both "historical" and "more-than-historical." It is structurally ambiguous vis-à-vis our history. But this ambiguity is not one of weakness. It is a result of "excess," as we shall see in the following chapter.

As a preliminary grammatical rule, then, we can say the following: any use of resurrection language that ignores either its "historical" or its "more-than-historical" aspect is no longer speaking resurrection language with sufficient competence, at least not in the way the New Testament speaks and teaches.

Put in somewhat different terms, terms we will need to progressively unpack throughout our study: *Jesus' resurrection from the dead is the proleptic (or "anticipatory") disclosure and definitive inauguration of history's fulfillment.* It is "historical" insofar as it irrupts within our history and produces a history of effects. It is "historical" insofar as it reveals (and proleptically accomplishes) the ultimate future of salvation history. We may therefore speak of it as the grammar of history, the governing narrative and logic by which Christians are to interpret history. On the other hand, the resurrection is "more-than-historical" insofar as it cannot be plotted within time as just one temporal link in an indefinite succession. It stands as God's definitive act of salvation *for* history; thus it comes to us from *beyond* history. Though it marks the inmost promise and fulfillment of history, the word of resurrection is spoken by God across an infinite, qualitative "distance" that history itself can never close. Seen in this way, the resurrection of Jesus from the dead remains Other to history, not as something alien or opposed to it, but as its im-possible Gift: as that which frees history from its own weight; as a self-investing promise by God, in Christ, and through the Spirit, to lead history through its many vicissitudes, sufferings, and disasters towards final "salvation."

The commitment to the category of history here is not in service of apologetics. Bultmann correctly argues that the resurrection cannot be the miraculous proof for faith, as so often alleged by Christian apologists who, eager to defend the faith, frequently end up adopting the very metaphysical presuppositions of their historical skeptics. The commitment to history, rather, is a commitment to the basic claim of Christianity itself, its very content: namely, that salvation is not salvation *from* the world, history, and the body, but *of* the world, history, and the body. Christian faith inspires what we might call an "eschatological imperative." Because it takes history with fundamental seriousness, even to the point of looking towards its absolute consummation in "resurrection," Christianity must resist every temptation to make of faith only an existential and private reality. From a Christian point of view, history cannot be thought of as a linear and immanently generated extension of causes and effects. Neither can human knowing be subject only to the "conditions of the possibility." Both may be the heirs to radical novelty, the irruption of the im-possible, the ultimate new thing — the *novum ultimum*.[20] This is why the appeal to existentialist hermeneutics for approaching Christian eschatology tends to work against its own intentions. By collapsing the interruptive character of eschatology into the "eternal now" of individual decision, so that every moment becomes a repetition of the same, the positivist's view of history, which would reduce all novelty in history to immanent laws of causality, is left uncontested. History becomes a "totality," unbreachable from anything beyond itself. Whatever account of freedom that the existentialist interpretation thinks it secures for Christian faith, it tends to be individualistic and apolitical. And this is the main point of Moltmann's quote above: Christian eschatology, properly understood, is anything but individualistic and apolitical. It concerns the transfiguration of the entire created order. The "resurrection of the body" is as social and political a doctrine as one will find in Christian theology.

THREE APPROACHES TO THE RESURRECTION

I now take the opportunity to examine three other ways of assessing the historical significance of Jesus' resurrection. Doing so will help us to set up the next chapter where I shall pursue a more or less phenomenological mode of inquiry. The following approaches, which I will call "methodologically agnostic," "historically argumentative," and "functionalist," do not exhaust the possibilities. I cannot possibly provide anything like a comprehensive survey, although we can get at least a general sense of the landscape.²¹ All three are concerned with the sort of questions raised by Bultmann and the Kantian problematization of eschatology. In addition to setting up the next chapter, the following approaches (or models) grant us a threefold opportunity: (1) to clarify my own use of the term "history" in relationship to Christian eschatology; (2) to gain insight into the non-foundational and self-involving character of the claim "Jesus is risen"; and (3) to show the inadequacies of a "functional" (or "expressive") approach that refuses to take seriously the objectively corporeal reality of the resurrection, i.e., its bodiliness.

Methodological Agnosticism

Perhaps no aspect of the New Testament is more sensitive to the theory-laden character of human knowing than Jesus' resurrection from the dead. Towards the conclusion of his exegetical and systematic study of the resurrection narratives, Edward Schillebeeckx writes, "the objective cannot be separated from the subjective aspect of the apostolic belief in the resurrection." Highlighting a point I shall take up at length later, Schillebeeckx reminds us that Jesus' resurrection can never be approached as a brute fact by a neutral observer. It is inextricably bound up with apostolic testimony and thus mediated by a historical community. Moreover, the kind of event it is purported to be — an eschatological event of paramount salvific importance — brings to the fore a host of commitments (theological and philosophical) about the ultimate character of reality itself. "Apart from the faith-motivated experience it is not possible to speak meaningfully about Jesus' resurrection. It would be like talking about 'colours' to somebody blind from birth."²² Even those who develop historical arguments for its actuality are obliged to acknowledge, as N. T. Wright readily does in his own exhaustive historical study, the self-involving and self-committing nature of its affirmation.²³ Such raises the question whether resurrection belief can ever be "verified" or "grounded."

Understandably, the complex epistemological and ontological questions involved in any consideration of the resurrection make some historical critics wary of entering into the fray. Whether an act of scholarly prudence, or a lack of nerve, a certain methodological agnosticism prevails in certain quarters of "historical Jesus" research. A "methodological agnosticism" says nothing about what the historian personally believes, but only something about the method adopted by the historian *qua* historian. Because Jesus' resurrection is so manifestly a faith-claim, so the argument goes, it remains outside the competence of historical reason to render judgments. The details of the resurrection narratives may be discussed, submitted to textual and literary analysis. But, as E. P. Sanders puts it in the epilogue of his *The Historical Figure of Jesus* (appropriately placed, it would seem), "the resurrection is not, strictly speaking, part of the story of the historical Jesus, but rather belongs to the aftermath of his life."[24] In reviewing the discrepancies of the narratives Sanders summarily states, "we cannot reconstruct what really happened.... I do not see how to improve on the evidence, or how to get behind it."[25] Sanders is willing to state in passing that apostolic fraud is unlikely, since several of those who testified to encountering the risen Jesus would meet violent ends precisely for their beliefs. Besides, deliberate deception would have resulted in greater unanimity in the accounts. Neither does mass hysteria seem sufficient given the diversity of extant traditions. Still, none of this provides grounds for a positive historical judgment about the *reality* of Jesus' resurrection. "That Jesus' followers (and later Paul) had resurrection experiences is, in my judgment, a fact. What the reality was that gave rise to the experiences I do not know."[26]

John P. Meier shares Sander's methodological agnosticism: "Since the Jesus of history is by definition the Jesus who is open to empirical investigation by any and all observers, the risen Jesus lies outside the scope of such investigation."[27] The Kantian restriction of historical knowledge to the empirical and universal ("any and all observers") is hard to miss here. The thought experiment guiding Meier's multi-volume work, *A Marginal Jew: Rethinking the Historical Jesus,* prescinds from all theological commitments to determine what any rational person, believer and non-believer alike, could affirm about the "historical Jesus."[28] The "historical Jesus," Meier insists, is not to be identified with the "real Jesus." The former is a historical reconstruction using the scientific tools of modern historical research. The latter is the ontological person Jesus of Nazareth. The "historical Jesus" is therefore an abstract construction of scholarship and can only provide a fragmented mosaic of the "real Jesus."[29] Carefully distinguishing empirical knowledge from knowledge of the thing-in-itself, Meier adds: "We cannot know the 'real' Jesus through historical research, whether we mean his total reality or just a reasonably complete biographical portrait. We can, however, know the 'historical Jesus.'"[30]

Meier complains that, all claims to neutrality notwithstanding, historians and exegetes frequently pursue theological or anti-theological ends that color and contaminate their conclusions. Confident in the ideal of a value-free form of knowledge, one that can shake metaphysical and theological prejudices, Meier's project "stubbornly restricts itself to empirical evidence and rational deductions or inferences from such evidence."[31]

He therefore assiduously avoids any appeal to the "supernatural" in his examination. When considering the sensitive case of Jesus' miracles, for example, his aim is not to determine whether Jesus performed miracles and by what power he performed them. Neither does he reject the possibility of miraculous phenomena a priori. Instead, the goal is modest and precise: to understand the historical circumstances of Jesus' ministry that led many to attribute the title of miracle-worker to him and what significance these alleged miracles had for Jesus, his companions, and his opponents. As for the question, "Was God acting in Jesus to bring about miracles?," the historian *qua* historian cannot respond. The historian may note that something extraordinary and inexplicable has taken place, eluding explanation according to intramundane factors. "But to move beyond such affirmations and to reach the conclusion that God indeed has directly caused this inexplicable event is to cross the line separating the historical from the philosopher or theologian."[32]

Such procedural agnosticism is identical to the sort we find in certain scientific quarters regarding the possibility of God's involvement in natural processes. For example, Stephen Jay Gould describes the respective domains of scientific method and religious belief as "non-overlapping magisteria," for which he provides the acronym NOMA. Stated somewhat superficially, science is concerned with discernable facts while religion is concerned with ultimate purpose:

> [T]he net, or magisterium, of science covers the empirical realm: what is the universe made of (fact) and why does it work this way (theory). The magisterium of religion extends over questions of ultimate meaning and moral value. These two magisteria do not overlap, nor do they encompass all inquiry (consider, for example, the magisterium of art and the meaning of beauty). To cite the old clichés, science gets the age of rocks, and religion the rock of ages; science studies how the heavens go, religion how to go to heaven.[33]

Borrowing Gould's NOMA principle we might say that the methodological agnosticism of Sanders and Meier situates "historical Jesus" studies within the plane of the empirically verifiable whereas the resurrection occupies the plane of "ultimate meaning" and "moral value." The former is the jurisdiction of the historian, the latter the purview of philosophers and theologians.

This relatively benign approach has the merit of greater restraint and consistency than many of the speculative reconstructions of Christian origins in recent decades. Compared to the crude scientism and relentless historicism that would reduce religious experience and truth-claims to mere epiphenomena, the careful delineation and strict adherence to methodological agnosticism regarding the resurrection event can seem an act of scholarly prudence. And yet, when we think about the matter further, we may find the restricted scope of such an approach less benign than first imagined. At the very least, theologians may find its usefulness extremely limited for a constructive and hermeneutical theology, since the bracketing out of Jesus' resurrection from the dead necessarily requires that we dismantle the narrative shape of the gospels into isolated fragments that no longer relate to one another in a coherent manner. Jesus' resurrection is not a kind of "gloss," a superadded layer imposed upon the historically retrievable "facts" of his life-ministry. Of course, we can readily grant that the composition of the gospels involves a complex and multilayered process of gathering and weaving together diverse oral and textual traditions that emerged after Jesus' death. I am by no means asserting that the gospels do not reflect extensive editorialization in their composition by authors who reflected on the meaning of Jesus' life, death, and resurrection within diverse historical and cultural milieus. In fact, I insist on it. That is the precise point of my suspicion regarding methodological agnosticism.

Serious questions may be asked about any method seeking to dispense with the narrative frameworks of the gospels, especially those claiming to operate free from theory-laden frameworks themselves. One need not accept a relativistic version of post-modern reflection to be skeptical of any claim to neutral observation of data. The attempt to break down the gospel portraits into atomized elements abstracted from the resurrection hermeneutic that envelops and configures them into a narrative *gestalt* inevitably, if subtly, substitutes an alternative framework for determining their significance. In the rigorous application of the various criteria arming a project like Meier's (the criteria of embarrassment, discontinuity, multiple attestation, coherence, etc.), inferences are necessarily drawn and overarching patterns constructed towards what Luke Timothy Johnson calls a "creeping certitude." The historian, argues Johnson, is not merely content with facts but "above all with the why and the how of things. But if the narrative framework that has placed the pieces in a certain meaningful pattern has been abandoned, then the remaining pieces cannot by themselves form a new pattern.... Meaning derives from the interpretation of the facts rather than the facts themselves. And such interpretation depends on story."[34]

In the approach adopted by Meier and Sanders, theological "interpretations" must be treated with methodological suspicion and winnowed away from the historical "facts," or at least historical probabilities. We must attempt to go "behind" the text's narrative framework in order to uncover what can be historically verified by the tools of historical research. The theological interpretations that house (and maybe even obscure) the data are left to theologians to analyze and debate. But it is precisely here where we must ask about the possibility of doing this in a value-free way, as though there were no implicit narratives (or worldviews) that govern the ideals of historical research. (The Enlightenment is nothing if not a "story" or *mythos* about the world; and it is out of the Enlightenment that such ideals in historical research emerged.) The belief that one is engaged in historical remembrance without built-in assumptions about things like "truth" and "probability," much less about how the various "parts" relate within a larger pattern of meaning, suffers from an inadequate appreciation of the hermeneutical character of knowledge. It may turn out that there are no "facts" without "interpretations." It may also be that ongoing theological interpretation in the development of the gospel traditions reflects a deepening of understanding, a process of clarification, a congealing of perspective that allowed Christians to remember and retell the story of Jesus in very specific ways. Obviously not everything about Jesus was important for the early Christians to remember. The gospels are notably selective in their presentations. They do not include or even seem to be concerned about certain "facts" about which we might be curious. From beginning to end the story of Jesus is told as "good news." They are relentlessly biased, if by this term we mean they were meant to inform through persuasion. They intend to portray Jesus as the Son of God who was crucified and risen from the dead. As John puts it, such was written "so that you may believe." But we must especially note the following: it is only in an act of retrospection that they do so. The resurrection is the hermeneutical lens through which the various episodes of Jesus' life and death take shape. As we shall argue later, the resurrection does something more than add an exclamation point to the end of the story. It is the reason why there is a story at all. It is the reason why the story takes the shape it does. Even more, it is the resurrection that transformed the memories of the earliest Christians so that what might have been regarded as a "fact" was reinterpreted in a radically new way. Originally obscure sayings that would have otherwise been ignored or forgotten began to make sense. Various deeds would begin to look different in the light of Easter. This is above all true regarding Jesus' death. How differently would Jesus' death and the details surrounding it be remembered if it weren't for the fact that days afterward he was believed to be vindicated by God and delivered from death's abysmal silence. The overarching pattern within which the various elements are found confers upon them a qualitatively new character so that when isolated from that pattern they become different sorts of "facts." As far as the gospels are concerned, peeling away their narrative patterns is somewhat like surgically removing various organs from a living, breathing person. While the parts between a body-person and a corpse appear to be the same, the animating spirit that emerges from the irreducible complexity of a living organism cannot be identified with the mere sum of its parts. The gospels, we maintained, are narrative constructions vivified by the reality of Jesus' resurrection from the dead and therefore premised upon a certain way of knowing. The gospels do not mean to provide mere information. Their narrative structures invite and instruct the reader into a world of meaning, to risk a different way of perceiving and interpreting whatever we might identify as common "facts."

We may be justified in asking whether Meier's reconstruction of the "historical Jesus," however incomplete and fragmentary it is, however removed it may be from the "real Jesus," will be too atomized, colorless, and thin to be of indispensable service for understanding *who* Jesus is — which, from a theological point of view, presupposes a much richer form of knowing than just the empirically verified and rationally deduced. As Johnson rightly points out: "That which can be verified historically is not at all necessarily what is most central or pivotal or essential to Jesus' ministry.... [W]e may determine that Jesus said or did certain things, but it does not follow that these things that we can determine were more central or more *determinative of who Jesus was* than the things we cannot historically verify."[35] If it is true that Jesus' resurrection is not historically verifiable (and this we must assert if we acknowledge the historical *aporia* — it "is" and "is not" historical), this will hardly mean that it is unimportant. It stands as centrally important since the gospels insist that Jesus' identity is only fully disclosed as God raises him from the dead. The resurrection must therefore become the *presupposition* for truly knowing Jesus. This is the strong claim the gospels make; and it is a claim we can only describe as "non-foundational," which is to say, a form of understanding that takes the perspective of belief. As Augustine puts it, "If you are not able to understand, believe, that you may understand. Faith goes before; understanding follows after" (Sermon 68).

In sum, my principle objection to the methodologically agnostic approach is not that historical critical inquiry is impossible or without a certain benefit to theology, but that it is impossible to do without a prior commitment to a narrative framework which already and always is theory-laden. The resurrection of Jesus in particular is not a discrete "object" of consideration that one may well dispense with when approaching the gospels. It is an event which proposes a world to be in-habited, a *habitus* within which a radically new manner of speaking, thinking, feeling, and acting is implied. The resurrection as "event," as "hermeneutic" and "structure," invites the self to a point of decision and a process of conversion. Only that presentation of Jesus with narrative integrity, i.e., one disclosive of Jesus as the crucified-and-risen One, will be able to give itself in this way — as Gift.

Jesus' Resurrection as Historical Event

While some scholars may find Meier's methodological neutrality refreshingly sensible, others see it as an evasion. Wolfhart Pannenberg argues that although Jesus' resurrection is not strictly a historical event, it nevertheless occurs within history and produces a history of effects open to fair-minded analysis. More than this, the patterns of evidence demand historical (not just theological) judgments about the events surrounding Easter, even judgments about the plausibility of the New Testament's claim regarding their origin. The historian is "obligated to reconstruct the historical correlation of the events that has led to the emergence of primitive Christianity."[36] Similarly, N. T. Wright declares that if anything in the New Testament is worthy of historical inquiry it is the resurrection. To skirt its investigation on a priori grounds is an abrogation of both the theologian and the historian's task.[37]

Other scholars are just as emphatic, if considerably less sanguine than Pannenberg and Wright about the implications for traditional Christian claims. Gerd Luedemann declares, for example, that the objections to treating Jesus' resurrection from a historical point of view usually amount to "apologetic manoeuvers to evade history."[38] In such cases, "the historical question is demoted to a question which is marginal compared with theology...or the concept of the historical is completely transformed into that of eschatology and thus elevated into the speculative sphere."[39] Robert Funk agrees, complaining that scholars "employ various strategies to keep the resurrection of Jesus out of reach," like insisting on its eschatological character, which by definition, or at least some definitions of it, remains "out of range for empirical and historical investigation."[40] Funk detects ideological motives in such a move. Since the appearance narratives in the New Testament serve to invest certain persons with apostolic authority, Peter and (less easily) Paul for example, they are "fundamentally self-serving."[41] The resurrection narratives are legitimating formulae, not descriptive accounts of an event "out there." By keeping the historical Jesus shrouded in the mystery of his resurrection and deity, church authorities continue to pose themselves as an *ersatz* presence, thereby blocking the "popular heart of Christianity," which, for Funk, is retrievable only through scientific and historical research. "Of this I have become increasingly certain: There is nothing we can exempt, or should exempt, from scientific and historical review either as Christians or human beings."[42] With the chutzpah of a man on a mission, Funk implores his readers to "break the Easter barrier" by coming to terms with its strictly mythological character.[43] Although this may be initially difficult for some, it is ultimately liberating for all. The relentless "hermeneutics of suspicion" is restorative in the end, for it allows Christians to become reacquainted with the real Jesus of history, not the one of ecclesiastical dogma.

We are obviously very far here from Meier's methodological agnosticism.[44] Funk essentially identifies what Meier seeks to meticulously distinguish: the "historical Jesus" and the "real Jesus." But Funk's views are more extreme (or at least more transparent in agenda) than others who otherwise share his negative historical judgments about the reality of the resurrection. To return to the work of Luedemann, a fellow of the Jesus Seminar co-founded by Funk and John Dominic Crossan, we find perhaps a less supercilious attempt to explain the rise of Easter faith, yet one doggedly committed to sensibilities of an Enlightenment worldview where things like "resurrections" do not and cannot take place. Like Bultmann, Luedemann declares that "the literal statements about the resurrection of Jesus...have lost their literal meaning with the revolution in the scientific picture of the world."[45] The sort of realism traditional theology has attributed to it "has been untenable since Kant."[46] Unlike Bultmann, however, Luedemman is prepared to explain "what really happened" rather than consigning the resurrection to the a-historical. The theory he proposes is that the tomb was not empty but unknown or forgotten. Moreover, the "appearances" of Jesus were the result of complex psychological factors explainable with the help of Jungian depth-psychology and Freudian analytical psychology. Peter's vision, we are told, originated out of his profound guilt and grief for having denied and forsaken Jesus during his most desperate hour.[47] Paul's vision was induced as the resolution of an unconscious "Christ complex." A zealous and violent persecutor of the Christian faith, Paul was apparently working out his aggression and unconscious attraction to Jesus' messianic mission (attraction and aggression being often connected in the fanatic); and, as is not uncommon among hysterics of this sort, he hallucinated an encounter with the one he so desperately hated/loved.[48] As for the case of "the more than 500 bretheren" mentioned by Paul who testify to "seeing" the risen Jesus (1 Cor. 15:6), we apparently have "a historical phenomenon" that "can plausibly be represented as mass ecstasy" induced by a sort of "religious intoxication" — a variety of those episodes of mass hysteria well documented in psychoanalytic literature.[49] So as to ensure us that we are on solidly scientific grounds in this admittedly complex hypothesis — while also throwing a bone to his Christian readers that such "hallucinations" are not simply spurious but potentially cathartic and meaningful — Luedemann approvingly quotes the medical dissertation of Peter Simon: "Visions are optical appearances of persons, things or scenes which have no objective reality... Visions or auditions do not reach their recipients... by the sense organs as defined anatomically but are the products of imagination and the power of ideas."[50]

Even a generous reading of Luedemann will be unable to dispose of the feeling that in spite of the appeal to psychoanalysis and medical literature for "scientific" support, the hypothesis demands of the reader an exceptionally high degree of confidence (one might call it "faith") in the explanatory power of depth-psychology.[51] Moreover, the sheer complexity of the hypothesis demands a robust commitment to a worldview in which Easter *must* have some alternative explanation to the one found in the New Testament. Mark Allen Powell notes that among the various criteria many historical critics adopt in assessing the authenticity of the gospel accounts, perhaps the most influential is the one least explicitly articulated: "the adoption of a post-Enlightenment worldview."

> In short, material is more likely to be regarded as historically reliable if it does not require acceptance of ideas that contradict modern views of reality. Some historians seem to operate with a prejudice that determines some things reported in the Bible not to have happened because they could not happen. An a priori judgment about what is possible transcends any consideration of how many sources attest to the event, whether it was potentially embarrassing for the church to report it, or anything else. The case is closed before it opens.[52]

Of course, those who defend the historicity of the resurrection are no less exempt from a priori judgments about the character of reality. Pannenberg and Wright, already mentioned above, fully embrace the challenge presented by Funk and Luedemann (among others) and claim to use the same historiographical principles and critically realist epistemology to arrive at radically different conclusions. Both are convinced that when thoroughly examined the historical facts surrounding the Easter event, if not capable of providing "proofs" for its actuality, will nevertheless provide strongly converging patterns for its probability. In their defense of the empty tomb traditions and critique of the subjective vision hypothesis, both Pannenberg and Wright argue that the empty tomb and appearances together provide the sufficient and necessary grounds for Christianity's claim that Jesus was bodily raised from the dead. While certainly a faith-claim, only it makes the best sense of the data. Only it adequately explains the rise of the primitive Christian movement from the utter disaster of Jesus' violent demise. "If the appearance tradition and the grave tradition came into existence independently," argues Pannenberg, "then by their mutually complementing each other they let the assertion of the reality of Jesus' resurrection...appear as historically very probable, and that always means in historical inquiry that it is to be presupposed until contrary evidence appears."[53] Similarly, Wright: "The empty tomb and the 'meetings' with Jesus, when combined, present us with not only a *sufficient* condition for the rise of early Christian belief, but also, it seems, a *necessary* one. Nothing else historians have been able to come up with has the power to explain the phenomena before us."[54]

If Pannenberg and Wright are both convinced that despite their complexities, ambiguities, and several incongruities, the New Testament accounts solidly withstand the historian's scrutiny, both readily acknowledge that considering the possibility of Jesus' resurrection from the dead for their explanation requires, at the very least, a far more open view of reality than modernity's closed system of linear causes and effects. On the one hand Pannenberg challenges those who say the modern scientific view of the world will not permit of things like resurrections by countering that recent advances in physics have outstripped the limitations assumed by the Newtonian-mechanistic view of the world. Only a part of nature's laws are ever known. Moreover, the conformity of events to known or unknown laws of nature is only part of the equation since from another perspective all events also bear a factor of contingency. And if natural science is right to express the general validity of natural laws, it can only be a self-correcting science by remaining open to genuine novelty, which is to say, it must constantly "declare its own inability to make definitive judgments about the possibility or impossibility of an individual event."[55] While this is undoubtedly true, and while there currently exists an interesting engagement between theologies of resurrection and contemporary science,[56] Pannenberg also acknowledges that a certain framework of understanding is ultimately necessary for Jesus' resurrection to become intelligible — the very framework Bultmann flatly ruled out:

> [T]he primitive Christian motivation for faith in Jesus as the Christ of God, in his exaltation, in his identification with the Son of Man, is essentially bound to the apocalyptic expectation for the end of history to such an extent that one must say that if the apocalyptic expectation should be totally excluded from the realm of possibility for us, then the early Christian faith in Christ is also excluded.... One must be clear about the fact that when one discusses the truth of the apocalyptic expectation of a future judgment and a resurrection of the dead, one is dealing directly with the basis of the Christian faith. Why the man Jesus can be the ultimate revelation of God, why in him and only in him God is supposed to have appeared, remains incomprehensible apart from the horizon of the apocalyptic expectation.[57]

The importance of this apocalyptic matrix of resurrection will become crucially important in later chapters as we explicate, more thematically, the meaning of Jesus' vindication. But here we must ask: where does this apocalyptic expectation come from? If, as Pannenberg asserts, the possibility of affirming Jesus' resurrection is bound up with an apocalyptic-eschatological imagination, is it not necessary to say that only a prior commitment to a particular narrative framework enables one to look at the New Testament witness from a historical point of view and determine that Jesus' bodily resurrection makes the best sense of the data? It is perhaps for this reason that Pannenberg quickly supplements his historical evaluation with other kinds of arguments, e.g., anthropological and transcendental.[58] There is nothing wrong with this, but one suspects that even these arguments will only be compelling to those already congenial to a particular worldview in which the hope for the whole human person, body and soul, and the hope for universal history already makes sense. In short, if Pannenberg rightly notes the negative prejudice (literally, "pre-judgment") some historians have in evaluating the New Testament witness to Jesus' resurrection from the dead, he will have to admit his own positive prejudice.[59]

In Wright's exhaustive study of the resurrection narratives we find a sustained argument as forceful and impressive as one is ever likely to find, but one that must admit that its conclusions cannot be derived from a neutral standpoint. His work, as he understands it, is "a historical challenge to other explanations, other *worldviews*. Precisely because at this point we are faced with worldview-level issues, there is no neutral ground, no island in the middle of the epistemological ocean, as yet uncolonized by any of the warring continents."[60] Wright is not naïve about this. He has written extensively about his own method as an attempt to straddle the Enlightenment goals of critical-realism and the post-modern sensitivity to the theory-laden (and thus constructed) character of all knowing.[61] Perhaps most helpfully, Wright attempts to integrate both historical-critical methods and literary-narrative approaches to the gospels. This implies that we must not only be interested in *what* actually happened but *why*. This latter question "opens up to reveal the full range of explanations available within any given worldview, including (in the case of answers available within first-century Judaism) the intentions not only of humans but of Israel's god."[62] Put differently, there are no historical facts that are not also interpretations; but just because there are interpretations (even theological), we should not disqualify them from being historically valid. To take up the gospels from a historical point of view means also engaging their interpretive frameworks as meaningful and potentially disclosive of truth.

In a move that may only arouse the charge of eclecticism (or worse) among his critics, Wright declares that approaching the New Testament will require unique epistemological tools. "Just as the gospels and epistles embody genres somewhat apart from their closest non-Christian analogues, so the study of them, and of their central figures, are tasks which, though they possess of course several analogies with other closely related disciplines, require specialized tools, that is, a theory of knowledge appropriate to the specific tasks."[63] One cannot simply apply any theory of knowledge to the gospels. One must be prepared to allow the gospels themselves to provide instruction for how they are to be read. Their content and form are so bound together that the procedure of extracting meaning from the distinctive manner of presentation will yield seriously deficient results. At the very least, argues Wright, the Enlightenment allergy to eschatology and its rigorous distinction between the "subjective" and "objective," the "empirical" and "spiritual," will require serious revision if not complete abandonment.[64]

This last statement is as apposite to Jesus' resurrection as anything else in the New Testament. To reiterate a point made above, Jesus' resurrection is an "event" which, because of its very nature, so thoroughly transgresses distinctions of subjective/objective, this-worldly/other-worldly, life/death, within/without, bodily/spiritual, historical/eternal that not only is it impossible to adequately consider it without reflecting upon worldviews; if taken seriously, it proposes to thoroughly reshape any worldview in which distinctions like these are its defining characteristic. Any consideration of Jesus' resurrection is therefore unavoidably theological, whether it remains agnostic, skeptical, or assenting. To say this is not an evasion, or a sleight of hand to keep the "real Jesus" out of reach of critical scholarship and in the firm grip of theologians. It is simply a frank recognition that Jesus' resurrection elicits a decision of the most fundamental kind:

> [O]ne cannot say "Jesus of Nazareth was bodily raised from the dead" with...minimal involvement. If it happened, it matters. The world is a different place from what it would be if it did not happen. The person who makes the statement is committed to living in this different world, this newly envisioned universe of discourse, imagination and action. In the same way — this is not so often noticed, but it is just as important — for someone to say "Jesus of Nazareth was *not* bodily raised from the dead" is equally self-involving.[65]

It is the burden of this book to show why and how such a claim is self-involving, how saying "Jesus of Nazareth was bodily raised from the dead" engenders a unique discourse and imagination. But about this we must be initially clear: no matter how committed the Christian must be to history, what history *is*, what history *means*, and what in history we may ultimately *hope for* can never be determined from a putatively disinterested point of view; it is only known within an eschatological framework, a self-implicating story which has no external or neutral "ground." To put the matter boldly: the resurrection of Jesus from the dead *is* this ground. It gives birth to and provides structure for a world of imagination, discourse, and praxis that cannot be derived from anything else, even if it reaches out to encompass all else. If you like, it is *the condition of its own possibility*. There is, it must be admitted, an inevitable circularity in saying this, perhaps not unlike the kind of circularity we find in Paul: "If Christ has not been raised, your faith is futile and you are still in your sins" (1 Cor. 15:17). But as I hope will become clearer, such circularity is not vicious. It does not demand abandoning oneself to irrationality, though it will mean constantly thinking "otherwise."

As stated above, we are opting for a non-foundational approach to Jesus' resurrection, which is to say, an approach that, while ever hospitable to interaction with other forms of knowledge and discourse (philosophical, sociological, historical-critical, scientific, etc.), can never be grounded or colonized by them. The statement "Jesus is risen from the dead" is a public statement, indeed, as public as any statement could be. But its publicness and possibility for assent is not grounded by a universally shared reason or set of first principles that may be empirically secured or deduced through transcendental analysis. There is no "foundation" upon which to fix the reality of Jesus' resurrection. It *is* its own foundation. Engagements with historical-critical and literary approaches will be beneficial for articulating its cogency and meaning, but they can only be appropriated in an *ad hoc* fashion, never as formally constitutive of resurrection faith and knowledge.

"Studying Jesus... might lead to a reappraisal of the theory of knowledge itself."[66] In a single statement Wright highlights the exact point I am making, just as he points to an unavoidable tension within his own work — more tension than perhaps he would like to admit. If, on the one hand, we approach the study of Jesus with an array of methods, analogies, experiences, intellectual horizons, and best guesses, we must be prepared, on the other hand, to have all these critiqued and transformed, perhaps even radically. And so, as Wright attempts a historian's defense of the New Testament witness to Jesus' resurrection, it is evident that the defense is deeply invested from beginning to end. The converging patterns of historical probability may be impressively presented, but ultimately one will have to admit that the patterns gain their persuasive power within a particular worldview. What this demonstrates, perhaps more than anything else, is that coming to faith in Jesus' resurrection will look a great deal more like progressively learning a new language and acquiring a new set of skills within a faith community than it will assenting to a historical argument or a proposition. That might not make historical argumentation pointless, but it will mean that faith is never something to be apologetically secured. It remains a self-involving risk.

The Functionalist Approach:
Jesus' Ongoing "Cause" in History

In the conclusion of this chapter I will say more about the proper way to think of Jesus' resurrection vis-à-vis history. But for now we must consider one last possibility for understanding the event-character of Jesus' resurrection. If, so far, I have spoken in a somewhat abstract way about Easter as "event," we must come to appreciate that Jesus' resurrection is meaningless if it lacks any sense of relationality to persons in history. The resurrection is, above all else, an interpersonal event: the eschatological fulfillment of persons-in-communion. It is the unmerited and unanticipated self-givenness of a person to the Other that essentially defines Easter. Any theology of resurrection that does not attain to the level of personhood in its understanding, that is to say, of *embodied relationality*, remains grammatically deficient.

Deep into his book, *The Resurrection of Jesus of Nazareth*, Willi Marxsen explains his title in the following manner: "The designation 'of Nazareth' is intended to bring out the fact that faith after Easter (faith in the risen Jesus) was no different in substance from the faith to which Jesus had already called me before Easter."[67] To say that the post-Easter faith of the disciples is "no different in substance" from their pre-Easter faith is as revealing as it is problematic, and it highlights the profound difference between two very different ways (functionalist and personalist) of appropriating resurrection language. We may begin illuminating this difference by first allowing Marxsen to describe more precisely the substance of Easter faith as he understands it: "*all of the evangelists want to show that the activity of Jesus goes on*. It goes on in spite of his death on the cross; and it remains the activity of the same Jesus who was active on earth."[68] We must take note here that the stress is on the continuity of Jesus' *activity*, not his person. Jesus' disciples continue "to do" after his death what Jesus "did" during his life: his mission "goes on," Jesus is "risen." "Jesus is risen in that his offer [of faith] meets us today and in that, if we accept it, he gives us this new life."[69] Only a functionalist interpretation of resurrection language permits Marxsen to make this rather odd statement: "I could equally well put it in this way: Jesus lived and gave a resurrection into new life even before his crucifixion. One could even say that Jesus was risen before he was crucified."[70] If this seems to get things backward, that is exactly the point. Jesus' "resurrection" is not what we have come to conventionally think. In fact, we are exhorted at the beginning of Marxsen's book to check the prejudices of the subsequent Christian tradition in order to appreciate with an open mind what the New Testament witness is really saying. Marxsen cites centuries of preaching and catechesis as clouding our vision, since they habitually tend to identify the core of Easter faith (Jesus' "cause" and "offer of faith") with its secondary metaphors and concepts ("ascension," "resurrection," "second-coming," etc.).[71] As he makes clear, or at least as clear as it apparently can be, belief in Jesus' resurrection is not the result of an encounter with the risen person of Jesus after his death, at least not an encounter that bears any sort of inter-subjective quality, certainly not in a way involving quasi-physical "appearances"; rather, Jesus' "resurrection" is a later interpretation and inference from the disciples' faith-experience that survives Jesus' death — "an inference derived from personal faith."[72] The "venture of faith" that Jesus of Nazareth offered during his life-ministry is "alive" even today. Hence, he is "risen." To be sure, the disciples were interpreting a miraculous reality, and so this is not to imply that Easter faith is fanciful projection plain and simple. But Marxsen emphasizes the precise nature of this reality: "the reality of *personal faith*. This reality was felt to be a miracle: here God was at work. In order, now, to express this divine activity — in order to hold fast to God's preeminent part in the birth of one's personal faith — it was interpreted with the help of the statement: Jesus is risen."[73]

If we describe this approach as "functionalist," we could as easily describe it as "expressivist." The reason is that Jesus' "resurrection," so interpreted, is a *function* of the disciples' faith, an interpretive *expression* about their (and our) faith, but in a way that says little or nothing about the post-Easter reality of Jesus himself. Marxsen presumes Jesus is "alive," it would seem, that he has survived death and is with God in some way. But this is as much as he is willing to suggest, doubtless because saying anything more would risk mythological thinking. In fact, Marxsen shows almost no concern for the personal destiny of Jesus. At times he seeks to account for something like Jesus' ongoing "presence," but it always falls short of any sense of subjective integrity and relationality, any sense of the risen One's alterity and sovereign presence. By reducing "resurrection" to the perpetuation of cause, the category of person is lost to functionality. Again, notice the way Marxsen describes the content of Easter faith as an inference from *my* faith, but in a way that works hard to avoid speaking of the post-Easter Jesus himself:

> For "Jesus is risen" simply means: today the crucified Jesus is calling us to believe.... How did people come to use this phraseology [of resurrection]? I do not think that this is very hard to understand. If (in whatever way) a man came to believe in Jesus after Good Friday, he knew himself to be called to faith by the same Jesus who performed an earthly ministry, who called men to faith, and who died on the cross. But if this Jesus was still *able* to call men to faith (and that he *was* able was clear from the reality of the believer's own faith) then it followed that he was not dead but alive. And that could be expressed by saying: "He is risen."[74]

Or, again:

> Jesus is dead. But *his* offer has not thereby lost its validity. That fact was experienced at the time and it can equally well be experienced today. Because the subject is *his* offer, I have tried to formulate this reality in the phrase "still he comes today."[75]

The logic seems to be thus: because faith survives Jesus' death, this can be expressed as his "resurrection," though this is not the only kind of expression adequate to carry the content of faith. The purpose of Easter kerygma, argues Marxsen, is not so much to pass along information about the status of Jesus. It is to awaken faith. And since Jesus offered this very faith before his death, he was "risen" before his death. "[T]he question of the resurrection of Jesus is not that of an event which occurred after Good Friday, but that of the earthly Jesus."[76]

By saying Jesus' "cause" persists after his death among his disciples — and that herein lies the substance of resurrection faith — Marxsen comes quite close to Bultmann's conflation of signified and signifier: Jesus is "risen into the kerygma." Both find resurrection language problematic as traditionally understood; and both deny that Easter can take on an "eventful" character independent of the subject's faith without resulting in mythology. But there remains a key difference between them. Whereas Bultmann prefers the kerygmatic Christ with little reference to the "historical Jesus," Marxsen prefers a Jesuology without much of a christology.[77] Bultmann identifies the "event" of resurrection in the preaching of the cross's saving efficacy, while Marxsen identifies the "event" of resurrection with the earthly Jesus' offer of faith and the perpetuation of his life-ministry.

But if this is all "Jesus is risen" means (Jesus' "offer of faith" or "cause" continues), not only is resurrection language shorn of all eschatological and personal content, which would make the expression a matter of equivocation and intellectual dishonesty if knowingly used in this way. It would indeed also be impossible to understand why it ever became indispensable for Christian discourse in the first place. Christianity is not a religion that simply includes within it *a* belief in resurrection. It is a "religion of resurrection."[78] Among the most problematic aspects of Marxsen's approach is his inability to account for the way resurrection language has historically and logically operated as the grammar for Christian faith. Though he acknowledges its historical importance, and though he admits that a Christian cannot totally dispense with it — apparently because of the sheer weight of almost two millennia of usage — he seeks to relativize it as just "one interpretation among others."[79] But it is just this view that cannot withstand historical and theological scrutiny.

Marxsen harnesses his position to a commonly repeated but never substantiated argument, viz., that the language of resurrection, almost as a matter of historical accident, only later won ascendancy over other viable kerygmatic expressions, such as Jesus' "exaltation," that emerged independently in the primitive Christian movement and do not presume

Jesus' post-mortem existence as being in any way bodily. Although the New Testament eventually harmonizes these various kerygmatic strands and metaphors in a way that clearly favors resurrection language, analysis reveals a much more complex and fluid process that led to this canonical preference. Pointing to the descent-ascent (*katabasis-anabasis*) motif preserved in John, Hebrews, and in particular the pre-Pauline Philippians hymn, where Jesus is said to have been "exalted" without explicitly mentioning resurrection, Marxsen concludes that resurrection language is interpretive only in a weak sense — it bears no essential connection with the content of Easter faith, at least no connection that is not sufficiently (and perhaps more fittingly) expressed in other ways.[80] The essence of Christian faith is that Jesus is "alive." The specific mode of Jesus' post-mortem existence is irrelevant. Only later, when resurrection language became more prominent, did the bodiliness of Jesus' aliveness become a preoccupation. This thesis gives Marxsen permission to opt for other expressive forms, particularly because resurrection language, with all the confusion it seems to conjure up for the imagination, especially its naïvely graphic and bodily aspects — telltale signs of mythology — tends to obscure the meaning of Easter for people today rather than illuminate it. "Once we recognize that originally the ideas familiar at any give time were used to express one and the same reality, it should be clear that we not only have the right but even the duty (if we want to be comprehensible *today*) to make this reality comprehensible — which means expressing it anew in *our* concepts."[81] Obviously this historical reconstruction is itself already committed to an expressivist view of language — where what is outwardly "expressed" or "objectivized" in conceptual-linguistic form is translatable into many other forms without altering the content, for the interior "experience" always remains the same.[82] This is quite evident as Marxsen writes:

> [The New Testament authors] came to believe in Jesus after Good Friday. They express this in pictorial terms. [This is what "myth" does, according to Bultmann.] But what they want to say is simply: "We have come to believe." Because they make this reality their starting-point they can externalize it in different ways, without feeling any contradiction thereby. It really is possible to visualize the same reality in different ways.[83]

Marxsen identifies a "faith experience" as the common core for the diverse kerygmatic forms and narratives in the New Testament. We are instructed to go behind the texts to properly interpret them. And because the faith experience of the disciples is available to us (we are utterly contemporaneous with the disciples), *our* quest for contemporary expressions is warranted, even if this might mean choosing alternatives to resurrection language for the sake of comprehensibility. What is more, because this experiential core remains constant between past and present, Marxsen can help the New Testament authors say more clearly what *they* really mean: "We have come to believe." "Jesus' cause continues." Incidentally, one wonders why the New Testament authors couldn't have said as much — or as little.

Aside from the dubious hermeneutics of going "behind" a text in order to retrieve its "essential" and "experiential" meaning — this, rather than reading "in front" of the text as it gives itself for meaning, a point to which we shall return later[84] — Marxsen's historical reconstruction is problematic in several ways. One can certainly accept that the New Testament is quite diverse, that a highly complex evolution and layering of traditions produce significant plurality within the canon. But the argument that resurrection language only comes later in that evolution, or that other kergymatic expressions like Jesus' "exaltation" emerged independently from resurrection language, has never been demonstrated, though it is frequently repeated. In point of fact, the thesis has been convincingly discredited by numerous critics who argue that resurrection language is very early, established in the tradition not as a matter of historical accident, or because it was the only anthropological-cosmological framework available to the earliest Christians to describe Jesus' postmortem existence.[85] It is early and well-established in the tradition because the events on the ground called for the kind of communicative and metaphorical work that only the language of resurrection could provide. Raymond Brown states quite frankly that Marxsen "is bending the evidence to fit a theory."[86] Having examined the very passages cited for evidence, Brown concludes as a matter of historical judgment (that is, before any considerations for contemporary meaning) "it is not really clear that any of the 'alternative' language for Jesus' victory over death existed in Christianity independently of a belief in Jesus' resurrection from the dead."[87] Brown further notes that the choice of resurrection "was not an inevitability for the early Jews who believed in Jesus," since there were several other options available to them. Its choice must therefore be explained, which is what Marxsen fails to do.[88] We must ask why, in the face of the massive challenge entailed in saying that this *one man* Jesus of Nazareth is *now* risen from the dead, the early Christians would adopt this peculiar expression. In the first century, among those who held a belief in the general resurrection of the dead (and not all Jewish groups did) no one anticipated that a single person would rise before everyone else, in the midst of a history still-in-the-making. If the purpose of the early Christians was simply to arouse faith, the proclamation of his resurrection would have been an extremely poor, even bizarre choice. Certainly not a ready-to-hand concept, the claim, if seriously maintained, would have presented more of a stumbling block than a rhetorical and metaphorical aid. If all they had wanted to say was Jesus' "cause" continues, they could have saved themselves a great deal of trouble by avoiding resurrection language altogether. (Paul in particular might have appreciated knowing this for all the effort expended in speaking of the "spiritual body" in 1 Corinthians 15.) May it be, then, that the stories of incredulity and misunderstanding recorded in the New Testament actually reveal something of the challenge that the disciples themselves had to face as they progressively came to terms with the kind of "event" they were interpreting? N. T. Wright is quite to the point:

> *The fact that dead people do not ordinarily rise is itself part of the early Christian belief,* not an objection to it. The early Christians insisted that what had happened to Jesus was precisely something new; was, indeed, the start of a whole new mode of existence, a new creation. The fact that Jesus' resurrection was, and remains, without analogy is not an objection to the early Christian claim. It is part of the claim itself.[89]

What the early Christians were saying was not simply that Jesus' offer of faith continues, or that his cause continues, but that the *person* Jesus of Nazareth continues. *He* lives. And because *he* lives, we too might live. Resurrection language is hopelessly disfigured if it is appropriated in a functionalist and expressivist way. Such would amount to imposing limiting "conditions of the possibility" on what is actually given. Resurrection language requires that we speak of *persons,* of *bodies.* What is given in Jesus' resurrection is the im-possible Gift of his person, the offer of an eschatologically transfigured body. Only a basic misunderstanding of Easter can propose to separate Jesus' function (what he "does") from Jesus' person (who he "is"). To say "Jesus is risen" means, quite precisely, the indissoluble unity of act and identity. The perpetuation of his cause is forever bound up with the inexhaustible gift of his person, and vice versa. Resurrection language operates grammatically for Christian faith, for by binding together the "cause" of Jesus with his "person" in the closest possible unity, it establishes the parameters within which Christian discourse may authentically unfold, which affirms that Jesus *is*

God's offer of salvation. Jesus' resurrection is axial, a gravitational force for all christological statements.[90]

Just what are the events, then, that would invite, no, demand the earliest Christians to use resurrection language? What would compel them to say "He is risen" when such a statement could only gain assent through an extensive process of conversion in speech and imagination? Why should they adopt a turn of phrase so vulnerable to falsification through the production of Jesus' corpse or skeleton?[91] (After all, belief in the resurrection in the first century meant the transformation of *bodies*.) And why, if one could use resurrection language metaphorically to describe the ongoing cause of an important prophetic figure, was it not predicated of John the Baptist by his disciples? (Jesus of Nazareth was hardly the only candidate for such language by Marxsen's own standards.) The answer to these questions is very simple: the earliest Christians actually believed that a profoundly new "event" took place after Jesus' death. The shocking *absence* of a body and the surprising *self-attestation* of the crucified Nazarene together led the disciples into a process of saying something they knew was intensely challenging to understand: "He is risen; he is not here." The character of the event itself created the conditions of the possibility for such language.

Even a superficial reading of the New Testament reveals that *because* "Jesus is risen" there is faith — not the other way around. One is certainly entitled to disagree that an eschatological "event" after Jesus' death took place, but only with exegetical violence can one conclude that the New Testament itself is not fundamentally interested in what happens to Jesus after Good Friday. If we can agree that saying "Jesus is risen" is an interpretive faith-claim, and thus not an objective event "out there" observable from just any perspective, we must be willing to recognize that the *prima facie* testimony of the New Testament, no matter how pluriform its narratives and metaphors, is unified in its proclamation that something new and radical occurs after Jesus' death, and that Christian faith, while ever remaining in continuity with the pre-Easter Jesus, is also transformed and given new content and form by it. The *manner* of Jesus' aliveness, far from being accidental to the Easter event, was crucially important to provide perspective on the far-reaching scope of the divine action involved. To say "resurrection" was to say something far more specific and consequential than that Jesus was "alive to God." It was a way to say that the totality of his concretely lived existence (his "body") is transformed; the power of death has been overcome; God's promise of salvation is now being accomplished; the condition of personal and social exile is over.

HISTORY *IN EXCESS*

To conclude this chapter we can now more formally state in what way Jesus' resurrection from the dead is a "historical event." We may put it this way: Jesus' resurrection *is* and *is not* a historical event. Or better, it is *both* a historical *and* more-than-historical event, where the "more-than" means transcendent-yet-inclusive of history. Speaking of the resurrection in this way requires simultaneous acts of saying and un-saying, a balancing and ceaseless succession of affirmations and denials.

As for the former, Jesus' resurrection must be affirmed as *historical* in at least two senses. First, when we affirm Jesus' "resurrection," we are saying that his entire embodied-historical existence is fulfilled, transformed into its ultimate finality. Such an act is God's definitive vindication of Jesus of Nazareth — his historical life and ministry in all its particularity, its concrete reality and form. By raising him from the dead, God has inaugurated the fulfillment of universal history. The Easter event causes the reality it signifies — the fulfillment of creation, the eschatological realization of embodied life — and so stands at the center of any Christian theology of history. Were Jesus' resurrection to be regarded as a non- or a-historical event, one that has nothing to do with Jesus' embodied history (there is no "history" for human beings that is not embodied), then the continued use of "resurrection" language would be quite misleading, fatally severed from the semantic field of its original proclamation. In short, Christianity affirms the salvation *of* history and *of* the body, not *from* them.

Second, if Jesus' resurrection is historical in the above sense, it must also generate a history of effects. If it did not, it would remain unknown and irrelevant. Like an underwater seismic event producing waves expanding in every direction, the Easter event leaves traces upon and within history, beginning with those events associated with the disciples' coming to faith — the discovery of the empty tomb and the various encounters with the risen and self-attesting Christ — and continuing its widening impact through the emergence of diverse ecclesial communities formed by worship, proclamation, and ethical praxis. Though we should not equate this extending history of effects with the original and originating reality of Jesus' resurrection (as Bultmann does with the *kerygma* and Marxsen with Jesus' ongoing "cause"), such effects should not be regarded as merely epiphenomenal, but co-constitutive of resurrection faith.

On the other side of this affirmative language we must also speak in denials, saying that Jesus' resurrection *is not a historical event* (or, is a "more-than-historical" event), and this for at least two reasons. First, because it stands as the inauguration of God's eschatological transformation *of* history, and so is God's sovereign action *upon* history, Jesus' resurrection cannot be regarded as simply one among other historical events. Though intimately related to all of history as its inmost promise and goal, it cannot be plotted within a continuum of events, but enfolds history within itself just as it supercedes it. As the proleptic disclosure of history's ultimate end, it saturates any single moment or horizon within history. It is *sui generis,* irreducibly unique in its eventfulness. As Karl Rahner puts it, Jesus' resurrection cannot be, nor intends to be, *a* historical event, for "otherwise it would not be the assumption of the fruit of our ongoing history into its final and definitive state."[92] It is, after all, a rupturing through the chasm between being and non-being. Jesus is not "resuscitated" so as to extend his personal existence within time's course, but is risen *from* the dead, and thus from time's contingency and futility, as its "Lord" (Acts 2:36; Phil. 2:9–11).

Secondly, because of the *sui generis* character of Jesus' resurrection, those historical signs pointing to and disclosing it cannot do so exhaustively, but only as traces of an event exceeding their manifestory power.[93] The oral and textual traditions associated with the empty tomb and appearances may be submitted to critical analysis, of course, but their testimonial capacity remains saturated, and so destabilized, by the transcendent reality inspiring them. This does not grant theologians a pass to evade historical inquiry, as some have charged theologians of doing (an "eschatological proviso"); but the necessary conclusion to be drawn, once Easter is granted its eschatological character, is that no historical testimony, and thus no historical analysis of that historical testimony, will be able to coincide with its ultimate referent. Thus, and perhaps paradoxically, a more faithful and authentic historical testimony to the eschatological presence of the risen Christ will self-efface just as it declares, will un-say in the midst of its saying, will renounce linguistic, conceptual, and ideological objectification in the midst of its proclamation. That is to say, as it makes present and near, it will do so while manifesting absence and distance.

Herein lays the gift and wisdom of the empty tomb and appearance narratives in their extant form and complexity. While it has become customary to treat these narratives, when critically examined individually or together, as posing a historical "problem," we ought rather to consider the way they are disclosive of "mystery." The historical *aporia* to which they testify and in some way impart may provoke the need to explain, which is typically the approach taken in critical-historical analysis (and even much fundamental/systematic theology) today; but it is possible, and far more illuminating, to "read off" this historical *aporia*, to think from it and with it as it gives itself to thought, rather than regarding it as something to master or ignore. Another way to present the thesis is to say the following: *precisely in their ambiguities, swerves, and paradoxes — and not despite them — are the empty tomb and appearance narratives revelatory of a "presence" whose eschatological character also presents itself as "absence," an absence that does not imply a lack in givenness, but an excess that cannot be measured or contained by its historical testimony.* Approaching the New Testament witness in this way requires a hermeneutics of hospitality rather than one of unrelenting suspicion. It requires a contemplative attitude that would allow the given "to be," a beholding of the given *as it gives itself*. In a word, it requires a phenomenological approach.

Chapter Two

THE IM-POSSIBLE GIFT

But silence is ordered to that final utterance. It is not an end in itself.
　Our whole life is a meditation of our last decision — the only decision that matters.
　And we meditate in silence. Yet we are bound to some extent, to speak to others, to help them see their way to their own decision, to teach them Christ. In teaching them Christ, our very words teach them a new silence: the silence of the Resurrection. In that silence they are formed and prepared so that they also may speak what they have. "I have believed, therefore have I spoken" (Ps. 115:1).
　　　　　　　— Thomas Merton, *Thoughts in Solitude*[1]

But just as the death that is refused according to the justice of love matures into Resurrection, so silence nourishes infinite proclamation.　　— Jean-Luc Marion, *The Idol and Distance*[2]

Remarkably, at the most dramatic moment in their narrative accounts, the gospels remain perfectly silent. No omniscient voice, no objective portrayal, no imaginary dramatization: God *raising* Jesus from the dead is never actually described.

This is a most telling silence.

The beginning of resurrection faith comes by way of encounter, as a surprising disclosure in the midst of an unintelligible and unspeakable vacuum. The crucified-and-risen One "appears" (*ophthe*). By his own free initiative Jesus manifests himself to the grieving women at the grave, to a misunderstanding Peter, to a skeptical Thomas, to the bewildered travelers to Emmaus, to a violently zealous Saul. Grief is met with alarming joy, panic with disarming peace. Incredulity is replaced with personal assurance, confusion with insight, sin with forgiveness: in a word, absence with a new presence. And yet, this new presence only deepens the absence. For as often as the risen One is recognized as the selfsame Jesus of Nazareth he is misidentified. The women at the empty tomb are said by Mark to be alarmed at what they see — or what they do not see. "Terror and amazement" seize them. In Luke's Emmaus story, just as the disciples "see" the risen One in the breaking of the bread with the stranger, the stranger is recognized only to suddenly disappear from their sight. John's account includes Mary Magdalene's confusion with the gardener, of all things. And upon his final commission to the disciples in Matthew, the risen Christ promises to be with them until the end of the age and forthwith parts from them, "ascending" into heaven from their view.

Resurrection faith is never one of pure immediacy. Not only do the readers of the gospels never gain the absolute perspective of seeing Jesus *being raised* from the dead in the darkness of the tomb, but those who are witnesses to Jesus' appearances experience an overwhelming presence which also, and for that very reason, is an absence — a seeing which is a not-seeing. Always in the structure of resurrection belief and language is there appearance and empty tomb, identity and non-identity, fulfillment and subversion of desire. To properly speak of the resurrection requires a certain skill in saying and un-saying. The emptiness of the tomb inspires a speechlessness, but one that does not merely reflect a lack of something to say. The absence of Jesus' body generates a superabundance of speech. Jesus' "transfigured body" induces the transfiguration of language itself. There is no Christian discourse without the primal, twofold proclamation: "He has been raised; he is not here" (Mark 16:6).

◆ ◆ ◆

This chapter approaches the resurrection narratives with a phenomenological style of reading, by which I mean a style of reading that allows the narratives "to be" or to "give themselves" in the manner of their actual givenness, as revelatory narratives that do not simply carry an inner content of information that can be extracted from its form, but as textual traces of a revelatory event that manifests itself in such a way that the form of its self-presentation is inextricably bound up with its content. We resist the dominant tendency to go behind or underneath the narratives in order to unearth a substrate that might provide an explanation for their extant shape. Instead we intend to "read off" their complexities, ambiguities, and swerves under the assumption that their present form communicates a reality in a mode uniquely suited to that reality. If I describe this as a phenomenological style of reading, we need not have in our minds an overly systematic method for its execution. Surely I do not mean by this some sort of "objective" reading that presumes to bracket out the interpreting subject. I am not suggesting that the following approach is the purest or most orthodox way to read the resurrection narratives. All I am attempting to achieve in this process is the expansion of the rather narrow aperture through which we are accustomed to approaching something like the empty tomb and appearance narratives. The following is an experiment designed to put in question our a priori assumptions about what we think in advance is possible or intelligible. I am invoking an act of intellectual purgation in order "to see" that which can only be seen when we become attitudinally hospitable to what is Other. Of course, some may think that the following represents an act of calculated obfuscation, so that by producing smoke and mirrors we could commend almost anything to be believed. I cannot concern myself with that particular criticism here, except to say this: it is of the very nature of the resurrection of Jesus Christ from the dead that we have no stable analogy or historical precedent to help us gain mastery over it. It is the condition of its own possibility; or rather, it is an im-possible Gift that can only be received in faith. The rigor of our task here is not to think behind this Gift by building up a structure of plausibility around it that fits rather comfortably with what we have already come to expect. Our task is to think *with* the Gift, to be responsive *to* it, to allow thought itself to become pierced by the mystery of divine love that takes the form of a risen body.

I will proceed by first invoking recent trends in phenomenology, particularly the work of French philosopher Jean-Luc Marion, to consider the ways Jesus' resurrection from the dead is the "saturated phenomenon" *par excellence*, i.e., an event which exceeds the cognitive-linguistic capacities of the subject, an event which appears simultaneously in the mode of "presence" and "absence," as that which reveals in the mode of concealment. We shall consider the saturated phenomenon of the resurrection under four major aspects:

1. *The resurrection is the unexpected ("unforeseeable") fulfillment of salvation history; it serves as the climax of Israel's story, and indeed, the climax of the story of creation, but it does so with a surprising twist.* "Resurrection" is the language the earliest Christians used to speak of the Easter event; and yet, while this language is deeply rooted in the grammar of the Hebrew scriptures, the way the earliest Christians used this language evidences radical novelty. Jesus' resurrection both fulfills yet transforms the language and expectations of the people of Israel.

2. *The empty tomb and appearance narratives together establish a phenomenology of Christian experience by showing that the risen Jesus (who is "unbearable") becomes "present" in the mode of "absence."* The revelatory event of Easter is "unbearable" — it saturates or overwhelms the perceptual horizons of those who are its witnesses. As presented in the canonical narratives, Jesus is both identifiable and a stranger, tactile and transcendent, intimately involved in history yet never something to be domesticated or grasped. This "both-and" structure forever constitutes Christian language as a ceaseless modulation between saying and un-saying ("He has been raised; he is not here"); and it is precisely this structure that corresponds with the eschatological ("trans-historical") character of the Easter event.

3. *Because the Easter event transgresses our linguistic and conceptual capacities for representation ("unnamable"), testimony to it will necessarily be pluralistic: the Easter event pluralizes our horizons.* Hence, the diversity in the New Testament canon, which results in (creative) tensions between the narratives, is not the result of a lack but an eschatological fullness.

4. *The resurrection of Jesus is not something that can be apprehended by a self-constituting subject ("unconstitutable"); rather, it is an event whose beholding transforms the human person into a "new creation" within the body of Christ.* The resurrection is radically self-involving, and this involvement implies the reformation of desires and habits within a living community. This community is ecclesial.

THE "SATURATED PHENOMENON"

I now return to the observation C. F. Evans makes in his study of the resurrection. Noting the "almost fortuitous character" of the traditions that support the central message of the New Testament, Evans conjectures that the Easter event, whatever kind of "event" it was, must have been the sort to give rise to these traditions in their present form at whatever distance.[3] To restate this conjecture in the form of a question, I ask: What is it about Jesus' resurrection that would generate the kinds of historical, textual, and conceptual complexities we actually find in the New Testament? Is there something about the peculiar character of the New Testament witness that is uniquely disclosive of the kind of event that Easter purports to be? Put simply, what is the relationship between the *form* and *content* of resurrection proclamation?

Reginald Fuller astutely observes that the silence and timidity found in the resurrection narratives, particularly in their resistance to pictorially portray Jesus being raised from the dead, is appropriate to the eschatological event they nevertheless proclaim. Precisely because it "took place at the boundary between history and meta-history, between this age and the age to come," the resurrection "as such cannot be narrated but only proclaimed." In itself, the resurrection is "not accessible to witnesses," for any witness "would have still been standing within history, and that which is at the end of history is not open to direct observation."[4] It can therefore be known only by "indirect revelatory disclosure within history."[5] If it were objectively narrated, as the late first-century *Ascension of Isaiah* and second-century apocryphal *Gospel of Peter* do, the narratives would then more tidily fall into the category of myth.[6] But passing over in silence the "event" of Jesus' resurrection, and withstanding perhaps the strong temptation to fill in the unnerving gap, the New Testament witness already stands "demythologized." It only narrates the arousal to faith through the discovery of the empty tomb and the encounters with the already risen Christ. Resurrection faith is therefore never one of pure immediacy, but one of "mediated immediacy." It comes by way of "eschatological signs" and apostolic testimony.

The silence in the gospels certainly reflects a withdrawal, a historical absence, an inability to gain perspective and lay hold of "it" like a quasi-object; but in no way does this silence signify a simple absence or deficiency of phenomenality. The silence reflects the "dazzling darkness" of a hyper-givenness, not the endless desert of non-givenness. Words cannot finally say it, images cannot re-present it, narratives cannot fully render it. Jesus' resurrection is *sui generis*.[7] It is a "God-sized event," one which "none better or greater could be conceived."[8] It is the *novum ultimum*, the ultimate new thing.[9] Or, as the New Testament puts it, Jesus' resurrection is a "new creation." We may also speak of it as Gift, as the "saturated phenomenon" *par excellence*. Here I enlist the work of Jean-Luc Marion whose study of givenness and sketches of saturated phenomena will prove helpful in exploring the eschatological signs of Jesus' resurrection, i.e., how they are uniquely disclosive of a "presence" that, in its eschatological (excessive) givenness, remains "absent" from the witnesses whose capacity for representation remains saturated.[10]

In setting up a strategy for sketching the characteristics of saturated phenomena, Marion adopts Kant's categories of quantity, quality, relation, and modality to show how each becomes overexposed. A broader concern for Marion is to show how the a priori conditions for experience and thought in Kant's philosophy (and by extension much modern thought) are too restrictive to account for phenomena that, rather than conforming to the subject's power of knowing, greatly exceed it. Marion is troubled by how the "turn to the subject" so frequently valorizes the knowable over the un-known, the visible over the in-visible, the objectifiable over the non-objectifiable, the conditions of the possibility over the im-possible.

The saturated phenomenon, according to Marion, refers to "the impossibility of attaining knowledge of an object, comprehension in the strict sense," not "from a *deficiency* in the giving intuition, but from its *surplus*, which neither concept, signification, nor intention can foresee, organize, or contain."[11] As a result of its excessive givenness to perception and intuition, the saturated phenomenon makes definitive and stable conceptualization impossible.[12] It is always "more than," disclosive of a depth dimension or in-visibility that cannot be fully grasped by the subject's objectifying intentionality. Such phenomena would require rethinking the "subject" as our primary starting point — particularly its pretension to self-constitution and conceptual mastery — and to begin instead with the givenness of phenomena as they give themselves to intuition.[13]

But what phenomena might we imagine as saturating the subject in this way? Kant himself provides an initial clue with the experience of the beautiful. Whereas Kant typically regards intuition the weaker in arriving at conceptual knowledge, aesthetic experience is said to engulf the power of thought so that the "representation of the imagination furnishes much to think, but to which no determinate thought, or concept, can be adequate."[14] Marion comments: "The impossibility of the concept arranging this disposition comes from the fact that the intuitive overabundance no longer succeeds in exposing itself in a priori rules, whatever they might be, but rather submerges them. Intuition is no longer exposed in the concept; it saturates it and renders it overexposed — invisible, unreadable not by lack, but indeed by an excess of light."[15]

Take the example of listening to music. In the opening moments of Mozart's "Jupiter" Symphony, even though the listener has settled in to enjoy the musical performance, and while the listener may already be quite familiar with the piece, the first reception of its givenness to the senses is truly magical. A sudden upsurge of intuition floods comprehension and leaves the listener without the ability to fully comprehend, though the effect is delight. The "sonorous mass...comes upon me and submerges me," leaving me "belated" to the "deployment of this becoming."[16] The actual event of music is always surprising, something I cannot fully anticipate. It is something to which I respond and follow. "I" am not coincident with the piece as listener but a witness to its givenness. To be sure, I discern patterns and intelligence. I follow the musical story it tells through tonal and temporal tensions and resolutions. Without being able to describe it in the least, the piece of music may be remarkably satisfying in its supreme musical sense. It is not unintelligible but inexhaustibly intelligible. It generates much greater intuition than I can possibly objectify through concepts and words. Herein lays the delight of its astonishing, beautiful unfolding. I am "caught up" in the piece, "outside" of my self in ek-stasis. What is occurring is an event in which I am transported. In the "play" of music I am moved to a kind of "self-forgetfulness," with self-forgetfulness being the "positive possibility of being wholly with something else."[17]

Or consider the event of beholding the beautiful form presented in painting. Although it may be possible to consider a painting as a "thing," made up of elements like wood, gold leafing, canvas, paint, and so forth, it is not primarily the painting's thingness in which the beauty consists. The beautiful form does not present itself as merely something ready-to-hand, an object for instrumental use, but gives itself as an appearing of unsuspected depth. Beauty discloses itself in the visible but never as strictly visible or completely objectifiable. It remains in-visible in its "crossing of the visible":

> [T]o see it as a painting, in its own phenomenality of the beautiful, I must of course apprehend it as a thing (subsisting, ready-to-hand), but it is precisely not this that opens it to me as beautiful; it is that I "live" its meaning, namely its beautiful appearing, which has nothing like to it, since it cannot be described as the property of a thing, demonstrated by reasons, or hardly even be said. What is essential — the beautiful appearing — remains unreal, an "I know not what," that I must seek, await, touch, but which is not comprehensible.[18]

The beautiful, writes David Bentley Hart, is objective, not in the sense that it concerns "things," but in its precedence to the response it evokes. "There is an overwhelming givenness in the beautiful, and it is discovered in astonishment, in an awareness of something fortuitous, adventitious, essentially indescribable; it is known only in the moment of response, from the position of one already addressed and able now only to reply."[19]

Beauty appears in "distance," or better, it *gives* distance. What is beautiful opens up a space for its inexhaustible beholding, an infinity of perspectives. "And because the surplus of 'meaning' in the beautiful consists in and urges attention toward this infinite content of distance, it allows for ceaseless supplementation: it is always unmoored, capable of disrupting stable hierarchies of interpretation, of inspiring endless departures and returns, and of calling for repetition and variation; it releases a continual distribution of meaning across the distance."[20]

But what seems exceptional here, at least in terms of saturating the conceptual and linguistic capacities of the subject, is quite paradigmatic. Take for example a well-known and important event of recent history, the First World War. Marion wants us to consider that determining the cause of this war and securing its meaning in an act of total comprehension is not possible. There is no shortage of generative factors or means to explore them — geographic, demographic, economic, technological, ideological, psychosocial, etc. "Troops of archivists and the curious have elaborated information; squads of researches have treated it and organized it into objects; generations of historians have interpreted it in terms of so many causes and systems of possible and often probable causes." And yet it is "precisely this overabundance that forbids assigning it a cause, and even forbids understanding it through a combination of causes." This is not to say that World War I prohibits all analysis and understanding, as though we should stop reflecting upon it in our narrations of history. Marion does not suggest that "explanation" is illicit; but it can always be supplemented and further revised. Explanation never finally grasps the event. Even when, in an act of retrospection, we come to see patterns that appear to converge towards the war's actual irruption, and thus understand it in terms of a network of causes, the actual irruption of the war and the concrete shape it took could never be predicted or calculated. Its "irrepressible bursting into the tranquil air of popular enthusiasm in the summer of 1914 does not arise from its causes to come, but from itself, from its unpredictable landing and its incident."[21] Only subsequent to its eventfulness may one respond with inquiry and interpretation. And even then inquiry and interpretation never succeed in finally coinciding with the event it seeks to understand. The event saturates the capacities of thought and representation through an ever-emergent complexity of perspectives and meanings. One is reminded here of Leo Tolstoy's postscript to *War and Peace,* perhaps the most imaginative attempt to understand war in literature:

Why did millions of people begin to kill one another? Who told them to do it? It would seem that it was clear to each of them that this could not benefit any of them, but would be worse for them all. Why did they do it? Endless retrospective conjectures can be made, and are made, of the causes of this senseless event, but the immense number of these explanations, and their concurrence in one purpose, only proves that the causes were innumerable and that not one of them deserves to be called the cause.[22]

There are many other examples of saturated phenomena Marion examines in his works, including memory, birth, death, the experience of one's own body, erotic love, and the interpretation of a text. But we should briefly consider one more, since it strikes important ethical keys.

Drawing upon the work of Emmanuel Levinas, Marion shows how the encounter with another person, "the face" of the Other, is saturating in its givenness. Visible yet in-inexhaustible in its irreducible depth, the face of the Other (his or her *alterity*) breaks in upon my egoic self-sameness (*ipseity*) and calls me to hospitality and responsibility. The Other is no objectifiable thing, something to be comprehended within a conceptual category such as humanity, society, ethnicity, gender, or nationality. To reduce the Other to strict visibility or comprehension in this way constitutes an act of violence. Persons are not "things," "commodities," or "parts" within a broader totality. The Other is an unsubstitutable revelation, illimitable and irrepressible in his or her self-gift. The Other reverses my gaze in a "counter-experience." In beholding the Other, I see one who sees *me*, as thus one who returns my gaze through different eyes. Here I am not a self-constituting "subject" regarding some "object," but a "witness" to an Other who calls me into an ethical relationship. "For as face, he faces me, imposes on me to face up to him as he for whom I must respond....I have received (and suffered) a call *[un appel]*. The face makes an appeal *[un appel]*; it therefore calls me forth as gifted."[23] My very sense of self is in fact given to me by the Other. My "being" is a "being given." The pretension to immediate self-presence is an illusion. I encounter myself only in mediation, in a multitude of face-to-face relations with Others who call me from the confines of egoic existence. Despite our persistent efforts to think of ourselves in terms of a transcendental ego gazing upon the world from a position of nowhere, the order of manifestation which phenomenological research unveils shows again and again that *alterity* precedes and radically conditions every sense of "mineness."

THE RESURRECTION AS "SATURATED PHENOMENON"

Although much more could be said about Marion's sketches of saturated phenomena, we now turn to an examination of Jesus' resurrection and its eschatological signs by adopting Marion's fourfold analysis. Accordingly, the resurrection of Jesus from the dead is the saturated phenomenon *par excellence* in being unforeseeable, unbearable, unnamable, and unconstitutable by the subject.[24]

In contrast with approaches to the resurrection that proceed from a predetermined foundation that sets forth what is historically possible, intelligible, or existentially meaningful in advance, we proceed here with what might be described as a hermeneutics of hospitality, by which I mean a style of reading that seeks to prioritize the given. To borrow from Paul Ricoeur, I am opting for a strategy that rather than going *behind* the text to find some sort of historical substrate or causal explanation that accords with the pre-understanding of the reader *stands in front of the text* and allows it to propose a world we might inhabit.[25] "As a reader, I find myself only by losing myself.... The metamorphosis of the world in play is also the playful metamorphosis of the ego."[26] Such a strategy does not pretend to be neutral, as though we could wrest ourselves from all presuppositions. Rather, it serves as an attempt, however tentative and experimental, to allow the phenomenon of Jesus' resurrection to give itself in the play of textual presence and absence, to allow the narratives to appear as "traces" or textual analogues of an event that both saturates and summons the reader to become a "witness" and, perhaps, a "new self" — a "new creation."

Unforeseeable: The Resurrection as Unexpected Fulfillment

Jesus' resurrection is the fulfillment of salvation history, the eschatological fruition of creation. And yet Easter does not always conform to prior expectations. Its truth comes by way of transforming our expectations, by opening up hitherto unknown horizons of possibility and meaning. The revelation of the risen victim is a reality to which we must accustom ourselves. It summons *us*. It offers new expectations and desires. What it would teach us is something we cannot fully grasp on our own, even if we may glean aspects of it here and there. To put a fine point on it, the resurrection of Jesus from the dead is something we must *learn*. The gospels consistently present Jesus' appearances as events that catch their recipients off guard, in various modes of misunderstanding, surprise, and sometimes fear. However much enthusiasm attended the early Christian

The Im-possible Gift

proclamation "He is risen; he is not here," its initial in-breaking upon the hearts and minds of Jesus' earliest followers came as a jolt that initiated a shift in understanding. This shift is evident in the story of scripture itself. Though eventually regarded by Christians as the fulfillment of salvation history (the ultimate antitype to the exodus), the irruption of Easter was not wholly foreseeable but only subsequently seen as "necessary." As Marion puts it: "The phenomenon of Christ gives itself intuitively as an event that is perfectly unforeseeable because radically heterogeneous to what it nevertheless completes (the prophecies)."[27]

In Accordance with the Scriptures?

The earliest Christians regarded the resurrection of Jesus as the fulfillment of the scriptures. "He was raised on the third day in accordance with the scriptures" (1 Cor. 15:4). The New Testament portrays Easter in the broadest and richest terms possible: as nothing less than the "culmination of the Biblical story of human captivity and God's deliverance."[28] The stories of creation, exodus, and covenant together form the matrix out of which resurrection language would emerge. Jesus' resurrection is described as the "new creation," the new and final exodus from the powers of sin and death, God's eschatological salvation. It therefore makes sense within an existing framework of meaning. It is "in accordance with the scriptures."

However, Jesus' resurrection is not quite foreseeable within this matrix. It is not the inexorable outcome of a prior narrative context. Neither is its meaning exhausted by the preceding metaphorical elements that nevertheless help us to make sense of it. The centrality of the resurrection in the New Testament is "in some respects puzzling," notes Evans. "There is no straight road here from the Old Testament to the New."[29] The centrality of the resurrection in the New Testament makes the relative absence of resurrection symbolism in the Old Testament quite surprising. In contrast to the numerous Old Testament passages adduced for establishing prophetic connections with Jesus' birth and death, the New Testament writers use very little scriptural argumentation for demonstrating his resurrection as the fulfillment of (predictive) prophecy, undoubtedly because there are only a few passages in the Old Testament that speak of the resurrection of the dead, and only one unequivocally (Daniel 12).[30] This is not to suggest that the New Testament presents Jesus' resurrection as an extraneous feature of Israel's original hope, quite the contrary. But as the early Christians searched the scriptures for illuminating the meaning of this *novum ultimum* in terms of creation, exile, and restoration, they were very much reinterpreting these terms from the new perspective given by this *novum ultimum*. The resurrection established for them a new hermeneutic that helped them to creatively re-envision the governing plot of the Jewish scriptures.[31]

To help explain the shift in emphasis from the Old to the New Testament, scholars quite naturally search for mediating influences from the apocalyptic literature of the Old Testament and several intertestamental writings. The metaphor of "rising" or "being raised," taken from the ordinary experience of "waking up" from sleep, became code for God's vindication of the persecuted righteous in particular and the restoration of Israel from exile in general. As in Daniel, written in response to the horrific mid-second-century persecutions of Jews during the reign of Antiochus IV, these writings use resurrection language to speak of a counter-factual hope in the midst of personal and national crisis. God's vindication of the martyrs who died defending their faith and the judgment of their oppressors constitute the dual focus. The resurrection of the dead here becomes the precondition for God's final judgment:

> At that time Michael, the great prince, the protector of your people, shall arise. There shall be a time of anguish, such as has never occurred since nations first came into existence. But at that time your people shall be delivered, everyone who is found written in the book. Many of those who sleep in the dust of the earth shall awake, some to everlasting life, and some to shame and everlasting contempt. Those who are wise shall shine like the brightness of the sky, and those who lead many to righteousness, like the stars forever and ever. (Dan. 12:1–3)

One of the uniquely apocalyptic features of this portrayal is the shift from a "horizontal" to a more "vertical" hope in which God's triumph is no longer primarily one over Israel's pagan enemies in history but the establishment of a new order of reality for the righteous beyond death — a "cosmic restoration."[32] Though this hope was ultimately rooted in a trust in Israel's creator God as faithful and just, the context of national crisis and the (sometimes extreme) violence of this time gave resurrection language a fiercely conflictual structure. As we shall see in chapter 5 more clearly, this dynamic of counter-factuality will greatly influence the early Christian proclamation of Jesus' resurrection as God's *vindication* of the righteous sufferer. This vindication motif provides a crucial foundation for affirming divine justice in the face of innocent suffering and injustice. However, it is important to observe the striking metamorphoses of meaning when we compare early Christian proclamation to the apocalyptic eschatology that helped to inspire it. I will briefly mention three of the most significant.

First, Jesus' resurrection is not merely the precondition for God's judgment of the righteous and unrighteous but the very content of God's offer of universal salvation. As Edward Schillebeeckx explains, the resurrection of the crucified Jesus is the shape of our salvation, the concrete realization of God's reconciliation with humanity:

> The difference between the New Testament and late Jewish ideas of resurrection is immediately obvious. Jesus' resurrection is a saving act *per se*, not a condition for appearing alive before God's throne in order to be judged. His resurrection itself is interpreted directly as the "amen" of God upon the person of Jesus. Even in the older, non-apocalyptic books of the Old Testament we hear of a resurrection that is a salvific event, but then in a spiritual sense (the "resurrection of the people of Israel," Isa. 26:19; 25:8). The idea of Jesus' bodily resurrection is more akin to that than to the apocalyptic, neutral concept of resurrection. "Resurrection" is God's eschatological, saving activity, accomplished in Jesus.[33]

In Part Two I shall explain in much greater detail just how and why Jesus' resurrection could be thought of in this way. But here I wish to point out a second shift in meaning which provides a preview.

If Jesus' resurrection is the vindication of a victim and divine *judgment* upon those "principalities and powers" that wreak havoc in the world — this is the apocalyptic motif in essence — it is also, quite remarkably, an offer of *forgiveness* to those responsible for Jesus' death. The murdered victim returns to his oppressors as their savior, as God's concrete gesture of reconciliation with the whole of humanity. The fundamental shift in meaning here is that the dialectical opposition between victim and victimizer found in much apocalyptic eschatology, and which at a certain level is preserved within Christian proclamation insofar as Easter announces with striking clarity God's justice for victims, is transformed through a counter-intuitive twist. The combative structure of apocalyptic that would keep the "righteous" and "unrighteous" poles apart has been subverted through a gracious offer which fundamentally reconstitutes the relationship. The victim has now become the oppressor's ultimate hope and salvation. The violence that locks victims and victimizers into endless spirals of recrimination has been thwarted by an *excess*. Retribution has given way to eschatological hospitality. This is not to suggest, incidentally, that no resources existed in the Old Testament to support this vision, on the contrary. As we shall see in chapters 7 and 8 especially, there are many thematic lines that shape the Easter proclamation in profound ways. Here too Jesus' resurrection should be understood as "in accordance with the scriptures." On the other hand, the New Testament makes a truly unforeseeable claim: God has become *our* victim in order to save us from the death-dealing totality in which we have enclosed ourselves. God has become radically self-involved in our plight, deigning to become one of us in order to release us from the cyclical violence and scapegoating to which we are subjected and in which we are complicit. We have made God our victim, but through the tenacious love of the resurrection God has returned to us to offer a new economy of relations based upon self-donation — the im-possible Gift — revealing to us once and for all that peace, not violence, is original to creation.

The third major transformation comes with the affirmation that one person has *already* been raised prior to the general resurrection. Of course, we should recall from the previous chapter that no uniform eschatology prevailed that would make resurrection language an inevitable choice among Christians when speaking of Jesus' post-mortem fate. First-century Judaism was quite diverse. The resurrection of the dead was an expectation among some Jewish groups, but not all. The dispute recorded in the gospels between Jesus and the Sadducees makes this clear (Mark 12:18–27; Matt. 22:23–33; Luke 20:27–40). Some groups, particularly those more thoroughly influenced by Greek thought and culture, anticipated a disembodied existence after death. Philo of Alexandria's blending of Jewish and Greek thought provides a clear preference for "immortality" over "resurrection" in matters eschatological. Still other groups, such as the Pharisees, looked forward to a general resurrection of the dead — a re-embodied existence that included a new physical creation. However, little to no thought was given to the notion of a single person being raised from the dead within the midst of history. The belief in resurrection was a matter of general eschatology. It concerned the resurrection of all the dead at the end of the age (*anastasis nekron*), not one person *from* the dead before the end of the age (*anastasis ek nekron*). "For if the dead are not raised, neither has Christ been raised" (1 Cor. 15:16). Here we see Paul drawing upon his previous hope as a Pharisee to illuminate the nature of Jesus' post-mortem existence. And yet the mutation in meaning is striking as he immediately adds, "and if Christ has not been raised, your faith is vain; you are still in your sins" (v. 17). Jesus has *already* been raised — something not foreseen within any eschatological hope — and this is God's definitive pledge of salvation. "For just as in Adam all die, so too in Christ shall

all be brought to life" (v. 22). Every eschatological horizon is fulfilled in, yet reshaped by, the singular event of Jesus' resurrection. Pheme Perkins puts the matter this way: "The Christian image of resurrection, because a new age was seen as having begun with Jesus... initiated a metaphoric shift with the symbolic patterns of the apocalyptic code.... Whether the first Christians were entirely conscious of this shift or not, their attachment of resurrection symbolism to Jesus collapsed the [apocalyptic] scheme."[34]

Unforeseeable to Jesus?

Why, we can continue to ask, does resurrection language become so dominant in the New Testament? If its explicit thematization is somewhat rare in the Old Testament and significantly altered when compared to the apocalyptic literature of the intertestamental period, what is the reason for this large-scale metaphorical emphasis and shift? Could it be that its centrality and peculiar significance in the New Testament comes from Jesus himself, say, from a substantial, characteristic block of teaching delivered during his historical ministry and which was obediently disseminated by his disciples after his death? Can we fully account for this shift by looking at the historical Jesus? The simple answer to this question is "no." If the sayings of the "historical Jesus" provide a necessary condition, they are not by themselves sufficient to account for Easter faith.

Although the gospels were written from the point of view of the resurrection — Easter is both the climax of their narrative presentations and the hermeneutical lens through which Jesus' life, ministry, and death are retrospectively viewed — Jesus is portrayed in the gospels as having relatively little to say about the resurrection, at least directly. Even if we were to determine that all the references to resurrection in Jesus' ministry were his *ipsissima verba* they would be notable by their infrequency when compared to his words about the Kingdom of God.[35] This is not to suggest that resurrection is incompatible with or incidental to Jesus' mission.[36] There is every reason to conclude that Jesus himself maintained a belief in the resurrection. Indeed, it is hard to imagine that any eschatologically driven movement within first-century Judaism, especially one that adopted the Kingdom of God as its prime metaphor, would not have included within it a hope for resurrection as a formal element.[37] Even so, we must acknowledge that the resurrection only occasionally appears as an explicit focus in Jesus' historical ministry. The debate with the Sadducees proves exceptional in this regard.

Quantity should not overshadow the importance of this passage, however. This "unique and precious relic," as John Meier calls it, provides several important clues for understanding Jesus' mission.[38] In this pericope, the Sadducees attempt to corner Jesus in a patently absurd predicament:

> Some Sadducees, who say there is no resurrection, came to him and asked him a question, saying, "Teacher, Moses wrote for us that if a man's brother dies, leaving a wife but no child, the man shall marry the widow and raise up children for his brother. There were seven brothers; the first married and, when he died, left no children; and the second married the widow and died, leaving no children; and the third likewise; none of the seven left children. Last of all the woman herself died. In the resurrection whose wife will she be? For the seven had married her."
>
> Jesus said to them, "Is not this the reason you are wrong, that you know neither the scriptures nor the power of God? For when they rise from the dead, they neither marry nor are given in marriage, but are like angels in heaven. And as for the dead being raised, have you not read in the book of Moses, in the story about the bush, how God said to him, 'I am the God of Abraham, the God of Isaac, and the God of Jacob'? He is God not of the dead, but of the living; you are quite wrong." (Mark 12:18–27)

This captivating exchange, which Meier argues as authentic by even the most rigorously applied criteria of historical criticism, is revealing in several ways. First, it shows that Jesus believed God's eschatological drama would culminate in an unprecedented transformation of the present world, not only an indefinite extension of it. Resurrection is not strictly continuous with the present order, as the Sadducees (mockingly) supposed it to be. Though very much a fulfillment of this world, it is also the rupturing of something presently unimaginable, a new reality transcending human relationships as we ordinarily think of them (marriage, sexuality, etc.). Second, the resurrection is shown to be consistent with the God of creation and covenant, the God of Abraham, Isaac, Jacob, and Moses (Exod. 3:6). Resurrection has to do with God's character. He is a God "not of the dead, but of the living." It is therefore intelligible and credible within the grammar of scripture. Third, and somewhat surprisingly, the supporting scriptural passage from Exodus does not actually mention the resurrection. In point of fact, a teaching about the resurrection (or about any manner of life after death) is entirely absent from the Torah, which was the exact point made by the theologically conservative

Sadducees who did not include the Prophets or the Writings within their canon of scripture.[39] Such a strange proof-text![40] Perhaps Jesus knew that citing a few prophetic writings with more *prima fasciae* support for the resurrection would fall on deaf ears anyway. In any event, Jesus shows that the resurrection is entirely in keeping with the Torah. The creator-covenant God who brings new life out of exile will surely not leave humanity abandoned to the ultimate exile of death. Resurrection is "in accordance with the scriptures," in continuity with the grammar of exodus and covenant, even if, as the lack of specific mention in Exodus 3:6 indicates, it is not quite foreseeable within the very scriptural grammar that nevertheless helps us to speak of it.

Which brings us to the fourth and final telling feature of this pericope: Jesus' appeal to the Torah in this case is, indirectly at least, christological. He approaches scripture with a freedom and authority that scandalizes the Sadducees. It is Jesus himself who proclaims this to be the proper interpretation of scripture. Meier explains:

> Jesus proclaims this particular view both of the manner of the resurrection and of the scriptural proof of the resurrection not on the basis of some hallowed tradition but simply on the basis of his own authority. Without any precedent in Jewish tradition, Jesus flatly asserts that Exod. 3.6 proves the truth of the general resurrection of the dead. He knows that this is so, he teaches it is so, and that is the end of the matter. We have here the peremptory, authoritative, it-is-so-because-I-say-it-is-so style that is typical of the charismatic leader.... One can understand why the Sadducees in particular and the Jerusalem establishment in general would find this Galilean upstart difficult to take or tolerate.[41]

Behind the force of this observation it is tempting to claim that the New Testament emphasis on resurrection directly follows from Jesus' vigorous affirmation of it in the face of those who directly opposed him. After all, the Sadducees among the various Jewish parties at the time were the most instrumental in bringing Jesus' life and ministry to a swift end. And there are, of course, several instances in the gospels in which Jesus predicts his death and subsequent vindication. Many scholars believe, however, that these predictions evidence formulization at the hands of the gospel writers. Meier himself maintains that while Jesus very likely expected to be vindicated by the Father, the form of this vindication probably remained vague to him. In celebrating his final farewell meal with the twelve disciples, Jesus expresses a palpable sense of his impending death — something that would not have required supernatural insight given the typical fate of Israel's prophets, and most recently John the Baptist — and an unwavering trust that the Father would bring about the Kingdom *despite* his death. "Truly I tell you, I will never again drink of the fruit of the vine until that day when I drink it new in the kingdom of God" (Mark 14:25). But the primary focus, argues Meier, is on the Kingdom, not his own personal destiny. Meier therefore agrees with one current of scholarship that regards the passion predictions and their soteriological framing as early church constructions after the fact, *vaticinia ex eventu*.[42]

It is not necessary here to say with exactitude what Jesus thought would occur immediately following his death, though there are good reasons to be much more confident than Meier (et al.) that Jesus believed his death and hoped-for vindication were central to his Kingdom message. Even if we can readily detect editorialization in the passion predictions, and thus see them reflecting a post-Easter hermeneutic, they faithfully portray Jesus' own sense, however inchoate, that his personal fate was utterly bound up with the Kingdom of God — that his person was intimately connected to Israel's final restoration from exile. G. B. Caird draws the sensible conclusion:

> Jesus believed that Israel was called by God to be the agent of His purpose, and that he himself had been sent to bring about that reformation without which Israel could not fulfil its national destiny. If the nation, so far from accepting that calling, rejected God's messenger and persecuted those who responded to his preaching, how could the assertion of God's sovereignty fail to include an open demonstration that Jesus was right and the nation was wrong? How could it fail to include the vindication of the persecuted and the cause they had lived and died for? "Shall not God vindicate His elect, He who listens patiently while they cry to Him day and night? I tell you, He will vindicate them speedily. Nevertheless, when the Son of Man comes, will he find faith on the earth?" (Luke 18:7-9).[43]

Especially when one takes into consideration the special significance the Danielic "Son of Man" title had for Jesus, we can conclude along with Ben Witherington that "whether Jesus predicted his resurrection, he did expect vindication of his cause beyond the grave. That vindication was spoken of both in terms of his assuming divine power and authority as world judge and in terms of his coming to earth to perform that final judgment."[44]

But even if we take a maximalist position on this issue and argue that Jesus explicitly hoped God's vindication would take the form of his resurrection, and furthermore that this unprecedented act would deliver God's eschatological judgment and salvation for Israel; even so, his resurrection — its actual occurrence, its incident and attestation to others, its impact and history of effects — would necessarily remain unforeseeable to Jesus himself. Let this be properly understood.

Ultimately Jesus submits to his own death. The New Testament frequently speaks of Jesus being "handed over" to death, which at once implies a network of religious and political powers as the agent of death and Jesus as its passive recipient. The New Testament also speaks of Jesus as the recipient of the Father's vindicating action. Although some later texts suggest Jesus as the agent of his own resurrection, by far the most usual ascription of agency is to God alone.[45] God *raises* — Jesus *is raised*. "But God raised him on the third day and allowed him to appear" (Acts 10:40; cf. 2:32; 3:15; 4:10). "And God raised the Lord and will also raise us by his power" (1 Cor. 6:14); "the power of God, who raised him from the dead" (Col. 2:20).[46] The significance of this is that the event of resurrection is not something Jesus can "do" but is something he receives. The event of resurrection could hardly be a *fait accompli* within his life, but only something subsequent, if at all — how could he possibly know with any certainty? — to his falling victim to religious and political powers. Only in the obscurity of faith could he face the rejection of his mission and person with the hope for vindication. "My God, my God, why have you forsaken me" (Mark 15:34)? Jesus encounters the incomprehensible mystery of God through the incomprehensible mystery of death. As Marion writes, Jesus submits himself to his own unforeseeable eventfulness just as he submits to the Father. "As a result, the end of the world is as unforeseen by him, by him the Son, as his own coming as the Christ surprises those who inhabit this same world. The unforeseeability comes to an end only for the Father: 'As for the day and the hour, no one knows them, neither the angels in heaven, nor [even] the Son, except the Father' (Mark 13:33), 'except the Father alone' (Matt. 24:36)."[47] This, according to Marion, is "expectation without foresight." It "defines the phenomenological attitude appropriate to the event — vigilance: 'Open your eyes, be vigilant, for you do not know when the [right] moment [*kairos*] will come' (Mark 13:33)."[48] Jesus may hope, even expect his vindication *via* resurrection, but such expectation was without foresight, for its intention could have no perceptible terminus. It could only extend indefinitely into the non-doing and non-being of death, and ultimately into the silent incomprehensibility of the Father. "Father, into your hands I commend my spirit" (Luke 23:46).

The Unthinkable Notion

Let us then return to the questions that inspire this portion of our study: What prompted the earliest Christians to adopt resurrection language specifically, doing so while also transforming its meaning in strikingly original, if not unlikely, and perhaps even strange ways? Why risk the initial incoherence of declaring Jesus *already* risen? Why unnecessarily invite the linguistic and conceptual difficulties in proclaiming God's eschatological future as already having taken place within a history still very much in the making? If this shift in focus and meaning is not quite foreseeable within the Old Testament, or the apocalyptic literature of the inter-testamental period, or even Jesus' historical ministry, then what? According to the New Testament, two kinds of eschatological signs converged in a way to elicit something from language and thought that, left to themselves, would not have been said or thought: the one, a historical *absence* — the empty tomb; the other, a saturating *presence* — the appearances. "But God raised him on the third day and allowed him to appear."

Although this cannot amount to a proof for resurrection faith, I am suggesting here that only the phenomena "on the ground" prompted the disciples to make specific claims about Jesus' post-mortem existence; that unless they were witnesses to, and participants in, a radically novel series of events following Jesus' death, their counter-intuitive claims regarding his resurrection from the dead would not have been made or gained traction; that unless they were filled with overwhelming conviction that, indeed, Jesus' tomb was empty and that he was alive and present to them in the mode of perceptible self-attestation, the process that resulted in transforming the early Jesus movement into a "religion of resurrection" would have never been made in the comprehensive way it was. Of course, the earliest followers of Jesus may have gotten it spectacularly wrong. Just because they claimed to have seen, heard, and felt certain things after Jesus' death does not make their testimony true. No matter how impassioned their behavior and bold their speech, there remains the possibility that the early Christian movement systematically misunderstood what took place after Jesus breathed his last on Golgotha. As I have said, believing in the resurrection today is a self-involving risk that remains dependent upon apostolic witness. Even if we can vigorously argue for the coherence, goodness, and beauty of this testimony, our embrace of the Easter message remains "non-foundational" insofar as we accept it as a Gift, as a summons, as a way of richly imagining ourselves and God in a particular way. Alas, believing in the resurrection is a gift of faith. And yet we may say precisely within this faith-formed context that only the actual event of Jesus being raised from the dead, and being made to appear to his followers, constitute the condition of the possibility for faith's assent. It cannot be arrived at through transcendental deduction or historical argumentation, but *gives itself* to us precisely in the mode of its own self-giving. It is *sui generis,* the im-possible Gift.

With obvious caution Evans writes that because the doctrine of resurrection was not firmly fixed in first-century Judaism, it might "be suggested that only this *event,* whatever it may have been, could have brought it about that there emerged in Christianity a precise, confident and articulate faith in which resurrection has moved from the circumference to the centre."[49] N. T. Wright puts the matter more forcefully:

> The early Christians did not invent the empty tomb and the "meetings" or "sightings" of the risen Jesus in order to explain a faith they already had. They developed that faith because of the occurrence, and the convergence, of these two phenomena. Nobody was expecting this kind of thing; no kind of conversion-experience would have generated such ideas; nobody would have invented it, no matter how guilty (or how forgiven) they felt, no matter how many hours they pored over the scriptures.... The early Christians insisted that what had happened to Jesus was precisely something new; was, indeed, the start of a whole new mode of existence, a new creation. The fact that Jesus' resurrection was, and remains, *without analogy* is not an objection to the early Christian claim. It is part of the claim itself.[50]

In response to an unexpected, yet palpably real series of events after Jesus' death, the earliest Christians were compelled to *adopt* and *adapt* an existing vocabulary to speak of what stimulated their newfound faith. On the one hand, no other language was more fitting than "resurrection" to announce what had happened to Jesus. Nothing else could come close to accounting for both the bodily absence of the tomb and Jesus' personal appearances to the disciples. On the other hand, the previous usage of that language could not contain the full scope of the event. Its semantic banks burst. The "new creation" of Jesus' resurrection from the dead brought about a new event in language. The transfiguration of his body inspired the transfiguration of language itself. As Eberhard Jüngel states, Easter causes "an immense disturbance in the sphere of language.

It reaches the very limits of incomprehensibility." It fights to express an "unthinkable notion": that the *absolute future* of creation, the resurrection of the dead *has already taken place*.[51] That the earliest Christians actually risked making this claim should astonish us. Although Christians have used resurrection language for many centuries, as if its meaning were self-evident (habitual usage can give the impression of inevitability and the presumption of comprehension), this should not obscure the fact that its usage in the first century to describe what happened to Jesus would have been met with surprise and incredulity. To reiterate, it is extremely difficult to imagine the circumstances under which the earliest Christians would have risked affirming Jesus' "resurrection" if the events on the ground did not conspire together to urge them to do so. It is important that Christians appreciate this disturbance in the field of language as a permanent feature of Christian discourse. To do so is to learn to think *from* and *with* the historical *aporia* that is Jesus' resurrection from the dead.

Unbearable: Easter and "Bedazzlement"

The eschatological signs of Jesus' resurrection cannot be borne by those who are its witnesses, but saturates and "bedazzles" their capacities of perception and comprehension. "In terms of quality," writes Marion, "the figure of Christ obviously attests its paradoxical character because the intuition that saturates it reaches and most often overcomes what the phenomenological gaze can bear."[52] Easter's unbearable character is evident in two related modes: the empty tomb and the appearances.

The Empty Tomb as Christological Apophasis

In the empty tomb stories, the saturation of intentionality (the "gaze") occurs through a striking absence. In the original ending of Mark's gospel (16:1–8) we are told that upon their discovery of the empty tomb the women were seized by "terror and amazement." Instructed by the mysterious "young man" in a white robe to tell the disciples in Galilee what they see, or rather what they do not see, they leave post-haste, saying nothing to anyone "for they were afraid" (*ephobounto gar*). This abrupt ending has given rise to endless speculation.[53] Did Mark intend to end his gospel this way? If so, what does he mean by it? Was the original ending removed by later editors, perhaps even lost? If original, does it assume an appearance tradition associated with Galilee ("there you will see him, just as he told you")? Or is Mark simply unaware of an appearance tradition? Naturally related to these questions are those concerning the historicity of the empty tomb traditions altogether. Are they later theological embellishments of a more primitive tradition, or

The Im-possible Gift

do they point to a tradition as old as the very first proclamation of the resurrection? Such questions are not my primary concern here.[54] Rather, I am interested in the eschatological signification of this fragmentary and suggestive "ending."

The narration of bodily absence in Mark is constructed to provoke its readers. "Do not be alarmed; you are looking for Jesus of Nazareth, who was crucified. He has been raised; he is not here. Look, there is the place they laid him" (v. 6). It may be, as Robert Gundry observes, that Mark's Hellenistic-Gentile audience would have been sufficiently impressed with an immortalizing of Jesus without bodily resurrection. "But no, compensation for crucifixion demands and gets more. The σωμα, 'body,' and the πτωμα, 'corpse,' that was taken down from a cross and entombed has been raised to new life with the result that Jesus is going ahead of his disciples in re-embodied and therefore visible form." The ostensible crudity of such bodiliness "is exactly what Mark wants his readers to understand."[55] The expectation of the women (and thus the reader's) is thwarted, even the mournful expectation that expected to see and anoint a corpse. Having arrived with the purpose of offering final acts of ritual hospitality to the body, a process customary for Jewish women to fulfill, their grief suddenly shifts to alarm at the sight of an absence (v. 5). The loss here is a double loss: for in addition to having lost Jesus to death (and their expectations associated with him and his Kingdom ministry), now his body has been taken away from his family and followers with the disconcerting effect of interrupting the grieving process. We can assume that the alarm is not primarily focused on Jesus' death as such but the inability to properly bury and prepare the body for the future resurrection of the dead and the messianic age.[56] John's recounting makes this second loss more apparent: "They said to her, 'Woman, why are you weeping?' She said to them, 'They have taken away my Lord, and I do not know where they have laid him' " (John 20:13).

But this "nothing" the women "see" is no mere lack. It is the negative impress of an excessive "something" that cannot be borne by intentionality. In verses 6 and 7 we are introduced to an oppositional structure in which geography functions as a kind of phenomenology. "He has been raised; he is not here.... But go, tell his disciples and Peter that he is going ahead of you to Galilee; there you will see him, just as he told you." The "there" of Galilee, which is where the risen Jesus *is*, is opposed to the "here" of the tomb in Jerusalem, where Jesus *is not*. What stretches from Jerusalem across to Galilee is more than a geographical distance. It is a perceptual and affective distance, a "space" that elicits anticipation and yearning, an attitudinal openness for beholding the as-yet recognizable form of the bodily risen Lord. As Gundry notes, the use of asyndeton quickens the pace of narration to dramatize the earlier prediction in 14:28.[57] But it intensifies the geographical opposition just as much. Whether Mark is motivated by an implicit judgment upon Jerusalem as the city of Jesus' rejection is of secondary significance. Of primary importance is the way present "absence" signifies a "presence" that is "going ahead" of them, drawing them, luring them towards an unimaginable encounter ("there you will see him") and a mission to proclaim ("tell his disciples and Peter"). The narrative itself seems to rush forward in anticipation of its conclusion. But precisely here the page goes blank! Careening towards a "solution" to the problem of the would-be messiah's crucifixion, Mark only intimates what *will be seen*, not what manifestly *is seen*. The reader is left, like the women, with dizzying, breathless expectancy. "So they went out and fled from the tomb, for terror and amazement had seized them; and they said nothing to anyone, for they were afraid" (v. 8).

Francis Watson warns against reading the fragmentary character of this "ending" as somehow accidental to Mark's overall meaning. Helpfully, Watson calls for a style of interpretation that reads all of the resurrection narratives "precisely *in* their fragmentariness, and not *in spite of* it."[58] Such a view, so closely aligned with my own, presumes that the narratives and the traditions from which they stem are "included within the sphere of the event itself, so that the generation of an appropriate testimony to itself would be integral to the event."[59] In the case of Mark 16:1-8, the reticence in not narrating the resurrection is complemented by the non-narration of the post-resurrection encounters. The story of the women at the tomb is thus framed by two non-narrated events — "events" that nonetheless stand as the gospel's climax. What we are left with is not an "object" that would satisfy intentionality but the hollowing out and intensification of desire for the crucified-and-risen One who becomes "present" by "going ahead" of them. That is to say, we are left without stable images or concepts that would comport with the capacities of the intending subject, but only the phenomenological attitude appropriate to an event that manifestly overwhelms those capacities — "terror and amazement."

Along with the geographical opposition between Jerusalem and Galilee just mentioned, Mark creates temporal displacements that prevent the resurrection from becoming "present" or "immediate." It is either in the future (14:28) or in the past (16:6). The women arrive at the tomb "very early" on the first day of the week (16:2). While the reader is likely expecting the kind of meaningful coincidence that narratives frequently employ — a "fortuitous arrival at the precise moment when something momentous is taking place" — here instead, "just as the coincidence is about to occur, this narrative swerves away from it; the women are very early, but Jesus rose earlier still, and they encounter not Jesus himself, but a surrogate with whom he has left a message."[60] Resurrection faith is always, from its inception, after the fact: a delayed response that welcomes what it never knew it always desired. The temporal displacements, like the geographical relays and buffering herald, act as so many veils for the *mysterium tremendum* of Easter which is made manifest precisely to the extent that it fascinates and eludes the gaze. With only the command to proclaim to Peter and the disciples what they have (not) seen, the women depart overwhelmed with the fear and silence characteristic of other theophanies and commissions found in scripture (Exod. 3:3; Jer. 1:6–8; Luke 1:29–30). The refusal to explicitly narrate therefore reveals the narrator's own "reticence in the face of the mystery of the divine act."

> To narrate an event is to enclose it within a verbal structure that aims to make it intelligible and imaginable; narrative presupposes the *reproducibility* of the event in the mind of the reader by way of the words on the page. In speaking of this event only in the form of non-narration, the Marcan narrator indicates that the divine act of raising Jesus from the dead is not intelligible, imaginable, and therefore reproducible as other events. Narrative testimony to it must therefore be indirect and fragmentary.[61]

This is *negative christophany*. Mark's empty tomb narrative performs a contemplative distance: through non-seeing, non-grasping, non-reproducing, non-narrating — yet ever intimating — the reader is drawn into the awful, expectant silence of the women that will eventually burst forth with kerygmatic speech. There is no contradiction here between the command to proclaim and the silence that presently holds back their tongues. Only a misunderstanding of the relationship between word and silence could suppose that the women do not ultimately fulfill their task. Here we must disagree with those who interpret the fear and silence of the women as an indication of failure.[62] While Mark describes the disciples at several points as fearful in order to highlight their misunderstanding or failure (9:6; 9:32; 10:32), the women's response of "terror and amazement" in the face of divine revelation is far more akin to the sort of reaction provoked by Jesus' miraculous signs, such as when the crowd was "overcome with amazement" upon witnessing the healing of Jairus's daughter (5:42).[63] It is within this silence — the Silence of the resurrection — that they are formed and prepared to speak of what they shudder to believe.

This contemplative distance is also, and for that very reason, a critical distance. Just as the empty tomb story opens up a necessary and preparatory "space" for beholding in the future the transfigured "form" of the risen Jesus (a properly theological aesthetics understands such "space" as the positive gift of the beautiful form, not a falling away from a primordial immediacy that we now mourn or resent or seek to overcome[64]), we also have here a critique of any attempt to domesticate the risen Lord or transform "presence" into something transferable or manipulable. Whether or not we can say Mark is challenging particular Christian communities or leaders who have improperly co-opted the appearance traditions to legitimate their authority, there is little question that his skeptical portrayal of the disciples throughout his gospel, now coupled with the stark non-image of the empty tomb, provides a critical function that effectively warns against any attempt to make Jesus' resurrection a matter of ownership or self-justification. The fact that the women are the first to receive the news of Jesus' resurrection is remarkable in many important ways, not least because women in first-century Judaism did not possess the legal status to give testimony. Perhaps this gives the empty tomb story a certain boost in credibility, historically speaking, since this was not the sort of thing likely to be fabricated due to its potential embarrassment. (Celsus in the second century pointed to this fact as yet another chink in the credibility of resurrection faith.[65]) But more important for our present purposes is that the first reception and proclamation of the Easter message comes in a way that would undermine every pretense to authority and possessiveness. It is first given to those who mourn, to women, those of lowly rank. The resurrection narratives in general, but the empty tomb stories in particular, remain "ideologically under-determined," writes Rowan Williams.[66] "[T]he empty tomb tradition is, theologically speaking, part of the Church's resource in resisting the temptation to 'absorb' Jesus into itself, and thus part of what its confession of the divinity of Jesus amounts to in spiritual and political practice."[67] Among other reasons, this is why the notion that Jesus is "raised into the kerygma" (so Bultmann) or raised into Jesus' ongoing "cause" (so Marxsen) bears the potential of ideological distortion. Every appropriation of Easter faith that does not take seriously the absence of the empty tomb, and thus would conflate signified and signifier without remainder — Jesus "rises into" the church, into ethical-political praxis, into proclamation, etc. — is subject to critique. By saying, "He has risen, he is not here," resurrection faith most certainly affirms that Jesus has been transformed into an eschatological mode of existence that enables him to be "present" in a qualitatively new way; but it says this precisely while acknowledging the freedom of the risen Jesus who remains eschatologically Other and thus "absent" from any and every effort to manipulate or subsume into an agenda. "The freedom of Jesus to act, however we unpack that deceptively simple statement, is not exhausted by what the community is doing or thinking — which allows us to say that Jesus' role for the community continues, vitally, to be that of judge, and that those who are charged with speaking authoritatively for or in the community stand in a very peculiar and paradoxical place."[68] There remains a structural "distance" or "difference" between the risen Jesus and the community, which is precisely the Gift. This gift of "distance" does not, as we shall see, lead to a kind of indifference, but a responsibility rooted in a liturgical and ethical praxis free from the false immediacy and utopianism that would reductively historicize Easter. As previously stated, Easter *is* and *is not* historical. Only this unity-in-difference prevents Easter from becoming bad ideology, either through a-historical abstraction or historical immanentization.

The Appearances as Christological Kataphasis

If the empty tomb story in Mark performs a contemplative and critical distance, we should not conclude that the appearance traditions, which narratively permit us to "see" the transfigured Christ, enclose or negate this distance. If the Marcan empty tomb is more *apophatic* in character, and the appearances more *kataphatic*, we should understand both of these modes as very closely linked. They are distinctive yet complementary attestations to the one eschatological Gift of Jesus' resurrection from the dead. Just because the risen Jesus becomes communicative and interpersonally "present" to Mary Magdelene, the disciples, Paul, and the five hundred, revealing himself in ways that include visual, auditory, and even tactile aspects, never is this presence something ready-to-hand or fully comprehensible. For all their diversity the appearance traditions are remarkably coherent in articulating that the witnesses "see" and "touch" precisely in the midst of their "not-seeing" and "not-grasping." They recognize the risen Jesus as a "stranger." They identify him through a process of initial mis-identification, frequently coming to faith through doubt, and thus through the purgation and transformation of their surface desires. In each of these vignettes, and through the sum of them, the risen Christ becomes epiphanous while overshadowing their perceptual and cognitive horizons. The perceived absence here is the result of an excessive presence, an extreme surplus of givenness that cannot be anticipated or absorbed by those who will nevertheless become its transformed witnesses.

The New Testament adopts a variety of expressions to describe the appearances of the risen Jesus. He is "revealed" to Paul (*apokalypto*; Gal. 1:16); the disciples and the five hundred "see" him (*horao*; 1 Cor. 15:5–8); he "appears" to the disciples (*optanomai*; Acts 1:3); Jesus "meets" the women at the tomb (*hypantao*; Matt. 28:9); he "shows" or "manifests" himself to the disciples (*phaneroo*; John 21:14).[69] Among these various expressions, *ophthe*, the aorist passive of *horao* ("to see"), has taken on the greatest significance in the tradition.[70] Literally translated as "was seen," *ophthe* implies much more than ordinary ocular vision, as though the risen Jesus were visible in the same way a tree or a rock are visible in casual observation. This does not mean however that the appearances lack an "objective" character.

> They put him to death by hanging him on a tree; but God raised him on the third day and allowed him to appear, not to all the people but to us who were chosen by God as witnesses, and who ate and drank with him after he rose from the dead (Acts 10:40).

> After his suffering he presented himself alive to them by many convincing proofs, appearing to them during forty days and speaking about the kingdom of God (Acts 1:3; cf. 9:17; 13:31; 26:16).

> They were saying, "The Lord has risen indeed, and he has appeared to Simon" (Luke 24:34).

> [H]e appeared to Cephas, then to the twelve. The he appeared to more than five hundred brothers and sisters at one time, most of whom are still alive, though some have died. Then he appeared to James, then to all the apostles. Last of all, as to one untimely born, he appeared also to me (1 Cor. 15:5–8).

As these passages emphasize, there remains a defining *alterity* to the encounters. The order of manifestation is made clear by the dative: Christ appears *to* them. The emphasis is on the transcendent Giver-Given (God-Christ) rather than the experiences of the recipients.[71] We must therefore disagree with those tendencies in scholarship that psychologize the appearances as subconscious "projections," likening them to mystical "visions" that only later become laden with quasi-empirical features. If we are prepared to believe that Jesus' entire embodied existence is transfigured by the power of God so that he becomes cognizable to his disciples as the self-same Jesus of Nazareth, and not a totally alien presence, it is reasonable to accept that such revelatory encounters were more than private, subjective insights later dramatized in graphic terms, but were encounters that, for all their transcendent nature, were communicated in historically and sensually mediated ways. There is no good reason here to exclude a priori the possibility that the risen Jesus appeared to the disciples within our concrete history, without however being reducible to those historical factors.

In surveying the New Testament appearance traditions we find consistent emphasis on at least four points. The appearances:

1. originated from the free initiative of the risen Christ in the power of God;

2. were unexpected by the witnesses, and thus not manufactured from their conscious or subconscious feelings of anxiety, hope, guilt, or fear;

3. involved historically and sensually mediating factors of embodied human experience, including sight, sound, and tactility; and

4. occurred during a circumscribed period of time before Jesus' ascension, and thus do not keep on occurring throughout history.

In sum, the manifestations bear the quality of *alterity*. They are arresting, revelatory *events*: "in-breakings" that originate from beyond the witnesses, penetrating and reorienting their fields of perception, expectation, and understanding. These are saturated phenomena *par excellence*. As is evident in the various reactions of the witnesses (surprise, confusion, intense joy mixed with fear, and often enough the immediate impulse to worship) what is given to intuition floods the witnesses' capacities for comprehension. Such *alterity* does not mean that the witnesses do not participate imaginatively (and thus "subjectively") in the revelatory event, as if their background understanding and previous relationship with Jesus leading up to his death had nothing at all to do with how they would come to "see" him in his appearances. Quite importantly, the risen Jesus does not appear to just anybody, but to those with whom he had shared his ministry.[72] This pre-existing relationship is exactly what allows the witnesses to eventually identify him as the self-same Jesus, even if, now in the blinding light of the Easter experience, they will come to see this Jesus in a profoundly new way. The structure of the experience here, at least in broadest outline, is a complex and mutually conditioning relationship of familiarity and strangeness, light and darkness, continuity and discontinuity, intimacy and otherness — just the sort of "both-and" dynamic that parallels the historical/trans-historical character of the resurrection itself.

But we should not understand this "both-and" dynamic as implying some sort of equality between these two sets of terms. The relationship is not linear, as though presence stands "side by side" with absence in equal measure, or with the same significance. The mis-understanding and mis-identification described in the narratives result from an unreservedly positive givenness that, by its antecedent and extreme intensity, produces a "negative" impress due to the perceptual limitations of the witnesses who cannot fully absorb it. Like the blindness that results when unadjusted eyes are flooded with intense light, the appearances of the risen Christ in his glorified corporeality "bedazzle" witnesses. The perceptual obscurity here is the subjective correlate to the objective surplus of givenness. *Apophatic* "formlessness" is a modality derivative of the inexhaustibly beautiful "form" of Christ.[73] This in essence is what Jean-Luc Marion means by "bedazzlement."

> Bedazzlement characterizes what the gaze cannot bear. Not bearing does not amount to not seeing; for one must first perceive, if not see, in order to experience this incapacity to bear. It is in fact a question of something visible that our gaze cannot bear; this visible something is experienced as unbearable to the gaze because it weighs too much upon the gaze; the glory of the visible weighs, and it weighs too much. What weighs here is not unhappiness, nor pain, nor lack, but indeed glory, joy, excess.... Intuition gives too intensely for the gaze to be truly able to see what already it can no longer receive, nor even confront.... Because the saturated phenomenon, due to the excess of intuition in it, cannot be borne by any gaze that would measure up to it ("objectively"), it is perceived ("subjectively") by the gaze only in the negative mode of an impossible perception, the mode of bedazzlement.[74]

For Marion, the paradoxical character of bedazzlement reaches its apogee in the revelation of the resurrection, since "it by definition passes beyond what this world can receive, contain, or embrace."[75] The resurrection is "absolute theophany."[76] Not only is it the manifestation of Christ in his eschatological beauty (his "glory," or *kabod*), but the revelation of the Father.

What blindness interprets as simple obscurity must be understood at base as a bedazzlement, in which, in the revelatory figure of Jesus

Christ, the Father enters into absolute epiphany, though filtered through finitude. If blindness sees nothing there and does not even suspect bedazzlement, the fault lies not with revelation, but with the gaze that cannot bear the evidence.[77]

If the witnesses are to see what is initially given in obscurity, the witnesses themselves will need to be converted to and transformed by the given. "Seeing" the risen Jesus entails a progressive accommodation to the Gift, an *ek-static*, Other-centered movement, a "self-forgetfulness" that allows one to be wholly with the Other. As Walter Kasper puts it, in the appearances "we have before us a total state of being possessed by Jesus, a state of impact and absorption, the awakening of faith."[78] Though such encounters are remembered as sudden jolts of awakening, they undoubtedly touched off a conversion process — how lengthy it is impossible to know — to a new manner of perception, understanding, judgment, and action. Such was not the project of any self-constituting subjectivity but the progressive acquisition of a new "self" (a "new creation") given by the crucified-and-risen Lord. In a word, such responses were responses to Love. "In effect, if what reveals itself is always summed up in Love, then only the gaze that believes, and thus only the will that loves, can welcome it. Thus only the conversion of the gaze can render the eye apt to recognize the blinding evidence of love in what bedazzles it."[79] Let us briefly look at this bedazzlement and conversion in a few key vignettes.

Luke-Acts

In Luke's Emmaus Road story the two disciples come to identify the risen Jesus just as he disappears from their field of vision. Having not recognized him while walking towards the village of Emmaus ("their eyes were kept from recognizing him"), and even speaking with him about the events that had recently transpired, they at last come to recognize the stranger in the blessing and breaking of the bread — an act of symbolic-sacramental mediation — at which point Jesus abruptly withdraws from their sight: "Then their eyes were opened, and they recognized him; and he vanished from their sight" (Luke 24:31). What kept them from recognizing him before? What sign was lacking in the initial encounter? "None whatsoever," writes Marion. "In fact, they kept themselves from recognizing him. Why were they denying the evidence? Not because it was deficient — it wasn't lacking in the slightest — but because it contradicts their entire comprehension (their miscomprehension, or at the least, their pre-comprehension) of a phenomenon that is nevertheless patently beneath their eyes, and in their ears."[80] The transition from non-recognition to recognition came as a process of understanding anew Jesus' life and crucifixion from the point of view of his vindication and resurrection. What they had not understood in "real time" became retrospectively intelligible through the Easter experience. Their memory was, as it were, reconstructed: "They said to each other, 'Were not our hearts burning within us while he was talking to us on the road, while he was opening the scriptures to us?'" (v. 32).

Just a few verses later the risen Jesus appears among the rest of the disciples who become "startled and terrified" by what they see, or what they think they see. Is it a ghostly apparition (v. 37)? Jesus, seeking to reassure them in their shock and confusion, speaks a word of *shalom* ("Peace be with you") and offers to reveal himself with yet greater determination: "Look at my hands and my feet; see that it is I myself. Touch me and see; for a ghost does not have flesh and bones as you see that I have" (v. 39). Despite this, the disciples remain disbelieving, even if they can barely hold back their initial joy, and so they offer him a piece of broiled fish. While there is a broader theological significance to the meal sharing that Luke intends to communicate, for our limited purposes here we can note that this is no ordinary tactility, as though Jesus has simply returned to his previous state of existence. Just as this vignette begins with Jesus' sudden and mysterious appearance among the gathered disciples, it ends with his withdrawal in ascension (v. 51). Quite paradoxically, the sensible absence of Jesus' risen body, now ascended, draws the disciples to a new and mediated presence of Christ in the eucharistic body of the bread and in the ecclesial community.

In keeping with this theme of presence and transcendence, the beginning of the Book of Acts (Luke's sequel) relates: "as they were watching, he was lifted up, and a cloud took him out of their sight. While he was going and they were gazing up toward heaven, suddenly two men in white robes stood by them. They said, 'Men of Galilee, why do you stand looking up toward heaven? This Jesus, who has been take up from you into heaven, will come in the same way as you saw him go into heaven'" (Acts 1:10–11). As if to wake them from a trance that keeps them gazing heavenward, stupefied, the buffering heralds direct the disciples to the apostolic task that now awaits them. The departing "presence" of the risen Jesus is by no means abandonment but a generous and creative "distance" that opens up an arena for the disciples to carry on Jesus' mission *in persona Christi*. The departure is a summons.

Matthew

In Matthew's gospel, which also ends with the summons of the Great Commission, Jesus' visibility on the mount in Galilee prompts the disciples to worship him. This appearance fulfills the earlier prediction adopted from Mark 14:28 that in Galilee they will see him (Matt. 28:7). However, "seeing" in this instance is not simply empirical or disinterested, as though anyone could casually become aware of the revelatory event presently unfolding. Jesus' visibility is never coincident with the horizons of those who would behold him, for as the narrative immediately adds, "some doubted" (v. 17). This theme of doubt, which is found in most of the resurrection narratives, bears a number of important features that will concern us in later chapters. But for our present purposes it reflects the historical memory of Jesus' transcendent otherness and the epistemic gap that existed between previous expectation and the saturating eventuality of Easter. What is suggested here is not that doubt and mis-identification were the result of a weakness in the phenomenon given. Jesus' self-attestation did not lack sufficient intensity for the more incredulous. Rather, the doubt and mis-identification arose from the "more than" (or *in*-visible) depth dimension of the given, a disruptive surplus of intuition that required the conversion of the witnesses. What the Easter event initiates here is a process in which the disciples will become progressively attuned to the *given*. As I shall stress in Part Two, this process entails a revolution in their view of God and each other on the basis of the risen victim. The encounters with the risen Jesus as the stranger reveal that, far from being a "projection of the community's own belief," the earliest Christians had to " 'learn' him afresh, as from the beginning."[81] The affirmation of Jesus' Lordship was not constructed from a simple recollection but through a dramatic encounter with one who eluded and yet undertook to transform their surface perceptions and desires.

John

This dynamic is evident in John's gospel as well. In one instance we find Mary Magdalene confusing the risen Jesus with a gardener at the tomb. In the midst of her mourning the loss of a body (mourning here is presented as both the precondition and barrier to seeing Jesus) Jesus asks her, "Woman, why are you weeping? Whom are you looking for?" Mary replies, "Sir, if you have carried him away, tell me where you have laid him, and I will take him away" (John 20:15). Even though the risen Jesus is speaking to her, it becomes apparent that she will never recognize him within her present frame of reference. Her perception remains obscured by a restricted horizon, by a former way of relating and understanding. At last Jesus calls her by name. "Mary!" Only then does she recognize him. "Rabbouni" (v. 16)! Despite her having a previous relationship with Jesus, her capacity for recognition is not something she possesses on her own. It is given to her by the crucified-and-risen One through his gratuitous address. In being recognized *by* the Other she comes into recognition *of* the Other. The One who first appeared through a "distance" as the stranger has revealed himself as incomprehensibly near, calling her by name. Her recognition does not annul this "distance" but, strangely, deepens it. Reaching out to grab the risen Jesus in the joy of recognition — not unlike the women in Matthew who take hold of Jesus' feet in worship (Matt. 28:9) — Jesus forestalls her attempt: "Do not hold on to me, because I have not yet ascended to the Father. But go to my brothers and say to them, 'I am ascending to my Father and your Father, to my God and your God" (John 20:17). Mary does what is commanded, telling the disciples, "I have seen the Lord" (v. 18). As Sandra Schneiders has brilliantly shown, this act of "touching" but "not grasping" narratively recounts a process of transformation in which Mary Magdalene learns to relate to the risen Jesus in a different way than in the previous dispensation. Rather than grasping onto Jesus as "Rabbouni," relating to him as she did before his death, the risen Christ directs her to the disciples and to his sacramentally mediated presence in the community. "The place where Mary will now encounter Jesus as he really is, glorified and risen, is the community. Mary must pass over from the pre-Easter to the Easter dispensation. Her proclamation to the other disciples makes clear that she has indeed made that transition. She no longer speaks of 'Rabbouni.' As the first apostle of the resurrection she proclaims 'I have seen the Lord.' "[82]

The ecclesial community now serves as the body of Christ in the world — "the corporate person who is the organ of Jesus' salvific action in the world." Resurrection faith produces life in *ecclesia*. But we should not conclude that the risen Jesus is wholly subsumed therein, as if Jesus has "risen into the Church" without remainder. This would make Jesus' resurrection strictly immanent, something the empty tomb and appearance narratives both preclude by their insistence on Jesus' *bodily* resurrection. The community is capable of bodying-forth Christ in history "only...if Jesus himself, the principle of that ecclesial body, is actually alive in the full integrity of his personal humanity." As Schneiders makes clear, "this is the significance of maintaining that Jesus is *bodily* risen from the dead (i.e., that what body signifies, namely, numerical identity, personal subjectivity grounding interpersonal presence and effective action in the world) is verified in him after his death on the cross."[83] This affirmation of the integrity and *alterity* of Jesus' body-person is one of the chief concerns of the two-part vignette that immediately follows.

In the first part, the disciples (minus Thomas the Twin) have locked themselves in a house out of fear. And not an unfounded fear, since they might be recognized as accomplices in the subversive movement led by their recently crucified leader. But such partitions, be they physical or spiritual, will not confine the risen Jesus who in his deathless freedom suddenly appears among them. As in Luke, Jesus offers a word of *shalom* in an address ("Peace be with you"). Such words allow the disciples' panic, now intensified by the im-possible appearance of a stranger, to be transformed into joy. "After he said this, he showed them his hands and his side. Then the disciples rejoiced when they saw the Lord. Jesus said to them again, 'Peace be with you. As the Father has sent me, so I send you'" (20:20–21). What they "see" is not a totally alien presence. Though unrecognizable at first in his eschatological transcendence, this is also the self-same Jesus of Nazareth who is identifiable by the marks of his death. As elsewhere in the gospels, the encounter involves a complex relation of visibility and in-visibility, tactility and transcendence, familiarity and strangeness. But this dynamic of the disciples' post-paschal faith was not one Thomas was prepared to accept, at least not on the authority of his fellow disciples. When Thomas later reunites with them after Jesus' departure, they say to him, "We have seen the Lord." But Thomas refuses to believe: "Unless I see the mark of the nails in his hands, and put my finger in the mark of the nails and my hand in his side, I will not believe" (v. 25). It is not just that Thomas doubts. He deliberately rejects the post-paschal dispensation. "He insists that he will believe only if he can touch the very wounds of Jesus, only if he can return to the dispensation of pre-Easter faith, only if he can continue to relate to Jesus in the flesh."[84]

When Jesus appears to the disciples again a week later, and this time with Thomas present, he extends a remarkable invitation: "Put your finger here and see my hands. Reach out your hand and put it in my side. Do not doubt but believe" (v. 27). We are never told whether in fact Thomas did as he was invited, but it is important to note that the invitation is not exactly what Thomas had previously demanded. Rather than physically probing the wounds for physical verification, "the invitation reaches deeper. Jesus commands Thomas to put his hand into his open side from which had issued the lifegiving blood and water, symbol of the gift of the Spirit in baptism and the Eucharist which Jesus had handed over in his death and had focused in the gift to the community a week earlier when Thomas was absent."[85] Thomas's response is not to touch in a strictly empirical way — again, we are never told that Thomas does what he originally set out to do — but to make a bold acknowledgement only possible in faith: "Thomas answered him, 'My Lord and my God'" (v. 28). This is among the clearest affirmations of Jesus as "God" in the New Testament, and it comes as a response to an unanticipated upsurge of insight into the meaning of Jesus as the crucified-and-risen One. The theme of Jesus' unity with the Father is found throughout John's gospel (1:49; 4:42; 6:69; 9:37; 11:27; 16:30; 20:17); but here we have an affirmation from a disciple who discerns the reality of God in Jesus' crucified-and-risen "form." To "see" this form is to "see" the Father. In response to Thomas's acclamation, "Jesus said to him, 'Have you believed because you have seen me? Blessed are those who have not seen and yet have come to believe'" (v. 29). In other words, blessed are those who enter into this structure of faith as a response to apostolic testimony: "We have seen the Lord."

All told, both episodes in John reflect a historical memory of the risen Lord as tactile and transcendent, familiar and surprising — historically "present" in his eschatological freedom, and thus in a way that also confers "distance." But they also reflect, as indeed all the resurrection narratives do, a catechetical aim. Written "so that you may come to believe that Jesus is the Messiah, the Son of God, and that through believing you may have life in his name" (v. 31), the gospel of John imparts a knowledge of the risen One that requires something far more demanding than the assimilation of a piece of information within a pre-established framework of intelligibility. "Jesus is risen" is not merely a proposition. It is something to be "lived-into." It entails a profound shift in perception, judgment, and action on the part of those who would be its witnesses. It requires a conversion to a new way of "making sense." Reading these narratives as they are intended, as catechesis, just may set off an interpretive process in which the reader imitates Mary Magdalene and Thomas. Taken together, these two episodes lay out the proper parameters for this transformation by showing the relationship between the bodily risen Jesus and the ecclesial community that now bodies him forth in history:

> The purpose of these two episodes of "touching" is to help the reader make the same transitions that Mary Magdalene and Thomas the Twin had to make, from a romantic fantasy of contemporaneity with

the pre-Easter Jesus through the Paschal experience of death and new life to faith in the glorified and risen Lord. But in making this transition two extremes must be avoided. One is to see the Church not as a mediation of the risen Jesus himself but as an exhaustive substitute for a Jesus who no longer exists. The other is a Gnostic attempt to relate to Jesus in a purely spiritual Jesus-and-I spirituality that rejects the sacramental structure of the ecclesial body of the Lord as a merely human organization that plays no necessary or essential role in our encounter with Jesus. Mary Magdalene had to realize that the Church is the *body* of Christ (Jesus is not a corpse) and Thomas had to realize that the Church is the body of *Jesus* (not an unsatisfactory substitute for him).... If Jesus is not a real, distinct, personal subject, a real bodyperson, there is no ontological foundation for the Jesus mysticism that has been a constant feature of the church's spirituality, at least from the stoning of Stephan who saw *Jesus* standing at the right hand of God and Paul who learned that it was *Jesus* whom he was persecuting, down to our own day. But if Jesus is merely physically resuscitated, if he is still in the flesh, then he cannot be mediated by a community from which he becomes not only distinct but separate.[86]

As is becoming increasingly evident in this study, any attempt to properly understand the resurrection narratives requires that we discern their performative character. They are not simply descriptive. They are instructive, a "showing how." And as we shall see more clearly in a moment, this performative character implies a particular "space" for their being lived-into, a *habitus* where knowledge of the risen One may be propagated and practiced — the ecclesial community. But first we must draw some broader conclusions about the appearances traditions as a whole.

The "Both-And" Structure of the Resurrection Narratives

Whatever the precise circumstances of the original encounters that gave rise to these narratives in their present, diverse forms — including others I have not analyzed here, but shall elsewhere — they are remembered as simultaneously possessing aspects of familiarity and *alterity*, tactility and transcendence, visibility and in-visibility, presence and absence. The risen Christ is eventually recognizable as the self-same Jesus of Nazareth, and yet he is only recognizable and remembered in his eschatologically fulfilled corporeality, in his "bedazzling" form. Although it may be difficult to say more precisely "what" this reality consists of, at least in ontic terms, the narratives provide a grammar to help us think and speak between two extremes.

On the one hand, the empty tomb and appearance traditions together will not permit us to speak of the risen Jesus as simply returning to his former state of existence. The resurrection is not resuscitation. That Jesus first appears as a stranger, as one not limited by the partitions of ordinary space-time existence, as one who ascends from view in glory, etc., reveals the error of this extreme — one that would simply annul Jesus' death. The resurrection is more-than-historical. It cannot be plotted within history without remainder.

On the other hand, the risen Jesus has not been transposed into a reality completely discontinuous with his embodied history, as though his humanity were only the penultimate stage in his bid for a formless eternity. His resurrection is not a disembodiment but the admission of his total historical-embodied humanity into eschatological fullness. The empty tomb tradition makes this point abundantly clear. That we are instructed to speak of continuity in the midst of discontinuity is evident in the narratives' insistence on the familiarity and tactility of the risen Jesus, in ways that even include the identifying marks of his death.

Jesus' resurrection *is* and *is not* historical, and this requires simultaneous acts of saying and un-saying. With this "both-and" structure, the narratives present us a set of grammatical rules to help us speak of the resurrection with relative adequacy, with proper ballast. We are not granted a stable and definitive mental picture that would allow us to identify the risen body's quiddity. But this we do not need, nor should we expect it. We are however given the sufficient parameters that allow us to avoid misspeaking and misunderstanding (without fully comprehending) so long as we stay within them. Through their memorable imagery and dialogue, the narratives serve a technical and negative function by screening out extreme tendencies that would distort the nature and meaning of the Easter event. Thus, whenever we speak of the risen Jesus in himself, or of his relationship to the ecclesial body, we must be resolved to do so by affirming continuity and discontinuity, presence and absence, familiarity and *alterity*, concrete history and deathless transcendence, the memory of his death and the inauguration of history's ultimate future in his vindication and glorification. "He is risen; he is not here."

Though it may be difficult to grasp, the risen Lord is "simultaneously the dead-and-risen Lord." As James Alison observes, "the resurrection was the giving back of the life and the death at the same time.... [T]he resurrection life... is able to include both the life and death which concludes it, precisely because it is the free giving and giving back of both."[87]

As we shall see in chapters 7 and 8, this simultaneity is exactly what makes Jesus' resurrection God's definitive and non-violent offer of forgiveness. It is also what makes the resurrection God's victory *over* death as opposed to its mere negation. But what Jesus' resurrection and ascension most radically mean is "the introduction of a novelty into heaven: human nature. Being human was from then on permanently and indissolubly involved in the presence of God."[88] This insight, which is the very boldest of Christian insights, means that the body, particularly the body of a risen victim, is the very site of God's self-communication. The flesh (*caro*) is the hinge (*cardo*) on which salvation turns, so declared Tertullian in the third century.[89] Echoing it in the twentieth is Karl Rahner:

> Jesus, the Man, not merely *was* at one time of decisive importance for our salvation, i.e. for the real finding of the absolute God, by his historical and now past acts of the Cross, etc., but — as the one who became man and has remained a creature — he is *now* and for all eternity the *permanent openness* of our finite being to the living God of infinite, eternal life; he is, therefore, even in his humanity the created reality for us which stands in the act of our religion in such a way that, without this act towards his humanity and through it (implicitly or explicitly), the basic religious act towards God could never reach its goal. One always sees the Father only through Jesus.[90]

This is ultimately the meaning of Thomas the Twin's acclamation: "My Lord and my God!" Seeing the "form" of the crucified-and-risen One is to "see" the Father. He is the image (icon) of the in-visible God. This is also why we must speak of Jesus' resurrection in a theological aesthetics, as "bedazzlement." Christian revelation is true by being supremely beautiful, for it confers infinite value upon "form." The movement towards God's infinite transcendence by no means requires the dissolution of form — the body, the earth, history, temporality, relationality, particularity — but rather a deeper penetration into and affirmation of form in its iconicity. Hans Urs von Balthasar puts the matter this way:

> As we pass through Jesus' finitude and enter into its depths we encounter and find the Infinite, or rather, we are transported and found by the Infinite. Indeed, through the mysterious dialectic whereby Jesus' external, spatially and temporally conditioned finitude is transcended (which is the condition for the coming of the

Holy Spirit), but transcended in a way that is replaced by the "eternal finitude" of Jesus' resurrected flesh, all that is interior, invisible, spiritual and divine becomes accessible to us. If there were no such thing as the resurrection of the flesh, then the truth would lie with gnosticism and every form of idealism down to Schopenhauer and Hegel, for whom the finite must literally perish if it is to become spiritual and infinite. But the resurrection of the flesh vindicates the poets in a definitive sense: the aesthetic scheme of things, which allows us to possess the infinite with the finitude of form (however it is seen, understood or grasped spiritually) is right.[91]

Unnamable: The Resurrection Pluralizes Horizons

As I have argued thus far, the empty tomb and appearance narratives are "eschatological signs": historical vestiges and afterimages, revelatory traces of an "event" which, because of its historical and trans-historical reality, leaves its impress upon history, imbuing it with eschatological promise and dynamism, yet transcending the historical effects it continually shepherds. Such a reality could only be signified with relative adequacy to the extent that it includes complementary acts of saying and un-saying, rendering while not-grasping, disclosing while self-effacing. The presence-absence structure of the narratives echoes and analogizes the historical *aporia* of Jesus' bodily resurrection from the dead. Their style of presentation (their form) is marked unmistakably and uniquely by the *sui generis* "event" they seek to reveal (their content). Far from reflecting a deficiency in the risen Christ's self-attestation, the tensions, ambiguities, and plurality of the resurrection narratives result from a brimming excess that produces harmonic, serializing patterns in the oral and textual traditions that enshrine without ever encompassing it.

While it is customary for apologetic defenses of the resurrection to emphasize the points of convergence between the resurrection narratives, no doubt because non-contradiction and multiple attestation are regarded as among the most important criteria for historical reliability, the differences and asymmetries between the narratives are just as important for appreciating their peculiar nature. Certainly patterns across the traditions do emerge. For example, most of the appearance traditions describe a process that works something like this: (1) the disciples find themselves in a state of desolation and shattered expectations; (2) Jesus appears to them, typically under the aspect of initial obscurity and shock; (3) Jesus greets his followers, offering them a word of *shalom*; (4) the disciples come to recognize him, sometimes worshipping, sometimes still doubting; (5) Jesus gives the disciples a word of command and/or mission; and, finally, (6) Jesus withdraws from their field of perception.[92] Despite this general coherence, however, important differences emerge, just as they do with the empty tomb narratives. For example, it is impossible to pin down a single chronological ordering of events. Neither can we map them consistently according to geography. Whereas Mark includes no appearance tradition in Jerusalem, focusing on Galilee instead as the place where the women and the disciples will see the risen Jesus, Matthew, Luke, and John all relate appearance traditions associated with Jerusalem. (Though the longer ending of Mark does include Jerusalem as a setting for the appearances.) While Mark, Matthew, and John exclusively associate the tomb area with the women, Luke includes an episode of Peter running to the tomb, "stooping and looking in," where he "saw the linen cloths by themselves; then he went home, amazed at what had happened" (24:34). Matthew's commission narrative occurs on a mountain in Galilee, while John focuses on the Sea of Tiberius. Luke's three appearances in and around Jerusalem — Emmaus (24:13–32), to Peter (v. 34) and the eleven (vv. 36–53) — all occur on the same day and concludes with his departure on Easter night. But the beginning of Luke's sequel, Acts, indicates that Jesus appeared over a forty-day period (1:3). Meanwhile, John extends the appearances over the period of a week. To complicate matters further, Paul tells of an appearance to five hundred brothers and sisters, not mentioned in the gospels, and of his own encounter with the risen Christ two years later (1 Cor. 15:6–8). While some of these differences are open to some harmonization, overall the various traditions resist a single sequence. This is by no means a concession to incoherence, as if the sometimes-irreconcilable aspects of the narratives yield unreliable testimony. Indeed, several critics have noted that the divergences and disagreements serve to support their reliability, historically speaking, since they show the witnesses are not in collusion to make it up. As N. T. Wright points out, "it is precisely this imprecision, coupled with the breathless quality of the narratives, that gives them not only their unique flavor but also their particular value. Despite the scorn of some, lawyers and judges have regularly declared that this is precisely the state of the evidence they find in a great many cases: this is what eyewitness testimony looks and sounds like. And in such cases *the surface discrepancies do not mean that nothing happened; rather, they mean that the witnesses have not been in collusion.*"[93] Wright also reminds us of the complex and layered processes that brought about the narratives in their present form, beginning with oral traditions that circulated from region to region, picking up this or that accent according to the particular exigencies of each community, and concluding with the textual traditions that formalized these transmissions within new narrative patterns, providing new thematic emphases, reflecting each gospel writer's authorial goals and historical context. Even in their final redactions, the gospel writers allow the asymmetries to stand "warts and all: this was how their community had told the story from the very first days."[94] But this plurality is more than a consequence of surface factors of historical and textual transmission. We will find in it a deeper theological significance.

In the Philippians hymn, God is said to have exalted Jesus, giving him "the name that is above every name" (Phil. 2:9). As Marion observes, this exaltation above every name reproduces "the property of God himself admitting all names and refusing each of them...the property of summoning an infinity of nominative horizons in order to denominate he who saturates not only each horizon, but the incommensurable sum of the horizons."[95] Christ, just as the Father, cannot be properly named within a single horizon, or the sum of them, but draws all perceptual and linguistic horizons towards himself, transcending and pluralizing them. His Kingdom remains "not of this world," even if it is always irrupting within and through it. He neither conforms to our categories, nor do the christological titles finally manifest his essence. Citing the end of John's gospel, where we are told that the whole world cannot contain the books necessary to describe all that Jesus did (21:25), Marion points to the plurality of the gospels and christological titles as traces of an eschatological excess. If the New Testament canon is "closed," it remains internally diverse and inexhaustible:

> The writers who attempt to offer witness to the paradox they have seen are at least four and necessarily in partial disagreement on account of the finite aspect and horizon that each was able to take into view and put into operation. Scripture itself traditionally admits four concurrent meanings, something that recent exegesis confirms by according it an unlimited number of different literary genres, each of which in fact offers a new horizon in order to welcome a new aspect of the one and only paradox.[96]

The incommensurability of the gospels may create certain difficulties for their historical valuation, at least the kind of valuation that is the hallmark of so much modern criticism, but no independent substrate can be extracted. No homogenized version of the gospels is possible, even if it were desirable. Such pluralization does not however lead to deconstructive undecidability, as though the differences in scripture result in endless *différance*. Viewed post-critically, and in recognition of the semantic surplus involved in all interpretation, the plurality within the canon is theologically pregnant.[97] In the multiplication of textual bodies that arise in the "space" of a gracious withdrawal (Christ's bodily "resurrection" and "ascension"), we glean something of the boundless fecundity of their ultimate referent. The multitude of images in the appearance traditions, rather than providing different pieces for a single, puzzle-like image that would work together to satisfy our desire for conceptual stability, instead generate an ungovernable turbulence that renders each and every image incomplete and overexposed. Here *apophasis* and *kataphasis* are virtually indistinguishable. "The images surround an inaccessible mid-point," writes von Balthasar, "which alone has the magnetic force to arrange around itself, in concentric fashion, this image-garland.... In the event of the Resurrection all previous schemata come to their fulfillment and suffer their breakdown at one and the same time."[98] Again, Christ's overwhelming proximity manifests in "distance." As the icon of the invisible God, the risen Christ is inexhaustible form and beauty. Such overabundance generates an infinity of perspectives and meanings. The form of Christ, writes David Bentley Hart, is not a truth recognizable apart from its aesthetic character, which, as the supreme moment of beauty, "is always *situated* in perspectives, vantages, points of departure, but is never fixed, contained, exhausted, or mastered."[99] To the extent that theological truth finds in beauty something more than a cosmetic overlay, it may learn to not be suspicious of the plurality of perspectives but welcome it as the consequence of beauty's playful extravagance.

Michel de Certeau describes Jesus' bodily withdrawal in death and resurrection as a "making room," a "permission" for new bodies of language, community, and praxis to arise in fruitful pluralization, as opposed to linear, self-same replication. The founding event of Christianity is a generative kenosis that "lets be" in history what continuously manifests that event without ever coinciding with it. This is not a lamentable "falling away" from an original, undifferentiated unity that we should attempt to overcome or recreate. It is a generous and creative absence that installs difference and otherness within origins, and thus to any proper Christian understanding of unity. The manifold images and narratives in the New Testament hang together as a *complexio oppositorum*, a patchwork of suggestive fragments, narrative strands, and image clusters sedimented over time and reflecting the countless factors that shaped the communities who orally and textually transmitted them through catechesis, prayer, and praxis. While the closing of the canon certainly rules out some traditions as insufficient to the grammar of Christian language and praxis — this is not, after all, a hapless collection of texts where any and everything goes — the canon also preserves diversity within it, thereby placing a premium on unity-in-multiplicity.[100] "They are a collection of texts which do not say the same thing. The Gospel of Mark cannot be reduced to that of John any more than to the Epistles of Jude or Paul. Non-identity is characteristic of the language of the New Testament." This "network of texts," argues de Certeau, reflects a different understanding of coherence and unity than what we might find in metaphysics. "It does not reduce the many to the one. On the contrary, the plural is maintained. Differences permit the other."[101] There is no single testimony, but *testimonies*, and this serves a critical function: it prevents a single image or representation to stand as stable (and thus opaque) before its referent. Such would be idolatry. "Indeed, there is the disappearance of an 'idol' which would freeze our view and give us the truth in a singularity. There is a fading away of any 'primitive' object capable of being delimited by a knowledge and possessed as in an ownership.... On the contrary, *the 'kenosis' of presence gives rise to a plural, communitarian language.*"[102] And so, rather than a single, conceptually permanent picture of origins, which might submit to a single schema of chronology, geography, and *dramatis personae*, we discover a plurality of times, places, and people who share in the "event" — in a way that permits differences to be acknowledged as more than a matter of historical accident, but as a constituting mark of Christianity as dynamic and communitarian:

> Christian language has (and must have) a communitarian structure. This connection of witnesses, of signs or different roles announces a "truth" which cannot be reduced to unity by one member, or by a particular function.
>
> Because this "truth" belongs to no one individual or group (even theological), it is proclaimed by several. Because this truth is the ungraspable condition of that which it makes possible, it leaves behind only a multiplicity of signs: a historical network of interconnected places, rather than a hierarchical pyramid.[103]

Unconstitutable: Resurrection as the Giving of a "Self"

We have at last reached the fourth and final characteristic way Jesus' resurrection reveals itself as the saturated phenomenon *par excellence*. In the first three, we have examined the following:

1. Jesus' resurrection from the dead is not foreseeable but fulfills all expectation through subversion and transformation;

The Im-possible Gift

2. The historical vestiges of Easter (the empty tomb and appearances) are bedazzling effects of an "event" that overwhelms the affective, linguistic, and conceptual capacities of those who become its witnesses, thus requiring complementary acts of saying and un-saying as its grammar;

3. Jesus' resurrection generates a dynamic plurality in the oral and textual traditions that enshrine it, thereby establishing within Christian origins a creative diversity and complementarity among the various communities formed by it.

The fourth and final aspect is directly related to the first three, but allows us now to focus more clearly on the ecclesial and apostolic dimension of the resurrection narratives. We may put it this way: Easter faith is not constituted by the "subject" who believes, but rather gives birth to a new "self" that may be received only in hospitality to the crucified-and-risen Other. The emergence of this new self follows a process of conversion within a new contextual setting, a new *habitus* in which Jesus' resurrection is embodied through proclamation, worship, and ethical praxis. This *habitus* is the church — the "body of Christ." And it is only in the realm of the church, through participation in the community's mission of "being sent" into the world, that Jesus' resurrection "makes sense." Here again the presence-absence structure of the resurrection narratives plays a key role.

Jesus' resurrection and ascension mark a new and saturating "presence" in the community that simultaneously manifests itself under the aspect of a generative "absence." Jesus' body, now risen and withdrawn, is to be found in the ecclesial body. Paul's metaphors of organic growth and bodiliness are most apt. New believers are "grafted" onto Christ (Rom. 11:17). Baptized into his death and resurrection they become members of his body. Though many, they become "one body in Christ, and individually we are members of one another" (Rom. 12:5). In him "all things hold together. He is the head of the body, the church; he is the beginning, the firstborn of the dead" (Col. 1:18). The resurrection/ascension represents a "logic of birthing," or a "logic of opening. The withdrawal of the body of Jesus," writes Graham Ward, "must be understood in terms of the Logos creating a space within himself, a womb, within which (*en Christoi*) the Church will expand and creation be recreated."[104] The metaphor of the body is especially important since bodiliness *is* mediation and relation. Just as embodied human beings are never absolutely and immaterially self-present, but outwardly extended in endless dynamic relations — even our inmost interiority is bodily mediated, and so inhabited by the Other — so too is the presence of Christ never to be found absolutely in immaterial identity but always in and through the mediation of sacrament, language, community, and praxis. The body *is* presence-in-mediation. "The body of Jesus Christ, the body of God, is permeable, transcorporeal, transpositional. Within it all other bodies are situated and given their significance."[105]

This insistence on the corporeality of Christian faith presents a stumbling block to many. Just as human bodiliness has proven to be a source of trouble for metaphysics, many find in the bodily and ecclesially mediated character of resurrection faith a scandal. As Louis-Marie Chauvet points out, Christian faith demands that we think God, not according to the immaterial and a-historical, but *according to corporeality*.[106] Christian existence is sacramental existence, a matter of mediated-immediacy. It is relational, historical, and pragmatic. In a brilliant reading of Luke 24, Chauvet shows that "seeing" the risen Jesus in the post-paschal dispensation requires that we relinquish the desire to see him with Gnostic immediacy: "for now he allows himself to be encountered only through the *body of his word,* in the constant reappropriation that the *Church* makes of his message, his deeds, and his own way of living. Live in the Church! It is there that you will discover and recognize him."[107] Just as we saw above in John's resurrection narratives, where Mary Magdalene and Thomas the Twin are directed to the ecclesial body and its apostolic mission as the place where the risen Jesus may be found, Luke affirms the church "as the fundamental sacramental mediation within which alone the believing subject can emerge." This is key: there is no "subject" who constitutes resurrection belief; rather, the ecclesial body gives birth to a new self. My identity as a Christian is not something I create. It is something I receive as a response to an invitation. This recognition may not come easily. Indeed, it requires a conversion. But it is precisely this point that Luke makes as he recounts the journey of the disciples from mis-understanding to understanding in the shared breaking of the bread.

If we acknowledge that knowing Jesus as risen is fundamentally bound up with the body of Christ — the New Testament permits no alternative to this — we must ask some basic questions about the nature of the statement: "Jesus is risen from the dead." What sort of statement is it? How is it possible to make such a statement? What is the relationship between the one who refers and the referent? In what way does it "make sense?" In chapter 1 I noted that Jesus' resurrection raises fundamental questions about worldviews and the nature of knowing itself. If we understand the resurrection narratives in their catechetical and ecclesial character, and if we can appreciate the conversion process that the witnesses to the resurrection were invited to undertake, we will find that affirming "He is risen; he is not here" or "Jesus is Lord" is far more like learning a new language and acquiring a new set of skills within a communal context than it is assenting to a single proposition. Just as all knowledge is socially webbed, generative of and generated by an array of social practices and shared discourse, knowing Jesus as risen implies a distinctive locality, a cultural-linguistic structure in which a broad array of sentiments, presuppositions, beliefs, and practices converge in sometimes thematic (but often tacit) ways, thereby engendering a meaning-field in which something like "resurrection" is intelligible, coherent, and productive. Coming to know Jesus as risen implies participation in a social-theoretical-practical space where Jesus is already affirmed as the risen One and where the act of knowing Jesus as risen is sourced through a constantly renewed memory, materialized in performance, and propagated through the instruction and "showing how" by its more competent members. In short, knowing Jesus as risen means knowing *ecclesially*, as church. Resurrection belief is not reducible to an isolated proposition about a single "event" that allegedly occurred some two thousand years ago. Such an approach already rests upon a deficient understanding. The meaning and significance of Jesus' resurrection, rather, *gives itself* or *manifests itself* (one might say, "appears") in the manner of a *worlding*. It cannot be conjured up in a discrete intellectual act. To be sure, "Jesus rose from the dead" has a propositional content. It refers *to* an "event" that precedes any recognition thereof. But this referentiality gains its "sense" from *within* a social-linguistic complex in which its meaning is lived, shared, and performed. This is not to deny the possibility of making truth-claims about some state of affairs "out there." We need not opt here for a completely non-referential understanding of truth. But we must recognize that knowing, believing, imagining, and speaking are also a doing, living, relating, and producing: socially generated and generative. Resurrection belief cannot simply be apprehended. It is *given*. It *manifests itself*. It *presents itself* as a possibility through apostolic witness. It invites. It summons. Responding to it will entail some kind of self-dispossession, a leaving behind, but also a new welcoming and in-habitation. Faith comes *ex auditu*, as Gift. "Blessed are those who have not seen and yet have come to believe" (John 20:29).

It is true, however, that resurrection language cannot simply be a "private language," utterly unintelligible and inaccessible to those "outside." As all language is porous to the Other — language *is* this porosity — even the unique world of meaning that is the resurrection's will necessarily be exposed to and interact with other conceptual-linguistic horizons. If Jesus' resurrection is the condition of its own possibility, giving birth and providing structure to a world of imagination and praxis that cannot be ultimately derived from anything else, still it reaches out in hospitality to all else. Resurrection faith is one of mission, of "being sent" into the world. Christianity's prophetic potential demands the exercise of a public and critical role, allowing even its most unique doctrinal claims and practices to interact with and give shape to a broader public. If, therefore, we speak quite emphatically of the ecclesial presupposition and configuration of resurrection belief, and thus assume here a non-foundational approach in which resurrection belief cannot be secured by an extra-textual foundation, this will not lead to some sort of fideism. In coming chapters, we shall explore the public and critical significance of Jesus' resurrection from the dead — its "productive force" not only *within* the church but beyond it. In the same way that doors and partitions cannot bind the risen Christ, the church is called to body Christ forth in the world through proclamation, dialogue, and praxis.

Ultimately the resurrection narratives are commission narratives, narratives of sending and receiving, narratives that reveal the structure of being as "being given," "being risen," and "being sent." Nearly every appearance story includes a word of command and commission. In Mark the women are commanded to "go, tell his disciples and Peter," "so they went out" (16:7). In Matthew the eleven are told: "Go therefore and make disciples of all nations" (28:19). And in Luke: "You are witnesses of these things. And see, I am sending upon you what my Father promised...and, lifting up his hand, he blessed them" (24:49, 50). The empty tomb narrative in John includes Jesus' instructions to Mary Magdalene to "go to my brothers and say to them, 'I am ascending to my Father and your Father, to my God and your God'" (20:17). As we saw above, her announcement to the disciples ("I have seen the Lord") indicates a fundamental shift in her understanding, just as it did for the eleven. She has received a new self from the crucified-and-risen One who, in the midst of her grief and misunderstanding, calls her by name and directs her to the community of disciples who will embody him and extend his mission in the world: "As the Father has sent me, so I send you" (20:21). To Peter, Jesus says "feed my sheep," "follow me" (21:17, 19). This connection between resurrection and apostolic mission is immediately evident in Paul's self-understanding as well: "Paul an apostle — sent neither by human commission nor from human authorities, but through Jesus Christ and God the Father, who raised him from the dead" (Gal. 1:1). All of this shows just how intimately the church's identity is bound up with mission, how being reconciled and being-in-community is, for the New Testament, "being sent" in the world as an agent for justice, reconciliation, and peace. Mission in proclamation and praxis is not a secondary movement of the church, coming as a consequence of an identity already established within itself, but as the very way that identity comes about.

Chapter Three

BODIES *IN ABSENTIA*

THE SCANDAL OF THE EMPTY TOMB

The Christian doctrine of bodily resurrection is a stumbling block for thought, the empty tomb a scandal for speech. For much modern theology, the proclamation of Jesus' bodily resurrection from the dead creates a certain embarrassment, a compulsive need to explain. Although the specific language of "resurrection" may be retained, and Jesus affirmed as "alive to God," the empty tomb narratives and the anthropology they seem to assume are among the first casualties of a demythologizing program, dismissed out of hand as reflecting an outmoded cosmology. Modern theologians frequently seem eager, as if carrying an intellectual burden in need of urgent confession, to disabuse their readers of the idea that Jesus' resurrection involves anything like the resuscitation of a corpse. If the point is necessary to make, it is frequently attended by an anxiety regarding the claim more generally. The challenges in affirming the doctrine of bodily resurrection are not just present in academic theology. They present a genuine pastoral problem. As previously mentioned, Paul Avis contends that while many Christians can maintain the central affirmation that "God was in Christ reconciling the world to himself" (2 Cor. 5:19), they find the "miraculous accompaniments" of virginal conception, exorcisms, bodily resurrection, and ascension "not only utterly incredible but also totally meaningless."[1] For such Christians Avis envisions a faith in which the fate of Jesus' body — "and it is that approach to the Resurrection which constitutes the *stumbling block for many*" — plays no real role, "for the empty tomb provides neither proof nor meaningful content for the Resurrection. In itself it is ambiguous and inconclusive. It may be an eloquent symbol, but it is not the reality of Resurrection."[2]

Notwithstanding Avis's laudable concern that theology be crafted with pastoral sensitivity, we might ask whether the doctrine of bodily resurrection and the empty tomb narratives that give this doctrine a specific meaning are so dispensable. Avis's disassociation of "symbol" and "reality" is most telling, and problematic. If we can grant the necessary caution that no symbol can be identified univocally with the reality it symbolizes, while conceding that an empty tomb proves nothing in itself, the assertion that the empty tomb bears no "meaningful content" is dubious on several counts. In the first place, such a position assumes either that the empty tomb stories have no historical basis whatsoever or that the data is so ambiguous that only agnosticism is warranted.[3] Avis gives the impression that biblical scholarship has come to a general consensus that history is not a meaningful category for thinking about the empty tomb. To some extent he is correct. It is not uncommon to find statements among historians and theologians alike that the empty tomb and appearances narratives are only later, legendary embellishments of a more primitive tradition. But to assume scholarly consensus on this matter would be hasty. An impressive number of scholars affirm an enduring historical kernel to them.[4] One of the most significant factors in considering their historical worth is the emergence of resurrection language in the early Christian communities. Once we appreciate that a considerable diversity of opinion existed in the first century regarding eschatology, the specific choice the earliest Christians made in adopting resurrection language to speak of Jesus' post-mortem existence is highly significant. To reiterate a point previously made, had the disciples only wished to affirm that Jesus was miraculously "alive to God" after his death, without in any way referring to the disappearance of a corpse, without suggesting that he was transformed into a new corporeality, there were ample resources to assist them. "The idea of a soul separable from the body," observes N. T. Wright, "with different theories as to what might happen to it thereafter, was widespread in the varied Judaisms of the turn of the eras."[5] Given this availability of options, the assertion made by some, that the early Christians developed stories about an empty tomb or adopted resurrection language as an inevitable outcome of a monolithically Jewish anthropology, is mistaken. No single conception of life after death was mandated within first-century Judaism. And so, the deliberate *choice* made by the earliest Christians to speak of Jesus as "risen from the dead" must be better clarified. Raymond Brown puts the matter this way:

> It is suggested that somehow a genuine faith in Jesus' victory over death emerged and that this faith was conceptualized as bodily resurrection, not on a factual basis (whether by encounter with the risen Jesus or by interpretation of the empty tomb) but simply because *the Jewish mind had available no other concept for*

expressing a victory over death. This contention is inaccurate, for we know of several other models of victory over death were current in Judaism and might have been employed by Christians, models that did not involve the resurrection and/or appearances of the one raised from the dead.... Thus the choice of resurrection language was not an inevitability for the early Jews who believed in Jesus. To the contrary, its choice must be explained; for, while there was an expectation among many Jews of the resurrection of the dead in the last times, there was no expectation of the resurrection of a single man from the dead, separate from and preliminarily to the general resurrection.[6]

There is no reason to suppose that the affirmation of Jesus' bodily resurrection from the dead was any less scandalous in the first century than it is today. Great risk attended the early Christians who embarked upon such a claim. Even among those who believed in the general resurrection of the dead, there was no good reason, much less a known precedent, to expect that a single person would be risen from the dead prior to the end of the age. The idea would have appeared counterintuitive at best, and quite possibly incoherent. With remarkable candor the gospels recount the considerable difficulty the disciples themselves had coming to terms with such a conclusion. Their risk was only heightened by the fact that had a body or a skeleton been produced it would have been "difficult, if not impossible, to understand how the disciples could have preached that God raised Jesus from the dead, since there would have been irrefutable evidence that He had not done so."[7] Resurrection language in the first century had to do with bodies, with creation in its concrete corporeality, not with immaterial spirits. There is no evidence that resurrection in the first century, either before or after Paul, could have meant something non-bodily.[8] If Jesus' dead body had been produced, the disciples may have still proclaimed him being present to God, but they would not have done so using the language of resurrection. While resurrection language is metaphorical, given to varying inflections of meaning within and beyond the New Testament, it is not without semantic anchorage. To say Jesus is "risen from the dead" cannot be translated without remainder into the more colorless expression, "alive to God." "Resurrection" and "resurrection of the body" are tautologous. For this reason, Geza Vermes, a non-Christian historian, has concluded:

> When every argument has been considered and weighed, the only conclusion acceptable to the historian must be that the opinions of the orthodox, the liberal sympathizer and the critical agnostic

alike — and even perhaps the disciples themselves — are simply interpretations of the one disconcerting fact: namely that the women who set out to pay their last respects to Jesus found to their consternation, not a body, but an empty tomb.[9]

Please notice the argument I am *not* making here: we are not arguing that because the tomb was empty, therefore Jesus is risen. We cannot make the transition from a historical absence to an affirmation of Jesus' risen presence without an act of faith, an act that remains dependent upon apostolic testimony. By itself the empty tomb remains ambiguous. It "is" not the reality of resurrection. (Avis is entirely correct on this point.) But this does not mean that the empty tomb is without meaningful content. Without a bodily absence the early Christian proclamation would have taken a substantially different form. The appearances of Jesus to his followers by themselves did not necessitate the use of resurrection language. The Hebrew scriptures with which the earliest Christians were intimately familiar teems with examples of spiritual visions and locutions. The encounters with Jesus after his death could have been interpreted in such terms without any recourse to resurrection language. Only a peculiar convergence of factors provoked the earliest Christians to adopt a form of discourse with the semantic capacities uniquely suited for their accounting. The empty tomb without the appearances, just as the appearances without the empty tomb, does not mandate resurrection language. But their mutual interaction *does*.[10] The appearances help us to interpret the empty tomb, and the empty tomb helps us to interpret the appearances. The "symbol" and the "reality" cannot be disassociated.

The rigor of our theological task is to reflect upon this historical absence. If the empty tomb is not later poetic ornamentation to Christian proclamation but the stimulus for that proclamation, we must weigh its significance for the whole range of Christian theology, particularly for anthropology. The project for theology is not to strip away the naïve mythology enshrining but now obscuring the "inner essence" of Christian truth, to cut through the clumsy media of the empty tomb and appearance narratives to arrive at more palatably generic affirmations. The proclamation of Jesus' bodily resurrection does not represent "mythology" in this pejorative sense. It does, however, run counter to some of the most deeply entrenched intellectual habits that shape our understanding of the human person. The scandal of the empty tomb, like the scandal of the incarnation, is not something we should dismiss simply because it doesn't easily comport with our prior assumptions about *theos* and *anthropos*. Pastoral sensitivity requires that we think within the scandal of the empty tomb, to allow it to be the starting point of our anthropology.

The scandal of the empty tomb, it turns out, is the *body*. But why should the body be a scandal? What is it that provokes a sense of offense or intellectual resistance when we think about risen bodies? That is the primary question I want to pursue in this chapter before, in the next, working towards a more constructive theology of bodily resurrection.

Francis Watson, in a most insightful essay, offers our initial clue: "The empty tomb story is a stumbling-block to all forms of theological docetism, and since docetism has proved the most pervasive and insidious of all the temptations that have afflicted Christian theology, resistance to the doctrine of the bodiliness of Jesus' resurrection is only to be expected."[11] My contention is that this theological docetism is a symptom of a broader tendency in our Western intellectual tradition to regard the body as non-constitutive of personal identity, to subordinate or instrumentalize the body in favor of immediacy and "self-presence." In christology, docetism refers to a heretical tendency to regard Jesus' bodily humanity as only an "appearance," somewhat like an external and instrumental "mask," of his internal, incorruptible, and immaterial deity. The Logos does not really suffer or die in the flesh. The Logos does not really enter into the flesh but only appears to do so in order to show the way of liberation to other souls tragically embodied and yearning for their final escape. To say that docetism remains a pervasive temptation for theology means that embodiment presents a constant challenge to how we imagine our personal identities. The oldest christological heresy reveals the single greatest challenge to theology — to think the Logos as flesh, not only for a time, but for all eternity. Although I would not care to label all who deny the meaningfulness of the empty tomb narratives "docetists," there is a creeping docetism or "essentialism" in the move to relativize them and diminish the stubbornly corporeal character of Jesus' resurrection.

"The doctrine of Jesus' bodily resurrection," adds Watson, is "of a piece with the doctrines of creation and incarnation; the culmination of the biblical narrative of creation, fall, and redemption is in fundamental conformity with the beginning."[12] As Watson shows, bodily resurrection is intertwined with the whole range of Christian affirmations. Together they form an internally coherent field of meaning, and together they cut across every attempt to identify the human person with an abstract, monadic essence. Because bodiliness is constitutive of the human person's eschatological fruition, and because bodiliness is just that which bonds "me" to the human and cosmic Other, the doctrine of bodily resurrection serves as the most direct challenge to every form of dualism.

A CLAIM UPON THE WORLD

"For what sort of human soul would have any further desire for a body that has rotted?" This question, posed by the second-century physician and philosopher Celsus, expresses more than curiosity, more than puzzlement at his Christian opponents. It expresses moral revulsion and aesthetic offense:

> But, indeed, neither can God do what is shameful nor does He desire what is contrary to nature. If you were to desire something abominable in your wickedness, not even God would be able to do this, and you ought not to believe at all that your desire will be fulfilled. For God is not the author of sinful desire or of disorderly confusion, but of what is naturally just and right. For the soul He might be able to provide an everlasting life; but as Heraclitus says, "corpses ought to be thrown away as worse than dung." As for the flesh, which is full of things which it is not even nice to mention, God would neither desire nor be able to make it everlasting contrary to reason. For He himself is the reason of everything that exists; therefore He is not able to do anything contrary to reason or to His own character.[13]

Among the most challenging doctrines early Christian apologists felt obliged to defend against their cultured despisers was unquestionably "the resurrection of the body." As the above passage attests, much more was involved in this debate than whether such a thing is possible. Even if we grant that for God anything is possible, says Celsus, we must ask whether it is desirable, whether it is in keeping with nature, whether it is consistent with God's character to raise bodies from the dead. It would seem here that it is more precisely the nature of the *body,* "full of things which it is not even nice to mention," which provokes the intellectual, moral, and aesthetic offense.

Brian Daley has argued that the emergence of Christian theological debate in the sub-apostolic period finds its roots in questions over eschatology.[14] While undoubtedly true, one might suggest that the question of the body more specifically drives these debates. More than any century before or since, debates over bodily resurrection raged at a fever pitch throughout the second century. Of course, the gospels evidence some apologetic motivation in various additions and redactionary decisions in order to emphasize that Jesus' body was *really* raised.[15] Paul's letter to the Corinthians shows the apostle at pains to correct those tendencies in the community that interpreted Jesus' resurrection in an overly spiritualized manner.[16] But in the second century the question of the body was particularly alive, undoubtedly the result of the growing conflict between Hellenistic and Hebraic attitudes towards the body. As the primitive Christian movement expanded throughout the broader Mediterranean world it was bound to encounter conflict with Hellenistic ideas. Generally speaking, the apologetic movement of the second century was inspired by the need for Christian theology to respond to a double accusation: (1) Christianity is intellectually indefensible, a bad mixture of mythology and philosophy; and (2) Christianity is a threat to the Roman Empire. As Paul Tillich observes, both accusations come together at their sharpest point in the polemical works of Celsus, for whom Jesus' resurrection becomes the central focus of attack. I have already noted Celsus's moral and aesthetic disgust for bodily resurrection. Tillich points out the other edge: if Jesus' resurrection meant the overcoming of the "principalities and powers," and if the risen Jesus is to be regarded as "Lord," this can only be viewed as a threat to the Roman Empire and its rule.[17] For Celsus, Jesus' bodily resurrection was not only philosophically incoherent and aesthetically objectionable; it was politically dangerous. Jesus' resurrection (read: the divine vindication of a criminal crucified under the rule of law) represents a narrative of subversion that might only embolden others who, with the hope of being vindicated in their practice of the faith, even unto death, might sound the same kind of revolutionary song as their so called "king." Wright puts the point well, saying that the resurrection "launched a claim on the world":

> a claim at once absurd (a tiny group of nobodies cocking a snook at the might of Rome) and very serious, so serious that within a couple of generations the might of Rome was trying, and failing, to stamp it out. It grew from an essentially positive view of the world, of creation. It refused to relinquish the world to the principalities and powers, but claimed even them for allegiance to the Messiah who was now lord, the *kyrios*.... The resurrection of Jesus, in the fully bodily sense I have described, supplies the groundwork for this: it is the reaffirmation of the universe of space, time and matter, after not only sin and death but also pagan empire (the institutionalization of sin and death) have done their worst.[18]

Wright's statement reinforces the point that the Christian view of salvation put the status of the body squarely in view.[19] And it was just this emphasis that was so difficult for the Hellenistic mind to accept.[20] Within a Hellenistic context the affirmation of the body's "resurrection" would seem naïvely materialistic, a mere "hope of worms." Little within Platonic, Stoic, Epicurean, Aristotelian, or neo-Platonic streams of thought could lend support to the attribution of "immortality" to the human body. "For this perishable body must put on imperishability, and this mortal body must put on immortality" (1 Cor. 15:53). The very idea would have been viewed as a category mistake, a confusion of ontically distinct realities, absurd, if seriously maintained.

It cannot be said that the early Christian apologists of the second and third centuries developed a uniform response to the various philosophical objections to bodily resurrection. Diverse are the metaphors and conceptual models for conceiving of such a reality.[21] Certain patterns do emerge, however. For example, Justin, Athenagoras, Irenaeus, Tertullian, and Origen all asserted the *reasonableness* of bodily resurrection on the basis that, because God originally fashioned human beings as a composite of body and soul, the fulfillment of the whole person logically required the fulfillment of the body.[22] This argument, which still demands thoughtful consideration, perhaps does little to convince someone who does not already affirm the body's constitutive role in personal identity. But it does reveal the internal relationship between eschatological and anthropological statements, a fact to which we shall return.

Many of the apologists also sought to demonstrate the *coherence* of bodily resurrection within the broader complex of Christian beliefs. Irenaeus of Lyons, for example, summarizes and systematizes a hundred years of theology as he correlates the significance of bodily resurrection with: (1) God's covenantal goodness and concern for material creation; (2) the incarnation of the Logos, who ontogenetically recapitulates and transforms the phylogenetic saga of human history; (3) Jesus' miracles of physical healing; (4) the indwelling of the Holy Spirit in the body as a temple; and (5) the sacramental practices of the church in which matter communicates and is bonded with what is most spiritual, not least in the Eucharist.[23] Bodily resurrection, argues Irenaeus, gains its meaning and coherence within the entire economy of salvation, an order in which the body plays a fundamental role. As Tertullian would memorably put it, the flesh (*caro*) is the very hinge (*cardo*) on which salvation turns. As the second-century apologists attempted to articulate how and why the body participated in the *eschaton,* they were in fact coming to terms with something that, from the point of view of Greek philosophy, demanded a transvaluation of ideas about *anthropos* and *theos:* the body is the very "site" of salvation, and is so because God has assumed a body, a piece of creation, not just for a time, but for eternity. Celsus was quite correct to point out that bodily resurrection bears upon God's nature. His understanding of God would, "according to reason," have little or nothing to do with the body. Christian theology, however, informed as it is by the shocking kenosis of a God who is found in a crucified-and-risen body, is obliged to think God and body in direct, not inverse proportion: to think God according to corporeality.[24]

In her major study of the doctrine of bodily resurrection from the sub-apostolic to the mid-fourteenth century, Carol Walker Bynum convincingly shows that despite the multitude of theological metaphors and images used to describe the resurrection of the body throughout the centuries, and despite the fact that Western Christianity has at times manifested a suspicion of the body, the sensuality and realism of its eschatology, as imagined by its theologians, artists, poets, and mystics, expresses a conviction of the self as a psychosomatic unity. The idea of "person" generated by belief in bodily resurrection was "not a concept of soul escaping body or soul using body; it was a concept of self in which physicality was integrally bound to sensation, emotion, reasoning, identity — and therefore finally to whatever one means by salvation.... Indeed, person was not person without body, and body was the carrier or the expression... of what we today call individuality."[25] Bynum's study confirms in a historical way the significance of Karl Rahner's statement that Christian eschatology is Christian anthropology in the future tense.[26] Anthropological and eschatological statements are mutually reinforcing. Deeply embedded in the debates over bodily resurrection from the second to the fourth centuries are questions about the human self and the self's relation to other selves within the material cosmos. Is there an "I" that survives the changes in the body, even its dissolution? Is there an identifiable substrate underlying biological flux? Is my body "me," strictly speaking, or is my body in some sense "other"? What is the relationship of my body with the rest of the material universe? Am I a "closed system"? Does my "me" stop where my skin meets the world, or is the body, and therefore my very self, ever ecstatically open outward, communicable, permeable, and thus structurally ambiguous? If understood aright, even the most apparently speculative (and perhaps most peculiar) reflections in eschatology have such issues squarely in mind. For example, Gregory of Nyssa's consideration of the dispersed "bits" of the decomposed body, or Augustine's thoughts on the size and age of the risen body, and whether it will have hair, nails, and entrails, are as much about eschatology as they are about anthropology: In what way is my body really "me"?[27]

If we take for granted that eschatological and anthropological statements are mutually reinforcing — that how one imagines the eschatological fulfillment of the person has much to do with how one imagines the nature of personhood at present, and vice versa — then it is possible to suggest that the scandal provoked by the idea of bodily resurrection reflects attitudes about the human body as such. More than any other Christian doctrine, the doctrine of bodily resurrection, if it is not to be simply written off as a bad mixture of mythology and philosophy, demands that Christians affirm the body as more than a temporary vehicle for personal identity — a disposable and instrumental "expression" of an immaterial and substantial "self" or "soul" — but as the very way personal reality is accomplished in the world, *permanently* constitutive of identity. I do not simply *have* a body, but I *am* my body. Or, to cast it within an eschatological perspective, which is the most fitting of all, I *will be* my body.

BODILY RESURRECTION AND LATE ANTIQUITY

Even among Christian theologians who defended and thought through the doctrine of bodily resurrection, its scandal is clearly felt. Gregory of Nyssa, for example, took the Christian doctrine on its face, yet expressed a certain sense of vertigo and even horror when contemplating the body as the self's eschatological future. The vertigo resulted, in part, from considering the body's insubstantiality and flux. Echoing Heraclitus, Gregory asks: "Who does not know that human nature is like a stream, proceeding from birth to death perpetually in motion and ceasing from motion only when it ceases from being?" How can my body be "me," Gregory asks, if the body is without stability and self-sameness? If my body is "me," then how could I possibly survive the body's decomposition? "Our nature is like the fire on a wick which seems to be always the same because the continuity of its motion shows that it is inseparably united with itself, but in truth it is always replacing itself and never remains the same... [Y]ou cannot take hold of the same flame twice."[28] The body is the portal of an interminable biological process, a process Gregory would like at times to freeze. The body is like a rushing river with a "downward flow": "human life is overflowing with disturbances and anomalies and is always pouring forth from the precipitousness of its nature and never restrains itself and is never sated, but contaminates everything it happens upon and runs over everything it touches."[29] To counteract this downward flow, the ascetical life "hardens" the naturally entropic body through the ordering of the passions, sculpts it more and more into the purified and crystalline body of the future resurrection. Asceticism generally, and virginity more particularly, prepares the body for and anticipates the eschatological body. Virginity is an eschatological sign of death's vanquishing, since it transcends (or at least disconnects itself from) the procreative process. "For the bodily procreation of children (let no one be displeased by this argument) is more an embarking upon death than upon life for man. Corruption has its beginning in birth and those who refrain from procreation through virginity themselves bring about a cancellation of death by preventing it from advancing further."[30] Peter Brown notes that Gregory is here very much influenced by the body-image of the desert ascetic movement in the fourth century, where the body, increasingly freed from biological processes and the drive of the appetites, is crafted into an "autarkic system," an "exactly calibrated instrument," or a "finely tuned engine" capable of idling indefinitely.[31]

Ascetical training for Gregory is fundamental to Christian ethics, the reordering of the passions key to any form of discipleship. But as Gregory praises the ascetical life, an unmistakably Platonic sensibility emerges: "Indeed, the person who removes himself from all hatred and fleshly odor and rises above all low and earthbound things, having ascended higher than the whole earth and in his aforementioned flight, will find the only thing that is worth longing for, and, having come close to beauty, will become beautiful itself."[32] Though Gregory never goes so far as to suggest the total desertion of the bodily — this is exactly what the stubbornly "earthly" doctrine of bodily resurrection forbids — there is a drive in his view of the philosophic life to become increasingly liberated from the partiality and limitation of sensuality so as to achieve a more serenely objective viewpoint, almost as if spirit and body stood in inverse relation. Gregory's asceticism here reflects something of philosophy's "training for death," a "training to die *to one's individuality and passions*, in order to look at things from the perspective of universality and objectivity."[33] If death is the separation of the soul from the body, then the increasing attunement of the body towards the soul is the pedagogy of death, i.e., learning to die well. For Gregory, and much of the anthropology of the ascetic movement, sexual renunciation becomes a central feature of this pedagogy.[34]

But death is not simply the separation of the soul from the body. The doctrine of bodily resurrection, and the obstinately corporeal character of Christian thought and practice, ultimately prevents the movement towards strict dualism in ascetical literature and the theology it influences. The centrality of the body in the economy of salvation served as a divine proscription against the soul's craving for clean flight. Gregory's thinking on the body and the resurrection is thus striking for its fierce ambivalence. His thought reflects the deep tensions that occur when Greek philosophical anthropology and the more Hebraic anthropology of the New Testament interact. Such turbulence characterizes a great deal of the ascetical literature in late antiquity that influenced him. "Seldom, in ancient thought," writes Brown, "had the body been seen as more deeply implicated in the transformation of the soul; and never was it made to bear so heavy a burden."

> For the Desert Fathers, the body was not an irrelevant part of the human person that could, as it were, be "put in brackets." It could not enjoy the distant tolerance that Plotinus and many pagan sages were prepared to accord it, as a transient and accidental adjunct to the self. It was, rather, grippingly present to the monk: he was to speak of it as "this body that God has afforded me, as a field to cultivate, where I might work and become rich."[35]

Brown observes further that those theologians trained in the ascetical traditions were all the more attendant to the issues raised by the debates surrounding the incarnation since they had experienced much more intensely the "haunting emblem of the enigmatic joining of body and soul within themselves."[36] This relationship between doctrine and experience is no more applicable than in Gregory's grappling with the doctrine of bodily resurrection.[37]

For Gregory, the close relationship between death and the biological process heightens the mystery of this haunting emblem. The body is where death happens. The force of this realization makes Gregory prepared to say what he knows will be so disturbing to his readers ("let no one be displeased by this argument"): that the procreation of children is the perpetuation of death itself. As he exhorts his readers to the life of virginity, he adumbrates the inconveniences and heartaches that may be avoided. Marriage distracts the soul, diffuses one's energies and the singleness of attention necessary for the life of prayer. "For having elevated his soul above the whole world, and considering his only precious possession to be virtue, [the virgin] will lead a life that is untroubled and peaceful and without dissension."[38] The difference between virginity and married life is the difference between heaven and earth.[39] While marriage brings its own blessings, so often it results in grief. There is the grief of one's child dying, fear for their future, the threat of losing one's mate. Giving birth (so much more precarious in the ancient world than today) invited death as a distinct possibility for both the mother and child.[40] The pain of childbirth is a portent of future grief. A parent's soul is divided into as many parts as the number of his or her children, particularly for women, "since she experiences in her own being whatever happens to them."[41] So when a child dies, something of a parent's very being dies. Why would one with spiritual aspirations invite this upon him or herself?

As rhetorically extreme as these views are, something of their truth cannot be denied. To enter into marriage and to have children as an outpouring of conjugal love is to give oneself over to a biological process that we neither originally fashioned nor ultimately control. (Though it would seem that the frenzied drive for genetic manipulation and total control over conception seeks to entirely remove the contemplative "letting be" of this process.) To have children, it is true, is to introduce unpredictability in life and risk profound grief. Throughout Gregory's extended treatise on the resurrection, *The Soul and the Resurrection,* which takes the form of a dialogue with his sister Macrina as she is preparing for her own imminent death, the shared pain of losing their parents, and Gregory's anxiety over his sister, is most palpable. As Gregory later reflects upon seeing his parents' corpses when their tomb was opened for Macrina's burial, he writes: "How, I ask myself, will I be spared...condemnation if I look at the common shame of human nature in the bodies of my parents, which are certainly decomposed, disintegrated, and transformed into an appearance unformed, hideous, and repulsive?" As Bynum emphasizes, a great deal of Gregory's anthropology and theology of bodily resurrection is stirred by the horror of decay. This is nowhere more despairingly expressed than in Gregory's homiletic commentary *On Ecclesiastes.* There is a time for weeping over our bodily nature, for there is "illness, mutilations, amputations, putrefying diseases, impairment of sense-organs, derangement due to demons, and all such things as our nature is prone to...The frenzy of sexual lusts, and the stinking filth in which this kind of passion results...the unpleasantness associated with food through defecation": all showing "how our nature is a dung-heap."[42] Even Celsus's protest did not reach this pitch. All of those things, "of which it is not even nice to mention," are here mentioned. The doctrine of bodily resurrection forces thought to not only face the specter of death in the abstract (as non-being), but death in the concrete—putrefaction, burial, and dissolution. "And death was horrible," writes Bynum, "not because it was an event that ended consciousness, but because it was part of oozing, disgusting, uncontrollable biological process. Such process, beginning at conception and continuing in the grave, threatened identity itself."[43]

It is all the more remarkable, therefore, that Christians tenaciously clung to this doctrine, even at the risk of intellectual incoherence. "To ask why people in late antiquity had the stubborn courage to face the putrefaction that joins death to life is to ask for causal explanation at a level no modern theory addresses."[44] Thought flinches when it thinks death. Sensibility winces at the sight of putrefaction. And yet Christians in antiquity, compelled by the doctrine of bodily resurrection and belief in the *absence* of Jesus' tomb — no other "causal explanation" will do — faced this putrefaction in a variety of ways. For example, Christian burial practices, the martyr cult, and the emerging relic cult of late antiquity would gradually restructure the symbolic construction of sacred space and time throughout many a late Roman town. Whereas earliest Christian worship often took place underground, most commonly in places of death, the catacombs, late antiquity saw this underground movement emerge to light of day and steadily reshape calendar and topography. Christians projected salvation "on the ground."[45] Places of death, once partitioned off from the cities to their perimeters, began to merge with the world of the living to blur and even join together those categories that had been "meticulously contrasted" for a thousand years in the minds of Mediterranean people.[46] By the early fifth century, Christian bodies, particularly those of the martyrs, returned to the cities to occupy places of worship. While the sight may have still aroused "fears of pollution and rouse a pagan mob to fury," the return of the martyrs' bodies to the cities "brought the dead back among the living. Not merely in thought and feeling, nor in strengthening the sense of their presence in time and in worship, but in their earthly reality, into the space of daily existence."[47] Eventually the prohibition of burial within the walls of numerous cities would be dropped. And with the distribution of relics to various sacred shrines extending outward from the cities into the suburbs and rural areas, a new sacred geography of pilgrimage was forming. As Robert Markus observes: "Late Roman towns were thus becoming spatial reflections of the ancient Christian belief that the Church was a single community embracing all the saints, alive or dead."[48] The body of the saint and the martyr was charged with eschatological potency. The once polluting and polluted corpse now intersected the world of the living. Death's abysmal absence was inscribed by a new kind of eschatological presence. The martyr's body became a point of contact with the future resurrection of all the dead, the concrete promise or eschatological sign of God's overcoming of death and decay. The saint's body was a piece of realized eschatology.

That the corpse was seen in antiquity as a site of pollution has much to do with the intellectual, moral, and aesthetic offense at the doctrine of bodily resurrection. Gregory's horror at the body's decay was widely shared.[49] But Gregory's lamentation raises a number of other reasons for this unease, reasons that begin to explain the persistence of dualism in its many guises. Though bodily nature is, according to Gregory, a fundamental good, created by God from the beginning, to be eventually restored through resurrection to its original condition, the body seems also a "dung heap" because of its vulnerability to dysfunction: illness, mutilation, physical pain, disease, sense impairment, mental derangement, lust, and so forth. Such things inhibit clear perception, the pleasantness of unobstructed sensation, longevity of life, unity of will, and the simplicity of intellect. Gregory is not a dualist; but from an existential perspective, that is, from reflection upon the *lived body,* the body can seem the soul's antagonist and foil, particularly when in a state of dysfunction. It is here where the temptation to some form of theoretical dualism becomes very great, to translate this experience of inner division and ambiguity into ontic categories: hypostasizing into "soul" all that is simple, agreeable, self-present, and transcendent, while identifying "body" with all that is ambiguous, painful, self-diffusive, and quotidian.

THE BODY AS "THING" AND MODERNITY'S "DISENGAGED SELF"

Before probing further into the underlying reasons for the tendency towards theoretical dualism — as we shall see, these reasons are actually rooted in our bodily experience — it is well worth considering, even if briefly, the tendency in our contemporary culture to think of the body as a "thing" and the way this situates the self in a disengaged position vis-à-vis the body.

Much of our thinking about the body remains dominated by a Cartesian paradigm. The body has become increasingly rationalized, mechanized, medicalized, and commodified. Despite the explosion of literature on the body in the past 20 or so years in phenomenology, cultural anthropology, gender studies, and social theory, we remain addicted to the idea that our bodies are not *really* ourselves but the insensate matter in and through which "I," as self-present subject, am "expressed." Although Descartes's philosophical project has often enough become the object of severe critique in theory, in point of fact the body remains an "object" for thought, quite thing-like, the *res extensa* of "soul" or "mind," the instrumental material through which the subject self-manifests and operates in a spatio-temporal setting. The body is, as it were, a "container." Such a view is only perpetuated, but now in an eschatological modality, as the body is described as the transitory shell of the soul that, upon death, takes leave of its body to enter into its original and beatific state, free of bodily encumberment, ambiguity, dysfunction, and corruptibility. To the extent that contemporary Christians unreflectively speak in this way, and many do, they are adopting a form of soul/body dichotomization that is more idiomatically Platonic than Christian. The almost self-evident ring of a passage from Plato's *Phaedo* will do well to illustrate the point:

> For the body is a source of endless trouble to us by reason of the mere requirement of food; and is liable also to diseases which overtake and impede us in the search after true being: it fills us full of loves, and lusts, and fears, and fancies of all kinds, and endless foolery, and in fact, as men say, takes away from us the power of thinking at all. Whence comes wars, and fightings, and factions? whence but from the body and the lusts of the body?... and, last and worst of all, even if we are at leisure and betake ourselves to some speculation, the body is always breaking in upon us, causing turmoil and confusion in our inquiries, and so amazing us that we are prevented from seeing the truth. It has been proved to us by experience that if we would have pure knowledge of anything we must be quit of the body — the soul in herself must behold things in themselves: and then we shall attain the wisdom which we desire, and of which we say that we are lovers; not while we live, but after death; for if while in company with the body, the soul cannot have pure knowledge, one of two things follows — either knowledge is not to be attained at all, or, if at all, after death. For then, and not till then, the soul will be parted from the body and exist in herself alone. In this present life, I reckon that we make the nearest approach to knowledge when we have the least possible intercourse or communion with the body, and are not surfeited with the bodily nature, but keep ourselves pure until the hour when God himself is pleased to release us. And thus having got rid of the foolishness of the body we shall be pure and hold converse with the pure, and know ourselves the clear light everywhere, which is no other than the light of truth.[50]

The body is thematized here as the scene of biological necessity, the exposure to pain and suffering, the origin of unruly passions, and the primary obstacle to genuine knowledge. Conversely, the soul enjoys the attributes of simplicity, agility, luminosity and virtue. While this "logocentric" view of the human person is one of the hallmarks of classical metaphysics, its modern manifestation takes on a peculiarly instrumentalist and even mechanical character. In Stoicism, for example, the soul could still be conceived as some kind of subtle "stuff" pervading the physical body, just as the cosmos was imbued with divine reason (*logos*). Though the physical body could be disparaged by the Stoa, the whole cosmos was seen as a vast living organism of body and soul.[51] Even in Platonism's more severe dichotomization of soul and body, the cosmos is never viewed as mere "nature," but a harmoniously ordered cosmos endowed with soul (the World-Soul).[52] But the Cartesian (modern) "subject" becomes an immaterial observer looking through the window of the body upon the world — a "disengaged self," to borrow Charles Taylor's phrase, which abstracts itself from the body and the world in order to take an instrumentalist stance towards them.[53] The body and the world are rendered to the thinking subject through objective representation, quite like a mental picture. Now viewed as mindless or soulless matter, the world is portrayed, not as a living organism, not as a World-Soul, but as a vast mechanism whose inner workings and laws can be revealed through science and harnessed by technology. The rise of the "disengaged self" is concurrent with the modern "disenchantment of nature"[54] (or as Carolyn Merchant puts it, the "death of nature"[55]), where "nature," now viewed under the aspect of efficient causality, becomes the raw material for instrumental ends, i.e., for production.[56] Matter is neutral, a dough-like substance, and the world filled with inert objects whose value is primarily determined by calculative thinking and the potential for technical transformation. Dualism in the modern, Cartesian sense has very little to do with any sort of "otherworldly" asceticism, a spiritual flight from the body/world in an ascending movement of participation in the supersensible. Rather, what is sought is an "innerworldly liberation" of the subject that uses a body from the disengaged stance of instrumental reason in order to gain technical mastery over itself and the world within which it is lodged.[57] For this reason, scientific reductionism and dialectical materialism should not be thought of as the opposite of dualism; they are intramundane versions of it.[58]

Importantly, this disengagement of the subject and the instrumental-technical knowledge it yields dovetails with the calculative and productionist thinking that informs much modern economic life in our "late capitalist" context. The body is not only an instrumentalized object for rational control, but the locus of individualistic expression and acquisitive desire. Quite paradoxically, modern life reveals an obsession with body-image and body-manipulation. This is no return to a more integrative anthropology of the person. It represents the facile aestheticization of the body that now becomes the material canvas for expressing individual "personality."[59] Body-images are produced, marketed, and sold. Certain body types become objects of mass desire as they are reified and displayed as commodities in advertising, other media, and the celebrity cult. In the astonishing rise of pornography in recent years — assisted by the "disengaged" portal of the Internet — the depth and invisibility of the body-person become utterly visible, and thus depersonalized, to the possessive gaze of the eroticized observer. The modern hedonistic construction of the body makes it a manipulable and expressive thing, but also an acquisitive thing designed for the ever-variable pleasures of consumerism, part of the ephemeral material of commercial exchange among "consumers."[60] The "consumer self" has in many ways become our default anthropology:

> The compulsion to consume has become for us as deep as the exigency to survive because the Commodity Form reveals our very being and purpose as calculable solely in terms of what we possess, measurable solely by what we have and take. We are only insofar as we possess. We are what we possess. We are, consequently, possessed by our possessions, produced by our products. Remade in the image and likeness of our own handiwork, we are revealed as commodities. Idolatry exacts its full price from us. We are robbed of our very humanity.... [I]f persons can be known only in terms of the mechanical, external, and instrumental, and if their interpersonal behavior is most adequately expressed in manipulation, force, and violence, then the world of personhood is replaced by the world of objectness. And if the human person is an object, the dominant form of body-consciousness in that world will be thing-consciousness. The body is a commodity. The body is a thing.[61]

The "disengaged self," the "expressive self," the "consumer self": by abstracting the self from the body, each enforces a highly individualistic and instrumentalist outlook. Standing "behind" the body, or "using" the body as an external apparatus, the "subject" becomes atomized and abstracted from the world of social and material relations. Such an outlook threatens to view the Other only in terms of utility. Because the body is the corporeal bond between "me" and "world," the reduction of the body to a thing-like status creates conditions for reducing the "Thou" to a mere "it." The reduction of corporeality to mere entity leads to the comprehension of the Other within a scheme of objectness.

The difficulty in our contemporary context for making intelligible the Christian belief in bodily resurrection has a great deal to do with the pervasive logocentrism and instrumentalism that characterizes it. If the body is not really "me," but a thing I provisionally use, bodily resurrection can only appear like a strange appendage to the fulfillment of my true (read: "spiritual") identity. For this reason, we must ask that when certain theologians who, in the service of a demythologizing program, seem eager to dispel the notion that Jesus' resurrection has anything to do with a body, or that the empty tomb narratives are anything more than artifacts of a primitive anthropology, their point ought rather to be that bodily resurrection issues a radical challenge to the disengaged subjectivity of modernity. When theology circles around the doctrine of bodily resurrection, or attempts to explain it away out of embarrassment, it is only reinforcing, rather than critiquing and transforming, those culturally generated habits that can only imagine the body as a quasi-object. It thereby fails to grasp the claim resurrection belief makes upon the world: namely, that salvation is not salvation *from* the body and *from* the world, but *of* the body and *of* the world.

THE ABSENT BODY

I have maintained that the scandal of bodily resurrection is rooted in longstanding intellectual and cultural habits. But why do these habits endure? Does their persistence testify to their truth, or is their persistence a matter of accident, so that only through the force of habit they have taken on a self-evidential aspect to them? For the remainder of this chapter I hope to answer this question with the help of phenomenology. Drawing upon the work of Maurice Merleau-Ponty and Drew Leder in particular, the argument advanced here is that the tendency towards theoretical dualism is actually rooted in our body experience. This is not to suggest that all dualisms are the same. Neither do I dismiss the many factors that contribute to how we construct our views of the human person, including intellectual, cultural, economic, political, etc. The point rather is to show that, while the construal of the human person in dualistic terms is a false construal, dualism in its various guises is not just an arbitrary habit of thought but is funded by aspects of our body experience. Leder in particular is helpful in identifying what he calls a "phenomenological vector," or a structure of experience, that can lead reflection in particular interpretive directions. Leder's argument, succinctly stated, is that several aspects of our body experience can conspire together to lead us to interpret the body as an appendage to the human person, when in fact corporeality is at the core of the human person. Dualism interprets and projects onto an onto-valuational screen the ways in which: (1) the body recedes or becomes "absent" in much of our perceptual experience, and (2) the body becomes thematically "present" under circumstances of pain, dysfunction, and limitation. In other words, while it is the body that actually enables persons to be-in-the-world, to be intentional and self-directing, to be in relationship with the Other within a broader corporeal horizon, the body rarely becomes explicitly thematized in our experience until we encounter some form of internal antagonism with our corporeal limitations. The body is, in fact, a multivalent reality: ecstatic and recessive, visible and invisible, self-concealing and self-presenting. And yet we tend to identify the body with only some of these aspects. We frequently assign to "the body" that which curtails freedom, rather than what facilitates it; with what hinders us from achieving self-identity, rather than what enables us to be persons in the world and in relation with other corporeal beings; with what ultimately brings about the demise of identity through death, rather than what enables life to be lived in the first place; with what causes epistemological and moral error due to the faultiness of sensual perception and subterranean drives and desires, rather than what gives us the capacity for cognition and will. In short, theoretical dualism tends to assign to "the body" all that presents limitation or ambiguity while assigning to "the soul" or "mind" what enables self-direction, reflection, and the sense of self-presence.

Leder's work is indebted to the phenomenological research of the twentieth century, though he advances it in crucial ways by offering a richer analysis of bodily "absence." He is able to provide a counterstatement to dualism while better accounting for its persistence. With particular indebtedness to Merleu-Ponty, Leder highlights the incarnational structure of human experience and reflection. Accordingly, "mind" or "consciousness," though very much a great mystery, should not be thought of as a separate entity, subtle or immaterial, standing "behind" or "within" a bodily shell. The human person is somatic through and through. Even the most subtle and transcendent dimensions of the human person are bound up with our corporeality. But notice what this last assertion means: it means that we must revise and expand our narrow conceptions of embodiment. Leder's position is not reductionistic. He is not attempting to "explain" the human person in a way that reduces what we tend to associate with "mind" or "spirit" to the sum of "parts," or as mere epiphenomena that have no relationship to the real. "The body itself proclaims spirit in our lives, that is, transcendence, mystery, and interconnection."[62] In saying this, Leder is attempting to reclaim a view of the person as a psychosomatic unity. Far from amounting to a rejection of the mystery of the human person, or denying the spiritual dimension of our experience, such a view roots the profoundest realities of human existence within embodied life. For this reason, the phenomenological approach to the human person is much closer to the portraits of the human person deriving from the biblical tradition than it is to any form of dualism.[63]

The Ecstatic Body and the Habit Body

As stated, Leder maintains that the body is a multivalent reality. It is self-revealing and self-concealing, visible and invisible in our conscious experience. Although the body is the seat of perception and cognition, of relationship and identity, our bodiliness often remains "absent" (or unthematized) in our experience. This is one of the several ways the structure of our bodily experience can incline us to construe the human person in dualistic terms.

The body is the *Nullpunkt* (Edmund Husserl) of perceptual experience. As I take in the world through my senses, my sensing body recedes into the background, becomes transparent or "invisible" to what gives itself. I do not so much directly experience my body as a quasi-object when encountering something; rather, I traverse my body *towards* that something. When I taste an olive, I do not taste my tasting; I taste the olive. When I touch the bark of the tree, it is the bark that gives itself to me in perception, not my own fingers. When I see a cloud formation overhead, I am drawn away from myself towards the given phenomenon in a "from-to" relationship. As the *Nullpunkt* of perception, the lived body comes to be "felt" only in "feeling," "seen" in "seeing," self-revealed in perceptual transitivity towards the given. "My being-in-the-world," writes Leder, "depends upon my body's self-effacing transitivity."[64] If I were to directly perceive my perception — that is, if my organs of sense were to become the sole and immediate objects of their sensation — I would never encounter otherness, or be-in-the-world, but would remain inescapably locked up into solipsistic auto-affectivity. Nothing would ever appear *to* me or *away* from me. The perceptual body, in order to be receptive to what is given, is structurally ek-static, literally, a "standing outside" or away from itself in self-traversing momentum towards the given. To "take in" a phenomenon is to "take leave" of my body-self in the intertwining act of perception. For this reason, the body frequently remains unthematized in experience. If later I reflect upon my experience of tasting an olive or watching a cloud formation, my reflection will rarely reflect upon the body as such but will focus on the given phenomenon. I "forget," as it were, my body in the remembrance of the given. Or, rather, it stands in the background of my experience and reflection, even if it is the condition for the possibility of that experience and reflection:

> The body always has a determinate stance — it is that whereby we are located and defined. But the very nature of the body is to project outward from its place of standing. From the "here" arises a perceptual world of near and far distances. From the "now" we inhabit a meaningful past and a futural realm of projects and goals. In this ecstatic nature of corporeality can be discovered the first reason that the body is forgotten in experience.... The body conceals itself precisely in the act of revealing what is Other. The very presencing of the world and of the body as an object within it is always correlative with this primordial absence.[65]

As this quotation indicates, the self-concealing nature of the body in perception is not to be thought of only in spatial terms. Bodily "absence" also occurs through temporal projection. As we move through space in a from-to manner, so do we move through time as though leaving our body in our wake. This occurs at a variety of levels. One of the most subtle is the way we develop skills and habits over time that eventually become "second nature." For example, the ordinary development of a human person from infancy involves the acquisition of a breathtaking array of skills for just basic motility. As one develops the skills of reaching, pointing, sitting, turning one's head, walking, balancing, eating, etc. (all so seemingly difficult to acquire at first!) they recede into the background of experience as the "toddler," so aptly named, moves on to acquire yet new skills, building on top of them, layer after layer, in a living process of corporeal sedimentation. What was once an action that required persistence in self-application becomes "natural." What was once a direct object of manipulation has now become part of the enabling background for future experience. The same occurs in language acquisition. Only by being long-immersed in a pre-existing world of spoken language — sound, however subtle, is still phonetic material — does the child begin to speak, to imagine, to think. We inherit the very thing that enables us to become self-reflective and communicative, and we do so only through imitation and habituation. The complex (and usually unspoken) rules of discourse that govern everything from basic statements and questions to inflections in voice and bodily gesture are internalized only through extensive practice. In learning to read with increasing efficiency, the child no longer focuses on letters, individual words, or sentences, but follows the storyline at a fluid pace. It is the content of the story that becomes the immediate object of attention, not the variety of skills of reading or the facilitating media of the text.

Or consider the example of the accomplished musician. When a pianist plays a well-rehearsed piece of music, or improvises within a given set of musical parameters, the complex rules of music (rhythm, melody, harmony, mode) have become so thoroughly internalized through habit-forming practice that the performer is now capable of creating in "real time." Good improvisation is hardly random. Only after assimilating countless skills and experimenting with potential voicings over years of tedious practice can improvisational freedom unfold. When a drummer is playing with all limbs a-go, tacit rhythms and patterns in the forms of somatic memories are expressing themselves from visceral regions to create audible rhythms and patterns. The drummer's action does not so much stand "in front" of him, like an object, but "behind" him as subject. The rhythm, as it were, plays *through* him. There are not four distinct operations taking place, but a single, coordinated movement radiating from an invisible (but no less corporeal) depth dimension. He does not think what he plays. He *is* what he plays, or rather, he is *playing*. Only through repetition comes this independence. Only through habit comes this spontaneity.

This process of the becoming absent (or "second nature") of learned skills and habits Leder calls "incorporation," meaning a "bringing within the body." Such skills and habits become "absent" in their actual performance. "Over time they simply disappear from view. They are enveloped within the structure of the taken-for-granted body from which I in*habit* the world."[66] Merleau-Ponty speaks of the paradox between the "habit-body" and the "body at this moment." In the acquisition of skills, what once was a thing "manipulable for me" becomes a thing "manipulable for itself," an "*almost* impersonal existence, which can be taken for granted, and which I rely on to keep me alive." An expansive, if largely tacit world of somatic habits allows me to be self-directing *through* them. It is an in-habited world "to which one must first of all belong in order to be able to enclose oneself in the particular context of a love or an ambition."[67]

This last point is of considerable significance, though space does not permit extensive elaboration. It is only through the lived process of habit formation that a human person develops "character." Just as the accomplished musician incorporates a broad array of practices in order to project a "style" in the event of musical performance, so too can we think of a person's character as the performance of a life projected from a multitude of calibrated perceptions, emotions, and attitudinal patterns that have developed over an extended period of time. The lived human body is not just a physical thing, an appendage to the self, as it were, but the "fleshing out" of a personal story, just the way the self unfolds within a dynamic nexus of relations. The body is the spatio-temporality of the self, the interval of emergent character-identity. The character of the person involves deeply entrenched habits — of varying moral significance, intentionally developed or uncritically assimilated from one's social-cultural context, and most certainly some mixture of the two — and an ongoing, improvisational performance in view of ever new experiences and shifting matrices. Just as a paradoxical relationship abides between the "body at this moment" and the "habit body," there is a paradoxical relationship, sometimes felt as a blend of freedom and necessity, perhaps describable as the interaction of conscious awareness and the unconscious, between the "self at this moment" and the "habit self." A person's character-identity is not, therefore, some immutable essence standing "over" or "within" the body, as if the body were its container, but is the complex and irreducibly unique style or personal form emergent from bodily life. The self is somatic through and through, even if the *soma* disappears from our immediate intentionality in the project of our becoming.

"Not only is the body the self in manifestation," writes Hans Frei, "it *is* the self. The body is I, or rather I am the body occupying this particular, unsubstitutable space. This is why we say 'I' (and not 'my body') walk from here to the corner. There is no way to state more simply the identity of the self as manifest in and yet identical with its embodiment."[68] Because I *am* my embodiment, my "me" is temporal, which is to say, an unfolding narrative set within, and partly encompassing, a dynamic set of relations that extend indefinitely in a receding, omni-directional horizon. Selfhood is an event, an open and ongoing dialogue, and thus it calls forth the category of the dramatic for its attestation and description. The "unity" of the self so conceived does not demand we search for numerical sameness. Even if we identify personhood with embodiment, this will not require us to locate a kind of incorporeal substrate that endures throughout the changes of the body. The compulsive need to rivet selfhood to an unambiguous "substance" is one we must renounce as the harbinger to reducing the body to a thing-like status. But to identify personhood with embodiment does not lead to Heraclitean flux either. This is the either/or error of metaphysical approaches to identity. Far more helpful is to think of identity as an unfolding narrative in which "unity" consists of a blend of persistence *and* elusiveness, focal dramatic action *and* non-focal subplots and horizons that, while often "absent," are nevertheless constitutive. Stanley Hauerwas observes that descriptively "the self is best understood as a narrative.... The unity of the self is therefore more like the unity that is exhibited in a good novel — namely, with many subplots and characters that we at times do not closely relate to the primary dramatic action of the novel. But ironically, without such subplots we cannot achieve the kind of unity necessary to claim our actions as our own."[69] A more organic style of thinking is called for here, not an essentialist style. Frei is helpful in this regard.[70] *Persistence* refers to self-continuity and self-ascription over a period of time, from action to action. Persistence allows for some degree of narrative cohesion and characterization. And yet, this cohesion is not unambiguous. Due to its complexity, relationality, and temporality, the self is also elusive. *Elusiveness* refers to the inability of the person to become fully "present" and self-coincident, for the self is always in dynamic relation. As finite and temporal, the totality of a person's lived narrative cannot become simultaneous, but is always receding into the past, just as its future is always not-yet.

We must resist associating *persistence* with "soul" and *elusiveness* with "body," which is just what metaphysics frequently strives to do, with the ultimate result of making the body the soul's representational and instrumental object. We should say rather that my body is just the way I am accomplished in the world. Just as the philosophical "turn to language" has shown that subjectivity comes to be in and through a given world of language — that we do not so much "use" language instrumentally as we are founded in language — so too must we say that the human body is erroneously thought of as instrumentally extended "stuff" for the operating "soul" or "mind," but, far more appropriately, understood and appreciated as the corporeal manifestation of personal becoming. My body is in-formed and in-habited with absences, which I may often forget in my self-directing activity, but which continuously project my "self" in time, bodying it forth. Personhood should not be thought of atomistically (out of relation) or anachronistically (out of time), but as an emergently complex and constantly modifying/modified *gestalt* of relation and duration. The fluidity and saturating richness of narrative communicates much more ably the multivalence of an embodied self who cannot be reduced to entity without some form of violence. "Self-manifestation in both word and body suggests that the elusive and persistent subject can only be described indirectly." Adds Frei, this "indirectness does not mean failure by any means."[71]

Although I shall further explore these thoughts in the following chapter, I can at least preliminarily state that the "resurrection of the body" means something quite different than the resurrection of some sort of "object." (This is the way we often think of it, given our tendency to objectify the body.) It means, more precisely, the eschatological transformation of a person's character-identity as embodied. The human body does not so much exist *in* time and *in* space (we must get beyond this kind of container model) but is an in-habitation *of* spatio-temporality.[72] The "risen body" is the absolute fruition of the whole human person who only comes to be in a corporeal way. Resurrection is the subsuming of a person's temporality into an eschatological fullness, where what is elusive and sequentially extended over time will become present in simultaneity. Bodily resurrection envisions a future for the human person that in no way entails the dissolution of concrete, bodily temporality. It affirms its transfiguration. However difficult to imagine, eternity is not the absence or opposite of time, but its fullness. In addition to the extraordinary dignity such a hope bestows upon the human body, and indeed, all of creation, such a view frees Christian anthropology from the need to secure personal identity in terms of some stable essence, which almost always leads to projecting the self as some kind of entity standing over the body. Human life is really contingent and open, a blend of persistence and elusiveness. Who I *am* is never present to me, but can only be *given*. Because the resurrection is totally gratuitous, a "new creation," my personal identity can never be secured or hoarded, but only lived *towards* in the hope of the resurrection. And, so, while it is quite proper to say, "I *am* my body," it is more theologically profound to say, "I *will be* my body."

The Recessive Body and the Dysfunctional Body

If the lived body is an ecstatic body, involving an array of absences in perception and bodily performance, there is another dimension of bodily absence continually funding our sense of bodily *alterity*. Leder describes this as the recessive body.

Much of my bodily life necessarily eludes my awareness and control. Inarticulate regions of visceral depth are not governed by my conscious intentionality but operate automatically. Eating, for example, includes both intentional and non-intentional aspects. I may choose what, when, how, and with whom I eat. To some extent, I may even choose why I eat. Eating can take on all manner of meaning — personal, social, religious, and cultural. Food is never *just* food. However, once food passes my mouth, a complex and involuntary process of digestion assumes control. Not only *must* I nourish my body to remain alive, but an impersonal and marvelously orchestrated series of automatic processes takes over to transform what I eat into nutrients and excrete what is harmful or unnecessary. I no more direct this process than I direct the vital activities of my kidneys, liver, colon, heart, and lungs. An immense and intricate world of the most basic vegetative and biological processes sustains my lived experience and recedes from my view, literally disappears underneath the very conscious intentionality it supports. This is no unfortunate or tragic aspect of a "divided self." If the visceral body seems to complicate identity and restrict freedom from being absolute, the autonomy of the viscera, as Leder well explains, actually sets me free for novel and self-directing activities. To be responsible for managing blood flow, breathing, cellular division, digestion, and so on, would demand competencies and energies I could not consciously provide. Conscious intentionality must trust and cooperate with the recessive regions of the body, be in tune with their visceral rhythms.[73]

At the very core of bodily life, therefore, is a fundamental ambiguity. Though a total organism, the human person, who may identify the "self" with the more surface experience of self-reflection and intentionality, is already "othered" by a vast, recessive realm: a "foreignness" which supports and institutes a world of "mineness." I experience being other to my own self as a structural aspect of bodily life. In contrast to the ecstatic body, which stands away from itself in the perceptual act, there is a recessive body of non-intentional depths. These are not ontic statements about different bodies but a phenomenological description of the *one, multivalent body*. The recessive body in particular can produce a sense of "alienness-from-within," as Leder puts it. Not only would I be unable to recognize my own viscera. The very sight of them can be quite repulsive. Furthermore, bodily life embeds me in the realm of the necessary. Whereas I typically associate my identity with what I consciously make of my freedom (the "I can"), the recessive body, which I often do not even sense within me, except for under the circumstances of limitation or dysfunction, can appear as a curtailment to freedom. The recessive body contrasts the "I can" with an impersonal "I must."

It is not difficult to see here how a certain kind of resentment or sense of self-alienation can result as the self seeks to expand its freedom over against its own bodily strictures. The body that enables the self to live ecstatically outward is the very body that exerts a gravitational pull from within. It is precisely this impersonal "I must" which, in part, founds the temptation for casting the self in a dualistic picture. To the extent I identify my "self" with intentional activities in freedom, my own body can seem quite other as I become aware of its automaticities and necessities. The body's recessive character can touch off a reactive posture for surface awareness to define its autonomy and yearning for total self-presence over against its corporeal heteronomy. The quote above from Plato's *Phaedo* describes the body as a source of endless trouble because, among other things, it requires food. The point has less to do with eating, *per se,* than it does with a broader existential condition: of being embedded in the realm of the involuntary, being subject to the non-luminous, being consigned to facticity.

As we saw earlier, Gregory of Nyssa too recoils at the awareness of impersonal forces pulsing through his body, some of which may be more or less innocuous, while others, such as hormonal drives originating below the level of surface consciousness, exert pressures on his moral compass. For Gregory the biological process appears to threaten the self's identity in its precipitous and riotous "downward flow" towards non-being, towards what has no stable form. The body is a "river, made turbulent by winter floods"; it is "dangerous and hazardous and flows heedlessly beyond its boundaries"; the "human flower... declines in winter and begets old age" and will eventually be "covered by forgetfulness."[74] This contemplation of bodily facticity is comparable to Heidegger's analysis of anxiety over the self's "thrownness" (*Geworfenheit).* Being-in-the-world does not permit absolute freedom, for *Dasein* is conditioned by its being delivered over to contingency and death. What Gregory describes as the entropic, downward flow of the body is surprisingly similar to Heidegger's *Verfallen:* where *Dasein* is implicated in a "falling" or "downward plunge" towards "the groundlessness and nullity of inauthentic everydayness."[75] Gregory reads the biological process as the impending absorption of identity into nothingness. Inauthentic life is the mindless capitulation to the monotonous rush of the body's anonymous demands. Virginity, which would "plug up" the biological process, is hailed as one of the privileged practices for averting this "falling" into inauthenticity. Just as facticity and death are rendered thematic to *Dasein* under the aspect of anxiety, Gregory's reading of the biological process arouses in him existential angst, as if he is staring into a bottomless abyss.

Adding further to the sense of the body's alterity is the experience of bodily dysfunction. When properly functioning, the body is taken for granted. The highly transitive nature of sensual perception can make the body seem translucent to the given. When healthy, my body seems to more or less flow with my intentions and activities. But in circumstances of dysfunction what is experientially tacit enters into sharp focus. Physical discomfort and pain draw attention to one's own body in an incisive way. If ordinary perceptual experience is ecstatic, pain grips attention with suffocating immediacy. I never feel more compactly localized and constrained than when I am "in" pain. Of course, pain is a vitally important aspect of bodily life. We could not properly function without it. We would not receive those necessary messages that alert us to eat or drink, to attend to certain stimuli in a way appropriate to our survival. And yet physical suffering and disease render my bodiliness intensely present to me under the aspect of estrangement. I no longer feel "at home" in my own body when afflicted by pain; rather, I seem to "have" a body that threatens me. Dysfunction presents the body to the self as a fragmenting and impersonal other, an "it." "I no longer simply 'am' my body, the set of unthematized powers from which I exist. Now I 'have' a body, a perceived object in the world.... Aversive, involuntary, and disruptive, the painful body emerges as a foreign thing."[76] Whereas unobstructed perception invites a more contemplative enjoyment of what is given, pain broadcasts urgent demands for its cessation.[77] This "telic demand," as Leder calls it, sets up an internal antagonism. The person acts *towards* the body in pain which now arises to conscious awareness as obstacle, negativity, and contradiction. The feeling of "I can" runs up against the "I no longer can."

Bodily deterioration is one of the most direct ways we become aware of our mortality. Whereas times of robust health can inspire a sense of invincibility, the aging process inevitably leads to complications of the many bodily functions once taken for granted. For persons who experience advanced disability, whether due to the natural course of aging or through an unexpected disruption of life due to accident or sudden illness, the body can indeed seem a "prison house." The dysfunctional body is the way death becomes "visible" to us, not only in the corpse of those who die before us, but in an experiential way as we feel quite palpably within ourselves the descending arc of our lifespan.

> Though none of us has ever experienced our death it ever seeds our body, waiting to blossom. It is foretold from within by episodes of pain, injury, and illness, by the body's gradual changes and loss of function with age. And in death lies the ultimate mode of dys-appearance. The body in its aspects as that-which-must-die can

constitute a threat to all of one's goals. It can sever or transform all relations, bring all projects to a halt, threaten one's very existence as an "I." This body thus emerges as an ego-alien force that demands thematization.[78]

Trapped in a Picture

To sum up thus far, because the body is often self-effacing in perception and performance, the body remains largely unthematic until it presents the "I can" with various necessities and strictures — the impersonal "I must." This twofold aspect of the body as ecstatic and recessive in part founds the inclination to theoretically construe experience in a dualistic way, i.e., to thematize the body in terms of necessity and limitation while identifying with the "soul," "self," or "spirit" all that is creative and self-directed. This inclination is only intensified in the experience of bodily dysfunction, when the body seems to be a threat to what we normally take for granted. Although some form of dualism is not an inevitable theoretical stance, the self-concealing nature of the body, along with its association with dysfunction, can, quite paradoxically, lend experiential support for such a view. A "positive feedback loop" can set in between our body experience and self-interpretation. "A dualistic metaphysics, first suggested by aspects of body experience, in turn feeds back to alter that experience, shifting it further in dualist directions."[79] Leder believes that this feedback loop has become intensified since the emergence of the modern "subject." Borrowing a metaphor from Ludwig Wittgenstein, Leder claims that we have become trapped in a picture. "A certain dualist picture has limited our self-development and self-relation. Moreover, this picture of onto-valuational dualism has deeply influenced our relations with others, emphasizing hierarchical opposition."[80] Leder is referring here to: (1) the hierarchical contrast of male and female, who have been associated with, respectively, mind/thought and matter/feeling; (2) class stratification between those who are knowledge workers and those who are laborers; (3) a cultural hermeneutics and epistemology where rational and scientific forms of thinking are regarded as superior or "higher" to the perceptual, intuitive, and symbolic; and (4) the ontological distinction between rational beings and "mindless" nonhuman creatures who lack any inherent worth.

Modern people are instinctively inclined to think of mind (or soul) as immaterial and the body as its instrument, an extrinsic relationship that deeply impacts how we view non-human reality. The body as "mechanism" is reinforced by much of our modern medicine and science, while the body as "commodity" is reinforced by our economic practices. In many of our intellectual traditions, we tend to valorize "clear and distinct ideas" over the ambiguities of metaphor, narrative, and intuition. In Descartes's epistemology, for example, the *cogito* strains to liberate itself from the ambiguity of the body. Attainment of genuine knowledge requires systematic doubt of the external senses in order to arrive at the rational and self-evident. As Leder amply demonstrates, Descartes consistently speaks of the body in terms of ambiguity and dysfunction throughout his works. Significantly, the motivation for Descartes is not only to arrive at secure knowledge (which is related to his proof of God's existence), but is also to secure the knowledge "that the human soul does not perish with the body."

> As a matter of fact, when one comes to know how greatly [mind and body] differ, we understand much better the reasons which go to prove that our soul is in its nature entirely independent of body, and in consequence that it is not liable to die with it. And then, inasmuch as we observe no other causes capable of destroying it, we are naturally inclined to judge that it is immortal.[81]

Descartes's epistemological project is thus a theological one. What is fundamentally at stake is the problem of self-knowledge, permanence, and identity. The postulate of God's existence becomes the security of the knowing subject. As Taylor puts it, it becomes the means by which "I achieve a clarity and a fullness of self-presence that was lacking before."[82] The fullness of this self-presence coincides with grasping the "ontological cleft" between mind and body, by understanding one's proper self as that which "objectifies" its body. "Clarity and distinctness require that we step outside ourselves and take a disengaged perspective."[83] Again, Descartes is not advocating a mystical flight from the body or the world. His is an "innerworldly" asceticism. Modern forms of dualism tend in a horizontal direction through the advancement of technical mastery over extended, soulless matter. "No longer is nature conceived of as fundamentally subjective and alive," says Leder. "It is simply *res extensa*, a plenum of passive matter moved by the operation of mechanical forces. The human soul is a small corner of experience dwelling within this vast inanimate universe. The modeling of the human body on the corpse is part and parcel of this larger shift to the primacy of the lifeless within modern cosmology."[84]

Although a Cartesian-style dualism is by no means an inevitable theoretical stance — the "disengaged subject" is, after all, very much a cultural, economic and technological production — the tacit and self-concealing structure of the body can lend experiential support for it.

When compounded with the assumptions that the body is the primary source for ambiguity for individual-identity, and the experientially driven sense of one's own body as threatening when in a state of dysfunction, some version of theoretical dualism (whether sharp or more subtle) may become compelling and, paradoxically, self-validating. Indeed, the act of thinking itself can, in its subtlety and considerable transitivity, seem quite disembodied.[85] Not coincidentally, perhaps, reason in Western tradition is most frequently associated with sight.[86] As Leder helpfully points out, of all our senses vision is the most delicate and elusive. When looking at an object, or gazing upon a landscape, the body and the eyes themselves recede into the background. Vision "looks away" from the body. When coming to new understanding, we instinctively say, "I see." We have "insight." Smart people are "bright." Truth is an "illumination." *Nous,* for Plato, is the "eye of the soul." Reason, in his allegory of the cave, is drawn out from cavernous and visceral depths into the broad light of lucid ideality. Intellect, for Descartes, is the "eye of the mind." Quite significantly, the principle seat of "mind," the human brain, itself participates in bodily absence.

> This invisibility of the brain is one experiential source for the notion of the human mind as immaterial. Our principle organ of mentality seems nowhere to register in the physical world. When I look into the eyes of another, they are like windows that lead inward to a place of consciousness and desire. Yet this place continually escapes direct apprehension.... This sense of mind-as-invisible is reinforced from the first-person perspective. I can no more discover from whence my acts and words emanate than can the Other. A song runs through my head. One thing "comes to mind" rather than something else. I discover I have finally mastered a skill. Different organs of my body seamlessly synthesize their motions. But I myself apprehend no material basis for this intelligence and coordination. My brain, as that which I exist from within, manifests no physical presence for me directly to know... Human mentality can thus seem immaterial, disembodied, as if of another order of things. An experiential disappearance is read in ontological terms.[87]

It is the nature of "logocentrism" to valorize the transitivity of vision, to privilege what is "clear" and "transparent," and to suppress or attempt to control the surplus ambiguity of the corporeal. The primacy of soul or the immaterial mind in so much metaphysics makes the body an external sign, a value or a thing to be mastered. There must be that which stands "behind" or "above" or "within" the body as permanent, stable, and more *real* — an original "self-presence" and "immediacy." As logocentrism valorizes the mental content (or "idea") over its ambiguous expression into language or writing, so does it oppose the substantial soul against its materially ambiguous expression in the body. The body is seen as the compulsory "writing" of the soul, its exteriorization and dilution, its supplement and trace. This necessity may produce resentment, maybe even a sense of the tragic. In any case, the body's writing scandalizes every yearning for total self-presence and immediacy. "All dualisms," writes Jacques Derrida, "all theories of the immortality of the soul or of the spirit, as well as all monisms, spiritualist or materialist, dialectical or vulgar, are the unique theme of a metaphysics whose entire history was compelled to strive toward the reduction of the trace."[88]

THE OTHERED SELF

So again I ask wherefore the offense to bodily resurrection? Why does the empty tomb so scandalize? Why is it that the proclamation of Jesus' resurrection from the dead, to the extent that we affirm the corporeality of this affirmation, is a stumbling block to sensibility?

The answer has less to do with whether one thinks God could do such a thing, if God so chose, but more to do with a variety of intellectual and cultural habits, in part funded by our own body experience, that lead us to view our own bodies as appendages to self-identity. Particularly in an intellectual-cultural milieu that treats the body as "thing" or "container," the idea of bodily resurrection can seem a rather strange and even disconcerting one. More than any doctrine within the whole range of Christian theology, the doctrine of bodily resurrection demands that we understand our corporeality as the very way selfhood is achieved. What is more — and here is yet another aspect of the stumbling block — this doctrine affirms that my self-identity is never unmediated, can never be seen as a monadic essence standing in disengaged relation to the Other; for through my body the Other is installed within me, co-constitutive of my identity. Bodies are relational and permeable, intertwined with other bodies in a corporeal field. My body is never just "my own." Because the body makes the human person ambiguous, permeable, and relational, the instrumental subjection of the body is one of the ways personal identity is inauthentically enforced. By dissociating the self from the body, the ambiguous self attempts to shore up its identity over against the Other. But the body is the self-as-othered. The body is the presence of the Other as co-constitutive of the self. I am not wholly "me" in any separative way. My "me" is primordially conditioned by the Other, whether this Other is seen as beneficent or threatening. To the extent that dualism seeks to assert a separative stance towards the body, essentially scapegoating it for all the troubles it presents to the unity of "soul," it is in fact a defiant assertion of *ipseity*, a resistance to coming to terms with the relational nature of the self.

The significance of this conclusion is immediately obvious for the doctrine of bodily resurrection: the affirmation of bodily resurrection is the affirmation of the relational self, the human being who comes into being corporeally as a being-with and a being-for, as one whose very existence is given by the Other. There is no properly human fulfillment (or "salvation") that is not also the fulfillment of the Other. The resurrection of the body is a doctrine that forever bonds individual and general eschatology, and thus the self with the entire community of creation, with which it shares a single body in the body of Christ. It is to this more constructive view of bodily resurrection we now turn.

Chapter Four

I WILL BE MY BODY

The idea of the immortality of the soul is based on the experience of man's indomitable spirit. The idea of the resurrection of the body is based on the experience of God's unspeakable love.
— Frederick Buechner, *Wishful Thinking: A Theological ABC*[1]

A PROFOUNDER MATERIALISM

The Future Festival of the World

Christians are "the most sublime of materialists," writes Karl Rahner. "We neither can nor should conceive of any ultimate fullness of the spirit and of reality without thinking too of matter enduring as well in a state of final perfection." Those who adopt the moniker "materialist" usually mean by it something reductionistic. But a more profound and reaching materialism may be affirmed by the Christian, one that sees in the resurrection of the body the transposition of our corporeality into its ultimate fruition, which is another way of affirming the eschatological fulfillment of the whole community of creation.

> We recognize and believe that this matter will last for ever, and be glorified for ever. It must be glorified. It must undergo a transformation of the depths of which we can only sense with fear and trembling in that process which we experience as our death. It continues to perform its function for ever. It celebrates a festival that lasts forever. Already even now it is such that its ultimate nature can survive permanently; and such too that God has assumed it as his own body.... And already for this world as a whole the process of fermentation has already commenced which will bring it to this momentous conclusion. It is already filled with the forces of this indescribable transformation. And this inner dynamism in it is called, as Paul boldly confirms for us in speaking of the resurrection of the flesh, the holy Pneuma of God.[2]

It is appropriate that Rahner should describe this eschatological fulfillment in terms of festival. The image is richly developed in scripture and in Christian liturgy, with the consummation of all things described variously as the eternal Sabbath and everlasting banquet.[3] The Easter hymn of Hippolytus gives it beautiful expression.

> O thou leader of the mystic round-dance! O thou leader of the spiritual marriage feast! O thou leader of the divine Pasch and new feast of all things. O cosmic festal gathering! O joy of the universe, honour, ecstasy, exquisite delight by which dark death is destroyed... and the people that were in the depths arise from the dead and announce to all the hosts of heaven: "The thronging choir from earth is coming home."[4]

Festivals are communal events of a celebratory and commemorative nature. Orchestrated yet ultimately unpredictable events of conviviality and pageantry, feast and festival joyously display creation in its abundance. Feast is pure affirmation. Festal time is time released from the constraints imposed upon it by "ordinary time." Through dancing and colorful dress, music and game, extravagant food and drink, festival sets time apart for experiencing afresh the basic stuff of life through its adornment and intensification. It is creation at play, bodies at play; but this play is also rest, since only from abundance can the laborer hovering over necessity be lifted up into the sphere of spontaneous self-expression. A festival cannot be had alone. Nor does it arise from a simple aggregation of people. By drawing those present into the unfolding of its event, so that the spectators become part of the spectacle, a festival can transform the sense of personal dispersion that often comes with being a part of a social mass into the feeling of genuine *communitas*.

It is also significant that Rahner should refer to Paul to speak of the future festival of the world. There is hardly a more rhapsodic moment in all of Paul's writings than when he speaks of the resurrection of the body in 1 Corinthians 15:

> Listen, I will tell you a mystery! We will not all die, but we will all be changed, in a moment, in the twinkling of an eye, at the last trumpet. For the trumpet will sound, and the dead will be raised imperishable, and we will be changed. For this perishable body must put on imperishability, and this mortal body must put on immortality. When this perishable body puts on imperishability, and this mortal body puts on immortality, then the saying that is written will be fulfilled: "Death has been swallowed up in victory.

Where, O death, is your victory? Where, O death, is your sting?" (vv. 51–55)

The festival of resurrection inaugurated by the last trumpet is a celebration of God's victory over death and decay. It is that moment when what is sown in dishonor is raised in glory, when what is weak and subject to dysfunction is raised in power, when what is sown as a "soulish" body (*soma psychikon*) is raised a spiritual body (*soma pneumatikon*) (vv. 43–44). The resurrection institutes radical change. Like the juxtaposition between ordinary time and the extraordinary time of festival, there is a qualitative difference between the present state of bodily existence and future eschatological life. In order to get at this difference, Paul establishes a heuristic framework within which to work.

Anticipating an objection, Paul rhetorically asks: "How are the dead raised? With what kind of body do they come?" (v. 35). To answer this we must, in the first place, consider that not all bodies are alike. The panoply of creatures in the present world shows forth many different kinds of corporeality: one for human beings, one for land animals, another for birds, yet another for fish. The moon, sun, and other stars are also representative of distinctive bodies. God has given each of these a body according to God's own choosing (vv 38–41). Each possesses its own form and integrity, even if, like a seed that eventually becomes wheat or some other grain, a body may undergo remarkable change throughout the course of its existence. And this brings us to the second feature of Paul's heuristic. Having observed that the world is already filled with many different kinds of bodies, and therefore we should not balk at the idea that God can create for us a new body in the *eschaton*, Paul employs an organic metaphor to show that the spiritual body is at once continuous and discontinuous with our present state of existence. Just as the fruit arises from the seed, yet by all appearances is utterly different from its humble origin, so too will this physical body be transposed into a reality dramatically different from its present mode. The seed and the fruit are not two independent realities, but neither are they the same. The former transcends itself into the latter, becomes more of itself through the full actualization of its potential. The organic metaphor has the benefit of holding identity and change in tension. It connotes that resurrection life is the fulfillment of present life while delivering it into a profoundly new modality.

The animating power for this transformation is not something we possess. Here there is greater discontinuity than the organic metaphor can suggest. When Paul speaks of the *soma pneumatikon*, he is not asserting that the *soma psychikon* bears within it the resources of its own self-transcendence into resurrection life. It is God's Spirit (*Pneuma*) which alone brings this transposition to pass. Thus, while the adjective "spiritual" is intended to indicate a qualitatively new state of bodily life, one freed from corruption and alienation, it is meant especially to emphasize God's pneumatic action upon and within creation. And this pneumatic action is already at work. While Paul's contrast between the *soma psychikon* and *soma pneumatikon* falls along lines of present and future, weakness and power, dishonor and glory, Adam and Christ, such a contrast by no means asserts a blunt opposition. Because Christ is already raised, and because the same *Pneuma* that raised him from the dead also dwells presently within our mortal bodies, we are emboldened to say that the future is breaking in upon the present, vivifying and fermenting creation in a progression towards that day when we will experience the full redemption of our bodies (Rom. 8:11, 22–23).

But can we say more about the resurrection body as conceived by Paul? If we can at least ascertain from his writings that the *soma pneumatikon* is both continuous and discontinuous with our present bodily existence, can we say something more precise about the nature of this transformation? Some kind of clarification seems necessary since Paul at times makes rather strong statements contrasting the "flesh" (*sarx*) and the risen body. For example, in the very Corinthians passage under consideration, Paul emphatically asserts "flesh and blood cannot inherit the kingdom of God, nor does the perishable inherit the imperishable" (1 Cor. 15:50). Some interpreters conclude from this statement that the pneumatic body of the resurrection has nothing at all to do with the outward physical body of fleshly existence. This position may seem initially strange because modern people are accustomed to think of the "body" as material and "spirit" as immaterial. What could a non-physical (or non-"fleshly") body possibly be? But as was noted in the previous chapter, dualism in antiquity differs from modern dualism in many crucial respects. Dualism in ancient philosophy does not typically make hard-and-fast distinctions between materiality and immateriality like we find in Cartesian dualism, but hierarchicalizes bodies along a scale from the grosser to the more subtle. In Stoic cosmology, for example, the soul was thought of as a higher and more refined substance. To be sure, the soul was regarded as superior to the physical body, but the soul was still a kind of "stuff." And it is within this kind of cosmological-anthropological context, argues Dale Martin, that we should situate Paul.

Transphysicality

Martin rightly warns against projecting our modern notions of materiality vs. immateriality into ancient texts. Doing so might, in the case of Paul, lead us to think that the resurrection is for him an immaterial existence when in fact it is a material existence, albeit in a different mode than we currently experience. Martin agues that the best way to understand Paul's meaning is to see his broader discussion of earthly and celestial bodies in 1 Corinthians 15 in terms of the philosophically sophisticated view held by many educated people in the Greco-Roman world, including those upper-class members of the Corinthian church to whom the letter is addressed. The list Paul provides (human, animals, birds, fish) is not random but most likely representative of a sliding scale (in this case downwards) of bodily forms.[5] Such a hierarchy was a fairly common way to conceive of various earthly entities. Moreover, when Paul cites the example of celestial bodies (sun, moon, stars) to illustrate God's resourcefulness in creating diverse bodies, this serves to establish a key distinction between the pre- and post-resurrection body. Celestial bodies were of a subtler variety, "lighter" and more "heavenly" than the "coarser" bodies of earthly composition. Crucial to Dale's argument is that when Paul speaks of the first group (human, animal, bird, fish), he uses the term *sarx,* or "flesh," whereas when speaking of celestial bodies he uses the term *soma,* or "body." Thus, when Paul asserts that "flesh and blood" shall not inherit the kingdom of God, but the risen person will become a *soma pneumatikon,* he apparently means that the human being will become a subtle body analogous to celestial bodies. The "fleshly" part of the human person, i.e., the gross body of physical existence, will be "sloughed off" while the *pneuma* of the person will be preserved. "For Paul, the current human body is made up of sarx [flesh], psyche [soul], and pneuma [spirit]. The resurrected body will shed the first two of these entities — like so much detritus — and retain the third, a stuff of a thinner, higher nature.... What human beings have in common with heavenly bodies is, in Paul's system, incorporation as a 'pneumatic body' — that is, a body composed only of pneuma with sarx and psyche having been sloughed off along the way."[6] Martin's conclusion is that the risen body, according to Paul, is not *sarx* and *psyche* transformed into something new, but the *pneuma* of the person freed from the encumberment of the former. This is a non-physical bodiliness, a subtler corporeality. "According to Paul, the resurrected body is stripped of flesh, blood, and soul (*psychē*); it has nothing of the earth in it at all, being composed entirely of the celestial substance of pneuma."[7]

If this is indeed what Paul means — and I shall argue differently — then this would put Paul at considerable odds with other New Testament writings as well as the patristic authors of the second century. As Martin argues, whereas the gospels tend to emphasize the "resurrection of the flesh," Paul seems specifically to preclude it. And when, in the second century, "Christian authors insist explicitly on a resurrection of the actual flesh and blood of the dead body," they are speaking of the very *sarx* Paul asserts will be shed.[8] Paul therefore stands unaccompanied on this particular matter, with the essential difference being the following: whereas the gospel traditions and patristic theology of the second century claim that the physical body will be transformed into something new, retaining yet transcending the physicality of the human body, Paul's understanding of the *soma pneumatikon* is that upon the resurrection "the immortal and incorruptible part of the human body will be resurrected — or, to put it more accurately, that the body will be raised, constituted (due to divine transformation) only by its immortal and incorruptible aspects, without its corruptible and corrupting aspects such as sarx."[9] Some interpreters, such as Marcus Borg, argue that this apparent preclusion, along with the lack of an empty tomb narrative in Paul, establishes within scripture enough interpretive room for modern Christians to elect for a non-physical view of the resurrection.[10] This is most likely what Paul Avis envisions, as when in the previous chapter I quoted him as saying that the contemporary Christian may still maintain a belief in the resurrection of Jesus Christ without the "miraculous accompaniment" of the empty tomb.

But there are strong reasons to resist Martin's interpretation here and argue, on the contrary, that Paul envisions the preservation and transformation of the whole human person, including the physical body. First of all, many commentators maintain that the phrase "flesh and blood" is not a physiological designation referring to the physical body as distinguished from "soul" or "spirit" but a Semitic phrase referring to the whole human being, most usually in contexts emphasizing creatureliness, weakness, and, in this particular case, alienation from God due to sin.[11] This latter meaning is most probable given the parallel passage in 1 Cor. 6:9–11 in which Paul adumbrates the vices preventing participation in the Kingdom of God.[12] Paul does not often employ Kingdom of God language. In the two instances he does in 1 Corinthians, the reference is used negatively to say that wrongdoers (6:9) and "flesh and blood" (15:50) will not enter the Kingdom. The significance of this parallel is that the former alerts us to the meaning of the latter. The point is paranetic, not anatomic. Paul is urging for appropriate behavior in view of the coming resurrection. What we do with our bodies matters quite precisely because it is our bodies that will be raised. "The continuity between the present body and the future resurrection body is what gives weight to the present ethical imperative."[13] Hence the strong statement: "The body is meant not for fornication but for the Lord, and the Lord for the body. And God raised the Lord and will also raise us by his power. Do you not know that your bodies are members of Christ?" (6:14–15). So when Paul asserts that "flesh and blood" will not inherit the Kingdom of God, he is saying that the weakness and corruptibility of our present condition of existence stands in need of transformation, a "new creation in terms of full deliverance from sin to a disposition of holiness."[14] The point then is that the human beings under domination by sin shall not be admitted to God's glory. It is a statement regarding the existential state of the whole person before God. Anthony Thiselton insists that much patristic theology is actually very close to Paul's own meaning when it interprets "flesh and blood" as referring to a state of alienation due to sin, not as a description of some discrete aspect (in this case the outwardly physical) of the human being.[15] Gregory of Nyssa captures just this meaning as he comments upon 1 Cor. 15, arguing that when human nature "abandons to death all the properties which it acquired through the state of subjection to passion ... [it] does not abandon itself. Instead, as if ripening into an ear, it changes into incorruptibility, glory, honor, power, and every kind of perfection."[16]

Second, neither is the contrast between the *soma psychikon* and *soma pneumatikon* intended to distinguish between different parts or layers of the human person. It is used by Paul to distinguish between two modes of existence of the one human person who *is* human only in a somatic way. Robert Gundry summarizes the meaning of *soma* in Pauline literature in the following way:

> The *sōma* denotes the physical body, roughly synonymous with "flesh" in the neutral sense. It forms that part of man in and through which he lives and acts in the world. It becomes the base of operations for sin in the unbeliever, for the Holy Spirit in the believer. Barring prior occurrence of the Parousia, the *sōma* will die. That is the lingering effect of sin even in the believer. But it will also be resurrected. That is its ultimate end, and major proof of its worth and necessity to wholeness of human being, and the reason for its sanctification now.[17]

The difference between the *soma psychikon* and *soma pneumatikon* is a question of what animates the one *soma* of the human being. This is crucial to emphasize. When Paul speaks of the *soma psychikon*, which translates literally into the "soulish body," he is speaking of the embodied human person living under its own power. It is ordinary human life, the kind of life lived by Adam — "from the earth, a man of dust" (15:47). The *soma pneumatikon*, which the risen Christ exemplifies, is the same *soma* but wholly indwelt by God's *pneuma* (v. 45). The adjectival use of *pneuma* does not refer to the "whatness" of the risen body (e.g., that it is made of the same "stuff" as celestial bodies) but refers to the pneumatic action of God upon and within the human person who, now fully under the influence of God's Spirit, has become a new somatic reality. "Spirit is not an anthropological category but a gift of God."[18] Or, as Peter Lampe writes: "The word 'spiritual'... does not say anything about the material or energetic structure of this new body. It does not try to describe a *Lichtleib*, some sort of concentration of light or other energy. Nor does it convey that this new body is composed of miniature particles of matter, as the Stoics would have described the *pneuma* (spirit)." Speculations about the risen body's quiddity are quite beyond Paul's interests. "For him, the term 'spiritual' emphasizes that God's Spirit is the *only* force that creates the new body. The creation of this new body is totally *beyond* all the possibilities of the present nature and creation. That is all he wants to convey with this term."[19]

Thirdly, the contrast between the *soma psychikon* (= perishable, dishonor, weakness) and *soma pneumatikon* (= imperishable, glory, power) is formulated to show that the former will become the latter through God's transforming *pneuma*. When in v. 53 Paul writes that "this perishable body must put on immortality," the emphasis on continuity is quite clear. "The same identifiable, recognizable, and accountable identity," writes Thiselton, "is transfigured into a *radically different form*, but remains this *created being in its wholeness*."[20] Our present earthly existence, however much under the sway of those powers in the world that mete out death and destruction, is precisely what is transformed by the resurrection into a new mode of life. With notably similar language, Paul assures us in his Philippians correspondence that our earthly bodies shall be glorified and share in the exalted corporeality of Christ himself. "He will transform the body of our humiliation that it may be conformed to the body of his glory, by the power that also enables him to make all things subject to himself" (3:21). This is what makes the resurrection a victory. Indeed, if the resurrection were only the ejection of a pneumatic (or "astral") body from a coarser physical husk, then the language of victory in 1 Cor. 15:54–56 would make no sense.[21] Such would amount to a philosophical truce with death. Death and decay would be left entirely intact and earthly existence would remain subjected by sin. Paul's meaning is much stronger than this. He means that resurrection accomplishes the *reversal* of death and decay.[22] It is the liberation of the earthly body from those antagonizing powers that dominate present existence. Resurrection is thus a cause for celebration, for festival. It gives him the boldness to taunt death ("Where, O death, is your victory?") while celebrating the God "who gives us the victory through our Lord Jesus Christ" (vv. 55, 57). The *soma*-person will thus become more truly him- or herself in the resurrection. The "resurrection mode of existence," writes Thiselton, is "constituted by (the direction, control, and character of) the (Holy) Spirit" in a way that the body is not "reduced in potential from the physical capacities which biblical traditions value, but enhanced above and beyond them in ways that *both assimilate and transcend them.*"[23] Resurrection existence in the Holy Spirit "is more than physical but not less." "Heaven is not *Sheol,* where earthly existence is perceived to be 'thinned down.'" Rather, it is the fullness of our earthly physical life transformed into "the 'more' of the agency of the Holy Spirit and the love of the Creator God."[24]

N. T. Wright speaks similarly, but ventures a neologism to express the point. Though difficult to describe or imagine, we may speak of the risen body as a *transphysical* reality. Such a term "is not meant to describe in detail what sort of a body it was that the early Christians supposed Jesus already had, and believed that they themselves would eventually have. Nor indeed does it claim to explain how such a thing can come to be. It merely, but I hope usefully, puts a label on the demonstrable fact that the early Christians envisaged a body which was still robustly physical but also significantly different from the present. If anything . . . we might say not that it will not be *less* physical, as though it were some kind of ghost or apparition, but more."[25] Wright obviously reads Paul as consistent with the rest of the New Testament.

Here we may observe that the term "transphysical" is at once a positive assertion and a gesture of negative theology. It affirms and denies at the same time. On the one hand it affirms that the risen body is inclusive (not exclusive) of the physical body. Resurrection is not decreation or dematerialization, but material creation most fully realized. The resurrection enfolds the entirety of our bodily life, frees it from its susceptibility to death and decay, and subsumes it into a modality that is yet "more than." This "more than" truly transcends our ability to imagine or name. Thus, on the other hand, speaking of the resurrection must include within it acts of unsaying. We cannot express "what" the risen body is in a way that allows us to objectify it to ourselves. "Listen, I will tell you a mystery" (1 Cor. 15:51). There is a richness and depth to resurrection life that is not amenable to full comprehension. Its reality is *in excess* of our present mode of existence, though it stands as the definitive fulfillment of that existence.[26] Here we find that the relationship between affirmative and negative statements is consistent with the gospel accounts of the risen Christ's self-attestation in the mode of presence and withdrawal, as the saturated phenomenon *par excellence.* He is capable of revealing himself in the historically mediated experience of the disciples in such a way that they are able to identify him, yet he does so in a manner that exceeds and transforms their intentionality, and thus by imparting "distance." Christ's glorified corporeality is at once continuous and discontinuous with their present experience; and this relationship of continuity and discontinuity is accounted for in the gospel narratives variously, as we have seen: in the ways he appears as the stranger, as one who dis-appears at the moment of recognition, as one who leads the women filled with terror and amazement from Jerusalem to Galilee to proclaim "He is risen; he is not here."

"We cannot really imagine the 'how' of this bodily consummation," writes Rahner. "In the last analysis, therefore, we can merely say in St. Paul's language of paradox: it will be a spiritual body (1 Cor 15:44), i.e., a true bodily nature which, however, is pure expression of the spirit become one with the *pneuma* of God and its bodily existence, and is no longer its restricting and abasing element and its emptiness. It will be a bodily nature which does not cancel again the freedom from the earth here-and-now gained with death, but will, on the contrary, bring it out in its pure form."[27] Rahner too works the dialectic of affirmation and denial with such a statement, maintaining all the while the Pauline view of the resurrection as the definitive fruition of embodied-historical existence.

THE CORPOREALITY OF GRACE

Now that we have examined Paul's theology of bodily resurrection, we turn to a more constructive theology of bodily resurrection in light of the issues raised by the previous chapter. There I maintained that theoretical dualism frequently results when we project into discrete ontic categories the multivalence of our bodily experience. Because the body is both self-revealing and concealing, both present and absent in our experience, and because the body frequently becomes more focal in our experience when we run up against restraint, either through the meeting of basic necessities or, more sharply, through physical pain, dysfunction, and death, the body is liable to becoming objectified in our conscious reflection and interpreted as only an outer trace of our inner identity, an external instrument or façade, or worse, as the foil to transcendence, when in fact our corporeality is the condition of the possibility of identity, relation, and transcendence. Here we are opting for a view of the human person as a psychosomatic unity. This view is not only supported by a phenomenological account of human existence; it is mandated by a theological anthropology that takes Jesus' resurrection from the dead with adequate seriousness. Ultimately, christology is the criterion for Christian theological anthropology. Jesus Christ is the paradigm for humanity, and his resurrection from the dead the proleptic realization of our fulfillment in him. Because of this we are obliged to say, among many other things, that *we are our bodies*. The body is the site of salvation. Personal identity is thoroughly corporeal, not just for a time, but forever, inasmuch as the resurrection affirms the eternal integrity and absolute consummation of bodily life. Moreover, because personal identity *is* embodied identity, and because my body, as an "open system," is woven into the fabric of other bodies, social and cosmic, the fulfillment of my existence is coextensive with the eschatological destiny of other persons — indeed, all of creation. My body is the intertwining of self and Other, the bond or "chiasm" that makes my identity an identity-in-relation. Hence, individual and general eschatology are really two aspects of the same reality. Finally, the resurrection obliges us to think of our identities-in-relation as an openness to the future, to God's absolute future. While it is correct to say we *are* our bodies, it is more theologically perceptive to say we *will be our bodies*. The fullness of eschatological life remains an outstanding reality. However much we may presently participate in that reality by grace, we await our final fulfillment when God will be all in all. Hence, there is no need to compulsively secure or hoard our identities. In truth, we become more fully ourselves — and therefore more fully who we shall be in the resurrection — to the extent that we lovingly open ourselves to the Other and to that future when God's Holy Spirit shall transform what is sown in death into pneumatic life.

I shall develop these lines of thought by explicating the doctrine of bodily resurrection in a fourfold way: in terms of the I-body, the social-body, the cosmic-body, and the ecclesial-body. From a Christian perspective, these bodies mutually subsist and together must be seen as the site and mediation of God's saving activity.[28] The imagination and praxis inspired by the resurrection distinguishes itself from every implicit and explicit dualism. More positively, it helps to support a holistic vision of salvation — a profounder materialism.

The I-Body

"It has always struck me," writes Edward Schillebeeckx, "that the Greeks have criticized Christianity for being a *genos philosomaton,* i.e. a kind of people who attach too much importance to corporeality.... [B]ut what can human consummation ultimately mean for human beings if it leaves out the corporeality which is so familiar to us? In that case I am no longer 'I,' and this 'I' has not achieved definitive salvation."[29] It is just this type of argumentation that many of the early Christian apologists adopted to defend their faith against many of their Greek philosophical critics, arguing that because human beings were originally created to be embodied beings, and that therefore the body is constitutive of personal identity, is indeed an expression of the original goodness of creation, only the fulfillment of our bodily existence can bring about genuine human beatitude. To be an embodied creature is not an ontological deficiency. Corporeality is not the result of a fall from an aboriginal unity which we must recapture. My body is not an appendage to my innermost self, but is, rather, generative of the "I." My *own body* is the only way I come to be, the way my personal identity is accomplished in the world. Even if, as explained in the previous chapter, my lived bodily experience is made up of many profiles, a multitude of presences and absences, so that I am capable of ignoring or objectifying my own body, even taking an instrumental attitude towards the very body that enables me to have existence, I can never take leave of my body, never finally wrestle myself away from my installation in the world's corporeal expanse. But the affirmation of bodily resurrection is much more than a begrudging consent to our bodily existence as an unavoidable arrangement. Properly understood, resurrection faith is the most radical affirmation of our bodily existence. It *releases us into our corporeality.*

The doctrine of bodily resurrection affirms the created contingency of human existence as an eschatological good. Resurrection gives us the freedom to *not* be God. This may seem like an unusual point to stress, but it must be thoroughly grasped. As I shall explain in later chapters, resurrection means full participation in God, the divinization of creation, the fullest expression of creaturely becoming in God. God is the inmost possibility and ultimate end of creation. But such divinization is not a matter of absorptive unity with God. Instead of negating our created contingency, our participation in divine life brings the particularity and diversity of creation into definitive expression. Resurrection is creation most united with God and, at the same time, creation maximally itself. It is a differentiated unity, a unity-in-difference, which is the eschatological goal of creation. To borrow a phrase from John Macquarrie, we must understand the resurrection as God's definitive "letting-be" of creation. Such a phrase is not intended to indicate indifference or separation. It intends to affirm the way God empowers creation to enjoy the maximal range of its created existence. God's love for creation is a "letting-be" insofar as it confers, sustains, and perfects the being of creatures.[30] Divine love for creation is unitive, and this *unity preserves difference within itself as a positive reality.* Love presupposes a creative and pacific "distance" between lovers. The qualitative difference between God and creation should not be thought of in any way as privation. There is no supra-creaturely status we must attain, no ontological alienation from ourselves or from God we must finally surmount. Too often notions of human transcendence involve some kind of expressed or implicit problematization of the body since it is through our bodiliness that we most immediately experience the contingency and finitude of our existence. The resurrection affirms that our finitude is blessedness. Resurrection faith releases us *into* our finitude, sets us free to be ourselves rather than something else. "To enjoy and love what is worldly in the world, what is human in man, is to enjoy and to love what makes God God. God's glory lies in the happiness and the well-being of mankind in the world."[31] "Eternal life," writes Schillebeeckx elsewhere, "is God's complete assent to our own love-filled temporality."[32]

Related to this "letting-be" of the resurrection is the powerful and dignifying affirmation of the human person as unsubstitutably unique. The I-body eternally abides in the order of salvation.[33] For a Christian anthropology that reads off the resurrection of Jesus in order to make assertions about the nature of personal identity, the only consistent affirmation can be that the historically concrete manifestation of personal individuation is really and truly the "I." Any projection of the self that situates the "I" in alienated relationship with its bodily manifestation betrays what I called in the previous chapter a creeping docetism. The body is not the negativity or dispersion of the "I." Although the body opens up the self to the Other in such a way that we must say that the self is othered from within — a point I shall clarify momentarily — the body is not the distorted manifestation of the true self; it is the self in self-manifestation and self-mediation. The body is the concrete symbol of the person: living, breathing, feeling, thinking, and communicating flesh. Such identification stresses the historicality of human existence. It is this emphasis that helps us to avoid some of the theological dead ends that are reached when we speculate over the "whatness" of the risen body. It is not possible, nor is it necessary, for us to state more precisely how, in ontic terms, the risen body remains in continuity with our present existence. Some trends in ancient and medieval theology spoke directly to these questions, as for example when Augustine, who along with Athenagoras, Tertullian, and Jerome, offered explicit descriptions of the risen body while weighing in on such questions as to whether it shall have hair, entrails, fingernails, what age and gender the body shall be, and what happens in the case of cannibalism when a living person eats the flesh of another. (Augustine in particular set the tone for medieval discussions of the resurrection.[34]) While questions like these may strike the contemporary reader as immodestly conjectural and perhaps less than sufficiently attendant to the radical discontinuity of resurrection life, they nevertheless speak to God's providential care for creation, as Book XXII of *De civitate Dei* demonstrates. "Far be it from us to fear that the omnipotence of the Creator cannot, for the resuscitation and reanimation of our bodies, recall all the portions which have been consumed by beasts or fire, or have been dissolved into dust or ashes, or have decomposed into water, or evaporated into the air."[35] Augustine's primary concern is to show that God's love for the human person upholds the particularity of the human person while restoring humanity from dysfunction and decay.[36] This strong affirmation of human particularity does not depend, however, upon the "anthropology of composition" that we find in those theological writings, like Augustine's, that speak of the resurrection in terms of the reconstitution of "parts" or indivisible "atoms" of the human being.[37] We may opt instead for an approach that speaks of the *soma pneumatikon* as the total integration and transfiguration of the embodied history of the human person in union with God.[38] The spiritual body is all-inclusive of the human person who only comes to be in a corporeal way, though we should remember that this inclusivity is also a healing, transformation, and perfection of the person by God's creative *Pneuma*. Here again the *pneuma* does not tell us "what" so much as "how": through the transformative power of God who alone is capable of bringing creation into its absolute fruition. The totality of our lived histories, our countless relations, our sufferings and our loves, the personal identities that have emerged throughout our lives with all their focal plots and non-focal subplots, the impact of our free decisions, the nexus of those desires that most characterize who we are: all that has contributed to the shape of our lives as lived up to the time of our death are the corporeal gifts we offer to God's eschatological artistry.

"Hope for 'the resurrection of the body,' " writes Jürgen Moltmann, "permits no disdain and debasement of bodily life and sensory experiences; it affirms them profoundly, and gives greatest honour to 'the flesh,' which people have made something to be despised."[39] Moltmann insists here that resurrection faith is in essence a creation faith. It inspires the human person to see his or her own life incarnationally and eschatologically: incarnationally, insofar as we are to cultivate richly the full range of our corporeal experience by embracing the senses, embracing our earthiness, embracing the particularities of our bodily identities, honoring the dignity and beauty of bodily form; eschatologically, insofar as we are to attend and respond to bodily affliction in ourselves and others, seeking to meet the bodily needs of those who suffer from hunger, abuse, and oppression, building up those interpersonal and social bodies for the purpose of enhancing human flourishing and creativity, all in active anticipation of the general resurrection. To live incarnationally and eschatologically in this way means understanding human identity (the "self," or I-body) in relational terms. Identity is not something to be secured over against the mediation of the body; it is something we discover in and through our corporeality, in and through our relationships with others, including non-human creation, which the body opens us out unto. Moltmann speaks of a "resurrection dialectic" in the formation of the Christian self. "In this resurrection dialectic, human beings don't have to try to cling to their identity through constant unity with themselves, but will empty themselves into non-identity, knowing that from this self-emptying they will be brought back to themselves again for eternity. Human beings find themselves, not by guarding themselves and saving themselves up, but through self-emptying into what is other and alien. Only people who go out of themselves arrive at themselves."[40]

It is just this releasement into our corporeality that should guide our understanding of personal identity. To put the matter succinctly, *we are beings-unto-resurrection.* Such a phrase might mean many things, but here we stress that as we live unto the resurrection we are able to release ourselves from attempting to build up our personal identities in any way that occurs through clinging and dividing. This is in no way to deny the important task of gaining self-understanding and self-integration, of attempting to organize one's feelings, thoughts, and behaviors in a coherent and healthy way. Rather, I am speaking of the act of establishing self-definition through polarization, particularly through the identification of one's "inner self" over against the body and the countless relations with the Other that bodily life involves. The formation of a fully embodied self who lives unto the resurrection is one freed to live *kenotically,* ecstatically, as one freely disposed to and for the Other in a movement of loving communion. I find myself through losing myself.

I will be my body. "I shall live *wholly* here, and die *wholly*, and rise *wholly* there."[41]

The Social-Body

In the previous chapter I noted that among the reasons why modern people have difficulty with the doctrine of bodily resurrection, the logocentrism and individualism that characterize modern views of the body figure prominently. While the doctrine has proved challenging to defend and articulate from the very origins of Christian theology, the distinctively modern tendency to view matter as a vast reservoir of inert "stuff" to be seized for technical mastery, including our own bodies, which are frequently reduced to commodity, surveillance, and facile aestheticization — as so many mechanical, expressive and libidinal "things" — has made it especially difficult to render bodily resurrection in an intelligible and compelling way for people today. Such difficulty extends to Christians, no less, particularly those who object that the notion is naïvely mythological and in need of translation into something more agreeable to contemporary sensibilities. Such objections, I argued, only serve to confirm rather than critique and transform the "disengaged subjectivity" of our time. To the extent that we imagine the subject to be an immaterial and immediate self-presence enveloped by a bodily shell, with the latter occupying the realm of objectness, the subject stands atomized and alienated from the broader web of corporeal relations in which we live, move, and have our being. The doctrine of bodily resurrection stands as a powerful rejoinder to any such dichotomization because it requires that we understand the eschatological fulfillment of the individual in relationship to the eschatological fulfillment of the Other. Individual and general eschatology are two aspects of the same reality, and both are anthropology in the future tense.

"The body is the *binding*, the space in the middle where both identity and difference are symbolically connected under the authority of the Other."[42] Louis-Marie Chauvet articulates here an understanding of the human body as at once individuating and relational, as the intertwining of interiority and exteriority. While it is manifestly true that the human body individuates one person from another, and thus it is entirely correct to say that my own body is my *proper* body — the unrepeatable manifestation of my person — I am yet a being-in-the-world and a being-with-the-Other in the most profound sense. Personhood is relational. Indeed, I am a being-*from*-the-Other insofar as the advent of my "me" is given from maternity and paternity. The navel symbolizes this relationship:

The navel is a good representation of this *liminal* position of the body, at the frontier between me and the non-me under the authority of the Other. This umbilical scar is the *trace* of the inaugural sewing up of the child in its "sack of skin" and thus of its delivery into the autonomy of a place which nobody else can occupy; but it is also the trace of a primordial opening through which it communicates the exterior and especially with the others-who-are-bodies, that, as both closed and open, permit it to experience every communication with the universe as a speaking.[43]

Leder too provides a meditation upon the givenness of our birth as a sign of this liminality:

[M]y lived body was formed from within that of another. I arose out of Viscerality, hidden from the gaze of my mother and preceding the birth of my own vision. Even my genes came not from perceptual but visceral chiasm. In the sexual act, my parents' bodies and cells intertwined, an identity-in-difference giving rise to me. My embryonic and fetal development then proceeded through a series of visceral *écarts:* the mitosis of my cells differentiating one from another, then giving rise to discrete but interrelated organ systems. The maternal/fetal relation is another chiasmatic identity-in-difference. While separate, we are enfolded together, sharing one pulsing blood-stream. Even after birth, through the act of breast-feeding, one body is nourished directly from the visceral production of the other.[44]

Selfhood is emergent from, dependent upon, and finds the possibility of self-reflectivity in and through *corporeal difference and mediation.* The very body I am is anterior to my ability to say, "I am." Psychogenesis is not *causa sui,* but formed from an original heteronomy. To be born is to-be in a way in which what I will eventually claim as my own — my proper body, my proper desires, my sense of interior depth — is *given* from an originating *exteriority.* Subjective spaciousness involves a kind of "involution" of the flesh. My interior monologue is already dialogical, an in-corporation of a world of language always-already spoken to me. Even as I assert some kind of autonomy, this is only possible because of a pre-reflective and unthematic heteronomy founded in intercorporeity. To be *born* is to *be given to corporeality.* For this reason every sort of essentialism valorizing self-presence and immediacy requires some sort of amnesia, a forgetfulness of natal beginnings. The subject's pretense to transcendental mineness assumes that its "outward expression" in the body is subsequent to an original "self-presence" when in fact the condition of its very possibility is its being-given to corporeality. "Metaphysical subjectivity," writes Jean-Luc Marion, might well be defined as the "denegation tripped up by the always already accomplished fact, *fait accompli,* of my birth."[45] The project of selfhood is a temporal delay, a response to a prior "call." The embodied person is emergent from the givenness of language, sociality, culture, and desire. Relation logically and temporally precedes identity. "Before my birth, words were said around me and I heard them without understanding; even before my conception, words were exchanged by others, words ranging from joy to violence and from which I no doubt come. I therefore was said and spoken before being; I am born from a call that I neither made, wanted, nor even understood."[46] Being — like faith — comes *ex auditu.*

To be bodily is to be communicative, is at once a self-concealedness and a self-revealing, an interiority and an exteriority. "Through our bodies we act, express ourselves, relate and communicate. Without our bodiliness," continues Gerald O'Collins, "there would be no language, no art, no literature, no religion, no industry, no politics, no social and economic relations, and none of that married love in which verbal and non-verbal communication reaches a supremely intense level. In short, without bodies we could have no human history." Again we have the affirmation of the essential historicality of human existence, but here with an emphasis on our *shared* history. "Through our bodies we build up that whole web of relationships with other human beings, the material universe and God which constitutes our story. Our bodies enable us to communicate, participate and play the human game."[47] That we share a common corporeality and history means that for Christian faith, which affirms the transformation of this corporeality and history into its definitive fulfillment through resurrection, salvation is inherently social. It makes a "claim upon the world," as stated in the previous chapter. Individual and general eschatology are necessarily linked. Though we must continue to emphasize individual responsibility for our lives before God, such responsibility is bound up with the web of relationships that intersect and sustain our lives. With such an insight in mind we can better grasp the resurrection as divine judgment — how it makes a claim upon us.

It is not possible here to enter into a discussion of traditional eschatological themes such as hell, purgatory, heaven, and the intermediate state. And yet we can penetrate to the core of these themes, if very briefly, by underscoring that the resurrection situates the eschatological fulfillment of the self within a broader interpersonal nexus. The truth of my existence before God is related to the shape of that existence as lived among others. There is no "I" without including the impact my life has made upon others, for good and for ill. Even at the moment of my death the reality of my "I" is not yet complete, since the impact of my life continues to extend in the lives of those with whom I have been in relation, whether I have been fully conscious of these relations or not. Here I refer to the point made in the previous chapter that the unity of the self is best thought of in narrative rather than metaphysical terms. A narrative style of thinking allows us to view the human person as positioned within a *complexus* of plots and subplots, with focal and non-focal dramatic actions. It allows us to ascribe a certain self-persistence of character over time while yet allowing for the self to be seen as ambiguous and changing due to constantly shifting relationships and contexts. The resurrection of the body should therefore be conceived of in terms of the completion of a person's narrative history as such. It is that event in which the totality of our lived existence achieves final determination, where what has extended over time and through a multitude of relationships becomes fully integrated. Eternal life is not the absence of temporality. It is time's fullness, its consummation, its ripening, to intone the Pauline theme. So conceived, the resurrection means quite precisely that the truth of my existence is not resolvable only in terms of my own death. As a being-unto-resurrection, and not just a being-unto-death, the truth of my life includes the effective history of my life upon others; and this truth is only resolvable in the general resurrection of the dead. Joseph Ratzinger (now Pope Benedict XVI) puts the matter this way:

> Every person exists in himself and outside himself: everyone exists simultaneously in other people. What happens in one individual has an effect upon the whole of humanity, and what happens in humanity happens in the individual. "The Body of Christ" means that all human beings are one organism, the destiny of the whole the proper destiny of each. True enough, the decisive outcome of each person's life is settled in death, at the close of their earthly activity. Thus everyone is judged and reaches his definitive destiny after death. But his final place in the whole can be determined only when the total organism is complete, when the *passio* and *action* of history have come to their end. And so the gathering together of the whole will be an act that leaves no person unaffected. Only at that juncture can the definitive general judgment take place, judging each man in terms of the whole and giving him that just place which he can receive only in conjunction with all the rest.[48]

It is crucial that we appreciate the dimension of justice and judgment that resurrection language entails. Earlier in this chapter I noted that Paul explicitly connects the resurrection with the moral order, arguing that the future resurrection bears upon how we live our lives in the present. So far from being an other-worldly doctrine that essentially casts a shadow over the present life as insignificant, the resurrection places enormous significance on the present world, our present history, and the quality of our desires, relationships, and free decisions insofar as the resurrection of the dead renders their truth before God. Only at the general resurrection will we see God "face to face" and know ourselves fully as we are known (1 Cor. 13:12). "Only in the 'universal resurrection,'" writes Bernard Prusak, "when the material world and its history will have achieved the fullness of finality, will our contributions and relationship to that world be finalized and fully realized, and integrated into our identity, which will thereby have achieved fullness."[49] Properly understood, the relationship between individual and general eschatology necessitates in Christian theology an acknowledgement of an "intermediate state" between our individual deaths and the general resurrection. The reality of a person's individual existence is not fully accomplished upon death but will continue to generate effects in the broader social body long afterwards. There exists a considerable diversity of opinions within theology, both over the centuries and today, regarding the "how" of the intermediate state, e.g., whether a person remains "asleep" from the time of their death until the general resurrection, whether the soul is reunited with the body on the Last Day, or whether a person "dies into resurrection" immediately at the termination of his or her life. Speculation on this subject would take us too far afield from our present study, which is content to affirm that the fulfillment of a person's individual existence is bound up with the fulfillment of the Other. The statement, "I will be my body," intends to express this point by emphasizing that our corporeality is what establishes this relationship. Human existence is set within an eschatological milieu: as an opening unto God's absolute future, when God shall be all in all and the truth of our existence shall be revealed; as an opening to the human Other who casts every human life in a situation of dependence and responsibility.

I shall say more about this dependence and responsibility in Part Two. Chapters 5 and 6 will focus on the theme of justice in the social order, while chapters 7 and 8 will focus on the theme of reconciliation. As we shall see, justice and reconciliation belong together in the closest possible unity, and both themes are found at the heart of resurrection theology.

The Cosmic Body

I have spoken of the body as the "binding" between self and Other, particularly in the interpersonal and social realm. Such an analysis would be incomplete without a consideration of our relationship to the broader community of creation. Bodily existence is ecstatic and recessive, relational and permeable, a subsistence from and vulnerability to the non-human Other. It is a cosmic body that we all share. The human person is in some sense a microcosm of the whole insofar as we bear the imprints of the entire material universe, including the biological and social history of humankind. While it is habitual for many of us to see the world as in some sense "out there," as a mere backdrop in the theater of a human play, such anthropocentrism fails to grasp that the subject-object distinction rooted in intentional consciousness is comprehended within a broader, cosmic milieu. However much we must insist upon the irreducible uniqueness of the human person (the I-body), and however much we can ascribe unique qualities to the *humanum* more generally (the social-body), we fundamentally misrepresent ourselves as persons and human communities if we do not see ourselves as the world itself coming-to-be. We are manifestations of the one world as it *worlds itself*. My perceptions and reflections upon the world "out there" are in reality a unique folding or coiling of the world upon itself. We are "the world that thinks itself." "[T]he world is at the heart of our flesh."[50] The cosmos comes to unique expression in and through the *humanum*. Our relationship to the world is characterized by an "intertwining" or "chiasm," as Maurice Merleau-Ponty puts it. Human perception and activity involves the enjoining and mutual inherence of perceiver and perceived. "Flesh," or *la chair*, according to Merelau-Ponty, is not limited to the human body. It is a communion of identity-indifference.[51] I am made of the same corporeality that I encounter and engage. *La chair* in this sense is the interaction or exchange of perceiver and perceived, knower and known in mutual exteriority and interiority, the binding between me and the Other which both differentiates and unites. My flesh is the flesh of the world; and it is only because I share in this flesh that I can perceive and know the world. Leder describes this mutual inherence in an exhilarating passage:

> In the perceptual chiasm, body and world reach out to each other from across an ineradicable space.... Yet in addition to this perceptual communion of the flesh, I am sustained through a deeper "blood" relation with the world. It is installed within me, not just encountered from without. The inanimate, calcified world supports

my flesh from within in the form of bones. A world of organic, autonomous powers circulates within my visceral depths. Science tells me that some ten quadrillion bacteria live within my body. I cannot even claim my own cells fully as my own. In all probability, they evolved out of symbiotic relations between different prokaryotic cells, one living inside another. My body everywhere bears the imprint of Otherness.

This encroachment of the world is renewed at every moment by visceral exchanges with the environment. In sleep I give myself over to anonymous breathing, relinquishing the separative nature of distance perception. Even waking perception is ultimately in service to the visceral.... As I eat, the thickness of the flesh that separates self from world melts away. No longer perceived across a distance, the world dissolves into my own blood, sustaining me from within via its nutritive powers. I am not just gazing upon the world but one who feeds on it, drinks of it, breathes it in.[52]

In a very real, if incomplete, sense we already exist in a state of "communion" with our world through this blood relation. We can even speak here of a "eucharistic communion of creation," as does Moltmann, to underscore the mutual giftedness of life. "I am" only to the extent that I receive. I receive my "me" from the Other, both human and non-human; and as I do, I have the choice of resisting and resenting this relationality in a separative movement, which is ultimately self-alienating, or I can accept this gift with hospitality and gratitude, thereby more fully realizing the human vocation of becoming a "eucharistic being."[53]

But as we know, our dependence upon the Other is a vulnerability that opens us up to the possibility of both nourishment and diminishment. There are experiences we endure that do not elicit spontaneous thanksgiving but instead prompt us, sometimes quite sharply, to recoil from dependence. Particularly when we take into account the pain and suffering due to bodily dysfunction and death, or the violation of bodies in situations of interpersonal and social violence, including war, sexual abuse, torture, slavery, and the scourge of poverty, we will need to give equal emphasis to themes of justice and reconciliation should we continue to insist upon the centrality of our corporeality in the order of salvation. That is, while we speak of the resurrection in terms of the *fulfillment* of our corporeality, as a transformative and "divinizing" reality that uplifts our humanity and the whole community of creation into everlasting communion with God, we must also speak of the resurrection as a *reversal* and triumph over those realities that destroy creation.

We do not look for a fulfillment beyond our corporeality; rather, we look for a fulfillment *through* and *of* it. For the resurrection to be a fulfillment in this way it must also be corrective and reconciling. Paul speaks directly to this fulfillment through reversal and reconciliation: "We know that *the whole creation* has been groaning in labor pains until now; and not only ourselves, who have the first fruits of the Spirit, groan inwardly while we wait for adoption, the redemption of our bodies" (Rom. 8:23). Christ's lordship is cosmic. He is "the firstborn of all creation.... all things were created through and for him. He himself is before all things, and in him all things hold together" (Col. 1:15–17). The cosmicity of Paul's christological-eschatological vision logically follows from his insistence on Jesus' bodily resurrection, and indeed flows out of the Jewish eschatology (both its apocalyptic and sapiential strains) which anticipate nothing less than a new heaven and a new earth (Isa. 66:22; see also Rev. 21:1). For Paul, such cosmic fulfillment is linked with the overcoming of those forces within creation that wreak suffering and alienation, including death itself. In 1 Corinthians 15 Paul speaks of God's triumph over "every rule and every authority and power" as the enabling condition for God to become "all in all" (vv. 24, 26, 28).

It is crucial that we understand the bodiliness of Christ's resurrection as that which makes this triumph possible and real. God's becoming "all in all" is precisely related to the particularity of Christ's risen body. Gustave Martelet notes this well, emphasizing that because the human body is the bond between the *humanum* and the cosmos, the transfiguring fulfillment of the one, in Christ, necessarily implies the transfiguring fulfillment of the other:

> Christ's resurrection, then, is *neither* mere reanimation of a corpse, *nor* abandonment of the body in so far as it is *relationship with the world;* on the contrary, it is the radical transformation of that relationship ... its absolute *metabolism*. In the Resurrection, *the relationship to this world* which defines Christ's body, as it defines man's, remains *the same in absolute value,* but it undergoes *a change of characteristic sign*. During his life it was ambivalent; inseparably both dominant and dominated; in death it became purely dominated and negative; then, finally, it becomes, and asserts itself as, entirely positive and purely dominant in his resurrection. We then see the Resurrection as the *radical reverser* of direction at the level of death, and as the beginning of a completely new relationship which revolutionizes man's real development in his *world* and thereby in his *body*.[54]

The resurrection is the liberating, anticipatory realization of creation's absolute future. Although we experience our present cosmic embeddedness as a mixture of *action* and *passio,* life and death, fruition and dysfunction, the resurrection is the concrete promise that the cosmos shall become a "new creation," freed entirely from all that diminishes it, a pure openness to God's *Pneuma.* Easter opens up the possibility for unlimited and unending communion throughout the whole of creation. "The Christ of the Resurrection represents such a revolution in the development of the universe that he is in very truth a new origin from which all things are born again; he is a second creation, he is entry into new times, which are transformed beyond recognition even though passionately awaited; he and he alone is truly the potential transfigurer of the world whose full revelation will be the parousia."[55]

Here again it is difficult, if not impossible, for us to conceive of this cosmic transfiguration in the *parousia.* That the general resurrection shall be a festival in which creation achieves its definitive fruition: this is something Christian eschatology emphatically affirms. That God's Holy Spirit shall transform our mortal bodies into a glorified corporeality, enabling us to become "the perfect expression of the enduring relation of the glorified person to the cosmos as a whole": this is a hope borne out of its actuality in the risen Christ, who already, in himself, has entered into a relationship with the world as its Lord and inner impulse.[56] "He is there as the innermost essence of all things," writes Rahner, "and the most secret law of a movement which still triumphs and imposes its authority even when every kind of order seems to be breaking up... [H]e is there, the heart of this earthly movement and the secret seal of its eternal validity. He is risen."[57] That the Spirit of the risen Christ is already operative in the world as that empowering dynamism leading it towards its ultimate goal — the "press of the divine from within creation":[58] this is a truth affirmed by Christians who take the wisdom traditions of Israel and the cosmic christology of the New Testament with the seriousness they deserve. But exactly what shape this transformation will take and when it will take place is unknown and unknowable to us. Here again Christian theology, in the face of holy mystery, must exercise a humility appropriate to the reality of which it speaks. The new creation remains *in excess* to all that we can envision and speak. However daring we can and must be in speaking of the future resurrection of the dead, such a reality finally saturates our capacity for imagination. "No one knows about that day or hour, not even the angels in heaven, nor the Son, but only the Father" (Mark 13:32).

There is, however, one important practical correlate that we should draw from this reflection, even while standing in the midst of mystery. Especially in this time of massive ecological degradation, which poses a threat to human and non-human creatures alike, and which is largely fueled by the rapacious instrumentalism that reduces the earth to a vast warehouse of resources for technical manipulation and production, the hope for bodily resurrection should help motivate Christians to develop attitudes and engage in practices that contribute to the honoring and protection of creation. Denis Edwards sees in the doctrine of bodily resurrection a call to an ecological imagination and praxis that promotes genuine reverence. "The material universe will itself be transformed," he writes. "The coming of the kingdom will be God's deed, but it will also be the self-transcendence of our cosmic history. Our own action and our own living have eternal significance." We should note that the moral reasoning here is quite similar to Paul's. What we do with our bodies in the present is morally significant, for it is our bodies (and here, by extension, our cosmic body) that shall be raised. "The human task of caring for and completing creation has final salvific significance."[59] Because the personal hope for resurrection is set within a broader context of the community of creation, that praxis which seeks the liberation and well-being of creatures, whether human or non-human, may be seen as partial realizations of God's future for creation.[60]

The Ecclesial Body

"For just as the body is one and has many members, and all the members of the body, though many, are one body, so it is with Christ. For in the one Spirit we were all baptized into one body — Jews or Greeks, slaves or free — and we were all made to drink of one Spirit" (1 Cor. 12:12–13). For Paul, the symbol of the body particularly commends itself when considering the dynamics of the *ecclesia*. The image suggests a vigorous corporate life in which unity and diversity are organically related and constantly nourished by the Spirit of the risen Christ, the church's animating principle. The risen body of Christ "passes into" (or extends itself in) the communion of the baptized, establishing it as an eschatological community anticipating and sacramentally embodying the ultimate future of creation.[61] The risen body of Christ, without being identified with the ecclesial body, since otherwise we will have ignored the creative liberty of the risen Christ as this is well attested by the empty tomb and appearance narratives ("He is risen; he is not here"), nevertheless finds historical mediation in our world through the corporate life of discipleship. The church is a leavening agent. It shares in and helps to perpetuate in our world, even if embryonically, and certainly not always perfectly, the transformative energies unleashed by Jesus' resurrection. The church is thus more than what can be described in purely functional-social terms. The Easter event requires that we not understand God's self-offering in Christ only in a verbal sense. We must understand it in a sacramentally and historically effective sense. The church must be understood as a unique and divinely willed mediation of God's self-giving to the world. To use somewhat traditional terminology, the church, as a visible society of men and women, is a visible sign of the invisible grace of the risen Christ. If Christ is the "primordial sacrament" of our encounter with the invisible God, the church is the "sacrament of the risen Christ."[62]

Following chapters will emphasize that in order for the salvific impact of Jesus' death and resurrection to become concrete and humanly meaningful, there must be a living, breathing community of people who commemorate and proclaim it, while living out its implications. The church is the church precisely by signifying and manifesting the justice, reconciliation, and divinization that the paschal event confers.

At present, we must content ourselves with just a few, brief observations regarding the sacramental economy of the church. First, the symbol of the body is uniquely suited to speak of the new identity persons receive upon entering the ecclesial community through baptism. It is an identity of "we." Incorporation into the body of Christ (Paul speaks of our being "grafted") entails a pronominal shift in which the "I" becomes a "we."[63] This is not, let it be understood, the dissolution of the "I" into a collectivity. It is the transformation of the "I" through participation in a reconciled community. Love in such a conception is a unity of mutual self-bestowal: dependence, vulnerability, dialogue, admonition, encouragement, and embrace. The ecclesial "we" constitutes the "I" in such a way that we are justified in saying that "the church precedes the individual."[64] Through our baptism we are incorporated into a reconciled and reconciling body of many members. By it we become children of God, "clothed" with Christ. "There is neither Jew nor Greek, slave nor free, male nor female, for you are all one in Christ Jesus" (Gal. 3:26–28). The process of this reconciliation, which I shall spend more time analyzing in chapters 7 and 8, is one in which those divisions polarizing human beings into discrete groups according to ethnicity, social status, gender, nationality, ideology, and so forth, are transformed from their exclusivistic (and frequently violently delineated) forms into a catholic (or "universal") communion of persons. Baptism and incorporation into the church more thoroughly transform *individuals* into *persons*. "Differences are no longer partitions; on the contrary, they offer to the 'body of Christ' this rich diversity of members and functions which any body needs. The other is no longer to be considered a rival or a potential enemy, especially on the religious plane; the other must be welcomed as a brother or a sister."[65] The *ecclesia* lives by its hospitality to the Other; and such hospitality is possible only if, rather than viewing the "I" atomistically and in terms of opposition to other "I's," it is transformed by the gift of the Other. The Other co-constitutes me, nourishes me from within, and I the Other. The church is called to be the place where this co-inherence is lived out intentionally and peacefully. For it to possibly hope for this, the church must live eucharistically.

"The cup of blessing that we bless, is it not a sharing in the blood of Christ? The bread that we break, is it not a sharing in the body of Christ? Because there is one bread, we who are many are one body, for we all partake of the one bread" (1 Cor. 10:16-17). In the communal celebration of the Eucharist, the presencing/absencing Spirit of the risen Christ forms a corporate personality out of its individual communicants — forms a constituted body or "complex person."[66] This happens at all levels. "It is performed," writes Ward, "through the reception, the eating, the digestion of the elements: the physiological absorption of the one Body of Christ within the body of the believer, so that the two become one flesh." The Eucharist brings about a "complex corporeality," or a "transcorporeality."[67]

The Eucharist signifies the mutual subsistence of bodies in a most remarkable way. The wine and bread are symbols of the earth's nourishing bounty as food and drink. Our relationship to the earth is one of dependence. We hunger. We thirst. The earth provides, yielding itself in the fruit of grain and grape. But bread and wine also reflect human activity. They come to be through human ingenuity, through *techne*. Hand and instrument plow, knead, prepare, break, and serve. Hand and instrument gather, press, store, bless, and pour. We do not just eat; we humanize what we eat. Bread and wine are "humanized nature," symbols of the creative interaction between cosmos and *anthropos*.[68] These are the gifts we bring to the altar: the gifts of the earth, the gifts of our labor, the gifts of ourselves. And because this altar is also a table, the Eucharist is a meal sharing. It is a communal event, a microcosm of the social macrocosm. The Eucharist institutes *communitas*, even if, at times, its celebration brings inequities within the human community, and the *ecclesia* more particularly, to light (1 Cor. 11:20-22).

The Eucharist is not just *our* supper. More primordially, it is the Lord's Supper. It is through the presence of the risen Christ in the Eucharist that such a supper truly becomes ours. "I am the bread of life.... Whoever eats of this bread will live forever; and the bread that I will give for the life of the world is my flesh" (John 6:31). It is in Christ that we are consecrated and constituted as a "we." Through this being-constituted we are enabled to participate, even here and now, in a sacramental way, in Christ's resurrection. "Those who eat my flesh and drink my blood have eternal life, and I will raise them up on the last day; for my flesh is true food and my blood is true drink. Those who eat my flesh and drink my blood abide in me, and I in them. Just as the living Father sent me, and I live because of the Father, so whoever eats me will live because of me" (vv. 54–57). In the Eucharist, the cosmic, the human, and the divine converge. The Eucharist is "cosmotheandric."[69] Irenaeus of Lyons gives potent expression to this convergence by showing the inner relationship between creation, salvation, and eschatological hope:

> Those who reject the whole "economy" of God, deny the salvation of the flesh and reject its regeneration, saying that it is not capable of receiving imperishability, are absolutely vain. If this flesh is not saved, the Lord did not redeem us by his blood (Col. 1:14) and the cup of the Eucharist is not communion with his blood and the bread we break is not communion with his body (1 Cor. 10:16). For blood comes only from veins and flesh and the rest of the human substance, which the Word of God became when he redeemed us by his blood. As his Apostle says, "In him we have redemption by his blood, the remission of sins" (Col. 1:14). And because we are his members (1 Cor. 6:15) and are nourished by means of the creation... he declared that the cup from the creation is his blood, out of which he makes our blood increase, and the bread from the creation is his body, out of which he makes our body grow.[70]

I WILL BE MY BODY

To bring this chapter (and Part One) to a close, we return to the statement, "I will be my body." Such a phrase emphasizes the point that eschatology is anthropology in the future tense. How we envision the future fulfillment of the human person will shape our view of the human person at present, and vice versa. Anthropological and eschatological statements are mutually conditioning, which is why the doctrine of bodily resurrection gives enormous significance to our present bodily life in all its many profiles and dimensions. But we must be careful to stress a certain prioritization in the order of Christian theological reflection. For while it is appropriate to say that anthropology and eschatology are mutually conditioning, and that therefore we can, to some extent, extrapolate from our present human experience to say something meaningful about the eschatological fulfillment of the person — this is how more transcendental approaches typically operate, with uneven success — the resurrection of the body is a doctrine that frequently cuts across our a priori horizons of intelligibility and meaningfulness. Jesus risen from the dead is a datum of revelation that is startling and saturating in its phenomenality: it exceeds our capacities for imagination and reshapes many of our preconceived notions about human fulfillment. If bodily resurrection were something we could simply extrapolate from our present experience, then the scandal frequently provoked by the doctrine would be difficult to explain. The resurrection of Jesus is both the fulfillment and subversion of desire: it reveals to us the content of eschatological hope and salvation while transfiguring the horizons of our expectations. The real theological challenge here is to not measure Jesus' resurrection according to the presuppositions of a prior anthropology, but to "read off" the resurrection for the starting point for a genuinely *theological* anthropology.[71] It proposes a world of meaning for us to learn and inhabit.

The phrase "I will be my body" also intends to emphasize that human identity is relational and eschatological. I cannot simply associate my identity with who I presently am. Nor can I be an authentic human person by securing my identity in polarized relationship to the many bodies from which I subsist. As a being-unto-resurrection, I am a being unto-the-Other, a being from- and unto-corporeality, a being-unto-God's absolute future. This being-unto is not a negative deferral of present existence. Of course, it is true to say that my fulfillment is an outstanding reality. It can only finally be achieved through God's transfiguring pneumatic action upon and within the whole of creation. Only in the *eschaton* will I know as I am known. But such a realization endows present existence with extraordinary richness and meaning. To live life consciously as a being-unto-resurrection is to know true freedom in the present: freedom from the compulsion to hoard existence, afraid that life is draining away into an impersonal abyss; freedom from every attempt to interpret our creaturely contingency as a barrier to immediacy to God; freedom from the alienation that comes when we isolate ourselves from the body's vulnerability to the Other; freedom for self-giving to and for Other; freedom for that joyful *releasement* into our common corporeality as the site of God's salvation.

PART TWO

INTRODUCTION: GRAMMARS OF RESURRECTION

We now move to an extended analysis of Jesus' resurrection as a soteriological event. Whereas Part One dealt with matters typically associated with fundamental theology, Part Two deals with matters pertaining to systematic theology. This distinction, however, is problematic if rigidly drawn. For our purposes it is a distinction that signifies a thematic shift, not a methodological one. Indeed, it has been my contention that resurrection faith cannot be grounded by external criteria for validation but instead invites us into a world which shapes imagination and desire. While we have engaged common objections to resurrection belief on historical, epistemological, and anthropological grounds, and therefore at a certain level Part One provides a case for reconsidering those assumptions that would close off the possibility for assent — we have been learning to become hospitable to an im-possible event that challenges us to a new way of perceiving, thinking, and acting — the effort was more presentational than disputational, in a word, confessional. Part One explicitly presumed the reality of Jesus' resurrection rather than elaborating a series of arguments to arrive at it. Already we have been exploring in its inner meaning and practical significance. The traditional distinction between fundamental, systematic (and even practical) theology can scarcely be recognized in the present effort, and its somewhat perfunctory mention here represents, perhaps, only a vestige of a time in theology when it was thought possible or even necessary to clearly indicate.

In any case, Part Two further explores the self-involving character of Jesus' resurrection by taking up standard themes in soteriology. We will proceed by developing three major thematic lines which together form a more multifaceted view of salvation: justice, forgiveness, and divinization. As we shall see, each of these themes relates to a characteristic pattern of Christian speech, or what I will be describing as a "grammar." The overall purpose of Part Two is to show how each of these thematic lines, along with the grammatical modes they exhibit, are distinct yet interrelated aspects of the one saving event we call Easter. My intent is to develop a more comprehensive statement regarding the salvific impact of Jesus' resurrection from the dead, which at once brings about justice for victims, forgiveness for victimizers, and participation for all ("divinization") in the trinitarian life of God. Along the way I shall advocate for a view of the atonement which rejects all notions of God's involvement in the violence of Jesus' death. In contrast to certain views of the atonement that explicitly or implicitly affirm God's endorsement of the scapegoat process the led to Jesus' crucifixion, I present a non-violent view of the atonement that highlights the dismantling of the scapegoat mechanism entrenched (if frequently hidden) in human relations. By making the resurrection much more central in how we envision God's salvific activity in the world, we are in a better position to see how God's forgiveness of sinners relates to justice for the sinned against. Moreover, the resurrection, when seen in close relationship with Jesus' life and death, reveals to us the divinizing impact of the atonement which, more than just bringing about some kind of juridical reconciliation with God, transforms the human personality through participation in divine life. A more thoroughly integrated vision of salvation views justice, forgiveness, and divinization in the closest possible relation. It therefore coordinates the major grammars of scripture to be mutually corrective and clarifying.

ON AVOIDING GRAMMATICAL ABSOLUTISM IN CHRISTIAN THEOLOGY

The Confluence of Time

Resurrection language, like the soteriological language of the New Testament more generally, cannot be confined to a single grammatical mode. It is not just a future or past reality. Neither is it wholly present. It is past, present, and future. It is "already" and "not yet." This concentration and stretching of time, and the pressures it puts on language in any attempt to speak of it, is strikingly evident in one of the most celebrated passages in the New Testament:

> But in fact Christ has been raised from the dead, the first fruits of those who have died. For since death came through a human being, the resurrection of the dead has also come through a human being; for as all die in Adam, so all will be made alive in Christ. But each in his own order: Christ the first fruits, then at his coming those who belong to Christ. Then comes the end, when he hands over the kingdom to God the Father, after he has destroyed every ruler and every authority and power.... When all things are subjected to him, then the Son himself will also be subjected to the one who put all things in subjection under him, so that God may be all in all.... When this perishable body puts on imperishability, and this mortal body puts on immortality, then the saying that is written will be fulfilled: "Death has been swallowed up in victory. Where,

O death, is your victory? Where, O death, is your sting?" The sting of death is sin, and the power of sin is the law. But thanks be to God, who gives us the victory through our Lord Jesus Christ. Therefore, my beloved, be steadfast, immovable, always excelling in the work of the Lord, because you know that in the Lord your labor is not in vain (1 Cor. 15:20-23, 28, 54-58).

As with many other soteriological summaries in the New Testament, this passage reflects a highly complex relationship between verb tenses.

- Salvation has happened once and for all: "*has been raised,*" "the resurrection of the dead *has* also *come.*"
- Salvation will happen conclusively in the future: "so all *will be made alive* in Christ," "then [*will come*] the end," "so that God *may be* all in all."
- Salvation is presently happening: "God, who *gives* us the victory," "therefore *be* steadfast, immovable, *always* excelling in the work of the Lord, because you know that in the Lord your [*present*] labor is not in vain."

As G. B. Caird has shown, this threefold pattern is amply illustrated in the Pauline literature, though by no means is unique to it. It characterizes the New Testament as a whole. Salvation has already come (Rom. 8:24; 10:10; 11:11; Eph. 2:8; Luke 2:30; 19:12; 2 Tim. 1:9; Titus 3:5; Heb. 5:9). We are in the process of being saved as we work out our salvation (1 Cor. 1:18; 15:2; 2 Cor 2:15; 6:2; Phil 2:12; Acts 4:12; 1 Pet. 1:9; 3:21; 4:18). Final salvation is yet to come (Rom. 13:11; Phil. 3:20; Heb. 2:8; 1 Pet. 1:5). This threefold pattern is never rigidly presented in the New Testament. Hence, we cannot completely associate our modern theological categories with it. Justification is not just in the past. Sanctification is not restricted to the present. Nor is glorification only a final goal we await. No "grammatical absolutism" is possible. "All that logic can claim is that there are differences of emphasis."[1]

Resurrection language is, of its very nature, confluential. The Easter event "overarches" our time, as Karl Barth puts it. Though it is something that has already occurred, the resurrection of Jesus is the absolute future of God made present here and now. "*Recollection* of this time must also be *expectation* of this same time."[2] Easter is not a-temporal. It is trans-temporal. It is time's fullness. Consequently, we must think of the present moment as intersected and saturated by this fullness. "Little wonder human language begins to stammer at this point even in the

New Testament," remarks Barth.[3] Little wonder indeed, yet this is the challenge Christian theology must face.

Three Grammatical Modes:
Reversal, Double Reversal, Fulfillment

There is another type of grammatical absolutism we must avoid when speaking of the resurrection and its salvific impact. Here I am speaking of grammar in a different, more expanded and comprehensive sense. I mean a deep structural tendency in expression or thought; a characteristic and coherent pattern of understanding; an identifiable and habitual mode of articulation which results in relatively consistent thematization. Conceived in this way, we can identify three major grammatical modes in the resurrection language of scripture and subsequent theological tradition.

The first grammatical mode is one of *reversal*. According to this modality, the resurrection is a reversal or overcoming of some negative situation. The grammar of reversal is counter-factual. It speaks to and out of an environment of conflict. It is more dialectical and agonistic in idiom. It projects a sense of urgency, of pressing anticipation. Here especially the prophetic and apocalyptic strains in the biblical traditions are in play. Resurrection language so construed favors the theme of *vindication*, i.e., the vindication of the victim or martyr before his or her oppressor. Vindication here presupposes a situation of injustice and an empowering belief in God's sovereignty over it. By raising the victim from the dead, God passes judgment *against* the oppressor and *for* the oppressed. This against-for dialectic is most poised to articulate salvation in terms of divine *justice*. And because it typically speaks out of situations of present conflict, it tends to favor the "not yet" pole of the eschatological spectrum. It looks forward to God's future in-breaking into the world to bring about a new order, a new reality in which past and present injustices are rectified. Appealing to Walter Brueggemann, we can describe this modality as arising out of grief, criticism, and hope. Criticizing assails the pretensions of the *status quo* and every ideological-political totality by embracing the negativity of experience — its refractoriness — and expressing grief. "So the prophet speaks his grief at the lack of resolution. He cannot cry enough."[4] Such grief is ultimately rooted in a sense of hope in God's sovereignty over the chaos of suffering and injustice.

The second grammatical mode is one of *double reversal*. This more complex mode presupposes the first reversal but transforms it by giving emphasis to *reconciliation* between oppressed and oppressor. Whereas the first reversal highlights the theme of vindication by setting off oppressed and oppressor in a dialectical relation (of "us" vs. "them"), the mode of double reversal emphasizes the reconciliation that occurs when the oppressor seeks and/or receives the offer of forgiveness from the oppressed. While in no way undermining the theme of justice from the first reversal, the double reversal complements and transforms the theme of vindication *over* the oppressive Other by emphasizing reconciliation and peace *with* the Other. The only way this is possible is through *forgiveness*. Resurrection language in this modality speaks of salvation for both victim and victimizer. The victimizer is reconciled to the victim through recognition and repentance. To see one's victim *as* victim requires a transformation in perspective, a transformation made possible when the victim, quite despite the violation, offers hospitality to the victimizer so as to release the victimizer from his or her untruth and violence. We may think particularly of the "suffering servant" motif in Isaiah and much of the New Testament as reflective of this double reversal: the victim bears the sin and violence of the Other in a way that brings about redemption *for* the Other. The innocent victim has become the salvation of the victimizer, is "risen" out of suffering, violence, and death to both reveal and absolve guilt. The against-for dialectic of the former grammar is thus recontextualized and transfigured as justice and mercy embrace.

The third grammatical mode is one of *fulfillment*. Here the emphasis is on the resurrection as the completion and final fruition of creation. While the grammar of fulfillment too is oriented towards the future, since it sees the future as the full realization of a promise, the fulfillment motif is more inclined to emphasize the "already" pole of the eschatological spectrum. It sees the present moment more in terms of *continuity* with the future, whereas the grammar of reversal typically thinks in terms of discontinuity and interruption, given its agonistic character. The biblical and theological traditions most representative of the grammar of fulfillment are sapiential and contemplative. The wisdom traditions of Israel, more so than its prophetic and apocalyptic traditions (though we should be wary of making overly rigid distinctions), tend to speak the language of *manifestation* and *participation*. The created order manifests the eternal and creative Wisdom of God, which human beings glean and reflect. Creation is God's ultimate work of art and this creativity is something human beings participate in as images of God. The gospel of John, more so than the austere and urgent gospel of Mark, renders resurrection language in a manifestory and aesthetic modality, one that speaks far more readily of the *present realization* of divine glory through resurrection. "I am the resurrection and the life." With its modal emphasis on the present as the time of fulfillment, John's gospel speaks of salvation in terms of our participation in the life of God as this is made possible by the "exalting" and "divinizing" effect of Jesus' resurrection from the dead. To refer again to Brueggemann, we may speak of this grammatical mode as doxological: it represents an energizing releasement, a divine "Yes" to creation which, from the beginning, was made for eschatological fulfillment — "eternal life."

Toward an Integrated Soteriology

If a theology of the resurrection wishes to be comprehensive (without presuming to be exhaustive) it must integrate the multiple grammatical modes above with sufficient adequacy. Such integration requires understanding each mode on its terms and in relationship to the others. It requires weighing the relative strengths and weaknesses of each grammar while coordinating them for the purpose of mutual clarification, correction, and amplification. We might ask, however, why are there multiple grammars in the first place? And why do we have this particular diversity rather another one? Furthermore, what is it about these three grammars (and the major soteriological motifs they support) that demand the attention of the theologian who wishes to develop a more comprehensive and integrated theology of the resurrection?

To answer these questions we can say, first of all, that because Jesus' resurrection from the dead is the saturated phenomenon *par excellence*, it cannot, of its very nature, be fully represented in language. It cannot be schematized within a particular grammatical mode without overflowing its banks. The Easter event gives rise to a surplus of meaning, and thus it destabilizes any and every perspective that would envisage it. This "bedazzling" surplus is not a result of revelation's weakness or incoherence; it is a result of an objectively excessive positivity that manifests itself subjectively in the mode of presence and absence, light and darkness, nearness and distance. Its givenness in our history is many-profiled. It pluralizes our linguistic-cognitive horizons. The diversity of grammars (or soteriological motifs) to speak of such an event is the necessary corollary to the kind of event it is.

The second reason is that we are still in the middle of the story, *in medias res*. Being in the middle of the story means being "in between" the times, being in a complex eschatological situation. We cannot abstract ourselves from this story (our history) to speak from an absolute point of view. There are multiple grammars because we still await the fulfillment of the absolute promise made by God through Jesus Christ. Recollection of the Easter event is also an act of anticipation. Salvation has occurred; it is presently occurring; and it will definitively occur in the *parousia,* when God will be all in all. No grammatical absolutism is possible. Because the resurrection "overarches" our time it requires that we see it within our history in terms of "already" and "not yet." Speaking of the resurrection with sufficient competence requires keeping these poles of the eschatological spectrum in creative tension and interaction.

Thirdly, because we live in a complex eschatological situation, there are limitations and potential dangers that arise when one or another grammatical mode is emphasized at the expense of the others. For example, excessive emphasis upon the "already" pole of the eschatological spectrum runs the risk of ignoring those aspects of present existence that demand critique and transformation. Collapsing the future-orientation of eschatology into an "eternal present," or in a protological direction, may only lead to the acceptance of the world's present state as necessary and divinely ordained, when in fact much in our history maligns the well-being of the *humanum* and is manifestly opposed to the will of God. To the extent that evil and suffering maintain a hold on our history, Christians must be inspired by an "apocalyptic imagination" that anticipates and helps to usher in a "new creation" in which evil and suffering are vanquished. To speak of the resurrection without the critical dimension of vindication and justice ignores crucial aspects of the biblical tradition, while threatening to make Easter's transformative capacities mute and ineffective. The resurrection is not the legitimation of the *status quo*; it is its rupture and judgment. The resurrection, as we shall see, is a political reality that inspires a critical memory and a liberating praxis on behalf of victims.

On the other hand, emphasis upon the grammar of reversal risks its own dangers if unaccompanied by other aspects of resurrection faith. For example, while uniquely effective in bringing the themes of vindication and justice to the fore, the dialectical structure of apocalyptic thinking, if not properly balanced by the motif of reconciliation, can lock persons and groups within binary and conflictual terms — in an "us" versus "them" relationship — and thus perpetuate antagonism within the *humanum*. As presented in the New Testament, the resurrection of the victim is vindication and justice; but vindication and justice are always rendered in ways that bring forth reconciliation between victim and victimizer, oppressed and oppressor. Indeed, it is the surprising forgiveness of the would-be avenger that most uniquely characterizes the soteriological impact of Easter: the risen Jesus is raised for our "justification," for the remission of sins, for our reconciliation with God, whom we have persecuted as *our* victim. The double reversal retains the theme of justice within it but now integrates it within a broader context to reveal the transformative reality of non-violent forgiveness and love. Forgiveness without justice is facile, to be sure; but justice without love is blind. The proclamation of the risen victim from the dead as our forgiveness expresses the "logic of excess" that most characterizes God's amazing grace.

Moreover, without the vivifying "Yes" of realized eschatology, the grammar of reversal can become desolate. The resurrection is not only an outstanding reality; it is a present reality that we may discern and participate in, even if in a fragmentary way, through the Spirit's divinizing work in the world and the church. The resurrection is an ontological reality. It reaches to the very core of the created order. Easter proclamation asserts that our world has been assumed and uplifted into the very bosom of God, never to be let go, never to be deserted to its own contingency — "glorified" and "divinized." Herein lays the ground for a Christian mysticism without reserve: the resurrection reveals that what passes through the cross of disfigurement and non-being in death shall be given an eschatological destiny and form. Consequently, the Christian ascent to the infinite mystery of God is also a deeper penetration into the world. Because the world has been divinized by God through the incarnation, life, death, and resurrection of Jesus Christ, we will find God at the heart of creation, and creation in the heart of God. Resurrection faith promotes an integral mysticism in which the infinite and form abide in eternal communion. Christian theology should therefore be as much concerned with beauty as with justice, with the mystical as with the prophetic, with the "Yes" of contemplation and ecstasy as with the dialectical "No" to suffering and injustice.

To get a sense for how these three themes are embedded in the resurrection kerygma of the early church, we turn to a striking example in Acts 2 — Peter's speech to the Sanhedrin in Jerusalem. Here we will not only be able to identify each of the three grammatical modes outlined above, but we will begin to see how they work together to present a dramatic and multifaceted vision of salvation.

THE RESURRECTION PROCLAIMED

The setting is Jerusalem, the place where Jesus of Nazareth was judged and condemned to die. Peter's audience is at once general and specific. On the one hand his speech is addressed to "You that are Israelites." Peter clearly asserts the guilt of his audience: they, and particularly their leaders, Caiaphas and the Sanhedrin, have murdered an innocent man, handing him over to "lawless men" (Roman Gentiles) to be crucified as a political revolutionary and religious blasphemer. In this impromptu court scene, Peter boldly proclaims the miscarriage of justice:

> You that are Israelites, listen to what I have to say: Jesus of Nazareth, a man attested to you by God and with deeds of power, wonders, and signs that God did through him among you, as you yourselves know — this man, handed over to you according to the definite plan and foreknowledge of God, you crucified and killed by the hands of those outside the law. (vv. 22–23)

The indictment here is a "structural one," as Rowan Williams points out: "the people of Jerusalem, and 'in' them 'all the house of Israel,' acting for them the rulers and elders — these are the ones whom the narrative identifies as the judges and killers of Jesus."[5] As the parallel formulation in Acts 4:27 makes clear, the indictment is all-inclusive in its "apocalyptic sweep."[6] Both Jews and Gentiles and all "the kings of the earth," including Herod and Pontius Pilate, have "gathered together against [God's] holy servant Jesus, whom [God] anointed." This "gathering together" of peoples and earthly powers against a victim in order to preserve social order is nothing less than the mechanism of scapegoating unmasked by the gospels. (In the gospel of John, Caiaphas reasons thusly: "it is better for you to have one man die for the people than to have the whole nation destroyed" [John 11:50]. In following chapters I shall say much more about this mechanism.) But Peter declares the injustice, stating further that this innocent victim has not been left to death. God has raised him from the dead, vindicating him, even exalting him to the right hand of God. The dynamic involved here is re-active. Like the Exodus testimony of the Old Testament that proclaims God's counter-factual activity in the face of external domination, Peter's speech affirms that the victim has received justice through divine vindication (you did *this*, but God has done *this!*). Such testimony is rendered with apocalyptic urgency and scope:

> But God raised him up, having freed him from death, because it was impossible for him to be held in its power.... This Jesus God raised up, and of that all of us are witnesses. Being therefore exalted at the right hand of God, and having received from the Father the promise of the Holy Spirit, he has poured out this that you both see and hear. For David did not ascend into the heavens, but he himself says, "The Lord said to my Lord, 'Sit at my right hand, until I make your enemies your footstool.'" Therefore let the entire

house of Israel know with certainty that God has made him both Lord and Messiah, this Jesus whom you crucified. (vv. 24, 32–36)

The roles of accused and accuser are now apocalyptically (impossibly) reversed. The original verdict has been overturned. The victim has returned from death's dominion as the judge of his judges.[7] Acquitted of all false charges by his resurrection, Jesus, at once made nameless and faceless, stands in a face-to-face relationship with his oppressors in an eschatological counter-gaze, forever disturbing any solace they may have taken in the mute anonymity of their victim's death. Death can no longer obscure injustice but is made to speak a new word — "He is risen; he is not here." Mediated through apostolic testimony ("all of us are witness") the victim again speaks, but now as God's own word of apocalyptic judgment upon the entire system that conspired to put Jesus to death. The proclamation thus asserts divine victory over the ruling "principalities and powers" of the world. This is not just a historically provincial happening. Its significance is epochal; for what is undone by Jesus' resurrection is death as such. When the powers of this world have done their absolute worst by putting to death an innocent man whose life and ministry were uniquely disclosive of God's will for humanity, divine justice reasserts itself to show that death, and the structural violence swirling about it, is as nothing to God and God's messiah.

The grammar of reversal is remarkably potent in the first part of Peter's proclamation. But it should be understood that this reversal is not simply a negation. It is also the fulfillment and eschatological "amen" upon Jesus' mission and person. However significant Jesus' resurrection may be in itself, there is yet a more specific content to it. It is not just *any* victim whom God has raised, but Jesus of Nazareth — one "attested to you by God with deeds of power, wonders, and signs." God's deliverance is at once *against* the structural violence that put Jesus to death and *for* Jesus himself. His mission and person form a unity. (Again, the functionalist distinction between "cause" and "person" is woefully inadequate for grasping Easter's significance.) All that Jesus said and did, including his claims to authority, is legitimated by God in an eschatologically definitive way. God is shown, retrospectively, to have been the "author" of Jesus' ministry. As we shall see in chapter 9 especially, the resurrection is *the* linchpin for all christological statements. Only from the perspective of Jesus' resurrection will his followers come to perceive the true significance of his *person*. The resurrection forms the essential framework for knowing who Jesus was and who he is. Indeed, the resurrection sparks the christological process that will result in the affirmation of Jesus as the very presence of God in the world. As Wolfhart Pannenberg puts it: "Only because the end of the world is already present in Jesus' resurrection is God himself revealed in him."[8] Even though we are still at an early stage in the evolution of christological formulations, the motif of "exaltation," which broadens the motif of "vindication" to affirm Jesus' status as Messiah and Lord, is moving in the direction that logically culminates in the incarnational theology of John's gospel. As Pannenberg shows, once the apocalyptic matrix of Jesus' resurrection proclamation interacts with the wisdom tradition and begins to thoroughly absorb Hellenistic terminology and conceptuality, the meaning of Easter becomes this: "[I]n Jesus, God himself has appeared on earth. God himself — or God's revelatory figure, the Logos, the Son — has been among us as a man in the figure of Jesus."[9]

But something further must be said about the reversal as framed by Acts 2. At issue is yet a deeper reversal, a second reversal which transforms the apocalyptic framework. As the narrative proceeds, the response of those listening to Peter's impassioned speech is one of compunction. "Now when they heard this, they were *cut to the heart* and said to Peter and to the other apostles, 'Brothers, what shall we do?' " (v. 37). Peter's response is not one of condemnation. He does not declare or call for God's retribution. In noticeable contrast with the accusatory speech that frequently attends apocalyptic discourse, Peter responds with an invitation to receive the gift of salvation through the remission of sins:

> Peter said to them, "Repent, and be baptized every one of you in the name of Jesus Christ so that your sins may be forgiven; and you will received the gift of the Holy Spirit. For the promise is for you, for your children, and for all who are far away, everyone whom the Lord our God calls to him." (vv. 38–40)

Remarkably, the victim who has become the judge of his judges has also become their Gift, their grace, the agent of their reconciliation with God and with their sisters and brothers. And it is not just a gift for some; it is the Gift for the whole world: "This Jesus is 'the stone that was rejected by you, the builders; it has become the cornerstone.' There is salvation in no one else, for there is no other name under heaven given among mortals by which we must be saved" (4:11–12).

The social duality that might pit the Jesus movement in an over-against relationship with those who murdered its leader has been transformed by a stunning offer of hospitality. The resurrection does more than bring vindication and justice to the innocent victim Jesus; it brings forgiveness to those responsible for his suffering and death. It is important to note the order of manifestation here — the offer of forgiveness *precedes* the decision made by his oppressors. The offer of forgiveness is what prompts and opens up the possibility for recognizing guilt. The resurrection is the framework for understanding, retrospectively, their implication in sin and violence. As a concrete gesture of this reconciliation, the victimizers are invited to become part of the paschal community which has formed out of the *memoria* of the crucified-and-risen One and hope in his imminent return in the *parousia*. "So those who welcomed [with hospitality] his message were baptized, and that day about three thousand persons were added. They devoted themselves to the apostles' teaching and fellowship, to the breaking of the bread and the prayers" (vv. 41–42). Here again, and here especially, we see the ecclesial presupposition for resurrection belief. It is the witness of and participation in the reconciled community that makes it possible "to see" the crucified-and-risen Jesus.

The rudimentary elements of this proclamation thus far include a *reversal* and a *double reversal.* In the first place, God *vindicates* the innocent victim Jesus. His resurrection reveals that justice for victims will ultimately prevail. Those who presently cry out for justice have been (and will be) heard by God, who *is* justice. It also highlights the justice-character of resurrection in the Christian community. Living in accordance with such faith implies participation in God's own "preferential option" for victims in history. The grammar of reversal which issues from the apocalyptic imagination of scripture inspires a hermeneutics of history that takes the "view of victims" as its perspectival center. It calls for solidarity with those who are history's "losers" — the poor, the powerless, the victimized, those scapegoated for the purpose of maintaining power and social identity.

On the other hand, the resurrection of Jesus is God's concrete offer of *forgiveness* to those directly and indirectly involved in the rejection and lynching of God's own Son. Unlike the intense social duality in much apocalyptic literature that situates "insider" and "outsider" in a relationship that may only perpetuate, rather than resolve, rivalry, God's re-action of raising Jesus from the dead is non-reciprocal to the original violence. It does not represent a "logic of equivalence," to borrow Paul Ricoeur's phrase, but a "logic of abundance."[10] This hospitality *in excess* is what Christian theology calls "grace." God's offer of non-violent hospitality to the Other, even the violent Other, completes a revelatory process in the Bible in which the human perception of God is finally purged of all violence. God "absorbs" the world's sin and violence in the cross by becoming its victim, and opens up through the resurrection a new economy that overcomes rivalry and exclusion through forgiveness. It is this *reversal upon reversal* that constitutes a critical mutation of apocalyptic eschatology.

Now, about this hospitality *in excess* we must be very clear: God's forgiving grace is by no means cheap or free of demands. It is in fact a "costly grace," for it is a call to discipleship.[11] Though pardoning, it does not promote a convenient and selective amnesia. The two aspects of this double reversal (vindication and forgiveness) are internally linked. Only in the re-cognition of and return to the victim may this forgiveness be encountered. The hospitality offered by God is one that calls for *metanoia,* and this involves a great deal more than a simple admission of guilt. It means allowing one's perceptions, desires, and actions to be transformed by resurrection grace so as to actively participate in history for its transformation. At its most fundamental level, the proclamation of the resurrection is "an invitation to *recognize one's victim as one's hope.* The crucified is God's chosen: it is with the victim, the condemned, that God identifies, and it is in company of the victim, so to speak, that God is to be found, and nowhere else."[12] This absolutely stunning insight forms the indispensable starting point for every soteriological statement. It comprises the essence of the Christian theology of salvation. As "primary theology," the story of the crucified victim's return cannot be reduced to a more fundamental level, and any soteriological statement that would become detached from its dramatic and practical character consigns itself to becoming a meaningless abstraction.

Finally, in addition to the *reversal* and *double reversal* that inspire the themes of justice and forgiveness respectively, there is yet another characteristic theme expressed in Acts 2. Jesus' vindication is simultaneous with his exaltation, which is to say, the eschatological *fulfillment* of his person. Already I have indicated that the resurrection is not only a reversal of some negative situation; it is the restoration and final fruition of a human life. Resurrection faith is a creation faith insofar as it affirms the eschatological destiny of the whole human person within the broader community of creation. As Peter asserts, "He was not abandoned to Hades, nor did his flesh [*sarx*] experience corruption" (v. 31). It is eternal life that God confers through resurrection. "Being therefore exalted at the right hand of God, and having received from the Father the promise of the Holy Spirit, he has poured out this that you both see and hear" (v. 33). Here we see the trinitarian form of the Easter event, which will be examined more closely in chapters 9 and 10. God the Father raises Jesus from the dead and pours forth the Holy Spirit so as to open up to humanity a new and remarkably rich participation in divine life. Peter's resurrection proclamation, it should be noted, is presented as occurring in the midst of a Pentecostal gathering in which members of the primitive Christian community have become saturated with the presence of the Spirit, plunged into a trinitarian milieu that enables them now to say and do as Jesus instructed them. Boldness of speech, proclaiming the good news to all nations and tongues, enduring persecution, offering hospitality to enemies, healing persons with physical and spiritual affirmities, sharing goods and possessions in common with others, distributing to those in need: these are the signs of the human personality animated by Spirit of the risen Christ so as to become God-like. These are the signs of eternal life breaking in upon and transforming the present age. However much the resurrection of the dead remains an outstanding reality that we anticipate with eager longing, it is also real and effective through the ongoing work of the Holy Spirit. Here we may speak of *theosis,* or "divinization," by which I mean the progressive transformation of the whole human person who, now liberated from the cycle of those social mechanisms that perpetuate sin and violence in the human community, is freed for genuine human flourishing, for realizing more fully the original vocation of humanity. The Christian life is a life of freedom, creativity, and gratitude. The resurrection of Jesus, which presages our own, releases us for embracing the beauty of creation with an ecstatic "Yes." Like the lame man in Acts 3 who upon being healed begins "walking and jumping and praising God," the resurrection of Jesus from the dead sets us free for the fullness of life.

Chapter Five

SUFFERING, *MEMORIA,* AND VINDICATION: RETRIEVING THE APOCALYPTIC IMAGINATION

We turn now to an extended study of the grammar of reversal in resurrection language, first by exploring the major aspects of apocalyptic eschatology that inform its use, then by examining their creative appropriation in political and liberation theology. The present chapter focuses on the "apocalyptic imagination" in important biblical traditions and the development of this imagination in the political theology of Johann Baptist Metz, accompanied by Edward Schillebeeckx. In chapter 6, I will continue this line of inquiry by examining the work of liberation theologian Jon Sobrino. To conclude that chapter, we will look at several key ways the apocalyptic imagination is both presupposed and transformed by other aspects of early Christian proclamation, not least by the double reversal illustrated in Acts 2.

RETRIEVING THE APOCALYPTIC IMAGINATION

Resurrection language is not properly intelligible outside of the apocalyptic matrix from which it historically emerges. Although the Easter event cannot be subsumed within apocalyptic eschatology without remainder, since it also brings about important mutations in several of its defining features, understanding the dramatic and universal significance of Jesus' resurrection requires retrieving the "apocalyptic imagination."[1] Summoning apocalyptic eschatology entails risk, however, since many condemningly associate it with end-of-time speculation, rigid sectarianism, and historical determinism. Theologians sometimes prefer the more general term "eschatology" to "apocalyptic" for these reasons.[2] Karl Rahner, in his influential essay "The Hermeneutics of Eschatological Assertions," writes that eschatological language, in contrast to apocalyptic language, is concerned with the future of humanity as this can be extrapolated from the present. It looks forward to the "definitive fulfillment of an existence *already in an eschatological situation.*"³ Rahner clearly favors a more sapiential eschatology, as we shall see in chapters 9 and 10. This is not, it should be noted, the same as Bultmann's existentialist interpretation of eschatology in terms of the "eternal now" of individual decision, which Rahner explicitly rejects as unacceptable.⁴ And yet, Rahner recoils from apocalyptic as a genre. If "eschatology" looks from the present toward the future, "apocalyptic" interpolates from the future into the present. Apocalyptic tends towards "phantasy" and "gnosticism." Concerned with speculation about end-of-time events, it focuses on "supra-temporal existence, of which history is only the projection on the screen of worthless time, and that time is not the real ground from which the eternal validity of man emerges, but a nothingness which is unmasked and really eliminated in this gnostic contact with the truth of reality."⁵ Rahner proposes that while Christian theology may not be "de-eschatologized," since this would cut at the very heart of the Christian faith, it may be "de-apocalypticized" for the interests of communicating the faith with intellectual credibility in the modern world.⁶ However pastoral in motivation this seems, the excision comes with a significant cost.

By "de-apocalypticizing" eschatology, Rahner has not abandoned resurrection language, but he has restricted its meaning primarily to only one of its grammatical modes — the *grammar of fulfillment.* Although he develops this modality to extraordinary effect, he cannot adequately account for the prophetic and political magnitude of resurrection language. This is generally true for other theologians who would ignore or relativize the apocalyptic matrix of resurrection faith. The motivations for this de-emphasis, one suspects, rest on mistaken assumptions about the nature of apocalyptic itself. We must take care therefore to define our terms and provide a constructive overview of apocalyptic eschatology in order to reinstate its rightful place in the Christian theology of Jesus' resurrection from the dead.

Apocalyptic as Genre

To begin, we may distinguish between an *apocalypse* as a literary genre and *apocalyptic eschatology* as a worldview.⁷ As a literary genre, an *apocalypse* is a vehicle for communicating a message revealed from the heavens to an earthly seer.⁸ (The Greek *apokalypsis* means "revelation.") While the content of this revelation may vary widely, most often the message adopts complex symbolic imagery and a narrative framework to speak of a divine judgment upon the present world and the creation of a new world to come. Some apocalypses take the form of "otherworldly journeys," or visions, in which recipients of divine communications are ecstatically drawn up into a transcendent realm to learn about matters of cosmological import.[9] Other apocalypses are more "historical" in focus in that they include reviews of historical epochs culminating in a future crisis of ultimate, eschatological consequence. The Book of Daniel is a historical apocalypse, as is the Book of Revelation, though both books contain some elements of the otherworldly journey. We may include the "little apocalypse" in Mark 13 (par. Matt. 24:3–36; Luke 21:7–36) in this category as well.[10] While the symbolism and speculative character of these writings may strike some as bizarre, impenetrable, or even "gnostic," as Rahner alleges, we should not overlook one of their chief goals: they were written to console and motivate during times of historical upheaval and institutional collapse. The cosmic symbolism sought to bring about a revolution in the imagination that could affirm the enduring reality of an alternative, transcendent order in the face of large-scale chaos in the social-cultural world, usually as the result of domination from an external, imperial power. As John J. Collins helpfully suggests, we should approach these writings, not in terms of a correspondence theory of truth, as though they provide pieces of information to be taken with wooden literalism, but as a critical *poesis* that dares to name a hope for transcendence and justice in spite of all evidence to the contrary.[11] This implies that apocalyptic language is not primarily metaphysical but poetic and pragmatic in character. It comforts and exhorts. It is *"commissive* in character: it commits us to a view of the world for the sake of the actions and attitudes that are entailed."[12] It is this aspect of apocalyptic that many theologians have not adequately appreciated, argues Collins, especially those troubled by its graphic imagery. But for those theological styles more concerned with social and political transformation (e.g., political and liberation theologies), the value of apocalyptic literature for inspiring imagination and praxis in situations of extreme oppression becomes more evident.[13]

Apocalyptic as Eschatology

The genre of the apocalypse is an expression of *apocalyptic eschatology*. However, apocalyptic eschatology should not be identified with a single literary genre. This is a crucial distinction since it allows us to identify apocalyptic motifs in a variety of texts that do not use the conceits of otherworldly journeys or predictive prophecy (*vaticinia ex eventu*). For example, although Paul does not write in the genre we typically associate with apocalyptic literature — his letters reveal very little speculative interest in historical timelines, angelic visitations, heavenly battles, or scenes of the last judgment — Paul's thought as a whole is imbued with apocalyptic motifs. Indeed, to the extent that his contextually specific letters can be said to exhibit a coherent structure, apocalyptic eschatology must be found at their core.[14] Certainly after his conversion there were important transpositions in the eschatology Paul inherited as a Pharisee, but these transpositions only confirm the indispensable role of the apocalyptic in his interpretation of Jesus' resurrection as the dawning of the "new age," the overcoming of "the principalities and powers," the renewal of creation, the universal offer of salvation, and the harbinger to the coming of Christ in glory.[15]

We cannot hope to define apocalyptic eschatology in a way that covers all the perspectives incorporating it in some form or fashion, but there are a few characteristic motifs that we can briefly outline. Some of these motifs have very ancient lineage, going as far back as the second millennium B.C.E. of Mesopotamian religion and culture.[16] The apocalyptic eschatology found in several Old Testament and inter-testamental writings is peculiarly shaped by Israel's theology of exodus and covenant, however, particularly as filtered through the prophetic traditions. Perhaps the most important distinction between the *prophetic* and *apocalyptic* modes of expression has to do with social setting. Whereas the former tended to flourish within the context of nationhood, apocalyptic eschatology emerges with greater definition during times of national disaster. With the destruction of Jerusalem in 587 B.C.E., the subsequent exile of the Jewish people to Babylonia, and later the intense persecutions of the Second Temple period, particularly in the mid-second century, the actuality of God's promises appeared to be jeopardized, if not demonstrably falsified. In the vacuum left by shattered social and religious institutions, and in response to the assault upon Israel's cultural memory through assimilation and persecution at the hands of seemingly invincible adversaries, eschatological hope modulated into a more dualistic idiom: one that looked forward to a decisive and all-encompassing (cosmic) *reversal* of circumstances. Apocalyptic eschatology is marked by a counter-factual view of the world in the face of overwhelming social and cognitive dissonance. But it would be incorrect to think of this simply as the wishful projection of a disenfranchised people. Apocalyptic beliefs, writes Wayne Meeks, "do not merely constitute a compensation in phantasy for real want of power, goods, and status, but first of all provide a way of making sense of a world that seems to have gone mad."[17] Apocalyptic eschatology reads a given historical situation, not simply on the basis of what *is*, but in light of what *should be*. At times, the difference between "is" and "should be" appears tragically incongruent. Nevertheless, apocalyptic enacts a "symbolic inversion," one linked with the memory of God's previous acts of deliverance: it seeks to bring about a change or renewal in the field of perception and language with the ultimate hope that historical and cosmic reality will also be transformed. As Walter Brueggemann writes of the post-exilic writings of Second Isaiah, this leap in imagination "is a seizure of power" that "carries with it the delegitimizing of all other claimants and definers of reality." The poet, whose power we should never underestimate, "speaks about the inversion even in exile and the images tumble out."[18]

Divine Faithfulness and Vindication

Apocalyptic eschatology may be outlined according to four major motifs.[19] The first and most important is *divine faithfulness and vindication*. The counter-factual view of the world proposed by apocalyptic eschatology is founded upon the affirmation of God's sovereignty over the world and the vindication of God's covenantal people. Despite every appearance to the contrary, that is, in the situation of exile and persecution, it boldly declares that God will not leave the people of Israel to ruin, and along with them the covenantal promises made to their ancestors. The creator God will deliver Israel from the threat of annihilation in a new and definitive exodus. If apocalyptic eschatology bears an urgent forward-looking perspective, this is because of its tenacious memory. Through an "exodus memory" it looks urgently towards the exercise of God's power over current and future situations of domination. "[T]he Exodus grammar of Yahweh saturates the imagination of Israel," writes Brueggemann. "Exodus recital, either as a simple declarative sentence enacting Israel's primal theological grammar or as a fuller narrative, becomes paradigmatic for Israel's testimony about Yahweh."[20] This testimony is "agonistic." It reflects Yahweh's active opposition to implacable forces. Within this "exodus grammar" — which is the ultimate foundation for what I am describing here as the *grammar of reversal* — the character of God (YHWH) is revealed as the subject of Exodus verbs. For example:

> Yahweh "brings out": ("... the Lord *brought you out* from there by strength of hand..." [Exod. 13:3]);
>
> Yahweh "delivers" and "brings up": ("... I have come down to *deliver them* from the Egyptians, and to *bring them up* out of that land to a good and broad land, a land flowing with milk and

honey..." [Exod. 3:8]; "I declare that I will *bring you up* out of the misery of Egypt...." [Exod. 3:17]);

Yahweh "frees," "delivers" and "redeems": ("...Say therefore to the Israelites, 'I am the Lord, and I will *free you* from the burdens of the Egyptians and *deliver you* from slavery to them. I will *redeem you* with an outstretched arm and with mighty acts of judgment..." [Exod. 6:6]; "every firstborn of my sons I *redeem*" [Exod. 13:15]).[21]

"Israel's testimony to Yahweh as deliverer," writes Brueggemann, "enunciates Yahweh's resolved capacity to intervene decisively against every oppressive, alienating circumstance and force that precludes a life of well-being. Yahweh is more than a match for the powers of oppression, whether sociopolitical or cosmic."[22]

It is well worth observing that when Jesus appeals to Exodus 3:6 to rebut the Sadducee's denial of the resurrection ("I am the God of your father, the God of Abraham, the God of Isaac, and the God of Jacob"), the broader context of this passage, replete as it is with Exodus grammar, reveals its deeper significance. Though we find no explicit affirmation of the resurrection in the Book of Exodus, the conviction that God will "raise the dead" coheres with the testimony to Yahweh as one who "delivers," "frees," "redeems," "brings up," and "brings out." "He is God not of the dead, but of the living" (Mark 12:27).

Apocalyptic eschatology reflects an idiomatically intensified style of this testimony. What most distinguishes it from the prophetic tradition is that the dramatic reversal hoped for comes less through human agency and more through a "sovereign incursion of Yahweh, whose newness is not extrapolated from the present."[23] This does not mean that human agency has no accompanying role. Rather, it reflects a situation of such extreme desperation that only God can ultimately accomplish it. "For I am about to create new heavens and a new earth; the former things shall not be remembered or come to mind" (Isa. 65:17). In this adoption of cosmic language ("new heavens and a new earth") we find a precursor to the apocalyptic rhetoric of Ezekiel, Zechariah, and Daniel. It is not just that God will affect a change within an already existing state of affairs. The transformation will be all-encompassing and enduring.

The motif of vindication becomes particularly evident in the metaphor of "resurrection." In a passage that almost certainly influenced Daniel 12:2 (the only place in the Old Testament where a full-fledged doctrine of personal resurrection beyond death is articulated), Isaiah 26 speaks of cosmic renewal and the vindication of Israel from the living death of exile:

> O Lord, in distress [the people of Israel] sought you, they poured out a prayer when your chastening was on them. Like a woman with child, who writhes and cries out in her pangs when she is near her time, so were we because of you, O Lord; we were with child, we writhed, but we have given birth only to wind. We have won no victories on earth, and no one is born to inhabit the world. Your dead shall live, their corpses shall rise. O dwellers in the dust, awake and sing for joy! For your dew is a radiant dew, and the earth will give birth to those long dead. (Isa. 26:16–19)

The metaphors of corpses "rising" and dust dwellers "awakening" are not yet pointing to the individual's survival beyond death, but to the hope for the concrete restoration of the whole people of God: the return to the promised land, the recovery of national sovereignty, the revitalization of the Temple, etc. That is, the language of resurrection first emerges in the Old Testament as a metaphor for Israel's *corporate* deliverance. We find the same kind of meaning in a remarkable passage from Ezekiel, where he retells his vision of the valley of dry bones:

> The hand of the Lord came upon me, and he brought me out by the spirit of the Lord and set me down in the middle of a valley; it was full of bones. He led me all around them; there were very many lying in the valley, and they were very dry. He said to me, "Mortal, can these bones live?" I answered, "O Lord God, you know." Then he said to me, "Prophesy to these bones, and say to them: O dry bones, hear the word of the Lord. Thus says the Lord God to these bones: I will cause breath to enter you, and you shall live. I will lay sinews on you, and will cause flesh to come upon you, and cover you with skin, and put breath in you, and you shall live; and you shall know that I am the Lord."
>
> So I prophesied as I had been commanded; and as I prophesied, suddenly there was a noise, a rattling, and the bones came together, bone to its bone. I looked, and there were sinews on them, and flesh had come upon them, and skin had covered them; but there was no breath in them. Then he said to me, "Prophesy to the breath, prophesy, mortal, and say to the breath: Thus says the Lord God: Come from the four winds, O breath, and breathe upon these slain, that they may live." I prophesied as he commanded me, and the

breath came into them, and they lived, and stood on their feet, a vast multitude.

Then he said to me, "Mortal, these bones are the whole house of Israel. They say, 'Our bones are dried up, and our hope is lost; we are cut off completely.' Therefore prophesy, and say to them, Thus says the Lord God: I am going to open your graves, and bring you up from your graves, O my people; and I will bring you back to the land of Israel. And you shall know that I am the Lord, when I open your graves, and bring you up from your graves, O my people. I will put my spirit within you, and you shall live, and I will place you on your own soil; then you shall know that I, the Lord, have spoken and will act, says the Lord." (Ezek. 37:1–14)

What functions more metaphorically in Ezekiel will eventually crystallize into a more metonymic affirmation of bodily resurrection in the second and first centuries B.C.E. Martyrdom provides the immediate context for this shift. In the Book of Daniel, an unambiguous account of bodily resurrection is found, one that includes the apocalyptic themes of tribulation, cosmic judgment, and divine vindication:

There shall be a time of anguish, such as has never occurred since nations first came into existence. But at that time your people shall be delivered, everyone who is found written in the book. Many of those who sleep in the dust of the earth shall awake, some to everlasting life, and some to shame and everlasting contempt. Those who are wise shall shine like the brightness of the sky, and those who lead many to righteousness, like the stars forever and ever. (12:1–3)

By the time of Daniel's composition in the mid-second century, a belief in bodily resurrection had established itself among various Jewish groups. The "resurrection of the dead" increasingly functioned as the precondition for God's eternal vindication of the righteous and judgment of the wicked. The transposition to a more cosmic understanding of resurrection is also evident here, particularly in the likening of the righteous to the bright stars of heaven that will shine forever and ever. But the cosmic imagery does not imply the splitting away from history, as though this were ultimately an escapist hope. The belief in resurrection served to support those who faced martyrdom as a consequence of remaining steadfast in their faith. "Belief in vindication beyond death undercuts the greatest threat at the disposal of the tyrant."[24] Though it may seem paradoxical at first blush, belief in divine vindication *beyond* death can embolden those who would defy tyrannical powers that presume absolute dominion over *present* existence.

Daniel 12 specifically reflects the situation of persecution in the mid-second century under the rule of Antiochus Epiphanes IV. According to the account given to us in 1 and 2 Maccabees, Antiochus had launched a systematic campaign in 167 B.C.E. to eradicate the Jewish people of their national sovereignty and cultural memory. He outlawed many Jewish customs and practices, including Sabbath observance and circumcision. He built numerous temples and shrines to foreign gods and made sacrifice to them obligatory. He also desecrated the temple in Jerusalem by installing an altar to Zeus in the Holy of Holies — the ultimate act of ritual pollution (1 Macc. 1:54). Such an assault ignited various acts of resistance and even violent rebellion among the Jewish people, including the revolt led by Judas Maccabeas that succeeded in reclaiming and rededicating the temple. Judas was no doubt emboldened by his own belief in the resurrection (2 Macc. 12:43–45).

But a very different act of resistance is recounted in 2 Maccabees, one immediately preceding the Maccabean revolt (2 Macc. 7). Seven brothers and their mother are arrested for defying Antiochus's mandates. One by one the seven brothers are tortured and killed as their mother was forced to look on. The means of torture were ghastly, including the burning and stripping of flesh, dismemberment and disembowelment. And yet, one by one, the seven brothers resist recanting their faith as they affirm their ultimate vindication against Antiochus in the resurrection: "You accursed wretch, you dismiss us from this present life, but the King of the universe will raise us up to an everlasting renewal of life, because we have died for his laws" (v. 9); "I got these [hands] from Heaven, and because of his laws I disdain them, and from him I hope to get them back again" (v. 11); "One cannot but choose to die at the hands of mortals and to cherish the hope God gives of being raised again by him. But for you there will be no resurrection to life!" (v. 14); "Because you have authority among mortals, though you also are mortal, you do what you please. But do not think that God has forsaken our people. Keep on, and see how his mighty power will torture you and your descendants!" (v. 16–17); "But do not think that you will go unpunished for having tried to fight against God!" (v. 19).

We are told that the mother "was especially admirable and worthy of honorable memory":

> Although she saw her seven sons perish within a single day, she bore it with good courage because of her hope in the Lord. She

encouraged each of them in the language of their ancestors. Filled with a noble spirit, she reinforced her woman's reasoning with a man's courage, and said to them, "I do not know how you came into being in my womb. It was not I who gave you life and breath, nor I who set in order the elements within each of you. Therefore the Creator of the world, who shaped the beginning of humankind and devised the original of all things, will in his mercy give life and breath back to you again, since you now forget yourselves for the sake of his laws." (2 Macc. 7:20–23)

As in Daniel, the belief in the resurrection serves here to undermine the tyrant's claim to dominion over bodies. It looks towards divine justice beyond a violent oppressor. Its agonistic rhetoric undercuts Antiochus's claim upon his victims as temporary and ultimately self-condemning. Notably, the belief in resurrection does not only operate within a grammar of reversal here. It is explicitly connected to faith in God as *creator*. The mother's assurance that justice awaits her sons flows from a conviction that God will be faithful to creation over and against every power that would destroy it. ("Therefore the Creator of the world.") The motif of reversal is thus also a fulfillment, since what is reversed is the destruction *of* creation, not creation itself. Underwritten by a belief in God as faithful creator and deliverer, the language of resurrection, like the Exodus grammar that supports it, affirms that no tyrannical power or dominion, not even death, will prevail against God's purposes.

Universal Cosmic Expectation

The second major motif of apocalyptic eschatology is *universal cosmic expectation*. As we have already seen, apocalyptic eschatology shifts the horizon of Jewish eschatological hope into cosmic terms. Whereas the prophetic writings tend to focus more specifically on Israel and its immediate neighbors, apocalyptic writings expand the scope to include *all* peoples and beings. The "Day of the Lord" in Amos, which was to be a day of final judgment upon Israel (Amos 5:18–20), takes on a more explicitly universal reach in the proto-apocalyptic writings of Isaiah:

Draw near, O nations, to hear; O peoples, give heed! Let the earth hear, and all that fills it; the world, and all that comes from it. For the Lord is enraged against all the nations, and furious against all their hordes; he has doomed them, has given them over for slaughter. Their slain shall be cast out, and the stench of their corpses shall rise; the mountains shall flow with their blood. All the host of heaven shall rot away, and the skies roll up like a scroll. All their host shall wither like a leaf withering on a vine, or fruit withering on a fig tree. (Isa. 34:1–4)

Out of this judgment and wrath will come a new creation, a new heaven and a new earth, where there will be no more weeping, want or violence, for the "wolf and the lamb shall feed together" (Isa. 65:25). Salvation shall be all-embracing: "For as the new heavens and the new earth, which I will make, shall remain before me, says the Lord; so shall your descendants and your name remain. From new moon to new moon, and from sabbath to sabbath, all flesh shall come to worship before me, says the Lord" (Isa. 66:22–23).

Eschatological universalism is certainly not unique to apocalyptic thought. It is an outcome of the most basic of Israel's beliefs. The one God of all *creation* has a purpose for that creation and *elects* the Hebrew people to realize it. When this purpose for Israel is threatened, so too is God's purpose for the whole created order. (Universality and particularity go hand in hand.) The hoped-for vindication/restoration of Israel is therefore an *eschatological* hope. Monotheism and election, taken together, demand eschatology.[25] When ultimate restoration occurs, Israel will, according to Isaiah, be a "light unto the nations" and draw Jews *and* Gentiles from all over the earth to witness and participate in the fulfillment of God's saving purposes:

> Nations shall come to your light, and kings to the brightness of your dawn. Lift up your eyes and look around; they all gather together, they come to you; your sons shall come from far away, and your daughters shall be carried on their nurses' arms. Then you shall see and be radiant; your heart shall thrill and rejoice, because the abundance of the sea shall be brought to you, the wealth of the nations shall come to you. ... I will appoint Peace as your overseer and Righteousness as your taskmaster. Violence shall no more be heard in your land, devastation or destruction within your borders; you shall call your walls Salvation, and your gates Praise. The sun shall no longer be your light by day, nor for brightness shall the moon give light to you by night; but the Lord will be your everlasting light, and your God will be your glory. (Isa. 60:3–5, 17–19)

Apocalyptic eschatology works within this narrative framework, but amplifies it in at least two ways: (1) it broadens the scope to include the more-than-human reality of creation (demons, angels, and other heavenly hosts); and (2) it anticipates a wide-scale conflagration among these cosmic forces as the harbinger for the "new age." This is sometimes described as a transition from a "horizontal" to a "vertical" eschatology, i.e., a transition from a more historically concrete to a "supra-temporal" (or "mythical") mode. But about this distinction we must be extremely careful.

It is sometimes assumed that the cosmic and "mythic" imagery is a retreat into a metaphysically dualistic view of the world. There is no question that the dramatic structure of apocalyptic eschatology thinks in terms of *dualities,* but it does not represent *dualism* in a metaphysical sense. I shall say more about this in a moment, but here I must point out two important aspects of this metaphoric shift. The first is that the cosmic imagery serves to inscribe into the *whole of creation* what Israel has come to experience of God within its particular history. All of creation participates in the story of exodus and covenant. Creation is not the "raw material" or neutral background to God's saving purposes. (We must resist projecting back upon these writings the disenchanted view of the world bequeathed to us by modernity.[26]) Creation is integral to God's saving purposes for Israel. When apocalyptic writings describe God's judgment and deliverance on a cosmic scale, its soterio-logic includes the whole created domain within the order of salvation.[27]

The second important aspect of the cosmic imagery reveals an indispensable insight into the larger-than-life forces operative in the human life-world. While many theologians have busied themselves with "demythologizing" (or "de-apocalypticizing") scripture for the purposes of intellectual credibility in the modern world, they have neglected critical resources for grasping how scripture gives name to the *structural* dimensions of evil, sin, and salvation. The modern preoccupation with the autonomous self who relates to other persons, social groups, institutions, and cultures subsequent to self-constitution, a subject whose identity first takes shape within an inner sphere of freedom and is "expressed" outwardly into the world: such a view has little in common with one that sees the human person woven into and profoundly shaped by social, institutional, and cultural "powers." If apocalyptic eschatology adopts cosmic imagery to characterize the world in terms of a conflict between extra-mundane forces (YHWH and "the Satan"), this is not because it takes flight from the world, but because it penetrates more deeply into the human life-world where structural forces of oppression, violence, and sin take on a seemingly autonomous profile, transcending the sum of individuals as an encompassing, self-perpetuating force, often in ways that do not submit to rational reflection or direct influence by human beings. When the Book of Daniel likens the four kingdoms of Assyria, Media, Persia, and Macedonia to four beasts coming up from the sea

(Dan. 7), or when the Book of Revelation addresses the angels of the seven churches to declare the imminent overcoming of the primordial chaos and defeat of "the Satan" by the subversive power of the slain lamb, the larger-than-life forces in the world that co-constitute human existence are in the process of being named, unmasked, and engaged.[28] This apocalyptic imagination is found everywhere in the New Testament: in Jesus' confrontation with "the Satan" and his exorcism of demonic powers; in Paul's theology of "sin" and the "principalities and powers"; in John's theology of "the world" (*kosmos*) that ignorantly murders the *Logos* made flesh. As we shall see later, the resurrection of the victim Jesus (the "lamb slain from the beginning of the world") unmasks and overcomes the "system" of rivalry, exclusion, and violence that entangles human beings, often despite themselves, from realizing the true purpose of creation. The resurrection of the victim unveils the economy of violence of the "present age" and throws open a new economy, a "new age" of reconciliation and peace. Important to this thesis is the transformation of apocalyptic eschatology itself.

Duality (Cosmic, Temporal, and Social)

We have already observed the agonistic character of Exodus grammar. Yahweh "delivers" ("brings out," "brings up," "frees," "redeems") the people of Israel from circumstances of domination, and thus actively opposes all forces antagonistic to God's purposes for creation. Resurrection language is informed by this grammar, expanding the motif of vindication to include the vanquishing of death itself. This over-against dynamic seizes upon the rift between what "is" and what "ought to be" and stimulates the strong tendency in apocalyptic eschatology to characterize the world according to a series of dualities. There are at least three: (1) a *cosmic* duality between "heaven" and "earth"; (2) a *temporal* duality between "this age" and the "final age to come"; and (3) a *social* duality between the "righteous" and the "unrighteous."[29]

Regarding the first two, apocalyptic eschatology interprets the disjunction between present exile and hoped-for reconciliation in spatio-temporal terms. Whereas the grammar of fulfillment favored by sapiential eschatology thinks more in terms of a *continuous* arc extending from origins, through the present, and to the future, the grammar of reversal favored by apocalyptic eschatology focuses on *interruption* and *discontinuity*. The present situation of dominated existence (the evil of "this world," of "this age") demands a reversal so thoroughgoing (a "new creation") that only a divine incursion into the present can ultimately bring it forth. Such duality does not imply a metaphysical dualism, however. Apocalyptic eschatology does not look toward the dissolution of the space-time universe.[30] It does not yearn for a blissful emancipation of the soul from the body. (This is precisely what *bodily* resurrection forbids.) Neither does its emphasis on divine intervention preclude human agency. Rather, it looks towards the definitive in-breaking of God's absolute future that at last establishes a total manner of life (material, interpersonal, cosmic) of enduring justice and peace. It was the promise of this absolute future that enabled people to name and resist oppression. As Richard A. Horsley explains, the dualities of apocalyptic simply magnify the broader biblical tradition that thought in terms of a "double level of historical action — i.e., action in the heavens determining or prefiguring that in the struggles of earthly life." It should therefore not be surprising "that apocalyptic visionaries would symbolize the historical situation in terms of superhuman demonic agents temporarily wreaking havoc in opposition to God."[31]

As for the allegation that apocalyptic eschatology implies ethical passivity, Horsley responds:

> Far from an "abandonment of historical responsibility" and "a retreat into a vision of the 'higher' reality," apocalyptic visions and literature attempt to make sense of and to respond to concrete historical situations of oppression and even persecution. Far from providing an escape, apocalyptic visions apparently helped people to remain steadfast in their traditions and to resist systematic attempts to suppress them.... The apocalyptic imagination thus had a strengthening effect on the people's ability to endure, and even a motivating effect toward resistance or revolt.[32]

Along with the spatial and temporal dualities, Jewish apocalyptic eschatology asserts a social duality between the "righteous," who are to be vindicated, and the "unrighteous," who are to be punished. This insider/outsider distinction explains why apocalyptic eschatology can support revolutionary acts of resistance while also providing a socially constructive (or "conservative") function for the marginalized group.[33] Of course, the sense of distinction, or being "set apart," is basic to Jewish self-understanding. It emerges from the theology of election and through the observance of the law. But in the context of apocalyptic, this social duality gains an eschatological vector. As Johan Beker points out, when the two themes of vindication and universalism combine, as they do so powerfully in apocalyptic, the distinction between "insider" and "outsider" can become quite rigid. Thus, even as Israel looked forward to a messianic era that would draw forth the Gentile nations to Jerusalem, Israel's thinking remained "introverted." "Although Israel can conceive of a new covenant with God in the messianic era, it finds the notion of a new Torah or its abrogation abhorrent. Thus there is a close connection between the identity of Israel as a people and God's apocalyptic vindication. 'The divine wall of the law' (Eph. 2:14) marks Israel's ethnocentricity: It signifies a sharp distinction between us, 'the insiders,' and them, 'the outsiders.' "[34]

But it is just this apocalyptic motif, among others, that Jesus' resurrection from the dead will subvert and transform. In Paul's theology, for example, the barrier between those who faithfully adhere to the law and those who are Gentiles is overcome. The death of Jesus reveals that *all* have sinned and fallen short of God's glory. God's apocalyptic judgment is upon all people, not just some (Rom. 3). And yet, by raising Jesus from the dead, God has ushered in the "final age" to offer salvation to all, even to those proximately responsible for Jesus' death. Through Christ's death and resurrection, every distinction between "insider" and "outsider" is dismantled.[35] "There is no longer Jew or Greek, there is no longer slave or free, there is no longer male and female; for all of you are one in Christ Jesus" (Gal. 3:28).

The importance of this mutation in meaning cannot be overstated, and I shall spend considerable time drawing out its implications as we proceed. But already now we can anticipate something of the transformation that Jesus' resurrection brings about to apocalyptic eschatology. Jesus is risen from the dead *now:* God's absolute future has been proleptically realized in the present ("this age" and the "new age" are converging); the "new creation" is already irrupting within and transforming the old ("heaven" and "earth" are enfolding); and the innocent victim has been vindicated, revealing in most dramatic fashion that God's justice will ultimately prevail over all injustice. At the same time, the *vindication* of Jesus is also the offer of *forgiveness* to victimizers and an expression of self-donating love. The social duality that would pit victims against victimizers in a scheme of retributive justice has given way to a new economy: one of non-violent and non-reciprocal reconciliation. The resurrection of the innocent victim, Jesus, marks the ultimate "revelation" (*apokalypsis*) of those hidden processes of rivalry, exclusion, and scapegoating that contaminate human relations and our perception of God, even those that might unwittingly perpetuate social dualism in the name of justice. It is the victim who, in the power of the living God, returns to his victimizers to offer them (us) *shalom*. Their (our) victim has become their (our) salvation. This is the im-possible Gift.

Historical Imminence

The final motif of apocalyptic eschatology reflects the hope in the *imminent coming of God's reign*. The present time is not simply one link in a smooth and indefinite succession of moments. Time is not running a flattened, linear course (*chronos*) but is "heaping up" with tension and meaning (*kairos*). In these "last days" the apocalyptic imagination looks forward to the final dénouement of God's plan for history. "The time is fulfilled, and the kingdom of God has come near" (Mark 1:14). These words inaugurating Jesus' ministry reflect his own conviction that Israel's story was at last reaching its decisive conclusion, that God's rule would soon be established "on earth as it is in heaven." The sense of urgency that underlies Jesus' message and ministry is entirely in keeping with the diverse apocalyptic movements dotting the landscape of first-century Palestinian Judaism, including the movement led by his mentor John the Baptist.[36]

It is important to note that although Jesus' resurrection from the dead means God's absolute future has *already* come, and therefore we must speak of a *realized eschatology*, the theme of futurity in apocalyptic thinking cannot be resolved into an *eternal now*. It is true that the presence of the risen Christ presently *dwells within* the world, transforming it at its very roots. (The resurrection is nothing if not ontological). God has sent the Son in the "fullness of time" to bring about our redemption and adoption as sons and daughters of God (Gal. 4:4-7). Those who enter into the "body of Christ" through baptism already participate in this new economy ("participation" and "dwelling" are key terms for the grammar of fulfillment). This form of life is "life in the Spirit" (Rom. 8). Yet we still urgently await the *completion* of what God has inaugurated in Christ, the "first born of the dead" (Col. 1:18). Flanked by two great eschatological events — Jesus' resurrection, and his *parousia* in the general resurrection of the dead — the present moment teems with eschatological urgency. "For the present form of this world is passing away" (1 Cor. 7:31). It is therefore more accurate to say that the realized eschatology of Jesus' resurrection *intensifies* apocalyptic longing.[37] The "already" does not cancel the "not yet," but brings it into greater relief. In a remarkable passage that captures the Christian sense of time as an "in-between" time, Paul masterfully weaves the apocalyptic themes of universality, vindication, present tribulation, and historical imminence:

> I consider that the sufferings of this present time are not worth comparing with the glory about to be revealed to us. For the creation waits with eager longing for the revealing of the children of God;

for the creation was subjected to futility, not of its own will but by the will of the one who subjected it, in hope that the creation itself will be set free from its bondage of decay and will obtain the freedom of the glory of the children of God. We know that the whole creation has been groaning in labor pains until now; and not only the creation, but we ourselves, who have the first fruits of the Spirit, groan inwardly while we wait for adoption, the redemption of our bodies. For in hope we were saved.... For I am convinced that neither death, nor life, nor angels, nor rulers, nor things present, nor things to come, nor powers, nor height, nor depth, nor anything else in all creation, will be able to separate us from the love of God in Christ Jesus our Lord. (Rom. 8:18–24, 38–39)

As we shall continue to see throughout the rest of this study, resurrection language in Christian imagination and praxis requires that we keep all three grammars (reversal, double reversal, fulfillment) in the closest possible unity. In this "in-between" time, they remain irreducible and mutually corrective for a fuller understanding of the Easter event.

TIME, *MEMORIA*, AND JUSTICE

In order to further explore the significance of the apocalyptic imagination for Christian theology — and how the grammar of reversal brings out the practical-political character of Jesus' resurrection from the dead — I turn now to the work of Johann Baptist Metz and, as a clarifying accompaniment, the work of Edward Schillebeeckx. Even if, as I will continue to argue, Easter proclamation brings about important mutations within apocalyptic eschatology, the latter remains indispensable for grasping the justice-character of the former. I will extend this line of thematic development into the next chapter where we will look more carefully at the work of Jon Sobrino.

Resurrection as "Dangerous Memory"

Previously I noted the aversion in much contemporary theology to apocalyptic. Karl Rahner, it will be recalled, contrasted "eschatology" with "apocalyptic" in such a way that, rather than being acknowledged as one of the indispensable grammars within Christian eschatology, the latter was deemed a distorted case of the former and problematic for contemporary Christians. It is hoped that the previous analysis dispels some of the commonly mistaken assumptions that might have led Rahner (or others) to dismiss apocalyptic as unworthy of serious attention. In any case, Metz, Rahner's most influential student, argues that the dismissal of apocalyptic eschatology in his mentor's (or any theologian's) thought comes with an unacceptable cost: the diminishment of the critical and political force of biblical Christianity. It is worth pointing out that Rahner himself once affirmed Metz's critique of his theology as the only one he took seriously.[38]

Metz argues that at the core of the Christian narrative-worldview is a "dangerous memory" that disrupts our evolutionary sense of time and summons us to be in solidarity with those who suffer. Funded by the memory of the exodus and the passion of Jesus Christ, this critical *anamnesis*, which also stimulates a hope in a just future that cannot be fully deduced from the present, is a *practical knowing*: it urges Christians to denounce and transform those social, institutional, and cultural realities responsible for oppression and suffering as a formal part of discipleship.

Metz provides a helpful summary of political theology as a "practical fundamental theology":

> The faith of Christians is a praxis in history and society that is to be understood as hope in solidarity in the God of Jesus as a God of the living and the dead who calls all men to be subjects in his presence. Christians justify themselves in this essentially apocalyptical praxis (of imitation) in their historical struggle for their fellow men. They stand up for all men in their attempt to become subjects in solidarity with each other. In this praxis, they resist the danger both of a creeping evolutionary disintegration of the history of men as subjects and of an increasing negation of the individual in view of a new, post-middle-class image of man.[39]

The assertion that Christianity is "political" means that faith cannot be reduced to the private experience of individuals; it means that "sin" and "grace" are not concepts referring to the guilt and reconciliation of persons isolated from their historical, social, and cultural environments; it means that the distinctions we presume as children of modernity (e.g., individual/society, private/public, spiritual/material, eternal/temporal) do not easily apply, if at all, to the biblical worldview wherein they form a complex whole. Put broadly, we may assert with Metz that "any theology which tries to bring about the process of transference between the kingdom of God and society is a 'political theology.'"[40] This does not mean that there is only one style of political theology, or that the methods employed by Metz represent the sum of approaches available. And it certainly does not mean that Christianity can be identified with a political party, ideology, or economic philosophy. It does mean however that Christianity is necessarily concerned with the *polis,* and that any authentic realization of the Christian faith must live out its apostolic mission to transform the culture and society ("the world") within and for which it exists.[41]

Apocalyptic Time versus Evolutionary Time

According to Metz, apocalyptic eschatology forms an indispensable foundation for any theology concerned with social transformation. For those who might regard apocalyptic as an instance of metaphysical dualism or a world-weary inclination toward ethical passivity, this claim can only seem strange. But for Metz, who regards apocalyptic as "the hem to my theological approach," it is invaluable because of its commissive and practical character, especially as this arises from the memory of past suffering and injustice.[42] Apocalyptic views history in terms of hope and justice, certainly; but these terms are given a dialectical structure because history is seen as a "history of suffering," not as the inexorable working out of an evolutionary time-line that enables us to forget or theoretically justify past sufferings and injustices. Suffering, especially innocent suffering, cannot be assimilated into a "system." It presents a scandal to metaphysics. It uncovers disturbing regions of human experience that teleological views of history tend to ignore. Refractory to thought, innocent suffering destabilizes every attempt to orchestrate the whole of history into a single pattern of intelligibility. Against all forms of historical "logocentrism," Schillebeeckx, with whom Metz shares a great deal, writes:

> There is, in point of fact, un-meaningful history; there is non-sense in our history: violence, lust for power, coveting at the expense of others, enslavement and oppression — there is Auschwitz, and goodness knows what else in the private sphere and in our own personal life. All of that does indeed fall outside the "logos" which the historian looks for in history — so much the worse for the varieties of concrete historical experience!...Human history is ambiguous, with flashes of light and clouds of impenetrable darkness, a realm of knowing and unknowing. The co-existing of meaning and unmeaning in this history — and so history itself — is not capable of complete rationalization; the "reason for" history is not accessible to theory.[43]

Metz's appeal to apocalyptic eschatology cannot be fully appreciated without seeing his theological project as a response to the horrors of the Holocaust. Having lived through the frightful reign of Nazism as a German Catholic, Metz's theology, which might well be described as a theology of catastrophe, has continuously asked in one form or another how it is possible to speak of God after Auschwitz.[44] But it is not just this event that so possesses Metz, as important and unimaginably awful as it is. It is the whole history of suffering, most of which is not recounted in what passes for "history," that haunts his theology at every turn. This is the reason why he repudiates the notion that theology can be a "system." If it heeds the cry of suffering and injustice as its point of departure, theology too will become a cry of "suffering unto God" — a fragmentary, rhetorical, and practical enterprise that seeks to awaken the conscience of the church and the broader human community to respond and transform those social conditions that produce unjust suffering.[45]

Among the most pervasive and pernicious ideologies of the modern age, argues Metz, is its view of time and history as a "closed system" or "totality," something fully luminous to theory or subject to technical mastery. It is this view of time Metz calls "evolutionary": "Man's understanding of reality, which guides his scientific and technical control of nature and from which the cult of the makeable draws its strength, is marked by an idea of time as a continuous process which is empty and evolving towards infinity and within which everything is enclosed without grace."[46] The flattened cosmology of modernity has no "outside." It yearns for nothing eschatologically exterior or Other to what it already possesses from "within." It is a totalizing scheme of representation and production. The modern conception of historical progress has thoroughly immanentized the future-orientation of its Judeo-Christian heritage into an indefinite "now" so that time runs its course with fluid, monotonous inevitability. Nothing is really "new," but all things, including human beings, are seen as increasingly measurable and predictable. Because its horizon of meaning is largely determined by functionality and manageability, the modern image of the human person produces a sense of fatalism rather than a sense of genuine freedom and creativity. With the ascendancy of technical rationality in our political discourse, we are more likely to approach human problems in terms of productivity and efficiency. What is "good" is "useful," and vice versa. With its trust in the scientific-technical picture of the universe, modernity's cosmology only reinforces the sense of fatalism that comes with the oft repeated conclusion that life is the product of hapless cosmic processes. Such disenchantment with the cosmos finds its practical correlate in the way "nature" is viewed as a vast storehouse of raw materials for usage and consumption, for the upkeep of an economic system that depends on the never-ending increase in desire for manufacturing and obtaining goods. And yet our insatiable craving for "more" and our unstoppable urge to gain technical mastery over the world — including outer space, no less — stands in ironic contrast with the creation of technological and economic systems that operate beyond our immediate control, often in ways inimical to human well-being. In Metz's view, the sense of human worth has not grown with our putative progress but has become weaker and more damaged.[47] Because modernity's horizon is not attendant to interruption and surprise, because its implicit eschatology views time in terms of an endless, anonymous continuum, a self-generating process that operates strictly from within — "non-dialectically," as Metz frequently puts it — we have lost what from a Christian point of view is so basic to human well-being: hope.

Hope is another name for apocalyptic expectation. Hope is not continuous or symmetrical with the present, but oriented towards things unseen. Apocalyptic time, as opposed to the linear time of evolutionary time-consciousness, is disruptive and discontinuous, open to the un-thinkable and un-predictable — to the *novum ultimum*. "Eschatology," writes Emmanuel Levinas, is a "breach of totality." To think eschatologically is to think with and after "*a surplus always exterior to the totality.*"[48] It is to allow thought itself to be disturbed by the Other — *as* Other — and not as something I may surmise and assimilate within a framework of intelligibility. With its crying out for God's in-breaking into the circle of the same, apocalyptic eschatology situates the "now" in tension with, and under the judgment of, a future that cannot be measured out from the present. Put in terms more familiar to biblical theology, apocalyptic time emphasizes the "not yet" pole of eschatology (and less its "already" pole) and does so, not in a world-weary negation of the present, but in agonistic response to the negativity within history that it yearns to overcome.

As we saw above, the forward-looking expectation of apocalyptic eschatology is a working out of critical *anamnesis*. It remembers God's incursion into past situations of suffering and injustice as the grounds for hope in an ultimately just future. Such interruptions *of* time shake time's monotony, its obliviousness to past suffering and death. Time is not self-grounded; neither can it be possessed in the end as the instrument of a dominating power. God's acts of deliverance breach time to reveal both its contingency and redeemability. It is "God's time."

In the apocalyptic's subversive vision, time itself is full of danger. Time is not just that evolutionarily stretched-out, empty and surprise-free endlessness that offers no resistance to our projections of our future. Time belongs not to Prometheus or to Faust, but to God. For the apocalyptic, God is the one who has not yet fully appeared, the still outstanding mystery of time. God is not seen as that which transcends time, but as the end which is pressing in upon it, its delineation, its saving interruption. For in the view of the apocalyptic, time appears first and foremost as a time of suffering.[49]

Innocent Suffering and God-Talk

The apocalyptic view of time as non-linear (or without metaphysical necessity) is crucial for clarifying God's relationship to evil and suffering. "The history of man's suffering has no goal," writes Metz, in obvious rejection of any "soul-making" theodicy, "but it has a future."[50] By distinguishing "goal" and "future," Metz rejects any attempt to rationalize, and thus permit, innocent suffering as an inevitable feature of the world-process, as having a teleological or educative "purpose," as fitting into a predetermined divine plan. Of course, some suffering can be made purposeful, and we could even say that some suffering is warranted. I am not suggesting that no wisdom, no moral good or personal growth can come from suffering. But I am not speaking here of that sort of suffering. Rather, I am speaking of *innocent suffering:* that which is unmerited and non-purposive, that which remains disproportionate (and often enough, radically so) to the personal guilt to whom it befalls. In a word, unjust suffering. To speak of innocent or unjust suffering does not require that we presume the absolute moral innocence of the one who suffers. It means that we acknowledge the non-meaningful *surplus* of evil and suffering in our world: that human beings are subject to physical, emotional, and spiritual affliction in ways that exceed personal guilt or defy any constructive purpose.[51] Again, Schillebeeckx: "[T]here is an *excess* of suffering and evil in our history. There is barbarous excess, for all the explanations and interpretations. There is too much *unmerited* and *senseless* suffering for us to be able to give an ethical, hermeneutical and ontological analysis of our disaster. There is suffering which is not even suffering 'for a good cause,' but suffering in which men, without finding meaning for themselves, are simply made the crude victims of an evil cause which serves others."[52]

To adopt the language from chapter 2, the realities of evil and innocent suffering *saturate* our powers of conceptual representation. The encounter with radical evil traumatizes language and fragments our horizons of understanding. The Kantian categories of understanding that structure, if only as a foil, Marion's sketches of saturated phenomena are surely no less subject to saturation by the kinds of phenomena that arouse in us moral indignation and lament. Where is the metaphysics that can render Krakow, Buchenwald, and Auschwitz intelligible? What theodicy is appropriate to the senseless slaughter presently taking place in Darfur and North Korea? What language can truly name the raging AIDS pandemic in Africa that has laid waste to entire generations of people and left millions of children orphaned? What teleological goal is advanced when millions of children are bought and sold everyday in the sex slave industry? "Our task," writes Gustavo Gutiérrez, "is to find the words with which to talk about God in the midst of the starvation of millions, the humiliation of races regarded as inferior, discrimination against women, especially women who are poor, systematic social injustice, a persistent high rate of infant mortality, those who simply 'disappear' or are deprived of their freedom, the sufferings of peoples who are struggling for their right to live, the exiles and the refugees, terrorism of every kind, and the corpse-filled common graves of Ayacucho."[53]

If *theo*-logy is the act of speaking words about God, how can we do so while honestly facing our moral catastrophe? If we acknowledge that evil and suffering overwhelm our capacities of representation and give lie to all attempts to provide exhaustive theological explanations, whether these be in terms of God's "permissive will" or the consequence of "original sin," what words shall we use and how shall we use them, assuming that there are even words to be used?[54] This is not to deny some legitimacy to these reasons given for evil and suffering. But the problem we are attempting to face here is not whether *some* evil and suffering can be attributed to the divine respect for human freedom or the accumulating effects of human sin in history. The problem is whether such reasons provide adequate theoretical solutions to the disturbing pervasiveness of evil and suffering in our world, especially as we continue to affirm God's providential care for creation. The disquieting question of Dostoevsky's Grand Inquisitor has not been given an adequate explanation by theology, but compels us to raise our voices in painful and even questioning lament before the creator-covenant God as an indispensable act of theologizing. For Metz, the only appropriate words are not explanatory in nature but *apocalyptical, commemorative*, and *commissive*. More specifically, Christians must be resolved to think, speak, and act within the narrative context of the *memoria passionis, mortis et resurrectionis Jesu Christi*.

The Apocalyptic Cry

Just as Jesus on the cross cried to God, "Father, why have you forsaken me?," those who suffer unjustly in history cry out with an "apocalyptic cry." Crying unto God, or what Metz calls "suffering unto God," presupposes a very different God than the philosopher's. "If one does not begin with a Greek or neo-Pagan way of thinking about being, but rather proceeds from biblical thinking — in terms of covenant and justice — in which every statement about being has a temporal mark ('I will be who I will be'), then one must also hear the Johannine statement 'God is love' as a statement bearing the character of a promise: God will prove Godself to us as love."[55] God appears in the biblical tradition as the God of the unprecedented *future*, the absolute promise for its fulfillment, not as the timeless Absolute under which temporality becomes a ceaseless and directionless flow unto infinity. "Rather God must be thought of as the one to whom time belongs, as the end that sets its bounds."[56] "God 'is' in coming."[57] The apocalyptic view of God, urges Metz, is not a-historical or a-cosmic, as some allege, but an attempt to speak of God in the mode of radical *alterity*, in terms of event and interruption, in a way that time gains its definition against the One who "appears in his eschatological freedom as the subject and meaning of history as a whole."[58] Before such a God evil and suffering cannot be theoretically justified but only protested with an apocalyptic cry. Those who suffer injustice cry out to a God who promises to "redeem the time"; they summon a God whose creative power and capacity to hear is determined to be actual and not just imagined. Such a cry is more than a lamentation; it is a petition and even a penetrating question put to God in the obscurity of faith. It is the question of Job. "Even Christian theology, drawing on its doctrine of creation, cannot eliminate the apocalyptic cry, 'What is God waiting for'? Not even Christian theology can allow Job's question to God, 'How long yet'? to fall silent in a soothing answer. Even Christian hope remains accountable to an apocalyptic conscience."[59]

Metz invites us to consider that among the most vital acts of theology is to continue speaking words about God and to God precisely in the midst of catastrophe, not in order to convince ourselves through consoling autosuggestion that despite evidence to the contrary all is well with the world, but to bring grief and bewilderment to concentrated expression. This is not catharsis, or a kind of linguistic therapy. It is a gritty (and as we shall see, a praxis-inspiring) language-act that asserts in faith and hope, even if stammering, that things should not be this way, that God's purposes for creation and the human community have been violated by a parasitical power whose frightful grip on history cannot be ultimate, cannot be metaphysically necessary or divinely sanctioned, but is subject to imminent disruption and vanquishing by the God of exodus and covenant, by the God of the living and the dead. Again, this is not a self-soothing act. It is a performative language that unflinchingly faces the abysmal contrast between what "is" and what "should be," particularly as this contrast appears in the light of a belief in God as the Lord of history. According to Metz, such language is "mystical" in a prophetic-apocalyptic sense. In contrast to a form of mystical theology that speaks ecstatically of God's boundless glory, this style of mystical theology represents a passionate and restless crying out to God in lamentation, questioning, and protest, what Metz dubs a "mysticism of suffering unto God." Such language, far from being a deviation from biblical faith, is rooted in its key traditions:

> It is found particularly in Israel's prayer traditions: in the Psalms, in Job, in Lamentations, and last but not least in many passages in the prophetic books. This language of prayer is itself a language of suffering, a language of crisis, a language of affliction and of radical danger, a language of complaint and grievance, a language of crying out and, literally, of the grumbling of the children of Israel. The language of this God-mysticism is not first and foremost one of consoling answers for the suffering one is experiencing, but rather much more a language of passionate questions from the midst of suffering, questions turned toward God, full of highly charged expectation.... What occurs in this language is not the repression but rather the acceptance of fear, mourning and pain; it is deeply rooted in the figure of night, in the experience of the soul's demise. It is less a song of the soul, more a loud crying out from the depths — and not a vague, undirected wailing, but a focused crying-out-to.[60]

According to Metz, we find just this "God-mysticism" in Jesus' cry from the cross.

> His is in an exemplary way a mysticism of suffering unto God. His cry from the cross is the cry of one forsaken by God, who for his part had never forsaken God. It is this that points inexorably into Jesus' God-mysticism: he holds firmly to the Godhead. In the God-forsakenness of the cross, he affirms a God who is still other and different from the echo of our wishes, however ardent; who is ever more and other than the answers to our questions, even the

strongest and most fervent — as with Job, and finally with Jesus himself.[61]

The prophetic-apocalyptic stream of the biblical tradition is here fully unfurled. Resurrection language, particularly when spoken out of the grammar of reversal, is a language of "suffering unto God" in just this way. To appreciate how resurrection language functions thusly, we must resist every temptation to read Jesus' resurrection backwards into the cross in any way that would blunt or rationalize the scandal of his suffering and death. (Often enough this occurs in certain atonement theories that interpret the cross as "necessary" for appeasing divine wrath or for the "satisfaction" of human sin. The proper way to understand the theme of necessity in the passion and resurrection predictions, as we shall see more clearly in the following chapters, is opposed to atonement theories presupposing God's complicity in violence.) "Suffering unto God" is a performance of faith that urgently yearns for the definitive completion in history what God has already accomplished for Jesus of Nazareth. God's response to Jesus' suffering and death does not retrospectively confer upon it cosmic necessity. The resurrection is counteractive, a work of vanquishing and eschatological vindication. It is just this reversal dynamic that opens up the narrative space within which Christians may cry out in grief, protest, and hope as an appropriate and faithful response to evil and suffering.[62] As Christians remember the life, death, and resurrection of Jesus Christ in liturgy and word, they inhabit a narrative space that encourages the acknowledgement of pain and bewilderment while also clinging to apocalyptic hope, especially because Jesus' resurrection from the dead reveals God's ultimate response to all that afflicts human beings. Among the very earliest prayers of the primitive Christian community was itself an apocalyptic cry: "Our Lord, Come (*Marana tha!*)" (1 Cor. 16:22; Rev. 22:20). This prayer, which also happens to be one of the earliest christological confessions in the New Testament, is anticipatory in its affirmation of Jesus' resurrection. Something of its urgency is also reflected in the abrupt ending of Mark's gospel. The women are summoned to go and speak of what fills them with "terror and amazement." The narrative ends with the accent placed on an unforeseen future, on the "not yet" pole of eschatological expectation. The sense of apocalyptic danger here likely serves Mark's purposes to speak appropriately to the situation of his persecuted community.

To state more precisely what I mean: Jesus' resurrection, although not providing an *explanation* for innocent suffering and death, is nevertheless God's *response* to the "apocalyptic cry" in the form of an active, self-committing *promise*. The distinction between these two terms ("explanation" and "promissory response") implies a fundamental difference in theological reasoning. We are not asserting what *must be* the case in order to justify the existence of evil and suffering in the world. Rather, we are reading from and within the narrative of Jesus' life, death, and resurrection to say something about God's relationship to evil and suffering in light of their eschatological *future*. We may not be able to explain to our satisfaction why evil and suffering exist in the way and degree they do. At this point, theology must be willing to plead a certain ignorance, just the sort of plea expressed in Jesus' cry from the cross: "Why have you forsaken me?"[63] And yet we can say, on the basis of Jesus' resurrection, that such negativity in our history is *opposed* to God's purposes for the human community. Why? Because the culmination of these purposes in Christ are revealed precisely in the *overcoming* of evil, suffering, and death. What God has promised for the future of humanity reveals what God has intended for humanity from the beginning. The resurrection reveals once and for all that evil, sin, and unjust suffering are an aberration.

God is a God of "pure positivity," asserts Schillebeeckx, not an ambivalent reality with a double will. "*Negativity* cannot have a cause or a motive in God."[64] How can we assert this as Christians? Or better, why *must* we assert this as Christians? Not from a general concept of God arrived at by philosophical reflection, but from God's definitive self-communication in the Easter event: "from the 'God of Jesus,' namely from Christian belief in the *resurrection* of Jesus. For it emerges that God transcends these negative aspects in our history, not so much by allowing them as *by overcoming them,* making them as though they had not happened. By nature, and in addition to other aspects and meanings, the resurrection of Jesus is also a corrective, a victory over the negativity of suffering and even death."[65] It is from this standpoint that Schillebeeckx's somewhat controversial statements regarding the cross make the greatest sense. Schillebeeckx describes God's offer of salvation to humanity in terms of a great despite: "we are not redeemed *thanks to* the death of Jesus but *despite* it."[66] The "despite" signifies here the denial of any attempt to rationalize Jesus' death as "necessary" for assuaging divine wrath against humanity, as a necessary "payment" to restore the honor due to God, or as "satisfaction" for human sin as demanded by the standards of retributive justice. It signifies the denial of any attempt to attribute salvific value to Jesus' suffering and death in isolation, or in a way that presumes the violence perpetrated upon him was caused by God. God is not the agent of Jesus' suffering and death but the agent of his vindication and resurrection. As with Jesus, so with us: "God does not want mankind to suffer.... God wants *men's salvation,* and in it victory over their suffering."[67]

In following chapters, I shall attempt to explain more clearly why, in fact, we can and must continue to say that we are redeemed "thanks to" Jesus' death. While fully acknowledging the concerns of Metz and Schillebeeckx to avoid attributing divine complicity in Jesus' death, there is yet a redemptive significance to Jesus' passion that the language of "despite" does not fully penetrate. This redemptive significance is found in the motif of double reversal, which places emphasis on the divine offer of forgiveness from the risen victim to sinners.

Memoria and Praxis

With explicit reference to the work of Metz, Schillebeeckx calls for a transition from theoretical theodicies to a *practical theodicy:*

> In theory, people may not be in a position to *explain* suffering and evil, but the *remembrance* of what has happened in very specific suffering in a particular historical context also belongs to the structure of human reason or critical rationality. The history of these specific remembrances therefore remains an inner stimulus for practical reason which seeks to be liberating and active. Human reason may not simply brush aside these admonitory remembrances if it still wants to remain *critical* reason.[68]

If the "apocalyptic cry" finds explanatory discourse grossly inadequate for confronting the reality of evil and suffering, and opts instead to approach it as a genuinely theological *mystery* — as that which saturates the subjective capacities of representation while arousing the question (even if in the mode of protest) of God — this by no means renders the process of rational reflection inappropriate or unnecessary. From a theological point of view, the "learned ignorance" called for when approaching the mystery of God is not a license for irrationality. Reason itself, properly understood, is grounded in mystery. All human comprehension is always a *reductio in mysterium.*[69] "Learned ignorance" in theological reasoning is still very much *learned.* The problem of evil and suffering demands all of the resources that rational reflection can give to it. But in this case we are speaking more particularly about *critical* reasoning rather than speculative reasoning, i.e., reasoning dedicated to the critique of society and culture in view of the emancipatory interests among those who suffer from injustice. To the extent that unjust suffering in history becomes a formal part of rational reflection, it gives such reflection a much greater chance of becoming critical and liberating, of becoming practical for humanizing ends. Critical reasoning of this sort is not an alien imposition upon Christian theology. To the extent that it thinks and speaks within the narrative structure of Jesus' life, death, and resurrection, Christian theology is compelled to interpret history from the point of view of the victim.

"Do this in memory of me." Central to the enactment of Christian identity is the commemoration of an innocent victim who "suffered and died under Pontius Pilate," and so under a political power charged with the task of maintaining the existing political order for all, even if this should result in suffering for some. Caiaphas's statement reflects quite bluntly the reasoning of political expedience: "It is better for you to have one man die for the people than to have the whole nation destroyed." Such sacrificial reasoning is quite adept at muffling the disturbing voice of the prophet or victim in order to maintain extant political structures. To achieve its self-validating timelessness, the totality of empire must remain oblivious to the disturbing past of injustice and suffering, either by ignoring it altogether, or by synthesizing it into the present as a necessary consequence of its alleged achievements. It is not by chance that every totalitarian regime seeks to refashion or destroy a people's memory. "The enslavement of men begins when their memories of the past are taken away. All forms of colonialization are based on this principle."[70] But this is also why the act of remembering past suffering can be so dangerous. "Every rebellion against suffering is fed by the subversive power of remembered suffering. The memory of suffering continues to resist the cynics of modern political power."[71] The memory of suffering, like the "time" of apocalyptic, is interruptive. It disorients and motivates. It challenges us to consider alternatives to prevailing attitudes and practices. It cannot be included in our narrations of history without provoking questions about how we continue to make it:

> We tend, consciously or unconsciously, to define history as the history of what has prevailed, as the history of the successful and the established. There is hardly any reference in history as we know it to the conquered and defeated or to the forgotten or suppressed hopes of our historical existence. In history, a kind of Darwinism in the sense of the principle of selection tends to prevail. [But] it is of decisive importance that a kind of anti-history should develop out of the memory of suffering — an understanding of history in which the vanquished and destroyed alternatives would also be taken into

account: an understanding of history *ex memoria passionis* as a history of the vanquished.⁷²

Christians are summoned to think "otherwise" about history. Whereas most accounts of history trace its development and meaning according to its "victors" — those who have exercised political, economic, military, and cultural power — the Christian community, whose primary narrative takes the perspective of an expelled *victim* (indeed a narrative in which *God* has accepted the role of the victim as the ultimate expression of love), is charged with the task of critically reflecting upon history from the point of view of history's victims. The problem of unjust suffering must be structural for Christian reasoning, determinative of its hermeneutics of history. Easter is God's efficacious act of memory that brings to life what was violated and destroyed by the cross. It is God's remembrance of Jesus of Nazareth in the particularity and form of his total human existence as lived unto death — his "body" — and in a way that death itself has been overcome. It therefore thrusts into the Christian's awareness the contradictoriness of human life, for it reveals to us what God's ultimate purposes for human beings truly are. Faith in Jesus' resurrection from the dead possesses a "critically liberating force." As Metz puts it, resurrection faith "acts 'contra-factually' in making us free to bear in mind the sufferings and hopes of the past and the challenge of the dead. It allows not only a revolution that will change the things of tomorrow for future generations, but a revolution that will decide anew the meaning of our dead and their hopes. *Resurrection mediated by way of the memory of suffering means: The dead, those already vanquished and forgotten, have a meaning which is as yet unrealized.*"⁷³ This is why Jesus' resurrection from the dead cannot be dismissed as an "otherworldly" hope. It is not a hope for a future that dispenses with history, or one that splits history into categories of "secular" and "sacred." The apocalyptic scope of resurrection faith looks urgently towards definitive justice for the whole of history:

> Such an understanding of the unity of the *memoria passionis* and *memoria resurrectionis* is ... opposed to the attempt to make the conventional distinction between a worldly history of suffering and a history of glory transcending the world, in fact between secular history and salvation-history in the usual sense of the words. Secular history and salvation-history are not two factors that can be equated by means of theological speculation, nor can they (nor ought they to) be merely paradoxically contrasted. Salvation-history is, instead, secular history in which a meaning is conceded

to obscured and suppressed hopes and sufferings. Salvation-history is that secular history in which the vanquished and forgotten possibilities of human existence that we call "death" are allowed a meaning which is not recalled or cancelled by the future course of history.[74]

Lest we imagine that this reading of resurrection language is not biblically warranted, we only need to recall the apocalyptic matrix in which resurrection language was forged, first metaphorically to speak of the corporate destiny of the people of Israel in its history, and later metonymically to speak of the vindication of victims in the face of political domination over bodies and cultural assimilation by imperial power. This is one of the reasons why the Easter event, when stripped of its apocalyptic character in the interests of a "demythologizing" program, presumably in order to make it more palatable to modern sensibilities, not only loses much of its historically productive and practical force, but actually ensures its irrelevance in our contemporary situation. The interpretation of Jesus' bodily resurrection in terms of his ongoing "spiritual presence" in eternity, or as the verification that beyond death we too may be "alive unto God," serves to undermine the social and political character of Easter. N. T. Wright puts it well: "The resurrection, in the full Jewish and early Christian sense, is the ultimate affirmation that creation matters, that embodied human beings matter. That is why resurrection has always had an inescapably political meaning."[75]

Just as the earliest Christians spoke of Jesus' resurrection as God's victory over principalities and powers, even assigning to the crucified-and-risen One a title of Caesar's — *kyrios*, "Lord" — so too are Christians empowered by the "subversive memory" of Jesus' resurrection to resist the temptation "to idolize cosmic and political powers and make them absolute."[76] Such memory summons Christians to denounce and resist all forms of totality while actively contributing to the emancipation of those who suffer injustice in their bodies. Such solidarity with those who suffer, and praxis in the world for their well-being, is intrinsic to "knowing" Jesus in discipleship. It is a knowing as doing, a knowing in the form of imitation in discipleship. "It is only when they imitate Christ that Christians know who it is to whom they have given their consent and who saves them." There is no subordination of narrative ("theory") to commandment ("praxis") in the New Testament. "These New Testament stories of the imitation of Christ are in themselves *appellative* and *imperative*. They attempt to *change the listening subject* in the telling of the story and to make him ready to imitate Christ."[77]

As was stressed in chapter 2, the resurrection narratives are not merely descriptions of an isolated "event" with a static meaning. They are narrative performances of a practical sort that attempt to "show how" the risen Jesus may be known. They are performative and self-involving. As commission narratives they do not simply relate information regarding the aftermath of Jesus' death. They open up a narrative *habitus* and invite a "living-into" among Christians whose own narrative identities become grafted onto the narrative form of Jesus' life, death, and resurrection. This means that to the extent that we participate in Jesus' mission we are *already*, in fragmentary but very real fashion, participating in the future of creation.

Chapter Six

TRANSFIGURING THE VICTIM

We now transition to the work of liberation theologian Jon Sobrino to further explore the apocalyptic matrix of Easter faith. If the work of Metz (along with Schillebeeckx) allows us to outline the relationship of temporality, suffering, and memory within the agonistic structure of resurrection proclamation, Sobrino's work allows us to analyze other crucial aspects.[1] Sobrino's theology of the resurrection, particularly as presented in the second volume of his two-part christology, *Christ the Liberator: A View from the Victims,* represents one of the most original and compelling retrievals of the apocalyptic imagination in contemporary theology.[2] As the subtitle indicates, the work adopts a selective viewpoint for appropriating resurrection language and the subsequent christology of the classical period. This is not arbitrary, argues Sobrino. It reflects the testimony of apocalyptic hope, which heralds above all else the themes of vindication and justice for the vanquished. In Sobrino's estimation studies of Jesus' resurrection have grown stagnant in recent decades for two main reasons: they focus on the future, while saying little about how Easter faith practically impacts the present; and they ignore the partiality that is fundamental to the eschatological hope — a partiality for victims.[3]

As we engage Sobrino's work we are afforded a twofold opportunity. First, we shall see how the task of bringing justice to victims is essential for any adequate account of Christian hope; how Christians are called to participate in the resurrection here and now by becoming "co-raisers" with God in history. Rightly understood, the Christian practice of bringing justice to victims proleptically anticipates the future resurrection of the dead. Such an understanding coheres with the narrative-practical approach to the problem of unjust suffering in history. Secondly, but as a point of critical assessment, we shall see that the themes of vindication and justice in resurrection theology, if emphasized to the diminution of other crucial themes, particularly that of forgiveness and reconciliation, begin to reveal limitations and even court potential dangers. As I will continue to argue, Jesus' resurrection *fulfills* apocalyptic eschatology through its *transformation*. This especially pertains to the tendency in apocalyptic thinking to assert distinctions between the just and unjust. Although we can only support Sobrino's "view from the victims" as faithful to the agonistic testimony of Easter, there is a risk that the opposition between "victims" and "victimizers" in Sobrino's work perpetuates the social dualities that Jesus' resurrection overcomes in the offer of reconciling grace. The critical question we will need to keep in mind as we move towards the conclusion of this chapter is this: to what extent does the "view from the victims" in Sobrino's theology of the resurrection adequately reflect the risen victim's offer of forgiveness and hospitality to his victimizers? In short, does Sobrino's emphasis on the resurrection in terms of justice do enough to account for the double reversal outlined by Acts 2?

A VIEW FROM THE VICTIMS

Universality and Partiality

We have noted on several occasions the cosmic and universal significance of Jesus' resurrection from the dead. While this is essential for understanding how by its very nature the resurrection discloses God's ultimate purposes for the entire community of creation, there is a risk that all talk of "universality" fails to take into account its dialectical character. For example, when theologians like Wolfhart Pannenberg emphasize the apocalyptic scope of Easter in order to show how the earliest Christians could interpret it as the definitive self-revelation of God in history, Sobrino asks whether its agonistic structure, which heralds *justice* for victims while issuing a call to *conversion* for oppressors, has become muted. If our interest in apocalyptic remains concerned primarily with the evolution of formal christological claims about Jesus' relationship to God,[4] or with elaborating theses for a general theology of revelation,[5] however valid the undertaking in itself, we must not fail to underscore the difference in implication this revelation will bear depending upon the situation of the addressee. As is quite typical in contemporary theology, Pannenberg develops transcendental arguments to demonstrate the intelligibility and meaningfulness of Jesus' resurrection as the fulfillment of the human desire for ultimate meaning in history. Pannenberg speaks of a universal hope that all human beings share as the intellectual-affective horizon within which the proclamation of Jesus' resurrection may be initially grasped as meaningful. But according to Sobrino, this hope, while universal in scope and significance, is by no means generic. Neither is it without demands.

If we are to speak *apocalyptically* about this hope, and not just transcendentally, we must say that hope in the resurrection is a "qualified hope." It stands "in the midst of and in the face of the negative aspect of history, a hope against injustice and death suffered unjustly."[6] Hope in apocalyptic terms is dialectical, which means that it is formed in an over-against relation to negativity in history. It does not just look toward the end of history, but the end of history in terms of theodicy.[7] It is a hope for *victims* and a denunciation of the injustices that produce them. Rather than the egoistic perspective of transcendental argumentation that yearns for "my" survival beyond death, Easter faith calls for a *"de-centered hope."*[8] The Christian hermeneutical principle should not have the transcendental ego as its perspectival pivot. Transcendental hope may be a necessary condition for understanding Jesus' resurrection, but it remains insufficient. Transcendental hope may be well suited for speaking of individual survival beyond death in terms of "immortality," but if we are to speak of "resurrection" we will need to retrieve the apocalyptic matrix within which such language emerged, which specifically means understanding hope in terms of eschatological justice. Coming to grips with the biblical account of hope requires a process of *conversion*, of accommodating ourselves to its startling specificity: "We have to *slot ourselves* into this hope, and by doing so we can rebuild — with different, though ultimately similar, mediations — the process followed by Israel's faith in a God of resurrection."[9] As hearers of the word of resurrection we must be willing to allow our egoistic perspectives to become transformed by the hope of the Other, especially that of the victim. "[S]uch a hope is difficult; it requires us to make the hope of victims, and with it their situation, our own."[10] But this difficulty is only the difficulty of the "evangelical precept that forgetting oneself is the condition for rediscovering oneself in Christian terms; hope of one's own resurrection depends on hope in the resurrection of victims."[11]

"In the earliest Christian preaching," declares Sobrino, "Jesus' resurrection was expressed in a dialectic-antagonistic framework."[12] Citing Acts 2 and its parallel formulations (Acts 3:14ff.; 4:10; 5:30; 10:39ff.; 13:28ff.), Sobrino seizes upon its grammar of reversal to characterize God's salvific activity in terms of eschatological liberation. As in the Exodus, where God's advocacy for the enslaved Hebrew people comes about *"dialectically* and *confrontationally* in battle with other divinities," the resurrection of Jesus from the dead reflects "the *struggle of the gods."* Though Peter's bold words speak of Easter's universal significance, they

are notable for their agonistic framing: "'This man...you...killed....
But God raised him up' (Acts 2:23f.). God's life-giving action is reaction
to the death-dealing action of the gods (through their agents)."[13] Sobrino
insists we miss something fundamental about the resurrection if we do
not take note of this conflict. The power of God revealed in it is not the
expression of God's omnipotence in the abstract but the concrete realization of God's power as healing and transformative. It is more than the
overcoming of death in general. It is the overcoming of *unjust death* as
wielded by social and political powers. If Christians have extrapolated
from this event the broader significance of God's lordship over life and
death, this is perfectly legitimate only if such universality is understood
as radiating out from its liberating particularity. "What is specific about
Jesus' resurrection is...not what God does with a dead body but what
God does with a victim.... God is the God who liberates victims."[14] The
"founding act of the New Testament" is a "*liberating* act: doing justice
to a victim."[15]

Along with this address of hope to victims comes a word of apocalyptic judgment for those who produce them. When Peter declares,
"This man...*you* crucified and killed," those responsible for the death
of Jesus are named and confronted with their guilt. We should not think
of these agents as representing only a handful of people. The accusation and judgment in Acts is apocalyptic in its sweep. The scope of the
"you" is alarmingly inclusive, encompassing a network of people and
powers who together mediate the "anti-Kingdom" that rejected Jesus'
ministry and person with violence: the religious and political leaders in
Jerusalem motivated by temple politics and the preservation of social-economic order; the "lawless Gentiles," including Pilate and the military
apparatus of the *pax romana;* the maddening crowd ("You who are
Israelites") under the sway of collective impulses for self-preservation
through scapegoat violence. While this apocalyptic judgment comes
through the testimony of an apostle, it bears the pattern of Jesus' own
prophetic ministry. Only this adequately explains why Jesus found himself the victim of such powers to begin with. As Sobrino makes clear in
his earlier volume, *Jesus the Liberator: A Historical-Theological View,*
what is "good news" for all human beings will be received differently
according to the situation of the addressee. "Jesus offered God's love
to all, but not in the same way."[16] "Blessed" are the poor, the hungry,
those who mourn, those who are persecuted; but "woe" to you who
are rich, who are full now, who are laughing now, who are spoken well
of (Luke 6:20–23). Though Jesus excluded no one from the Kingdom
(Jesus was not sectarian), his message of "good news" turns out to be

a provocation and call to conversion, especially for those who benefit from social and religious privilege. Had Jesus' Kingdom ministry not exhibited such partiality, had it been an irenic call to love one another without the uncomfortably pointed insistence that we give up security to love our enemies, give up false conceptions of purity to associate with the unclean, give up wealth to elevate the poor, and give up power to serve the powerless, it is unlikely that when Jesus arrived in Jerusalem he would have attracted notice, much less get crucified as a blasphemer and enemy of the state.

By speaking of God's "liberating partiality" in this way, Sobrino gives forceful expression to one of the characteristic dualities in apocalyptic literature — the *social duality* between the just and the unjust. But apocalyptic is only an amplified rendering of the same theme throughout the Old Testament, so Sobrino insists.

> God taking sides in this way seems to me to be a constant element of revelation. It is clearly shown by the choice God makes in support of some as opposed to and against others.... Abel is opposed to Cain, Moses to the Pharaoh, the leaders of the Jewish people to the poor majorities. In the New Testament, the *Magnificat* contrasts the lowly with the powerful; Jesus contrasts the poor, those who hunger and thirst, with the rich, who laugh and have their fill; children with the wise; sinners with the just; publicans and prostitutes with Pharisees and scribes and so on.[17]

As Sobrino states repeatedly, God is revealed as on the side of the poor *"simply because they are poor."*[18] This does not mean that salvation is only for the poor. Salvation is for the rich and the powerful too. Those who are well-fed and laughing now are not excluded; but their offer of salvation comes with the command to turn toward the poor and oppressed with compunction and mercy, to enter into solidarity with those who are the primary addressees of Jesus' words of blessing, and thus to share in that blessing as actors *in persona Christi*. Those who are recipients of Jesus' words of "woe" encounter revelation as a dramatic "counter-experience," to adopt Marion's terminology, since the experience occurs in the mode of contradiction — as a call to conversion from a state of life incompatible with the Kingdom of God. In the story of the rich young man, for example, the reversal is acute, a "saturation upon saturation." Told to sell his goods and give the proceeds to the poor, Jesus' encounter with him implies a "redoubling: one must not only respect the gaze of the poor (not objectify them, but recognize their originarity) and, in doing that, come to stand before the irregardable gaze of Christ; one must also annul all possession and all originarity in order to 'give [oneself] to the poor,' therefore to the first among them."[19] In the (non-objectifiable) face of the poor is found the "counter-gaze" of Christ himself. "Truly I tell you, just as you did it to one of the least of these who are members of my family, you did it to me" (Matt. 25:40). Sobrino's meditation upon the poor as the "crucified people" in history takes this identification with absolute seriousness. The poor and oppressed of our world bear the marks of injustice, and in their bodies suffer the world's iniquities; they mediate, painfully and protractedly, the crucified body of Christ in our history. At the same time, they serve as a "light to the nations" by offering, in a quasi-sacramental way, the gift of salvation to those who help create or tolerate the circumstances of their oppression. By bringing life to the victims of injustice, life may also be received.[20]

If Sobrino vigorously presses into service the social duality between poor and rich, oppressed and oppressor, victim and victimizer, even articulating this duality to a degree not often seen in theology, we must appreciate that his purpose is not to incite conflict between social groups or to keep the righteous and unrighteous separated by an eschatological divide delineated by an inverted purity system. His purpose is to help create conditions for solidarity among persons. To the extent that Sobrino adopts the trope of partiality, he intends that it give those who contribute to the suffering and oppression in our world a new frame of reference — a "view from the victims" — as the first step in bringing about the necessary revolution in human affairs for global justice. The purpose is not to reverse the role of oppressor and oppressed, or to intensify *resentiment* (Nietzsche) among those who occupy the unfortunate echelon of a socio-economy hierarchy. The purpose is to establish the kind of blessed mutuality that can only begin when justice and reconciliation embrace.

> The crucified people are prepared to forgive their oppressors. They do not want to triumph over them, but to share with them, and offer them a future.... When the crucified people allow the oppressors' world to approach them, they make it possible for this world to recognize itself for what it is, sinful, but also to know that it is forgiven. In this way they introduce into the oppressors' world the humanizing reality so absent from it, grace: becoming something not only through what you achieve, but also through what is given to you, unhoped for, undeserved and gratuitously.[21]

We must pause to appreciate this modification of the sometimes rigid social duality that frequently attends apocalyptic literature. What

Sobrino articulates here will become especially important in the following chapter as we explore how Jesus' resurrection from the dead opens up a new economy, a new set of relations (one might say im-possible) between victims and victimizers which peacefully overcomes the dialectic of "us" and "them" through the Gift.

In pursuing this issue, however, we shall have to ask whether Sobrino has given adequate attention to the resurrection on precisely this point, i.e., whether he has sufficiently accounted for the way Jesus' resurrection from the dead is also the definitive offer of *forgiveness* to victims *and* victimizers. Quoting Karl Rahner approvingly, but perhaps not quite penetrating its full significance, Sobrino states: "At the same time the miracle described in Karl Rahner's phrase, 'Only the forgiven know they are sinners,' now takes place."[22] Sobrino speaks personally here of the way he has witnessed the willingness of the poor to forgive their oppressors, how forgiveness brings about a new relation that breaks cyclical violence.[23] But what makes such forgiveness possible? What enables a victim to forgive his or her oppressor even before the latter has expressed any compunction? Why should a victim forgive an oppressor who may not even desire forgiveness or respond positively to the victim's call for justice? From a Christian point of view, such is possible (even commanded) because of God's prior offer of forgiveness to all of us, whether we understand ourselves to be "victims" or "victimizers." Jesus' resurrection is more than justice, though it surely is that; it is the gratuitous offer of hospitality to sinners even before the awareness of sin, indeed, as the precondition for such awareness. Only from the perspective *of* this forgiveness can sinfulness become visible (or "remembered") in its radicality. "The ultimate and radical nature of guilt itself," writes Rahner, "lies in the fact that it takes place in the face of a loving and self-communicating God, and only when a person knows this and makes this truth his own can he understand the depths of guilt."[24] The resurrection acts to recreate memory and identity; and herein lays the deepest possibility for the kind of solidarity of which Sobrino speaks. For what produces divisions in the human community runs deeper than any economic or sociological factor. At the heart of every person — and here we must include both victims and victimizers — is the possibility of a conflict, a mimetic rivalry with the Other that easily leads to exclusion and violence, and which can justify itself with even the noblest of reasons, including that of "justice." Justice without the primacy of love, without forgiveness, too easily begets new forms of injustice as each side in a conflict can claim the status of victim.

The Idols of the Anti-Kingdom

In keeping with another important theme developed in his first volume, Sobrino presents the resurrection as God's confrontation with and triumph over the powers of sin and evil — the "idols" of the "anti-Kingdom."[25] This apocalyptic rhetoric should not be dismissed as *mere* rhetoric, as though providing a cosmetic flourish that only intensifies heat in language without adding any light. Such rhetoric serves to illuminate the social-structural dimensions of sin and evil, i.e., their objective, semi-autonomous reality; the way they gain systemic influence in the human life-world. Without overlooking the individual responsibility of persons involved, such an understanding allows us to outline the reality of evil and sin in its *impersonal* manifestation, as it courses through the complex mediations of institutions, economic systems, class structure, ideology, and culture. Racism, for example, represents sinfulness on both a personal and structural level, for it is not only reflected in the attitudes and actions of individual persons; it becomes sedimented in and self-perpetuating through economic conditions, legal systems, political policies, educational systems, city planning, cultural images, and so forth. While the level of participation in such structures (and thus culpability) will vary from person to person depending on their realm of influence, sinfulness in the human community can take on some of its most comprehensively destructive forms when "it" is allowed to exist unnamed and uncontested, almost as if "it" had become "second nature." For Sobrino, whose immediate context is the crushing poverty and subhuman squalor found throughout Latin America, the sheer magnitude of injustice cannot be attributable only to the sum of those individuals who may be more or less directly responsible for maintaining a situation of oppression; it is evidence of a malevolent force of irreducible complexity that subsists in the mode of predation, inscribing itself at a visceral level in the human life-world.

If many in the "first world" find the apocalyptic language of the New Testament a source of embarrassment, many in the so-called "third world" find it all-too-intelligible. This is not because they have yet to undergo the intellectual enlightenment that comes with scientific progress, so that what once was regarded as demonic can now be explained in terms of physical or psychological disease. It is because they experience life in terms of a great conflict between tectonic, social-spiritual forces. For those caught within the gears of a history that seems bent upon their annihilation, the New Testament's language of the "principalities and powers" possesses unmatched descriptive potency. "For our struggle is not against enemies of blood and flesh, but against the rulers, against the authorities, against the cosmic powers of this present darkness, against the spiritual forces of evil in the heavenly places" (Eph. 6:12).[26] This aspect of New Testament theology has remained largely neglected in modern theology, though recent currents in biblical theology, as well as political and liberation theology, have shown the importance of this language as a crucial first step in naming and unmasking the reality of sin and evil. While there are many differences between the first century and our contemporary context, a "structural similarity" in social-spiritual climate exists between the world of the poor today and the world of those who were the first recipients of Jesus' "good news."[27]

> We know that in our own day there are thousands of people whose deaths are like Jesus' and the causes of whose deaths — as alleged by their executioners — are similar to the cause alleged against Jesus. These lives that today lead to this type of death have essentially the same structure as that claimed for the life of Jesus: proclamation of the Kingdom to the poor, defense of the oppressed and confrontation with their oppressors, the proclamation of the God of life and the condemnation of idols.[28]

As is especially evident in Sobrino's work, the appropriation of "historical Jesus" studies in liberation theology differs in method and interest from the typical Anglo-European approach. The latter is fueled by the Enlightenment suspicion of tradition and myth and focuses on questions of historical *veracity*. The former tends to focus on the liberative power of Jesus' life and mission in the face of historical *conflict*. "Depacification," rather than "demythologization," is the main interest of political and liberation theology.[29] And so, when the New Testament portrays the dramatic action of Jesus' Kingdom of God ministry in apocalyptic terms — as a direct and extended confrontation with the sum of those conditions (physical, social, and spiritual) that oppress human beings; as a battle with the unifying source ("the Satan") of these forces — those who are themselves victims of complex systems of oppression find in such language descriptive adequacy and motivating power.

Sobrino's language of the "anti-Kingdom" is strikingly similar to Walter Wink's analysis of the "Domination System." More than anyone else in recent biblical scholarship, Wink has sought to retrieve the language of "the powers" as indispensable for theology.[30] According to Wink, the principalities and powers, whether they be social groups, public institutions, corporations, schools, churches, nations, cultures, economic systems, legal systems, etc., possess a spiritual (depth) dimension as well as a material-historical dimension. Just as a corporate personality emerges from the complex interactions of individuals, yet is not reducible to the sum of individuals — one can think of the *ethos* of a people, the "spirit of an age," the tacit-level knowledge and habits of an organization — the principalities and powers are socio-spiritual structures that help sustain and give shape to human life. Such structures are *originally* good. From a Christian theological point of view, human beings are by nature both social and personal. Social structures are not a "necessary evil," but part of the fabric that sustains the *humanum*. And yet such structures can deviate from their original purpose and become hostile to human well-being, in which case they exhibit *fallenness* and stand in need of *redemption*.[31] When multiple powers collude to mutually reinforce their destructiveness in the human community, they can bring about large-scale social transformations to produce a system of domination. Just as converging atmospheric factors can produce a massive weather system of qualitatively new complexity, so that, as a system, it takes on a life of its own, so too can the powers in the human life-world converge to produce a climate of oppression. As Wink helpfully points out, those who are in the grip of a system of domination, whether they be victims or perpetrators (or some combination thereof), are often unaware of its spiritual reach. We can become entranced by the way things are that we are no longer capable of envisioning alternatives. "Like addicts who cannot tell how distorted their perceptions have become until they get off drugs, we too cannot recognize the depth of our alienation from life until we are well on the way toward healing.... [W]e cannot redeem ourselves from a system whose malignancy we scarcely recognize and whose blandishments we have come to crave. We need revelation, to see our state, and liberation, to be freed from it."[32] Wink is articulating here a full-blooded doctrine of "the fall." He is not suggesting that we imagine the fall taking place in some mythic time that is transmitted to us through procreative generation. Neither is he suggesting that human beings are utterly destitute of the *imago Dei*. He is saying that fallenness is a condition that takes on a social-cultural as well as a personal form in human life, a condition that has existed from time-immemorial in our collective history, and that one of its chief characteristics is its power to mesmerize, to warp the field of our perception so that we grow incapable of actually perceiving our sinfulness. What is required in this situation is a revelation, an *apocalypsis,* an "in-breaking" into the circle of our illusion.

For Sobrino, one of the primary ways the negative power of the anti-Kingdom takes spiritual root among the poor and oppressed is by producing the feeling of historical (cosmic) impotence. For those who have been oppressed and marginalized for so long that it has become "normal," simply the way things are — "metaphysically necessary," to use a philosophical locution — despair has burrowed itself so deeply into their consciousness that they have difficulty even knowing how to hope, how to dare envisioning a reality alternative to the one the powers that be have established for them. Sobrino offers a basic definition of such poor: "The poor are those who have all the powers of this world against them: oligarchies, government, armed forces, party politics and, sometimes, churches and cultural institutions."[33] The apocalyptic framing of "the powers of this world" is unmistakable, as is the way Sobrino speaks of a growing conflict in history between human and anti-human forces, between God's Kingdom and the anti-Kingdom.[34] The crisis of our situation, according to Sobrino, is deepening. Those who we may describe as "the poor," "the victims," "the crucified peoples" (these terms are synonymous for Sobrino[35]): such persons find it difficult simply to survive, much less to actualize the fuller potential of their humanity in a healthy social, cultural, and economic environment. The number of such persons is growing rapidly, as is the gap between those who possess wealth and power and those who do not.[36]

In the face of such historic-cosmic calamity, the apocalyptic praxis of the liberation theologian proceeds first by *naming a hope* in the midst of widespread despair. "The deepest impact of liberation theology, I believe, lies in helping the poor to overcome this feeling of helplessness and powerlessness, to believe that liberation from oppressive forces is possible."[37] In contrast to those renderings of eschatology that take exception to apocalyptic, such a project names a hope that cannot be extrapolated from the present. Whereas a more sapiential-oriented eschatology interprets the present moment as *already* participating in the eschatological future, so that hope comes from a depth dimension *within* the present, an apocalyptic-oriented eschatology interprets the present moment from the perspective of a future that, while the genuine fulfillment of history, and not its simple negation, nevertheless appears as the *interruption* of the present. The agonistic logic of apocalyptic eschatology moves *from* the unforeseen future *to* the present, rather than the opposite. What Collins says of apocalyptic texts more generally is quite applicable to Sobrino's formulation of hope. "In [apocalyptic] texts, while the present experience of righteousness gives rise to the hope of final vindication, it is also true that the hope of final vindication confirms and even makes possible the present experience of righteousness and divine approval."[38] Thus the present moment stands under the corrective judgment of God's absolute future; and it is because of this apocalyptic future that persons within present situations of domination may hope, are given the strength to endure, are emboldened to resist and fight against injustice, even if it means that violent death may await them for doing so.

> Jesus' resurrection is hope, first of all, for those crucified in history. God raised a crucified man, and since then there is hope for the crucified. They can see the raised Jesus as the firstborn from among the dead, because they truly — and not just intentionally — see him as their elder brother. This gives them the courage to hope in their own resurrection, and they can now take heart to live in history, which supposes a "miracle" analogous to what happened in Jesus' resurrection.[39]

Again, we must notice the modal emphasis of this hope. The logic is less *from* the present *to* the future, as we find in sapiential readings ("projections of hopes experienced in the present"[40]); it is the reverse. Though Sobrino will speak of "analogies" of Jesus' resurrection in our history — and thus we shall find a more than tenuous hinge between the "already" and "not-yet" poles of eschatology — the circumstances faced by the poor and oppressed require an imaginative leap into a future that present experience does not readily corroborate, if at all. Framed in this way, we must say the following: *because* Jesus is risen from the dead; *because* his resurrection anticipates the future resurrection of the dead, victims may "take heart to live in history." Such hope "breaks in" as a saving interruption, as a breach of totality — a "miracle." This is the Gift of apocalyptic: it throws open an im-possible future for victims, both living and dead.

In addition to naming hope, the apocalyptic rhetoric of the liberation theologian seeks to bring crisis to consciousness and put before the reader a *decision*.[41] In a manner similar to Peter's structural indictment ("You that are Israelites"), or Moses' farewell speech to the Israelites — "I call heaven and earth to witness against you today that I have set before you life and death, blessings and curses. Choose life so that you and your descendants may live" (Deut. 30:19) — Sobrino testifies on behalf of victims ("the poor," the "crucified peoples") and calls upon all who participate, directly or indirectly, in their victimization to recognize personal guilt and begin adopting attitudes and practices that, on both the personal and social order, will bring justice and life. In a move that highlights the practical dimension of the resurrection narratives, Sobrino argues that the hermeneutical key for understanding the content of Easter proclamation is entering into the praxis of liberation. As a reader I am not only in-formed but invited into a process of trans-formation that proceeds by seeing the crucified-and-risen Jesus in all those who suffer as a result of the way I live my life, whether through my activity or negligence. I am summoned to see in my victim my hope. I am called to become a "co-raiser" with God.

Becoming "Co-raisers" with God

In chapter 2, I maintained that the presence/absence structure in the resurrection narratives represents a "logic of birthing" (G. Ward). The withdrawal of Jesus' body in resurrection and ascension is a generative absence that initiates a process in which the witnesses of Easter accede to the body of Christ. Through a creative and gracious "distance," the followers of the risen Jesus are afforded the "space" to analogize in history, through community and apostolic mission in the world, the form of Christ. "Jesus *effaces himself*," writes Michel de Certeau, "to give faithful witness to the Father who authorizes him, and to 'give rise' to different but faithful communities, which he makes possible."[42] Though it would be improper to assert that Jesus "rises into the community of disciples" without remainder, or that his "resurrection" is simply the continuation of his "cause" within the apostolic community — such a functionalist approach, as I have argued, fails to account for the *alterity* and bodiliness of the risen Christ — it is nevertheless important to appreciate how the revelation of Jesus' resurrection from the dead gives birth to a history of effects that manifests its character. Were this not true, the resurrection would be the great exception to history, not its proper fulfillment.

Sobrino's treatment of the resurrection narratives as commission narratives stands as one of the more arresting and important of such treatments in contemporary theology. While affirming the necessarily apostolic character of Easter faith as "something handed down to us as an offer to be accepted — which is what the New Testament states — on the basis of the credibility of the disciples," Sobrino asserts that such an assent remains reasonable and even "experiential" in an analogous way today.[43] Though an "act of faith," which at least negatively implies assenting to that which is not verifiable with certainty, there are sufficient convergent factors that allow Christians to trust the content of apostolic testimony. As is characteristic of most contemporary theological approaches, Sobrino reviews some of the most important historical-critical problems related to the empty tomb and appearance narratives and argues for their general historical reliability.[44] What is most unique about Sobrino's approach, however, is the way he adapts techniques of transcendental approaches in fundamental theology for a practical end. Key to this adaptation is the category of analogy.

To begin with, Sobrino consistently affirms the *sui generis* character of Jesus' resurrection. "The resurrection of Jesus is an eschatological event, the irruption of the ultimate into history. It is, then, a sort of overall reality, and as such it is not accessible directly but only from a particular point of view."[45] The self-disclosure of the risen Christ is without precedent, beyond schematization, non-objectifiable. Easter is trans-historical, and thus it saturates every horizon within history. Sobrino also affirms the uniqueness and non-repeatability of the original appearances of Christ to the disciples. He therefore distances himself from those who so generalize the appearance narratives that the qualitative difference between the disciples' encounter with the risen Christ and our own is collapsed.[46] All subsequent encounters with the presence of Christ throughout history "are referred back to the original Easter experience."[47]

Such insistence on uniqueness of the original Easter experiences does not imply that apostolic testimony is to be received only in an extrinsic fashion, however. We too may "share in the experience of the first witnesses."[48] The very character of the resurrection is such that it generates effects in our history so as to grant participation in it in a real, if partial, way. While retaining its transcendence *over* history, it brings forth *within* history vestiges that reproduce its original power and significance. Were this not true, if Jesus' resurrection did not continue to generate novelty in our world, if it did not insinuate and analogize itself in our history, transforming and continually shepherding it toward its ultimate purpose, then we would have to say that Easter is only incidentally related to our world. We would fall into what Sobrino calls a "deism of the resurrection, according to which the presence of the eschatological was made manifest in history at the beginning but not afterward."[49] We would therefore fail to account for the New Testament's insistence on the continuing presence of the risen Christ in the Spirit.

This relationship of Easter's historical transcendence and immanence, its otherness and radical nearness, is what enables us to affirm the analogical nature of Christian praxis. If we take the resurrection/commission narratives with the seriousness they demand, we must say that we are called to become "co-raisers" with God in history. God's act of raising Jesus from the dead is a *praxis,* not merely an idea. It is an eschatological act that overflows into history. One of the ways it does so is through the praxis of liberation and reconciliation in history. Sobrino is careful to denote the qualitative difference between God's eschatological act and our co-operative participation in it. It is not as though the latter reproduces Jesus' resurrection as such. Yet it does so *analogously*, in a historically mediated fashion. Thus, when we are engaged in acts of mercy towards victims, when we bring new life to those written off by history as dead, we imitate the eschatological action of God towards the crucified Jesus. We become "co-raisers" in history. We take the crucified people down from the cross.

Sobrino speaks of an "eschatological fullness" to Jesus' resurrection that "reverberates" through history in "analogous form."[50] Such reverberations are manifold, including joyous celebration in liturgy and ecclesial community;[51] proclamation of the gospel of life without fear;[52] experiences of gratitude for life and love in the midst of death; experiences of hope in situations of extreme desperation;[53] encounters of unsuspected joy in the midst of despondency; sharing that joy with others;[54] experiences of freedom to die to oneself for the Other, and thus, by grace, "rising again" in the Spirit of the risen Christ which pours itself out in selfless love.[55] But above all, when justice is brought about in situations of domination, when the victims of history are brought down from the cross of their political, economic, and social oppression, something of the eschatological surplus of Jesus' resurrection from the dead is mediated in our world as anticipations of that world to come. "Putting oneself at the service of the resurrection means working continually, often against hope, in the service of eschatological ideals: justice, peace, solidarity, the life of the weak, community, dignity, celebration, and so on. And these partial 'resurrections' can generate hope in the final resurrection, the conviction that God did indeed perform the impossible, gave life to one crucified and will give life to all the crucified."[56]

Toward the conclusion of *Jesus the Liberator*, in a moving meditation upon Isaiah's "suffering servant" motif, Sobrino quotes Ignacio Ellacuría, which he does often: "Ask yourselves: what have I done to crucify them? What do I do to uncrucify them? What must I do for this people to rise again?"[57] These are haunting questions. They come to us to disturb and awake. In them we can hear the apocalyptic cries of those who suffer injustice in our world. And just maybe we will be impacted by them in the way those listening to Peter's words were impacted: "[A]nd they were cut to the heart and said to Peter and the other apostles, 'Brothers, what should we do?'" (Acts 2:37). This close connection between *hearing* and *heeding* the word of resurrection, of responding to its proclamation through conversion and praxis, shows that in their appropriation today the resurrection narratives come in the form of "creative witness. This desire and intention to bring something new to the world is the common horizon which is shared by both text and interpreter and which makes it possible for us to comprehend the resurrection. Only in that case will the interpreter be following in the footsteps of the texts." In short, "the hermeneutics of the resurrection is the apostolate itself."[58] In a move that shifts the hermeneutical circle of understanding from a primarily ideational to a practical axis — without, however, denying the cognitive element — Sobrino (and the political-liberationist approach in general) argues that understanding the resurrection entails living out its summons. "[T]he hermeneutics designed to comprehend the resurrection must be political. This means that it is possible to verify the truth of what happened in the resurrection only through a transforming praxis based on the ideas of the resurrection."[59]

This conviction that praxis should "verify" resurrection belief (or any Christian belief, for that matter) is shared by Edward Schillebeeckx and Jürgen Moltmann, both of whom figure prominently in Sobrino's work. Schillebeeckx argues that while no direct verification of faith-motivated claims is ever possible, evaluating their personally and socially transformative character can provide an "indirect test."[60] The response to the history of suffering and evil is a "practical exercise of resistance to evil, not a theory about it." If history in all its refractoriness is not amenable to theoretical explanation, we can nevertheless bring about meaning, even if in fragmentary fashion, "in a course of action that tries to overcome evil and suffering in the strength of the religious affirmation that things can be otherwise."[61] Easter is therefore something we can "make true." We do not mean this literally, of course. We mean it analogically, in the sense that we may co-operate with God's eschatological act to "extend" the risen body throughout history — through the non-identical repetition made possible by the generative "distance" of his resurrection and ascension. The Christian belief in resurrection gains its credibility in the world by the performance of those who profess it in faith, by their "showing how," by embodying its palpable goodness. The concern within fundamental theology to somehow justify resurrection belief through argumentation misses the mark. The point should be to make our proclamation persuasive by "bodying-forth" the presence of the risen Christ in community and in the world. "In other words," writes Schillebeeckx, "the question whether Christian belief in the resurrection, through which death unmistakably takes on another meaning, opens up a real future for man, will have to be 'proved' again and again, here and now, from corresponding behaviour on the part of Christians, from their activities in this world. Without such consistency, what Christians assert is in fact incredible; furthermore, it has no power of attraction, and above all gives no hope to the world."[62]

Similarly, Moltmann speaks of the resurrection as an ongoing historical process. "Belief in resurrection is not summed up by assent to a dogma and the registering of a historical fact. It means participating in this creative act of God."[63] Moltmann makes the important observation that Paul often links the perfect, present, and future tenses when speaking of the resurrection. "If the Spirit of him who raised Jesus from the dead dwells in you, he who raised Christ from the dead will give life to your mortal bodies also through his Spirit that dwells in you" (Rom. 8:11). We may add to this Paul's frequent exhortations to diligence in the present work for the Kingdom, knowing that nothing gained for it will ever be lost, for Christ has been risen from the dead: " 'Death has been swallowed up in victory. Where, O death, is your victory? Where, O death, is your sting?'... [T]hanks be to God, who gives us the victory through our Lord Jesus Christ. Therefore, my beloved, be steadfast, immovable, always excelling in the work of the Lord, because you know that in the Lord your labor is not in vain" (1 Cor. 15:54–58).[64] For Moltmann, participation in the historical process of resurrection involves co-operation with the power of God "that quickens into life, that makes the poor rich, that lifts up the humble and raises the dead. Faith in the resurrection is itself a living force which raises people up and frees them from the deadly illusions of power and possession, because their eyes are now turned towards the future of life."[65] It thus has "mobilizing, revolutionizing and critical effects upon history."[66]

It must be observed that should we participate in the ongoing history of the resurrection, should we take the commission narratives to heart and thoroughly work through the process of critical reflection that translates into concrete action, we may very well be putting ourselves in danger. If Jesus' death shows us anything, it shows us how costly the work of the Kingdom can be. It also reveals the ultimate idol of the anti-Kingdom — death. Fear of death, especially when propagated by the public display of extreme violence, which was the precise purpose of the perverse liturgy of crucifixion, is the "last enemy." Weaponized and made into spectacle, death becomes the instrument by which the powers arouse shock and awe among a populace they wish to remain compliant. Sobrino reads Jesus' ministry as one that drew the anti-Kingdom's ultimate weapon in a kind of "duel."[67] Because Jesus offered a stark alternative to the system of domination, he quickly attracted its attention... and ire. Jesus' death is therefore the *consequence* of his mission, not its primary goal. He "got in the way" of "a world that is anti-Kingdom, which acts against the Kingdom."[68] Contrary to Bultmann's judgment that Jesus' death was a kind of historical accident — which only further illustrates the apolitical tendencies of existentialist hermeneutics — Sobrino asserts that from a historical and theological point of view it was a necessity. This necessity was not, as is assumed by certain atonement theories, due to a system of (retributive) justice requiring God to discharge wrath upon an innocent victim as an appeasing sacrifice for sin. It was a necessity in the sense that it reflects the perfunctory and predictable way the anti-Kingdom disposes of those bold enough to challenge it. "Jesus' death was not a mistake. It was the consequence of his life and this in turn was the consequence of his particular incarnation — in an anti-Kingdom which brings death — to defend its victims."[69]

The power of the resurrection is that it unmasks the anti-Kingdom's idolatry of death. Despite its ostensible finality, death as such has been broken through by God's eschatological word. The Easter event throws open an im-possible future for those who engage in the praxis of the Kingdom, even unto death.

Such was Ellacuría's fate. A personal friend and colleague of Sobrino's, Ellacuría was one of eight people (six Jesuit priests and two employees of the Jesuit house at the University of Central America) murdered by the Salvadoran army in 1989 for activities deemed threatening by the government.[70] It was Ellacuría who, during a homily some twenty years before his death, spoke words that deeply affected Sobrino (who was in attendance) and which continue to resonate in his work: we must "live as risen beings in history."[71] Living in anticipation of the resurrection sets us free to work towards the goals of the Kingdom with abandonment, without the fear that death will consume and annul all in the end.

Incidentally, it is for this reason why the Sadducees were deeply suspicious of the belief in resurrection. To be sure, there were theological arguments against this "newfangled" idea, including the fact that nowhere in the Torah was the doctrine explicitly articulated. But another reason — one that turned out to be quite prescient — was that those who believed in God's vindication *via* resurrection were more likely to risk their lives fighting against established powers and become martyrs for the sake of righteousness. The resurrection was, as N. T. Wright states, "from the beginning a revolutionary doctrine.... It had to do with the coming new age, when the life-giving god would act once more to turn everything upside down — or perhaps, as they might have said, right way up. It was the sort of belief that encouraged young hotheads to attack

Roman symbols placed on the Temple, and that, indeed, led the first-century Jews into the most disastrous war they had experienced." The logic here is simple: "People who believe that their god is about to make a new world, and that those who die in loyalty to him in the meantime will rise again to share gloriously in it, are far more likely to lose respect for a wealthy aristocracy than people who think that this life, this world and this age are the only ones there ever will be."[72]

TRANSFIGURING THE VICTIM

In this and the previous chapter we have explored the soteriological significance of Jesus' resurrection in terms of justice. By raising an innocent victim from the dead, a man whose life's mission it was to proclaim and concretely realize the Kingdom of God, God has been revealed as one who sides with victims, as one who promises to bring forth justice to the poor and oppressed, the weak and the outcast, and thus a God who summons persons directly and indirectly responsible for oppression to convert and actively participate in the coming Kingdom. By taking the crucified people down from the cross, by uplifting the poor and oppressed in our history to a human wholeness that God intends for us all, we anticipate the future resurrection of the dead. Our praxis has eschatological bearing and significance. We become "co-raisers" with God in history.

This theme of justice is crucial to any adequate account of Christian salvation, and much of what gives this theme its unique character and urgency is the apocalyptic dimension of Christian faith. The resurrection is more than a redundancy element here. It is not just the validation and continuation of Jesus' historical ministry, i.e., his "cause," though it surely includes this. The resurrection of Jesus from the dead constitutes God's dramatic in-breaking into the real and imagined totalities in which we are enclosed. Because it breaks through the barrier of death to speak a word of *eschatological* justice, it reveals that, after all, time is God's time, that all our machinations for closing off the interruptive grace of the divine Other, which would only make our own programs (and pogroms) of progress seem self-validating and inevitable, stand under God's judgment. It is not for us to slot the reality of the resurrection within our preconceptions of what constitutes "history." The resurrection of Jesus from the dead establishes for Christians a distinctive hermeneutics of history that is not defined or limited by any scientific, historicist, ideological, evolutionary, or bourgeois ordering of knowledge: it is a history open to God's eschatological justice for the victims of history. From this confessedly "partial" point of view — a "view from the victims" — we are called to not only help redeem the time by bringing justice to victims in our history to the extent this is possible; we are also called to interpret our history with a critical *memoria,* to review our history as a history of suffering, to not allow history to be the province of its self-professed victors. "History" is never a self-evident thing: it is an interpreted thing. And so as Christians look *from* and *through* the resurrection of the victim Jesus to give shape to a worldview — and this worldview cannot be deduced from anything else — we come to see it more and more from the perspective of the sufferings and hopes of the poor and oppressed, both living and dead. This requires imagination because our histories are so proficient at screening out those sufferings and hopes. But this is the very imagination that the apocalyptic dimension of resurrection faith would install within us.

◆ ◆ ◆

As we conclude our study of the justice-character of Jesus' resurrection, we must now ask some leading questions in anticipation of upcoming chapters. Specifically, we must begin inquiring into the ways Jesus' resurrection from the dead brings about important mutations within apocalyptic eschatology, leading it towards its "transfiguration." About this transfiguration we must be very clear: we cannot possibly mean that the apocalyptic imagination is negated. We mean that the broader significance of Jesus' resurrection cannot be expressed within an apocalyptic framework alone. It requires amplification and correction from other thematic trajectories in scripture.

For example, the grammar of reversal is accompanied by a grammar of fulfillment, which highlights the restorative and divinizing impact of Easter. Accordingly, God creates out of an infinite fecundity and brings creatures into being to share in divine life. Such participation is made possible by the "going out" of God's Word into the world, the Word's "returning" to the Father through resurrection, and the outpouring of the Holy Spirit of the risen Christ. The resurrection is situated here within a continuous pattern of descent and ascent, and comprises that moment in which the human creature passes through death in order to realize its final, eschatological form. Together, the grammars of reversal and fulfillment support the prophetic-apocalyptic and mystical-aesthetic dimensions of Christian faith. They are mutually illuminating and corrective. Gustavo Gutiérrez puts the matter concisely: "Mystical language expresses the gratuitousness of God's love; prophetic [apocalyptic] language expresses the demands this love makes. The followers of Jesus and the community they form — the church — live in the space created by this gratuitousness and these demands. Both languages are necessary and therefore inseparable; they also feed and correct each other."[73]

I shall say more about the grammar of fulfillment in chapters 9 and 10, but here we must observe something about the double reversal in preparation for the following chapter. We must consider some of the problems that emerge when we make the apocalyptic matrix overly determinative in resurrection theology. With respect to Sobrino's project in particular, we must again ask whether he has given adequate account of its forgiveness-character. Granted that the dialectical-antagonistic framework of resurrection kerygma in the New Testament gives potent expression to divine vindication and judgment (themes well attested in the biblical tradition), there is reason to believe that Sobrino's presentation does not sufficiently reflect the full range of the double reversal in the very passages he cites in support of his analysis. The limitation of Sobrino's focus is most evident in the rather static (and sometimes abstract) relation that distinguishes "victims" and "victimizers." While it is necessary to articulate some such distinction — indeed, it is morally imperative that we name injustice and innocent suffering — we must ask whether situating persons or groups into categories of "victims" and "victimizers" runs the risk of distorting more complex situations of conflict. Such categories, when left unmodified by another way of envisioning human relations, may only perpetuate conflict in the human community.

Miraslov Volf argues, correctly in my view, that narratives of history which take as their defining plot a dialectical schema of victims/victimizers (oppressed/oppressors) exhibit serious limitations when applied indiscriminately. Particularly in situations of reciprocal violence between groups, where conflict spirals to form complex patterns of reprisal, each side can find new ways to invoke the status of "victim" in order to justify a variety of attitudes and actions towards their "victimizer." Volf by no means advocates dispensing with these categories altogether. Such would "be a mockery of the millions who have suffered at the hands of the violent — battered women, exploited and dehumanized slaves, tortured dissidents, persecuted minorities." "The categories cannot be given up"; and yet, insists Volf, "the *schema* 'oppression/liberation' remains beset with unresolved and deeply disturbing problems."[74]

As Volf sees it, there are at least two problems that demand our careful attention. The first is that while certain situations of oppression allow for more discernable sides in a conflict, conflicts are often morally ambiguous and resistant to clear-cut assignations of guilt and innocence. "How will we disentangle those who are innocent from those who are blameworthy in the knotted histories of individuals, let alone the narratives of whole cultures and nations?"[75] Especially when conflicts between groups are long-standing and characterized by cyclical violence — where even if one side initiated the conflict, the other side engages in reprisals that only introduce new wounds of suffering and injustice, and on and on — each side becomes increasingly entrenched in its own assertion of innocence, locked in a cycle of recrimination and defensiveness. The potential for self-deception in conflict is very great since assertions of innocence, whether contrived or authentic, can deflect attention away from one's own implication in present or future guilt. As we shall see in the following chapter, the formation of one's identity over against the Other, even if this Other is regarded as an oppressor, produces strong incentives for projecting one's own inner violence upon the Other. To the extent that my own identity as "victim" is largely defined in antagonistic terms vis-à-vis my "victimizer" — an "us" versus "them" polarization that presumes conflict as the basis of the relationship — the potential for violent rivalry becomes very great indeed. Because violence is a highly contagious phenomenon, the sense of moral indignation towards one's oppressor can unleash reprisals that only mimic the original injustice. This problem requires that we understand the mechanism of scapegoating that frequently embeds itself in human relationships, and which the gospels thoroughly unmask.

The second major problem that concerns Volf is this: what happens once liberation has been achieved? How do those who fought for liberation live in reconciled relationship with their one-time oppressors? How is it possible to resist simply reversing the relation of oppressed and oppressor once victory has been achieved? Because the categories of oppressed/oppressor presuppose conflict, what categories are available when conflict ceases? As Volf points out, the idea of liberation tends to be defined negatively. It seeks to "overcome" alienation, to "unmask" ideology, to "resist" oppression, and so forth. Even if a positive vision of human wholeness is implied in these terms of "negative contrast" (Schillebeeckx), the dialectical framework within which they are articulated remains insufficient for sustaining reconciled relationships between persons and/or groups previously polarized by conflict. Granted that justice is a basic presupposition for reconciliation, the ultimate goal of justice, Christianly speaking, is not victory *over* the

Other but reconciliation and peace *with* the Other.[76] Only the practice of forgiveness can make peace possible.

Here, above all, we must appreciate the crucial significance of God's offer of forgiveness and hospitality to *both* victims and victimizers. Jesus' ministry, it should be well noted, included an offer of forgiveness and call to conversion to victims too. This offer would be unintelligible and even offensive without understanding the cyclical nature of violence. In the end, it is impossible to clearly divide Jesus' audience into two groups so that one group, the oppressed, is called to hope, whereas the other, the oppressor, is called to change. As challenging as it may be, the gospels call all to repentance. Victims too are called to repent, and herein lies the truly revolutionary character of Jesus' message to the poor and oppressed. What is the nature of this repentance? It is not repentance for the original injustice, of course, but of becoming "shaped in the mirror image of the enemy" — of imitating, in intention, if not in deed, the very violence now implanted in the heart which would fester as indignation and enmity. It is "being released" (forgiven) from the bondage of resentment and hatred for the Other. "Pray for your enemies and love those who persecute you" (Matt. 5:44). Imitation of the risen victim here means being unmoved (mimetically) by the violence of the Other. "If victims do not repent today," writes Volf, "they will become perpetrators tomorrow who, in their self-deceit, will seek to exculpate their misdeeds on account of their own victimization."[77] This divine offer of forgiveness to the "sinned against" is not, it must be stressed, an insult to injury. Forgiveness and conversion in fact restore dignity and freedom to the victim, so that he or she is no longer primarily moved by the injustice and violence of the Other. It is an invitation to a transformation which alone makes reconciliation with one's oppressor possible. It is to this invitation that we now turn.

Chapter Seven

MIMESIS, SCAPEGOATING, AND THE CRUCIFIED

> *Western theology, in rejecting the idea of Satan tricked by the Cross, has lost a pearl of great price in the sphere of anthropology.*
> — René Girard, *I See Satan Fall Like Lightning*

The following two chapters represent an extended study of the resurrection event as God's non-violent offer of forgiveness. The present chapter focuses more on the problem of mimetic and scapegoat violence in human interpersonal relations, and how the dynamic of such violence is operative in Jesus' crucifixion. The following chapter addresses more specifically the grammar of *double reversal* in resurrection kerygma. There I shall state more formally, behind the force of the preceding analysis, the inadequacy of atonement motifs that explicitly or implicitly assume God's endorsement of the violence leading to Jesus' death. Appeal shall be made to the patristic theme of *Christus Victor* as the most effective response to sacrificial atonement theory.

THE BIBLE AND VIOLENCE

The Bible is one of the most violent books in all of sacred literature. There is hardly a subject given more attention in the Bible than the problem of violence. "No other human activity or experience is mentioned as often," writes Raymund Schwager, "be it the world of work or trade, of family or sexuality, or that of knowledge and the experience of nature. For the biblical authors, the most impressive and distressing experience seems to have been that human beings war with and kill one another."[1]

By at least one count, the Old Testament alone contains over six hundred passages involving violence among nations, kings, individuals, and groups, some of which is explicitly sanctioned by YHWH.[2] Nearly one thousand passages speak of YHWH's anger and judgment, including threats to take revenge or bring about total annihilation.[3] No wonder some view the God of the Old Testament as a disturbing character. No wonder many Christians find ways either to ignore or dispense with such images. The church in the second century struggled with this issue in its own way as the theologian Marcion proposed a canon that excised the entire Old Testament (along with distinctively Jewish influences in the New) under the conviction, notably dualistic, that the God of Jesus Christ *replaced* Israel's capricious demiurge. The canon that gradually emerged within Christianity was formed in large part as a response to Marcion and included the writings of the Old Testament as essential for providing a full presentation of salvation history with internal "order and continuity," as Irenaeus of Lyons put it.[4] The previous dispensation was not negated by the new, as Marcion supposed, who sought to "circumcise the scriptures."[5] The new dispensation of Christ fulfills by "recapitulating" the story of Israel. Christ embodies the one creator God in history.[6] "Thus men were taught to worship, not a different God, but the same God in a new way."[7] But the temptation of Marcionism remains a strong one. It is common to hear Christians and non-Christians alike contrast the God of the Old Testament with the New as though we were dealing with such contradictory views of the divine that they may as well represent different gods. But should we flee to the New Testament for reprieve from violence we will find ourselves confronted with an even starker and more shocking dose of it. The passion narratives relate a truly horrifying and gruesome story. Even if these narratives exhibit no voyeuristic interest in the graphic details of Jesus' suffering, they are forthright about the circumstances that led to the brutal torture and death of a man condemned for religious blasphemy and political ambition. That such could somehow be "good news" is not just counter-intuitive; it may seem bizarre and even sadistic.

In an essay entitled "Enlightenment and Crucifixion," D. T. Suzuki, a mid-twentieth-century populizer of Zen Buddhism in the West, expressed bafflement that the crucified Jesus could ever become a symbol for salvation. "Whenever I see a crucified figure of Christ, I cannot help thinking of the gap that lies deep between Christianity and Buddhism.... Christ hangs helpless, full of sadness on the vertically erected cross. To the Oriental mind, the sight is almost unbearable."[8] Having lived in a culture where the symbol of the cross had not deeply permeated its history, literature, and art, Suzuki saw with fresh eyes what many in nominally Christian environments must struggle to appreciate — the scandal of the cross. To show just how scandalous it can be, Suzuki, who engaged extensively and appreciatively in dialogue with psychologists, philosophers, and theologians from the West, nevertheless could only say this as he attempted to wrap his head around this central Christian symbol: "The crucified Christ is a terrible sight and I cannot help associating it with the sadistic impulse of a physically affected brain."[9] For all his training in the art of paradox, Suzuki could find little more to say about what Christians hail as the "victory of the cross" than that it possibly exhibits the symptoms of a collective neurosis. This is not uncharitable of Suzuki. The essay reflects a genuine struggle to understand. And just because the cross may not strike us in the same way does not mean we have come to understand it.

Why is violence so prominent in the Bible? This may seem an especially difficult question for those who argue that the revelation of Jesus Christ is the revelation of a non-violent God and the irruption in our world of a new "economy" or "dispensation," a new possibility for human beings to live a reconciled existence freed from rivalry and violent conflict. What could possibly be the meaning of so much violence in the Bible if it is indeed a story about the establishment of a set of relations between human beings and God founded in reconciliation and peace? Would it not be better if the Bible exhibited considerably less conflict and violence? Would it not be advisable to disregard or maybe allegorize the violence in the Bible in order to craft a more constructive view of God and humanity? What about those passages which speak of God's wrath and agency in violence? What about the "victory of the cross," if indeed a victory it can be called? Does all this undermine any honest attempt to be faithful to the canon of scripture while advocating a view that maintains God's unreserved and consistent non-violent hospitality?

But let us ask questions like these from a different angle. May it be that the conflict and violence in the Bible reflect a deep truth about human existence that could not be revealed without a penetrating and sustained exploration of its darkest and most recalcitrant regions? Might we view the Bible as a revelatory account of how human life is mired in complex dynamics of conflict and violence, which at times appeal to God to justify their existence? Could it be that whatever we come to say about revelation from a Christian point of view has everything to do with the problem of violence, that the "process of revelation is thus technically identical with the overcoming of violence among men and women?"[10] S. Mark Heim puts it this way:

> What is violence doing in the Bible? It is telling us the truth, the truth about our human condition, about the fundamental dynamics that lead to human bloodshed, and most particularly, the truth

about the integral connection between religion and violence. There is no way to be truthful without exhibiting these things. If we complain that the tales of Genesis and the bloody sacrifices of Leviticus, and the fire for revenge in the Psalms, are too sordidly, familiarly human to have any place in religious revelation, we make an interesting admission that they reveal our humanity all too well. We always knew this was the way things were, we claim. We don't need a religious text to tell us so. We need cures, not diagnosis. But is that true? What if our cures need diagnosing?[11]

This last question is the precise issue of our interest. What if our methods of curing the problem of conflict and violence themselves need diagnosing? What if our remedies are themselves poisonous? What if our attempts to overcome or at least contain violence only perpetuate violence in a special and concentrated form?

René Girard, whose work on violence and religion exerts considerable influence on the work of Schwager and Heim, as well as my own, has noted the double meaning of "cure" in Greek. *Pharmakon* can mean both "cure" and "poison." If not administered properly, the antidote for poison can itself become poisonous. Medicines themselves often are concentrated forms of poisons that produce other ailments as they work to cure. Not long after Jacques Derrida published his famous essay "Plato's Pharmacy" exploring the same paradox in Plato's *Phaedrus*, Girard published his landmark work *Violence and the Sacred* in which he analyzed the dynamics of scapegoat violence in mythology, literature, and culture.[12] The "scapegoat" (*pharmakos*) appears in myths, tragedies, and cultic practices as both a "cure" and a "poison" by being both the cause and remedy for social crisis. To state the theory very briefly, during times of crisis within a social group, when conflict and even outright violence threaten to become all-consuming due to competing desires, focused and measured acts of violence towards an "outsider" (a surrogate, a scapegoat victim) can function to restore unity and order. As a group projects upon a surrogate the inner discord and rising violence within the group (an inner "chaos" that the group may characterize as "pollution" or "contamination"); and as this surrogate is expelled from the community, often enough through sacrificial violence, a cathartic and calming effect can descend upon those associated with the violence as a temporary cure. The inner discord or contamination is "purged" as the ritual violence induces a sense of *tremendum* and *fascinans*. As the group becomes unanimously polarized over against the expelled Other, tensions within the group are eased. Order and peace are restored. The role of the scapegoat (*pharmakos*) is thus a paradoxical one: the surrogate is seen as the "poison" but also part of the "cure"; or, the poison of violence is medicinally used to prevent a more dangerous poison from becoming deadly for the group as such. By harnessing the power of sacrificial violence, a greater and indiscriminate violence can be averted. The scapegoat victim is something repellent, since the victim symbolically represents the contamination within the group. And yet, the victim is strangely fascinating because the victim's violent expulsion is a powerfully restorative act. Such cathartic fascination is evident in our own cultural obsession with violence. "Whether it is a public hanging, a war, or a televised glorification of violence," writes Gil Ballie, "a culture's righteous violence will fascinate its onlookers. It will be a spectacle. Regardless of the rhetoric and details of its justification, if a society can heighten that fascination and bring it to a cathartic sacrificial conclusion, then the sacrificial violence will be a pharmacological cure for the society's internal animosities."[13] As the group defines itself as an "us" against the "it" of the Other — this Other, as we shall see, must be seen as "monstrous," stripped of certain human-like qualities that might elicit sympathy and thus thwart the scapegoat process — the group achieves a sense of inner coherence and purity. The logic of scapegoating is thus rooted in cyclical (but preventative) violence. It bonds people together within a group, and thus acts as a founding principle.

Girard argues that the origin of the sacred emerges in human culture out of the *tremendum* and *fascinans* associated with the sacrificial process. As conflict and potential violence arise within a group, enough to threaten its existence, the sacrifice of a victim, upon whom the group has transferred its inner discord, serves to placate hostilities. The combination of awe, dread, and unanimity generated by sacrificial violence constitutes the primordial sense of the holy.[14] Indeed, one of the chief functions of religion in human history has been to restrain violence from becoming all-consuming. Though we need not assert this as the sole purpose of religion, and while we must resist an overly functionalistic reading, the sacrificial practices ubiquitous in human culture from time-immemorial (though increasingly ineffective for reasons I shall explain) have provided an unparalleled source of cohesion among groups precisely by channeling and restraining violence. (The Latin *religio* means "to bind together," and is possibly related to *religare*, "to restrain.") "Good violence" — its enactment or ritual remembrance — helps to prevent the "bad violence" that threatens to snowball out of control into a violence of *all against all*. "The resulting violence of all against all would finally annihilate the community if it were not transformed, in the end, into a war of *all against one,* thanks to which the unity of the community is reestablished."[15]

As we continue unpacking the dynamics of human relationships that lead to the scapegoating process just described, I will adopt the anthropological insights of Girard, some of his most important interpreters, and other thinkers who, though not "Girardian" in any strict sense, provide complimentary insights.[16] These dynamics are not restricted to ritual sacrifice in religion, though they are powerfully concentrated there. These dynamics can be found in human relationships in their many defining characteristics: interpersonal, religious, ethnic, cultural, and ideological. As we proceed in our analysis, I will attempt to understand how the resurrection of Jesus unveils the dynamics rivalry, conflict, and violence in the *humanum* — above all, how in the eschatological act of raising a scapegoat victim from the dead, God offers us forgiveness, peace, and freedom from the sin of the world that keeps us ensnared in webs of rivalry and violence, often without our even knowing it. God not only vindicates a scapegoat victim from the dead in order to reveal what human beings could not fully understand without it; but we come to find out, retrospectively *from* the resurrection, that *God* has become *our* victim. In the strange triumph of God, God has become our victim in order to give us a life free from making and becoming victims. This is the basic insight of the most characteristic soteriological models of the early church, what Gustav Aulén describes as *Christus Victor.* On such a view, God, through Jesus Christ, enters into our world in an act of loving kenosis to reveal and overcome what remains hidden to us — our deceit, rivalry, and violence. God, as it were, "absorbs" our sin within God's self by becoming *our* victim, not in order to legitimate the violence through which we build our fragile identities, but to unmask the lie that the Other must be immolated in order to achieve individual or group identity. Here, the language of God "tricking" Satan ("the accuser") used by many of the early church fathers makes the greatest anthropological sense. Jesus' death by crucifixion is the apparent triumph of those semi-autonomous powers in human life that produce victims in order to maintain identity, order, and peace. "It is better that one man die than the entire nation perish," asserts Caiaphas, with words that give the clearest articulation of the scapegoat process. But this victory of the accuser is only apparent, for by raising him from the dead, and most remarkably, by offering forgiveness and eschatological hospitality to those complicit in Jesus' crucifixion, the scapegoat process has been revealed from the inside out — the ultimate *apocalypsis* — and its logic of reciprocal violence has been replaced by a logic of non-reciprocal, superabundant grace. The triumph of Christ is thus an event of divine irony. The resurrection transforms what was the ultimate victory of "the Satan" (the self-replicating and semi-autonomous cycle of reciprocal violence and scapegoating in human relations) into its ultimate defeat. God does not use violence in order to free us from the captivity of our deceit and violence, but love. Irenaeus speaks of God's "loving persuasion" as the means for this ultimate coup: "and He redeemed that which was His own, not by violence (as the apostasy had by violence gained dominion over us at the first, insatiably snatching that which was not its own), but by persuasion (*secundum suadelam*), as it was fitting for God to gain His purpose by persuasion and not by use of violence; that so the ancient creation of God might be saved from perishing, without any infringement of justice."[17]

This "good news" of Jesus' death and resurrection means, ultimately, coming to grips with hitherto unknown "bad news," i.e., that we are all bound and implicated in reciprocal relations of victimization. Only from the perspective of being forgiven by our victim can we finally see the depths of our guilt, and our true humanity. Only when we enter into a face-to-face relationship with the One we have lynched as our scapegoat will we come face-to-face with the truth about ourselves. But then, this would be an im-possible Gift. For the death of the victim means quite precisely the inability of the victim to speak or offer forgiveness. How shall a victim speak from death's abysmal silence, much less offer hospitality and forgiveness to victimizers? The resurrection *is* this im-possible Gift. By raising Jesus from the dead and allowing him to "appear," God graciously penetrates our invincible deception to speak a word of eschatological hospitality and forgiveness. The risen Jesus *is* this word, not merely a metaphor for it. This is why affirming the *bodiliness* of his resurrection is so crucial: this is the *self-same* Jesus who was crucified, whose victimized body-person is eternally remembered and transformed by God into eschatological fullness as the eschatological offer of grace to us in our common, concretely embodied history. Victimization occurs to and in *bodies*. Every notion of disembodied salvation is thus one that has not grasped the corporeality of sin and reconciliation. To look for salvation beyond the body is to look for peace by amnesia. The resurrection is the offer of salvation precisely in the warp and woof of our concrete human existence, through the reconciliation of memories and the restoration of violated bodies.

In order to see this dramatic fulfillment in its depth and universal breadth, we must understand the role of violence in scripture. The reason why the Bible *displays* so much violence does not actually mean that it is more violent than other sacred texts. The Bible documents a revelatory process in which human beings are progressively extricated from the conflict and violence very much present, yet submerged and obscured in other sacred texts and myths, indeed submerged in human culture as such. If the Bible is more explicitly violent, this is because it is more explicitly concerned with unveiling the dynamics of human relations that lead to conflict and ultimately to the temptation to resolve conflict through the production of victims.[18] On this reading, the violence at times ascribed even to God in the Bible reflects the all-too-human tendency to project upon God our own scapegoat violence, to appeal to divine sanction for the production of victims. But sacred violence is what the people of Israel are being led to *overcome*. The significance of scripture is thus found not only in the ultimate unveiling of scapegoat violence in Jesus' death and resurrection, but also in the tensions and ambiguities within scripture that document the revelatory process in all its fits and starts. The tensions within scripture should be seen as instructive, not ignored or written off. "The God described in the Bible appears in a variety of characterizations," writes Heim. "The God represented in the passage about collective stoning in Leviticus looks different from the God presented in Amos or Isaiah, for instance."[19] Perhaps we can interpret this variation with the help of historical criticism to explain that earlier, more "primitive" conceptions of God are outmoded or critiqued by later conceptions. But if we apply this approach too narrowly, argues Heim, it "might suggest that there is no truth revealed in the earlier or the contrasting pictures of God that would be lost when we pass on to later, preferred ones. And this leads us to wonder why the historically or theologically less valued elements should have a place in scripture at all."[20] This is no doubt what Marcion wondered, and perhaps many others after him. "But at least in some cases this variety embodied in the biblical narrative may be a crucial part of the truth that it has to impart."[21] What Heim means by this is that as we come to see how the Bible reveals with growing precision a view of God purged from the sort of mythological entrapment that appeals to divine sanction for the creation of victims, we can look back in scripture for instances in which God has been used precisely for that purpose. Scripture itself helps us to decode scripture, and the resurrection of the victim its ultimate hermeneutic.[22] Rather than reading scripture monochromatically, as though all its images of God must be set side-by-side and viewed with equal significance, we must read it as a richly layered chronicling of how the people of God are led through a process of discovery to a new economy of human relations where we no longer need to produce victims in order to establish and protect our identities, where we can see through the terrible deception that the Other must be objectified and immolated in order to placate inner rivalries and violences, where our "cures" for the disease of sin can finally be seen as perpetuating its "poison" in concentrated form.

It is important to reject the idea that the Old Testament is only a staging area for the New. If we come to affirm the death and resurrection of Jesus as the ultimate fulfillment of the story of Israel, this by no means implies that what is prior serves only a negative condition for what is its positive counterpoint. It is just this sort of flawed thinking that has led Christians at times to not only oppose the Old and New Testaments, but foster anti-Semitic attitudes and activities.[23] This is the ultimate perversion of the gospel since it stands in such explicit contradiction with what it unveils so clearly: the projection upon and lynching of a victim in order to maintain group identity. What reaches its fulfillment in Jesus Christ is exactly what is of ultimate concern in the story of Israel, even if its "recapitulation" in him comes with an unthinkable twist. "The Old Testament is an antimyth," asserts Heim. By saying "antimyth," he means something different from the more neutral *mythos,* or "story," as I have used this term elsewhere. He means it in a pejorative sense, i.e., as the divine sanctioning of human violence and the obscuring of the innocence of scapegoat victims. The Old Testament is "thick with bodies, the voices of victims and threatened victims."[24] Indeed, this is what makes the Bible so remarkable: it constantly draws our attention to the *innocence of victims.* By innocence I do not mean that such victims are without any moral culpability whatsoever. I mean that the guilt their accusers project upon them in order to justify violence is shown to be deceptive and unjust. In order to keep the scapegoat process intact, it is vitally important that the guilt of victims be secured. They really must be responsible for what threatens security, identity, and purity. The victims must not be thought of as "victims" at all, not in the way we have now come to understand this term, thanks to scripture. To see the victim as innocent, and thus as one whom I have unjustly accused as the source of my inner conflict and violence, is the first step in unmasking the scapegoat process. This is why much of the Bible's razor-sharp focus on the innocent victim is so culturally subversive, even if it involves an almost repulsive focus on violence in human affairs. It threatens to undermine the ways individuals and groups habitually fashion identities through some form of definitional polarization that assumes the non-innocence of the objectified Other. The Bible's violence is not for sadistic curiosity; and neither is the cross of Christ an object for a cult of violence. The story of the Bible is a story about what we are freed from; and the only

DESIRE, *MIMESIS,* AND SCAPEGOAT VIOLENCE

The Triangularity of Desire

According to Aristotle, one of the chief characteristics of poetry lies deep within our nature. Poetry *imitates* life. It is creative *mimesis*. It renders human life in a distinctive linguistic medium (one with harmony and rhythm) that allows us to contemplate it, to say of humanity, "Ah, that is us." Whereas Plato views the mimetic representations of poetry in terms of diminution, as copies removed from their original, Aristotle sees in poetic imitation something fundamental to the human animal, something with terminal value. The "instinct of imitation [*mimesis*] is implanted in man from childhood, one difference between him and other animals being that he is the most imitative of living creatures, and through imitation learns his earliest lessons; and no less universal is the pleasure felt in things imitated."[25] This truth is easily observable.

Anyone who has children, or who has observed them with the least bit of attentiveness, knows just how voraciously mimetic they are. Children mirror everything they see and hear. Their acquisition of skills in bodily motility comes as they imitate the bodily movements of others. Their acquisition of skills in language emerges from being long-immersed in a world of language and becoming increasingly proficient in imitating the patterns of speech that reverberate all around them, first by babbling, then with words and phrases, and finally with more complete utterances. The relationship between body and language is extremely close here — and so it remains — since language and thought are emergent from the world of perception.[26] The formation of the human person from the earliest stages of life involves an extended process of incorporating (literally, bringing *within* the body through habituation) the desires and behavioral habits of others, e.g., parents, siblings, extended family, peers, etc. Any anthropology that imagines the self to be originally self-constituting, or a "clean slate," is hopelessly naïve. My "me" is born as a response to the Other. Though I may make something of myself, as it were, this "me" arises from an antecedent givenness. Though I may forge a personal identity within a world of relationships and come to name certain desires as my own, my desires are in fact shaped by and reflective of the desires of others. My being comes *ex auditu*.

Mimesis is basic to the development of human beings, and thus is a necessary and fundamentally good thing. Not only is it essential for human formation, but it is what bonds human beings together. As my desires are formed by mirroring those of the Other, I find myself inextricably connected with this Other. Though we retain our unique identities (we are never mere replicas of the Other, and neither is my being "other" *to* the Other a diminution or "falling away" from primordial unity), still our respective senses of "mineness" (*ipseity*) is connected at the most fundamental level with the "non-mineness" (*alterity*) of the Other. A person's identity is an identity-in-relation, where "relation" is not something subsequent to identity, as if I come into relation with the Other only after self-constitution, but logically prior and ontologically constitutive of identity.[27] Human existence is thus an expanse of inter-individuality, or inter-givenness. The human being is a *being given* — contingent and relational despite our various attempts, subtly or overtly violent, to absolutize identity by gaining ascendancy over this givenness and contingency, by making *alterity* continuous with *ipseity,* by conforming the Other to the Same.

When the desires of persons-in-relation are concordant, a profound sense of belonging prevails. This sense of belonging is vitally important even as the emerging identity of a child occurs through growing differentiation from the Other. Parents know only too well how powerful the word "no" is to the child. Indeed, it can seem like the most powerful word in the whole universe. This "no," while it may create irritations and stresses within the parent-child relation, is also a kind of "yes." The emerging identity of the child is formed, not only by aping the desires of the Other, but by sorting through and defining the unique patterns of his/her own desires in relation with the Other — in *relative autonomy.* This "no" thus presupposes a prior relationality and belongingness. It occurs as an ongoing negotiation of identity-in-relation within a greater inter-personal world.

As children continue to develop their sense of "mineness," they do so also in negotiation with other children. This can lead to great companionship (children are instinctively fascinated by other children), but it can also lead to conflict as the desires of children mirror and compete with each other. Were we to place two toddlers in a large room with, say, 101 toys — toys of every conceivable shape, size, and color — with which of these toys will the two children play? Will it be the big one, the bouncy one, the furry one, or the one with flashing lights? Who knows, but of this we can be assured: it will be the *same* one. Why is this? This is not random, and neither is it unique to children. It reveals a structural feature of the human animal: our desires are generated by imitating the desires of the Other. Our desires mirror each other. The reason why I desire something has only a little to do with what I think are its innate properties. The reason why I take interest in something, the reason why I may want to possess it is not arbitrary. I come to find it interesting, desirable, something to possess or share in because others do as well. My desires are reflective of, woven into, and in constant negotiation with the desires of others — and this creates the possibility of both cooperation and conflict. It is what can bond human beings together; but it is also what can create rivalry and discord with the Other. And so to return to our two children in the room filled with all manner of toys, we can predict with great accuracy that the children will gravitate towards the same toy. Desire is mimetic, a centripetal force in human relations. (Indeed, the theory of desire elaborated here is to anthropology what the theory of gravity is to physics.) And as the children play with the same toy, their mutual desires interlock and begin to conflict. In all likelihood, the children will begin to claim ownership over the toy. As the conflict increases, the toy becomes increasingly desirable. What each child desires is not just the toy, but the toy of the other child's desire. If left unchecked, the amplification of desire can lead to a tug of war, either with competing refrains of "it's mine," or worse, with flailing limbs. The children have thus reached a "mimetic crisis."

Human desire is "triangular," writes Girard. "Rivalry does not arise because of the fortuitous convergence of two desires on a single object; rather, *the subject desires the object because the rival desires it.* In desiring an object the rival alerts the subject to the desirability of the object." This is why the innate qualities of the object are secondary in the triangulation of desire. The toy in the room of 101 toys could by *any* toy; but it will eventually be the *same* toy. In this inter-subjective relation, the Other becomes a potential rival, but a rival who is also a *model*. "The rival, then, serves as a model for the subject, not only in regard to such secondary matters as style and opinions but also, and more essentially, in regard to desires."[28] In some of his earliest work, Girard attempts to show the dynamics of triangular desire in literature, largely as a rejoinder to the deeply Romantic (or "expressivist") notion that human desire is spontaneous.[29] Obviously at the level of adolescent and adult relations, the dynamics at play are much more complex than what is more apparent in very young children. Mimetic desire, its cooperative and conflictive capacities, carries on in human affairs through love, friendship, hatred, envy, jealously, *ressentiment,* repression, and so forth.[30] We can also say that ritual and taboo in primitive culture has much to do with training and regulating desire, to routinize and/or proscribe certain kinds of desire from becoming actualized or so conflictive that the clan or tribe would come under internal threat. Law is also another crucial way human beings regulate imitation from becoming violent. But among the most enduring channels for controlling mimetic rivalry and contagious violence in human affairs is scapegoating. I have already discussed above some of the basic dynamics of scapegoat violence in sacrificial practices, but let us consider for a moment how some of these dynamics are present in everyday relational patterns.

To return once again to the maturation of the child, we know that as children begin to fashion their identities beyond the proximate sphere of the family, they normally do so in peer groups. The socialization process that occurs outside of the familial context is an important step in the process of individuation. *Mimesis* is no less important here, even if the dynamics are more complex. As children identify with peer groups their desires continue to mirror and shape those of others. Such emergent identities can be quite cooperative and wholesome; but, as is so obvious in observing interpersonal dynamics on playgrounds, school hallways, and in lunchrooms, peer groups gain their delineation in a contrastive relation with other groups. What creates identity *within* one group is often distinguished (with varying degrees of intensity) *from* the identity of another group. The characteristics that might polarize groups according to "us" and "them" can range from the arbitrary to the profound, e.g., clothing styles, types of extra-curricular activities, proficiency in sports, aptitude for learning, ethnicity, socio-economic status, and so on. (To put it in colloquial terms, the "jocks" are not the "nerds," the "goth" kids are not the "popular" kids, and so on.) And, of course, there is the potential that certain young people find no social niche. For whatever reason, a young man or woman may find no way to "fit in." He is the really "weird" kid, the loner, the subject of rumors. She is the "icky" kid, the butt of jokes, the victim of pranks. As it so often happens, young people who might otherwise identify with different peer groups can find sudden unanimity as they regard the "loner" or "outsider" as a *common* Other. Differences that had previously polarized groups can become lessened to the extent that a common "stranger" is objectified, i.e., "picked on." This is an example of social expulsion. Even if the "weird" kid is not sacrificed on an altar, by being verbally abused, implicated in strange rumors, or being identified with a peculiar physical feature (a big nose, speech slur, racial ambiguity, etc.), the basic dynamics of scapegoating are present. A similar dynamic is operative when, for example, two rival schools face each other in athletic competition. During a typical school day various peer groups will be differentiated only in relationship to each other; but when a rival team from across town comes to the home stadium for an important football game, a newfound and encompassing sense of identity ("school spirit") can temporarily allay differences as the home team defends its "turf" against a common opponent. Social distinctions among the groups become relativized, at least temporarily, by a more embracing distinction over against a greater Other.

This process of identification *within* groups by establishing distinction *from* other groups is so recurrent that it may seem unworthy of the attention I have given it. It may seem that by talking about toys, playgrounds, lunchrooms, and school sporting events I have trivialized our topic. But that would be the point: it *is* common. It is *so* common that we can describe it as an anthropological constant. We form our identities, individually or in groups, in contrastive interaction with the Other. As James Alison writes:

> [T]here is what might (with great care) be called an ontological need, a radical need to *be,* a need which draws us to others and to imitate them in order to acquire a sense of being, something felt as a lack. The better we are parented, the more that need is met by the "sense of being" being given. Yet, however well we are parented that need is never fully met. We grow up, in short, conflictual little animals, with a built-in mechanism for shoring up our fragile identity, for producing security and order, both as individuals and in groups. We learned this while we were building our "I," and as we continue to build it. We try to expel the "other" who is our rival. Our "I" is in fact built on that expulsion. It means that we often build up *over against,* rather than by serenely allowing the other to be a beneficent influence on our lives.[31]

Alison's language of "imitation," "rival," and "expulsion" is clearly influenced by Girard, but also by Jean-Michel Oughourlian, who has developed Girard's insights in the realm of psychology.[32] "Rivalry is resolved at all levels of human life by the expulsion of a victim. Here, in purely psychological terms, such an expulsion takes the form of an assertion of the incipient self over against the model, in order to take the model's place, or be him or her."[33] To possess what the Other possesses is equally a desire to *be* what the Other *is.* It is to become the one who is my model. To achieve this, the Other must be displaced (expelled or manipulated), made to conform to my project. To this extent, desire shifts from a pacific to an acquisitive and conflictual mode.

Importantly, this conflict with the Other is also, and necessarily, an inner conflict. As I seek mastery over the Other through various strategies, I am not only cutting myself off from the Other with whom I remain in relation — I cannot ultimately escape relationality, however much I may seek to control or deny it — but I am also in contradiction with the givenness of my being. It implies a negation of my original heteronomy. It is a denial of my being *received* from the Other through acts of *possession*. Rather than being-with-the-Other in a relation of mutual hospitality, in "original peace," the self seeks to overcome (and thus negate) heteronomy in acts that amount to the expulsion of the Other, as though my self and the Other were locked in a zero-sum relation. Instead of individuation taking place in a mutually beneficent way, in what Alison calls "pacific relation" with the Other — where the Other is welcomed as gift, and the Other welcomes me as gift — the self so frequently accomplishes its sense of identity by subtly or aggressively denying the Other, "which means that, as it takes the other as rival, so it becomes splintered, dissociated, and subject to pathological mechanisms."[34] And here we begin to perceive something of the anthropological depths of what the Christian tradition calls "original sin." "The relationship between the *être* as received and as acquired by more or less violent appropriation is at the heart of the theology of original sin."[35] We are "constitutionally heteronomous," but we often imagine and act as though this were not true, as though we are constitutionally autonomous, a self-constituting "I" that enters into relation with a "Thou" only as a secondary and exterior movement outside the self.

To widen the scope from the interpersonal to a more broadly social and cultural consideration, we can easily observe how the yearning to achieve unanimity with a particular social or cultural group is accomplished through the elaboration of symbolic borders, so that what is exterior is regarded as the source of inner ambiguity and disorder. The will toward social-cultural coherence often depends upon drawing hard and fast symbolic distinctions that highlight any number of distinguishing factors, e.g., ethnicity, language, ideology, religious identification, etc. The assertion of a collective "I" comes with a "politics of purity," as Miroslav Volf puts it, which would extract a particularly defined group of persons from the ambiguity that is nevertheless intrinsic to human existence.

> The blood must be pure: German blood alone should run through German veins, free from all non-Aryan contamination. The territory must be pure: Serbian soil must belong to Serbs alone, cleansed

of all non-Serbian intruders. The origins must be pure: we must go back to the pristine purity of our linguistic, religious, or cultural past, shake away the dirt of otherness collected on our march through history. The goal must be pure: we must let the light of reason shine into every dark corner or we must create a world of total virtue so as to render all moral effort unnecessary. The origin and the goal, the inside and the outside, everything must be pure: plurality and heterogeneity must give way to homogeneity and unity. One people, one culture, one language, one book, one goal; what does not fall under this all-encompassing "one" is ambivalent, polluting, and dangerous. It must be removed. We want a pure world and push the "others" out of our world; we want to be pure ourselves and eject "otherness" from within ourselves. The "will to purity" contains a whole program for arranging our social worlds — from the inner worlds of our selves to the other worlds of our families, neighborhoods, and nations. It is a dangerous program because it is a totalitarian program, governed by a logic that reduces, ejects, and segregates.[36]

These last words, "reduces," "ejects," and "segregates" represent different forms of the scapegoating process which arises from the triangularity of desire. We instrumentally use the Other, which we must objectify and expel, in the effort to delineate an internal domain, a collective "I," that is now free from ambiguity. Such expulsions allow those who occupy this collective "I" to sublate their differences. With a collective Other upon whom we project in an act of symbolic transference all that is dangerous, polluting, or evil, we can deflect our attention from the tensions and rivalries within the group.

Mimetic Rivalry and Violence

We return now to the problem of "mimetic crisis." Recalling the example above, the triangulation of desire among the two toddlers leads to an escalating conflict that, without some kind of intervention from the outside — say, from a parent who separates and redirects the children to share or "take turns" — promptly leads to verbal and physical aggression. Parents may stand aghast that their beloved children do this. They may say with embarrassment to other parents, "I don't know where little Trevor and Austin learned to behave like that!" But there is no doubt that they have learned it: they have learned it by imitating the desires of the Other. What would happen, however, were there not an intervention into the mimetic crisis from a third party, by someone outside the conflictual spiral, someone unmoved by the competing desires of the two children? What would happen if there was no constructive way to resolve the mimetic crisis that embroils the children, either by an appeal to an external authority ("mommy, mommy!") or through some externalization of the conflict toward some other activity that might lead to cooperation?

Violence is contagious. Left unchecked it can quickly swell to all-consuming proportions. There is no lack of recent examples in our world of such combustible, mimetic violence. We are all familiar with (and likely touched by) instances of mob violence at sporting events, riots in city streets, gang rivalry, ethnic clashes, civil war, terrorism, ideological warfare, etc. As conflict between individuals or groups irrupts into full fledged violence, the effect can be highly destabilizing. With just a single spark dormant tensions can abruptly express themselves in the most awe-inspiring acts of collective brutality. People who would normally never imagine themselves engaged in violence can suddenly find themselves swept into the waves of its heaving power, quite as though possessed by an external, willful force. Spiraling violence can take on a coherent life of its own. To refer to the analogy used in the previous chapter, mimetic violence can become a kind of self-perpetuating "system," rather like a furious weather system induced by a variety of atmospheric conditions that interact and morph into new and irreducibly complex patterns of phenomena. The semi-autonomous and quasi-personal character of mimetic violence is yet another way to retrieve the biblical language of the demonic. Walter Wink argues that, phenomenologically speaking, mimetic violence works in ways that suggest the language of "Satan" and "demons." Whatever we believe about the metaphysical status of such language (i.e., whether it refers to discrete entities), we can easily observe the self-generating and infectious character of violence that takes on semi-autonomous structures in human existence.[37] Just as computer viruses are "self-replicating and 'contagious,' behaving almost willfully even though they are quite impersonal," mimetic rivalry and violence can take on a level of complexity and sweep persons, groups, or institutions into ecstatic events of bloodshed. Wink uses the example of a riot at a soccer match. "For a few frenzied minutes, people who in their ordinary lives behave on the whole quite decently suddenly find themselves bludgeoning and even killing opponents whose only sin was rooting for the other team. Afterward people often act bewildered and wonder what could have possessed them."[38]

Gil Ballie draws our attention to the disturbing persistence of mimetic violence in our collective history and the pharmacological strategies we have adopted to resolve it. In just one of many illuminating examples, Ballie discusses the 1991 riots in Los Angeles in the wake of the Rodney King beating and subsequent verdict that acquitted the white police officers of their collective brutality against him. The first act of violence — the beating of King by the officers, which was videotaped by a bystander — bears all the marks of a spontaneous convergence of a mob on a victim. Though King led police on a car chase and actively resisted arrest once apprehended, the video shows quite plainly the disproportionate amount of violence used to subdue him, most egregiously the repeated bludgeoning by police in hysterical violence. In a front-page story in the *Los Angeles Times*, journalist Janny Scott summarized her conversations with psychologists and sociologists to understand the shocking brutality. Scott noted the strong inclination for "tightly knit groups" to "devalue and dehumanize outsiders and, under certain conditions, to commit terrible violence against them."[39] No matter how these groups identify themselves (family, race, profession, culture, religion, ideology, etc.), the building of morale *within* the group tends to arise in proportion to the self-definition *from* other groups. While this may occur in relatively benign ways, so that potential tensions between group identities remain tacit and only occasionally expressed, during times of crisis within or between groups the underlying structures of definitional contrast can become strongly determinative. Indeed, "in some groups, members manipulate the sense of 'us versus them' to bolster group spirit and divert attention from internal problems. A sense of identity forms from denigrating outsiders." This dynamic of allaying internal problems through intensifying "us versus them" is the governing dynamic of the scapegoat process. Important in this process is the magnification and caricaturization of what differentiates. Members within a group "tend to focus on whatever is unusual or different, just as one's eye is drawn to one part of a picture and the rest blurs. A group's attention centers on the rare thing, the outsider."[40] When tensions between groups become particularly strong, what is different becomes an all-consuming point of collective attention. Especially when a tight-knit group imagines itself threatened by the presence of the Other — a presence which disturbs or contaminates — conditions are ripe for reflexive outbursts of violence upon the Other. Members of such a group no longer see the Other as deserving respect or sympathy, but a monster deserving to be expelled or immolated.

Ballie argues that this dynamic of convergence of a mob upon a victim is the scapegoat mechanism in crystallized form. "There is a kind of algebraic formula at work here whose most irreducible formula is 'unanimity-minus-one,' a phrase René Girard uses to describe the cathartic moment of scapegoating violence." Noting the connection between archaic mythology and contemporary examples of mob violence, Ballie writes:

> When a modern mob experiences the nonhumanity of its victim, what it sees in the victim's stead is some deranged animal, a source of social pollution, a beast, a pervert. When a primitive mob experiences the nonhumanity of its victim, what it saw in the victim's stead was the demon-god who was the source of violence in life and the source of peace in death. In both cases, the human victim disappears, only to be transfigured into an icon in the sacred system that his victimization generated or regenerated. The victim becomes Dionysos or Tiamat, a god or goddess of mythical proportions whose killing was in accord with the divine plan.[41]

When, over a year later, the police officers were acquitted due to a hung jury, widespread rioting immediately irrupted in Los Angeles and continued for a four-day period. The riot resulted in 53 deaths, nearly 2,500 injuries, hundreds of fires, and massive looting. On the first day of the rioting, Reginald Denny, a white truck driver stopped at a street light, was randomly pulled out of his truck by a mob and nearly beaten to death. The beating, which was also televised, was a mirror reflection of the original mob violence against King. Denny had nothing at all to do with the original injustice, but because he superficially represented the Other by sharing the same skin color, he was a satisfactory surrogate. The question of his guilt was irrelevant as he became the cipher of a collective projection. Such reciprocal violence was, of course, an expression of the long-standing racial and economic tensions in South Central Los Angeles. It is just one of countless examples of how violence irrupts out of a sense of moral indignation. Ballie explains:

> Righteous indignation is often the first symptom of the metastasis of the cancer of violence. It tends to provide the indignant ones with a license to commit or condone acts structurally indistinguishable from those that aroused the indignation. When moral contempt for a form of violence inspires so explicit a replication of it, there is only one conclusion to be drawn: *The moral revulsion the initial violence awakened proved weaker than the mimetic fascination it inspired.*[42]

Miroslav Volf has analyzed the cyclical violence premised upon indignation in his extraordinary work on violence and reconciliation. As violence replicates itself, each side of the conflict can lay claim to being the other's victim. As each reprisal results in new wounds, so too do they produce new causes for indignation and recrimination. In the former Yugoslavia, where Volf was teaching during the war between Croats and Serbs, this exact cycle was at work with overwhelming magnitude:

> Nobody seemed in control.... there seemed to be an insatiable appetite for brutality among ordinary people. Once the war started and the right conditions were maintained, an uncontrollable chain reaction was under way. These were mostly decent people, as decent as most of us tend to be. Many did not, strictly speaking, *choose* to plunder and burn, rape and torture, or secretly enjoy these. A dormant beast in them was awakened from its uneasy slumber. And not only in them. The motives of those who set to fight against the brutal aggressors were self-defense and justice. The best in others, however, enraged the best in them. The moral barriers holding it in check broke down and it went after revenge. In resisting evil, they were trapped by evil.... Evil engenders evil, and like pyroclastic debris from the mouth of a volcano, it erupts out of the aggressor and victim alike.[43]

There are two aspects to Volf's statement that are of particular interest here. The first is that understanding the mimetic character of victimization is the condition for understanding the otherwise unintelligible and perhaps offensive nature of Jesus' ministry of *forgiveness to victims*. It is easy for us to understand why Jesus called oppressors to conversion, much less so his call to conversion to those who are oppressed. As noted in the conclusion of the previous chapter, the schematization of oppressed and oppressor is necessary to maintain at one level, yet it remains insufficient. It tends to underestimate how the originating violence replicates itself even in those who are its victims. It also pays inadequate attention to the subtle ways those who achieve their liberation from oppressors can themselves become oppressors, all the while bearing the mantle of justice. Part of the radical injustice of producing victims is the installation within the hearts of victims a violence that would replicate itself to transform them into potential victimizers. "It will not do," argues Volf, "to divide Jesus' listeners neatly into two groups and claim that for the oppressed repentance means new hope whereas for the oppressors it means radical change.... The truly revolutionary character of Jesus' proclamation lies precisely in the *connection between the hope he gives to the oppressed and the radical change he requires of them.*" What is this change? It is "release from the understandable but nonetheless inhumane hatred in which their hearts are held captive."[44] This is not merely a matter of personal feeling, or of some kind of psychological release. It is a process of healing with extraordinary social and political significance.

> Victims need to repent from the fact that all too often they mimic the behavior of the oppressors, let themselves be shaped in the mirror image of the enemy. They need to repent also of the desire to excuse their own reactive behavior either by claiming that they are not responsible for it or that such reactions are a necessary condition of liberation. Without repentance for these sins, the full human dignity of victims will not be restored and needed social change will not take place.[45]

Secondly, it is important to underscore that the mimetic rivalry and violence associated with the above instances of conflict is far more pervasive in everyday life than we would like to imagine or admit. We might convince ourselves that such examples really are extraordinary, not the norm in human life, certainly not the norm in *my* life. It may be difficult to imagine ourselves caught up in the orgiastic violence characteristic of ethnic cleansing, rabid nationalism, spontaneous mob violence, and so forth. But then, so too is it difficult for many who have actually participated in such violence to understand how it could have occurred to them. Often, those who have been involved in the worst forms of human brutality, and who survive it to later reflect remorsefully on their behavior, confess that they do not know why or how they could have engaged in such acts. As though waking from a dream, or a drug-induced stupor, they look back at their violence and stand aghast that they were swept up into its demonic power.[46] The most self-deceptive thing we can do is to imagine we are not vulnerable to mimetic rivalry and violence, or that we are not *already* involved in forms of exclusion and scapegoating in much subtler, though still very tangible, ways. In reflecting upon the admittedly extreme (yet disturbingly recurrent) examples of spiraling violence above, we might ask ourselves about how we construct our identities within the web of human relations in ways that easily translate into the objectification and potential immolation of the Other. Volf speaks of the "dormant beast" lying within all our hearts that can be awoken from its "uneasy slumber" in moments of mimetic crisis. Volf maintains that the kinds of conflict we see writ large in history are directly related to the "inescapable ambiguity of the self." Because the self is "dialogically constructed," so that the "other is already from the outset part of the self," the attempt to assert identity comes with it the danger that I reduce the Other to my project.[47] This is by no means to deny the importance of cultivating a healthy sense of independence within the web of personal relationships, i.e., a *relative autonomy*. The antidote to rampant individualism is not an equally dehumanizing conformism.[48] And yet, too easily the cultivation of the self results in acts of expulsion, where the Other, who is my model, becomes my rival. "[T]he tension between the self and the other is built into the very desire for identity: the other over against whom I must assert myself is the same other who must remain part of myself if I am to be myself." When I find resistance from the Other as a result of competing desires, or if the Other is not who I desire him or her to be, I will find myself inclined towards some kind of project to manipulate the Other. "Hence I slip into violence: instead of reconfiguring myself to make space for the other, I seek to reshape the other into who I want her to be in order that in relation to her I may be who I want to be."[49]

UNVEILING SCAPEGOAT VIOLENCE

"Dionysius versus the Crucified"

It may seem thus far in this analysis that I have presumed a view of the human person as congenitally violent: that human desire is necessarily acquisitive and objectifying; that the relationship between the I and Thou is necessarily conflictual; that should we learn to live in reconciled relationship with the Other in mutual giftedness, even if this were possible, this would require going against our "nature." If such were my view, then my analysis could rightly be numbered among those representing an "ontology of violence."[50] On such a view, conflict and violence are "normal," not only because so recurrent and predictable, but constitutive of existence as such. The perpetual reappearance of conflict and violence in interpersonal relationships, in cultures and institutions, is interpreted as a manifestation of the unalterable structure of "being." (Or, alternatively, there is no "being" but only the "becoming" of ceaseless strife.) "Difference" is privation, something to be overcome or mastered in a dialectical progression. Violence, not peace, is primordially generative — life's *arche*. Hence, Heraclitus: "War is father of all, king of all. Some it makes gods, some it makes men, some it makes slaves, some free." Or: "We must realize that war is universal, and strife is justice, and that all things come into being and pass away through strife."[51] It is also presumed by Nietzsche, for whom Heraclitus represents the Dionysian philosopher *par excellence*. "[Heraclitus'] affirmation of transitoriness *and destruction,* the decisive element in dionysian philosophy, affirmation of antithesis and war, *becoming* with a radical rejection even of the concept of *'being'* — in this I must in any event recognize what is most closely related to me of anything that has been thought hitherto." The doctrine of the "eternal recurrence," "that is to say of the unconditional and endlessly repeated circular course of all things — this doctrine of Zarathustra *could* possibly already have been taught by Heraclitus."[52]

We shall look more closely at the difference between the Dionysian "ontology of violence" and the Christian "ontology of peace." Crucial in this distinction is the issue of scapegoat violence, and this concerns us at present. The anthropology and soteriology I am developing here is in explicit repudiation of ontological violence, even if it gives a strong reading of "original sin." Human desire is not intrinsically violent. "Without mimetic desire there would be neither freedom nor humanity. Mimetic desire is intrinsically good."[53] Without *mimesis,* "we would not be open to what is human or what is divine."[54] The Christian doctrine of original sin is very different from any notion that human beings are "naturally" sinful, as though by our nature we are violent, or that the "distance" between God, others, and self constitutes a negative relation that must be overcome through ceaseless striving or through the production of victims in sacrificial violence.

The resurrection of Jesus from the dead reveals two things at once: first, how serious our predicament truly is, how deeply implicated we are in webs of sinful relations without our even knowing it; and second, how from the gratuitous offer of being forgiven by our victim, we discover our true humanity as created in and for original peace. Jesus' resurrection reveals at once the pervasiveness and non-necessity of violence. It allows us to look at our human situation with gripping honesty, while also allowing us to perceive it as Gift. Girard's thought, along with the work of James Alison, who has developed Girard's anthropology of the cross in more explicit interaction with resurrection theology, is our guide here. So too is Nietzsche, though for quite different reasons. Nietzsche's diagnosis of Christianity provides us a crucial starting point to see the revolutionary character of Jesus' death and resurrection, for it is Nietzsche who, according to Girard, "was the first philosopher to understand that the collective violence of myths and rituals (everything he named 'Dionysos') is the same type as the violence of the Passion. The difference between them is not in the *facts,* which are the same in both cases, but in their interpretation."[55] The difference in interpretation is found in the gospels' assertion of Jesus' resurrection — the vindication and exaltation of the innocent victim from the dead, and the return of this victim as forgiveness and eschatological hospitality to both victims and victimizers.

Nietzsche's reading of the Judeo-Christian tradition is one that sees in it an inversion of values that leads to cultural decadence. The morality presented in the Bible is a "slave morality," which among other things valorizes weakness by asserting the moral authority of "victims." It invents the language of victimization. It is a morality that trades on *ressentiment* against nobility and privilege. "Master morality," as opposed to the "slave morality," develops an ethic of virtue and personal excellence. Its value judgments "presuppose a powerful physicality, a rich, burgeoning, even overflowing health, as well as all those things which help to preserve it — war, adventure, hunting, dancing, competitive games, and everything which involves strong, free, high-spirited activity."[56] The master morality does not construe the world in terms of "good versus evil," as those possessed by *ressentiment* do against those who lord over them, but only in terms of "good and bad." "As I said, the pathos of nobility and distance, the enduring, dominating, and fundamental overall feeling of a higher ruling kind in relation to a lower kind, to a 'below' — *that* is the origin of the opposition between 'good' and 'bad.'" But those consumed with *ressentiment* towards their masters take an "imaginary revenge" by inventing "values," by developing a language of good versus evil. Above all, the inversion of the master morality comes by concocting the moral authority of the victim. This first occurs in the Hebrew scriptures.

> [T]he Jews, that priestly people who ultimately knew no other way of exacting satisfaction from its enemies and conquerors than through a radical transvaluation of their values, through an art of *the most intelligent revenge*. This was only as befitted a priestly people, the people of the most downtrodden priestly vindictiveness. It has been the Jews who have, with terrifying consistency, dared to undertake the reversal of the aristocratic value equation (good = noble = powerful = beautiful = happy = blessed) and have held on to it tenaciously by the teeth of the most unfathomable hatred (the hatred of the powerless). It is they who have declared: "The miserable alone are the good; the poor, the powerless, and low alone are the good. The suffering, the deprived, the sick, the ugly are the only pious ones, the only blessed, for them alone is there salvation. You, on the other hand, the noble and the powerful, you are for all eternity the evil, the cruel, the lascivious, the insatiable, the

godless ones. You will be without salvation, accursed and damned to all eternity!" There is no doubt as to *who* inherited this Jewish transvaluation.[57]

At least Nietzsche was able to see more clearly than Marcion the essential connection between the Old and New Testaments. The beatitudes in the gospels alluded to above carry on the "Jewish transvaluation" with "terrifying consistency." Nietzsche saw in the Bible's depiction of violence something remarkably different from that found in the epic and tragic poetry of antiquity. Instead of revering and celebrating the beauty of human struggle, where suffering presents the occasion for strength and heroism — the virtue of "hardness" that buoys life above hardship — the Bible problematizes suffering, names it "evil," and takes perverse comfort in elevating the status of those who are its alleged "victims." In so doing, it asserts the inviolability of the individual before the interests of the species. In a word, the Bible presents an anti-sacrificial logic.

> Through Christianity, the individual was made so important, so absolute, that he could no longer be sacrificed: but the species endures only through human sacrifice — All "souls" became equal before God: but this is precisely the most dangerous of all possible evaluations! If one regards individuals as equals, one calls the species into question, one encourages a way of life that leads to the ruin of the species: Christianity is the counterprinciple to the principle of *selection*.... This universal love of men is in practice the *preference* for the suffering, underprivileged, degenerate: it has in fact lowered and weakened the strength, the responsibility, the lofty duty to sacrifice men.... The species requires that the ill-constituted, weak, degenerate, perish: but it was precisely to them that Christianity turned as a conserving force.... Genuine charity demands sacrifice for the good of the species — it is hard, it is full of self-overcoming, because it needs human sacrifice. And this pseudo-humaneness called Christianity wants it established that no one should be sacrificed.[58]

Nietzsche is not literally calling for a return to cults of human sacrifice — though the National Socialism that appealed to Nietzsche's vision surely did — but a recovery of a Dionysian vision that accepts the mixture of strife, suffering, and beauty of human life *as it is,* as it *always will be;* hence, the doctrine of "the eternal return" is a heroic attitude, a "yes" to life and an affirmation of strife as original to existence. Like Christ, Dionysius is immolated, ripped apart by the Titans. But whereas

Christ's crucifixion is regarded by Christians as a radical affront to the inviolability of the human person, a breach of justice, the story of Dionysius's sacrifice suggests to Nietzsche that clinging to individual existence in resistance to participation in the whole is only a source of pointless suffering, a "no" to life as it is. The "resurrection" of Dionysius is the *end of individuation* by a "rebirth" into the whole — the species — a reabsorption into the ever-flowing cycle of human life. The "resurrection" of Christ, at least as interpreted by Christians (Paul's interpretation being the most influential and loathsome), represents a hypertrophying of the individual by lifting the human personality up and out of this eternal return, thus alienating it. The doctrine of bodily resurrection makes the individual person sacrosanct, and thus thwarts the logic of sacrifice for the group, and the heroism this requires, while suppressing the strife and suffering that humans must embrace in the *agon* of life. What Nietzsche overlooks in his Dionysian fantasy, according to Girard, is the scapegoat process lurking within. What passes as a heroic "yes" in Nietzsche's affirmation of the "eternal recurrence" is structurally identical to the myths it endorses, which at root legitimate (yet shroud) the endless cycle of groups producing victims for the establishment of their identity. This is in profound contradiction with Nietzsche's well-known repudiation of the "herd mentality." "He opposes, so he believes, the crowd mentality, but he does not recognize his Dionysian stance as the supreme expression of the mob in its most brutal and its most stupid tendencies."[59]

In a well-known passage from the *The Will to Power*, Nietzsche makes his case:

> Dionysos versus the "Crucified": there you have the antithesis. It is *not* a difference in regard to their martyrdom — it is a difference in the meaning of it. Life itself, its eternal fruitfulness and recurrence, creates torment, destruction, the will to annihilation. In the other case, suffering — the "Crucified as the innocent one" — counts as an objection to this life, as a formula for its condemnation. — One will see that the problem is that of the meaning of suffering: whether a Christian meaning or a tragic meaning. In the former case, it is supposed to be the path to a holy existence; in the latter case, being is counted as *holy enough* to justify even a monstrous amount of suffering. The tragic man affirms even the harshest suffering.... The god on the cross is a curse on life, a signpost to seek redemption from life; Dionysos cut to pieces is a *promise* of life: it will be eternally reborn and return again from destruction.[60]

Noteworthy here is that the death of Dionysius and Jesus exhibit the same mythical pattern. Both are destroyed by convergent powers and later "raised." Girard insists that we miss something vitally important if we do not see the relationship of the gospels and myth. (Myth for Girard has a crucial historical value; it illuminates the scapegoat process that is very real and recurrent in human culture.) Only by seeing their similarities can we see why they are worlds apart. Only by seeing the gospels within the context of mythology can we see precisely what they are repudiating. Nietzsche apparently saw this, noting that the deaths of Dionysius and Jesus are structurally identical but polar extremes in outcome. The former is tragic; the latter is anti-tragic. The former points us to the affirmation of suffering as an affirmation of life; the latter is the denial of suffering as original to life, and thus a rejection of life. The former sees the individual as something to be sacrificed for the species; the latter is anti-sacrificial by declaring the innocence of the victim and the injustice of Jesus' death. And it is the latter interpretation, according to Nietzsche, that has, to our detriment, won out over the former. The transvaluation inaugurated by the Jews and intensified by the Christians has gained ascendancy in Western culture. In his *On the Genealogy of Morals,* Nietzsche describes the difference between these two moralities in terms of "Rome versus Judea": "The Romans were the strong and noble men, stronger and nobler than they had ever been on earth, or even dreamed themselves to be.... The Jews conversely were the priestly people of *ressentiment par excellence,* with an innate genius in matters of popular morality." And yet, as improbable as it may seem, "there is no doubt that Rome has been defeated," — defeated by *"three Jews,* as one knows, and *one Jewess* (before Jesus of Nazareth, the fisherman Peter, the carpet-maker Paul, and the mother of the aforementioned Jesus, Mary)."[61]

Looking afresh at the *Magnificat* from Nietzsche's perspective makes this reversal all the more obvious, just as it shows its internal relationship with the Jewish scriptures:

> My soul proclaims the greatness of the Lord and my spirit rejoices in God my savior; because he has looked upon the humiliation of his servant.... He has used the power of his arm, he has routed the arrogant of heart. He has pulled down princes from their thrones and raised high the lowly. He has filled the starving with good things, set the rich away empty. He has come to the help of Israel his servant, mindful of his faithful love — according to the promise he made to our ancestors — of his mercy to Abraham, and to his descendants forever. (Luke 1:46–55)

Nietzsche saw quite clearly the legacy of this transvaluation in Western culture. The "slave revolt in morals," which the Jews began and the Christians inherited, "has a two-thousand-year history behind it and which has today dropped out of sight only because it — has succeeded."[62] This is how Nietzsche diagnoses the decadence of his contemporary world, and by extension ours: the success of the Judeo-Christian tradition in weakening and sickening Western culture by valorizing the victim and problematizing misfortune and suffering into "evil."

Girard agrees entirely with this historical assessment, but gives it a very different evaluation. "Our society is the most preoccupied with victims of any that ever was.... No historical period, no society we know, has ever spoken of victims as we do.... We are all actors as well as witnesses in a great anthropological first."[63] This does not mean that we do not continue to make victims, or that the process of scapegoating is without power in the world. What it means is that the *perspective of the victim* has achieved an authority in our era that is unthinkable without the Judeo-Christian tradition. Girard's thesis is that the unveiling of the scapegoat process in the Jewish and Christian scriptures has unleashed a remarkable historical process that, with fits and starts, and certainly with ironic mutations, has made the victim and the inviolability of the individual human person increasingly dominant in the construction of our moral and political imaginations:

> [S]ince the High Middle Ages all the great human institutions have evolved in the same direction: more human private and public law, penal legislation, juridical practice, the rights of individuals. Everything changed very slowly at first, but the pace has been accelerating more and more. When viewed in terms of the large picture, this social and cultural revolution goes always in the same direction, toward the mitigation of punishment, greater protection for potential victims.[64]

While some may regard the Enlightenment "emancipation" from the Judeo-Christian tradition as the possibility for elaborating such things as human rights, for example, Girard argues that only the unmasking of the victim mechanism allows for such a development. "The essential thing in what goes now as human rights is an indirect acknowledgement of the fact that every individual or every group of individuals can become the 'scapegoat' of their own community. Placing emphasis on human rights amounts to a formerly unthinkable effort to control processes of mimetic snowballing."[65]

This authority of the victim is so pervasive in our contemporary discourse that identifying oneself (or one's group) as a victim is one of the most effective ways to attract sympathetic attention and motivating action on behalf of one's cause. To understand the current preoccupation in our political and intellectual discourses with the Other — with peoples or histories at the margins, with those who are excluded, silenced, or ghettoized, whether according to gender, race, sexuality, class, religion, or irreligion — requires understanding the centrality of the victim in our language and imagination. Even the most obnoxious forms of "political correctness" that assiduously police our language are possible only because of the Judeo-Christian transvaluation. Gil Ballie puts it well: "[T]he empathy for victims — *as victims* — is specifically Western and quintessentially biblical. The burr under the saddle of 'Western' culture, the source of its moral uneasiness and social restlessness, is precisely this growing empathy for victims. Most of the West's political innovations are linked to it, and our most deeply held social and moral sensibilities are suffused with it."[66] Even if it is true that ours is a "post-Christendom" era, the Judeo-Christian concern for the victim continues to inspire our secular discourses, though these secular discourses rarely acknowledge this inspiration, or view religion itself as an obstacle to progress in humanitarian matters. In the West, the Judeo-Christian tradition is under particular attack, its canon of scriptures sometimes viewed as repressive in their ideological editorializing of alternative discourses and voices. The canonical limitation to just four gospels, we are told, excludes many other gospels that circulated in the first century in order to exert a theological hegemony that we must now deconstruct. What many of these would-be liberators fail to understand, or even acknowledge, is that the Bible's concern for the victim, its unmasking of the scapegoat process that obfuscates the voice of the victim by projecting upon him or her inner pollution and conflict — and supremely so in the New Testament, whose hermeneutic is uniformly shaped by the *resurrection of an innocent victim* — is in fact the only reason why they have become sensitized to search for marginalized voices in the first place. "We would not accuse the Gospels of victimization if we had not already been converted by them."[67]

The Keystone of Biblical Inspiration

The Bible relentlessly draws our attention to the *perspective of the innocent victim*. In its key narrative traditions, the perspective of the victim before the accuser takes on such a defining role that we might be justified in declaring that the "keystone of biblical inspiration" is found in the "reversal of the relation of innocence and guilt between victims and executioners."[68]

The brotherly rivalry which led to Cain's murder of *Abel* is told with the presumption of the latter's innocence. The first of several stories in the Old Testament centered upon mimetic rivalry among brothers, the story of Cain and Abel highlights the inclination to expel the rival-model as desires entangle in close proximity. After his murder, Abel's blood cries from the ground to YHWH, and thus the memory of the injustice sends out an eschatological echo (Gen. 4:10). Importantly, although Cain is driven from the land now saturated with his brother's blood, he is protected by YHWH from cyclical violence with a mark that distinguishes him as "set apart" by YHWH. "Abel is the first scapegoat," observes James G. Williams, "but then Cain, as the one who is 'signed' or 'marked,' is the substitute for Abel. He in turn would be murdered if it were not for the sign. The sign is thus a substitute for the victimization process that averts a new sacrificial substitution through the prohibition (i.e., 'thou shalt not murder Cain as he murdered Abel')."[69]

The expulsion of *Joseph* occurs as his older brothers throw him into an empty cistern and sell him into slavery out of jealousy. Covering for their crime, they allow their father to believe that his favored son had been eaten by a ravenous animal. Yet, Joseph eventually becomes their "salvation" as he provides protection for his entire family as an administrator in Egypt. With a characteristic biblical irony that reaches its climax in the passion and resurrection narratives, the victim again speaks after his expulsion and returns to his enemies as their gift. What was originally an act of scapegoating is subverted and transformed by God into an act of hospitality. Joseph says to his frightened brothers: " 'Come closer to me.' When they had come closer to him he said, 'I am your brother Joseph whom you sold into Egypt' " (Gen. 45:3–4). In other words, *I am your victim.* "God sent me before you to assure the survival of your race on earth and to save your lives by a greater deliverance" (Gen. 45:7). This "greater deliverance" is possible only because Joseph has broken the cycle of violence by offering his brothers forgiveness and hospitality. "The final triumph of Joseph," notes Girard, "is revealed at the point where pardon replaces the obligatory vengeance. It is only this pardon, this forgiveness, that is capable of stopping once and for all the spiral of reprisals, which of course are sometimes interrupted by unanimous expulsions, but violently and only temporarily."[70]

In the story of the *exodus,* God takes the side of a people suffering enslavement. Slavery, a distinctive form of expulsion through absolute social domination, was the Egyptian solution for containing the

Hebrew population that had grown too numerous to maintain imperial order. YHWH identifies with the innocent suffering of the Hebrews and, through a reversal of sacrificial expulsion, leads them out of their oppressor's hands into a new land for the establishment of a covenantal community. The "founding" of the Mosaic community thus comes through the experience of being liberated from the "domination system" that Pharaoh's Egypt represented. One of the crucially important elements of the exodus narrative is the cry of protest among the Hebrews, which is also the cry of innocence. Here there is not a voice of resignation, which would only legitimate the draconian measures undertaken by the Egyptians to reassert control of their empire-building, "but instead...a militant sense of being wronged with the powerful expectation that it will be heard and answered. Thus the history of Israel begins on the day when its people no longer address the Egyptian gods who will not listen and cannot answer." As Walter Brueggemann further observes, "bringing hurt to public expression is an important first step in the dismantling criticism that permits a new reality, theological and social, to emerge."[71] Putting the matter in more Girardian terms, the language of protest, and the innocence it presumes for those who are the victims of scapegoat violence, pierces the silence required for keeping the process intact.

In many of the *psalms,* the perspective of the victim emerges with striking clarity. The voice of the psalmist frequently speaks of unjust accusations, of being surrounded by enemy mobs that set traps and intend to carry out violence. Schwager notes that nearly 100 of the 150 psalms in scripture deal with threats from enemies, many of which demonstrate an explicit awareness of how collective violence towards individuals gains justification through false projections of guilt. Even if some of these psalms (the so-called "imprecatory psalms") give expression for revenge upon enemies, they speak from the point of view of one who stands to become the victim of frenzied mobs bent upon scapegoat violence.[72] Not surprisingly, the gospels frequently appeal to the psalms as particularly illuminating of the structural dynamics involved in Jesus' passion and death.

In the book of *Job,* which may be thought of as an extended psalm, we see the scapegoat process thwarted as Job consistently asserts his innocence before his accusers. "The book of Job is a failed sacrificial event," writes Heim, "where the victim inexplicably has the stage and is interrogating his persecutors, including the divine power appealed to as the foundation for sacrifice."[73] Job is a spectacular example of how one tradition can emerge to question and subvert others in light of new insights. The accusers of Job speak from a point of view that can claim support from earlier strains within scripture, particularly the form of theodicy associated with the Deuteronomistic history that attributes *all* suffering to guilt. As Job resists the interpretation of his accusers, he not only contradicts a form of theological reasoning that closes off the possibility of innocent suffering, but he emerges in the end as one who is vindicated of the projected guilt that is essential for the scapegoat process to properly function.

The *suffering servant* motif in Second Isaiah also speaks on behalf of an innocent, scapegoat victim. As the servant bears the iniquities of his own people, the principal features of scapegoating violence emerge in sharpest outline. As Gil Bailie writes, the "Suffering Servant Songs combine two insights: first, that the victim was innocent and his persecutors wrong, and, second, that his victimization was socially beneficial and that his punishment brought the community peace.... It has suppressed neither the moral offensiveness of the violence nor the social fact that the violence had beneficial cultural effects."[74] This combination provides us with an understanding of scapegoating "from within," as it were. It simultaneously acknowledges the *unjust* and socially *constructive* effects it can serve, i.e., both its poisonous and curative properties.

Thus, from the story of Cain's murder of Abel, Joseph's expulsion by his brothers into slavery, and the exodus's grammar of reversal reverberating throughout scripture, not least in the "apocalyptic imagination" of later writings; to the psalmist's cries of protests before gathering mobs, Job's resistance to false accusations among his so-called "friends," and the "suffering servant" who innocently bears the iniquities of his people: through these and many other plots and motifs, those who are victims of expulsion, objectification, and domination are shown to be innocent before their accusers who falsely project guilt upon them in order to justify their violence. By displaying in rich and varied detail the rivalries and crises among brothers, clans, nations, and kings in Israel's history, the Old Testament affords insights into the dynamics of mimetic desire while showing how such rivalries and crises so often lead to the production of victims.

That One Man Should Die

The *gospels* are entirely in keeping with this unveiling process, yet they penetrate the problem to its core, to the very heart of what Girard calls the "victim mechanism," i.e., the habitual tendency for humans to resolve mimetic conflict within groups by collectively polarizing themselves over against a common Other upon whom guilt and inner violence are projected, with the outcome of the Other's expulsion or lynching. If the dynamics of scapegoating can be found in subtler forms in interpersonal dynamics, that is to say, without explicit (or "hot") violence, Girard asserts that embedded within human culture — as evident in the ubiquitous practices of sacrifice, either actual or ritually memorialized, and the commonly recurrent structure of myths worldwide that depict order emergent from the slaying of primordial chaos — lies countless founding murders that have provided human beings pharmacological measures to keep the contagion of violence from spiraling out of control.[75] Important to Girard's thesis regarding the effectiveness of the victim mechanism is the belief that the victim truly is guilty, that the scapegoat is in fact responsible for the contamination or rising chaos within the group. This is fundamental to the deception, as is the temporarily curative effects of the victim's expulsion that give a self-validating structure of experience.

In the drama of Jesus' crucifixion all the tell-tale signs of the scapegoat process are visible, even if their true significance remains hidden to all but one of its *dramatis personae*. On one level there is nothing extraordinary about this drama whatsoever. If any form of evil deserved to be called "banal," the scapegoat process is it. The manner of Jesus' death reflects all too faithfully the mythic pattern observable in other persecution stories, most notably the convergence of multiple agents upon a victim who, despite the actual merits of the accusations leveled against him, including sorcery, blasphemy, inciting social unrest, and so forth, find him guilty of injecting chaos and instability between groups that might irrupt into uncontrollable, mimetic violence if they cannot reach unanimity by locking on a mutual Other, whose lynching serves to placate the rising hostilities. In the gospel of John, just after Jesus' "I am the resurrection" discourse and the raising of Lazarus, we see with mechanical precision the logic that leads to Jesus' murder.

> Then the chief priests and Pharisees called a meeting. "Here is this man working all these signs," they said, "and what action are we taking? If we let him go on in this way everybody will believe in him, and the Romans will come and suppress the Holy Place and our nation." One of them, Caiaphas, the high priest that year, said, "You do not seem to have grasped the situation at all; you fail to see that it is to your advantage that one man should die for the people, rather than that the whole nation should perish." He did not speak in his own person, but as high priest of that year he was prophesying that Jesus was to die for the nation — and not for

the nation only, but also to gather together into one the scattered children of God. From that day onwards they were determined to kill him. (John 11:47–53)

Here we begin to see both the exposure and subversion of the scapegoat process. With great clarity Caiaphas articulates the salutary effects for the group when a single victim dies. Jesus is identified as a menace, an outsider who figures to create controversy and anarchy by his mighty "signs." Left unchecked, the excitement generated by Jesus among the people will spiral out of control and mimetically attract the attention of Israel's occupiers, the Romans, who will engage in their own act of expulsion by destroying the temple and its cult, over which the Sadducees preside. Characterized as a perfect bind, Caiaphas's political calculus adds up to a single and serenely rational solution: Jesus must die.

"Caiaphas is the incarnation of politics at its best, not its worst. No one has ever been a better politician."[76] Indeed, how often has Caiaphas's line of reasoning served some politically expedient purpose! But Pilate is no less the politician. Pilate is even persuaded that Jesus is innocent of the charges leveled against him, and yet he still proceeds to have him scourged and crucified. He allows whatever better judgment he might have had to be drowned out by the voice of the mob bent upon Jesus' death without compelling reasons. Only the thought, suggested by the crowd/chorus, that Caesar will find him untrustworthy if he does not efficiently handle potential political insurgency, convinces Pilate to do what only he has the power to do (John 19:12, 10). Pilate therefore chooses *power* over truth. Even though this is a trial to find out the truth, the truth is a causality by scene's end, distorted in the pressurized exchange among groups in mimetic crisis. Only Jesus, who *is* the truth (14:6), is unmoved by mimetic violence. "Mine is not a kingdom of this world; if my kingdom were of this world, my men would have fought to prevent my being surrendered to the Jews. As it is, my kingdom does not belong here" (18:37). Jesus consistently resists being drawn into the violence that threatens him at every turn. Even when faced with the real possibility of his murder he does not resort to the means associated with the "kingdom of this world" to defend himself. The Kingdom of God is an alternative order to the one presently dominant in the *humanum*. This is something Pilate cannot comprehend. "Pilate said, 'So, then you are a king'? Jesus answered, 'It is you who say that I am king. I was born for this, I came into the world for this, to bear witness to the truth; and all who are on the side of truth listen to my voice.' 'Truth?' said Pilate. 'What is that?' " (vv. 37–38). Not surprisingly, perhaps, Nietzsche declared that only one figure emerges in the whole New Testament who demands respect — Pilate, the Roman governor. "To take a Jewish quarrel *seriously* was a thing he could not get himself to do. One Jew more or less — what did it matter?... The noble scorn of a Roman, in whose presence the word 'truth' had been shamelessly abused, has enriched the New Testament with the only saying which *is of value*... 'What is truth'!"[77] But the reason for Pilate's question is not because he is a philosopher-king pondering the nature of truth. His question is an expression of utter incomprehension. He does not comprehend because he is beholden to the truth of power, the *will to power.* Jesus' power, however, is the power of truth, and this truth entails the renunciation of the pseudo power of violence.[78] Jesus makes clear the nature of this renunciation in his farewell speech to his disciples: "I shall not talk to you much longer, because the prince of this world is on his way. He has no power over me, but the world must recognize that I love the Father, and that I act just as the Father commanded. Come now, let us go" (14:30–32). According to Volf, Pilate emerges as the most shrewdly deceitful of all, since he "manages to have a popular preacher and potential trouble-maker hanged and the Jewish religious leaders held responsible for the act; he succeeds both in having the Jewish religious leaders express publicly their allegiance to Caesar as their only king (19:15) and in making Jesus' fate a showcase to any pretenders to the title of Jewish king (19:21). The religious leaders seek to twist Pilate's arm, but he makes them executioners of his own hidden purpose. In both cases — religious leaders' pressure or Pilate's cunning — communication is a tool of violence, not an instrument of reasonable exchange."[79]

What makes the conspiracy of Jesus' execution and the trial scene that brings it to pass revelatory — a narrative deconstruction of the mythic illusion that reflexively presumes the guilt of the scapegoat — is the gospels' insistence on Jesus' innocence.[80] "They hated me without reason" (John 15:25, Ps. 69:4).[81] Those involved in the lynching are even convinced they are honoring God. "They will expel you from the synagogues, and indeed the time is coming when anyone who kills you will think he is doing a holy service to God" (16:2). But drawing God into the myth of sacred violence only shows ignorance of God. "They will do these things because they have never known either the Father or me" (v. 3). The innocence and guilt between accuser and accused is thus reversed. Those engaged in Jesus' execution, who would otherwise be seen as blameless, are shown to be guilty: "If I had not come, if I had not spoken to them, they would have been blameless; but as it is they have no excuse for their sin" (15:22).

What is most stunning about this last passage, and what enables us to properly understand the "necessity" of Jesus' death and resurrection, is that *if the Logos of God had not come* to enter into the web of mimetic rivalry and violence to speak to those ensnared by it, then its cycle would have continued unabated and the mythic illusion that keeps human beings hostage to the invincible deception — under the dominion of the "father of lies," the one who was a "murderer from the beginning" (8:44) — would have remained unbroken.[82] So ensconced are we in our sin that we cannot even perceive the truth when it appears before our very eyes. The "saturated phenomenality" of divine truth is perceived under the aspect of obscurity because we remain addicted to the untruth of violence and power. The *Logos* of God has come into the world, though we knew him not, and we proceeded to kill him. With an irony so extreme that it takes considerable time before we can properly begin to fathom it: God, in Jesus Christ, has become *our* victim. Humans have committed deicide. We killed God. And not just by accident, but because we believed we were doing God's will. And yet God has overcome our deicide in the resurrection of the victim. With a love both tenacious and vulnerable, God has used our deicide to save us from ourselves. The *Logos*, who was *with* God in the beginning and who *was* God (1:1), has allowed himself to be "handed over" to the powers of this world to be condemned and murdered in an act of self-donating love, not in order to legitimate our production of scapegoat victims, which *is* the great lie, but to release us from the endless cycle of producing them. Only by killing God, and only as this God offers us forgiveness in spite of our lethal self-deception, are we able finally to perceive the depth of our guilt. Only *from* the encounter with the risen victim, who *is* God — and thus in the recognition of the extreme contradiction between who God really is and who we falsely imagine God to be — can we begin the most important act of human recollection, the remembrance of guilt past.

God has subverted the scapegoat process from the inside out. This is the ultimate meaning of the last part of the passage from John above: "[Caiaphas] did not speak in his own person, but as high priest of that year he was prophesying that Jesus was to die for the nation — and not for the nation only, but also to gather together into one the scattered children of God." On one level Caiaphas expresses with great economy the essence of sacred violence. However, Caiaphas and all the other parties involved in Jesus' lynching do not understand what they are doing. Superimposed upon Caiaphas's words is another level of meaning, an ironic "prophecy." By murdering the *Logos* of God, the divisions that have kept the human family divided in mutual exclusion and hostility may at last be overcome. Jesus Christ is the universal victim whose death and resurrection make possible the gathering together of the whole human family.

The passages in the synoptic gospels that speak of the "necessity" of Jesus' passion and resurrection do not make the point that Jesus had to become a victim in order to appease God, as though God has an appetite for the murder of an innocent. (God is unmoved by our mimetic rivalry. This is the proper meaning of God's impassivity. God cannot be drawn into rivalry with human beings, but is agapic Love. God doesn't need scapegoats, we do — or so we believe.) In Mark 8, the structural center of the gospel, we see the first of three predictions of the passion and resurrection in a most remarkable exchange between Jesus and Peter. Immediately after Peter's confession of faith ("You are the Christ"), Jesus proceeds to teach his disciples that "the Son of man was destined to suffer grievously, and to be rejected by the elders and the chief priests and the scribes, and to be put to death, and after three days to rise again." Upon hearing this very strange utterance, Peter takes Jesus aside to rebuke him. Peter's prior understanding of messianic vocation has nothing at all to do with the scenario depicted by Jesus. A suffering, crucified messiah was to him quite unthinkable, patently scandalous. To the contrary, the messiah was destined to liberate Israel from its enemies, to restore the kingdom and vindicate God's purposes for his people. Victory, not demonstrable defeat, was the plan. What a dead messiah had to do with Israel's hope, not only could Peter not perceive this, but it struck him as worthy of stern rebuke. But Jesus responds with a rebuke of his own, the strongest of all Jesus' rebukes recorded by the gospels: "Get behind me, Satan! You are thinking not as God thinks, but as human beings do" (33). If Jesus' mission entails a radical inversion of expectation, this includes even the expectations of those closest to Jesus. Jesus intends to transform Israel's story and its hope. But it was not until the resurrection of Jesus from the dead that the disciples would fully perceive this. The perspectival tension between what Peter thought Jesus was doing in "real time," and what Jesus himself set out to accomplish, is nothing less than the epistemic gap between pre- and post-resurrection knowledge. As James Alison has so brilliantly put it, not until the disciples became witnesses to the risen victim did they inherit the "intelligence of the victim" that would allow them to retrospectively see the true significance of Jesus' ministry and death. "After the resurrection the disciples began to see the internal coherence between [Jesus'] teaching, and the way he had lived, leading up to his death. That is to say, the intelligence of the victim that had been in Jesus, passed to them. They began to be able to understand the story of Jesus' life from Jesus' own point of view."[83] From this point of view, the "necessity" of Jesus' death and resurrection appears only retrospectively to the disciples. Whether the passion predictions in their present form represent the *ipsissima verba* of Jesus, or give evidence of some formulization *ex eventu* — in all likelihood, a combination of both — they are important in revealing two things at once: first, only after the resurrection of the victim will the disciples grasp the true significance of Jesus' life-ministry and death; and second, the true significance of Jesus' life, death, and resurrection entails a fulfillment through the subversion of the disciples' expectations regarding Israel's hope.

The Non-Accidental Scapegoat

Before I pursue the "intelligence of the victim" further in the next chapter, I must briefly address the question of Jesus' own view of death. Although we discussed this briefly in chapters 2 and 3, here we must say something more, particularly given the tendency in some "historical Jesus" quarters to peremptorily dismiss the predictions of Jesus' death and resurrection to be of little or no historical value. As I have said, we can fully acknowledge that the present formulation of these predictions give evidence of formulization. But this does not mean they bear no historical value. It is most implausible that Jesus did not anticipate his death and interpret it as bearing crucial significance to his ministry. To the extent that Jesus styled his ministry, in part, along the lines of Israel's great prophets, including Jeremiah and John the Baptist, both of whom would become victims — one to his own people, the other (and more proximately to Jesus) to Roman political power — the outcome of violent death as a consequence of his ministry could only seem assured.[84] From beginning to end his ministry generated scandal, the nature of which is crucially important to understand.

Jesus' ministry was nothing if not a relentless transgression of social-religious distinctions, and thus a destabilization of extant order in the *polis*. The world of first-century Palestinian Judaism was a complex patchwork of groups, many of which sought explicit identification in definitional contrast with others. Although the specific configurations of group distinction in Jesus' day were unique to his time, the underlying dynamics involved are not that different from those in any other social setting. To draw upon my earlier analysis, the project of acquiring and maintaining identity within one group so often comes through the articulation of distinction *from* another. While Israel's identity as a people was similarly fashioned — a people elected or "set apart" by God to serve and worship the true God in fidelity to the law — the state of Judaism in the first century was characterized by deep divisions, particularly over issues of purity. As Marcus Borg explains, a purity system "is a social system organized around the contrasts or polarities of pure and impure, clean and unclean. The polarities of pure and impure establish a spectrum or 'purity map' ranging from pure on one end through varying degrees of purity to impure (or 'off the purity map') at the other. These polarities apply to persons, places, things, times, and social groups."[85] Purity systems are ubiquitous in human culture, but in first-century Jewish Palestine such a system was operative by way of distinguishing groups according to heredity, religious office, observance of purity codes, physical wholeness, and gender. Understanding Jesus' ministry, as well as the danger he quite consciously put himself in, requires that we see it as an unrelenting disruption of the boundaries of "pure" and "impure" as delineated by the dominant purity map of his day. A very significant proportion of his sayings and deeds involve bringing these distinctions into crisis: his words of rebuke to the Pharisees who fashion their strict adherence to purity, which also served to distinguish them over against the "impure"; parables like the Good Samaritan that show an "outsider" performing the work of the Kingdom; his deliberate breaking of specific purity laws, such as picking grain on the Sabbath to demonstrate that the Sabbath was made for humans, not for God; his denunciation of the temple system and its administrators who placed harsh burdens on ordinary Jews, and who compromised with Roman power to maintain their own; his constant association with "sinners," such as tax collectors and prostitutes; his table-fellowship with the ritually "unclean"; his touching and healing of the infirm who, because of their lack of physical wholeness, were denied full access to Jewish worship; his public association with and touching of women, which was regarded as taboo. Through these and many other sayings and deeds, Jesus undermines the subtle and overt ways human beings cultivate identity, individually or in groups, in contrastive relation to the Other. He thus brings scandal to identity. His is a ministry of healing through cauterization. (Hence the otherwise unintelligible statement, "I have not come to bring peace, but a sword" [Matt. 10:34; see also Luke 12:51–53; 14:26–27].) It painfully brings to light the underlying disease of mimetic rivalry and conflict. Such an operation is extremely dangerous. It plays directly, if calculatingly, into the dynamics of the scapegoating process: for when identity is threatened, when social distinctions are confused, when pollution is introduced into the system, the habitual reaction is to expel, to exterminate. As Girard has shown, persecution myths exhibit stereotypical patterns that lead to the scapegoat process. "The great social crises that engender collective persecutions are experienced as a lack of differentiation," a confusion or contamination of the distinctions deemed necessary for social order.[86] Such social chaos may be the result of institutional collapse, rivalry among groups, external domination, or natural disasters. What is notable in Jesus' case is that he aggressively brings crisis to distinction. He blurs the dominant purity map to such an extent that he can quite legitimately be regarded as the cause of social disorder. Jesus baits the very processes that lead to unjust persecution. "Through his message of the basileia," writes Schwager, "he himself had awakened the forces which concentrated against him, and he lured them out of their hiding-place by his judgment speeches. He was no accidental scapegoat, as is usually the case. By his claim expressed in the message of the basileia and by his relentless judgment sayings, he himself set in motion that process which was bound to turn against him."[87]

Did Jesus know that his ministry would end with his death? Did he foresee that he would eventually become a victim upon whom multiple forces would converge in an act of violent expulsion? For a man whose ministry was explicitly predicated upon bringing crisis to social-religious distinction, of upending the ways human beings, above all the powerful, operate with a politics of purity in order to maintain order, the question is, How could Jesus *not* think he would become such a victim? If his ministry exhibited such extraordinary intelligence regarding the conflictual dynamics of human relations, even drawing these dynamics out into the light, relentlessly exposing them through his sayings and deeds, why would Jesus remain so extraordinarily ignorant of the outcome that surely awaited him? But he was not ignorant of this. Jesus in fact drew the self-deception and projective judgment of his accusers upon himself, though he did not return their conspiring violence with violence. He orchestrated the scapegoat process, wicked it toward himself in a capillary action. He "triggered off a process which struck back at him and hit him: he became the victim of the sins of others, a scapegoat." In so doing, he brought the self-deception of his adversaries to explicit thematization; but their judgment was in the end an act of self-judgment:

> The self-judgment of humankind, in which people shifted their guilt onto Jesus in self-deception, became a judgment on him. But from his viewpoint this was a judgment of a completely different sort. He allowed himself to be drawn into the process of self-judgment of his adversaries, in order, through participation in their lot, to

open up for them from inside another way out of their diabolical circle and hence a new path to salvation. He did not pay back the lying judgment and violent attack with the same coin, but he turned around the intensified evil and gave it back as love redoubled. He made himself a gift to those who judged him and burdened them with their guilt.[88]

We need not imagine that Jesus *desired* to become a victim of human hostility as though such, by itself, possessed terminal value. Jesus' mission was not a sacred suicide.[89] To become just one among countless other victims would hardly be a satisfactory conclusion to a ministry dedicated to the overcoming of victimization. Neither should we draw the theological conclusion that God desired Jesus' death in a way that would underwrite the scapegoat process. The exact opposite is true. What we must say instead is that Jesus knew that the ultimate consequence of his Kingdom of God ministry was death, but his death would become centrally important in the final fulfillment of that ministry. He was not an accidental scapegoat, but, as the gospels insist, he "handed himself over" to this process with the ultimate goal of defeating it.

Chapter Eight

THE GIFT OF
THE FORGIVING VICTIM

RESURRECTION AS RECONCILIATION

In Part One we examined the revelation of the risen victim in terms of a "dazzling darkness," as a saturated phenomenon that is encountered in the mode of obscurity due to its excessive givenness. The risen Jesus "appears" as one who is both familiar and strange. The relationship of presence and absence in the gospels reflects the eschatological nature of the Easter event, which is both historical and more-than-historical. All this can be reaffirmed here, but now we can inquire more thoroughly into the soteriological significance of this mis-identification. The "risen stranger" is strange, not simply because finite human beings cannot fully represent in image or language the eschatological excess of Easter, but because our warped perception keeps us from recognizing the truth about how we build our identities through exclusions. "The delayed recognition of Jesus," writes Girard, "has nothing to do with a lesser visibility of his resurrected body due to the lesser reality of the shadowy afterlife to which he now would belong. The opposite is true. *This resurrection is too real for a perception dimmed by the false transfigurations of mimetic idolatry.*"[1] According to this interpretation, the tendency to view the stories of the disciples' doubt primarily in terms of apologetic intent is superficial. We are indeed correct to see in the gospels a frank acknowledgement of an epistemic gap. Nothing less than a revolution in how one views the world is entailed in the process of moving from a pre- to a post-Easter perspective. But the gap between these two perspectives is more than about metaphysical possibilities, e.g., whether we think that given the laws of nature something like Jesus' bodily resurrection is possible. The gap is one of *desire*.

James Alison speaks of the disciples' doubt as reflecting a process of conversion to what he calls the "intelligence of the victim." What he means by this is that affirming Jesus' resurrection implies much more than assimilating a discrete piece of information within a preexisting framework of knowing. It involves a transformation in knowing itself. This transformation is radical, though we should not imagine that it occurs all at once. Because it entails a thoroughgoing reframing of how we understand ourselves in relation to the divine and human Other, we will find that the true pedagogical value of the stories of apostolic doubt lay in their ability to guide us along the process of *metanoia*, even well after we have at least notionally assented to the proclamation that Jesus is "risen from the dead." The sort of radical transformation we are considering here is possible only when we enter into a *face-to-face relation with our victim* — with the One whose expulsion from our midst is reversed and overcome by God's eschatological forgiveness. Only from the knowledge of *being forgiven* can we fully perceive the depths of our guilt and see in sharpest outline the strategies we employ, often without our full comprehension, to fashion our identities through a succession of denials and expulsions. This offer of forgiveness from God is not a simple declaration. It is not a verbal absolution from afar. The special character of "resurrection" language is alone adequate to account for the true nature of God's eschatological hospitality to us. The offer of forgiveness comes to us in the mode of a *risen person*. Victimization has a *face*. In *being-faced* by our victim, our idolatrous and objectifying gaze is reversed in a counter-experience so that *we see ourselves from the perspective of our victim*. To begin seeing ourselves from the perspective of the victim is to awaken to the "intelligence of the victim."

God's Logic of Excess

Let us return once again to the double reversal in Acts 2. As noted in previous chapters, the first reversal is characteristically apocalyptic in its pronouncement of judgment and vindication. The improvised court scene, which mirrors the (mis)trial of Jesus, begins with an accusation all-inclusive in scope. It includes not only "You that are Israelites," but the Romans "outside the law" to whom Jesus was "handed over" to be crucified (Acts 2:22–23). In the parallel formulation in Acts 4, the accusation is more specific, yet equally embracing, and includes Israel's "rulers, elders, and scribes assembled in Jerusalem, with Annas the high priest, Caiaphas, John, and Alexander, and all who were of the high-priestly family." Indeed, the entire city of Jerusalem stands under judgment as the place where "Herod and Pontius Pilate, with the Gentiles and the peoples of Israel, gathered together against [God's] holy servant Jesus, whom [God] anointed" (vv. 5–6, 27).[2] This "gathering together" is most significant. It is the collective polarization of the *many against one*. The supporting psalm in the same chapter draws our attention to the underlying dynamic at work: "Why did the Gentiles rage, and the peoples imagine vain things? The kings of the earth took their stand, and the rulers have *gathered together* against the Lord and against his Messiah" (4:25–26, Ps. 2:1–2). There seems to be no one outside the sweep of Peter's indictment, including himself, who denied even knowing Jesus after his arrest. The recollection of the disciples' abandonment, as well as the accounts of their doubt before and after the resurrection, alert us to their own involvement in Jesus' lynching, even if their guilt is one of passive complicity.[3] The clear implication of this inclusivity is that *all* are entrenched in the dynamics that led to Jesus' death — including you, dear reader. The New Testament invites the reader into a process of self-interpretation from the point of view of this victim, so that even if we are not literally contemporaneous with the events that led to Jesus' crucifixion in first-century Jerusalem, we *are* contemporaneous insofar as the dynamics involved in his crucifixion are operative in our own lives. Had *we* been there, the text is urging, we would have done the same thing. The text draws us into its narrative world in order to deconstruct the stories we frequently tell about ourselves, but which are in fact rooted in self-deception and violence. Whether we see ourselves reflected in Caiaphas, the crowd, Pilate, Herod, Caesar, or the disciples — in all likelihood, some combination thereof — we are invited to see Peter's speech directed at *us*.[4] But this deconstruction of original naiveté does not leave us in the desert of disillusionment. It is offered with the possibility of a second innocence, a "resurrection" into a new story whose truth can set us free for full human flourishing.

True to apocalyptic form, Peter declares the injustice of Jesus' death and announces that God has countered with an act of eschatological vindication. The grammar of reversal is sharply wielded. "But God raised him up, having freed him from death, because it was impossible for him to be held in its power" (2:24). Of this resurrection "all of us are witnesses," which is to say, counter-witnesses to the injustice meted out to an innocent man. The juridical tone is quite deliberate as Peter speaks God's verdict. Yet more than compensation is involved here. God has conferred upon Jesus those titles that connote the sum of Israel's hope, quite despite the fact that this Jesus has been violently expelled from Israel's midst: "Therefore let the entire house of Israel know with certainty that God has made him both Lord and Messiah, this Jesus whom you crucified" (2:36). The victim Jesus has thus become the judge of his judges, and the entire network of peoples and institutions that gathered together to crucify him are charged with the guilt of murdering God's messiah.

The collusion is so widespread, the guilt so transparent, and the reversal of judgment so complete that one might expect at this moment God's righteous indignation to irrupt in an act of retribution worthy of the most phantasmagoric of displays. The agonistic rhetoric seems ready to burst into open threats of divine vengeance, such as those leveled against Antiochus IV by the righteous martyrs. "Keep on, and see how his mighty power will torture you and your descendants" (2 Macc. 7:17). But this is precisely what does *not* happen. Peter announces God's surprising verdict, one that collapses the apocalyptic duality of "righteous" and "unrighteous," indeed, every configuration of "us" and "them." Such is the nature of the second reversal. We might call it a reversal upon reversal, or the transfiguration of apocalyptic hope.

Rather than responding reciprocally to the original violence, God instead offers the risen victim as our Gift. In an act that utterly supersedes the "logic of equivalence" operative in conceptions of retributive justice, the resurrection of the victim, and his return in our midst as the concrete offer of reconciliation with God, manifests God's "logic of excess."[5] "Peter said to them, 'Repent, and be baptized every one of you in the name of Jesus Christ so that your sins may be forgiven; and you will receive the gift of the Holy Spirit. For the promise is for you, for your children, and for all who are far away, everyone whom the Lord our God calls to him" (2:38–39). Similarly: "The God of our ancestors raised up Jesus, whom you had killed by hanging him on a tree. God exalted him at his right hand as Leader and Savior that he might give repentance to Israel and forgiveness of sins" (5:30–31). According to the kerygmatic formulae in Acts, God has brought about the fulfillment to Israel's story through a twofold reversal. First, by raising Jesus from the dead, God has served eschatological justice to an innocent victim whilst unmasking the guilt of his accusers and murderers. The relationship between guilt and innocence has been reversed as the condemned Jesus has now become the judge of his judges. Second, by raising Jesus from the dead, God has acquitted those responsible for this death, using their own ignorance and sin as the very means to save them from self-condemnation, extending to them the Gift of hospitality to participate in a new community, the *ecclesia*, founded upon the *welcome* of the victim. Such a "surprising avenger."[6] Instead of acting within the parameters of reciprocity, where "this" is met with an equivalent "that," God's Gift of the risen victim floods the banks of our limited imaginations and distorted desires in a gesture of superabundance. The dynamic of mutual exchange proves inadequate to foresee and absorb the amazing "more than" of grace which pours itself out in self-donating hospitality, even while we were enemies of God (Rom. 5:10).

Such tenacious hospitality, it should be noted, is entirely in keeping with Jesus' historical ministry. The resurrection of Jesus is internally consistent with his most challenging though characteristic sayings and deeds. In the Sermon on the Mount, for example, the logic of "an eye for an eye and a tooth for a tooth" is supplanted with "do not resist an evildoer"; the response to being struck on the right cheek is to "turn the other also"; the saying "you shall love your neighbor and hate your enemy" is reformulated into "love your enemies and pray for those who persecute you, so that you may be children of your Father in heaven" (Matt. 5:38-44). How many times must we forgive? "Not seven times, but, I tell you, seventy-seven times" (18:22). Or consider the parable of the Prodigal Son, where the Father, filled with compassion, runs out to embrace and kiss his son whom he sees far off, even before the son has the opportunity to ask for forgiveness (Luke 15:20). "This logic of generosity," which Paul Ricoeur claims is present in virtually all of Jesus' parables, proverbs, and eschatological sayings, "clashes head on with the logic of equivalence that orders our everyday exchanges, our commerce, and our penal law."[7]

In the proclamation of the risen victim as forgiveness, this clashing of logics is all the more evident. The reason for this intensification is because the resurrection overcomes even the violent rejection of Jesus' Kingdom of God ministry as such. The expulsion of his *person* is tantamount to the rejection of his *cause*. Jesus' crucifixion stands as the ultimate expression of human sin and guilt. It is the most direct repudiation of divine truth and hospitality. So far from being heeded, God's eschatological prophet was met with a resistance so sharp, yet so emblematic as to stand as humanity's definitive "No." We should not see in Jesus' crucifixion God's rejection of Jesus, but our rejection of God. It is not God's condemnation of us, but our condemnation of God — and thus the ultimate act of self-condemnation. The cross is our guilt made totally visible for the first time. We have murdered the "author of life" (Acts 3:15). The face of the crucified Christ is the face of all our expulsions. But we can only "see" this crucified face by Easter's light. Had Jesus' death concluded his story, our original naiveté would have never been broken. Death is the ultimate keeper of secrets, its dark anonymity the best refuge for power relationships built upon expulsions. Rendered nameless, voiceless, and faceless, the casting out of the victim in the effort to delineate our tenuous identities goes on without protest. Had Jesus died without a sign of divine reaction, our collective "No" would have never been heard in its reality, but only drifted off into an infinite, echoless abyss. The counteract of God, which penetrates through this abyss, rebounds our "No" and enables us to hear it for what it really is. The resurrection of Jesus does something that was not possible within his historical ministry. It overcomes *death* itself. It transforms death's absolute non-presence into God's self-presence to us in the crucified-and-risen One. Death is no longer a barrier between humanity and God. It can no longer obscure the truth about ourselves. It can no longer conceal our exclusions, but has been "filled in" with God's luminosity. But if God brings the victim Jesus back *from* the dead (*anastasis ek nekron*) as an act of apocalyptic judgment — the divine "No" to the human "No" — such an act exceeds reciprocity in the surprising, encompassing "Yes" of divine forgiveness.

> And now, friends, I know that you acted in ignorance, as did also your rulers. In this way God fulfilled what he had foretold through all the prophets, that his Messiah would suffer. Repent therefore, and turn to God so that you sins may be wiped out, so that times of refreshing may come from the presence of the Lord, and that he may send the Messiah appointed for you, that is, Jesus, who must remain in heaven until the time of universal restoration that God announced long ago through his holy prophets. (Acts 3:17–21)

This passage begins by insisting on our ignorance. The nature of this ignorance is vitally important to understand, for it is the same ignorance that underlies the doubt and misunderstanding among the disciples throughout the gospels, both before and initially after Jesus' resurrection. It is the ignorance described in John that kept the world from "seeing" the *Logos* made flesh. It is the ignorance Jesus names in his prayer to the Father from the cross: "Father, forgive them; for they do not know what they are doing" (Luke 23:34).[8] We must understand that such ignorance is not a matter of insufficient information. It is not as though another piece of data would have helped to avert the crisis. When Jesus prays to the Father for his persecutors' forgiveness, he is naming the impregnable deception buried in our hearts that distorts our field of perception so that we cannot see the truth when it appears to us. The obscurity of Jesus' teaching and actions was not due to his attempt to communicate esoteric knowledge. His parables, aphorisms, apocalyptic utterances, and prophetic enactments were not attempts to impart secret *gnosis*. They were acts to jolt us out of the way we ordinarily perceive reality. They only appear oblique within our present horizons of intelligibility because our *desires* are disordered. "The disciples' understanding was (as ours is) formed by what Jesus was trying to change: that is, the constitution of our consciousness in rivalry and the techniques of survival by exclusion of the other."[9] Jesus' ministry is explicitly intent upon reversing these techniques, of extracting people from building identities over against the Other, e.g., the sinner, the unclean, the maimed, the leper, the prostitute, the tax collector, the enemy, the prisoner, the victim, "these little ones." Jesus' "intelligence of the victim" is one that relentlessly takes the perspective *of* the Other — my potential or real victim — as the only truly human way to be a person. This is possible for Jesus because, above all, he follows the will of the *divine Other*.

Here is the primordial root of Jesus' "consciousness," should we wish to use this term: the will of the Father. Because Jesus lives in total transparence to God the Father, Jesus is the one who lives utterly free from rivalry with the human Other. Since Jesus imitates God the Father, whose reality is utterly gratuitous, free from all rivalry as *agapic* Love — "unmoved" by mimetic rivalry, which is the true significance of God's "impassibility" — Jesus is able to live among his sisters and brothers with utter freedom *for* them, without concern for his own identity. Jesus' identity is not built upon contrasting relations with the Other, but in utter self-emptying (*kenosis*) for the Other. When Paul speaks of having the "mind of Christ" he is speaking of just this intelligence: "Let the same mind be in you that was in Christ Jesus, who, though he was in the form of God, did not regard equality with God as something to be exploited, but emptied himself, taking the form of a slave, being born in human likeness. And being found in human form, he humbled himself and became obedient to the point of death — even death on a cross" (Phil. 2:5–8). The "mind of Christ" is one freed from rivalry with God, translucent to the divine Other, whose Otherness is received as total Gift rather than an obstacle to the project of becoming a self. Such loving *kenosis* resulted in Jesus' death, not because death was positively willed by God as having value in itself, but because such unrestrained freedom in a world where rivalry and exclusion are rife is threatening and attracts resistance. The ignorance that led to the violent rejection of Jesus' Kingdom of God ministry was at root a nexus of desires that, so far from desiring to live wholly for and from the divine Other as the possibility for living for and from the human Other, was configured to assert identity over against the Other. Because Jesus set out to unmask and transform the underlying dynamics of human relations premised upon power and exclusions, drawing them out into the light through his sayings and deeds of hospitality and judgment, he himself became a victim. But the faithfulness of the Father would have the last word. It is the word of resurrection: "Therefore God also highly exalted him and gave him the name that is above every name, so that at the name of Jesus every knee should bend, in heaven and on earth and under the earth, and every tongue should confess that Jesus Christ is Lord, to the glory of God the Father" (vv. 9–11).

This is the transvaluation of "values" at its most extreme. The "victim" is "Lord." "This Jesus is 'the stone that was rejected by you, the builders; it has become the cornerstone'" (Acts 4:11; Ps. 118:22).[10] Jesus' total fidelity to the Father results in a loving self-sacrifice to end all sacrifice. By raising him from the dead, God subverts the sacrificial process from within. *This* is the im-possible Gift: forgiveness from our victim, who is our "Lord." "Christ sheds his own blood to end that way of trying to mend our divisions," writes Heim. "Jesus' death isn't necessary because God has to have innocent blood to solve the guilt equation. Redemptive violence is our equation. Jesus didn't volunteer to get into God's justice machine. God volunteered to get into ours. God used our own sin to save us."[11] As Heim further explains, we are entirely correct to say that "Jesus died for our sins," but we must properly understand this statement. Jesus "died for our sins" insofar as "his death exemplifies a specific kind of sin we are all implicated in and we all need saving from, and acts to overcome it." In other words, Jesus is the one upon whom our sin and guilt is projected — *from our side*. When in the New Testament God "hands over" the Son, we must keep the dialogical nature of this drama in view. It is not that God is the primary agent in Jesus' death. We are. Otherwise the declaration of Jesus' *unjust* death would make no sense. As Schwager explains, "judgment did not start from God but from humankind, and the will of the Father was only that the Son should follow sinners to the very end and share their abandonment, in order thus to make possible for them again a conversion from the world of hardened hearts and distance from God."[12] This conversion is only possible, adds Heim, through the "divine power of resurrection": "God was willing to be a victim of that bad thing we had apparently made good, in order to expose its nature and liberate us from it. In so doing, God made that occasion of scapegoating sacrifice (what those who killed Jesus were doing) an occasion of overcoming scapegoat violence (what God was doing)."[13] Jesus' death was a sacrifice *for our sins*, not as a "payment," as it were, but as a self-sacrifice to subvert sacrifice — a sacrifice to end all sacrifice.

The Hermeneutical Circle of Forgiveness and Sin

I shall say more about this subversion of sacrifice in the conclusion of this chapter, but first I return to Karl Rahner's statement that "only the forgiven know they are sinners." This deceptively simple statement alerts us to what might be called the hermeneutical circle between the experience of forgiveness and the awareness of sin. "It could be said," writes Rahner, "that an understanding of the real nature of guilt is not possible until we have discussed the absolute and forgiving closeness of God in and through his self-communication; or that the real truth about a person's guilt can come home to him only when he experiences forgiveness and his deliverance from guilt."[14] With similar meaning, but put in the terms used throughout this chapter, we can say the following: only by entering into a face-to-face relation with the risen victim as our forgiveness, and thus allowing ourselves to be fully embraced by the divine hospitality that absorbs and overcomes the mimetic rivalry and violence in which we are ensnared, can we begin to plumb the depths of our sin and learn to cooperate with divine grace so as to allow our identities to be reformed with new desires. The reason for this order of this manifestation — forgiveness, recognition of sin, and conversion — is that our sin is not perceptible to us in its true depths. One of the consequences of sin is that "it consists precisely in its blindness to its own false nature."[15] In a very real sense "sin" is a datum of revelation, something made explicable to us only from the encounter with God's gratuitous offer of grace. The forgiveness of the risen victim opens up our memory to illuminate the distorted nature of our desires. In accepting God's pardon — in welcoming the risen victim as the One in whom we allow our identities to be refashioned — we open ourselves to a purgative and transformative process (*metanoia*) that restores us to our true humanity.

Here again, the semantic distinctness and richness of resurrection language carries a range of meanings that cannot be translated into another kind of language without losing what is most vital to this process. The *resurrection* of the victim Jesus — his whole body-person, his "face" — is far more powerful and concrete, both in terms of its expression of divine justice and love, than the vague affirmation of his being "alive to God." Because "sin and its consequences are registered in bodies, and especially on faces," the bodily resurrection of Jesus from the dead and his "appearance" in our world focuses our attention and memory on the crucifixion as intrinsic to its meaning.[16] Christ's lordship, writes David Ford, "has his death, this tortured, bloody and dead face, always at its heart. To be dominated by this face is to be loved in a way which transforms our conception of what it is to be loved."[17] This is no doubt scandalous to contemplate. Particularly here we are reminded of D. T. Suzuki's sense of revulsion that Jesus' crucifixion would ever become iconic for the Christian understanding of God. The resurrection of Jesus demands this. It reorients our attention and reforms our memory by drawing us to stand before this crucified face to see in it God's self-donating love, which followed us down to the deepest nadir of our human existence ("for God so loved the world"), as well as our sin, our deicide. Suzuki may have been more illuminating than he realized in describing the Christian focus on the cross as the result of a collective neurosis. Though what he meant in employing such language was that it represents an unhealthy fixation on suffering and death, we can slightly shift his intention to say that the cross does in fact represent a collective neurosis — the "disease" of human sin that generates expulsions and violences, both subtle and overt, as a result of mimetic rivalry. The cross of Christ is human sin made visible, denuded of its secrecy, graphically displayed. To stand in a face-to-face relation with the cross is to allow our sin to face *us* in its stark reality, to see our sin in the face of the Other whom we have expelled. The cross is supremely revelatory, anthropologically speaking, because it bears witness to the deceptive and damaging pharmacological measures we employ to maintain our health. Wanting to be free of the poison we believe is introduced by the Other into our social, religious, and political bodies, we seek to heal ourselves by projecting upon a surrogate our inner violences. But this is only a concentrated reproduction of the poison.

The cross displays the victim mechanism in its most crude form whilst unmasking it. "His suffering on the Cross," writes Girard, "is the price Jesus is willing to pay in order to offer humanity this true representation of human origins that holds it prisoner. In offering himself in this way, he deprives the victim mechanism of its power in the long run."[18] Jesus' self-gift is therefore redemptive suffering, not redemptive violence. He does not utilize violence in any form as a part of his Kingdom of God ministry; rather, he absorbs our violence in his very person in order to transform those who are addicted to its intoxicating power. As we stand before the crucified Christ contemplatively and worshipfully, we worship the *person* who reveals to us in an act of total self-giving the full scope and nature of our untruth. Our worship opens us to a purgative process that begins once we see our self-judgment and self-condemnation in the face of a victim whose innocence and non-violent hospitality is absolute. The cross disabuses us of our naiveté. It is revelation in the strictest sense of the term.

That this is possible to affirm is because of the resurrection. God has traversed our alienation by giving back the crucified Jesus to us in our concrete history. God's forgiveness is not offered by a sort of divine fiat that renders our sin a matter of indifference. Because God allows the risen Jesus to appear in our midst with the marks of his rejection and crucifixion, such forgiveness allows us to adjust our eyes to see the full scope of our sin for the first time. The deepest mystery of the resurrection is found in God giving back to us the one we crucified. "The resurrection life *includes* the human death of Jesus," writes Alison. "He is always present after the resurrection *simultaneously* as the crucified and as risen Lord."[19] The significance of this simultaneity is this: as we stand face-to-face with the risen Christ, we stand face-to-face with our sin from the *perspective of divine forgiveness*. The light of the latter makes the darkness of sin visible by contrast. In John, for example, Thomas is instructed by the risen Jesus to "put your finger here and see my hands. Reach out your hand and put it in my side. Do not doubt but believe" (John 20:27). Thomas reacts to this remarkable invitation with a christological confession of the highest order. "My Lord and my God" (v. 28)! Whatever else we may want to say about the relationship of historical tactility and divine transcendence in this vignette, it gives elegant expression to the relationship between the risen victim and divine forgiveness. To "see" the crucified-and-risen One is to "see" the forgiving hospitality of God in its incomprehensible nearness. (And as I shall explain more fully in the following chapter, the event of Jesus' resurrection inaugurates the process of christological reflection that would lead the earliest Christians to confess Jesus as God's absolute *self*-communication, i.e., to see retrospectively from the Easter event that God was in Christ, from the beginning, as the means for our reconciliation with God.)

The resurrection awakens true memory. It unseals the collective amnesia that has allowed us to suppress the injustice of our violent exclusions and expulsions, showing once and for all that the effort to build our identities through the denial of hospitality to the human Other, with whom we are always in relation, no matter how much we willfully or casually deny it, is in fact a rejection of the divine Other. Again, it is crucial to understand that this awakening to sin — this awakening to authentic memory, the memory of guilt past — is not prompted by divine retaliation. Judgment, to be sure, does come (this Jesus *you* crucified); but such judgment comes first with a word of *shalom*, revealing that peace is prior to violence, that creation is "from the beginning" a Gift, not an "eternal recurrence" of violence and suffering to willfully embrace, or to which we must become passively resigned. Consistently the risen Christ appears in the midst of panic and despair with a word of peace. "While they were talking about this, Jesus himself stood among them and said to them, 'Peace be with you'" (Luke 24:36). "Do not be afraid" (Matt. 28:10). "Jesus came and stood among them and said, 'Peace be with you'" (John 20:19; vv. 21, 26). With their original hopes crushed upon his arrest and execution ("But we had hoped that he was the one to redeem Israel" [Luke 24:21]), the risen One appears to them in the midst of an unbreachable divide to restore communication with them and offer them a renewed innocence, a "second innocence."[20]

This new innocence is the offer of forgiveness. Just as Peter welcomes those responsible for Jesus' murder to embrace the forgiveness offered to them by God, so too do we find running throughout the New Testament the intimate association of resurrection, forgiveness, and newness of life.[21] In all of the appearance accounts the disciples are instructed with a ministry of baptism as the ritual-symbolic enactment of forgiveness. In Luke the risen Jesus charges the disciples with a ministry of "repentance and forgiveness of sins" to all nations, beginning from Jerusalem (24:47). Similarly, in John, Jesus establishes the community with a ministry of reconciliation: "If you forgive the sins of any, they are forgiven them; if you retain the sins of any, they are retained" (20:23). In Matthew: "Go therefore and make disciples of all nations, baptizing them in the name of the Father and of the Son and of the Holy Spirit, and teaching them to obey everything that I have commanded you" (28:19–20). For Paul, "if Christ has not been raised, your faith is vain and you are still in your sins" (1 Cor. 15:17). Christ has been "raised for our justification" (Rom. 4:25). Paul's own conversion experience shows quite dramatically the coincidence of revelation and the recognition of sin. Having set himself in violent opposition to the early Jesus movement, he discovers his self-deception and guilt as the risen victim speaks: "I am Jesus, whom you are persecuting" (Acts 9:5). Such revelation is encountered in the mode of initial obscurity — as a saturated phenomenon — on account of his distorted field of perception. "Saul got up from the ground, and though his eyes were open, he could see nothing.... For three days he was without sight, and neither ate nor drank" (vv. 8, 9). But then Paul is charged with a new way of life, one that extends God's hospitality to all nations: to preach the gospel of Jesus Christ to the Gentiles "so that they may receive forgiveness of sin and find place among those who are sanctified by faith in me" (26:18).[22]

Original Sin

Sin is a datum of revelation, its ultimate depths made visible only from the perspective of divine forgiveness. The formal articulation of this revelation in the Christian theological tradition comes with the doctrine of "original sin," which, as I have said, does not at all imply that human beings are intrinsically sinful or that human desire is innately violent. It affirms just the opposite: that our bondage to sin is in fundamental contradiction with our fulfilled nature. We can begin to plumb the richness of this doctrine, and the process of conversion entailed in it, by reflecting on the nature of mimetic desire.

As stressed earlier, long before we come to a moment in our development when we begin to name certain desires our own, and long before we achieve any sense of self-possession as an act of personal freedom, our desires have already been formed by the Other with whom we remain in constant relationship. We only come "to be" within the warp and woof of interpersonal, social, and cultural relations ("the world") that precede and continue to form us. From my natal beginnings my desires are given their shape and texture as I mimetically replicate (or "incorporate") the patterns of speech, affectivity, thought, and behaviors of others. Even as I acquire relative autonomy within the broader context of my environment to cultivate a sense of personal identity that comes with it the task of being responsible for my decisions, this is possible because of an original heteronomy from which I continue to subsist. "To be" is "to-be-in-relation," not just for a time, but permanently, whether I learn to live in peaceful relationship with the Other, or renounce this relationality through strategies of power and exclusion — undoubtedly a complex combination of both. The doctrine of original sin simply affirms that in the process of our formation within the human life-world, we are not only formed by peaceful desires through nurturing love and generosity, but also formed by the desires of others that are conflictual and violent, and which are socially and culturally transmitted throughout our common history. As Rahner puts it, the formation of the human person is "co-determined by the free history of all the others who constitute his own unique world of persons."[23] Hence the brokenness and alienation that constitute the guilt of others in part forms the milieu within which the individual person comes to be. "There are no islands for the individual person whose nature does not already bear the stamp of the guilt of others, directly or indirectly, from close or from afar."[24] We may therefore speak of original sin as "original" in two related ways. First, it extends indefinitely into our collective past. We cannot recollect a time when it was not the case. Sin has become a determining dimension of our human condition, even if this condition is not willed by God. Second, sin is antecedent to our individual existence, and therefore original to psychogenesis. Each of us is born into and shaped by a world that manifests both human flourishing and brokenness. Each of us ontogenetically "recapitulates," through *mimesis,* the phylogenetic condition of humanity. Sin is truly a corporate reality. Though we cannot identify "social sin" and "personal sin" without remainder, to the extent that the human person is intrinsically relational, neither can they be separated. The Christian theology of sin would have us consider that we are all implicated in the "sin of the world," not in the sense that some primordial sin has been transmitted through biological procreation (such a view has nothing to do with the position advanced here), but because of the way sin replicates itself through interpersonal, social, and cultural relations. Only by keeping the relational nature of the human person in view are we able to make the doctrine of original sin intelligible and meaningful.

We must also keep in mind the "alien" nature of sin, and here the understanding mimetic desire is again insightful. As Paul speaks of sin, he does so in terms of an alien power that operates within him in a semi-autonomous way. "I do not understand my own actions. For I do not do what I want, but I do the very thing I hate. Now if I do what I do not want, I agree that the law is good. But in fact it is no longer I that do it, but sin that dwells in me" (Rom. 7:15–17). Paul speaks of the tension that is felt when he notionally wills to do the good but is volitionally inclined to live in ways that contradict his intentions. As described here, sin is not a matter of lacking adequate information about the good. This the law provides. It is the result of being habituated into various attitudinal and behavioral patterns that contradict God's law. We should not understand the existential tension Paul describes here in ontic terms, as if the war between his "sinful flesh" and "inmost self" represents the struggle between "body" and "soul." After all Paul will speak of the Spirit of the risen Christ who indwells the temple of the body (8:11).[25] The dichotomy reflects the contradiction that is viscerally felt when distorted desires have inscribed themselves within the personality to form patterns of affectivity and activity that concupiscently draw the person away from the will of God. "So I find it to be a law that when I want to do what is good, evil lies close at hand. For I delight in the law of God in my inmost self, but I see in my members another law at war with the law of my mind, making me captive to the law of sin that dwells in my members. Wretched man that I am! Who will rescue me from this body of death?" (7:21–24). We should not dismiss as excessive rhetoric Paul's assertion of our being "slaves to sin" (6:17). He is identifying "the fundamental heteronomy of the human condition: we are slaves either to sin or to righteousness, which is to say that our 'I' is formed by our relationality with that which masters us, be it God or the sinful order following on from Adam's sin (5:12)."[26] Paul's anthropology views the human person as othered-from-within, not as a subject whose domain of "mineness" (*ipseity*) enters into relation with "otherness" (*alterity*) subsequently to self-constitution. The human person is structurally ambiguous, founded by an otherness that remains co-present in every act of self-determination. Given this ambiguity, which is only another way of describing the relational nature of the person, the question we must ask is this: By what are we "othered"? Who or what co-constitutes us? Is the presence of the Other within me contradictory or unifying? Is this Other something I may welcome as life-giving, or is its presence that which alienates and destroys?

For Paul, the transition from being dominated by sinful existence to genuine freedom is not a movement from heteronomy to complete autonomy. (The libertarian notion of freedom has nothing to commend it from a Christian point of view.) Neither is the internal struggle overcome by asserting one's will over the Other in order to make ambiguity unambiguous. (Such a strategy reflects quite precisely the very violence we are summoned to renounce.) The transition comes only by welcoming an Other whose *alterity* is not an obstacle to human flourishing but the condition of the possibility for it — *theonomy*, or, more particularly from the Christian point of view, theonomy in the mode of *christonomy*. By welcoming the crucified-and-risen Christ at the very heart of my identity, I welcome an Other who, so far from being my rival, comes to me in the mode of self-donating love. I welcome an Other whose love frees me from my violence through forgiveness. I welcome the victim I have crucified as a result of my sin, but whose return in the offer of hospitality raises me to new life, whose non-violent, nourishing presence heals the sickness of my violent desires so that I may become hospitable and forgiving to my brothers and sisters. "Who will rescue me from this body of death? Thanks be to God through Jesus Christ our Lord!" (Rom. 7:24–25). "We know that Christ, being raised from the dead, will never die again; death no longer has dominion over him. The death he died, he died to sin, once for all; but the life he lives, he lives to God. So you also must consider yourselves dead to sin and alive to God in Jesus Christ" (6:9–11). In much the same vein, Paul declares in Galatians: "I have been crucified with Christ; and it is no longer I who live, but it is Christ who lives in me" (2:19–20). The transformative process here entails the "de-possession of the 'I' formed by the world and the constitution of an 'I' that is possession by Christ."[27] This movement from "de-possession" to "re-possession" is the essence of Christian conversion.

Conversion and Catholicity

Here we can begin to see the very close relationship between what the Christian theological tradition calls "justification" and "sanctification." God's offer of forgiveness in the risen victim is what allows us to be freed from our implication in guilt (forgiveness, or *aphiemi,* means "to loose"). God's pardon in Christ is an objective reality in the sense that it comes entirely and gratuitously from God. Here again God's logic of excess is evident: "but where sin increased, grace abounded all the more, so that, just as sin exercised dominion in death, so grace might also exercise dominion through justification leading to eternal life through Jesus Christ our Lord" (Rom. 5:20-21). In being forgiven by our victim, whose presence we welcome in faith, we are "justified" and granted "peace with God" (5:1). We are "made right" with God, "reconciled." Even as we continue to struggle with the practical implications of our being forgiven, we can do so boldly, as Paul explains, because as much as we find ourselves estranged from God through sin, grace abounds all the more.[28] The barrier between humanity and God has been overcome by Jesus' death and resurrection once and for all, and the hospitality made concretely real to us in this event is boundless in its reach. "He who did not withhold his own Son, but gave him up for all of us, will he not with him also give us everything else?" (Rom. 8:32). Because it is God who justifies us, argues Paul, we have a secure hope: nothing — not sin, suffering, death, cosmic or earthly powers, nor anything else in all creation — can separate us from the love of God in Jesus Christ our Lord (vv. 33-39).

But should our understanding of reconciliation end here, as if justification were a onetime, forensic act with nothing for us to do except embrace it in faith, we would forsake the process of sanctification to which we are called. Sanctification, most fundamentally considered, is the ongoing process of conversion made possible by God's forgiving and justifying grace. It involves *metanoia,* i.e., the progressive revolution of our own entire framework of knowing, perceiving, speaking, and behaving through the Spirit of the risen Christ. In the same breath that Paul calls us to put on the "mind of Christ," he exhorts: "work out your own salvation with fear and trembling; for it is God who is at work in you, enabling you both to will and to work for his good pleasure" (Phil. 2:12). The point is not that we obtain our own salvation — salvation is a Gift we receive, it is "objective" — but we cooperate ("subjectively") with its re-creative capacities to become "new creations" in Christ. As we allow our narrative identities to be reshaped by the narrative of the crucified-and-risen One — the Christian tradition views baptism as the sacramental inscription of this new identity in our bodies, one that initiates us into the "body of Christ" as the primordial *habitus* for the formation of this new self (Rom. 6) — we die to our old selves and are risen into a new identity in Christ. *Metanoia* (or repentance) is thus trivialized if we imagine that it simply means "saying sorry." However cathartic and potentially transforming the experience of compunction may be, *metanoia* is an integrative reality that draws thought, affectivity, and action into closest unity. To know the risen Christ is a practical knowing. Our desires are reformed from their violent entanglements to peaceful relations; and this reformation entails learning through *imitation*. "We learn to imitate the self-giving victim, drawn on by the intelligence of the victim which both sets us free to act gratuitously, reveals to us our and other people's outcasts, the inconvenient ones, and empowers us to works of service, of solidarity with them and so on." The ministry of reconciliation is one that puts the Christian in a mode of service to the Other, to become highly sensitized and responsive to those social mechanisms that produce victims. By offering hospitality to those who suffer expulsion or want, we offer hospitality to Christ himself (Matt. 25:34–46). But because we are creatures of habit, formed in behavioral patterns that resist the self-expropriation involved in having the "mind of Christ," we can expect that the conversion involves a process of purgation, a *via negativa*. Conversion proceeds by allowing our distorted desires to be hollowed out and reformed through prayer, community, asceticism, and ethical praxis so as to allow our identities to become progressively refashioned in Christ. We become "possessed by the crucified and risen one, by a slow process of entrancement, or possession, which has to pass through concrete acts of increasing freedom and service."[29]

The resurrection of Jesus is thus self-involving and practical reality. To be sure, the affirmation "He is risen" refers to an event that occurred to *Jesus*. It is an objectively real happening — *because* Christ is risen, there is faith and forgiveness of sin, not vice versa. But such a declarative statement implies a manner of knowing which is performative. Its enactment allows the referent to become subjectively realized and meaningful in human life. The narrative presentations of Jesus' resurrection from the dead, and the proclamatory utterances embedded within them, extend to us an imaginative realm to in-habit, to in-corporate within ourselves — or better, for us to be incorporated within *it,* into the "body of Christ" — through the reformation of our behavioral patterns in imitation of the crucified-and-risen Christ. The point of Christian conversion is not, therefore, detachment from *mimesis*. Christian theology cannot advocate a view of human flourishing that depends upon the annihilation of desire. It advocates a revolution of desire and ongoing imitation of the crucified-and-risen Lord in community.

The risen victim is the foundation for true community, not the false unanimity created by the *all minus one* formula of the scapegoat process. "This Jesus is 'the stone that was rejected by you, the builders; it has become the cornerstone'" (Acts 4:11). The One who was expelled in order to manufacture the identity of the group has now become the foundation for a new kind of universality. The narrative in Acts shows God transforming the scapegoat violence that brought about false and temporary unanimity with true and lasting community founded upon reconciliation. The speaking of many languages at Pentecost suggests the reversal of Babel. "[I]n our own languages we hear them speaking about God's deeds of power" (2:11). The catholicity expressed here is not the conforming of all languages into one — into a totality where *alterity* is suppressed — but a unity-in-difference that welcomes the otherness of the Other as enrichment.

The resurrection of Jesus is presented by the New Testament as the fulfillment of Israel's story, but a surprising fulfillment it is. Though in "accordance with the scriptures" as the universal restoration of God's people — one that now decisively includes both Jews *and* Gentiles — the resurrection of the crucified messiah has shifted the story's axis. It is not at all by accident that the gospel message of the risen victim opened up the story of Israel to the Gentiles. If Israel's story can be described as the formation of an understanding of God who identifies with the victim, the New Testament radicalizes this story by declaring that *God* has become our victim — the universal victim. By returning to us in our history in the eschatological offer of hospitality and forgiveness, the story once identified with the people of Israel bursts open to embrace all people.

> It opened up the way for Judaism to be turned into a universal religion. The revelation of God as the forgiving victim at the base of all human exclusions was the condition which made possible the construction of a society which did not define itself over against anything at all. Any society which does define itself over against anything at all cannot, by definition, be universal. It limits God to its own frontiers. For it to be possible to worship the true, non-tribal, non-partial, transcendent God who created and sustains everything, God had to reveal himself as the forgiving victim.[30]

Resurrection language is most significant to this transition. As we saw in chapter 3, the apocalyptic matrix within which such language emerged spoke of universal-cosmic restoration. The restoration of Israel, according to Isaiah, would make it a "light unto the nations" and draw the Gentiles unto it (60:3–5). Crucial to Israel's hope for restoration was the forgiveness of sin. N. T. Wright reminds us that the writings of Jeremiah, Ezekiel, and Isaiah relate the return from exile with the forgiveness of Israel's sins very closely, so closely, in fact, that they are really two different ways of saying the same thing.[31] The implication is therefore clear: if the language of resurrection is cosmic in scope, and the language of the forgiveness of sins a sign of Israel's return from exile — the precondition for Israel becoming the "light unto the nations" — then the resurrection of Jesus from the dead *as* the offer of forgiveness to Israel is, within the logic of their own story, universal in its breadth.

In terms of the personal transformation entailed in this narrative fulfillment, we can say this: in welcoming the Gift of the risen victim, the human person learns to become a "catholic personality."[32] This felicitous phrase, borrowed from Miroslav Volf, means that as we allow the Spirit of the risen Christ to graciously penetrate our self-enclosed patterns of perception and behavior, and to disarm those many defenses that prevent us from allowing the Other to be welcomed as co-constitutive and the enrichment of the self, we become "a personal microcosm of the eschatological new creation."[33] Indeed, we anticipate (or "analogize") the general resurrection of the dead in which God will be all in all. The eschatological liberty of the risen Christ, whose self-giving presence is not restricted by any barrier, opens the self up to and for the Other in a movement of hospitality and generosity. In chapter 4, I enlisted Jürgen Moltmann to say much the same thing, and as such is worth quoting again: "In this resurrection dialectic, human beings don't have to try to cling to their identity through constant unity with themselves, but will empty themselves into non-identity, knowing that from this self-emptying they will be brought back to themselves again for eternity. Human beings find themselves, not by guarding themselves and saving themselves up, but through self-emptying into what is other and alien. Only people who go out of themselves arrive at themselves."[34]

CHRISTUS VICTOR REVISITED

Justice and Mercy Embrace

As we have seen, the proclamation of the resurrection in the New Testament, whose constitutive elements are exemplified in the kerymatic formulae of Acts, entail a double reversal. The first reversal emphasizes God's vindication of an innocent victim from the dead. Empowered by the apocalyptic framework within which resurrection language was first forged, the dialectical-antagonistic framework of the Easter message articulates God's triumph over those structural powers, including death itself, that led to the brutal death of God's eschatological prophet; thus, the message of Easter draws our attention to God's solidarity with the victims in our history, which inspires a critical hope among them, while also energizing an apocalyptic praxis of discipleship on behalf of victims, i.e., to become co-raisers with God. The grammar of reversal supporting the themes of vindication and justice is rendered in a narrative format that explicitly draws upon the Exodus grammar of the Old Testament. Such grammar reveals the reality of God as the subject of exodus/resurrection verbs. God is one who "lifts up," "delivers," "liberates," "draws out," "raises up," one who has heard and responded to the apocalyptic cry of those suffering oppression and exile. As Sobrino points out, such divine action is "partial," not in the sense that it lacks universal breadth, but that it reveals a God whose characteristic activity in history is liberating. Divine revelation is context-sensitive: for those who are victims of oppression, the word of resurrection comes as a word of hope and liberation; for those who are responsible for oppression, whether through direct agency or passive complicity, the word of resurrection also comes as a word of hope and salvation, but strongly characterized with a call to conversion and solidarity with victims, both attitudinally and behaviorally.

The second reversal, which does not negate the first, yet encompasses it within a new field of meaning, emphasizes God's universal offer of forgiveness to humanity in the risen victim whose death manifests the sin of the world in which *all* are implicated. The antagonistic dynamic of the first reversal, which denotes the apocalyptic theme of judgment, is reoriented within God's surprising verdict of acquittal. This acquittal is not a reckless disregard of human responsibility. On the contrary, the gratuitous offer of forgiveness in the crucified-and-risen Jesus opens up memory to a purgative process of healing. The eschatological counter-gaze of the forgiving victim awakens us to perceive those deeply engrained processes of obtaining identity, whether individually or in groups, through the expulsion of the Other. The divine logic of excess made manifest through forgiveness throws open a way of imagining relations premised upon gratuity, rather than reciprocity. By allowing our identities to be reformed through a movement of "de-possession" to "re-possession" in Christ — it is not "I" but Christ who lives within me — we allow our acquisitive and objectifying desires to be progressively reformed in peaceful imitation of the non-violent God.

Such imitation undermines every tendency to build our identities according to "us" and "them" in favor of a "catholic" identity that welcomes the Other in hospitality. The truly radical nature of this hospitality comes into focus when we consider that this Other may be our "enemy." In the same way that Jesus prayed to the Father for the forgiveness of his persecutors, even on the cross — and just as God extended saving mercy to us even while we were "enemies of God" — so too do we imitate the God of Jesus Christ when we engage with love those who persecute us. The significance of this mutation is not to undermine the call for eschatological justice, or our active participation in bringing it about; and yet, it requires us to be attentive to the ways victims too are vulnerable to becoming swept up into cycles of mutual recrimination, *resentment,* and violence. Here especially will we find Jesus' offer of forgiveness to *victims* to be the most challenging and, perhaps, offensive. But, as Volf explains:

> To repent means to resist the seductiveness of the sinful values and practices [of the oppressor] and to let the new order of God's reign be established in one's heart. For a victim to repent means not to allow the oppressors to determine the term under which social conflict is carried, the values around which the conflict is raging, and the means by which it is fought. Repentance thus empowers victims and disempowers the oppressors. It "humanizes" the victims precisely by protecting them from either mimicking or dehumanizing the oppressors. Far from being a sign of acquiescence to the dominant order, repentance creates a haven of God's new world in the midst of the old and so makes the transformation of the old possible.[35]

The resurrection of the universal victim is that event which unambiguously discloses to us *our* complicity in the production of victims, even when we believe ourselves to be victims. It should be clear that repentance among victims here is not for the original injustice inflicted. It is, instead, a process of "being loosed" from the violence now inscribed within the victim's heart that, left to fester or metastasize through the reflexive sense of righteous indignation, can lead to the dehumanization of the Other. When the Other is objectified as villain or perpetrator, the potential for scapegoat violence becomes very great indeed. I can now only see my perpetrator as my rival, as one I hate or envy, as one whose position vis-à-vis my condition I must displace or even destroy. Imitation of the risen victim here means learning how to be unmoved (mimetically) by the violence of the Other. "Though victims may not be able to prevent hate from springing to life, for their own sake they can and must refuse to give it nourishment and strive to weed it out. If victims do not repent today they will become perpetrators tomorrow who, in their self-deceit, will seek to exculpate their misdeeds on account of their own victimization."[36] It is this kind of repentance, asserts Volf, that is alone capable of purifying (not pacifying) human desire sufficiently for the kind of social transformation that allows victims and victimizers to live in the mode of embrace, rather than mutual exclusion: "[T]alk about the need for the victim's repentance has to do with *creating the kind of social agents that are shaped by the values of God's kingdom and therefore capable of participating in the project of authentic social transformation.*"[37]

It should be obvious that the above analysis of cyclical and scapegoat violence does much, in fact, to confirm the liberationist's concerns, not least in stressing the centrality of the victim in the biblical understanding of God. To the extent that, as Girard has stated, the keystone to biblical revelation is found in the reversal of perspective from persecutor to innocent victim, the "view of the victims" for interpreting history is given significant support. The Girardian reading we have adopted here views divine revelation as interruptive, as an in-breaking and unmasking, as something that puts our historical and cultural horizons in question. Revelation is not something that simply corresponds with our immediate expectations. It gives itself in our history in a counterintuitive manner. Our previous reflection on the importance of a "critical memory" that surveys history from the perspective of its "losers," i.e., those swept under the blanket of the voiceless, nameless, faceless anonymity made possible by death's inaccessibility, is corroborated insofar as the resurrection of the victim breaks death's power to fill it with the luminosity of God's truth. Death can no longer mask our expulsions; it has been given a verbal structure — it speaks a word of judgment that allows us to perceive the reality of our sin.

We can never lose sight of the fact that Jesus was crucified by a political power. Although his Kingdom of God ministry was not primarily political, if by this we imagine his objective was to obtain political power, his ministry was profoundly political insofar as it sought to reorient our social construction of reality. Jesus was crucified as a political criminal because he represented a thoroughgoing challenge to the way we order interpersonal and social relationships, above all the way we order our world through the production of victims. Jesus' "intelligence of the victim" is socially and politically subversive. When lived fully and freely, it attracts the powers of the world toward it with almost mechanical inevitability. The call to "take up your cross" is much more than a metaphor for bearing personal travails and grief. It is a realistic account of what occurs when people are moved to order their lives around the crucified-and-risen Jesus. Jesus' apocalyptic sayings make this point abundantly clear: "beware; for they will hand you over to councils; and you will be beaten in synagogues; and you will stand before governors and kings because of me, as a testimony to them" (Mark 13). We should understand from this that "the powers" of the world will not look kindly upon those who set out to participate in God's alternative Kingdom. The "clashing" of logics we spoke of earlier is evidently not hyperbole.

Embodying the risen victim in the world means being-with the victims of our world, living in solidarity with those who are deemed the outsiders, the contaminants, the monsters, the prisoners, the dispensable, and the unclean according to the dominant purity maps in any given social-cultural setting. It means associating ourselves with what "pollutes" — blurring and confusing the meticulously distinguished patterns that allow for the formation of identity in polarization against others. It means drawing attention to, while setting ourselves to the task of transforming, those interpersonal and social dynamics that depend upon ostracism and result in dehumanization. Especially if we understand the dynamics that led to Jesus' death — as a convergence of powers upon a surrogate for the reassertion of social-religious-political order — we must become particularly proficient in identifying, deconstructing, and refashioning our deeply entrenched tendencies to operate out of a "politics of purity" (Volf). "Do not judge, so that you may not be judged.... Why do you see the speck in your neighbor's eye, but do not notice the log in your own eye?" (Matt. 7:1, 3). Jesus' sayings about judgment and hypocrisy could hardly be more direct about the scapegoating process.

Christus Victor Revisited

One of the most remarkable features of Jesus' resurrection, is that it unravels the snares of mimetic and scapegoat violence. In this way it is truly an *apocalypsis,* a deeper *apocalypsis:* it unveils the hidden logic of exclusion that keeps human beings captive to webs of alienation and sin. God does not triumph over violence with a new and final act of retribution against enemies on behalf of the victim. Nor does God underwrite the original scapegoat violence exhibited in Jesus' death. "God is not 'with' the victim in order to make *us* victims; so the preaching of the resurrection affirms."[38] Instead, by raising Jesus from the dead, and allowing him to appear as the divine-human face of forgiveness, a frequently hidden but very real power inimical to human well-being has been unveiled and transformed. It is here especially where we can discover the extraordinary richness of the *Christus Victor* motif frequently used by the Greek Fathers.

This phrase, dubbed by Gustaf Aulén in his 1931 publication, *Christus Victor*, refers to what he calls the "classic" and "dramatic" idea of the atonement. "Its central theme is the idea of the Atonement as a Divine conflict and victory; Christ — Christus Victor — fights against and triumphs over the evil powers of the world, the 'tyrants' under which mankind is in bondage and suffering, and in Him God reconciles the world to Himself."[39] In this scenario, the power of evil, sin, and death is subverted through an ultimate coup: by becoming human, God covertly enters into the realm of "the enemy" to dismantle its power from within. Having freely become victim to evil's indiscriminate predation, God "baits" evil into its characteristic expression — violence and death — and through the resurrection transforms ostensible defeat into triumph. The cross and resurrection are here related in terms of act and counter-act: whereas Jesus' death displays violent victimization in undiluted form, the resurrection expresses God's most direct confrontation with all that destroys creation, revealing once and for all that life, not death, forgiveness, not insult, peace, not violence are original to creation and shall finally prevail.

Importantly, the language of "victory" here has nothing to do with force. The victory wrought is a *strange victory*. Recalling the language from chapter 2, where I described Jesus' resurrection as a *fulfillment that transforms expectations*, God's victory occurs precisely through the transformation of what we have come to think of as "victory." To get a sense for the sort of dramatic and ironic action involved, we can scarcely do better than to refer to Irenaeus of Lyons:

> Apostasy reigned over us unjustly, and, though by nature we belonged to almighty God, it alienated us against our nature, making us its own disciples. And so, in all things mighty, in His justice indefectible, the Word of God turned justly against this apostasy, redeeming from it His own property. He did not use violence, as the apostasy had done at the beginning when it usurped dominion over us, greedily snatching what was not its own. No, He used persuasion. It was fitting for God to use persuasion, not violence, to obtain what He wanted, so that justice should not be infringed and God's ancient handiwork not be utterly destroyed.[40]

Among the many noteworthy aspects of this highly compressed passage, we should first highlight its account of Jesus' death. Rather than attributing to Jesus' death a payment to God — as is customary in penal substitution theories — it is described as a ransom for the emancipation of humanity. Jesus does not die for the sake of God but for the sake of human beings who are held captive by a deceptive and death-dealing totality. The difference is crucial: Jesus does not die because God needed a final sacrificial victim to rectify an infringement of divine honor; rather, Jesus became a victim at the hands of humanity as a result of his provocative life-ministry. Divine agency is most definitively expressed in raising Jesus *from* the dead — in *overcoming* those colluding forces that brought about the violent rejection of Jesus' ministry and person. Jesus' death is indeed salvific, but only within a broader narrative sequence of events in which God, out of love, "absorbs" within God's self the ravenous power of sin, violence, and death in order to dismantle its pervasive influence. Irenaeus insists upon God's non-complicity in violence: God "behaved with justice even towards the apostasy itself"; "not by use of violence"; "without any infringement upon justice." As Aulén puts it, "God observes 'the rules of fair play.'... Evil is overcome not by an external use of force, but by internal methods of self-offering."[41] God does not underwrite the scapegoat violence that led to Jesus' murder, but through a radical gesture of self-giving (or "loving persuasion") that extends reconciliation to humanity, God reveals once and for all what it really is — the work of humanity's (and thus God's) adversary. The resurrection is central to this equation. It is through Easter that God fully exposes the deception of the enemy while allowing us to see, retrospectively, the true meaning of Jesus' life and death. Aulén notes this well: "Assuredly, then, the death of Christ holds a central place in Irenaeus' thought. But, we must add at once, it is not the death in isolation; it is the death seen in connection, on the one hand, with the life-work of Christ as a whole, and on the other with the Resurrection and the Ascension; the death irradiated with the light of Easter and Pentecost."[42]

Another important aspect of this account is the way it speaks of sin as a quasi-intentional influence in human affairs. Irenaeus writes of our being "snatched away" into a state of alienation from God. Through a primordial seduction we apostatized from our original human vocation and fell into a condition of alienation from God and each other. The deception regarding the true state of our existence became so entrenched that only a gracious act of God proved capable of delivering and restoring us. Irenaeus by no means denies human responsibility for our separation from God, on the contrary: "They who have fallen away from the Father's light, and transgressed the law of liberty, have fallen away through their own fault, for they were made free and self-determining."[43] And yet Irenaeus does not hesitate to speak of sin in more objective terms, i.e., as a parasitical and self-replicating presence capable of distorting human perception and desire. We can make the greatest sense of this objective aspect by recalling the social character of sin. While, for some, such an account borders upon the mythological — if it doesn't cross the border outright — the language of the "principalities and powers" is, for others, indispensable for naming the way sin and violence take on a systemic character through social mechanisms (such as scapegoating), institutions, and cultural habits. Again, this does not deny the human responsibility involved in their perpetuation, though we will have to acknowledge that participation (and thus culpability) frequently occurs at tacit levels of the human personality. As discussed above, the truth about ourselves is not fully perceptible to us. "Father forgive them, for they know not what they do." The depth of sin is that it forms a way of perceiving, knowing, and acting. One of the chief insights of *Christus Victor* is that it highlights the dynamic that takes place when God enters into our human condition in order to reveal the truth about ourselves. The theme of "divine trickery," however trivially it may be treated by those who regard the notion unbecoming of God, actually provides a penetrating insight into the "wisdom of God" and the drama of redemption.

As Paul writes in his First Letter to the Corinthians, "But we speak God's wisdom, secret and hidden, which God decreed before the ages for our glory. None of the rulers of this age understood this; for if they had, they would not have crucified the Lord of glory" (1 Cor. 2:7–8). The wisdom of God is "hidden," not because God employs an artificial ruse, but because violent power does not recognize the power of truth even when it appears at point blank. The "wisdom of the cross" is obscure in its givenness, not by a lack of phenomenality, but by a saturating excess that overflows the limited and distorted horizons of its would-be recipients. Understood in this way, the patristic notion that Christ's self-givenness "baits" the enemy into its own demise is in keeping with important New Testament themes that emphasize the saturated phenomenality of divine revelation, including the "messianic secret" motif in Mark, the "wisdom of the cross" in Paul, and the Johannine theme of the *Logos* who appears in the world but is not perceived as such. We may take the well-known example, most fully developed by Gregory of Nyssa in his *Great Catechism*, in which God is compared to a fisherman who hooks the unsuspecting devil with the bait of Jesus' humanity.

> [T]he Deity was hidden under the veil of our nature, that so, as with ravenous fish, the hook of the Deity might be gulped down along with the bait of flesh, and thus, life being introduced into the house of death, and light shining in darkness, that which is diametrically opposed to light and life might vanish; for it is not in the nature of darkness to remain when light is present, or of death to exist when life is active.[44]

Like Irenaeus, Gregory insists that divine action is non-reciprocal to the violence of the enemy. Rather than "tearing us away by a violent exercise of force from [the enemy's] hold," God freely enters into our condition to free us, illustrating that divine grace exhibits power through self-giving love.[45] It is only a "superabundant exercise of power" which is capable of descending "to the humility of man." Such is the counter-intuitive way of divine revelation — "Power conjoined with Love."[46] And it is just this kind of power — the power of self-donating love — that the enemy cannot recognize. Our emancipation comes as "the enemy," as it were, is hoisted on its own petard. The metaphor of divine trickery is not, therefore, a throw away contrivance. It is essential to illustrate the paradoxical character of divine grace which overcomes cyclical and scapegoat violence through self-gift. God enters into our human condition to free us from the dynamics of sacrificial violence operative in human relationships. God has transformed our deicide into our redemption.

Girard argues that if we understand "the enemy" here to be the mimetic contagion (or "satanic cycle") of violence which takes on a semi-autonomous character in human affairs, then the *Christus Victor* motif provides an extraordinary insight for theological anthropology:

> The Greek Fathers had it right in saying that with the Cross Satan is the mystifier caught in the trap of his own mystification.... The idea of Satan duped by the Cross is therefore not magical at all and in no way offends the dignity of God. The trick that traps Satan does not include the least bit of either violence or dishonesty on God's part. It is not really a ruse or trick; it is rather the inability of the prince of this world to understand the divine love. If Satan does not see God, it is because he *is* violent contagion itself.... Satan himself transforms his own mechanism into a trap, and he falls into it headlong. God does not act treacherously, even toward Satan, but allows himself to be crucified for the salvation of humankind, something beyond Satan's comprehension. The prince of this world

depended too heavily on the extraordinary power of concealment of the victim mechanism.[47]

As Girard stresses elsewhere, it is only the cross in light of the resurrection which makes this unmasking and pardon complete.

The Resurrection is not only a miracle, a prodigious transgression of natural laws. It is the spectacular sign of the entrance into the world of a power superior to violent contagion. By contrast to the latter it is a power not at all hallucinatory or deceptive. Far from deceiving the disciples, it enables them to recognize what they had not recognized before and to reproach themselves for their pathetic flight in the preceding days. They acknowledge the guilt of their participation in the violent contagion that murdered their master.[48]

Chapter Nine

THE GRAMMAR OF FULFILLMENT AND CHRISTOLOGY

Previously, in chapter 5, I criticized Rahner's rejection of apocalyptic in his eschatology, arguing (along with Johann Baptist Metz) that such a decision mutes vital resources for understanding the political reality of the resurrection. Apocalyptic eschatology, I further argued, is indispensable for discovering the meaning of Easter for the earliest Christians and for retrieving its liberating character today, since it articulates with unique power God's justice for victims. Its counter-factual imagination serves both to console and energize. In the context of "negative contrast experiences" (Schillebeeckx), resurrection language naturally modulates towards the "not yet" pole of the eschatological spectrum to speak dialectically of an unrealized future. But it would be inaccurate to say that political and liberationist approaches speak only of the future, or strictly in terms of an outstanding promise over against the present horizon of negativity. If we are to avoid a "deism of the resurrection" (Sobrino) we must affirm the ongoing impact of the resurrection event as a transforming reality made effective and present. Sobrino claims such participation occurs in a variety of ways: through liturgical celebration and the proclamation of the gospel, through experiences of gratitude, hope and self-giving love in the midst of catastrophe, etc. But among these analogous forms of Easter in history, Sobrino gives the greatest emphasis to the praxis of bringing justice to victims. We may become "co-raisers" with God and extend the resurrection in our history as we bring hope to the hopeless, memory to those forgotten, and life to those consigned to a living death. For Sobrino, the eschatological future intersects the present moment, even if this intersection often occurs in the mode of interruption, so that we can and must say that we *already* participate in the future of creation. We also noted in the conclusion of the same chapter that if the political and liberationist approaches to the resurrection are effective in retrieving the apocalyptic matrix of its meaning, they must remain in constant and creative interaction with other matrices.

One of the weaknesses in Sobrino's project is that it does not attend sufficiently to the cyclical nature of violence and the forgiveness character of the resurrection, which we examined in the previous chapters. Another weakness is that it does not attend fully enough to the grammar of fulfillment in Christian imagination and discourse. Whereas the grammar of reversal tends to be more pronounced among political and liberation theologians, the grammar of fulfillment is more pronounced among theologians concerned with the mystical and aesthetic dimensions of Christian faith. Instead of the agonistic response that yearningly reaches out to an apocalyptic horizon of unfulfilled meaning, the grammar of fulfillment tends to connect protology and eschatology in a more continuous way. Accordingly, the present moment is viewed in terms of our ongoing participation in renewed creation. Creation is situated within an *exitus-reditus* pattern of redemption in which its assumption into the Godhead occurs through the "descent" and "ascent" of the eternal *Logos*. It is not at all surprising that political and liberationist theologies generally prefer the more genetic presentations of the Christ event in the synoptic gospels, whereas the more ontological styles in christology take their orientation from the more identifiably "high" christologies of the New Testament, above all the gospel of John and the "cosmic Christology" of the Pauline literature. The crucial point we must make is that both of these orientations in christology, as well as the soteriological motifs they most directly support (liberation and divinization, respectively), must remain in very close relationship in any christology that wishes to integrate more thoroughly the major idioms of scripture.

In his essay, "On the Spirituality of Easter Faith," Rahner argues that the very nature of Easter requires that we keep the historic and cosmic dimensions of christology in the closest possible unity.

> The risen Christ is not merely the One who at some earlier time lived a human life, was crucified and died, but has now simply left all this behind him as the no-longer-existing past, and now leads a different, new life.... No, the risen Lord *is* the One who was crucified. This "is" does not merely indicate the identity of a substantial subject, who now sustains a different life from before. The "is" states that this very earlier life itself is completed and has found eternal reality in and before God.... His eternal life is rather the ultimate form of his earthly life itself.[1]

If christologies "from above" and "from below" can be distinguished according to their methodologies and thematic emphases, they must ultimately work in concert with each other. Easter demands this, for it is that christological moment in which history and transcendence, anticipation and memory, doing and being, function and person so completely conjoin. "[T]he resurrection means the ultimate, God-given form of the earthly life belonging to history. And this history has an ultimate meaning because in the incarnation and cross of the eternal Logos it is the history of God himself."[2] Although this insight does not dictate how a work in christology should proceed, when the resurrection is properly thematized and given a regulative role, such a work will necessarily attend to the relationship between the history of Jesus of Nazareth and the ontological considerations of his person as the self-manifestation of God in our world. Easter is the radiating center for a more integral (or "holistic") christology.[3]

In this chapter, I intend to show how the resurrection serves just this regulative role. The present chapter thus serves three overarching purposes: first, to demonstrate that the Easter event provides the historical impetus and internal logic for the subsequent christological reflection in Christian theology that led to the affirmation of Jesus as the very self-communication of God in history; second, to outline the grammar of fulfillment in resurrection language that is rooted in the wisdom/sapiential strain within scripture and which would become decisive in this christological assessment; and third, to show how this grammar is connected to and supports the soteriological theme of *theosis*.

"I AM THE RESURRECTION AND THE LIFE": MANIFESTATION AND PRESENCE IN THE FOURTH GOSPEL

Of the four gospels, the gospel of John has the most to say about the resurrection. Devoting more space to narrating the encounters with the risen Christ than the synoptic gospels combined, the Jesus of John also has considerably more to say about the resurrection throughout his ministry than the portraits provided by Mark, Matthew, and Luke. Not only is the theme of "eternal life" uniquely dominant in John's gospel as a soteriological theme, but its "compositional zenith" is the vignette of Jesus raising Lazarus, during which he delivers his "I am the resurrection and the life" discourse.[4]

> Jesus said to [Martha], "I am the resurrection and the life. Those who believe in me, even though they die, will live, and everyone who lives and believes in me will never die. Do you believe this?"

She said to him, "Yes, Lord, I believe that you are the Messiah, the Son of God, the one coming into the world." (11:25–27)

Whereas the synoptic gospels identify Jesus' cleansing of the temple as the immediate cause for his arrest, John places the temple cleansing at the beginning of Jesus' ministry and identifies the raising of Lazarus as the culminating "sign" (*semeion*) that finally compelled the religious leaders to have him put to death. The vignette functions as the turning point for the entire gospel. It is the structural hinge between the "book of signs" (chapters 1–12), which focuses on Jesus' seven miracles, and the "book of glory" (chapters 13–20), which centers on the paschal mystery. Of all the miracles in John the raising of Lazarus is the most revealing of Jesus' *person*. In giving life he gives himself; he *is* the resurrection and the life. The choice John makes in using this sign as the proximate cause for Jesus' death thus serves more of a pedagogical and theological purpose than a historical one.[5] (Most historians believe the temple incident is the likeliest reason for Jesus' arrest.) Its literary value is also significant, particularly as the episode represents a high point of Johannine irony: by raising Lazarus, the giver of life (5:25) is consigned to death (11:53); yet despite the intentions of his murderers, Jesus' death is his "glorious" return to the Father and the "gathering" of the dispersed children of God (vv. 49–52).

As many commentators have observed, the resurrection serves a very different role in John than it does in the synoptics. Some express difficulty in even defining what that role is. The difficulty arises for at least two reasons. First, whereas the synoptic gospels identify the resurrection as Jesus' vindication before his accusers and murderers, the motif of vindication via resurrection is subsumed into John's theology of Jesus' death. Jesus' death *is* his exaltation, simultaneous with his ascension to the Father in glory. Throughout the narrative we are told that as the Son of Man is "lifted up" on the cross, so too is he "lifted up" unto the Father in exaltation (3:13–14; 8:28; 12:32–33). Jesus' last words upon the cross ("It is finished!") convey that his death finally accomplishes the goal of his ministry (19:30), and thus whatever dramatic tension had been building up to this point has reached its resolution. By contrast, the narrative tension in the synoptic gospels is only heightened at the moment of Jesus' death as it anticipates God's response to the shocking and swift ending of the Nazarene's ministry. To some commentators, the Johannine descent-ascent motif, which begins with the Logos becoming flesh and concludes with Jesus' death, renders the resurrection accounts superfluous. "Strictly speaking," declares C. F. Evans, "there is no place in the Fourth Gospel for resurrection stories, since the ascent or exaltation has already taken place."[6] Evans echoes the judgment of Bultmann who states that "if Jesus' death on the cross is already his exaltation and glorification, *his resurrection* cannot be an event of special significance. No resurrection is needed to destroy the triumph which death might be supposed to have gained in the crucifixion. For the cross itself was already triumph over the world and its ruler."[7] Evans thinks the reason why John includes resurrection stories at all is "in deference to Christian tradition." Because they were well known by the time of John's composition, they were essentially tacked on, either by the Johannine author, or by a redactor, or both, which perhaps explains why, at least to Evans, they appear to lack integration with the rest of the gospel.[8]

The second difficulty in determining the role of the resurrection in John is christological in nature. Generally speaking the identity of Jesus as the Son of God progressively emerges in the synoptic gospels through his actions, words, and relationships as presented in narrative form. While there are "christological moments" (R. Brown) early on in the synoptic gospels that alert the reader to Jesus' identity as the messiah and Son of God, Mark, Matthew, and Luke tend to follow a more genetic line of development that leads to Jesus' death and resurrection as the climactic moment in which Jesus' identity is fully revealed. They therefore preserve something of the process of discovery that the disciples themselves underwent as they followed Jesus throughout his ministry. Even though Mark, Matthew, and Luke give ample evidence they were written from the point of view of Jesus' resurrection, they maintain a perspectival tension from the beginning that allows the reader to imaginatively retrace the steps of the disciples' own experience. In John, however, we begin with the preexistent Logos who was with God, who was God, and who entered into the world in a sovereign and loving movement of descent from a previously exalted position. From the outset the reader is drawn into a contemplative posture before a revelatory event of divine self-manifestation. Rather than tracing a process of discovery throughout the narrative which culminates in the resurrection of the Son of God, the Logos poem of John's gospel immediately lifts the gaze of the reader in a vertical direction to become witness to Jesus Christ as the eternal Son of God. Whereas most other New Testament writings give considerable emphasis to the resurrection to account for Jesus' filial relationship to God, in John "there is now *no thought of Jesus' status as Son being dependent on or even influenced by his resurrection.* Whatever it means for Jesus that is the Word become flesh," writes James Dunn, "it involves no diminution in his status or consciousness as Son. And whatever it means for Jesus that he is glorified and lifted up on the cross, in resurrection and ascension, it involves no enhancement or alteration in his status as Son."[9] We might put the matter this way: whereas the synoptic gospels suggest a process of Jesus "becoming" Son of God, a process which reaches its definitive conclusion in Jesus' resurrection and exaltation, the gospel of John affirms the eternal preexistence of the Word whose identity as the exalted Lord perdures throughout his life, death, and resurrection. The consequence of this is that the resurrection seems to lose the christological role it exercises in the synoptics, which immediately raises the question: what is the role of the resurrection in the fourth gospel?

Sapiential Eschatology

The best way to understand this role is to understand John's eschatology. We can generally contrast the eschatology in the synoptics with Johannine eschatology by describing the former as more apocalyptic and futuristic in orientation and the latter more sapiential and realized. Notwithstanding the real and important differences in inflection between Mark, Matthew, and Luke, compared to the Johannine predilection for realized eschatology, together they place greater emphasis on the future pole of the eschatological spectrum. It is important that we not think of this difference in emphasis as a matter of contradiction, or an arbitrary decision on the part of the gospel writers to emphasize one or the other. We should also avoid thinking that John is absent of all futuristic eschatology, or that the synoptic gospels lack all sense of realized eschatology. The difference is a matter of modal emphasis. Even in Jesus' own preaching there is a tension between future and realized eschatology, a tension which is not the result of conceptual imprecision but reflective of the multivalent reality of the Kingdom of God itself: it is already present, and palpably so in the ministry of Jesus, and yet its final manifestation is forthcoming, a reality that continues to press in upon the present from an as yet realized future. The New Testament writers "were not creating *ex nihilo* theories of realized or of [future] eschatology, but were applying to a particular situation one or the other strain already present in Jesus' thought."[10] As Brown further points out, strains of both types of eschatology (apocalyptic and sapiential) were available in the first century from which Jesus and the New Testament authors could readily draw.

The strain of sapiential eschatology which suffuses the Johannine imagination flows out of the wisdom tradition of Israel. This is not to suggest that apocalyptic themes are lacking in John. Some of the most important motifs in the fourth gospel give "intimations of apocalyptic," including the distinction of the two aeons, the interaction of the world above and the world below, those who are in the light and those who remain in darkness, and the fulfillment of the divine plan in history.[11] There are also several instances of futuristic eschatology embedded in John's gospel. For example, those who believe in Jesus may presently share in eternal life, yet they still await the future vision of glory in resurrection (11:25; 14:2–3; 17:24). The gospel also points toward a final judgment (5:28–29; 6:39–40, 54; 12:48). Possible allusions to a second coming and the precipitating tribulations can be found in chapters 14–16, though nothing like the synoptic "little apocalypse" appears in John.[12] Indeed, much of what constitutes the anticipated second coming in the synoptics gets telescoped backwards to the original descent of the eternal Word into the world. Some exegetes, like Bultmann, speculate that such instances of future eschatology must have been introduced later into John's gospel by a redactor in order to bring it into greater conformity with the broader church. Even if his hypothesis is highly debatable, it underscores the fact that whatever intimations of apocalyptic and futuristic eschatology are evident in John, they are assimilated within an eschatological imagination that is deeply contemplative and fixed upon the present moment of divine revelation.

As already noted, the theme of vindication via resurrection, which is crucial to the synoptic account of resurrection, is virtually absent in John. This absence is due to the difference in eschatological framework. Sandra Schneiders notes that John's theology of resurrection reflects an innovative appropriation of sapiential eschatology (or "exaltation eschatology," as she sometimes calls it). Developing in the second to early first century B.C.E. among Diaspora Jews living in the broader Hellenistic world, this form of eschatology gained some of its most characteristic features among faithful Jews who experienced persecution for their faith. Unlike the emphasis on a future judgment we find in Daniel or 2 Maccabees, where the resurrection of the body is the precondition for the vindication of the elect, sapiential eschatology, which had absorbed aspects of Greek philosophical anthropology (e.g., the immortality of the soul), saw the death of the martyr as simultaneous with his or her vindication. "The theme of exaltation-for-judgment is combined with the theme of entering into an intimate relationship with God in a nonterrestrial realm."[13] A classic example can be found in the deuterocanonical work, the Wisdom of Solomon: "But the souls of the righteous are in the hand of God, and no torment will ever touch them. In the eyes of the foolish they seemed to have died, and their departure was thought to be a disaster, and their going from us to be their destruction; but they are at peace. For though in the sight of others they were punished, their hope is full of immortality" (3:1–4).

What is striking about the language of this work is its emphasis on the soul (1:4; 2:22; 4:14; 8:19; 10:16; 15:8) and the soul's immortality (1:15; 2:23; 4:1; 6:18–19; 8:13; 12:1; 15:3). The influence of Greek philosophical anthropology is obvious, as is the emphasis on the moment of death as the attainment of immortality. (One clear difference however is that immortality is not the natural property of a preexistent soul, but a free gift of eternal life from God.) Whether this eschatology represents an alternative to bodily resurrection, or implies it, is still debated among scholars.[14] At the very least, bodily resurrection is not very explicit in this eschatological scenario. But as Schneiders hastens to point out, sapiential eschatology is not incompatible with bodily resurrection. If the gospel of John may be taken as an example, it is "fundamentally susceptible to it."[15]

Schneiders draws two important conclusions that can assist us in understanding the role of the resurrection in John's gospel. First, because sapiential eschatology is at least compatible with notions of bodily resurrection, the latter "*could* easily become explicit in this eschatology if the right pressures were brought to bear upon it, e.g., by the Easter experience of the first followers of Jesus."[16] This explication is quite obvious in John. Far from being a superadded, verbal gloss upon an underlying framework that can be extracted intact, John's gospel percolates with resurrection language. For all its emphasis on transcendence, it is tenaciously corporeal. Bodily resurrection serves an important role in the structure of revelation in the fourth gospel as a whole, a point to which we shall return. At the same time, and this is Schneiders's second conclusion, John's theology of resurrection necessarily takes on a distinctive set of meanings as it interacts with sapiential eschatology. The most obvious difference is that John's theology of resurrection is not preoccupied with the themes of vindication and the overcoming of death. Because Jesus' death *is* his vindication/exaltation, and because death is, in some sense, *already* relativized by the eternal Word (10:17–18), the grammar of reversal which characterizes the synoptic gospels recedes into the background. Instead, the resurrection of Jesus becomes for John "a manifestation of the meaning for the whole person of life in God now lived in all its fullness."[17] It is the self-manifestation of the glorified person of Jesus Christ to his disciples after his death, and their *participation* in that glorification, that is the chief preoccupation of John's account of the resurrection. Its grammar is one of *fulfillment,* not reversal.

In a telling inversion of the resurrection-exaltation sequence we find in the synoptic gospels, John presents Easter as the self-revelation of the *already* exalted Christ to his disciples.[18] Jesus has already returned to the Father in glory upon his death. Now he returns in a risen body to his disciples in order to make possible for them participation in divine life. "The resurrection narrative in John, therefore, is not really about what happens to *Jesus* after his death. That has already been narrated in the account of his glorifying death, namely, that he has *returned to God*. The resurrection narrative is about what happened to *Jesus' disciples* after Jesus' glorification, namely, that the Jesus who had gone to God has also *returned to them*."[19] C. H. Dodd puts the matter similarly, stating that the quasi-physical aspects of the appearance narratives in John are meant to convey the "epoch-making" nature of the Easter event which occurs "in this world," and not just in a supra-historical realm. The resurrection does not emphasize heavenly glory for Jesus as much as it emphasizes the "renewal of personal relations with the disciples" which enables them to body Christ forth as his church.[20] There are thus two distinct, but related moments in the paschal event according to John. The first is Jesus' glorification on the cross and his being "lifted up" to the Father. The second is the exalted Jesus' return to his disciples and the formation of a community that embodies the risen Christ in the world.

If this interpretation is correct, and I believe it is, the resurrection narratives should not be thought of as tenuously related to a self-contained movement of descent and ascent that completes its cycle at the moment of Jesus' death.[21] If Jesus' death does in fact coincide with his "going to the Father" (14:28; 16:10, 16), the resurrection remains absolutely central in John because it is that which allows *us* to participate in divine life. The resurrection of Jesus is his return to us as the possibility for our union with God, for our participation in the very life of God here and now. The Easter event opens up for us eternal life, a reality that is not just in our future but one that qualitatively transforms the life we are presently living.

"You are from below; I am from above"

Another way to understand the distinctive features of Johannine eschatology is to think in spatial-metaphorical terms. The gospel of John constantly orients the gaze of the reader in an upward direction, correlating events "down below" with the heavenly world "above." The organizing movement of the entire gospel forms an *exitus-reditus* pattern: though it pushes forward in a horizontal direction in its narrative unfolding, it originates and returns in a vertical direction as the Son of

Man "descends" and "ascends" to and from earth (3:13). Jesus' elaborate discourses throughout the "spiritual gospel," as it is often called, frequently speak in terms of spatial contrast along a vertical axis. "Jesus answered them, 'Very truly, I tell you, no one can see the kingdom of God without being born from above'" (3:3). "The one who comes from above is above all; the one who is of the earth belongs to the earth and speaks about earthly things. The one who comes from heaven is above all" (3:31). "He said to them, 'You are from below, I am from above; you are of this world, I am not of this world'" (8:23). This contrapuntal interplay between the heavenly and the earthly is not just one of contrast. For all the opposition between light and darkness (1:5; 3:19), Spirit and flesh (3:6; 6:63), living and ordinary water (4:10–14), heavenly and earthly bread (6:27), the relationship is not dualistic but analogical. Just as Jesus, the Word become flesh, makes manifest and visible the transcendent and invisible reality of the Father, so too do the sensible realities that point toward heavenly reality, which they cannot contain, nevertheless participate *in* that reality. The symbols of water, bread, wine, and body are incarnational in structure: they make present in sensible mediation what is above, drawing those who partake in them toward a transcendent reality that can only be encountered through their mediation, in "mediated-immediacy."

"For John," writes Hans Urs von Balthasar, "the Christ-event, which is always seen in its totality, is the vertical irruption of the fulfillment into horizontal time; such irruption does not leave this time — with its present, past and future — unchanged, but draws it into itself and thereby gives it a new character."[22] That the Christ event is "always seen in its totality" in John is a point to which we shall return in a moment. But here we can observe that compared to the more horizontal trajectory of the synoptic gospels, where God's activity operates through history in a more linear fashion that moves towards a definitive climax, the narrative in John takes on a meditative-poetic character where each stanza and line intones transcendence. Though John certainly retains aspects of horizontal directionality, not least in the narrative movement towards the "hour" of Jesus' passion, the narrative is a highly stylized act of theological contemplation where each moment in its unfolding suggests the whole narrative as such. The Logos poem, which in some sense is the entire gospel in miniature, is more than the beginning of the gospel: every new movement in the gospel "keeps reverting to the one beginning which contains the whole, so that every time [John] begins a new section he, as it were, starts all over again, though every time more and more can be taken for granted, and so a fuller and fuller picture is built up."[23] To read John by following its gestures and pace is to enter contemplatively into its textual world. "In John thought itself has found a mode of meditative, manifestory expression for this reality of unfolding, encompassing exaltation. The shock of beauty in that glory manifests the need for a meditative, a contemplative mode of thought — a mode common to both the contemplative mystical traditions of releasement and the more ordinary, everyday experiences of the giftedness of God and life itself."[24] If this makes John's eschatology more "mystical" in sensibility, it should be understood that this upward, spiral movement never absconds from the historical. Even if the vertical trajectory is dominant, the vertical and horizontal trajectories remain united in the Johannine view of salvation.[25] In notable contrast to, say, the Logos in Philo of Alexandria's philosophy, which obviously drew from similar intellectual resources as the Johannine author, the Logos in John became flesh and dwelled among human beings in a personal form. For Philo, the Logos is not personal, nor an object of personal piety. But for John, the Logos is manifestly a *personal* reality.[26] The incarnation and resurrection together affirm that human salvation is ultimately an *interpersonal* event that occurs within history. The Word who became flesh and whose glorified body became manifest to Mary Magdalene and the disciples as the possibility for their participation in the life of God shows that such participation is ultimately one of communion among persons, divine and human. "I will not leave you orphaned; I am coming to you. In a little while the world will no longer see me, but you will see me; because I live, you also will live. On that day you will know that I am in my Father and you in men, and I in you" (14:18–20).

"I came that they may have life, and have it abundantly"

Corresponding with its verticality, the temporality of John's gospel is noticeably different from the synoptic gospels. This is immediately evident from its opening lines. The beginning of the story, like the beginning of the Bible, harkens to time-immemorial. The Logos, who was in the beginning with God, and indeed, who was God, is the generative principle of creation. "All things came into being through him, and without him not one thing came into being. What has come into being in him was life, and the life was the light of all people" (1:3–4). The parallels with the wisdom writings, both canonical and deuterocanonical, are abundant (see especially Ps. 33:6; Prov. 8:27–30; Wisd. 9:9; Sir. 24:9) as are the parallels with non-scriptural sources.[27] Distinguishing John's Logos theology from these parallels is that the Logos becomes *sarx*. "And the Word became flesh and lived among us, and we have seen his glory, the glory as of a father's only son, full of grace and truth" (v. 14). What is notable about John's account here is that much of the language of future judgment and glory associated with apocalyptic eschatology extends backward in the narrative. "He was in the world, and the world came into being through him; yet the world did not know him. He came to what was his own, and his own people did not accept him. But to all who received him, who believed in his name, he gave power to become children of God" (vv. 10-12). Compared to Matthew, for whom Jesus' future coming will be the time of judgment (Matt. 25:31-46), the original descent of the Logos into the world in John — which is shown here to be "bedazzling" in its impact — marks the present time as the time of judgment. Those who reject the Word are already judged (John 3:18; 9:39). The defeat of the "ruler of this world" has already occurred (12:31). The offer of "eternal life" is made now. "Very truly, I tell you, anyone who hears my word and believes him who sent me has eternal life, and does not come under judgment, but has passed from death to life" (5:24).

As indicated above, the theme of eternal life suffuses the fourth gospel and is one of the chief ways its realized eschatology is expressed. "Life" (*zoe*) or "eternal life" (*zoe aionios*), which is frequently contrasted with natural life (*psyche*), is obviously much more than about duration. Eternal life is not natural life extending indefinitely, but the transformation of natural life into a qualitatively new reality. The fullness of resurrection life that is promised to those who are united to Christ certainly remains an outstanding reality, and yet that fullness saturates the present moment and may be participated in now by those who believe in Christ. To "believe" (*pisteuein*) here presumes an intimate relationship predicated upon love, commitment, and imitation. Believing is thus participatory, not merely the assimilation of information.[28] Salvation in John comes through the disciple's personal assent to the revelation of Jesus as the Son of God, an assent which is portrayed as possible even prior to Jesus' passion and resurrection. This is quite evident in the "I am the resurrection and the life" discourse: "Those who believe in me, even though they die, will live, and everyone who lives and believes in me will never die" (12:25-26). Recalling von Balthasar's statement above, namely, that John sees the entire Christ event in its totality, we find in this gospel a striking confluence of time so that what generally occurs in a chronological sequence in the synoptic accounts is concentrated into a perduring present that extends throughout the narrative. What we discover in the "I am the resurrection and the life" discourse, and the Lazarus episode accompanying it, is the apocalyptic future "transplanted into the historic ministry of Jesus," with the clear implication that the finality of the general resurrection is fundamentally connected to and present in Jesus' historical ministry.[29] One of the most significant outcomes of this backward extension of future eschatology in a protological direction — a movement naturally facilitated by the sapiential framework with which the evangelist is working — is the portrayal of Jesus in explicitly ontological terms. Jesus' resurrection is not just something that produces certain salvific effects, but is manifestory of Jesus' *person*. Person and function are identified throughout. He *is* the resurrection. He *is* the life. What Jesus gives in giving life is himself. Believing *in* the person of Jesus then is to acquire a qualitatively new form of life, "eternal life," a life characterized by a renewed relationship with God and with others that is no longer dominated by alienation, fear, and sin. Even though the individual Christian will die according to *psyche*, she already participates in the eternal life that will become fully realized in the resurrection of the dead. The Jesus of John "has not abolished final eschatology... but has given it a new dimension of depth, the experience of union with the risen Christ in this life, which constitutes the possession, here and now, of eternal life."[30]

Christophany and Participation

Earlier I stated that the primary purpose of the resurrection in John is one of revelation: it serves as the self-manifestation of the exalted Christ to his disciples and the reestablishment of his relationship with them for the purpose of their communion with God and each other. The resurrection is not so much about Jesus' return to God as it is about the return of the already exalted Jesus to his disciples in love. The whole of the Christ event is thus not an event merely "for itself" but "for the world" (3:16). The resurrection is that *ad extra* event which draws the disciples (and the implied reader of the text) into the *ad intra* event of Jesus' return to the Father. By it they (we) are incorporated into the glorification of the Son by the Father. It is what enables us to "dwell" and "abide" in God in the post-paschal era. The appearances of the risen Christ are thus best thought of as acts of love.[31] Such surprising, yet tender gestures of divine hospitality are offered as Mary Magdalene is called by her name ("Mary!") and out of her grief ("I have seen the Lord!") (20:11–18); as the risen Lord breaths upon the disciples to receive the Holy Spirit and the ministry of reconciliation (vv. 22–23); as Thomas is invited to trace with his fingers the wounds of self-donating love (vv. 24–29); and as Peter responds to Jesus' question, "Do you love me, Simon Peter?"

as many times as he previously denied him: "Yes, Lord; you know that I love you" (21:15–19). Such love for the risen Christ is to radiate out towards others ("feed my lambs," "tend to my sheep," "feed my sheep" [vv. 15, 16, 17]), thereby extending the circle of embrace between the Father and the Son: "The glory that you have given me I have given them, so that they may be one, as we are one, I in them and you in me, that they may become completely one, so that the world may know that you have sent me and have loved them even as you have loved me" (17:22–23).

Even though the whole gospel of John is christophany, the account of the resurrection is so in a special sense, for it reveals the possibility of acceding to a christic personality, to "become" *alter Christi* by enacting Christ's own ministry of loving hospitality and forgiveness to others.[32] The possibility of such participation, and the remarkable degree to which it is offered to the disciples, comes as a result of a new kind of "presence" among them. Here we must recall one of the important features of the resurrection narratives in general, though its particular significance is uniquely developed in John. The self-manifestation of the risen One takes place in the mode of "absence," or better, by imparting "distance." All of the appearance narratives, together with the empty tomb narratives, suggest that the manifestory character of the Easter event is so precisely as a movement of withdrawal, which so far from implying a merely negative relation that leaves the disciples in their various postures of mourning, despair, and alienation, transforms their perceptions and desires with a qualitatively new and *excessive* presence that is experienced, and can only be experienced, in the mode of absence. The absence is generative, fulsome. The resurrection and ascension of Jesus create an "opening" or "space" within which the disciples — and here, as readers of this text, we may wish to consider ourselves as such — may enter so as to participate actively, and not just as passive spectators, in the revelatory event.[33] In John, the withdrawal of the physical body of Jesus from any objectifying view or grasp is the conditioning possibility for the presence of the risen Christ in the community. As Mary Magdalene searches for the entombed body of Jesus, she is still caught within a pre-paschal imagination. Even when the risen Lord calls her by name, she reaches out to grasp him. To Mary Jesus says, "Do not hold on to me, because I have not yet ascended to the Father. But go to my brothers and say to them, 'I am ascending to my Father and your Father, to my God and your God'" (20:17). This "going away" in ascension is what enables Mary to transition to a post-paschal imagination, i.e., to encounter the risen Lord in the community of believers who will body him forth in the world.³⁴ Paradoxical though it may seem, the risen and glorified Christ is capable of being present in a variety of modes precisely by not being wholly identified with any one particular modality. Though the personal reality of Jesus is communicated in a way that allows the disciples to recognize him, his transfigured corporeality is not subject to the same kind of limitations prior to his death and resurrection. Though he can reveal himself in historically mediated modes to those who remain embedded in time and space, his presence reveals his transcendence *of* those historically mediated modes. He is revealed in his full, embodied humanity, but he is no longer in mortal flesh. His glorified body-person is, to use N. T. Wright's locution, "trans-physical," which is to say in full continuity with his historical-embodied existence but transformed into a reality that is more-than-historical, and thus capable of being present in gracious multivalence. "He can be present when, where, and how he wills," writes Schnieders: "in the community itself and in its actions of preaching the Word, celebrating the Eucharist, and ministering to the needy."³⁵

The resurrection of Jesus has the effect in John of conferring upon the disciples an unprecedented role vis-à-vis the risen Lord. They are not just to be ambassadors of a cause that comes with it a set of instructions that one may codify and report, but are, in a very profound sense, to *become* the reality they signify. They are to become analogies of the risen Christ, to body him forth in the world in a generative act that expands his embrace. The Easter event exhibits a "logic of birthing" (G. Ward). The withdrawal of Jesus' body in resurrection and ascension, though very much an absence, "announces the plenitude of God's presence" which communicates itself in and through a multitude of bodies, including those of the followers of Christ who together *are* the body of Christ in *ecclesia*. Drawing upon Gregory of Nyssa's theology of resurrection, which conceives of participation in divine life in terms of constant expansion or growth, Graham Ward maintains that the body of the church and the risen body of Christ together are "enfolded" within the Godhead. "The body of Jesus Christ is not lost, nor does it reside now in heaven as a discrete object for veneration (as Calvin thought and certain Gnostics before him) in and by the Spirit. The body of Jesus Christ, the body of God, is permeable, transcorporeal, transpositional. Within it all other bodies are situated and given their significance."³⁶ Hence, we are to think of God's ubiquitous presence in Christ, not as something that stands over and away from the body, but as mediated in and through bodily life. The resurrection and ascension, from a Christian point of view, is the way God's infinite (and non-localizable) presence continues to extend itself in the particularities and textures of embodied human existence. To hearken back to some thematic lines developed in Part One, the resurrection of Jesus from the dead, and the Spirit of the risen Christ that is imparted by God in the world as part of its ongoing influence, reveals the corporeality of grace.

RESURRECTION AND CHRISTOLOGY

With the gospel of John more squarely in view, we turn our attention to the relationship of the resurrection and the development of christology in the New Testament more generally. My purpose here is twofold. First, I intend to show that the resurrection gives momentum and shape to the development of christology which ultimately leads to the identification of Jesus Christ as the Son of God, and that without the revelation of Jesus as the risen Lord, the christological process that eventually affirms him as the very self-communication of God, and thus unsurpassably revelatory of God's personal reality, would not have acquired its ground or orientation. Resurrection is therefore grammatical in all christological discourse. Secondly, by showing the close relationship between resurrection and incarnation, we will be in a better position subsequently to consider the divinizing impact of the resurrection.

Christology in Retrospect

I have argued throughout this book that the resurrection of Jesus brought about a shift in perception among the disciples who had previously followed him throughout his ministry up until his death. In light of the Easter experience, Jesus' earliest followers began to recollect his life and death in a dramatically new way. What was familiar became strange, and what was strange became familiar. Cast within a new horizon, one distinguished by the surprising offer of forgiveness from a risen victim through whom reconciliation with God became possible, their memory was quite literally reformed. They now possessed the "intelligence of the victim," to again refer to James Alison's phrase, which is to say, they saw themselves and the reality of God from the perspective of the forgiving victim whose death and resurrection laid bare, while overcoming in a movement of gracious superabundance, their sin. The gospels are thus theory-laden through and through. They are explicitly theological reflections upon a past nexus of persons, encounters, words, and actions that gain their full meaning and coherence from the experience of the Easter event. Written "so that you may believe," the gospels seek to bring about the same kind of conversion in their readers that the disciples themselves underwent. Exhibiting a resurrection hermeneutic, the entire canon of the New Testament represents an act of recollection that is possible only *ex eventu*. Only subsequent to the revelation of Jesus of Nazareth as the crucified-and-risen Lord was it possible more fully to perceive the original purpose of his mission (soteriology), the nature of his personal identity (christology), and the implications of this revelation for those who seek to embrace it (spiritual, sacramental, and ethical praxis). Here I wish to look more directly at the christological impact of this resurrection hermeneutic.

It would be extremely difficult to surmount the widely elaborated argument that the resurrection (and parousia) christology of the primitive church is the source and mediating framework for the development of the early church's christology. Although we must acknowledge, without here attempting to analyze, the implicit christology of Jesus of Nazareth, i.e., the way he understood his identity and relationship to God before his death as this can be gleaned from his sayings and deeds — even if they can be cleanly sifted from the post-resurrection confession of the New Testament — there is little question that the experience of the risen Jesus as personally "present" in community, worship, and mission was singularly important in prompting the earliest Christians to attribute to him titles of honor explicitly thematizing his unique relationship to God. Before saying anything further about doctrinal development in the tradition, it is crucial to point out that as Christian reflection on the Christ event took shape, it did so as a response to the communal worship of the church, which it also intended to serve. Here we must acknowledge, if in passing, the mutual influence of *praxis* and *theoria*, prayer and reflection — *lex orandi, lex credendi,* the rule of prayer is the rule of belief. That the risen Jesus was both a *recipient* of worship and a *mediator* of worship to God the Father, as so many binitarian and trinitarian formulae in scripture attest, could only make an enormous impact on how Christians would come to assess his identity and relationship to God.[37] "The continuing practice of invoking the name of Jesus in worship," writes Maurice Wiles, "helped to ensure that when the time came for more precise doctrinal definition of his person it would be in terms that did not fall short of the manner of his address in worship."[38] But what gave the earliest and succeeding generations of Christians the confidence that Jesus, after his death, was a communicable reality? What allowed them to imagine there could be dialogue with him, that when they invoked his name in company with the Father and the Holy Spirit there was a personal reality to receive and respond in the manner of a transcendent and gracious presence? It was the conviction of Jesus' resurrection from the dead and the experience of encountering him in his "appearances" that filled the earliest Christians with this confidence and imagination. Peter Carnley is entirely correct when he says that "prior to all the Christological talk *about Jesus,* which eventually resulted at Chalcedon with the definition of the incarnation of God in Christ in terms of one person with two natures, there were Christian men and women whose fundamental affirmation of belief seems to have centered almost exclusively upon his resurrection from the dead."[39] Carnley further observes that the "really crucial, controlling category for Christian theology, is the idea of the *Christus praesens.* Resurrection theology is in turn the foundation of all theology in the sense that secondary affirmations of belief are drawn from it concerning Christ's messianic role and divine status. Eventually this leads on to incarnational talk of God's sending of his Son into the world."[40] Carnley is making a historical as well as a logical argument. Historically speaking, the affirmation of Jesus as the risen Christ precedes the incarnational theology of the church. Logically speaking, it is the resurrection which makes that incarnational theology conceivable.

We cannot obviously trace here the complex history of christological development in the New Testament, much less the christological controversies leading up to the fourth- and fifth-century conciliar definitions, though we can draw some general conclusions about this process in order to show, at least in barest outline, the internal coherence between resurrection and incarnation language. Generally speaking, first generation christology (that which we can associate with Christianity prior to 50 C.E.) was intensely focused on the resurrection and parousia as defining "christological moments." This phrase I adopt from Raymond Brown, who uses it in the following way: a "christological moment" is "a scene in the life of Jesus that became the vehicle for giving expression to NT christology (e.g., Jesus' conception, youth, baptism, death, resurrection, second coming)."[41] The resurrection as a christological moment is evident in some of the earliest Christian preaching: "This Jesus God raised up...[and] has made him both *Lord* and *Messiah,* this Jesus whom you crucified" (Acts 2:32, 36); "God exalted him at his right hand as *Leader* and *Savior* that he might give repentance to Israel and forgiveness of sins" (5:31); or as Paul is said to have addressed the synagogue: "And we bring you the good news that what God promised to our ancestors he has fulfilled for us, their children, by raising Jesus; as also it was written in the second psalm, 'You are my *Son;* today I have begotten you'" (13:32–33). Such titles as Lord, messiah, savior, and Son of God certainly drew their meaning from the Jewish tradition that preceded the early Christian movement; and yet the experience of Easter gave these titles a new significance and depth. That the crucified Jesus was risen to a heavenly and exalted status meant he exercised influence as a defining presence within the community of believers as well as dominion over life and death. Whatever significance the titles of Lord and messiah might have had prior to or during his lifetime, they could not but be deeply impacted by a new range of meanings that became possible by the Easter event. As Schillebeeckx puts it: "Only through his resurrection, exaltation and investment with power does it become apparent that he is the 'Lord of all' (Acts 10)."[42]

Implied in those New Testament passages identifying the resurrection as the key moment in Jesus' installation as Lord or his being "begotten" as God's Son (see also Rom. 1:4 and Phil. 2:8–9) is a sense of novelty in Jesus' relationship to God. Without evidencing any scruples about the sort of metaphysical questions that would dominate the christological controversies of the fourth and fifth centuries (e.g., whether it is proper to ascribe any "becoming" to the Logos), the first generation of christology typically affirms that God bestowed upon Jesus a new status through his resurrection and exaltation. Such early christology is sometimes called "two-stage" christology. The lowliness of Jesus' life, and his obedience to God unto death, is contrasted with his exalted status that comes with his resurrection and ascension into heaven, where from on high he reigns as Lord.[43] But as later generations of christology continued to reflect upon the work and person of Jesus, a discernable process takes effect in which the titles of Lord and Son of God extend backwards into the narrative presentations of Jesus' career. Whereas the earliest christological formulae highlight the resurrection as *the* defining christological moment, later traditions begin to adopt moments earlier and earlier in his life in order to express something important about Jesus' identity. Put somewhat simplistically, the later the christology in the first century, the earlier in the narrative presentations of Jesus' life do we find significant christological moments.[44]

For example, in Mark we find an important christological affirmation associated with Jesus' baptism. "And a voice came from heaven, 'You are my Son, the Beloved; with you I am well pleased'" (Mark 1:11). Such Son of God language, and its revelation in the form of *theophany*, represents a "backward extension" of the same language first used after Jesus' resurrection.[45] Reaching back further yet in the narrative sequence, but in all likelihood forward in the historical evolution of christology, we find the conception christology of the infancy narratives in Matthew and Luke.[46] In Matthew, Jesus is presented as the "Son of David" and the "Son of God" who is conceived of the Holy Spirit — the same Spirit that dawned upon the post-paschal community (Acts 2), and which Paul designates as the "Spirit of the risen Christ" (Rom. 8:9–11). In Luke, an angel tells the virgin, "The Holy Spirit will come upon you, and the power of the Most High will overshadow you; therefore the child to be born will be holy; he will be called Son of God" (Luke 1:35). Here again, the Son of God language says something about Jesus' identity towards the beginning of the narrative sequence, even if this christological moment is retrospective of the resurrection.

Such a process culminates in the preexistence christology of John. If in the synoptic gospels there is still a sense of "becoming" in Jesus' relationship with God, a process which, as I have said, reaches its climax in the resurrection and exaltation of the crucified Jesus, the sense of becoming fades entirely in the fourth gospel.[47] As stated earlier, the gospel of John tends to view the Christ event in its totality, whereas the synoptic gospels are more genetic in approach. Rather than following a line of dramatic development in which the death and resurrection of Jesus serve as culminating christological moments, when it is revealed most unambiguously to the disciples (and the reader of the text) *who* Jesus truly is, John's gospel concentrates such horizontality, without collapsing it, into a perduring present so that Jesus' identity as Son of God is explicit throughout, even from the first lines of the gospel which express in overtly ontological terms that Jesus Christ is the self-manifestation of God the Father as the eternal Logos of God. Whereas the synoptic gospels tend to "ascend" towards the revelation of the crucified-and-risen One in a continuous and more "history-like" movement, the gospel of John begins with his eternal identity and, adopting a more contemplative mode of reflection, renders the Christ event in terms of identity-manifestation, as an event in which the preexistent Logos, who shares in the divinity of God, "descends" to reveal himself as the Son of the Father, the One through whom union with God is possible.[48] If, in the synoptic gospels, Jesus is focused almost entirely on the Kingdom of God, so that his christology seems by comparison more "functional," i.e., related to his soteriological role as the bringer of God's salvation, the Jesus of the fourth gospel is highly self-reflective of his person, of his mediatorial role, and thus more ontological, more conscious of his "being." This is no more evident than in the many "I am" sayings woven throughout the book, including the "I am the resurrection and the life" discourse which represents the assimilation (not negation) of future eschatology into christology.

While some may argue that this development from a functional to an ontological christology imposes a foreign conceptuality upon the "Jesus of history," it is not at all unreasonable to argue that once one affirms the resurrection of the Jesus from the dead, the trajectory that leads reflection to affirm Jesus as the very *self*-communication of God is really incumbent upon one who makes it and understands it. "In the course of reflection," writes von Balthasar, "there is an enrichment...of the christologically determined experience of time.... Gradually, the whole life, activity and speech of Jesus in his days on earth had to be slowly thought out afresh on the foundation of the Resurrection and drawn into the light that would illuminate them once and for all."[49] From Brown's point of view, the christological development which results in the backward branching of christological moments in the gospels "is not illogical: The resurrection seen as God's intervention brought Jesus' followers to authentic faith in who he was, and *only in light of that faith did they turn to interpret the earlier aspects of his life.*"[50] The resurrection reveals who Jesus always was, from the beginning; but this knowledge was only possible for his earliest followers subsequent to the resurrection experience by which the full reality of Jesus' *person* was revealed to them. "His followers who saw the risen Jesus realized that he was even more than they had understood during his public ministry. The resurrection, therefore, makes it very difficult to explain away as romanticized creation the more explicit christology attested after the resurrection."[51] Just as the Easter event becomes the hermeneutical lens through which the disciples would come to understand the full soteriological significance of Jesus' life and death, so too does it provide the stimulus and context through which to understand, retrospectively, the full identity of this Jesus as the self-expression of God in history, which is what we mean by the term "incarnation."[52] Even if it would not be exactly accurate to think that the affirmation of the incarnation is the inevitable outcome of resurrection theology alone, since there are important co-mediating factors involved that led to such an affirmation, including the integration of the wisdom tradition of pre-Christian Judaism, which allowed Christians to speak of Jesus as the personal embodiment of God's eternal and creative wisdom, it is nevertheless true that the resurrection provided the catalyst and inner logic for this very development, that such conceptually mediating factors as the Jewish wisdom tradition and the various titles of honor appropriated from the Old Testament, including messiah, Lord, and Son of God, were like so many iron filaments magnetically attracted by the Easter event to bring them into mutual interaction to give support to the Christian conviction, constantly nourished in communal prayer and worship, that *in* Jesus Christ God's *very self* is encountered. By using the phrase "very self," I mean here that God's work of salvation in and through Jesus Christ was not imagined to be an act extrinsic to God, but contact and communion with the reality of God as such. How else to understand the proto-trinitarian formulae of Paul which speak of our participation in the risen Christ as the mutual indwelling with God? "If the Spirit of him who raised Jesus from the dead dwells in you, he who raised Christ from the dead will give life to your mortal bodies also through his Spirit that dwells in you" (Rom. 8:11).

It is just this perspective that John's gospel takes from its opening prologue, and which is sustained throughout. It is a "christology from above" insofar as it begins where the synoptic portraits end. Completing a backward extending arc from the resurrection to preexistence, so that the "coming" of the future parousia is shown to have "already" come in the Logos taking on flesh — a process which shows the intimate relationship between resurrection and incarnation, eschatology and protology — the fourth gospel represents a maturation in the christological process which, though it does not replace the synoptics' more genetic approach, complements them by expressing in more ontological terms the identity of Jesus Christ as the incarnation of God's eternal Word.

The Proclaimer and the Proclaimed

To appreciate further this internal coherence between resurrection and incarnation, it is crucial to understand that the resurrection reveals the indissoluble unity of Jesus' *mission* and *person*. The resurrection, as I have argued throughout, is not simply the perpetuation of Jesus' "cause." It is not just the ongoing moral influence of his ministry within the community of his followers. Certainly, by raising him from the dead, God has retroactively legitimized Jesus' life and concrete aims in an unsurpassable way. It is God's "amen" upon his ministry, which fills it with an authority bearing no strong analogy with any prophet before him. Jesus is God's "eschatological prophet," the one through whom the office of prophet is maximally realized. But such an understanding remains too limited by functional terms. For God raises Jesus from the dead and makes him epiphanous to his disciples as God's own self-presence. The self-manifestation of the risen victim is the concrete way God offers hospitality and forgiveness to sinners. The crucified-and-risen Lord *is* God's forgiveness, its "face" and "form." Thus, if the historical Jesus lived a life wholly for the Kingdom of God, and therefore did not make himself the primary object of his preaching and ministry, but only indirectly revealed his identity through self-emptying, the Easter event, because it is the transposition of Jesus' entire person into eschatological finality as God's definitive word, inserts Jesus at the very center of God's salvific action for humanity. If Jesus, heedless of self, proclaimed the coming Kingdom of God, the essence of that proclamation was retrospectively shown to be embodied in his total personal reality, in the sequence of his life, death, and resurrection. "Jesus may, within the Father's governance, have forgotten himself, but God 'remembers' the historical Jesus and of this divine remembrance and Parousia are the end result: God himself identifies the kingdom of God with Jesus of Nazareth, the crucified One." The Kingdom of God did indeed come, continues Schillebeeckx: "in the living One who was crucified. The selfless proclaimer becomes thus the One proclaimed, the centre of the Christian affirmation of belief."[53] Here we can begin to catch sight of the trinitarian action involved in the resurrection event, a point to which we shall return momentarily.

There is a marvelous way this transition from proclaimer to proclaimed is traced in the synoptic gospels. Hans Frei has highlighted the progression evident in Mark, Matthew, and Luke in which Jesus, who at once had been thoroughly engaged in intense prophetic activity, becomes less and less a direct agent in inverse proportion to the deadly opposing forces about him. Through his arrest, trial, and execution, Jesus' actions and words become increasingly terse, even enigmatic: "You say that I am." "You say so." To Pilate's amazement, "Jesus made no further reply" (Mark 15:5). Concurrently, we perceive a rising curve in God's activity on behalf of Jesus, not in the account of his death (God seems most withdrawn here — "My God, my God, why have you forsaken me?"), but most dramatically, yet elliptically, in his resurrection. When Jesus is at his most passive, God the Father is the most active. But God's activity is entirely focused on making Jesus epiphanous. God's decisive "act" is to manifest the "being" (or better, the risen "person") of the crucified Jesus. The "hand of God, though obviously dominant and alone efficacious and directly present in the raising of Jesus, remains completely veiled at this point of the story."[54] Such "veiling" is not without content. God's eschatological activity is concentrated upon the person of Jesus. The risen Christ marks the very presence of God's action. God *acts* — Jesus *is risen;* God *acts* — Jesus *is manifest.*[55]

The significance of this shift in agency is twofold. First, it shows the complete unity between the historical ministry of Jesus of Nazareth and the crucified-and-risen Christ, his *mission* and *person*. The gospels make it quite clear that we are not dealing with alternatives, as though Jesus of Nazareth were different from the risen Christ, as though one or the other is any more or less "real." The effect of the narrative, when read in its integrity, is to show that the risen Christ *is* the crucified Jesus of Nazareth, and none other.[56] He is not an alien presence. He cannot be converted into a myth. His life is not the illustration of an abstract principle. He is a person, unsubstitutably himself. All that he has enacted throughout his life up until his death is recapitulated and made manifest in its eschatological finality and full personal form in the resurrection. Here it is essential to observe that none of the christological titles associated with him coincide with his personal reality. It is his *person* which identifies the titles, not the other way around.[57] Secondly, because God's characteristic activity is so firmly associated with the raising of Jesus from the dead, the Easter event most fully reveals *God's* identity. The dovetailing of God's eschatological "act" and Jesus appearing in the fullness of his "person" reveals to us a now permanent and reciprocal identification between God and Jesus. From this point on in the history of divine revelation, *Who* this risen One is decisively informs our understanding *Who* God is, and vice versa. "Who is this man? He is Jesus of Nazareth who, as this man and no other, is truly manifest as the Savior, the presence of God."[58]

God's Definitive Self-Expression

In considering this relationship between Jesus' resurrection and God's presence further, we take note of Wolfhart Pannenberg's assessment that the apocalyptic eschatology which provides the indispensable (if insufficient) framework for understanding the Easter event bears within it the seeds for drawing just this conclusion, namely, that God was revealed in the person of Christ in an unsurpassable way. If, for the apocalyptic imagination, God was to be fully revealed at the "end of the world," when the ultimate destiny of creation and human history would be realized, the fact that Jesus has *already* been raised means that the end of the world has already begun and that God has been revealed in a way that possesses genuine finality. The distinction between the two aeons, which characterizes the "not yet" distinction of time, has been transformed by the in-breaking of the apocalyptic future here and now. This in-breaking comes in a unique and entirely unexpected modality: in the revelation of a person, the crucified-and-risen Jesus of Nazareth. The "presence" of the apocalyptic future, and the God who is the architect of that future, are encountered in the personal form of the living Christ. Pannenberg puts the matter thusly:

> If Jesus, having been raised from the dead, is ascended to God and if thereby the end of the world has begun, then God is ultimately

revealed in Jesus. Only at the end of all events can God be revealed in his divinity, that is, as the one who works all things, who has power over everything. Only because in Jesus' resurrection the end of all things, which for us has not yet happened, has already occurred can it be said of Jesus that the ultimate already is present in him, and so also that God himself, his glory, has made its appearance in Jesus in a way that cannot be surpassed. Only because the end of the world is already present in Jesus' resurrection is God himself revealed in him.[59]

So even if we remain within the framework of apocalyptic eschatology, already we find that the Easter message situates Jesus in an utterly unique role within salvation history, as the one in and through whom Israel's God is definitively revealed. At the very least, it becomes extremely difficult to avoid this conclusion, especially once we recall from the previous chapter that the resurrection of the victim was understood to be God's offer of eschatological forgiveness, the offer of reconciliation with God.

Pannenberg further observes that as the apocalyptic eschatology which supports this interpretation begins to interact with and more thoroughly integrate the wisdom traditions of pre-Christian Judaism, including the intellectual resources available in the broader Hellenistic world, the language of revelation increasingly takes on the mode of "epiphany" or "manifestation." The meaning of Jesus' resurrection thus modulated becomes as follows: "in Jesus, God himself has appeared on earth. God himself — or God's revelatory figure, the Logos, the Son — has been among us as a man in the figure of Jesus."[60] Implied in this assessment of Jesus' revelatory role is his divine sonship — though Christian theology would have to wait some time before defining more precisely the orthodox position on Jesus' divinity.[61]

Coming at the issue from a slightly different perspective, Karl Rahner offers an incisive account of the inner relationship between resurrection and incarnation. Noting that if the resurrection means that the "whole person" of Jesus belongs irrevocably to God, which is what the early Christians insisted upon by affirming the "bodiliness" of the event, then it is not difficult to envisage the later christological confessions of the church:

> Once we have, in a spirit of faith, seized upon the "Resurrection" of Jesus, then we have grasped the fact that the one and single history of the world as a whole can no longer fail, even though the question of how the personal history of the individual will turn out remains open, and belongs to the absolute future of God which

brings blessing indeed, but still at the same time remains at the level of inconceivable and indefinable mystery. But once the word of God's self utterance, in the case of a concrete individual in history, is present never again to be withdrawn, and accepted in faith as the absolute future of history, then that unity between God and man is present and believed in too which Christian faith acknowledges in the "hypostatic union."[62]

This passage is most interesting, for it attempts to show that while a person may not know what the "hypostatic union" of natures might precisely mean, the affirmation of the resurrection of Jesus implicitly contains it. This is so, according to Rahner, because of the eschatological finality of the resurrection. Easter means that Jesus is not just *a* word of God. He is *the* Word of God, the ultimate utterance of God in our history in which "God promises himself irrevocably." The irrevocable nature of this self-promise derives from the fact that God has spoken through the abyss of death. It is only in Jesus that God's revelatory word breaches "the demarcation line of death," which makes it, in comparison to the history of revelation prior to it, ultimate and unsurpassable.[63] Here again the trans-historical character of Jesus' resurrection is of crucial significance. The resurrection of Jesus reveals the inmost promise of history as its eschatological fulfillment, but it *is* this fulfillment precisely by also being more-than-historical. It liberates history from its contingency. It is "the event in which God irrevocably adopts the creature as his own reality, by his own divine primordial act"; an event in which God "divinizes and transfigures the creature"; an "ontological" and not only a "juridical" act that constitutes "the irreversible and embryonically final beginning of the glorification and divinization of the *whole* reality."[64] And again: "But Jesus lays claim to being God's definitive self-promise in a way that is unconditional and irreversible, and Jesus' self-interpretation and his claim are confirmed by God through the definitiveness of his existence in death and resurrection. Therefore Jesus' human reality, notwithstanding its historical and finite character, must be something that is not merely established by the God who is beyond the world, but it must be God's own reality."[65] Although in saying this we have not quite deduced a statement that asserts with metaphysical precision the Logos as "eternally begotten" of the Father, it is possible to see that when the time came for making such doctrinal statements in response to the controversies and confusions emerging in Christian antiquity, such terms were necessary within their context and faithful to the original and full meaning of the original Easter experience. "Unless it is untrue to itself," writes Rahner, "the simplest experience of faith with Jesus, the crucified and risen One, therefore leads inescapably to statements which in actual fact include an ontological Christology of descent and incarnation, but which also from the very beginning simultaneously include, seriously and effectively, the horizontal Christology of salvation history and fundamental theology."[66] One may wish to quibble with Rahner on this point, or object to what appears to be an overly simplified translation between incarnation and resurrection. On the other hand, that is precisely the point: such a possible swift movement means that these christological moments are (or at least should be) read as internally and integrally related in meaning.[67]

By way of concluding this brief foray into christology, here it would be helpful to call attention to an important distinction. If, in numerous strains of New Testament christology, the impression is given that Jesus ontologically "becomes" the Son of God at the moment of his resurrection and exaltation, subsequent generations of theological reflection increasingly took this to mean that Jesus was only revealed as such. The distinction to be made here is between revelation and ontology. On the order of revelation, Jesus' identity as the Son of God became known only subsequent to the resurrection. Only from the perspective of the Easter experience in which the crucified-and-risen Jesus became epiphanous in his total personal reality as God's eschatological justice and forgiveness was it possible to perceive that he was previously one with God, that from "the beginning" of his appearance in the world he was the self-expression of God in our history. This is what the evolution of christology in the New Testament increasingly clarifies as it looks from the resurrection back to ultimate origins — in a protological direction.[68] Thus, if the resurrection has historical and logical priority over the incarnation, the incarnation possesses ontological priority since, according to the mature reflection of the church, the resurrection completes and reveals what occurred in the incarnation of the Word. We may phrase it this way: without the resurrection, the revelatory process which led Christians to affirm the incarnation would not have occurred; without the incarnation, the resurrection, which led Christians to say that God was *in* Christ reconciling himself to the world, would be empty of meaning.

The Trinitarian Form of Easter

The resurrection of Jesus is ultimately a trinitarian event. Indeed, of all the events narrated in the New Testament, Easter reveals most distinctly a "trinitarian form."[69] Although we have not yet explored this trinitarian form at length, particularly the imparting of the Holy Spirit, it is timely now to do so since it is just this impartation which allows for the "mutual indwelling" of God and humanity.

We have already observed the near-exclusive emphasis on God's agency in raising Jesus from the dead: God *raises*—Jesus *is raised;* God *acts*—the risen Christ *is manifest.* "God raised him on the third day and allowed him to appear" (Acts 10:40; see also 2:32; 3:15; 4:10). "God raised the Lord and will also raise us by his power" (1 Cor. 6:14); "the power of God, who raised him from the dead" (Col. 2:20). With these and similar passages we discern a characteristic manner of naming God that, because of its notable consistency throughout the New Testament, "comes close to being a definition of God."[70] God is the One "who raises the dead" (2 Cor. 1:9), "who raised the Lord Jesus [and who] will raise us also with Jesus" (2 Cor. 4:14); "who gives life to the dead and calls into existence the things that do not exist" (Rom. 4:17; see also Rom. 4:24, 8:11, 10:9; Eph. 1:20; Col. 2:12; 1 Pet. 1:21). At times Paul specifies "God the Father," "who raised him from the dead" (Gal. 1:1). Other formulations in Paul and elsewhere in the New Testament indicate that God raises Jesus through the work of the Spirit: "[Christ] was declared to be Son of God with power according to the Spirit of holiness by resurrection from the dead" (Rom. 1:4); "He was revealed in flesh, vindicated [by the] Spirit" (1 Tim. 3:16; see also 1 Pet. 3:18). The parallels with Old Testament passages are numerous, particularly those emphasizing God's power over life and death and faithfulness to creation, a point to which we shall return. Yet such ascriptions in the New Testament are uniquely concentrated on the person of the risen Christ through whom the entire community of creation has (proleptically) achieved its fulfillment. Through him God's "glory" (*doxa*), and not just God's "power" (*dunamis*), is revealed: "just as Christ was raised from the dead by the glory (*doxa*) of the Father, so we too might walk in newness of life" (Rom. 6:4). By his resurrection we too, in company with the entire community of creation, will be "glorified with him" (8:17) through the "redemption" and "glorification" of our bodies (v. 23; see also 1 Cor. 15:43, 47–57; 2 Cor. 5:1–5; Col. 3:1–4; Phil. 3:21).

While this shared glorification is promissory, it is a reality made effective and present through the Holy Spirit. A key passage from Paul, previously quoted, accentuates the point: "If the Spirit of him who raised Jesus from the dead dwells in you, he who raised Christ from the dead will give life to your mortal bodies also through his Spirit that dwells in you" (Rom. 8:11). Paul presents the Easter event "stereoscopically," as it were. It is an encompassing reality in whose inner world we are plunged. Indeed, there is no "outside" or "inside" so much as there is a coinherence between its objective and subjective dimensions. The Spirit of the risen Christ is poured within our hearts, filling us from within, vivifying us, fructifying our work, drawing us beyond ourselves toward that eschatological goal — which we anticipate, along with all of creation, "with eager longing" — when "creation itself will be free from its bondage to decay and will obtain the freedom of the glory of the children of God" (vv. 19, 21). It is this Spirit also that bears witness within us as we cry "Abba! Father!" that we are children of God and will be glorified with the risen Christ (vv. 15–17). When, in the previous chapter, we observed the movement of "de-possession" from sin to "re-possession" in Christ, as the false heteronomy of the sinful "I" is transformed through christonomy, this is made possible by the indwelling Spirit of the risen Christ. It is what enables us to say Christ "lives in us" (Gal. 2:20; Phil. 1:21) or we can "put on Christ" (Gal. 3:26–27). Such language forms the biblical basis of what the later church fathers will call *theosis*.[71] Here there is no thought of the Spirit of God "replacing" our own, but rather the Spirit of Christ indwells within us so that we participate by grace, and with ever-increasing richness, in divine life. "Do you not know that you are God's temple and that God's Spirit dwells in you?" (1 Cor. 3:16).

So close is the relationship between the risen Christ and the Spirit in the Pauline literature that it is sometimes difficult to distinguish the two (see, for example, 2 Cor. 3:17). A clearer differentiation can be found in the gospels. For example, in Luke-Acts we find the language of "sending": God (the Father) raises Jesus from the dead and the risen Christ sends the Holy Spirit as promised by the Father (Luke 24:49). Early in Acts we discover the fulfillment of this promise: "This Jesus God raised up, and of that all of us are witnesses. Being therefore exalted at the right hand of God, and having received from the Father the promise of the Holy Spirit, he has poured out this that you both see and hear" (Acts 2:32–33). If Paul more fully expounds upon the Spirit's indwelling within the individual believer, the overarching plot of Luke-Acts naturally emphasizes the animating role of the Spirit in the church as it extends Christ's mission throughout the world. Similarly, Matthew ends with the great commission in which the risen Christ directs Jesus' followers to make disciples of all nations by baptizing them in the name of the Father, Son, and Holy Spirit (28:19). Here, as with Luke, the Spirit descending upon Jesus at his baptism is imparted to his disciples. Inscribed with a new identity and incorporated into Christ's body through the regenerating waters of baptism, the followers of Christ are bonded together to share in the common life of God.

In the farewell discourses of John (13:31–17:26), Jesus promises to send his disciples the Paraclete who will "abide" in them and guide them into all truth. The Holy Spirit is the Spirit of Truth, the Comforter, and the Advocate who testifies on Jesus' behalf to all that he said and did for the benefit of his disciples and to the glory of the Father. In these discourses we find a unique relationship between Jesus' withdrawal and the possibility of a new kind of presence that encompasses the disciples within a trinitarian milieu. The Paraclete, who comes from the Father at the request of the Son, does so only as Jesus returns in glory to the Father. "When the Advocate comes, whom I will send to you from the Father, the Spirit of truth who comes from the Father, he will testify on my behalf" (15:26). Jesus prepares his disciples for his coming absence and (qualitatively new) presence among them by drawing a comparison with a woman in labor who, in sharp pain because "her hour has come," at last gives birth to a child only later to forget her anguish "because of the joy of having brought a human being into the world. So you have pain now; but I will see you again, and you will rejoice, and no one will take your joy from you" (16:20–23). This return and the joy it brings is exactly the purpose of Jesus' resurrection in John. But here we can be more precise by saying that the resurrection is the revelation of the Holy Spirit and the dawning of a new dispensation — the post-paschal dispensation — in which the disciples carry on Christ's mission as they become *alter Christi* through the Spirit's vivifying power. The Spirit, as it were, "makes room" for the disciples to be drawn up into the life and work of the triune God so that they begin to do for the broader human community what Christ himself set out to do. Easter and Pentecost are therefore simultaneous in John. This is evident as the risen Christ breaths on the disciples, saying, "Receive the Holy Spirit. If you forgive the sins of any, they are forgiven them; if you retain the sins of any, they are retained" (20:22–23). Having now become his "friends," and not just his "servants" (15:15), the disciples, by carrying on his mission in the presence of the Spirit, who makes that mission truly worldwide (17:20–24), are able to "do the works that I do and, in fact, will do greater works than these, because I am going to the Father" (14:12).

Together the purgative and illuminative moments in John's resurrection narratives map out an itinerary for the mystical transformation the Christian must undergo in entering the post-paschal dispensation. Von Balthasar notes this well, stating that "the disciples had to be transformed and raised up from a *carnalis amor ad Christi humanitatem*... by being carried, entranced, into the sphere of the Spirit, to a *spiritualis amor ad eius divinitatem*."[72] This corresponds quite precisely with the observation made in chapter 2 that both Mary Magdelene and Thomas the Twin, each in their own way, had to "relearn" Jesus Christ by "rediscovering" him in the presence of the community of disciples who, in the presence of the Spirit, now body him forth in the world. Mary misidentifies the risen Lord with the gardener because she has not yet learned how to relate to him according to his glorified corporeality. When she does, she no longer calls him "Rabbouni" but "Lord" (20:16, 18). Thomas too had to undergo this transformation, but his first step towards christological faith passes through the absence differently. Needing to grasp at evidence, Thomas remains hampered by his pre-paschal imagination, which, in this context, we may interpret as a *carnalis amor*. Though the risen Christ lovingly makes the concession, and though Thomas will utter a christological confession of the very highest order, demonstrating that he too has acceded to a *spiritualis amor ad eius divinitatem* ("My Lord and my God!"), Jesus responds by saying, "Have you believed because you have seen me? Blessed are those who have not seen and yet have come to believe" (v. 29). In other words, blessed are those who come to faith, not through the kind of evidence required by Thomas, but through the signs of the gathered community in the Spirit, its witness, its sacramental life, its love. "The Resurrection appearances are themselves a training in just such a transformation," writes von Balthasar.

> [T]he disappearance is at the service of a deeper and more definitive presence — not that of a distant God, hiding himself anew from men, but, rather, that, in express terms, of him who became man and is the "heir" of all the Father's creating work, reflecting the "glory of God" and bearing "the very stamp of his nature" (Hebrews 1:3). "I am with you" (Matthew 28:20); "I will not leave you desolate; I will come to you...you will see me; because I live, you will live also" (John 14:18ff). Jesus speaks here of his presence in the Church. The appearances of the Risen One are a kind of down-payment towards this abiding presence, and indeed of the ceaselessly self-renewing advent (parousia) of the definitive Word of God in the Church.[73]

While it is true that the binitarian and trinitarian formulae in the New Testament do not permit complete systematization, and while we must avoid making anachronistic statements by declaring for the New Testament the more conceptually precise doctrinal formulations of the fourth and fifth centuries (though we can affirm the latter's appropriateness to the former), we can readily perceive emergent patterns in scripture that allow us to predicate distinctive roles to the Father, Son, and Holy

Spirit in the Easter event: God the Father raises the Son through the power of the Holy Spirit, allows the Son to "appear" to the glory of the Father, and together the Father and Son impart the Holy Spirit as the indwelling presence of the whole Godhead among and within humanity for our salvation. A trinitarian action with a single, sweeping economic progression, Easter opens up *for us* the life of God. By "assuming" our humanity in the incarnation and "transfiguring" through the resurrection, we have been united to God, in Christ, and through the Holy Spirit in such a way that, without losing what is essential to our humanity, we may become "divinized" through our participation in triune life. In the ultimate act of divine hospitality, the triune God welcomes the Other (in this case, that which is not-God) to partake in God's own life. The manner of this hospitality, as well as the intimacy of the communion between God and humanity it makes possible, is most remarkable: God, in a loving and utterly free act of self-donation, "goes out" of God's self to become united, through the incarnation of the eternal Logos, with that which is not-God, creation, thereby endowing it with unimaginable dignity; and, having become vulnerable to the brokenness of the human condition, "absorbing" our sin and violence in the cross, revealing our sin and violence through the risen victim whose eschatological pardon is made effective and epiphanous in the form of a face, God "raises" our humanity in Christ, through the power of the Holy Spirit, to usher us into permanent union with God who alone is our fulfillment. The whole of the Christ event is, of course, soteriological in impact and trinitarian in form. It must be seen in its totality to adequately grasp its true character. But here I might make the special point, in support of the christological analysis above, that it is the resurrection of Jesus which, historically and logically speaking, makes it possible to view the Christ event in just this way. "[O]nly with the Resurrection," writes von Balthasar, does the mystery of the Trinity "come forth openly into the light."[74] Although, ontologically speaking, the intra-trinitarian relations of God make possible the trinitarian order of the *oikonomia,* only subsequent to the resurrection event, which so uniquely discloses a trinitarian form, is it possible to retrospectively describe the entire Christ event, and, indeed, the entire history of revelation as the work of the triune God.[75]

We must therefore say, even if parenthetically, that the above description of Easter's trinitarian form eventually necessitates a full-blown trinitarian theology (something we cannot pursue here) for one basic reason: the God who is revealed in history *pro nobis* is none other than who God is *in se*. Rahner's axiom, which has become more or less paradigmatic in contemporary theology, holds true: the immanent Trinity is the economic Trinity, and vice versa.[76] Such an axiom does not imply their total conflation, as though God can only be trinitarian (and thus, can only be God) by self-emptying into that which is other than God, which would be tantamount to asserting the metaphysical necessity of creation. Rather, the possibility of divine kenosis *ad extra* is found in the eternal self-emptying of the Trinity. The Father eternally begets the Son, who receives his reality and the fullness of divinity through the Spirit, and through the Spirit returns himself wholly to the Father in one ecstatic movement of love. The ceaseless "emptying" and "filling" of the Godhead in the trinity of Persons is infinitely creative; and this creativity, which needs nothing in order to be itself, overflows from its boundless fecundity to bring forth creation in absolute freedom and love. Thus, the incarnation of the Logos and the outpouring of the Holy Spirit are economic movements corresponding to the eternal reality of the one God. God is not just relational and tri-personal in appearance to us; the phenomenality of divine revelation — its "form" — is really the *self*-communication of who God is *in se*. The God who is revealed in the Christ event "for us" in the economy of salvation is not different from who God really is "for God's self." Christ is God's *self*-communication, not a façade or a proxy. And as we shall see in the following chapter, the humanity of Christ remains the permanent means of contact in our relationship with the triune God, even in the beatific vision.

Chapter Ten

ORIGINAL PEACE, DIVINIZATION, AND BEAUTY OF FORM

On the one hand there is the absurdity of primordial chaos, the nothingness from which everything is supposed to emerge, which is said to engender being, the blind power which is supposed to bring forth the light of the Spirit: and on the other hand there is the source of Being—a certain "Point Alpha."

On the one hand there is the hopelessness and the final chaos of the ultimate defeat, of the Spirit finally overcome by the darkness of matter, unending death, or that mournful "eternal recurrence" in which all dreams finally vanish; on the other hand there is the Place where being recollects itself—a "Point Omega."

"I am the Alpha and the Omega," says the Lord.
—Henri de Lubac, *The Discovery of God*[1]

ORIGINAL PEACE: CREATION IN RETROSPECT

We have seen how the resurrection galvanized the process of christological reflection that led to the affirmation of Jesus' prior unity with God, and thus as the definitive self-communication of God in our world. Along with this new understanding of God eventually comes the reframing of Jewish monotheism in trinitarian terms. The trinitarian form of the Easter event, as characterized by the kerygmatic and doxological formulations of the New Testament, led Christian theology to an understanding of God's unity in terms of personal communion. To the extent that the resurrection plays a decisive role in such christological and theological reflection, historically and logically, we must accord to it a grammatical function. We can say the same for the Christian understanding of creation.

James Alison, in his study of original sin from a Girardian perspective, makes a striking and important observation. The "intelligence of the victim" imparted to the earliest Christians in their encounters with the risen Christ did more than transform their understanding of Jesus, God, and salvation; it allowed them to see the reality of creation in a new light. Cast within the perspective of the self-giving victim, they began to see that creation as such, from the beginning, came to be *in* and *through* Christ. If Easter reveals the eschatological future of creation, so the logic goes, it reveals the destiny given to it by God from the very beginning. We see just this logic operative in this remarkable passage from Colossians:

> He is the image of the invisible God, the firstborn of all creation; for in him all things in heaven and on earth were created, things visible and invisible, whether thrones or dominions or rulers or powers — all things have been created through him and for him. He himself is before all things, and in him all things hold together. He is the head of the body, the church; he is the beginning, the firstborn of the dead, so that he might come to have first place in everything. For in him all the fullness of God was pleased to dwell, and through him God was pleased to reconcile to himself all things, whether on earth or in heaven, by making peace through the blood of his cross. (Col. 1:15–20)

Here again we see the movement from eschatology to protology. In the same way the resurrection opens up the understanding that Christ was previously one with God, so does it reveal that the "firstborn of the dead" is also the "firstborn of all creation." The entire drift of creation is shown to be summed up in him. The end reveals the beginning, and both are present now in Christ, in whom the fullness of deity dwells. From this perspective it must be seen that Christ's appearance in the world is not a second thought or a stopgap measure for something inexplicably gone awry. The Son is original to creation itself, co-generative of creation with the Father and the Spirit. It must also be seen that the manner of creation is entirely free from the presence of violence. In contrast to many of the world's creation myths that depict cosmic origins in terms of the suppression of chaos, or through a founding murder in the realm of the gods, creation in Christ is shown to be the bestowal of existence from an original peace. The hospitality offered by the One whose death and resurrection brings forth reconciliation with God opens up a perspective upon creation as utterly gratuitous and originally free from the violence that has become parasitical upon it. The resurrection of Jesus thus permits the "definitive demythologization of God," as Alison puts it, since it fundamentally breaks with any view, ancient or modern, that envisions violence as anterior to or generative of the world. The resurrection of the victim — the "new creation" — shows that God's originally creative act is gratuitous and pacific. This perception is made possible by the complete unmasking of the scapegoat process.

There is yet another important dimension to the Colossians passage, directly related to the former, which will concern us in this chapter, though it may not be immediately apparent. This dimension is aesthetic. Christ is the "image of the invisible God." His humanity is manifestory of divine reality. He is, in his human form, iconic of the divine. The invisible traverses itself to become visible in him, and not just temporarily. The resurrection and transfiguration of his corporeality into its eschatological *doxa* and form has now become the permanent means for our relationship to the creator God. So far from remaining an inhibiting veil to our restless yearning for the infinite and invisible God, creation itself is in fact the mediatorial site for this communion. Having assumed a body for our salvation, and having "gathered" all things into himself, whether visible or invisible, God has given us access to divine life through Christ in a manner entirely appropriate to our created nature. The aesthetic significance of this is considerable. Without in any way undermining the contingency of creation, the resurrection endows creation with an eschatological destiny and dignity by drawing it into the bosom of the triune God, where eternally it manifests God's inexhaustible beauty. Even if all creation is subject to dissolution, God shall "remember" it in all its particularity to give what has passed through the cross deified life. It is for this reason, asserts Hans Urs von Balthasar, that Christianity is "*the* aesthetic religion *par excellence*."[2] The aesthetic sensibility that sustains such a vision stands in sharp contrast with the tragic sublime. The latter, as we shall see, tends to think of "difference" in terms of negation, privation, and force, whereas the former reads "difference" in terms of analogy, participation, and gift. The latter implies an "ontology of violence," the former an "ontology of peace."

Ontology of Violence, Ontology of Peace

We now pick up and expand upon a point made in chapter 7. There we observed that Nietzsche's valorization of Dionysius over the Crucified was, in effect, an affirmation of a sacrificial logic which presumes the primordial nature of violence, its originality and coextension with all life. Nietzsche illuminated the striking contrast in interpretation between two murders that nevertheless bear very similar patterns, structurally speaking. Whereas Dionysius's immolation represents the ceaseless generation and destruction of life, which we must learn to embrace if we wish to accept life as it is, Jesus' death and subsequent resurrection stand as a rejection of life as it is, above all because it appeals to an alternative reality, entirely fabricated out of *ressentiment*, to declare the "innocence" of the victim and the "evil" of the ordeal. Whereas Dionysius's "resurrection" constitutes his reabsorption into the processes of life and death, and thus represents a tragic wisdom which has learned to say "yes" to and endure even the harshest of suffering, the "resurrection" of the Crucified extracts him from the world's cyclical becoming, leaving him in a permanently unreconciled relationship with the strife intrinsic to it. For Nietzsche, the truth of the world is that it is a sphere of combat: "life itself is *essentially* appropriation, injury, overpowering of what is alien and weaker; suppression, hardness, imposition of one's own forms, incorporation and, at the least and mildest, exploitation."[3] Although Nietzsche might wish to claim for his view a break with metaphysics, as David Bently Hart rightly points out, the Nietzschean critique, and the narrative offered in its stead, cannot ultimately escape metaphysics. It is a metaphysics of violence in which ontic difference is viewed in terms of strife, antagonism, contrariety, force, and instinct; "indeed, difference is appreciably different precisely in the degree to which each force resists, succumbs to, or vanquishes another force: an ontology of violence in the most elementary form."[4] Hart is candid about the plausibility of Nietzsche's position, which, more than any other, has set the tone for the metaphysics of *difference* in much postmodern thought.[5] "Between Nietzsche's vision of life as an agon and the Christian vision of life as creation — as a primordial 'gift' and 'grace' — there is nothing... that makes either perspective self-evidently more correct than the other. Each sees and accounts for the violence of experience and the beauty of being, but each according to an irreducible mythos and a particular aesthetic."[6] Each, that is, narrates reality differently, and neither narration can claim a kind of self-evidence that dispenses with interpretation. Even if the things to be interpreted are the same (the world, life, death, beauty, violence, etc.), such things will appear differently as they are interpreted within different horizons of meaning. They are stories about the world with radically different aesthetic sensibilities — the one committed to the sublime, the other to divine *doxa* and the eschatological transfiguration of created form through Christ's incarnation, death, and resurrection.

The Nietzschean counter-narrative gives Christian theology a singular opportunity, then. Because it is a post-Christian interpretation quite deliberately proposed as an alternative to the Christian story, it "liberates theology from apologetical dialectic, in which it has no ultimate stake, and calls it again to its proper idiom: *a proclamation of the story of peace posed over against the narrative of violence,* a hymnody rising up around the form of Christ offered over against the jubilant dithyrambs of Dionysius, the depiction of an eternal beauty advanced over against the depiction of a sempiternal sublime."[7] Nietzsche does not intend to justify his vision of life by appealing to the sciences of his day. It is kerygma, story-telling, rhetoric, a presentation of life to be richly envisioned and heroically embraced. Nietzsche, like his Zarathustra, is an evangelist. So is Christianity fundamentally proclamation, rhetoric. Its ability to persuade comes through its account of the beautiful, an account which sees creation from the perspective of its eschatological fruition and glory, its goodness, its original peace. "The most potent reply a Christian can make to Nietzsche's critique is to accuse him of a defect of sensibility — of bad taste.... Nietzsche had atrocious taste."[8]

The ontology of violence we find in Nietzsche is not, for all its post-Christian polemics, entirely new. It is a retrieval, a neo-paganism that looks to the pre-Socratic philosophers, tragedians, and Homeric myths to exhume a vision of life from over two millennia of Platonic and Judeo-Christian sedimentation. Here again we recall Nietzsche's claim that, of all the philosophers dear to his message of the "eternal recurrence," Heraclitus is chief. "Opposition unites. From what draws apart results the most beautiful harmony. All things take place by strife." Being itself is ceaseless becoming, a cacophony of ephemeral and opposing forces. The *kosmos* is an "ever living fire, kindling in measures and being quenched in measures." Conflicting energies are what make the world possible, and this possibility means actual, incessant war. Order is to be won, achieved through strife, and always cyclically. "As the same thing in us are living and dead, waking and sleeping, young and old. For these things having changed around are those, and those in turn having changed around are these." On such a view, violence is normal, structural, primordial. "War is the father of all."[9] Peace, from this point of view, is a temporary armistice, an interlude between extended states of conflict, intelligible primarily in terms of war's absence. Hence, violence is "ontological."

We would be mistaken to imagine that this view is limited to a particular philosophical tradition. It just may be the most enduring of humanity's myths. As we saw with Girard, it is the essence of sacred violence, and it is precisely the subject matter of the gospels as well.

> Behind the Passion of Christ, behind a number of biblical dramas, behind many mythical dramas, and behind primitive rituals, we find the same process — the process of crisis and resolution founded on the same error, the same illusion. This illusion is the misunderstanding about the single victim who pays the price of the

"mimetic cycle." When we examine the great stories of origin and the founding myths, we notice that they themselves proclaim the fundamental and founding role of the single victim and his or her unanimous murder. The idea is present everywhere. In Sumerian mythology cultural institutions emerge from the single victim: Ea, Tiamat, Kingu. The same in India: the dismemberment of the primordial victim, Purusha, by a mob offering sacrifices produces the caste system. We find similar myths in Egypt, in China, among the Germanic peoples — everywhere.[10]

The mimetic rivalry which leads to violent conflict and, finally, the sacrifice of a surrogate for the placation of escalating hostility, serves in such myths as a founding moment, as the emergence of order from prevenient chaos. Quite often, as in the Sumerian-Akkadian theogonic myths predating and, in part, influencing Israel's creation stories, the original conflict takes place in the realm of the gods prior to the creation of the human realm. In the *Enuma Elish,* for example, we discover that before the creation of human beings, and, in fact, as the proximate cause for their existence, a fracas developed between the gods which ended in the slaying and dismemberment of Tiamat, the wife of Apsu, who himself was killed by one of their progeny, Ea, on account of the parental plot, discovered by the younger gods, to kill them because their noisy association kept their elders from sleep. As the mimetic rivalry between the gods escalated to bloodshed, the violence threatened to consume them all. Ea kills Apsu, and Tiamat threatens revenge upon all her progeny. Only the preemptive slaying of Tiamat — the mother of all the gods, whose name symbolizes the chaos of the ocean waters — kept total destruction at bay. Marduk, whose courageous act of slaying his mother earned him the supreme power in the assembly of gods, stretches Tiamat's corpse to form the cosmos. And, at last, human beings were formed from the blood of the slain Kingu for the purpose that they serve at the gods' pleasure.

> Blood I will mass and cause bones to be.
> I will establish a savage, "man" shall be his name.
> Verily, savage-man I will create.
> He shall be charged with the service of the gods
> That they might be at ease![11]

The upshot of this mythological picture, according to Paul Ricoeur, is that creation is a conquest over a more ancient enemy. Order emerges from chaos, peace from violence. Indeed, "Violence is inscribed in the origin of things, in the principle that establishes while it destroys."[12] This mythological picture also underwrites a particular political order, since the king serves at the bidding of the gods and has as his mission to destroy any enemy who, like the chaotic waters symbolized by Tiamat, threatens that order.[13] "In the final analysis," writes Ricoeur, "evil is not an accident that upsets a previous order; it belongs constitutionally to the foundation of order. Indeed, it is doubly original: first, in the role of the Enemy, whom the forces of chaos have never ceased to incarnate, although they were crushed at the beginning of the world; second, in the figure of the King, sent to 'destroy the wicked and evil' by the same ambiguous power of devastation and of prudence that once upon a time established order."[14] Walter Wink contends that the reason the mythical structure of the Babylonian creation story exported so easily to Syria, Phoenicia, Egypt, Greece, Rome, Germany, Ireland, and India was due to its ability to render evil unproblematic while supporting political arrangements based upon power. It is the archetypal story of *the will to power*. "The distinctive feature of the myth is the victory over chaos by means of violence. This myth is the original religion of the status quo, the first articulation of 'might makes right.'... Life is combat.... Ours is neither a perfect nor a perfectible world; it is a theater of perpetual conflict in which the prize goes to the strong. Peace through war, security through strength: these are the core convictions that arise from this ancient historical religion."[15]

One should add to Wink's assessment Girard's insight that the basic pattern of this myth supports and even emerges from the process of scapegoating, which possesses a self-validating structure. The scapegoat mechanism "works," even if its effectiveness depends upon the illusion of the victim's guilt. Sacred violence has proven successful in human culture for diffusing a greater violence that threatens to become all-consuming. By transferring upon a surrogate victim the "chaos" within the group now mired in mimetic crisis, and by expelling the victim in an act of violence that at once inspires dread and fascination — an experience that can be ritually represented and transmitted — order and peace are restored. The murder is thus a founding act. From Girard's point of view, however fantastic this theogony (and its variants) may seem to us, it should not be dismissed as a "mere" myth. The mimetic conflict and subsequent lynching of a victim for the establishment of order depicted in it fairly adequately describes the origins of some of the most durable and dominant infrastructure in human culture.

This is what makes its comparison to the biblical creation stories so striking. The Judeo-Christian scriptures thoroughly problematize evil and violence, as Nietzsche correctly observed. What is remarkable about the Adamic myth in Genesis, for example, is that it is "strictly anthropological" (Ricoeur). Rather than situating violence in an anterior relationship to the human realm, the etiological myth of Adam associates the origin of evil with a *human* ancestor. Rather than equating the reality of evil with the origins of all life, which endows it with metaphysical necessity, the Genesis account sharply distinguishes the anteriority of goodness from the posteriority of evil. Of the various mythical accounts of cosmic and human origins, the Adamic myth "is the most extreme attempt to separate the origin of evil from the origin of the good; its intention is to set up a *radical* origin of evil distinct from the more *primordial* origin of the goodness of things."[16] What violence there is in the world is non-necessary, parasitical upon a prior good, the result of a human moral catastrophe. The monotheism of the Hebrews, which was forged out of a prophetic-ethical imagination that consistently aimed its accusations against humanity to arouse it to repentance, simultaneously affirms God's unconditional goodness.[17] It therefore breaks through the mythological picture of divine/human origins that envisions chaos and order, evil and goodness, violence and peace as co-elemental and eternally recurrent. Jewish monotheism defines a time when evil was not; and it is just this imagination which necessitates the eschatological anticipation of a time when evil will be no more. The creational monotheism of Judaism logically implies eschatology, and vice versa.

On the strength of this observation, we pick up James Alison's suggestion, inspired by the work of Girard, that the revelation of the victim in the biblical tradition allows for an understanding of creation free from structural violence and necessity. "To the degree in which the arbitrary nature of victimization or persecution becomes apparent in the Old Testament, so it becomes possible to tell the story of a foundation or creation which does not involve a god in the suppression of chaos. It became possible to give a nonmythological account of creation, because it became possible to see that God is anterior to any human violence, and thus anterior to chaos."[18] The Priestly account of creation (Gen. 1:1–2:4), which was likely written during or after the time of the Babylonian exile, shows the influence of the *Enuma Elish,* but largely in terms of critical transformation. Like its Mesopotamian counterpart, the Priestly version describes the emergence of order from the chaotic deep (*tehom*) of the waters; but rather than order emerging through the violent subjugation of chaos, a wind sweeps over the deep as God proceeds to speak things into existence ("Let there be...."). The manner of this creation gives no indication of antagonism or conquest. It comes from an inexhaustible bounty and follows an ordered progression that reaches its apex in the creation of human beings who, as male and female, bear God's image. Whereas the *Enuma Elish* depicts the formation of human beings almost as a second thought, and even then from the blood of a slain god, the biblical portrait views the formation of the human being as the crowning jewel of God's generous creativity: "God saw everything that he had made, and indeed, *it was very good*" (1:31). After the six-day sequence of creation comes the Sabbath, the hallowing of creation, the day God allows creation "to be" in its contingent integrity, the day human beings are to rest and celebrate in the world's giftedness. It is thus possible to read the Priestly account as a critique and subversion of Babylonian theogony, the inspiration for which comes from the dismantling of the scapegoat mechanism which leads those in its grasp to represent the origins of order ("the world") in terms of primordial violence, i.e., a founding murder.

Alison suggests that the developing doctrine of the resurrection in post-exilic Judaism may have played a formative role in clarifying the biblical view of cosmic and human origins in terms of creation *ex nihilo*. Even if it might be difficult to verify such a causal connection, the internal coherence between the resurrection and creation *ex nihilo* is instructive to consider. To do so we must recall that although the creation stories in the Old Testament appear first in the narrative sequence, they were composed well into Israel's history, well after the exodus and covenant. Both creation stories in Genesis are retrospective accounts that look backwards through the exodus and covenant, back through the history of Israel and its evolving theological traditions to articulate a vision of origins indelibly shaped by that history and theological reflection.[19] The Priestly creation story was likely composed seven centuries after the liberation of the Hebrew people from Egypt, and probably four centuries after the Yahwist creation story. Alison sees in these stories subversive adaptations of key motifs in the Mesopotamian stories long predating them. In addition to their monotheistic refashioning, quite notable is the absence of any scene of originary violence. Though the chaos of the waters still appears in the Priestly story, the creative act is described in terms of divine *fiat*, not as a result of a conflict with a pre-existing impersonal force. Alison maintains that this subversive rereading represents the logical conclusion to the dismantling of sacred violence at the heart of the Jewish experience of God. As the belief in the resurrection became increasingly widespread during the Hellenistic period, so did the understanding of creation *ex nihilo* become increasingly prominent in Jewish theology. It cannot be a matter of happenstance that those few instances in pre-Christian writings in which the resurrection is an explicit theme also speak explicitly of creation. For example, 2 Maccabees: "Therefore the Creator of the world, who shaped the beginning of humankind and devised the origin of all things, will in his mercy give life and breath back to you again, since you now forget yourselves for the sake of his laws" (7:23). Alison explains:

> That is to say a perception of God [had] been developed as vindicating persecuted victims by raising them from the dead: belief in the resurrection is intrinsically linked with God as not allowing his persecuted ones to be forever silenced. This is simultaneous with the perception that the violent means by which social order is being maintained (by the persecutor) is just that, and no more: God is not involved. Now it is not an accident that the understanding of the noncomplicity of God in this victimary violence... permits the Jewish thinkers to see through the victimary illusion with sufficient clarity to be able to affirm *in the same period* the doctrine of creation *ex nihilo*.... [T]he intelligence of the victim has advanced sufficiently for it to be possible to separate the perception of God as Creator from any complicity with the suppression of chaos.[20]

Whatever is possible to say about the causal connection elaborated here — Alison admits his argument remains speculative and tentative — such is less important than seeing the internal coherence between the resurrection of the dead and creation *ex nihilo*.[21] The most obvious connection is that both affirm God's total sovereignty over nothingness. Neither pre-existing nor post-mortem formlessness present an obstacle to God's irresistibly creative power. God is the one "who gives life to the dead and calls into existence the things that do not exist" (Rom. 4:17; see also Heb. 11:3). Within a single phrase, Paul expresses their mutual significance, showing that God's primordially creative act of speaking things into being is entirely in keeping with the new creation of resurrection life. But we can say more than this: the resurrection of the dead is explicitly connected with the unmasking and dismantling of sacred violence, as the Maccabees passage above attests, along with the many passages in the New Testament examined in chapters 7 and 8. The theme of the victim's vindication witnesses to God's judgment of those religious-cultural structures that produce victims and obscure their innocence for the establishment of order. Likewise, God's primordially creative act is presented in scripture as having nothing at all to do with the underwriting of such violence. God calls into existence things that do not exist, and does so out of a boundless generosity that has no opposition with which to contend. What strife there is in the world is anthropological, not part of the very fabric of things endlessly recycled. God's relationship to creation is one of peace, not antagonism and strife. Here it is very much worth noting that the doctrine of creation *ex nihilo* (and the biblical view more generally) is not primarily about the first instant of creation. Creation within the biblical tradition concerns God's ongoing relationship to the creature. It affirms that this relationship is one "of purely gratuitous giving, without motive, with no second intentions, with no desire for control or domination, but rather a gratuity which permits creatures to share gratuitously in the life of the Creator. The relation of gratuity is anterior to what is and has ever been."[22]

When we look at the New Testament we find that the revelatory process well underway in Israel's history comes to its climax with an unforeseeable and even shocking twist, one that so thoroughly reverses the theogonic portrayal that we can only look at it in astonishment. Instead of creation emerging through the subjection of chaos and the expulsion of a victim whose dismembered corpse becomes the cosmic body — i.e., violence manufactures "the world," the social order, even the individual — the creator God in the New Testament summons things into being pacifically and with no other motive than love; and furthermore deigns to become a part of that creation in an act of self-donation, even unto death, so as to free creation from the bondage that has enveloped it. Having willingly become the victim to *humanity's* deicide, the resurrection of Jesus from the dead exposes the injustice and inhumanity of the scapegoating process and offers in its stead reconciliation with God through forgiveness. The creator God succumbs to a victimary death on a cross in order to reveal, through the resurrection of the victim, the lies, self-condemnations, and divisions that ensnare humanity. Though Jesus' resurrection is very much a vindication and vanquishing of those forces corrosive to the human community, God's response is non-reciprocal to what precipitates it. God does not apply violence to violence, force to force, tit for tat, but rather overcomes sin through eschatological pardon, violence through agapic hospitality, and death through the renewal of life. God redeems humanity by bringing justice to the victim, to be sure; but the peculiar manner in which this justice is rendered reaches out with loving vulnerability to the persecutor in a profound gesture of embrace, with the aim that the persecutor be converted and reconciled to his or her victim as the concrete (sacramental-historical) mediation of reconciliation with God. Justice and mercy embrace. The vindication of the victim is thus expressly in service of a *total* human salvation, not a vindication that leaves human beings in an over-against relationship. Having willingly become our victim in order to awaken us to and save us from our sin and violence, God has communicated God's very self to us whilst assuming our broken humanity for its restoration and divinization. God's "yes" to humanity proves infinitely *in excess* to humanity's deicidal "no."

From the perspective of this hospitality and pardon, it becomes possible to perceive that creation, rather than originating out of violence and remaining in antagonistic relationship to its creator, is in fact a drama of freedom, redemption, and participation in divine life. It shows unambiguously that God is non-complicit in violence — that whatever violence there is in the world is non-necessary, a privation of being. It therefore constitutes "the definitive demythologization of God." Writes Alison: "God, completely outside of human reciprocity, is the human victim. The Father is the origin of the self-giving of the human victim. Thus, far from creation having anything to do with the establishment of an order, what it reveals is that the gratuitous self-giving of the victim is identical with, and the heretofore hidden center and culmination of, the gratuitous giving that is the creation."[23] In sum, the very self-giving expressed in the Christ event is the very self-giving at the heart of God's originally creative act. The "first born of the dead" is also the "first born of creation." The peace brought about by the paschal event is the restoration of an original peace.

> In the beginning was the Word,
> and the Word was with God,
> and the Word was God.
> He was in the beginning with God.
> All things came into being through him,
> and without him not one thing came into being.
> What has come into being in him was life,
> and the life was the light of all people.
> The light shines in the darkness,
> and the darkness did not overcome it. (John 1:1–5)

The parallels between creation and resurrection are exquisitely drawn in John. "Early on the first day of the week, while it was still dark, Mary Magdalene came to the tomb and saw that the stone had been removed from the tomb" (20:1). When John specifies "the first day of the week," which he does again in verse 19, the allusion is quite clear: the resurrection of Jesus from the darkness of the tomb is the new creation. The darkness of the tomb has not overcome the Word made flesh, but yields to the manifestation of the Son's *doxa* in the world. The risen Christ returns to Mary Magdalene and the remaining disciples to free them from the darkness now curled around them in their misunderstanding, fear, and sin. It is significant that Mary's encounter with the risen Christ occurs in a garden, as it is suggestive of the encounter between God and the first couple in the garden (Gen. 2:15–17). "In this garden of new creation and new covenant," writes Sandra Schneiders, "Jesus, who is both the promised liberator of the new creation and the spouse of the new Israel, encounters the woman, who is, symbolically, the Johannine community, the church, the new people of God."[24] Paradise lost has become paradise restored: the enmity between human beings (3:15) that resulted from rivalry with God ("you will be like God" [3:5]), and which brought about separation from God by death, has now been reversed as the self-giving victim offers himself as eternal life.

Equally suggestive is the way the risen Christ imparts the Holy Spirit — by breathing upon them (John 20:22). This is an allusion to Genesis 2:7, where Yahweh "formed man from the dust of the ground, and breathed into his nostrils the breath of life; and the man became a living being." The primordially creative *ruah* in the Old Testament is now identified with the re-creative *pneuma* of forgiveness. "Receive the Holy Spirit. If you forgive the sins of any, they are forgiven them; if you retain the sins of any, they are retained" (John 20:22–23). The significance of this connection should not go unnoticed: the God who is revealed in the Easter event is creator, redeemer, and sanctifier, and these three aspects are intrinsically related. Now that God is encountered as the self-giving victim for our forgiveness and divinization, it is possible to see that God's original act of creation was (and is) one of pure gratuity and love. The peace that the risen Christ leaves his disciples (20:19, 21, 26; see also 14:21) is seen as the restoration of an original peace — "the primordial peace of the Creator from the beginning."[25]

TRANSCENDENCE, FORM, AND BEAUTY

Resurrection faith is at root a creation faith. When the New Testament speaks of Easter as the "new creation," this by no means implies that the original creation is discarded. Even if the resurrection cannot be thought of as time and space extending indefinitely, lest the discontinuity between the present and eschatological future be ignored, the resurrection is God's enactment of a promise that creation will never be abandoned to its own contingency but will be delivered to its final fruition and glory, freed from all corruption and alienation. "For the creation waits with eager longing for the revealing of the children of God...in hope that creation itself will be set free from its bondage and decay and will obtain the freedom of the glory of the children of God" (Rom. 8:19–21).

It is truly difficult to imagine what this fruition and glorification will ultimately be. Imagination strains and language buckles in the attempt to speak of the *eschaton*. But then all talk of God shares the same situation. Every subdiscipline in theology, whether it is anthropology, ecclesiology, christology, or sacramental theology, etc., ultimately flows from the same holy mystery. Once we penetrate through some of its more surface distinguishing features we will necessarily be immersed in the deep things of God. But just because our imaginative capacities are stretched to their limits, even painfully at times, we should not fail to speak of such things with courage and evangelical joy. The *reductio ad mysterium* of Christian theology is not an excuse for mutism. While contemplative silence is truly its wellspring, theology must risk advancing language and imagination into territory that cannot be adequately spoken or imagined. This entails a serious kind of play, the kind of which metaphor is uniquely capable.

If the case can be made that all theological language is metaphorical — one might go further to say that all language is metaphorical — eschatology will serve as one of its chief exhibits of evidence. Resurrection language, as we have seen, is metaphorical to its root. It takes something within our ordinary experience, waking up from sleep, to speak all manner of things: the restoration of God's people, the deliverance of creation from dissolution, the vindication of the righteous martyr; and in the New Testament, the vindication of Jesus, the offer of forgiveness through him, his exaltation unto God, his exercise of sovereignty over creation, the glorification of creation. Paul's discussion of the resurrection in 1 Cor. 15, which we examined in chapter 4, fundamentally depends upon the work of metaphor to indicate the relationship between the present and risen body (present body = seed; glorified body = fruit). Though there is continuity between them, what becomes of the seed will be a qualitatively different reality. Organic metaphors were frequently used through the early patristic period. Later, inorganic metaphors were favored to speak of the risen body's incorruptible form. The principle concern among those who adopted the imagery of precious jewels or reassembled vessels was to affirm that the totality of the human person, in all his or her corporeal uniqueness, will not be forsaken by the creator God, but will, in a way not fully imaginable to us, attain eschatological blessedness. God is a God of the particular and unrepeatable. Even when creation seems to fly apart in its wild display of mutability, the resurrection of Christ gives eloquent testimony to God's love for creation precisely as creation, which will at last be made wholly diaphanous to God's infinite beauty. Creation will, in the resurrection, be most fully itself because it will be fully united to God, sharing forever in the hypostatic union of natures in Christ.

Another common metaphor adopted in antiquity to speak of the divinizing effects of the resurrection is that of an iron in a fire. While the iron retains (ontological) distinction from the fire, when placed in the fire long enough it will eventually radiate in heat and light the properties of the fire that now wholly infuse it. The iron "is" not the fire, and yet through immersion it takes on the fire's nature by participation. Creation already evinces this divine fire, "like shining from shook foil" (Gerard Manley Hopkins). But with the resurrection, what is hidden will become manifest; what is slowly irrupting from within will exteriorize itself fully. Karl Rahner puts it memorably in one of his sermons:

> His resurrection is like the first eruption of a volcano which shows that in the interior of the world God's fire is already burning, and this will bring everything to blessed ardor in his light. He has risen to show that has already begun. Already from the heart of the world into which he descended in death, the new forces of a transfigured earth are at work. Already in the innermost center of all reality, futility, sin, and death are vanquished and all that is needed is the short space of time which we call history *post Christum natum*, until everywhere and not only in the body of Jesus what has really already begun will be manifest.[26]

These words are strikingly similar to those of Gregory of Nyssa: "The fire that is hidden and as it were smothered under the ashes of this world... will blaze out and with its divinity burn up the husk of death." Or again: "What is hidden within will cover up completely what is seen on the outside."[27]

It is interesting to observe that Rahner's use of resurrection imagery serves to emphasize the unity of transcendence and immanence. When we speak of Jesus being "raised," we naturally think of this in terms of a vertical movement. This is metaphorical, of course, and corresponds with much of the imagery of scripture and its ongoing representation in literature and art. When one looks at a typical iconographic depiction of the resurrection, for example, verticality nearly always provides the perspectival orientation. But here Rahner emphasizes that Jesus' death and resurrection is a deeper immersion into the interiority of the world. The risen body of Christ is not "lifted out," so to speak, from the world. Jesus' resurrection is (pan)cosmic in scope. It orients Christians to think of transcendence and immanence as correlative. The movement towards God is also, and necessarily — if the resurrection be our guide — a movement towards the creature so that ultimately we shall discover God *in* creation and creation *in* God. Among the most important works that the grammar of resurrection can accomplish, therefore, is the consistent coordination of this twofold movement within Christian imagination and language.

The Cosmicity of Easter

If we are to plumb further the immeasurable depths of Easter's significance, we must say that something in our world has changed. At the level of its "being," the world has been transformed by God who has become united with it. This unity, it should be well noted, is not an extrinsic one. God has become world, become body, become human, shared in the arc traced by all creatures that extends from life to death in order to transform the whole of creation from within. The resurrection, like the incarnation, means that God has taken on a body, that divine grace courses throughout the corporeal expanse that is our world, pressing out from within it, transforming its textures and rhythms, its spaces and ligatures. God has "recapitulated" within God's self the entirety of a human life, to intone the Irenaen theme, encompassing even death with divine presence. The resurrection thus adds something substantially new to the incarnation, while completing it. By it, death has been given a verbal structure. The Logos has overcome it and made it to signify divine love. However strange it may seem at first, this is what enables the Christian to view death as a means of *participation* in Christ. Though this does not take away the mystery of death, especially when death is so often attended by suffering, injustice, and alienation, the death and resurrection of Christ stand as the "great despite" to death's blunt negativity so that we may say, along with Paul the Apostle, that our death is a sharing in "newness of life." "For if we have been united with him in a death like his, we will certainly be united with him in a resurrection like his" (Rom. 6:4–5).

Through the resurrection of Jesus of Nazareth, a creature has become inmost to God. This means that the world has become inmost to God in a way quite unprecedented in the God-world relationship. As was emphasized in Part One, embodiment is relational. To be embodied means to subsist within and from a corporeal field. The human body is no isolated "thing." The human body is an unrepeatable manifestation of the one social-cosmic body we all share. The resurrection of the body is thus the affirmation of an all-encompassing salvation. A more creation-centered view of salvation could hardly be conceived. "A piece of this world," writes Karl Rahner, "real to the core...is surrendered...to the disposition of God, in complete obedience and love. This is Easter, and the redemption of the world." The bodiliness of the Easter event is central to its meaning. It is an event in which "God irrevocably adopts the creature as his own reality," an event of "real ontological participation": "the irreversible and embryonically final beginning of the glorification and divinization of the *whole* reality."[28] Rahner gives bold expression to the cosmicity of Easter, writing that "the world as a whole flows into his Resurrection and into the transfiguration of his body."[29] "For he rose again in his *body*. That means he has already begun to transform this world into himself. He has accepted the world forever. He has been born again as a child of the earth, but of the transfigured, liberated earth, the earth which in him is eternally confirmed and eternally redeemed from death and futility."[30] Rahner's reading of the resurrection in such robustly ontological terms is entirely in keeping with the doctrine of deification elaborated in much patristic theology. The oft repeated axiom, "God became human so that humans might become God," is no less applicable to Rahner's theology than it is to Irenaeus, Athanasius, Maximus the Confessor, and Gregory of Nyssa, to name just a few. Rahner argues that because the more juridical orientation of Western soteriology so focused on the eradication of sin through Christ's death, the resurrection was given a largely confirmatory role, namely, of assuring that the theological interpretation of Good Friday is correct.[31] Lacking much soteriological significance in itself, at least not any kind of significance that was not already accomplished by Jesus' death, the resurrection became a matter of interest only in terms of Jesus' personal destiny, or, as was noted earlier in the Introduction, increasingly confined in modern theology to questions of fundamental theology, e.g., the possibility of miracles, the nature of revelation, the question of history and its limits. Reinstating the proper role of the resurrection within the drama of salvation requires, according to Rahner, taking a lesson from the more ontologically explicit approaches of the Greek fathers, from what has been dubbed the "physical" or "naturalistic" theory of salvation, which may be characterized in the following way: God has entered the created order through the Logos made flesh in order to bring human persons forgiveness, incorruptible life, and participation in divine reality. The descending-ascending movement of this economic action reaches us at the level of our nature (our *phusis*, or "nature," hence the "physical" or "naturalistic" theory of salvation). It restores and uplifts the creature into an intimate relation with the creator so as to permit, through an increasing richness of participation, a growing likeness to the creator. Made in the image and likeness of God, human beings are enabled to become increasingly attuned to their proper nature precisely to the extent that they grow nearer to God. The unsurpassable expression of this direct proportionality is the hypostatic union of natures in Jesus Christ, the God-man. Jesus' humanity is most properly and fully human precisely because it is united to the divine — a unity which is personal (hypostatic). Read within these terms, the Christ event is something far more embracing than the more narrow approaches characteristic of much Latin soteriology: it points to the transfiguration of creation as such. God enfolds the human person and the broader community of creation within God's self, without in any way negating the distinctiveness of that creation, without effacing its diversity, its form, or what is unique to it. To be sure, this divine action is also an atoning one. Even if, by comparison to the more juridical approaches in theology, the dimension of forgiveness may appear secondary, this is in fact not the case, as Aulén rightly asserts against those who have suggested as much.[32] Nevertheless, as Rahner maintains, the inclination within theology in the East tended to view the drama of salvation as "a real ontological process which began in the incarnation and ends not so much in the forgiveness of sin as in the divinization of the world and first demonstrates its victorious might, not so much in the expiation of sin on the cross as in the resurrection of Christ."[33] Again, the theme of forgiveness is not secondary in importance, and neither, we might add, is the theme of justice; but both are seen as contributing to the ultimate purpose of the Christ event: the drawing of creation into the inner life of God for its eternal fruition.

Jesus' Self-Gift, the Father's Embrace

As we speak of the resurrection in more explicitly ontological terms, it is important that we keep the foundational narratives close at hand. Ontological considerations within Christian theology must take on a narrative shape. In order to see how Jesus' resurrection is pivotal to the "ontological process" described above, we must see it as the unity of a twofold dramatic movement.

In the first place, Jesus of Nazareth, a human person like any other human person, save sin, lived his life in total transparency to the Father, availing himself without reserve, completely abandoning himself to the Father's will, which, for Jesus, went hand in hand with his Kingdom of God ministry. It may be thought that such complete self-abandonment is dehumanizing, that by living utterly "outside" oneself in this way requires stripping away that aspect of our humanity which modern people are likely to determine as its most defining characteristic — freedom. The exact opposite is true: dependency and autonomy are not inversely but directly proportional in the divine-human relation. Precisely because Jesus lived his life in perfect self-givenness unto the Father he was the most human, the most capable of living in loving self-givenness to the human Other. He was therefore most truly *himself*. Because in him there was no rivalry with God, whom he did not regard as something to be grasped (Phil. 2:6), Jesus lived a life free from the distorted desires and mimetic rivalry with the Other that are in fact the root causes of bondage and dehumanization. However contradictory it may seem to a libertarian notion of freedom and selfhood, Jesus' perfect obedience is perfect freedom. The Father is not a now beneficent, now hostile force with whom to contend in the bid for healthy independence. Neither is the Father a delimiting horizon against which existence gains an inescapably tragic aspect. In the Father is an infinitely welcoming interiority, alone capable of providing the space for full human flourishing. "In my Father's house there are many dwelling places. If it were not so, would I have told you that I go to prepare a place for you?" (John 14:2).

Now it happens that the historical occasion of Jesus' self-giving is, in part, conditioned by alienation from God, sin. Because human beings have given themselves over to rivalry and violence, thereby betraying their original nature and vocation; and because such distortion within the human life-world has become so entrenched as to be deemed "normal" or "inevitable," when shown the truth of its alienated condition by one who exhibits no such distortion or rivalry, and indeed by one who seems quite intent on bringing this condition to crisis by artfully, though lovingly, transgressing those mechanisms of self-assertion and scapegoating that divide humanity — here we see the religiously and politically subversive nature of Jesus' radical obedience — such freedom will be interpreted as threatening, something that upsets the order of things, something requiring containment and, ultimately, expulsion. So when we speak of Jesus being obedient to the Father even unto death, implying all the while that living life with true freedom may very well incur a violent end, nothing at all morbid or inhumane should be imagined by this. God does not deal death to humanity. It so happens, however, that a life lived with genuine freedom, and with the fullness capable by the human personality, is subject to the danger of the cross in the context of a sinful world. Only this makes intelligible the many sayings in the gospels that speak of dying in order to live.[34]

The second aspect of this twofold movement is found in the Father's acceptance of Jesus' self-gift. Though it is improper to ascribe any sense of compulsion to the raising of Jesus — like creation, it is gratuitous — there is something entirely "fitting" about it, aesthetically speaking.[35] In this one man the human race has achieved its definitive form. Creation has become, in him, and for the first time, wholly diaphanous to its creator. "He is the image of the invisible God." This is the human being most fully alive, creation at its most beautiful. The truly elegant conclusion to a life thus lived is its eternal commemoration and transfiguration. If, from the side of creaturely existence, a life has been given to the Father so unreservedly, it is "fitting" that, from the other side of this drama and dialogue, the Father "accepts" this self-gift in a demonstrable way. If there is any way to salvage the language of sacrifice, it is here. Jesus exercised his freedom and love so fully that he was willing to sacrifice himself for the Other. Jesus' self-gift is not one demanded by the Father so as to channel divine violence. Jesus' self-gift is to liberate creation from the bondage of violence and victimization. The violent death incurred by Jesus becomes here the absolute expression of his fidelity and love for the Father. And it is just this expression of fidelity and love that is accepted by the Father by raising him from the dead.

The ontological depths of this dramatic exchange come into view once we allow the full range of resurrection language to be sounded. However metaphorical resurrection language is, and however multivalent it necessarily remains — this is its great strength, not its weakness — it cannot become detached from its affirmation of the body without rendering its usage a matter of equivocation. It cannot simply mean that the Father has accepted Jesus' self-gift by issuing a kind of verbal decree. It is not the same as saying that Jesus is now "alive to God" in some sort of "spiritual" sense. It means, rather, that the totality of Jesus' existence in its corporeal and narrative shape has been embraced and given its definitive reality by God. "The proffered gift," writes Rahner, "which is the man himself, in all its dimensions, in its whole concrete reality, must be at the absolute disposition of God, who has graciously accepted it. To be accepted totally and definitively, without restriction or reserve, by God who reveals and communicates himself: that is nothing else than being transfigured in the whole bodily reality, that is, being raised up from and finally exalted."[36] The conferral of the Father's "amen" upon Jesus is given its concrete expression in the transformation of his whole embodied existence. Such requires that we not think of corporeality as exterior or incidental to the person. The body is the real and living symbol of the person, the very way a human being comes to be in the world. It is also that which bonds the person to the world. Or, to put it another way, the body-person is a particular way the world comes to be. Through our bodies, we share in the cosmic body. Hence, while the resurrection of Jesus from the dead is unique to him, what is risen is the corporeality of our humanity and the world *in* him. This is why we can say that in him is the inauguration of the divinization of *all* creation. God has become eternally united with creation. The glorified body of Jesus is the future of creation.

THE ETERNAL SIGNIFICANCE OF JESUS' HUMANITY: THE HEART OF CHRISTIAN SPIRITUALITY

As we come to comprehend more fully the ontological significance of Jesus' resurrection, the most radical conclusion we can draw from it is this: *Jesus' risen and transfigured humanity is the eternal mediation of our relationship to the infinite God.* He was not just at one time "the image of the invisible God," but is now and will be forever the means of our communion with the invisible God. God's self-communication in the form of Christ's humanity is not suddenly withdrawn or made irrelevant by his death; rather, the form of risen Christ is, and remains, even in the *visio beatifica,* our mediated-immediacy to the ineffable mystery of God. While such a conclusion may seem somewhat speculative, it is in fact remarkably important for giving proper orientation to Christian imagination and life. Here we may consider its significance for Christian spirituality.

It is not uncommon to find tendencies within spiritual traditions (sometimes within Christianity) to imagine that growing proximity to God requires a corresponding movement away from creatures. It may be supposed that because God is infinite, unfathomable mystery — not *a* being among beings, but the "ground of being" or "beyond being," a bottomless depth from which all surface forms arise and descend, not *this,* not *that,* but the conditioning possibility for anything to exist at all — entering more deeply and completely into the mystery of God requires that we somehow surmount those creaturely mediations that present so many veils to that perfect immediacy which alone can satisfy transcendental desire. Perhaps an ascetical regime, complemented by techniques of non-discursive meditation, can help trigger unitive experiences of such purity that the sense of subject-object distinction normally conditioning intentional consciousness can at last, or at least for a while, be overcome. In such moments, should the aspirant be lucky enough to have them, the experience of the multiplicity of forms gives way to the Formless, particularity to the Absolute, and the conditioned to the Unconditioned. Here, at this mystical peak, there is neither this nor that, neither I nor Thou, but pure being, a vastness so deep and wide that all things have become consumed without a trace. Like a drop of water merging with the ocean, the soul has finally shed itself of sensual-bodily encumberment to become absorbed into the All. To the extent that one imagines human fulfillment in these terms it is difficult to describe it as "personal" since the distinction between I and Thou that makes interpersonal communion possible is viewed as an impediment to be sublated. Indeed, it is difficult to distinguish the impulse of such spirituality from nihilism, since it looks upon creaturely difference as a negativity to be transcended in the attainment of undifferentiated unity.

By no means do I wish here to undermine a genuine mysticism, or deny a proper place to asceticism and non-discursive forms of meditation. Neither am I suggesting that the apophatic strain within Christian spirituality and theology is nihilistic in bearing. Yet it should be understood that the apophatic mood in Christian spirituality and theology is not opposed to mediation and form, but one kind of response to the excessive givenness of God's self-communication. Negative theology is the subjective correlate to the objective unknowability of God, not in the sense that no knowledge of God is ultimately possible, but that no *exhaustive* knowledge of God is possible. The imagery and language of "divine darkness" is one that is yet "bedazzling." The form of God's self-communication in Christ is inexhaustible in its beauty, its luminosity unbearable and unconstitutable. Hence, the subjective experience of darkness is in fact just the other side of an excessive givenness. *Apophasis* and *kataphasis* are internally linked. Mark McIntosh puts the matter well:

> [A]pophatic mysticism ought not to be thought of as something undertaken by people who are absorbed by the unutterable *remoteness* of God. On the contrary, apophasis happens because, like Moses at the burning bush, persons have been drawn so *close* to the mystery that they have begun to realize how beautifully, appallingly, heart-breakingly mysterious God really is.... Thus apophatic speech might take the form of a quieting down, a stilling into hushed silence. But it might also take the form of an explosion of speech, a carnival of self-subverting discourse, language tripping over itself in paradox or fantastical repetition as it comes undone in the whirlwind of divine superabundance.[37]

In chapter 2 we looked more closely at the relationship of *apophasis* and *kataphasis* in the empty tomb and resurrection narratives. Phenomenologically speaking, the perceptual absence described in them is the result of a personal presence which, on account of its eschatological character, gives itself in a mode that overwhelms (though never inhumanely) the intentionality of its historical recipients. Only when the basic grammar supplied by these narratives is kept in view is it possible to really understand what Christian theology means when it speaks of God as the ever-receding horizon of human transcendence, the unconditioned ground for all that exists. Such a God is, to be sure, ungraspable; and yet this God is supremely communicative and personal. The abysmal silence of the Father has uttered itself (and eternally utters itself) in the Word, and this self-utterance returns the Gift of itself through the Spirit as the expression of love. God is at once perfect society and perfect unity. Thus, when the risen Christ reveals himself in the mode of distance, this has as much to do with affirming his transcendence as it does with affirming the mysterious personal nature of our union with God. The resurrection eschatologically affirms creation in its particularity. The distinction between God and creature is not a negative relation to be overcome in ecstatic absorption. It is a blessed "distance" that allows for unity-in-difference. Distance here is an expression of God's creative goodness, the "making room" for love.

In a seminal essay Rahner gives an account of Christian experience as permanently awash in the beauty of Christ's resplendent form.[38] Appropriating the classic tropes of Christian spirituality — no doubt given particular inflection by his Ignatian sensibilities[39] — Rahner speaks of the "ascent" towards God as simultaneous with a deeper "descent" into the world, a more profound penetration into the mystery of the world that manifests the glory of its creator. Of course, God and creation are not to be confused. In point of fact, the initial movement towards God in the spiritual life is frequently prompted by the recognition of the fundamental difference between God and creation — as we awaken to the hidden depth dimension of our human experience which, on account of our unreflective immersion in our everyday world and tasks, goes largely unrecognized and unthematized. Since God is not one thing among others, arriving at a more mature apprehension of divine mystery means recognizing the region of dissimilarity that pertains to the God-world relationship. God is not continuous with creation but the ever-receding horizon of the world, the non-objectifiable term of our transcendental desire. God is "the simply incomparable," the one "most radically distant."[40] Yet even the concept of distance can be misleading, for we are inclined to think of it in terms of an interval between two objects occupying the same plane. God's distance from the world is not spatial but qualitative. God is *absolutely* other-than-world.

Now, if the ascent to the unfathomable and unconditioned God is prompted by the knowledge of the difference between creation and creator, and thus in some sense requires our "taking leave" of the creature in a movement of transcendence, this is in fact only the initial ambiance and momentum for a deeper penetration into the world. In imitation of God's self-communication in Christ, those who encounter divine mystery become more and more "like" God to the extent they recapitulate this economic action of self-expropriation. The contemplative immersion into divine mystery is complemented by another (and horizontal) act of transcendence: the apostolic movement towards the Other in self-donating love. These two movements — interiority and exteriority, contemplation and action, ascent and descent — are not so much distinct "stages" as they are (or ought to be) two aspects of a single oscillating rhythm in the spiritual life. And both have as their ultimate aim the discovery of the creature *in* God, as Rahner explains:

> [T]o find the very creature itself, in its dependence and autonomy, *in* God, in the midst of the jealously burning inexorableness of His being-all-in-all; to find the creature even in the very midst of this — the small in the great, the circumscribed in the boundless, the creature (and the very creature itself) in the Creator — this is only the third and highest phase of our relationship to God. For there we who have gone out from the world to God, return with him in his entrance into the world, and are nearest to him there where he is furthest away from himself in his true love of the world; there and in this we are nearest to him because, if God is love, one comes closest to it where, having given itself as love to the world, it is further away from itself.[41]

There is an unmistakably trinitarian pattern to this way of describing the spiritual life, but Rahner stresses the unique contribution resurrection grammar makes to it. The resurrection of Jesus Christ means that human nature has become permanently united with the divine, and furthermore, that the humanity of Christ has become our eternal access to the ineffable mystery of God, even in the *visio beatifica*. It is the christic form, and this form alone, which enables the transcendentality of our human nature to meet the divine in a way proper to our humanity. Without this unity of the infinite and form, the self-transcending movement towards the Absolute would remain unattainable and impersonal. "We may speak about the *impersonal* Absolute without the non-absolute flesh of the Son, but the *personal* Absolute can be truly *found* only in him, in whom dwells the fullness of the Godhead in the earthly vessel of his humanity."[42] In contrast to certain notions of human transcendence that imagine unity with God in terms of pure immediacy, Christian eschatology envisions beatific life as inclusive and absolutely affirmative of creation in its differentiated integrity. It shall not become wholly God, but neither will it remain "mere" creation. It shall share, by grace, in the hypostatic union of natures, and thus be in union with God through a unity-in-difference, in *communion*. The risen, eternal humanity of Christ is the mediated-immediacy of God.[43] Pure immediacy would in fact amount to the liquefaction of what makes created existence what it is — particular, relational, conditioned by *alterity*. Only a relational and inter-personal communion with God is proper to creation. The risen humanity of Christ makes this possible:

> For, according to the testimony of the faith, this created human nature is the indispensable and permanent gateway through which everything created must pass if it is to find the perfection of its eternal validity before God. He is the gate and the door, the Alpha and Omega, the all-embracing in whom, as the one who has become man, creation finds its stability. He who sees him, sees the Father, and whoever does not see him — God become man — also does not see God.... Without him every absolute of which we speak or which we imagine we attain by mystical flight is in the last analysis merely the never attained, objective correlative of that empty and hollow, dark and despairingly self-consuming infinity which we are ourselves: the infinity of dissatisfied finiteness, but not the blessed infinity of truly limitless fullness. This, however, can be found only where Jesus of Nazareth is, this finite concrete being, this contingent being, who remains in all eternity.[44]

Notice here the distinction Rahner makes between an empty and blessed infinity. The former is nihilistic, the latter personalistic. The former is abstract, the latter committed to the eternal validity of form. The former entails a never-ending striving towards the unattainable, the latter is an inexhaustible richness that offers itself as the possibility for loving communion. The Christian vision of "the end" of all things is one that affirms the givenness of the created order. The notion of Christ's eternal mediation is simply another way of saying that salvation, so far from promoting a sense of alienation from our cosmic and personal embodiment, plunges us back into the heart of the world where Christ lives as its hidden center and inner vitality. In him material reality has become "wholly transfigured" as "the glorious body of God."[45] Here is the grounds for an unbridled Christ-mysticism: "He rose, not to show that he was leaving the tomb of the earth once and for all, but in order to demonstrate that precisely that tomb of the dead — the body and the earth — has finally changed into the glorious, immeasurable house of the living God and of the God-filled soul of the Son.... He has risen because in death he conquered and redeemed forever the innermost center of all earthly reality.... When we confess him as having ascended to God's heaven, that is only another expression for the fact that he withdraws from us for awhile the tangible manifestation of his glorified humanity and above all that there is no longer any abyss between God and world."[46]

In sum, the resurrection serves a regulative (or grammatical) role for an authentic Christian mysticism. It directs every movement towards transcendence back towards the world, and vice versa. "Easter faith," writes Rahner, "postulates an indissoluble unity between transcendence and history.... It demands, that is to say, that devotion should let the God of infinite, eternal and unassailed fullness of life be in truth the God of a history of abiding validity; and, conversely, that devotion should lay hold on the God of history ... as being the God of fullness of life and reality, already possessed from eternity to eternity."[47] Because Jesus' humanity is eternally significant for our relationship to God, our ultimate blessedness is finding creation *in* God. Christian faith is thus as much God-centered as it is creation-centered, for it is Christ-centered.

THE BEAUTY AND COMFORT OF THE RESURRECTION

The resurrection of Jesus is a reality that possesses wide-ranging aesthetic significance. It makes a singular contribution to the Christian sense of the beautiful since it affirms that form, though subject to dissolution, awaits an eschatological destiny. Although the world can seem a whirlpool of chaotic forces, and though it groans in travail as it awaits this destiny, creation as such shall be vindicated and fulfilled as it has *already* in Christ's transfigured body. Such a vision is radically different from those that look upon the world as a random collection of forces and atomized elements signifying nothing of enduring value, i.e., as so much ephemera. It contrasts with a conception of the world that inspires only pathos, the sense of unfulfilled longing. It is also different from a conception of the world that sees it only in instrumental terms, as something to be used and finally dispensed with in the effort to achieve some end, whether technical or spiritual. The world, from a Christian point of view, is creation—the very "site" of our salvation.

Such themes are sounded in Gerard Manley Hopkins's masterful sonnet, "That Nature is a Heraclitean Fire and the Comfort of the Resurrection."[48] In its first several lines, Hopkins gives dizzying expression to the volatility of nature:

> Cloud-puffball, torn tufts, tossed pillows | flaunt forth, then chevy on an air-
> Built thoroughfare: heaven-roysterers, in gay-gangs | they throng; they glitter in marches.
> Down roughcast, down dazzling whitewash, | wherever an elm arches,
> Shivelights and shadowtackle in long | lashes lace, lance, and pair.
> Delightfully the bright wind boisterous | ropes, wrestles, beats earth bare
> Of yestertempest's creases; | in pool and rut peel parches
> Sqaundering ooze to squeezed | dough, crüst, dust; stánches, stárches
> Squadroned masks and manmarks | treadmire toil there
> Foótfretèd in it. Million-fuelèd, | nature's bonfire burns on.

It seems we are to imagine the speaker walking along a countryside marked by a previous storm ("yestertemptest's"), entranced for the moment by the roiling atmosphere, the brilliant contrast of billowing clouds and sky, and the kaleidoscopic play of light and shadow upon the surface of the land, now dried and peeling. With all senses ablaze, he imagines the whole of nature a giant, ceaseless bonfire. (In the cosmos of Heraclitus, all things emerge from and resolve to fire; and the raucous display of nature just now does nothing to disconfirm this intuition.) It is an experience that brings him delight, initially. There is something exhilarating in witnessing the glittering cascade of it all, of feeling oneself a part of its mysterious heaving. For the moment, his reflexive self-consciousness has become relaxed and permeable. With senses filled to their brim, he is no longer a spectator but immersed in the play.

But as these first impressions congeal into thoughts, his delight gives way to another mood; perhaps quite suddenly, as when he notices the tire tracks and footprints ("manmarks") slowly succumbing to erasure by the relentless pounding of the elements. The initial feeling of expansiveness now contracts, and the speaker's thoughts turn inward. The human world, it turns out, is no less subject to volatility. It too shares in the endless flow and ebb that the landscape now awesomely displays, though with this difference (which in the end makes no difference at all): human beings are aware of their impermanence. The speaker's thoughts now fill him with a sense of the tragic.

> But quench her bonniest, dearest | to her, her clearest-selvèd spark
> Mán, how fást his firedint, | his mark on mind, is gone!
> Bóth are in an únfáthomable, áll is in an enórmous dárk
> Drowned. O Pity and indig | nation! Manshape, that shone
> Sheer off, disséveral, a stár, | death blots black out; nor mark
> Is ány of him at áll so stárk
> But vastness blurs and time | beats level.

Despair has now filled him as he comes to the suffocating realization that even human beings — nature's "clearest-selvèd spark" — shall become ash. No face, no love, no child, no human artifice, no thing is but is quenchable and quenched. All forms that manage to survive for a time are pulled back by their own weight to be submerged and forgotten. The words are frightful in their effect: drowned, sheer, sever, blot, blur, beats.

And yet, in mid-thought, literally mid-line, almost as if by a sheer act of will, the poem suddenly leaps from despair to hope, from a sense of the tragic sublime to a different aesthetic vision.

>   Enough! The Resurrection,
> A héart's-clarion! Awáy grief's gasping, | joyless days, dejection.
> Across my foundering deck shone
> A beacon, an eternal beam. | Flesh fade, and mortal trash
> Fáll to the resíduary worm; | world's wildfire, leave but ash:
> In a flash, at a trumpet crash,
> I am all at once what Christ is |, since he was what I am, and
> Thís Jack, jóke, poor pótsherd, | patch, matchwood, immortal diamond,
> Is immortal diamond.

It is tempting to accuse the speaker of being disingenuous, as though by declaring "Enough!" so peremptorily he has merely suppressed the real truth of his contemplation. But the beacon that lights his darkened mind gives him more than a contrived hope. He has not denied the truth of his original contemplation, for he still accepts the facticity of his existence, the sheer contingency of things. The "residuary worm" will yet have its prize, and the world's bonfire will leave its ash... but the Resurrection! With an allusion to the patristic maxim, the speaker identifies the substance of his hope: Christ is risen; and because I am what Christ was, I shall become what he is. Nature's flux is not, as it was for Heraclitus, eternal; it is the medium of God's creative art. From it shall emerge the new creation — eschatological Form. Like the theologians of antiquity who employed images of hardened, crystalline jewels or refashioned vessels to speak of the risen body's incorruptibility and fulfilled form, here we are given the image of an immortal diamond. The form possesses its own integrity and structure, but it is translucent to Christ's "eternal beam." The diamond remains itself, but the splendor its gives comes from another light that utterly fills it.

◆ ◆ ◆

With special emphasis given to the resurrection, von Balthasar summarizes the Christian aesthetic:

> In Jesus' finitude, and in everything that is given with and which pertains to his form, we hold the infinite. As we pass through Jesus' finitude and enter into its depths we encounter and find the Infinite, or rather, we are transported and found by the Infinite. Indeed, through the mysterious dialectic whereby Jesus' external, spatially and temporally conditioned finitude is transcended (which is the condition for the coming of the Holy Spirit), but transcended in such a way that it is replaced by the "eternal finitude" of Jesus' resurrected flesh, all that is interior, invisible, spiritual and divine becomes accessible to us. If there were no such thing as the resurrection of the flesh, then the truth would lie with Gnosticism and every form of idealism down to Schopenhauer and Hegel, for whom the finite must literally perish if it is to become spiritual and infinite. But the resurrection of the flesh vindicates the poets in a definitive sense: the aesthetic scheme of things, which allows us to possess the infinite within the finitude of form (however it is seen, understood or grasped) is right.[49]

The crucial distinction von Balthasar makes here is between the beautiful and the sublime. In the latter, finite form is dialectically set off against the infinite. Finite form may point to infinitude, but it does so only by pointing away from itself, by effacing itself. It does not participate in what it signifies as much as it cancels it out. Finite form is thus only a staging ground for empty transcendence. The spirit of the sublime is restless and tragic in aspiration. It yearns for what outstrips each and every form. It longs for the unrepresented and absolutely unrepresentable. Its preference is for an ever-elusive absolute, not the particular; the abstract, not the concrete.

But in the Christian imagination, Ground and Image, the Infinite and Form are not opposed; they are conjoined. Christian faith affirms that the fullness of deity has made itself epiphanous in the humanity of Christ. The form of Christ opens out to the invisible God, and thus facilitates transcendence; but the mediation of this movement abides. The "eternal finitude" of Christ is just the way the incommunicable is communicated, the way the most distant draws near to us as love. Christ's visibility is not an outer husk to an invisible content that can never adequately express it. God has traversed God's own inaccessibility to become accessible as Form, even if we did not recognize it at first. God has made our own humanity, and the corporeality of the world, the idiom of God's self-communication, eternally.

"The whole mystery of Christianity," writes von Balthasar, "is that the form does not stand in opposition to infinite light, for the reason that God has himself instituted and confirmed such form."[50] All created forms come into being from the boundless fecundity of the triune God. This instituting act, which the Genesis account describes as "very good," is not primarily a moral good. It is an aesthetic one. God takes delight in creation.[51] Such delight is perfect because God's creativity involves no necessity or striving. Creation is not the result of divine diremption. It is not the outcome of a violent conflagration, or the subjection of chaos. There is no pressing need, no irritating passion for God to create something other than God. Creation is not a vast Hegelian project so that the Infinite may finitize itself and return to itself through the sublation (or "sacrifice") of form.[52] There is not in God's creative act a libidinal and acquisitive process of objectification that restlessly tears through the panoply of evolving forms so as to close, through the self-consciousness of creatures, a strange loop. Creation does not "add" something to God missing before. All relationality, all possibility, all love, all movement, all form, all rest — is already perfectly realized in the triune God. Creation comes to be from an infinite abundance. It is imparted by an utterly pacific "distance," which is to say, instituted as world in original peace. God "lets be" what is, and what is is very good. This is how we are to apprehend creation. Such "letting be," so far from resulting in uncaring disregard, is a contemplative beholding, a taking delight in what is. Its gratuity inspires in us gratitude. Creation, in all its contingency and particularity, is beautiful.

There is no greater testimony to God's love for creation in all its contingency and particularity than the resurrection. What creation institutes, the resurrection confirms and completes. "And although, being finite and worldly, this form must die just as every other beautiful thing on earth must die, nevertheless it does not go down into the realm of formlessness, leaving behind an infinite tragic longing, but, rather, it rises up to God *as form,* as the form which now, in God himself, has definitively become one with the divine Word and Light which God has intended for and bestowed upon the world. The form itself must participate in the process of death and resurrection, and thus it becomes coextensive with God's Light-Word."[53]

Notes

Introduction

1. Augustine, *The Confessions*, trans. Henry Chadwick (Oxford: Oxford University Press, 1991), IV.19, 64.
2. Jean-Luc Marion, *The Erotic Phenomenon*, trans. Stephen E. Lewis (Chicago: University of Chicago Press, 2007), 46–47.
3. Walter Brueggemann, *The Bible Makes Sense* (Atlanta: John Knox Press, 1977), 45–46.
4. Walter Brueggemann, *Theology of the Old Testament: Testimony, Dispute, Advocacy* (Minneapolis: Fortress Press, 1997), 178.
5. Northrop Frye, *The Great Code: The Bible and Literature* (San Diego: A Harvest Book/Harcourt, 1982), 171–72.
6. Pheme Perkins, *The Resurrection: New Testament Witness and Contemporary Reflection* (New York: Doubleday, 1984), 18. Compare with Hans Küng's statement: "At least for primitive Christendom, Christian faith stands or falls with the evidence of Jesus' resurrection, without which there is no content to Christian preaching or even to faith. Thus Easter appears — opportunely or inopportunely — not only as the basic unit, but also as the permanent, constitutive core of the Christian creed" (*On Being a Christian*, trans. Edward Quinn [New York: Doubleday, 1984], 346). Similarly, Walter Künneth describes the resurrection as "the primal datum of theology, from which there can be no abstracting, and the normative presupposition for every valid dogmatic judgment and for the meaningful constructing of a Christian theology" (*The Theology of the Resurrection*, trans. James W. Leitch [London: SCM, 1965], 294).
7. Ibid.
8. C. F. Evans, *Resurrection and the New Testament*, Studies in Biblical Theology, Second Series, no. 12 (London: SCM, 1970), 1.
9. Brueggemann, *Theology of the Old Testament*, 147.
10. Walter Künneth, *The Theology of the Resurrection*, trans. James W. Leitch (London: SCM, 1965), 152.
11. Gerald O'Collins, *The Resurrection of Jesus Christ* (London: Darton, Longman & Todd, 1973), 118.
12. Karl Rahner, "Dogmatic Questions on Easter," *Theological Investigations* 4, trans. Kevin Smyth (London: Darton, Longman & Todd, 1966), 123. Rahner further states that "it can only be due to an accident of history and a shortcoming in the fulfillment of the task [of theology] that every text-book today offers a long treatise on Good Friday and disposes of Easter in a few lines" (ibid., 121).
13. Athanasius, *The Incarnation of the Word of God*, trans. a religious of C.S.M.V. (New York: Macmillan, 1957), V.26, 56–57.

14. Wolfhart Pannenberg, *Jesus — God and Man*, 2d ed., trans. Lewis L. Wilkins and Duane A. Priebe (Philadelphia: Westminster Press, 1977), 136–37.

15. James D. G. Dunn, *Christology in the Making: A New Testament Inquiry into the Origins of the Doctrine of the Incarnation* (Philadelphia: Westminster Press, 1980), 267.

16. Ibid., 267–68.

17. Walter Kasper, *Jesus the Christ*, trans. V. Green (New York: Paulist Press, 1976), 130.

18. Francis Schüssler Fiorenza, *Foundational Theology: Jesus and the Church* (New York: Crossroad, 1992), 6.

19. Gerald O'Collins notes that no empirical research has been done on this subject to his knowledge, but that it would nonetheless be interesting "to discover a posteriori why people in fact believe [in the resurrection], rather than insisting a priori why they ought to believe" ("The Resurrection: The State of the Questions," in *The Resurrection: An Interdisciplinary Symposium on the Resurrection of Jesus*, ed. Stephen T. Davis, Daniel Kendall, Gerald O'Collins [Oxford: Oxford University Press, 1997], 19).

20. Paul Avis, "The Resurrection of Jesus: Asking the Right Questions," in *The Resurrection of Jesus Christ*, ed. Paul Avis (London: Darton, Longman & Todd, 1993), 18.

21. This is not without resemblance to Friedrich Schleiermacher's contention that "the disciples recognized in Him the Son of God without having the faintest premonition of His resurrection and ascension, and we too may say the same of ourselves; moreover neither the spiritual presence which He promised nor all that He said about His enduring influence upon those who remained behind is mediated through either of these two facts" (*The Christian Faith* [Edinburg: T. & T. Clark, 1989], 418).

22. Avis, "The Resurrection of Jesus," 19–20. Such a view is similar to that of Marcus Borg, who argues that what happened to Jesus' body after his death is of no real importance. See his "The Truth of Easter," in *The Meaning of Jesus: Two Visions*, Marcus J. Borg and N. T. Wright (New York: HarperCollins, 1999), 129–42.

23. Ibid., 20.

24. See, for example, the collected essays edited by John Hick, *The Myth of God Incarnate* (London: SCM Press, 1977).

25. Rahner, "Dogmatic Questions on Easter," 129.

26. Louis-Marie Chauvet, *Symbol and Sacrament: A Sacramental Reinterpretation of Christian Existence*, trans. Patrick Madigan and Madeleine Beaumont (Collegeville, Minn.: Liturgical Press, 1995), 154–55.

27. Ibid., 161–89.

28. John Milbank, "Postmodern Critical Augustinianism: A Short *Summa* in Forty-two Responses to Unasked Questions," in *The Postmodern God: A Theological Reader*, ed. Graham Ward (Oxford: Blackwell Publishers, 1997), 277.

Chapter One

1. Evans, *Resurrection and the New Testament*, 130.

2. William C. Placher, *Unapologetic Theology: A Christian Voice in a Pluralistic Conversation* (Louisville: Westminster Press, 1989), 128.

3. Rowan Williams, "Between the Cherubim: The Empty Tomb and the Empty Throne," in *On Christian Theology* (Oxford: Blackwell Publishers, 2000), 195.

4. Ibid., 195–96.

5. See Matt. 28:15. Such early detractors would not be the last to use this hypothesis. This was one of the major arguments the second-century Celsus used to refute Christianity, to which Origen vehemently responded in his *Contra Celsum*. It would also be a central argument in Reimarus's *Fragments*.

6. Rudolf Bultmann, "New Testament and Mythology," in *Kerygma and Myth: A Theological Debate,* ed. Hans Werner Bartsch, trans. Reginald H. Fuller (New York: Harper & Brothers, 1961), 4.

7. Ibid., 41.

8. Quoted in Kasper, *Jesus the Christ,* 132.

9. Bultmann, "New Testament and Mythology," 42.

10. Ibid., 39.

11. John Thiel, "For What May We Hope? Thoughts on the Eschatological Imagination," *Theological Studies* 67 (2006), see 517–19.

12. Bultmann, "New Testament and Mythology," 10, n. 2. Italics mine.

13. Immanuel Kant, *Religion Within the Limits of Reason Alone,* trans. Theodore M. Greene and Hoyt H. Hudson (New York: Harper & Row, 1960), 119.

14. Kant regards eschatological statements as symbolic representations of an underlying moral imperative. The eschatological future of the "end of the world," or the "new heaven and earth," are "intended merely to enliven hope and courage and to increase our endeavors to that end." We are thus ensured that this "beautiful ideal of the moral world-epoch" presents "nothing mystical," since "everything moves quite naturally in a moral fashion" (ibid., 125–26).

15. Bultmann, "New Testament and Mythology," 39.

16. Ibid., 42.

17. Rudolf Bultmann, *History and Eschatology: The Presence of Eternity* (New York: Harper & Brothers, 1957), 155.

18. Jürgen Moltmann, *The Coming of God: Christian Eschatology,* trans. Margaret Kohl (Minneapolis: Fortress Press, 1996), 21.

19. Oscar Cullmann, "Immortality of the Soul or Resurrection of the Dead: The Witness of the New Testament," in *Immortality and Resurrection, Death in the Western World: Two Conflicting Currents of Thought,* ed. Krister Stendahl (New York: Macmillan, 1965), 33.

20. Moltmann, *The Coming of God,* 28.

21. For overviews of various interpretive models commonly adopted today in biblical criticism and systematic theology, the following are particularly useful: William P. Alston, "Biblical Criticism and the Resurrection," in *The Resurrection: An Interdisciplinary Symposium on the Resurrection of Jesus,* 148–83; John M. B. Barclay, "The Resurrection in Contemporary New Testament Scholarship," in *Resurrection Reconsidered,* ed. Gavin D'Costa (Oxford: Oneworld, 1996); Peter Carnley, *The Structure of Resurrection Belief* (Oxford: Oxford University Press, 1987); David Ferguson, "Interpreting the Resurrection," *Scottish Journal of Theology,* vol. 28, no. 3 (1985): 287–305; John P. Galvin, "The Resurrection of Jesus in Contemporary Catholic Systematics," *Heythrop Journal* 20 (1979): 123–45; Hans Kessler, *Sucht den Lebenden nicht bei den Toten. Die Auferstehung Jesu Christi in biblischer, fundamentaltheologischer und systematischer Sicht* (Düsseldorf: Patmos, 1987); Thorwald

Lorenzen, *Resurrection and Discipleship: Interpretive Models, Biblical Reflections, Theological Consequences* (Maryknoll, N.Y.: Orbis Books, 1995); Gerald O'Collins, *Jesus Risen: An Historical, Fundamental and Systematic Examination of Christ's Resurrection* (New York: Paulist Press, 1987); Kenan B. Osborne, *The Resurrection of Jesus: New Considerations for Its Theological Interpretation* (New York: Paulist Press, 1997).

22. Edward Schillebeeckx, *Jesus: An Experiment in Christology*, trans. Hubert Hoskins (New York: Crossroad, 1979), 645.

23. N. T. Wright, *The Resurrection of the Son of God*, vol. 3, *Christian Origins and the Question of God* (Minneapolis: Fortress Press, 2003), 717.

24. E. P. Sanders, *The Historical Figure of Jesus* (New York: Penguin Books, 1993), 276.

25. Ibid., 278.

26. Ibid., 280.

27. John P. Meier, "Jesus," in *The New Jerome Biblical Commentary*, ed. Raymond E. Brown, Joseph A. Fitzmyer, and Roland E. Murphy (Englewood Cliffs, N.J.: Prentice Hall, 1990), 1328.

28. John P. Meier, *The Roots of the Problem and the Person*, vol. 1 *A Marginal Jew: Rethinking the Historical Jesus*, (New York: Doubleday, 1991), 1.

29. Ibid., 25.

30. Ibid., 24.

31. John P. Meier, *Mentor, Message, and Miracles*, vol. 2, *A Marginal Jew: Rethinking the Historical Jesus* (New York: Doubleday, 1994), 511.

32. Ibid., 514.

33. Stephen Jay Gould, *Rocks of Ages: Science and Religion in the Fullness of Life* (New York: Ballantine, 1999), 6.

34. Luke Timothy Johnson, *The Real Jesus: The Misguided Quest for the Historical Jesus and the Truth of the Traditional Gospels* (New York: HarperCollins, 1996), 131, 133.

35. Ibid., 132.

36. Pannenberg, *Jesus — God and Man*, 97.

37. Wright summarily takes up the most common historical and theological objections to such an inquiry in the introduction to his own massive study (Wright, *Resurrection of the Son of God*, especially 12–31).

38. Gerd Luedemann, *The Resurrection of Jesus: History, Experience, Theology*, trans. John Bowden (Minneapolis: Fortress Press, 1994), 180. See also Gerd Luedemann, *What Really Happened to Jesus? A Historical Approach to the Resurrection*, trans. John Bowden (Louisville: Westminster John Knox, 1995); *Jesus' Resurrection: Fact or Fiction? A Debate between William Lane Craig and Gerd Lüdemann*, ed. Paul Copan and Ronald K. Tacelli (Downers Grove, Ill.: InterVarsity Press, 2000).

39. Luedemann, *The Resurrection of Jesus*, 180.

40. Robert W. Funk, *Honest to Jesus: Jesus for a New Millennium* (New York: HarperSanFrancisco, 1996), 258.

41. Ibid., 313. Quoting Elaine Pagels to make the point, the official doctrine of Jesus' bodily resurrection "legitimates the authority of certain men who claim to exercise exclusive leadership over the churches as the successors of the apostle Peter" (*The Gnostic Gospels* [New York: Random House, 1979], 6).

42. Ibid., 258.

43. Funk, *Honest to Jesus,* 303. For more on the missionary zeal with which Funk and several others from the Jesus Seminar approach their scholarship, see "Introduction," *The Five Gospels: The Search for the Authentic Words of Jesus,* Robert W. Funk, Roy W. Hoover, and the Jesus Seminar (New York: Macmillan, 1993), 1–38.

44. At the end of his book, Funk provides several theses for a Christianity that can no longer remain committed to its original symbolic world. "Since that symbolic world is crumbling or has crumbled, the times call for a wholly secular account of the Christian faith, not just for the sake of its appeal to the third world but primarily for the sake of those who inhabit the contemporary, scientifically minded Western world. For an embattled and embittered shrinking minority — yes, that is what it is — who want to retreat into contrived mental ghettos as a way of maintaining some hypothetical past, the issue does not matter. But for the rest of us, it does: we cannot continue to traffic in sedimented theological language, or in the ancient worldview at selected, discrete levels, chosen carefully as defensible religious preserves" (*Honest to Jesus,* 298). Undoubtedly statements like these are what Meier has in mind when he writes: "The problem is that, despite loud protests about a purely historical approach, most authors of books about the historical Jesus mesh their historical agenda with a theological one" (*A Marginal Jew,* vol. 2, *Mentor, Message, and Miracles,* 522, n. 2).

45. Luedemann, *The Resurrection of Jesus,* 180.
46. Ibid., 249, n. 678. See also, 16–19.
47. Ibid., 97–100.
48. Ibid., 82–84.
49. Ibid., 107.
50. Ibid., 221, n. 350.

51. This blending of historical and psychological explanation stands squarely within a tradition reaching back as early as David Friedrich Strauss in the nineteenth century. For another subjective vision hypothesis of the Straussian variety, see Michael Goulder, "The Baseless Fabric of a Vision," in *Resurrection Reconsidered,* ed. Gavin D'Costa (Oxford: Oneworld, 1996), 48–61.

52. Mark Allen Powell, *Jesus as a Figure in History: How Modern Historians View the Man from Galilee* (Louisville: Westminster John Knox Press, 1998), 50.

53. Pannenberg, *Jesus — God and Man,* 105. See also, Wolfhart Pannenberg, "Dogmatische Erwägungen zur Auferstehung Jesu," in *Grundfragen Systematischer Theologie: Gesammelte Aufsätz,* vol. 2 (Göttingen: Vandenhoeck & Ruprecht, 1980), 160–73; "Did Jesus Really Rise from the Dead?" in *New Testament Issues,* ed. Richard Batey (London: SCM, 1970), 102–17; "History and the Reality of the Resurrection," in *Resurrection Reconsidered,* 62–72; *Systematic Theology,* Volume 2, trans. Geoffrey W. Bromiley (Grand Rapids: Eerdmans, 1994), 343–63.

54. Wright, *The Resurrection of the Son of God,* 706. See also N. T. Wright, "Jesus' Resurrection and Christian Origins," *Gregorianum* 83/4: 615–35; *The Challenge of Jesus: Rediscovering Who Jesus Was and Is* (Downers Grove, Ill.: InterVarsity Press, 1999), 126–49; N. T. Wright, "The Resurrection of the Messiah," *Sewanee Theological Review* 41, no. 2 (1998): 107–56; Marcus J. Borg and N. T. Wright, *The Meaning of Jesus: Two Visions* (New York: HarperSanFrancisco, 1999), 111–27.

55. Pannenberg, *Jesus — God and Man*, 98. Elsewhere Pannenberg writes: "Though the idea of miracles as breaking the rules of natural law is still excluded by the very concept of natural law, that concept does not preclude the impact of contingency and hidden parameters that in particular cases may influence the actual occurrence of events without violating the presently known natural laws" ("History and the Reality of the Resurrection," 65).

56. See for example the collection of essays in *Resurrection: Theological and Scientific Assessments*, ed. Ted Peters, Robert John Russell, and Michael Welker (Grand Rapids: Eerdmans, 2002).

57. Pannenberg, *Jesus — God and Man*, 82-83.

58. Ibid., 83-88.

59. As Hans-Georg Gadamer has reminded us, the very idea that prejudices are *ipso facto* negative is part of the Enlightenment legacy. However, a hermeneutical understanding of knowledge affirms that prejudices are unavoidable, that all knowledge operates within the "effective history" of a tradition. So, the question is not whether one will work independent of a prejudice, but which set of prejudices is operative. This will of course lead to the necessary task of critiquing prejudices, determining their relative adequacy to be self-correcting and truthful, for example; but we shall not get very far in doing this by assuming we can be free of prejudices as such (*Truth and Method* [New York: Crossroad, 1986], 235-341).

60. Wright, *The Resurrection of the Son of God*, 717. Italics mine.

61. See N. T. Wright, *The New Testament and the People of God*, vol. 1, *Christian Origins and the Question of God* (Minneapolis: Fortress Press, 1992), 31-144.

62. Ibid., 96.

63. Ibid.

64. Ibid., 97. Wright makes this further point, which only highlights the fact that his consideration of "history" is already an incipient, if not explicit, ontology: "If we are eventually to mount a new theory of knowledge itself, we will also need a new theory of being or existence, that is, a new ontology" (ibid.). In my view, Wright is only making explicit here what is often implicit in any approach to "history."

65. Wright, *The Resurrection of the Son of God*, 714.

66. Wright, *The New Testament and the People of God*, 96.

67. Willi Marxsen, *The Resurrection of Jesus of Nazareth*, trans. Margaret Kohl (London: SCM Press, 1970), 125-26. This important volume continues the work of his earlier and more moderate essay, "The Resurrection of Jesus as a Historical and Theological Problem," in *The Significance of the Message of the Resurrection for Faith in Jesus Christ*, ed. C. F. D. Moule (London: SCM Press, 1968), 15-50.

68. Marxsen, *The Resurrection of Jesus of Nazareth*, 77. Italics original.

69. Ibid., 184.

70. Ibid.

71. Ibid., 22-24.

72. Ibid., 138.

73. Ibid., 139. Italics mine.

74. Ibid., 128.

75. Ibid., 147.

76. Marxsen, "The Resurrection of Jesus as a Historical and Theological Problem," 50.

77. Peter Carnley, *The Structure of Resurrection Belief,* 157–58.
78. Evans, *The Resurrection and the New Testament,* 1.
79. Marxsen, *The Resurrection of Jesus of Nazareth,* 138–48.
80. For more on the relationship between this *katabasis-anabasis* motif and resurrection language in John, see chapter 7.
81. Ibid., 147. Italics original. Other indications of Marxsen's expressivism may be observed in the following statement: "There is, after all, no specifically Christian language; the preacher simply takes the language that is available. Translating into another language does not mean a change in the message. Why should this be the case when prevailing concepts change?" (pp. 136–37).
82. George Lindbeck notes that the expressivist view of language that has dominated much modern theological literature is in part due to the breach left by Kant's critique of metaphysics (*The Nature of Doctrine,* 20–25, 31–32). The religious dimension, rather than being "out there," is relocated in the interior depths of the subject who externally expresses or thematizes religious experience in the ever revisable medium of language — this rather than language itself constructing experience. In such a climate, it is not difficult to see how the language of "resurrection" is reduced to a metaphor of interior "faith-experience," even if it gets used at all. My own approach has much in keeping with Lindbeck's "cultural-linguistic" alternative to expressivism on the one hand and propositionalism on the other. Resurrection language, I shall be arguing, constructs imagination, community, praxis and experience rather than just "expressing" them. However, I would want to say more clearly than Lindbeck's rule-theory approach does that resurrection language is public and referential.
83. Marxsen, *The Resurrection of Jesus of Nazareth,* 156.
84. In contrast to going "behind" a text in this way — a hallmark of Romantic hermeneutics — Paul Ricoeur helpfully suggests standing "in front" of the text in the process of appropriation: "to understand *oneself* is to understand oneself *in front of the text....* To appropriate is to make what was alien become one's own. What is appropriated is indeed the matter of the text. But the matter of the text becomes my own only if I disappropriate myself, in order to let the matter of the text be. So I exchange the *me, master* of itself, for the *self, disciple* of the text. The process could also be expressed as a *distanciation of self from itself* within the interior of appropriation" ("Phenomenology and Hermeneutics," 37).
85. In his widely respected and exhaustive analysis of the resurrection narratives, Reginald H. Fuller writes: "The resurrection of Jesus from the dead was the central claim of the church's proclamation. There was no period when this was not so" (*The Formation of the Resurrection Narratives* [Philadelphia: Fortress Press, 1971], 48). Gerald O'Collins argues for the original use of resurrection in which exaltation language "emerges as a comment on and subsequent interpretation of the resurrection" (*The Resurrection of Jesus Christ* [London: Darton, Longman & Todd, 1973], 51). Pheme Perkins indicates that rather than evidencing alternatives to resurrection language, the diversity of the New Testament shows diverse uses *of* it (*Resurrection,* 21). For more on the relationship between exaltation and resurrection language in biblical scholarship, see Evan's survey, *Resurrection and the New Testament,* 135–43.
86. Raymond E. Brown, *The Virginal Conception and Bodily Resurrection of Jesus* (New York: Paulist Press, 1973), 75, n. 125.

87. Ibid., 75.

88. Marxsen can only say this: "The fact that in the course of later developments confession in the form of the acknowledgment of the risen Lord acquired a central significance cannot be called mere chance; for the associated idea is particularly close to the statement that the one who was crucified *is alive*" (*The Resurrection of Jesus of Nazareth*, 148). But this only begs the very question again: Why was resurrection language uniquely disclosive of this when other options were available?

89. Wright, *The Resurrection of the Son of God*, 712.

90. We shall take up questions of christology in chapter 9.

91. Brown, *The Virginal Conception and Bodily Resurrection of Jesus*, 126.

92. Karl Rahner, *Foundations of Christian Faith: An Introduction to the Idea of Christianity*, trans. William V. Dych (New York: Crossroad, 1995), 277.

93. Ibid., 276–77.

Chapter Two

1. Thomas Merton, *Thoughts in Solitude* (New York: The Noonday Press, 1956), 90–91.

2. Jean-Luc Marion, *The Idol and Distance: Five Studies*, trans. Thomas A. Carlson (New York: Fordham University Press, 2001), 144.

3. Evans, *Resurrection and the New Testament*, 130.

4. Reginald H. Fuller, *The Formation of the Resurrection Narratives* (Philadelphia: Fortress Press, 1980), 22–23.

5. Ibid., 23.

6. For more on the resurrection in apocryphal literature, see Fuller, *Formation of the Resurrection Narratives*, 189–97; Perkins, *Resurrection*, 338–43; Wright, *Resurrection of the Son of God*, 494–500.

7. Rahner, *Foundations of Christian Faith: An Introduction to the Idea of Christianity*, trans. William V. Dych (New York: Crossroad, 1978), 277.

8. David F. Ford, *Self and Salvation: Being Transformed* (Cambridge: Cambridge University Press, 1999), 210.

9. Moltmann, *The Coming of God*, 27–29.

10. For a more extended treatment of Marion's christology in light of his analysis of the saturated phenomenon, see my "A Gift to Theology? Jean-Luc Marion's 'Saturated Phenomenon' in Christological Perspective," *The Heythrop Journal* 48.1 (2007): 86–108. Parts of that article appear in the present chapter.

11. Jean-Luc Marion, "In the Name: How to Avoid Speaking of 'Negative Theology;'" in *God, the Gift, and Postmodernism*, ed. John D. Caputo and Michael Scanlon (Bloomington: Indiana University Press, 1999), 39–40. Italics mine. This essay is substantially the same as "In the Name: How to Avoid Speaking of It," in *In Excess: Studies in Saturated Phenomena*, trans. Robyn Horner and Vincent Berraud (New York: Fordham University Press, 2002), 128–62.

12. "Givenness," or *donation* in the French, translates the German *Gegebenheit* of Husserl, and denotes the priority of what is given to the consciousness that would receive it. For more on this, see *Being Given: Toward a Phenomenology of Givenness*, trans. Jeffrey L. Kosky (Stanford, Calif: Stanford University Press, 2000), 62–70. For a brief summary of important themes explored in *Being Given*, see Jean-Luc Marion, "Sketch of a Phenomenological Concept of Gift," in *Postmodern Philosophy and*

Christian Thought, ed. Merold Westphal (Bloomington: Indiana University Press, 1999), 122–43.

13. As Heidegger puts it: "Thus 'phenomenology' means *aophainesthai ta phainomena* — to let that which shows itself be seen from itself in the very way in which it shows itself from itself" (*Being and Time,* trans. John Macquarrie and Edward Robinson [New York: Harper & Row, 1966], 58).

14. Immanuel Kant, *Critique of Judgment,* trans. J. H. Bernard (New York: Hafner Publishing Co., 1951), 157.

15. Jean-Luc Marion, *Being Given,* 198. See also Jean-Luc Marion, "The Saturated Phenomenon," in *Phenomenology and the "Theological Turn": The French Debate,* trans. Bernard G. Prusak (New York: Fordham University Press, 2000), 176–216.

16. Marion, *Being Given,* 216.

17. Gadamer, *Truth and Method,* 111.

18. Marion, *Being Given,* 46. For a more extended treatment of painting, see Jean-Luc Marion, *The Crossing of the Visible,* trans. James K. A. Smith (Stanford, Calif.: Stanford University Press, 2004).

19. David Bentley Hart, *The Beauty of the Infinite: The Aesthetics of Christian Truth* (Grand Rapids: Eerdmans, 2003), 17.

20. Ibid., p.19.

21. Marion, *Being Given,* 167–68.

22. Leo Tolstoy, *War and Peace,* trans. Louis and Aylmer Maude (New York: Simon & Schuster, 1942), 1359.

23. Marion, *Being Given,* 267.

24. Helpfully, Marion regularly crosses over to theology in his work. Even when he adopts a more strictly philosophical idiom, always is theology close at hand. Such parallelism will naturally raise the question about the relationship between phenomenology and theology — whether and to what extent the former functions as a kind of "pre-theological" enterprise, or under the pretense of philosophical autonomy, it smuggles in (not so subtly, some might say) an array of theological commitments. While this is an important question, our present purposes do not permit us to wade into the ongoing debate here as framed most notably by Dominique Janicaud; see his "The Theological Turn of French Phenomenology," in *Phenomenology and the "Theological Turn,"* trans. Thomas A. Carlson, ed. Dominique Janicaud (New York: Fordham University Press, 2000), 16–103. For a helpful overview of the problem, see Robyn Horner, *Rethinking God as Gift: Marion, Derrida, and the Limits of Phenomenology* (New York: Fordham University Press, 2001). We can briefly state here that Marion emphatically denies his phenomenology functions covertly as theology or apologetics. If one may speak of the possibility of revelatory phenomena whilst doing phenomenology, to speak of its actuality is to enter into the terrain of revealed theology (*Being Given,* 71ff., 114–15, 234–36, 296ff., 367 n. 90; see also Jean-Luc Marion, "Metaphysics and Phenomenology: A Summary for Theologians," in *The Postmodern God: A Theological Reader,* ed. Graham Ward [Oxford: Blackwell, 1997], 279–96). While these two projects can be stylistically homologous, they are not (nor can they be) substantively the same without compromising each discipline. Thomas A. Carlson, in my view, gets it right when he states: "At this level the structure of Marion's phenomenological vision and the structure of his theological vision are strikingly similar, if not isomorphic.... Such isomorphism would not mean, as

many argue or assume, that Marion's phenomenology is 'really' or 'only' an indirect means to advance theology. It could mean, however, that Marion's theology and phenomenology inform one another in more subtle and complex ways than Marion himself sometimes wants to allow" ("Converting the Given to the Seen: Introductory Remarks on Theological and Phenomenological Vision," Translator's introduction to *The Idol and Distance: Five Studies,* trans. Thomas A. Carlson [New York: Fordham University Press, 2001], xxxi.)

25. Paul Ricoeur, "The Hermeneutical Function of Distanciation," *From Text to Action: Essays in Hermeneutics,* vol. 2, trans. Kathleen Blamey and John B. Thompson (Evanston, Ill.: Northwestern University Press, 1991), 86.

26. Ibid., 88. The influence of Gadamer's phenomenology of "play" is quite evident here. We might add that such an approach does not prohibit critical approaches. I subscribe to Ricoeur's notion of "distanciation" as that which permits the sort of critical analysis assisted by an array of theoretical models (historical, semiotic, social-theoretic, psychoanalytic, etc.). I would simply add, rather vigorously, that such models can only be employed in an *ad hoc* way, never as a substitute for the more phenomenological style that reads scripture contemplatively, as the word of God. Scripture already possesses remarkable resources for self-critique. To this extent, I am sympathetic to the important critiques of correlational strategies (without wanting to abandon them altogether) of thinkers like George Lindbeck and Hans Frei.

27. Marion, *Being Given,* 236.

28. Perkins, *Resurrection,* 18.

29. Evans, *Resurrection and the New Testament,* 11.

30. In addition to Daniel 12, see Macc. 7:10–11 and Wisd. 2:21–25:23.

31. "Though later exegesis, both Jewish and Christian, became skilled at discovering covert allusions which earlier readers had not seen—a skill shared, according to the gospels, by Jesus himself—there is general agreement that for much of the Old Testament the idea of resurrection is, to put it at its strongest, deeply asleep, only to be woken by echoes from later times and texts" (Wright, *Resurrection of the Son of God,* 85).

32. Perkins, *Resurrection,* 40.

33. Edward Schillebeeckx, *Jesus: An Experiment in Christology,* 523–24.

34. Perkins, *Resurrection,* 23.

35. Evans, *Resurrection and the New Testament,* 32. "The paucity of resurrection language in the teaching of Jesus...and its use in ways that are apparently typical of other Jewish speakers of the period make it impossible to explain the centrality of resurrection in later Christian preaching by appeal to the teaching of Jesus" (Perkins, *Resurrection,* 75).

36. In later chapters, I will attempt to show how the resurrection is very much in keeping with Jesus' Kingdom of God proclamation, but in a way that does not make Jesus' resurrection a redundancy element. It is simply not true, as some have argued, presumably in order to combat what they perceive as an excessively "high" or "otherworldly" christology, that Jesus' resurrection does not add a new content and structure to Jesus' historical ministry.

37. Wright, *Resurrection of the Son of God,* 403.

38. John P. Meier, *A Marginal Jew: Rethinking the Historical Jesus,* vol. 3, *Companions and Competitors* (New York: Doubleday, 2001), 443.

39. We shall see later why the resurrection was also politically and religiously a dangerous notion to the Sadducees. More than arguments over canon and authority is at stake here.

40. "If Jesus' use of Exod. 3.6 as *the* scriptural proof for the general resurrection strikes us as strange, it apparently struck his Jewish contemporaries as well as later Christians in the same way. As far as we can tell from the sources available to us, there was no Jewish exegetical tradition before or after Jesus in ancient times that used Exod. 3.6 to argue for the general resurrection" (Meier, *Companions and Competitors*, 435–36).

41. Ibid., 443–44.

42. Meier, *Mentor, Message and Miracles*, 308. See Rudolf Bultmann, *Theology of the New Testament*, vol. 1 (New York: Charles Scribner's Sons, 1951), 29.

43. G. B. Caird and L. D. Hurst, *New Testament Theology* (Oxford: Oxford University Press, 1994), 365–66. See also Joachim Jeremias, *New Testament Theology*, vol. 1, *The Proclamation of Jesus* (New York: 1971), 277–86.

44. Ben Witherington, III, *The Christology of Jesus* (Minneapolis: Fortress Press, 1990), 262. See also N. T. Wright's, *Jesus and the Victory of God*, vol. 2, *Christian Origins and the Question of God* (Minneapolis: Fortress Press, 1996), especially 540–653; and his *Resurrection of the Son of God*, 408–49; Craig A. Evans, "Did Jesus Predict His Death and Resurrection?" in. *Resurrection*, ed. Stanley E. Porter, Michael A. Hayes and David Tombs, Journal for the Study of the New Testament Supplement Series 186 (Sheffield: Sheffield Academic Press, 1999), 82–97. Karl Rahner argues, rightly in my view, that while we do not know exactly how Jesus interpreted his death and resurrection, we must say as an exegetical minimum for dogmatic theology at least the following: that Jesus "faced his death resolutely and accepted it at least as the inevitable consequence of fidelity to his mission and as imposed on him by God" (*Foundations of Christian Faith*, 248). This minimally sufficient assertion entails two aspects: First, "by freely accepting the fate of death Jesus surrenders himself precisely to the unforeseen and incalculable possibilities of his existence; and, secondly, Jesus maintains in death his unique claim of an identity between his message and his person in the hope that in this death he will be vindicated by God with regard to his claim" (ibid., 254–55).

45. For the exceptional instances where Jesus appears to raise himself, see especially John 10:17–18, where Jesus is depicted as saying: "For this reason the Father loves me, because I lay down my life in order to take it up again. No one takes it from me, but I lay it down of my own accord. I have power to lay it down, and I have power to take it up again." It is possible to see in this and other passages an increasingly high christology. In patristic literature, the preference for speaking of Jesus' agency in his resurrection can be found as early as Ignatius of Antioch (*Epistle to the Smyrneans* 2) and becomes more common from the second century on.

46. See also Rom. 4:24–25; 1 Cor. 15:15; 1 Thess. 1:9; Eph. 1:20; 1 Pet. 1:21. For a helpful overview of the words and verb tenses associated with resurrection in the New Testament, see Matthew Brook O'Donnell, "Some New Testament Words for Resurrection and the Company They Keep," in *Resurrection*, ed. Porter, et al., 136–63. See also Evans, *Resurrection and the New Testament*, 20–27. For more on the trinitarian pattern in the resurrection, see chapter 9.

47. Marion, *Being Given*, 237.

48. Ibid.

49. Evans, *Resurrection and the New Testament*, 39–40. Italics mine. Perkins, *Resurrection*, 84–85, 102–3.

50. Wright, *Resurrection of the Son of God*, 707, 712. Italics mine.

51. Eberhard Jüngel, *Death: The Riddle and the Mystery*, trans. Iain and Ute Nicol (Philadelphia: Westminster Press, 1974), 85–86.

52. Marion, *Being Given*, 237.

53. For two helpful overviews of the extensive literature on this subject, see Robert H. Gundry, *Mark: A Commentary on His Apology for the Cross* (Grand Rapids: Eerdmans, 1993), 988–1021; and John Fenton, "The Ending of Mark's Gospel," in *Resurrection: Essays in Honour of Leslie Houlden*, ed. Stephen Barton and Graham Stanton (London: SPCK, 1994), 1–7. See also Gerald O'Collins's concise summary of scholarly approaches, "The Fearful Silence of Three Women (Mark 16:8c)," in *Interpreting the Resurrection: Examining the Major Problems in the Stories of Jesus' Resurrection* (New York: Paulist Press, 1988), 53–67.

54. I, in fact, presuppose the historical reliability of the empty tomb narratives. For more on this, and what I think is the deeper scandal of the empty tomb, see chapter 3.

55. Gundry, *Mark*, 993. I say ostensible, because it is clear that Mark does not have a strictly "materialistic" conception of Jesus' resurrection, as Gundry also points out. See also Fuller, *Formation of the Resurrection Narratives*, 56–57.

56. Marianne Sawicki, *Seeing the Lord: Resurrection and Early Christian Practices* (Minneapolis: Fortress Press, 1994), 255–57.

57. Gundry, *Mark*, 993.

58. Francis Watson, "'He is Not Here': Towards a Theology of the Empty Tomb," in *Resurrection*, ed. Barton and Stanton, 99.

59. Ibid.

60. Ibid., 101.

61. Ibid.

62. This position is advanced by Norman Perrin. See his *The Resurrection According to Matthew, Mark, and Luke* (Philadelphia: Fortress Press, 1977), 27–31.

63. It is along these lines that R. H. Lightfoot argues. See his *The Gospel Message of St. Mark* (Oxford: Oxford University Press, 1950).

64. "This presence of distance within the beautiful, as primordially the *effect* of beauty, provides the essential logic of theological aesthetics: one that does not interpret all distance as an original absence, or as the distance of differentiation's heterogeneous and violent forces, but that sees in distance, and in all the series and intervals that dwell in it, the possibility of peaceful analogies and representations that neither falsify nor constrain the object of regard" (Hart, *The Beauty of the Infinite*, 18).

65. "But who saw this? A hysterical female, as you say, and perhaps some other one of those who were deluded by the same sorcery, who either dreamt in a certain state of mind and through wishful thinking had a hallucination due to some mistaken notion (an experience which has happened to thousands), or, which is more likely, wanted to impress the others by telling this fantastic tale, and so by this cock-and-bull story to provide a chance for other beggars" (quoted in Origen, *Contra Celsum*, trans. Henry Chadwick [Cambridge: Cambridge University Press, 1965], II.55, 109).

66. Williams, "Between the Cherubim," 187.

67. Ibid., 192.

68. Ibid., 192. This is a far more effective theological critique than Robert Funk's critique, mentioned in Chapter One, that the appearance traditions merely "endow certain leaders with authority and position — authority to proclaim the gospel as they understood it and the position of reliable and exclusive witnesses to the resurrection." Such "circular credentials," argues Funk, are "fundamentally self-serving" (*Honest to Jesus*, 313). Funk's assessment is far more illuminating of his own relentless (and perhaps self-serving) hermeneutics of suspicion than it is about the resurrection narratives, which on inner-theological grounds provide resources for self-critique in the church. Even without the empty tomb narratives, the appearance narratives, as we shall see shortly, expose and undermine every pretense to ideological domestication.

69. Lorenzen, *Resurrection and Discipleship*, 128–29.

70. For some helpful discussions of *ophthe*, see Carnley, *The Structure of Resurrection Belief*, 223–65; Fuller, *Formation of the Resurrection Narratives*, 27–49; O'Collins, "What Were the Easter Appearances Like?" in *Interpreting the Resurrection: Examining the Major Problems in the Stories of Jesus' Resurrection* (New York: Paulist Press, 1988), 5–21; Perkins, *Resurrection*, 84–87; 95–103.

71. Fuller, *The Formation of the Resurrection Narratives*, 31.

72. "[B]ut God raised him on the third day and allowed him to appear, not to all the people but to us who were chosen by God as witnesses, and who ate and drank with him after he rose from the dead" (Acts 10:40–4).

73. "The form of Christ is the revelation of this final dramatic action between God and the world. It appears in the world with such a plenitude of meanings, with such an accumulation of all possible religious forms between heaven and earth, that Christ, as divine and as worldly divine synthesis, necessarily has on man the effect of an overwhelming superabundance and, hence, of a darkness from excess of light" (Hans Urs von Balthasar, *The Glory of the Lord: A Theological Aesthetics, I: Seeing the Form*, trans. Erasmo Leiva-Merikakis (San Francisco: Ignatius Press, 1982), 645.

74. Jean-Luc Marion, "The Saturated Phenomenon," in *Phenomenology and the "Theological Turn": The French Debate*, trans. Bernard G. Prusak, ed. Dominique Janicaud (New York: Fordham University Press, 2000), 200–201. Marion appropriates the term "bedazzlement" from Pseudo-Dionysius. For a more thorough study of this concept in Marion's thought, see his "The Distance of the Requisite and the Discourse of Praise: Denys," in *The Idol and Distance*, 139–95. Hans Urs von Balthasar's study of Pseudo-Dionysius exerts considerable influence on Marion's reading. See his in *The Glory of the Lord: A Theological Aesthetics, III: Studies in Theological Styles: Lay Styles*, trans. Andrew Louth et al. (Edinburgh: T. & T. Clark, 1986), 144–210.

75. Marion, *Being Given*, 238.

76. Jean-Luc Marion, "Evidence and Bedazzlement," *Prolegomena to Charity*, trans. Stephen E. Lewis (New York: Fordham University Press, 2002), 68.

77. Ibid., 66.

78. Kasper, *Jesus the Christ*, 139.

79. Marion, "Evidence and Bedazzlement," 66. Sarah Coakley suggests something similar in her "The Resurrection and the 'Spiritual Senses'" in *Powers and Submissions: Spirituality, Philosophy and Gender* (Malden, Mass.: Blackwell, 2002). Adopting the theology of the "spiritual senses," especially as developed by Origen and Gregory of Nyssa, she argues that the resurrection narratives portray a

conversion process that integrates cognitive, affective, and erotic dimensions (see especially 136–41).

80. Jean-Luc Marion, "They Recognized Him; and He Became Invisible to Them," *Modern Theology* 18:2 (2002): p., 147. See also Jean-Luc Marion, "The Gift of a Presence," in *Prolegomena to Charity,* especially 127–37, where Marion analyzes the role of "blessing" in Luke as the condition of the possibility for disciples' "seeing."

81. Rowan Williams, *The Resurrection: An Interpretation* (Harrisburg, Pa.: Morehouse Publishing, 1994), 83–84.

82. Sandra M. Schneiders, "Touching the Risen Jesus: Mary Magdelene and Thomas the Twin in John 20," *The Catholic Theological Society of America Proceedings* 60 (2005): 31. For a reworking of this article, see Sandra M. Schneiders, "The Resurrection (of the Body) in the Fourth Gospel: A Key to Johannine Spirituality," in *Life in Abundance: Studies of John's Gospel in Tribute to Raymond E. Brown, S.S.,* ed. John R. Donahue and Raymond Edward Brown (Collegeville, Minn.: The Liturgical Press, 2005), 168–98.

83. Schneiders, "Touching the Risen Jesus," 33.

84. Ibid., 27.

85. Ibid., 27–28.

86. Ibid., 33–34. For more of Schneiders's treatment of John's resurrection theology, see her *Written That You May Believe: Encounter Jesus in the Fourth Gospel* (New York: Herder & Herder/Crossroad, 1999), especially 180–207.

87. James Alison, *Knowing Jesus* (Springfield, Ill.: Templegate Publishers, 1993), 22–23. See also his *The Joy of Being Wrong: Original Sin Through Easter Eyes* (New York: Crossroad, 1998), 70–77.

88. Alison, *Knowing Jesus,* 24.

89. Tertullian, *De Resurrectione Carnis,* par. 8.

90. Karl Rahner, "The Eternal Significance of Jesus' Humanity for our Relationship with God," in *Theological Investigations,* 3, 44.

91. Von Balthasar, *The Glory of the Lord: Seeing the Form,* 155. Likewise, David Bentley Hart: "The resurrection vindicates the aesthetic particularity of truth over against the violences that seek to reduce particularity to nothingness, over against all economies of abstract wisdom, political, philosophical, social, or religious. After the crucifixion, which is the final word — the final proof — pronounced by the powers of the age in defense of their rule and final argument whereby the totality claims for itself foundations as old as the world, the resurrection suddenly reveals the form of Christ to possess an infinite power of expression, which the final word of the totality can do nothing to silence, or even to anticipate: the power of this world's 'final' word is exhausted even as God's Word is only just beginning to be pronounced with absolute clarity" (*The Beauty of the Infinite,* 333–34). As it turns out, a genuinely *theological* aesthetics is also prophetic to the extent that it resists every "totality" that would squelch particularity and form through violence. We shall explore the relationship of theological aesthetics and prophetic resistance in coming chapters, particularly as they relate to the grammars of fulfillment and reversal respectively.

92. This schema is adapted from C. H. Dodd, "The Appearances of the Risen Christ: An Essay in Form-Criticism of the Gospels," in *Studies in the Gospels: Essays in Memory of R. H. Lightfoot,* ed. Dennis Eric Ninehan (Oxford: Oxford University

Press, 1955), 9–35; and Raymond Brown, *The Virginal Conception and Bodily Resurrection of Jesus,* 107–11.

93. Wright, "The Transforming Reality of the Bodily Resurrection," 121–22. Italics original.

94. Ibid., 122.

95. Marion, *Being Given,* 240. "[W]hat we say about Jesus begins to take on more and more clearly the tone and character of what we say about God. Jesus is not to be tied down to any set of worldly configurations and constraints, although he is never a merely abstract term. He eludes and questions our predictions and projections, recedes and hides before our attempts to arrive at adequate, definitive statements.... A theology of the risen Jesus will always be, to a greater or lesser degree, a *negative* theology, obliged to confess its conceptual and imaginative poverty — as in any theology which takes seriously the truth that God is not a determinate object in the world" (Williams, *Resurrection,* 91).

96. Marion, *Being Given,* 239.

97. "[T]he fragmentary nature of the fourfold gospel resurrection tradition as a whole may similarly be seen not as subverting its own authority, but as essential to the peculiar nature of its testimony" (Watson, " 'He is not here' " 101).

98. Hans Urs von Balthasar, *Mysterium Paschale,* trans. Aidan Nichols (San Francisco: Ignatius Press, 1990), 200, 198.

99. Hart, *The Beauty of the Infinite,* 17.

100. Michael Welker speaks of a determinate, yet dynamic, "canonic memory" that is birthed by Jesus' resurrection from the dead: "On the one hand, the living cultural memory is bound by a certain stock of texts (e.g., the biblical traditions that grew for about 1,500 years). As a fixed stock of texts, the possibilities for change are limited. On the other hand, a pluralistic multitude of perspectives in the canonic traditions stimulates a liveliness, a liveliness of permanent exegesis and interpretation that functions like hot cultural memory but does not swallow up the historical basic stock of texts and does not devour the common identity. A canon and a canonic memory cannot be planned, launched, or constructed. They arise out of complex historical and cultural lives and patterns.... From a multitude of witnesses to the presence of the resurrected Christ, the unfolding of the full life of the pre-Easter Christ, his sayings and his deeds and intentions, arises and in all this a rich and living memory and doxology with respect to his person and his continuous effectiveness" ("Resurrection and Eternal Life: The Canonic Memory of the Resurrected Christ, His Reality, and His Glory," in *The End of the World and the Ends of God,* ed. John Polkinghorne and Michael Welker [Harrisburg: Trinity Press International, 2000], 287–88).

101. Michel de Certeau, "How Is Christianity Thinkable Today?," in *The Postmodern God: A Theological Reader,* ed. Graham Ward (Oxford: Blackwell, 1997), 148.

102. Ibid., 147.

103. Ibid., 148.

104. Graham Ward, *Cities of God* (London: Routledge, 2000), 113.

105. Ibid.

106. Chauvet, *Symbol and Sacrament,* 155.

107. Ibid., 166.

Chapter Three

1. Paul Avis, "The Resurrection of Jesus: Asking the Right Questions," 18. Italics mine.
2. Ibid., 20. Italics mine.
3. Avis's position is similar to Marcus Borg's, who writes: "Whether Easter involved something remarkable happening to the physical body of Jesus is irrelevant. My argument is not that we know the tomb was not empty or that nothing happened to his body, but simply that it doesn't matter. The truth of Easter, as I see it, is not at stake in this issue" ("The Truth of Easter," 131).
4. Gerald O'Collins offers such a list in one of his several books on the resurrection: "Berten, Blank, Blinzler, Brown, von Campenhausen, Delorme, Fitzmyer, Fuller, Grundmann, Jeremias, Künneth, Léon-Dufour, Martini, Moule, Murphy-O'Connor, Mussner, Nauck, Pannenberg, Rengstorf, Ruckstuhl, Schenke, Scmitt, Schubert, Schweizer, Seidensticker, Strobel, Stuhlmacher, Trilling, Vögtle and Wilkens. These scholars support the truth of the empty tomb traditions with different degrees of intensity and, sometimes, for differing reasons. But they converge in maintaining a kernel of reliable history in the narrative of the empty tomb" (*Jesus Risen,* 123).
5. Wright, *The Resurrection of the Son of God,* 142.
6. Brown, *The Virginal Conception and Bodily Resurrection of Jesus,* 76.
7. Ibid., 126. See also Wolfhart Pannenberg, "History and the Reality of the Resurrection," in *Resurrection Reconsidered,* 69–70; and James D. G. Dunn, *Jesus and the Spirit* (London: SCM Press, 1975), 120.
8. Wright, *The Resurrection of the Son of God,* 314–15. Some suggest that because Paul does not explicitly mention an empty tomb tradition he could have envisioned Jesus' resurrection in a nonbodily way. Indeed, some point to the absence of an empty tomb tradition in Paul as reason for its nonessential role for Christian theology. However, as N. T. Wright has argued, the neglect of a formal narrative tradition associated with the empty tomb in no way means that Paul knew nothing of it. Furthermore, the affirmation of Jesus' "resurrection" presupposes an empty tomb, since resurrection precisely means that the physical body has been *transformed* (not sloughed off) and is no longer susceptible to corruption. If Paul thought that upon Jesus' death he was immediately assumed into heaven in a non-bodily way, not only could he have avoided the Herculean effort of explaining the *soma pneumatikon* in his letter to the Corinthians, but his handing on of the tradition that Jesus was risen on the "third day" would make no sense, for why should Jesus have to wait (ibid., 322)? We will deal with Paul's theology of bodily resurrection further in the following chapter.
9. Geza Vermes, *Jesus the Jew: A Historian's Reading of the Gospels* (London: Collins, 1973), 41.
10. Again I refer the reader to N. T. Wright's strong argument regarding this mutual interaction (*The Resurrection of the Son of God,* 685–718).
11. Watson, " 'He Is Not Here,' " 106.
12. Ibid.
13. Quoted by Origen, *Against Celsus,* trans. Henry Chadwick (Cambridge: Cambridge University Press, 1965) 5.14, 274–75.
14. Daley, "A Hope for Worms: Early Christian Hope," 137. See also Brian E. Daley, *The Hope of the Early Church: A Handbook of Patristic Eschatology* (Cambridge: Cambridge University Press, 1991).

15. Matthew's version of the empty tomb story adds guards to Mark's version, perhaps indicating an attempt to head off opponents' claims that Jesus' body was stolen by his disciples. John's gospel includes the stories of Jesus eating fish and Thomas's incredulity to underscore Jesus' bodily resurrection.

16. 1 Corinthians 15:12-19; 35-58; 2 Timothy 2:18.

17. Paul Tillich, *A History of Christian Thought: From Its Judaic and Hellenistic Origins to Existentialism,* ed. Carl E. Braaten (New York: Simon and Schuster, 1967), 24-26. For Celsus the *daemons* deserve our acts of devotion since "the rulers and emperors among men" do not "hold their position without the might of the daemons" (Quoted by Origen, *Contra Celsus,* 8.63, 500).

18. Wright, *The Resurrection of the Son of God,* 729.

19. Pheme Perkins notes that the majority of the debates in the second century were less concerned with the fate of Jesus after his death than the eschatological destiny of all believers. While the direction of these debates concern the future, they press upon the present, since what is fundamentally at issue is the role of the body in the economy of salvation: "These arguments required evaluation of the place of the body in Christian soteriology" (*Resurrection,* 331-32).

20. In his characteristically insightful way, if often despite himself, Ludwig Feuerbach writes: "The resurrection of the body is the highest triumph of Christianity over the sublime but certainly abstract spirituality and objectivity of the ancients. For this reason the idea of the resurrection could never be assimilated by the pagan.... Thus did 'spiritual' Christianity unspiritualise what was spiritual" (*The Essence of Christianity,* trans. George Eliot [Amherst, N.Y.: Prometheus Books, 1989], 136).

21. For a handy typology of the theological approaches developed from the second to the fourth centuries, see Daley, "A Hope for Worms." See also Carol Walker Bynum, *The Resurrection of the Body in Western Christianity, 200-1336* (New York: Columbia University Press, 1995), especially 19-114; Harry A. Wolfson, "Immortality and Resurrection in the Philosophy of the Church Fathers," in *Immortality and Resurrection: Death in the Western World: Two Conflicting Currents of Thought,* ed. Oscar Cullmann (New York: Macmillan, 1965), 54-96; Perkins, *Resurrection,* 331-90; Wright, *The Resurrection of the Son of God,* 480-552.

22. J. N. D. Kelly, *Early Christian Doctrines* (New York: HarperCollins, 1978), 466-67. "It would probably surprise a good many modern Christians," writes Etienne Gilson, "to learn that in certain of the earliest Fathers the belief in the immortality of the soul is vague almost to non-existent. This, nevertheless, is a fact, and a fact to be noted, because it casts so strong a light on the point on which Christian anthropology turns and on the course of its historical development. A Christianity without the immortality of the soul is not, in the long run, absolutely inconceivable, and the proof of it is that it has been conceived. What really would be absolutely inconceivable would be a Christianity without the resurrection of the Man" (*The Spirit of Medieval Philosophy,* trans. A. H. C. Downes [New York: Charles Scribner's Sons, 1936], 172).

23. See especially Book V of his *Against Heresies.*

24. Chauvet, *Symbol and Sacrament,* 155.

25. Bynum, *The Resurrection of the Body,* 11.

26. Karl Rahner, "The Hermeneutics of Eschatological Assertions," *Theological Investigations* 4, trans. Kevin Smyth (London: Darton, Longman & Todd, 1966), 355.

27. See Gregory of Nyssa, *On the Soul and Resurrection,* trans. Catherine P. Roth (Crestwood, N.Y.: St. Vladimir's Seminary Press, 1993); Augustine, *The City of God,* bks. 13, 19–22.
28. Gregory of Nyssa, *On the Soul and Resurrection,* 111.
29. Gregory of Nyssa, "On Virginity," in *Gregory of Nyssa: Ascetical Works,* trans. Virginia Woods Callahan, Fathers of the Church (Washington, D.C.: Catholic University of America, 1967), 26.
30. Ibid., 48.
31. Peter Brown, *The Body and Society: Men, Women, and Sexual Renunciation in Early Christianity* (New York: Columbia University Press, 1988), 223. St. Anthony is the prototype of this ascetic body, which is a body that has already "received a portion of that *spiritual body* which it is to assume in the resurrection of the just" (Anthony, *Letters of Saint Anthony the Great,* trans. D. J. Chitty [Oxford: SLG Press, 1977], 5).
32. Gregory of Nyssa, "On Virginity," 40.
33. Pierre Hadot, *Philosophy as a Way of Life: Spiritual Exercises from Socrates to Foucault,* ed. Arnold I. Davidson, trans. Michael Chase (Oxford: Blackwell, 1995), 94–95.
34. Virginity, Gregory says at one point, is "the deadening of the body" ("On Virginity," 61).
35. Brown, *The Body and Society,* 235–36.
36. Ibid., 236.
37. Bynum argues that the relic cult and the doctrine of bodily resurrection were also complimentary to each other, and both complemented the asceticism of the fourth century to emphasize "the triumph of integrity over partition, of stasis and incorruption over decay" (*The Resurrection of the Body,* 108ff.).
38. Gregory of Nyssa, "On Virginity," 21.
39. Ibid., 13.
40. Ibid., 15.
41. Ibid., 16. It is for this reason that the life of virginity could also be very liberating for women, since they were not to be identified strictly with their maternal roles. Women who entered the desert could "become men": "For the perfect ascetic the question of male or female no longer exists, because he or she has risen above the limits determined by the body; asceticism means annihilation of sexual distinction" (Susanna Elm, *"Virgins of God": The Making of Asceticism in Late Antiquity* [Oxford: Oxford University Press, 1994], 267).
42. Gregory of Nyssa, Homily 6, in *Gregory of Nyssa: Homilies on Ecclesiastes: An English Version with Supporting Studies,* ed. Stuart George Hall, trans. Stuart George Hall and Rachel Moriarty (New York: Walter de Gruyter, 1993), 109.
43. Bynum, *The Resurrection of the Body,* 113.
44. Ibid.
45. Robert Markus, *The End of Ancient Christianity* (Cambridge: Cambridge University Press, 1990), 139.
46. Peter Brown, *The Cult of the Saints: Its Rise and Function in Latin Christianity* (Chicago: University of Chicago Press, 1982), 1–2.
47. Markus, *The End of Ancient Christianity,* 146.
48. Ibid.

49. See Jean-Marie Mathieu, "Horreur du cadavre et philosophie dans le monde romain: Le cas de la patristique grecque du Ive siècle," in *La Mort, les morts, et l'au-delà dans le monde romain* (Caen: Centre de Publications de l'Université de Caen, 1987), 311–20.

50. Plato, *Phaedo,* trans. B. Jowett (Roslyn, N.Y.: Walter J. Black, 1942), 95–96.

51. It is important to recognize that body/soul dualism (or hierarchy) in the ancient world is not identical to Cartesian dualism. Whereas the latter characterizes mind or "soul" as strictly immaterial, the former may very well conceive of "soul" as an ontically distinct and subtler *corporeality*. Dale Martin is quite correct to note the differences between body/soul hierarchicalization in the modern and ancient worlds. While this distinction is no doubt important, on one level the distinction is without an ultimate difference. If, as Martin writes, the soul was typically regarded as some sort of "stuff," a kind of subtle body, the onto-valuational hierarchy of Stoicism (which was more influential during the New Testament period than Platonism) still assumed the "the deprecation of the body," the "flesh-and-blood body of current human existence" (*The Corinthian Body* [New Haven: Yale University Press, 1995], 116–17). And it is precisely this "flesh-and-body of current human existence" that is risen from the dead, even if transfigured. This is what was so offensive to thought then, as it is often now. In the next chapter, we shall have to take up Martin's somewhat problematic interpretation of Paul's *soma pneumatikon.*

52. Plato, *Timaeus,* 34A-47E.

53. Charles Taylor, *Sources of the Self: The Making of Modern Identity* (Cambridge, Mass.: Harvard University Press, 1989), 155–56.

54. Max Weber, *Essays in Sociology,* ed. H. Gerth and C. Mills (Cambridge: Oxford University Press, 1948).

55. Carolyn Merchant, *The Death of Nature* (New York: Harper & Row, 1980).

56. Louis Dupré, *Passage to Modernity: An Essay in the Hermeneutics of Nature and Culture* (New Haven.: Yale University Press, 1993), 75.

57. Taylor, *Sources of the Self,* 146. In using the phrase "innerworldly liberation," Taylor is adapting Max Weber's phrase "innerworldly asceticism" to describe aspects of Protestant spirituality (Max Weber, *The Protestant Ethic and the Spirit of Capitalism,* trans. Talcott Parsons [New York: Scribner's, 1958]).

58. Mary Midgley, "The Soul's Successors: Philosophy and the 'Body'," in *Religion and the Body,* ed. Sarah Coakley (Cambridge: Cambridge University Press, 1997), 66–67.

59. Talal Asad, "Remarks on the Anthropology of the Body," in *Religion and the Body,* 43.

60. On the paradox of the mechanization and consumeristic hedonization of the body, see Bryan S. Turner, "The Body in Western Society," in *Religion and the Body,* 15–41. Perhaps the apogee of this mechanization and commercialization of the body is to be found in biotechnology and cloning. "Cloning," writes Jean Baudrillard, is the "last stage of the history and modeling of the body, the one at which, reduced to its abstract and genetic formula, the individual is destined to serial propagation... mechanical reproducibility... [reduced to] a stockpile of information and of messages, as fodder for data processing" (*Simulacra and Simulation,* trans. Sheila Faria Glaser [Ann Arbor: University of Michigan Press, 1994], 99). For more on the commercialization of the body in biotechnology, see the disturbing work of

Lori Andrews and Dorothy Nelkin, *Body Bazaar: The Market for Human Tissue in the Biotechnology Age* (New York: Crown Publishers, 2001).

61. John F. Kavanaugh, *Following Christ in a Consumer Society* (Maryknoll, N.Y.: Orbis Books, 2001), 37, 47.

62. Drew Leder, *The Absent Body* (Chicago: University of Chicago Press, 1990), 68.

63. This is not to say that there is a single anthropology in the Bible. And yet we can agree with Joel B. Green that "the New Testament is not as dualistic as the traditions of Christian theology and biblical interpretation have taught us to think"; for "the dominant view of the human person in the New Testament is that of ontological monism, with such notions as 'escape from the body' or 'disembodied soul' falling outside the parameters of New Testament thought," ("Bodies — That Is, 'Human Lives': A Re-Examination of Human Nature in the Bible," in *Whatever Happened to the Soul? Scientific and Theological Portraits of Human Nature*, ed. Warren S. Brown, Nancey Murphy, and H. Newton Malony (Minneapolis: Fortress Press, 1998), 173.

64. Leder, *The Absent Body*, 15.

65. Ibid., 21–22. The overtly Heideggerian themes in this passage highlight the essential relationship between the spatial and temporal dimensions of lived bodily experience (Martin Heidegger, *Being and Time*, trans. John Macquarrie and Edward Robinson [New York: Harper & Row, 1962], 377–80). Importantly for our purposes, this highlights that bodily resurrection is wrongly focused if focused on the body as a kind of spatial object; bodily life is temporal life. The resurrection of the body means the transfiguration of embodied histories.

66. Leder, *The Absent Body*, 32.

67. Maurice Merleau-Ponty, *Phenomenology of Perception*, trans. Colin Smith (New York: Routledge, 2002), 95.

68. Hans W. Frei, *The Identity of Jesus Christ: The Hermeneutical Bases of Dogmatic Theology* (Eugene, Ore.: Wipf and Stock Publishers), 140–41.

69. Stanley Hauerwas, "Character, Narrative, and Growth in the Christian Life," in *The Hauerwas Reader*, ed. John Berkman and Michael Cartwright (Durham, N.C.: Duke University Press, 2001), 245.

70. Frei, *The Identity of Jesus Christ*, 138–39.

71. Ibid., 141.

72. "We must therefore avoid saying that our body is *in* space, or *in* time. It *inhabits* space and time.... The body is to be compared, not to a physical object, but rather to a work of art" (Merleau-Ponty, *Phenomenology of Perception*, 161, 174).

73. Leder, *The Absent Body*, 48.

74. Gregory of Nyssa, *On Virginity*, 26–27.

75. Heidegger, *Being and Time*, par. 38, 223.

76. Leder, *The Absent Body*, 79.

77. Ibid., 78.

78. Ibid. 141.

79. Ibid., 152.

80. Ibid., 154.

81. René Descartes, quoted in Leder, 139.

82. Taylor, *Sources of the Self*, 157.

83. Ibid., 146.

84. Leder, *The Absent Body*, 143.
85. Ibid., 108.
86. Richard Rorty, *Philosophy and the Mirror of Nature* (Princeton, N.J.: Princeton University Press, 1979), 53.
87. Leder, *The Absent Body*, 115.
88. Jacques Derrida, *Of Grammatology*, trans. Gayatri Chakravorty Spivak (Baltimore: Johns Hopkins University Press, 1998), 71.

Chapter Four

1. Frederick Buechner, *Wishful Thinking: A Theological ABC* (New York: Harper & Row, 1973), 43.
2. Karl Rahner, "The Festival of the Future of the World," in *Theological Investigations* 7, trans. David Bourke (New York: Herder & Herder, 1971), 183.
3. Jürgen Moltmann provides an overview of this theme in his *God in Creation*, 276–96.
4. Quoted in Moltmann, ibid., 307.
5. Martin, *The Corinthian Body*, 125.
6. Ibid., 126, 128.
7. Ibid., 129.
8. Ibid., 124.
9. Ibid., 128.
10. Borg, "The Truth of Easter," in *The Meaning of Jesus*, 132–33.
11. See Matt 16.17; Gal 1.16; Eph. 6.12; Heb 2.14; also Sir 14.18. Joachim Jeremias makes this point in his essay, " 'Flesh and Blood Cannot Inherit the Kingdom of God' (1 Cor 15:50)," *New Testament Studies* 2 (1955): 151–59. Jeremias writes (in 1955) that after the 1896 publication of E. Teichmann's influential *Die paulinischen Vorstellungen von Auferstehung und Gerich* it became virtually commonplace in New Testament scholarship to argue that Paul had, by the time of his first Corinthian correspondence, "spiritualized" his earlier view of the resurrection under Hellenistic influences so that now the spiritual body was seen as entirely independent of the earthly body. This reading has been, in Jeremias's words, "disastrous" for New Testament scholarship. Whether or not Jeremias's own interpretation of the passage is adequate, namely, that "flesh and blood" refers to the transformation of those who are living at the time of the *parousia* and not those who have already died, the important point is that 1 Cor. 15:50 is not intended to tell us information about the nature of the risen body, what it is or is not.
12. Perkins, *Resurrection*, 306.
13. Wright, *The Resurrection of the Son of God*, 289.
14. Anthony Thiselton, *The First Epistle to the Corinthians: A Commentary on the Greek Text* (Grand Rapids: Eerdmans, 2000), 1291.
15. Thiselton refers to Novatian, John Chrysostom, and Augustine as chief examples (ibid., 1292).
16. Gregory of Nyssa, *On the Soul and the Resurrection*, 118.
17. Robert Gundry, *Sôma in Biblical Theology With Emphasis on Pauline Anthropology* (Cambridge: Cambridge University Press, 1976), 50.
18. Perkins, *Resurrection*, 306.
19. Peter Lampe, "Paul's Concept of a Spiritual Body," in *Resurrection: Theological and Scientific Assessments*, 108–9.

20. Thiselton, *The First Epistle to the Corinthians*, 1297. Italics original.
21. Wright, *The Resurrection of the Son of God*, 358–59.
22. Thiselton, *The First Epistle to the Corinthians*, 1272.
23. Ibid., 1279. Italics mine.
24. Ibid., 1277.
25. Wright, *The Resurrection of the Son of God*, 477–78. Wright expresses surprise that no one seems to have invented the word "transphysical" to date. In fact, Pope Benedict XVI, then Joseph Ratzinger, used just this expression ("einer transphysikalischen Wirklichkeit") in his *Einführung in das Christentum* (Munich: Kösel-Verlag, 1968), 298. Ratzinger makes the point that the present body, which can be conceived in chemico-physical terms, shall appear in the mode of a transphysical reality in the resurrection.
26. Drawing richly upon biblical language, the Second Vatican Council document, *Gaudium et Spes,* characterizes the relationship between continuity and discontinuity in this way: "We do not know the moment of the consummation of the earth and of humanity nor the way the universe will be transformed. The form of this world, distorted by sin, is passing away and we are taught that God is preparing a new dwelling and a new earth in which righteousness dwells, whose happiness will fill and surpass all the desires of peace arising in human hearts. Then death will have been conquered, the daughters and sons of God will be raised in Christ and what was sown in weakness and dishonor will become incorruptible; charity and its works will remain and all of creation, which God made for humanity, will be set free from its bondage" (Ed. Austin Flannery, O.P., *Vatican Council II: The Basic Sixteen Documents,* Revised Translation in Inclusive Language [Northport, N.Y.: Costello Publishing Company, 1996], par. 39, 204.
27. Karl Rahner, "The Resurrection of the Body," in *Theological Investigations* 2, trans. Karl-H. Kruger (London: Darton, Longman & Todd, 1963), 214.
28. Thorwald Lorenzen speaks to this holistic view: "By emphasizing the 'resurrection of the body,' and not the 'immortality of the soul,' the early Christians wanted to say that human beings have to be understood as a unity of body, soul, and spirit, together with their interwovenness in society, nature, and history. It is this total *humanum* in its ecological context that is graced with the promise of salvation.... Indeed, by analogy with the risen Christ being 'the beginning, the firstborn from the dead' (Col. 1:18; compare 1 Cor. 15:20–23; Acts 26:23), those who follow Christ are the ones 'who have the first fruits of the Spirit' groaning 'inwardly as' they 'wait for adoption as sons, the redemption of our bodies' (Rom. 8:23). And since with 'our bodies' we are woven into nature, history, and cosmos, this promise entails a universal thrust" (*Resurrection and Discipleship,* 266).
29. Edward Schillebeeckx, "I Believe in the Resurrection of the Body," in *God among Us: The Gospel Proclaimed,* trans. John Bowden (New York: Crossroad, 1983) 137–38.
30. John Macquarrie, *Principles of Christian Theology,* 2d. ed. (New York: Charles Scribner's Sons, 1977), 348–49.
31. Edward Schillebeeckx, "I Believe in God, Creator of Heaven and Earth," in *God among Us,* 94.
32. Schillebeeckx, "I Believe in Eternal Life," in *God among Us* 142.
33. See Karl Rahner, "The Body in the Order of Salvation," *Theological Investigations* 17, 71–89.

34. Bynum, *The Resurrection of the Body*, 94–114.
35. Augustine, *The City of God*, trans. Marcus Dods (New York: The Modern Library, 1950), XXII.20, 843–44.
36. Ibid., 842.
37. I borrow this phrase from Brian Daley, who notes that several models existed in patristic theology to speak of the risen body, one of which conceived of the resurrection as the "reconstitution" or "reassembly of the scattered material fragments ('atoms' in the ancient sense) into which the body has been reduced by death and decomposition, and the rejoining of those fragments with the surviving soul to constitute a single person — the same one who now exists. Underlying this notion is what one might call an 'anthropology of composition': a conception of the human person that has its roots in both common sense and in some traditions of ancient philosophy — especially scientific atomism and Aristotle's conception of the soul as intrinsically related to the material body" ("A Hope for Worms," 147–48).
38. For a helpful survey and synthesis of contemporary Catholic theologians who express general consensus for using these terms to speak of the risen body, see Bernard P. Prusak, "Bodily Resurrection in Catholic Perspectives," *Theological Studies* 61 (2000): 64–105.
39. Moltmann, *The Coming of God*, 66.
40. Ibid., 67.
41. Ibid.
42. Chauvet, *Symbol and Sacrament*, 147.
43. Ibid.
44. Leder, *The Absent Body*, 67.
45. Marion, *Being Given*, 289.
46. Ibid., 290.
47. O'Collins, *Jesus Risen*, 182–83.
48. Joseph Ratzinger, *Eschatology: Death and Eternal Life*, trans. Michael Waldstein, trans. Aidan Nichols, *Dogmatic Theology*, vol. 9, ed. Johann Auer and Joseph Ratzinger (Washington, D.C.: Catholic University of America Press, 1988), 190.
49. Prusak, "Bodily Resurrection in Catholic Perspectives," 104.
50. Maurice Merleau-Ponty, *The Visible and the Invisible*, trans. Alphonso Lingis (Evanston, Ill.: Northwestern University Press, 1968), 136.
51. *La chair* is "a relation of the visible with itself that traverses me and constitutes me as a seer, this circle which I do not form, which forms me, this coiling over of the visible upon the visible, can traverse, animate other bodies as well as my own" (ibid., 140).
52. Leder, *The Absent Body*, 66.
53. Moltmann, *God in Creation*, 69–70.
54. Gustave Martelet, *The Risen Christ and the Eucharistic World*, trans. René Hague (New York: Crossroad, 1976), 83–84. Italics original.
55. Ibid., 84.
56. Karl Rahner, *On the Theology of Death*, trans. C. H. Henkey (New York: Herder & Herder, 1961), 26.
57. Karl Rahner, "Hidden Victory," *Theological Investigations* 7, trans. David Bourke (New York: Herder & Herder, 1971), 158.
58. Denis Edwards, *Jesus and the Cosmos* (New York: Paulist Press, 1991), 106.
59. Ibid., 112.

60. Elsewhere, Dennis Edwards develops several basic principles that ought to be included in any Christian consideration of ecological praxis: (1) an understanding of the intrinsic value of all creatures, not just human beings; (2) an understanding of the value of the human person within the context of creation, especially those who are the most vulnerable to ecological degradation (the poor of the Earth); (3) a reverence for all forms of life; (4) an understanding of the interdependence of all living creatures, especially within the biological realm; (5) criteria of discerning between the competing interests of species; (6) a commitment to lifestyles and economic and political systems that promote ecological sustainability; and (7) cultivating a sense of our shared "poverty" (in the Franciscan sense) with all creatures (*Jesus the Wisdom of God: An Ecological Theology* [Maryknoll, N.Y.: Orbis Books, 1995]), 153–71. Regarding this last point, Michael J. and Kenneth R. Himes make a compelling case for being in solidarity with non-human creatures through an awareness of our shared "poverty" (or contingency) and the "sacramentality" of all creatures (see their *Fullness of Faith: The Public Significance of Theology* [Mahwah, N.J.: Paulist Press, 1991], 104–24.

61. We echo here the well-known words of Leo the Great, that "*quod conspicuum erat in Christo transivit in Ecclesiae sacramenta*" (Sermon 74, par. 2).

62. Edward Schillebeeckx, *Christ the Sacrament of the Encounter with God* (Kansas City, Mo.: Sheed & Ward, 1963), 47–89.

63. Ward, *Cities of God,* 153.

64. Louis-Marie Chauvet, *The Sacraments: The World of God at the Mercy of the Body* (Collegeville, Minn.: The Liturgical Press, 2001), 31.

65. Ibid.

66. Ibid., 32.

67. Ward, *Cities of God,* 153.

68. Martelet, *The Risen Christ and the Eucharistic World,* 35.

69. "The consecrated bread does not cease to be bread. On the contrary, it becomes integral bread, a bread that contains the entire reality, a bread that is divine and material and human at the same time. It is the revelation of the cosmotheandric nature of reality.... The Mystical Body does not mean just a small group of humans. It extends to the 'breadth' of the entire universe in its proper status" (Raimon Panikkar, *The Cosmotheandric Experience: Emerging Religious Consciousness* [Maryknoll, N.Y.: Orbis Books, 1993], 69).

70. Irenaeus of Lyons, *Against Heresies,* V.34.2, 180.

71. It is true that phenomenology has played an important role in these chapters to make the doctrine more intelligible. That being said, a certain kind of phenomenology has been selected and incorporated into these considerations because it is already congenial to some of the claims theological anthropology makes regarding the embodied nature of human existence. In other words, phenomenology has been internalized for explicitly theological purposes. Such an approach is not foundationalism. It is, rather, a more *ad hoc* appropriation.

Part Two

1. Caird, *New Testament Theology,* 118–20.

2. Karl Barth, *Church Dogmatics,* I/II, *The Doctrine of the Word of God,* trans. G. T. Thomason and Harold Knight, ed. G. W. Bromiley and T. F. Torrance (Edinburgh: T. & T. Clark, 1956), 115–16. Italics mine.

3. Ibid., 115.
4. Walter Brueggemann, *The Prophetic Imagination,* 2d. ed. (Minneapolis: Fortress Press, 2001), 51.
5. Williams, *Resurrection,* 8.
6. Ibid.
7. Ibid., 9.
8. Pannenberg, *Jesus — God and Man,* 69.
9. Ibid.
10. Paul Ricoeur, "The Logic of Jesus, the Logic of God," in *Figuring the Sacred: Religion, Narrative, and Imagination,* trans. David Pellauer, ed Mark I. Wallace (Minneapolis: Fortress Press, 1995), 279–83.
11. "An abstract Christology, a doctrinal system, a general religious knowledge on the subject of grace or on the forgiveness of sins, renders discipleship superfluous, and in fact they positively exclude any idea of discipleship whatsoever, and are essentially inimical to the whole conception of following Christ. With an abstract idea it is possible to enter into a relation of formal knowledge, to become enthusiastic about it, and perhaps even to put it into practice; but it can never be followed in personal obedience. Christianity without the living Christ is inevitably Christianity without discipleship, and Christianity without discipleship is always Christianity without Christ" (Dietrich Bonhoeffer, *The Cost of Discipleship* [New York: Macmillan, 1963], 63–64).
12. Williams, *Resurrection,* 11.

Chapter Five

1. The phrase is John J. Collins's from his *The Apocalyptic Imagination: An Introduction to Jewish Apocalyptic Literature,* 2d. ed. (Grand Rapids: Eerdmans, 1998).
2. Klaus Koch surveys the variety of allergic reactions to apocalyptic in the fields of critical exegesis and systematic theology in his *The Rediscovery of Apocalyptic,* trans. Margaret Kohl (Naperville, Ill.: Alec R. Allenson, 1972).
3. Karl Rahner, "The Hermeneutics of Eschatological Assertions," *Theological Investigations,* vol. 4, 334. Italics mine.
4. Ibid., 326, 336. For Bultmann's systematic treatment of eschatological themes, see his Gifford Lectures, *History and Eschatology,* especially 138–55.
5. Rahner, "The Hermeneutics of Eschatological Assertions," 337.
6. Ibid.
7. Paul D. Hanson suggests that we may distinguish between *apocalyptic* as a literary genre, *apocalyptic eschatology* as a theological worldview, and *apocalypticism* as a sociological phenomenon. Though all three may be present, they cannot be identified. Particularly pertinent to our present purposes is Hanson's assertion that *apocalyptic eschatology* does not necessarily adopt *apocalyptic* as its primary idiom of expression (*The Dawn of Apocalyptic: The Historical and Sociological Roots of Jewish Apocalyptic Eschatology* [Philadelphia: Fortress Press, 1979], 427–44). See also Paul D. Hanson, "Apocalypticism," in *Interpreter's Dictionary of the Bible,* supplementary volume (Nashville: Abingdon Press, 1974), 27–34.
8. The following is a widely used description of apocalyptic formulated by the Society of Biblical Literature Genres: It is "a genre of revelatory literature with a narrative framework, in which a revelation is mediated by an otherworldly being to

a human recipient, disclosing a transcendent reality which is both temporal, insofar as it envisages eschatological salvation, and spatial insofar as it involves another, supernatural world" (*Apocalypse: The Morphology of a Genre*, ed. John J. Collins [Semeia 14; Missoula, Mont.: Scholars Press, 1979], 9).

9. Better known examples are pseudepigraphal: *Apocalypse of Zephaniah, 3 Baruch, 1–3 Enoch, Testimony of Abraham*, etc.

10. Books that are neither canonical nor deuterocanonical include: *Jubilees, 2 Baruch*, and *4 Ezra*. For more on the category distinction between the "otherworldly journey" and "historical" forms of apocalypse, see Collins, *The Apocalyptic Imagination*, 2–11.

11. "Beyond the thresholds of life and of this world we can only see as in a glass darkly. The apocalyptic revelations are symbolic attempts to penetrate the darkness, which provide ways of imagining the unknown, not factual knowledge" (ibid., 282).

12. Ibid., 283.

13. Ibid.

14. As Johan Christiaan Beker has shown in his *Paul the Apostle: The Triumph of God in Life and Thought* (Philadelphia: Fortress Press, 1980); and *The Triumph of God: The Essence of Paul's Thought*, trans. Loren T. Stuckenbruck (Minneapolis: Fortress Press, 1990), 34–35. See also M. C. de Boer, "Paul and Apocalyptic Eschatology," in *The Continuum History of Apocalypticism*, ed. Bernard J. McGinn, John J. Collins, and Stephen J. Stein (New York: Continuum, 2003), 166–94.

15. Beker, *Paul the Apostle*, 135–81.

16. These include the "combat myth," heavenly journeys, and prophecy after the fact (*vaticina ex eventu*). For a helpful synopsis of this lineage, see Richard J. Clifford, "The Roots of Apocalypticism in Near Eastern Myth," in *The Continuum History of Apocalypticism*, 3–29.

17. Wayne A. Meeks, "Social Functions of Apocalyptic Language in Pauline Christianity," in *Apocalypticism in the Mediterranean World and the Near East*, 2d. ed., ed. David Hellholm (Tübingen: J. C. B. Mohr, 1989), 687.

18. Brueggemann, *The Prophetic Imagination*, 70, 74

19. In developing these four motifs, I draw explicitly from the work of Johan Christiaan Beker (*Paul the Apostle*, 136; *The Triumph of God*, 21). Beker himself condenses the eight motifs elaborated by Klaus Koch (see *The Rediscovery of Apocalyptic*, 28–35).

20. Walter Brueggemann, *Theology of the Old Testament: Testimony, Dispute, Advocacy* (Minneapolis: Fortress Press, 1997), 178.

21. Ibid., 174–76.

22. Ibid., 174.

23. Ibid., 172.

24. Collins, *The Apocalyptic Imagination*, 113.

25. Wright, *The New Testament and the People of God*, 247ff.

26. For more on this, see chapter 3.

27. "[S]ince the exodus had long been associated with the act of creation itself, metaphors from creation would likewise be appropriate. The sun would be turned to darkness, the moon to blood. This is to say: when the covenant god acts, it will be an event (however 'this-world' by post-enlightenment standards, and however describable by secular historians) of cosmic significance.... Within the context of creational and covenantal monotheism, apocalyptic language makes excellent sense.

Indeed, it is not easy to see what better language-system could have been chosen to articulate Israel's hope and invest it with its full-perceived significance" (Wright, *The New Testament and the People of God,* 283).

28. I am specifically invoking Walter Wink's trilogy on "the powers" here (*Naming the Powers: The Language of Power in the New Testament* [Philadelphia: Fortress Press, 1984]; *Unmasking the Powers: The Invisible Forces that Determine Human Existence* [Philadelphia: Fortress Press, 1986]; *Engaging the Powers: Discernment and Resistance in a World of Domination* [Minneapolis: Fortress Press, 1992]). For a more condensed version of the trilogy, see his *The Powers That Be: Theology for a New Millennium* (New York: Doubleday, 1998).

29. Meeks, "The Social Functions of Apocalyptic Language in Pauline Christianity," 689.

30. Wright, *The New Testament and the People of God,* 320–34.

31. Richard A. Horsley, *Jesus and the Spiral of Violence: Popular Jewish Resistance in Roman Palestine* (San Francisco: Harper & Row, 1987), 137.

32. Ibid., 139, 144. Horsley is responding here to Walter Schmithals, *The Apocalyptic Movement: Introduction and Interpretation* (Nashville: Abingdon, 1975), 108.

33. Meeks, "Social Functions of Apocalyptic Language," 687.

34. Beker, *The Triumph of God,* 25.

35. Ibid., 25–26.

36. According to Hanson, "apocalypticism" is a socio-religious movement latent in the perspective of apocalyptic eschatology, though the two cannot be simply identified. "At the point where the disappointments of history lead a group to embrace that perspective as an ideology, using it moreover to resolve the contradictions between traditional hopes and frustrating historical realities and to establish the identity of that group vis-à-vis other groups as well as the Deity, we can speak of the birth of an apocalyptic movement" (*The Dawn of Apocalyptic,* 432.)

37. Beker, *The Triumph of God,* 31–36; *Paul the Apostle,* 143–49.

38. See Rahner's introduction to James Bacik, *Apologetics and the Eclipse of Mystery: Mystagogy According to Karl Rahner* (Notre Dame, Ind.: University of Notre Dame Press, 1980), ix.

39. Johann Baptist Metz, *Faith in History and Society: Toward a Practical Fundamental Theology,* trans. David Smith (New York: Crossroad, 1980), 73.

40. Ibid., 102.

41. It is not possible to enter here into the current debates over the more precise relationship between Christian theology and the sort of political and social theories that inform the work of figures like Johann Baptist Metz, Edward Schillebeeckx, and Jon Sobrino. Neither is it possible here to outline Metz's "practical-fundamental theology" in a systematic way. For a more thorough treatment of Metz's project, the reader may refer to J. Matthew Ashley, *Interruptions: Mysticism, Politics and Theology in the Work of Johann Baptist Metz* (Notre Dame, Ind.: University of Notre Dame Press, 1998); Rebecca Chopp, *The Praxis of Suffering: An Interpretation of Liberation and Political Theologies* (Maryknoll N.Y.: Orbis Books, 1986); Roger Dick Johns, *Man in the World: The Political Theology of Johannes Baptist Metz* (Missoula, Mont.: Scholars Press, 1976); and Bruce T. Morrill, *Anamnesis as Dangerous Memory: Political and Liturgical Theology in Dialogue* (Collegeville, Minn.: The Liturgical Press, 2000). Our present interests concern the themes of apocalyptic

eschatology, suffering, and memory as sources for *any* theology concerned with the relationship between gospel and society, no matter its specific stance on available theoretical tools and practical solutions.

42. Metz acknowledges that while apocalyptic has preoccupied him throughout his career, "I have not learned to speak consistently and convincingly about it" (*A Passion for God: The Mystical-Political Dimension of Christianity,* trans. J. Matthew Ashley [New York: Paulist Press, 1998], 47). The reason for this surely has everything to do with the challenging character of apocalyptic discourse as one that attempts to speak "otherwise" about history.

43. Schillebeeckx, *Jesus,* 615. Similarly, Metz: "The slightest trace of senseless suffering in the world of human experience gives the lie to all affirmative ontology and all teleology and is clearly revealed as a modern mythology. Human suffering resists all attempts to interpret history and historical processes in the light of nature and nature as the subject of such historical processes" (*Faith in History and Society,* 108).

44. See especially his essay "The Church after Auschwitz," in *A Passion for God,* 121–32.

45. This does not mean that theology cannot be "systematic," insofar as theology attempts to coordinate various areas (or subfields) to illuminate their interrelationships and internal coherence. The critique of theology as a "system" means, rather, the critique of the attempt to secure theology within a universally valid theoretical foundation, especially one that interprets the world process in teleological terms.

46. Metz, *Faith in History and Society,* 170. See also Johann Baptist Metz, "Time Without a Finale: The Background to the Debate on 'Resurrection or Reincarnation,'" in *Reincarnation or Resurrection?,* Concilium, ed. Hermann Häring and J. B. Metz (Maryknoll, N.Y.: Orbis Books, 1993), 124–31.

47. Metz, *Faith in History and Society,* 6.

48. Emmanuel Levinas, *Totality and Infinity: An Essay on Exteriority,* trans. Alphonso Lingis (Pittsburgh, Pa.: Duquesne University Press, 1969), 22–23.

49. Metz, *A Passion for God,* 52.

50. Metz, *Faith in History and Society,* 108.

51. For a helpful clarification of innocent suffering along these terms, see John E. Thiel, *God, Evil, and Innocent Suffering: A Theological Reflection* (New York: Herder & Herder, 2002). Thiel provides a compelling case for affirming innocent suffering in the Christian theological tradition against various theodicies that would ascribe all evil and suffering to a primordial fall (Augustine), to the inevitable consequence of the world-process or human freedom (John Hick, Richard Swinburne), or to characterizations of God as compromised in power (process thought).

52. Schillebeeckx, *Christ,* 725.

53. Gustavo Gutiérrez, *On Job: God-talk and the Suffering of the Innocent,* trans. Matthew J. O'Connell (Maryknoll, N.Y.: Orbis Books, 1997), 102.

54. "To develop a *logos* on *theos* — a theology — today is to start by facing evil and suffering. To develop a theology today is to reject modern theodicies in their modern forms of purely theoretical solutions which, however finely tuned in argument and however analytically precise in concept, are somewhat beside the point — the point of facing with hope the horror while still speaking and acting at all by naming and thinking the God of genuine hope" (David Tracy, "Evil, Suffering, Hope: The

Search for New Forms of Contemporary Theodicy," in *Proceedings of the Catholic Theological Society of America* 50 (1995): 16.

55. Metz, *A Passion for God*, 70–71.
56. Ibid., 71.
57. Ibid., 82.
58. Metz, *Faith in History and Society*, 117.
59. Metz, *A Passion for God*, 71.
60. Ibid., 66–67.
61. Ibid., 67.

62. See the remarkable and deeply personal work of Alan E. Lewis which takes the perspective of Holy Saturday in order to read the narrative of Jesus' death and resurrection "from within" (*Between Cross and Resurrection: A Theology of Holy Saturday* [Grand Rapids: Eerdmans, 2001]).

63. As Thiel notes, every theodicy includes a plea of ignorance. "Believers meet a wall of ignorance when they question why the God of the legal explanation would bring the punishment of suffering and death on persons who seem so completely innocent. Believers meet a wall of ignorance when they question what purpose the God of the providential explanation might have in willing these or those circumstances of someone's suffering and death" (*God, Evil and Innocent Suffering*, 98). In this case, we plead a "learned ignorance" as to why suffering and evil exist in the way and degree they do while clinging to the promise of God made available to us in Christ that suffering and evil will not ultimately prevail.

64. Edward Schillebeeckx, *Christ*, 729.
65. Ibid.
66. Ibid.
67. Ibid., 724, 730.
68. Ibid., 726.

69. Karl Rahner, "The Concept of Mystery in Catholic Theology," *Theological Investigations* 4, 36–73. For Rahner's approach to the mystery of suffering and its relationship to the mystery of God, see his "Why Does God Allow Us to Suffer?" *Theological Investigations* 19, trans. Edward Quinn (New York: Crossroad, 1983), 194–208. Rahner criticizes several theoretical theodicies and argues that innocent suffering in the world presents a genuine scandal to theology. This scandal cannot be theoretically resolved, but only seen in relation to the incomprehensible mystery of God. "There is no blessed light to illumine the dark abyss of suffering other than God himself. And we find him only when we lovingly assent to the incomprehensibility of God himself, without which he would not be God" (p. 208). To some extent, Rahner's approach is similar to Metz's in that both repudiate theoretical resolutions to evil and suffering. And yet, Metz's apophaticism is different than Rahner's inasmuch as Metz approaches the incomprehensibility of suffering in terms of protest, which acts as a critical stimulus for praxis in history. Rahner's apophaticism is more sapiential than apocalyptic, and less explicitly related to the call for overcoming, to the extent that this is possible for us, those conditions in history that continue to produce innocent suffering.

70. Metz, *Faith in History and Society*, 110.
71. Ibid.
72. Ibid., 111.
73. Ibid., 113. Italics mine.

74. Ibid., 113–14.
75. Wright, *The Resurrection of the Son of God*, 730.
76. Metz, *Faith in History and Society*, 91.
77. Ibid., 52. Italics mine.

Chapter Six

1. For a helpful comparative study of apocalyptic eschatology in Metz and Sobrino, see J. Matthew Ashley, "Apocalypticism in Political and Liberation Theology: Toward an Historical *Docta Ignorantia*," *Horizons* 27/1 (2000): 22–43.
2. Jon Sobrino, *Christ the Liberator: A View from the Victims*, trans. Paul Burns (Maryknoll, N.Y.: Orbis Books, 2001). The first volume of Sobrino's two-volume christology focuses on the historical ministry and death of Jesus of Nazareth (*Jesus the Liberator: A Historical-Theological Reading of Jesus of Nazareth*, trans. Paul Burns and Francis McDonagh [Maryknoll, N.Y.: Orbis Books, 1993]). Sobrino's earlier major work in christology is very much worth consulting (*Christology at the Crossroads: A Latin American Approach*, trans. John Drury [Maryknoll, N.Y.: Orbis Books, 1973]), as is his more recent and popularly accessible *Jesus in Latin America*, trans. Robert R. Barr (Maryknoll, N.Y.: Orbis Books, 1987).
3. Sobrino, *Christ the Liberator*, 12.
4. Pannenberg, *Jesus — God and Man*, 69–72.
5. Wolfhart Pannenberg, "Dogmatic Theses on the Doctrine of Revelation," in *Revelation as History*, trans. David Granskou, ed. Wolfhart Pannenberg (Toronto: Macmillan, 1968), 125–58.
6. Sobrino, *Christ the Liberator*, 28. See the similar critique of Pannenberg in *Jesus the Liberator*, 112–17 and *Christology at the Crossroads*, 250–51. Sobrino follows Jürgen Moltmann's critique of Pannenberg's *Revelation as History* on this point ("Antwort auf die Kritik der Theologie der Hoffnung," in *Diskussion über die "Theologie der Hoffnung" von Jürgen Moltmann*, ed. Wolf-Dieter Marsch [München: Kaiser, 1967], 201–38).
7. Sobrino, *Christology at the Crossroads*, 243.
8. Sobrino, *Christ the Liberator*, 44.
9. Ibid., 45. Italics mine. Elsewhere, Sobrino states: "[W]e cannot assume at the start that we already know who God is and move from there to an understanding of resurrection. As was the case with the cross of Jesus, we can only learn who God is from the cross and resurrection of Jesus" (*Christology at the Crossroads*, 240).
10. Sobrino, *Christ the Liberator*, 45. See also the more condensed analysis in *Jesus in Latin America*, 148–58.
11. Sobrino, *Christ the Liberator*, 44.
12. Ibid., 84.
13. Ibid., 80–81.
14. Ibid., 84.
15. Ibid., 83.
16. Sobrino, *Jesus the Liberator*, 79.
17. Ibid., 83–84.
18. Ibid., 83. Sobrino frequently appeals to the statement made at the Third General Conference of the Latin American Episcopate (CELAM) held in Puebla in 1979: "[T]he poor merit preferential attention, whatever may be the moral or personal situation in which they find themselves. Made in the image and likeness of

God (Gen. 1:26–28) to be his children, this image is dimmed and even defiled. That is why God takes on their defense and loves them (Matt. 5:45; James 2:5). That is why the poor are the first ones to whom Jesus' mission is directed (Luke. 4:18–21), and why the evangelization of the poor is the supreme sign and proof of his mission (Luke 7:21–23)" ("Evangelization in Latin America's Present and Future," par. 1142, in *Puebla and Beyond: Documentation and Commentary*, ed. John Eagleson and Philip Scharper, trans. John Drury [Maryknoll, N.Y.: Orbis Books, 1979], 265).

19. Marion, *Being Given*, 241.

20. Sobrino does not suggest that the poor are the primary cause of salvation, which is God's prerogative alone, but a secondary or mediating ("sacramental") cause, inasmuch as salvation is mediated in and through history, without being reducible to history (*Jesus the Liberator*, 262).

21. Ibid., 263–64.

22. Ibid., 264.

23. See Jon Sobrino, "Latin America: Place of Sin and Place of Forgiveness" and "Personal Sin, Forgiveness, and Liberation" in *The Principle of Mercy: Taking the Crucified People Down from the Cross* (Maryknoll, N.Y.: Orbis Books, 1994), 58–68, 83–101.

24. Rahner, *Foundations of Christian Faith*, 93.

25. Sobrino, *Jesus the Liberator*, 160–92.

26. See also Eph. 2:1ff.; 3:10; Col. 1:16; 2:15; 1 Cor. 2:8; 15:24–26; Rom. 8:38.

27. Sobrino, *Jesus the Liberator*, 61.

28. Ibid.

29. Ibid., 50.

30. See chapter 5, n. 28.

31. This threefold, narrative pattern follows John Howard Yoder's similar analysis in *The Politics of Jesus: Vicit Agnus Noster*, 2d. ed. (Grand Rapids: Eerdmans, 1994), 134–61. See also the important work of Hendrikus Berkhof, who influences both Wink and Yoder, and who helped to usher in new interest in the powers in biblical theology (*Christ and the Powers* [Scottdale, Pa.: Herald Press, 1962]). For yet another influential work on the powers, see G. B. Caird, *Principalities and Powers: A Study in Pauline Theology* (Oxford: Clarendon Press, 1956).

32. Wink, *Engaging the Powers*, 73.

33. Sobrino, *Jesus the Liberator*, 94.

34. Ashley, "Apocalypticism in Political and Liberation Theology," 30.

35. See Sobrino, *Christ the Liberator*, 4–5; *Jesus the Liberator*, 254–71; *Jesus in Latin America*, 159–65; "A Crucified People's Faith in the Son of God," in *The Principle of Mercy*, 159–65.

36. Sobrino characterizes the situation in this way: "Poverty, *first and foremost*, is the situation in which by far the greater part of the human race lives, bowed down under the weight of life. For these people, survival is their greatest problem and death their closest destiny. Poverty means, then, grave difficulty in surviving as the human species, the situation in which, according to the 1996 report of the United Nations Development Program, some three billion human beings find themselves — and their numbers are growing in some places. Eighty-nine countries are now poorer than they were ten years ago, and some of those poorer than thirty years ago.... *In the second place,* the inequality within the species makes it impossible to use the metaphorical — but essential in Christian faith — language of the

family to describe it. The same report tells us that the gulf between rich and poor is growing. The combined wealth of the 358 individuals whose assets exceed one billion dollars is greater than the combined annual income of 45 percent of the world's population.... *In the third place,* the deepest roots of this poverty are historical: they lie in structural injustice. The 'poor' are impoverished; the 'indigenous' are stripped of cultural identity.... Poverty, *finally,* is the most lasting form of violence and the violence that is committed with the greatest impunity. Holocausts and massacres — sometimes — produce their Nurembergs, but not the depredations on the continent of Latin America or the exploitation of Africa. What court of appeal is there for the thirty-five or forty million people who die annually of hunger or hunger-related diseases? And the most maddening thing is that today it *is* possible to eliminate poverty.... This is where the victims view the matter from" (*Christ the Liberator,* 4–5).

37. Ibid.

38. John J. Collins, "Apocalyptic Eschatology as the Transcendence of Death," *Catholic Bible Quarterly* 36.01 (1974): 41.

39. Sobrino, *Christ the Liberator,* 43. "God has raised a crucified one, and from this moment forward there is hope for the crucified of history" (*Jesus in Latin America,* 151).

40. Collins, "Apocalyptic Eschatology as the Transcendence of Death," 41.

41. Ashley, "Apocalypticism in Political and Liberation Theology," 30.

42. De Certeau, "How is Christianity Thinkable Today?," 145.

43. Sobrino, *Christ the Liberator,* 67.

44. Ibid., 54–65.

45. Ibid., 11.

46. Ibid., 68–69. Elsewhere, Sobrino states that "between the reality of the resurrection, including the experience of the appearances, and ourselves, there is an inescapable abyss" (12).

47. Ibid., 70.

48. Ibid. Distinction does not negate the possibility of participation, quite the contrary. Analogical participation presupposes difference. Difference is the "space" that allows for non-identical repetition.

49. Ibid., 70. Sobrino speaks similarly of a "christological deism" in his *Jesus the Liberator* (25).

50. Sobrino, *Christ the Liberator,* 13, 14.

51. Ibid., 75–76. "The fact that life can be celebrated is basic to understanding the living resurrection of Jesus.... It is the joy of communities that, despite everything, come together to sing and recite poetry, to show that they are happy they are together, to celebrate the eucharist" (ibid., 77).

52. Ibid., 74–75.

53. Ibid., 71–72.

54. "It is the joy of Archbishop Romero, besieged on all sides and by all powers, who was filled with joy when he visited the communities, and who exclaimed — seemingly rhetorically but most truly — that 'with this people it costs nothing to be a good shepherd.' It cost him his life, but the people provided him with a joy no one could take away, and in this joy the triumph of the resurrection was made historically present to him" (ibid., 77).

55. Ibid., 76–77. One thinks immediately in this context of the famous words of Archbishop Oscar Romero spoken shortly before his assassination: "I have often been threatened with death. I must tell you, as a Christian, I do not believe in death without resurrection. If I am killed, I shall arise in the Salvadoran people. I say it without boasting, with the greatest humility" (quoted in James Brockman, *Romero: A Life* (Maryknoll, N.Y.: Orbis, 1989), 248.

56. Ibid., 49.

57. Sobrino, *Jesus the Liberator*, 262–63. See also Sobrino, "The Crucified Peoples: Yahweh's Suffering Servant Today," in *The Principle of Mercy*, 49–57.

58. Sobrino, *Christology at the Crossroads*, 254.

59. Ibid., 255.

60. Schillebeeckx, *Jesus*, 619. For more on Schillebeeckx's shift towards praxis in hermeneutics, see especially his "Towards a Catholic Use of Hermeneutics," in *God the Future of Man*, trans. N. D. Smith (London: Sheed & Ward, 1969), 3–49; and *The Understanding of Faith: Interpretation and Criticism*, trans. N. D. Smith (New York: Crossroad, 1974).

61. Ibid., 620.

62. Schillebeeckx, *Christ*, 801.

63. Jürgen Moltmann, *The Way of Jesus Christ: Christology in Messianic Dimensions*, trans. Margaret Kohl (New York: HarperCollins, 1990), 241.

64. See Beker's treatment of Paul's exhortatory discourses and their relationship to apocalyptic expectation and Jesus' resurrection (*Paul the Apostle*, 272–302).

65. Moltmann, *The Way of Jesus Christ*, 241.

66. Jürgen Moltmann, *Theology of Hope*, 48. See also Jürgen Moltmann, "The Hope of Resurrection and the Practice of Liberation," in *The Future of Creation: Collected Essays*, trans. Margaret Kohl (London: SCM, 1979), 97–114.

67. Sobrino, *Jesus the Liberator*, 196.

68. Ibid.

69. Ibid., 210.

70. Sobrino speaks personally of the murder of his fellow Jesuits and the way it shapes his theology of the cross in *Jesus the Liberator*, 235ff. See also his "The Legacy of the Martyrs of the Central American University" and "A Letter to Ignacio Ellacuría" in *The Principle of Mercy*, 173–85, 187–89.

71. Sobrino, *Christ the Liberator*, 12. See Sobrino's moving memoriam, written shortly after Ellacuría's death and read at Mass in November 1990 ("A Letter to Ignacio Ellacuría," in *The Principle of Mercy*, 187–89).

72. Wright, *Resurrection of the Son of God*, 138. In light of its explosive possibilities, we shall have to ask in the following chapter how the Christian appropriation of resurrection language did not lead Christians to engage in violent conflict with imperial power, even if the theme of vindication would continue to empower them to resist its domination.

73. Gutiérrez, *On Job: God-talk and the Suffering of the Innocent*, 95.

74. Miroslav Volf, *Exclusion and Embrace: A Theological Exploration of Identity, Otherness, and Reconciliation* (Nashville: Abingdon Press, 1996), 103.

75. Ibid.

76. Ibid., 105.

77. Ibid., 117.

Chapter Seven

1. Raymund Schwager, *Must There Be Scapegoats? Violence and Redemption in the Bible*, trans. Maria L. Assad (San Francisco: Harper & Row, 1987), 47.
2. Ibid.
3. Ibid., 55.
4. Irenaeus of Lyons, *Against Heresies*, I.8.1.
5. Ibid., I.27.4.
6. Ibid., V.14.1-4, 18.3, 19.1.
7. Ibid., III.10.2 (Von Balthasar, *The Scandal of the Incarnation*, 46).
8. D. T. Suzuki, *Mysticism Christian and Buddhist: The Eastern and Western Way* (New York: Collier Books, 1962), 98.
9. Ibid., 103.
10. Schwager, *Must There Be Scapegoats?*, 119.
11. S. Mark Heim, *Saved from Sacrifice: A Theology of the Cross* (Grand Rapids: Eerdmans, 2006), 101-2.
12. Jacques Derrida, "Plato's Pharmacy," in *Dissemination*, trans. Barbara Johnson (Chicago: University of Chicago Press, 1981), 63-171; René Girard, *Violence and the Sacred*, trans. Patrick Gregory (Baltimore: Johns Hopkins University Press, 1972), see especially 93-99, 297-308. For a comparative study of Derrida and Girard, see Andrew J. McKenna, *Violence and Difference: Girard, Derrida, and Deconstruction* (Urbana: University of Illinois Press, 1992).
13. Gil Ballie, *Violence Unveiled: Humanity at the Crossroads* (New York: Crossroad, 1995), 87.
14. Girard, *Violence and the Sacred*, 250-73.
15. René Girard, *I See Satan Fall Like Lightning*, trans. James G. Williams (Maryknoll, N.Y.: Orbis Book, 2001), 24. Girard states that this does not mean sacrificial religion is the worship of violence. It involves the limited use of a highly focused violence, symbolic and ritually remembered, to maintain peace. Sacrificial religion is "nothing other than this immense effort to keep the peace. *The sacred is violence,* but if religious man worships violence it is only insofar as the worship of violence is supposed to bring peace; religion is entirely concerned with peace, but the means it has of bringing it about are never free of sacrificial violence. To see in my theory some sort of 'cult of violence,' approval of sacrifice, or, at the other extreme, a blanket condemnation of human culture, is to miss the point entirely" (René Girard, *Things Hidden Since the Foundation of the World*, trans. Stephen Bann and Michael Metteer [Stanford, Calif.: Stanford University Press, 1987], 32).
16. It is not possible to provide a comprehensive overview of Girard's anthropology here, but neither is it necessary for my limited purposes. Nor will I be able to address some of the more sensitive areas of Girardian approaches to scriptural interpretation. In general I might say that while Girard's thought exerts considerable influence on my own approach in anthropology and soteriology, there are certain features of it that are still only now being fleshed out and absorbed. I am in agreement with many who argue that Girard's thought represents a staggering breakthrough in the humanities, not least in theology. Though there are certain aspects of his thought that will require ongoing modification and amplification, Girard's will likely be remembered as one of the most important contributions to theological anthropology and soteriology in the twentieth century. For some of the most helpful introductions

to and/or applications of Girard's thought in biblical, historical, and systematic theology, see the following (some have already been fully cited): Alison, *The Joy of Being Wrong*; Alison, *Raising Abel: The Recovery of the Eschatological Imagination* (New York: Herder & Herder/Crossroad, 1996); Gil Ballie, *Violence Unveiled*; Anthony Bartlett, *Cross Purposes: The Violent Grammar of Christian Atonement* (Valley Forge, Pa.: Trinity Press International, 2001); Chris Fleming, *René Girard: Violence and Mimesis* (Cambridge, Eng: Polity Press, 2004); Richard Golson, *René Girard and Myth: An Introduction* (New York: Routledge, 2001); Robert G. Hammerton-Kelly, *The Gospel and the Sacred: Poetics of Violence in Mark* (Minneapolis: Fortress Press, 1994); Robert G. Hammerton-Kelly, *Sacred Violence: Paul's Hermeneutic of the Cross* (Minneapolis: Fortress Press, 1992); Heim, *Saved from Sacrifice*; Michael Kirwin, *Discovering Girard* (Cambridge, Mass.: Cowley Publications, 2005); Robert Leo D. Lefebure, *Revelation, the Religions, and Violence* (Maryknoll, N.Y.: Orbis Books, 2000); Andrew J. McKenna, ed., *René Girard and Biblical Studies* (Decatur, Ga.: Scholars Press, 1985); Schwager, *Must There Be Scapegoats?*; Raymund Schwager, *Jesus and the Drama of Salvation: Toward a Biblical Doctrine of Redemption*, trans. James G. Williams and Paul Haddon [New York: Herder & Herder, 1999]; Willard Swartley, *Covenant of Peace: The Missing Peace in New Testament Theology and Ethics* (Grand Rapids: Eerdmans, 2006); Willard Swartley, ed., *Violence Renounced: René Girard, Biblical Studies, and Peacemaking* (Telford, Pa.: Cascadia Publishing House, 2000); and James G. Williams, *The Bible, Violence, and the Sacred: Liberation from the Myth of Sanctioned Violence* (Valley Forge, Pa.: Trinity Press International, 1991).

17. Quoted in Gustaf Aulén, *Christus Victor: An Historical Study of the Three Main Types of the Idea of the Atonement*, trans. A. G. Herbert (New York: Macmillan, 1969), 27 (*Against Heresies*, V., 1.1).

18. "Ask ten people what they think of the Hebrew Scriptures — the 'Old Testament' — and even if they've never opened it, eight of the ten will tell you that they are put off by its violence. The world over which myth presides with its majestic poise is no less violent. Its violence is simply better veiled and suffused with grandeur" (Gil Bailie, *Violence Unveiled: Humanity at the Crossroads*, 44).

19. Heim, *Saved from Sacrifice*, 102.

20. Ibid.

21. Ibid., 103.

22. "The Bible's anthropological distinction lies in the fact that in it an empathy for victims again and again overwhelms the Bible's own attempt to mythologize its violence and venerate it as divinely decreed" (Bailie, *Violence Unveiled*, 44). "The scapegoat critique in the biblical tradition emerges as a critique *of* that tradition. This is the weight of the prophetic voices, who reminded Israel that despite the calling of the new and true God they steadily fell always into old ways, doing so even in the name of God. The way the story is told to us who belong to it forbids that we should suppose we are exempt from the danger it discovers" (Heim, *Saved from Sacrifice*, 103).

23. See Heim's penetrating analysis of anti-Semitism from a Girardian perspective (ibid., 207–15). For some of Girard's writings dealing with both Christian anti-Semitism and inaccurate accusations of anti-Semitism in the gospels, see his "The Question of Anti-Semitism in the Gospels," in *The Girard Reader,* ed. James G.

Williams (New York: Herder & Herder, 2005), 211–21; René Girard, *The Scapegoat*, trans. Yvonne Freccero (Baltimore: Johns Hopkins University Press, 1986), 1–23; *Things Hidden Since the Foundation of the World*, 245–53.

24. Heim, *Saved from Sacrifice*, 103.

25. Aristotle, "Poetics," in *On Man in the Universe*, trans. Samuel Henry Butcher, ed. Louise Ropes Loomis (Roslyn, N.Y.: Walter J. Black, 1943), IV, 421.

26. See Merleau-Ponty, "The Body as Expression and Speech," 202–32.

27. According to Marion, phenomenology discloses an order of manifestation which reverses that assumed by transcendental analysis: "relation here precedes individuality"; "the interloqué, resulting from a summons, is taken and overwhelmed (taken over or surprised) by a seizure"; "I receive *my self* from the call that gives me to myself before giving me anything whatsoever"; "my sole individuation or selfhood is found only in the facticity imposed on me by the word originally heard from the call, not pronounced by *myself*" (Marion, *Being Given*, 267–71). The parallels with Levinas here are quite obvious.

28. Girard, *Violence and the Sacred*, 145.

29. For applications in the realm of literature, see René Girard, *Deceit, Desire and the Novel: Self and Other in Literary Structure*, trans. Yvonne Freccero (Baltimore: Johns Hopkins University Press, 1965); *Resurrection from the Underground: Feodor Dostoevsky*, trans. James G. Williams (New York: Crossroad, 1997); and *A Theater of Envy: William Shakespeare* (New York: Oxford University Press, 1991).

30. "If desire were not mimetic, we would not be open to what is human or what is divine. Mimetic desire enables us to escape from the animal realm. It is responsible for the best and the worst in us, for what lowers us below the animal level as well as what elevates us above it" (Girard, *I See Satan Fall Like Lightning*, 16).

31. Alison, *The Joy of Being Wrong*, 33.

32. Much of Girard's *Things Hidden from the Foundation of the World* is a dialogue between Girard and Oughourlian, with approximately the latter third of the book focused on Oughourlian's "interdividual psychology." See also, Jean-Michel Oughourlian, *The Puppet of Desire: The Psychology of Hysteria, Possession, and Hypnosis*, trans. Eugene Webb (Stanford, Calif.: Stanford University Press, 1991).

33. Alison, *The Joy of Being Wrong*, 30.

34. Ibid., 32.

35. Ibid., 30.

36. Volf, *Exclusion and Embrace*, 74. Volf's analysis here is in conversation with Henri Lévy, Julia Kristeva, and Donald Horowitz.

37. I am inclined to agree with Wink about this: "Do these entities possess actual metaphysical *being*, or are they the 'corporate personality' or ethos or gestalt of a group, having no independent existence apart from the group? I leave that for the reader to decide. My main objection to personalizing demons is that they then are regarded as having a 'body' or form separate from the physical and historical institutions of which, on my theory, they are the actual interiority. Therefore I prefer to regard them as the impersonal spiritual realities at the center of institutional life" (*Engaging the Powers*, 9). Mark Heim also puts the matter well: "The evil of sacrifice is a supernatural, transpersonal power, in the sense that no one who takes part in it fully understands or intends all that it involves. It is greater than the sum of its parts. But on the other hand it is an intensely personal reality, for it can subsist only within the subjectivity of interpersonal relationships as the host for its parasitic

activity. Between a New Testament vision of the power of Satan and the demons and a thoroughly depersonalized and secular view of evil as nothing but ignorance or selfishness, we would be advised to prefer the first as an empirical description" (*Saved from Sacrifice*, 149).

38. Wink, *The Powers That Be*, 27–28. See also, *Engaging the Powers*, 3–10.
39. Quoted in Ballie, *Violence Unveiled*, 47.
40. Ibid., 47–48.
41. Ibid., 50.
42. Ibid., 89
43. Volf, *Exclusion and Embrace*, 86–87.
44. Ibid., 114.
45. Ibid., 117.
46. On the flip side, there are many who find the spectacle of violent conflict, particularly war, to be sublime, the very essence of life, so much so that when its time has past they look back upon it with nostalgia and yearning. Violence is transcendent, an "event" that draws the person out of the self into the ek-stasis of pure action, and thus something that can be loved and even worshipped. For the sublimity and quasi-religious character of war, see James Hillman, *A Terrible Love of War* (New York: Penguin Books, 2004), especially 104–77.
47. Volf, *Exclusion and Embrace*, 91.
48. This, in fact, is one of the important contributions of feminist appraisals of original sin: that the doctrine has traditionally emphasized the sin of excessive autonomy (or "pride") to the exclusion of the sin of excessive heteronomy (or "sloth"). According to a number of feminist theological anthropologies, the former construal of sin tends to be a more typically male temptation, while the latter has been the imposed lot of many women in patriarchal cultures. Although we cannot explore this important line of thinking more here, one critical way of advancing the present work would be to understand better how the scapegoating process is operative in gender relations, both in the ways women have been objectified and vilified in terms of "impurity" or "temptation" by men, and in the way, in the effort of working towards equality between men and women, "masculinity" has at times become problematized and even demonized.
49. Volf, *Exclusion and Embrace*, 91.
50. John Milbank, *Theology and Social Theory: Beyond Secular Reason* (Oxford: Blackwell, 1990), 278–325.
51. Heraclitus, "Fragments," in *The First Philosophers of Greece*, trans. and ed., Arthur Fairbanks (Scribner, 1898).
52. Friedrich Nietzsche, *Ecce Homo: How One Becomes What One Is*, trans. R. J. Hollingdale (New York: Penguin Books, 1979), 81.
53. Girard, *I See Satan Fall Like Lightning*, 15. See also René Girard, "The Goodness of Mimetic Desire," in *The Girard Reader*, 62–65. Among other reasons, this is why Milbank's reading of Girard as exhibiting an "ontology of violence" is off the mark (*Theology and Social Theory: Beyond Secular Reason*, 392–98). Hans Boersma continues this misreading of Girard in his *Violence, Hospitality, and the Cross: Reappropriating the Atonement Tradition* (Grand Rapids: Baker Academic, 2004), 133–51. Chris Flemming writes that we must "be very careful to distinguish Girard's insistence on the socio-historical pervasiveness of violence, and its (again, socio-historical) centrality to cultural and social structuration, from the idea that

violence is an inescapable metaphysical absolute, somehow inscribed in the very 'nature of things.' This distinction is, unfortunately, lost on John Milbank, who complains that Girard's socio-scientific expalanations are predicated on an almost Hobbesian metaphycs of violence" (Flemming, *René Girard*, n. 32, 175). For an extended defense of Girard from Milbank's criticisms, see Fergus Kerr, "Rescuing Girard's Argument," *Modern Theology* 8:4 (1992): 385–99.

54. Girard, *I See Satan Fall Like Lightning*, 16.
55. Ibid., 171.
56. Friedrich Nietzsche, *On the Genealogy of Morals: A Polemic*, trans. Douglas Smith (Oxford: Oxford University Press, 1996), 19.
57. Ibid., 19–20.
58. Friedrich Nietzsche, *The Will to Power*, trans. Walter Kaufmann and R. J. Hollingdale (New York: Random House, 1967), 142.
59. Girard, *I See Satan Fall Like Lightning*, 173.
60. Nietzsche, *The Will to Power*, 543.
61. Nietzsche, *On the Genealogy of Morals*, 35–36.
62. Ibid., 20.
63. Girard, *I See Satan Fall Like Lightning*, 161.
64. Ibid., 166.
65. Ibid., 168.
66. Ballie, *Violence Unveiled*, 19.
67. Heim, *Saved from Sacrifice*, 113.
68. Girard, *I See Satan Fall Like Lightning*, 118.
69. Williams, *The Bible, Violence, and the Sacred*, 38.
70. Girard, *I See Satan Fall Like Lightning*, 111.
71. Brueggemann, *The Prophetic Imagination*, 11–12.
72. Schwager, *Must There Be Scapegoats?*, 91–109.
73. Heim, *Saved from Sacrifice*, 89.
74. Bailie, *Violence Unveiled*, 44.
75. Girard's argument is structural: "We assert that certain texts are based on a real persecution because of the nature and the disposition of the persecutor stereotypes they portray. Without this origin it is impossible to explain why and how the same themes keep recurring in the same pattern" (*The Scapegoat*, 28).
76. Girard, *The Scapegoat*, 113.
77. Friedrich Nietzsche, "The Antichrist," in *The Complete Works of Friedrich Nietzsche*, vol. 16, ed. Oscar Levy, trans. Anthony M. Ludovici (New York: Russell & Russell, 1964), 195–96.
78. Volf, *Exclusion and Embrace*, 266–67.
79. Ibid., 266. Volf is influenced here in part by David Rensberger, "The Politics of John: The Trial of John in the Fourth Gospel," *Journal of Biblical Literature* 103.3 (1983): 395–411.
80. "There is nothing unique about the persecution in the story of Passion. The coalition of all the worldly powers is not unique. This same coalition is found at the origin of all myths. What is astonishing about the Gospels is that the unanimity is not emphasized in order to bow before, or submit to, its verdict as in all the mythological, political, and even philosophical texts, but to denounce its total mistake, its perfect example of nontruth" (Girard, *The Scapegoat*, 114–15).

81. See also Pilate's threefold assertion of Jesus' innocence in Luke (23:4, 14–15, 22) and later the Roman centurion's (23:47).

82. The gospel of John is written, of course, subsequent to the resurrection of Jesus. Like all the other writings in the New Testament, it is thoroughly shaped by an Easter hermeneutic. It is suffused with what Alison calls "the intelligence of the victim," by which he means, among other things, a framework of understanding that takes as its point of departure, and its perspective from beginning to end, the point of view of a risen victim. If sometimes modern exegetes find the fourth gospel to be less "historical" compared to the synoptic gospels, largely because of its later composition and long, poetic discourses that evidence a thorough absorption of Hellenistic conceptuality, we should see in it a further distillation, in a more contemplative idiom, of the intelligence of the victim that suffuses all the writings of the New Testament. Thus, when in those discourses Jesus speaks in the mode of a more "realized eschatology," so that what was fully revealed only subsequent to Jesus' resurrection is rendered more in terms of "already," we should not think of this as a spurious literary act on the part of the author, but rather as a logical extension backwards into the narrative of the revelatory significance of Jesus' resurrection from the dead. We are obviously not seeing in "real time" a literal account of Jesus' life, death, and resurrection in John — or the other gospels, for that matter, though the synoptics are more genetic in character — so much as a concentration of its historical-narrative unfolding into a more poetic, contemplative rendering, much like a "sacred oratorio" or "verbal icon," as David Tracy has put it (*The Analogical Imagination: Christian Theology and the Culture of Pluralism* [New York: Crossroad, 1981], 285). In the following chapter, we will look more closely at this contemplative distillation in John, one that more fully draws explicit connections between creation and resurrection in a "grammar of fulfillment."

83. Alison, *Knowing Jesus,* 45–46.

84. Bultmann rather famously declared Jesus' death to be the result of a misunderstanding of Jesus' ministry: "What is certain is merely that he was crucified by the Romans, and thus suffered the death of a political criminal. This death can scarcely be understood as an inherent and necessary consequence of his activity; rather it took place because his activity was misconstrued as a political activity. In that case it would have been — historically speaking — a meaningless fate" (Rudolf Bultmann, "The Primitive Christian Kerygma and the Historical Jesus," in *The Historical Jesus and the Kerygmatic Christ,* ed. C. Braaten and R. Harrisville [Nashville: Abingdon, 1964], 23). In contemporary historical research, the allegedly apolitical nature of Jesus' mission is frequently gainsaid, not so much in favor of the exact opposite conclusion, namely, that Jesus was *primarily* motivated politically, but that his religious-prophetic actions were politically repercussive enough to run him afoul with both Roman and Jewish authorities. In Mark Allan Powell's survey of the major figures in recent historical Jesus studies (including, among others, John Dominic Crossan, Marcus J. Borg, E. P. Sanders, John P. Meier, and N. T. Wright), a consensus has emerged, despite the disparity in interpretation, that Jesus' life and ministry had socio-political ramifications enough to genuinely, not accidentally, bring him into conflict with the religious-civil authorities of his day (*Jesus as a Figure in History,* 174–76). Jürgen Moltmann puts it bluntly, asserting that Bultmann's distinction between religion and politics on this point is little more than a projection of a bourgeois restriction of religion to the private sphere (Jürgen Moltmann, *The Crucified*

God: The Cross of Christ as the Foundation and Criticism of Christian Theology, trans. R. A. Wilson and John Bowden [New York: Harper & Row, 1974], 137). For a helpful survey of this issue in contemporary theology, see John Galvin, "Jesus' Approach to Death: An Examination of Some Recent Studies," *Theological Studies* 41 (1980): 713–44. For an updated and more concise survey, see John P. Galvin's "Jesus," in *Systematic Theology: Roman Catholic Perspectives,* vol. 1, ed. Francis Schüssler Fiorenza and John P. Galvin (Minneapolis: Fortress Press, 1991), especially 281–97.

85. Marcus Borg, *Meeting Jesus Again for the First Time: The Historical Jesus and the Heart of Contemporary Faith* (New York: HarperCollins, 1994), 50.

86. Girard, *The Scapegoat,* 30. For more, see 12–44.

87. Schwager, *Jesus in the Drama of Salvation,* 92.

88. Ibid., 117.

89. "The climax of the story, of the battle for the kingdom, was therefore, inescapably, that Jesus would die, not as an accident, nor as a bizarre quasi-suicide, a manipulated martyrdom, but as the inevitable result of his kingdom-inaugurating career. But this death, as he conceived it, would be the actual victory of the kingdom, by which the enemy of the people would finally be defeated. Jesus would act out the role of the revolutionary, at the point at which it could no longer be understood. It is therefore not surprising, but entirely natural, to suggest that Jesus, in telling the story of Israel reshaped around himself, predicted his own death. It did not take much insight to see that it was very likely from the beginning. From within Jesus' retelling of the Jewish stories, such a death would carry an obvious, though shocking, interpretation" (Wright, *Jesus and the Victory of God,* 466).

Chapter Eight

1. Girard, *A Theater of Envy,* 342.

2. Luke includes an episode of Jesus before Herod Antipas (23:6–12). Pilate sends Jesus to Herod to be questioned, due to the latter's jurisdiction, during which the chief priest and scribes mock Jesus, as do the Roman soldiers. Herod puts an elegant robe on Jesus, with obvious irony, and returns Jesus to Pilate, having received no answer from Jesus during his questioning. Notably, this exchange of the accused Jesus creates unanimity between Pilate and Herod: "That same day Herod and Pilate became friends with each other; before this they had been enemies" (v. 12).

3. "Jesus is presented to us as the innocent victim of a group in crisis, which for a time at any rate, is united against him. All the subgroups and indeed all the individuals who are concerned with the life and trial of Jesus end up by giving their explicit or implicit assent to his death: the crowd in Jerusalem, the Jewish religious authorities, the Roman political authorities, and even the disciples, since those who do not betray or deny Jesus actively take flight or remain passive. We must remember that this very crowd has welcomed Jesus with such enthusiasm only a few days earlier. The crowd turns around like a single man and insists on his death with a determination that springs at least in part from being carried away by the irrationality of the collective spirit. Certainly nothing has intervened to justify such a change of attitude" (Girard, *Things Hidden from the Foundation of the World,* 167).

4. The liturgy of Good Friday, centered on the passion of John's gospel, makes this connection poignantly as the congregants speak the part of the crowd as well as the Roman soldiers who cast lots for Jesus' tunic.

5. Ricoeur, "The Logic of Jesus, the Logic of God," 279–83.
6. Markus Barth and Verne H. Fletcher, *Acquittal by Resurrection* (New York: Holt, Rinehart and Winston, 1964), 70.
7. Ricoeur, "The Logic of Jesus, the Logic of God," 281–82.
8. See the similar statement by Stephen as he was being lynched by a mob: "Then they dragged him out of the city and began to stone him; and the witnesses laid their coats at the feet of a young man named Saul. While they were stoning Stephen, he prayed, 'Lord Jesus, receive my spirit.' Then he knelt down and cried out in a loud voice, 'Lord, do not hold this sin against them.' When he had said this, he died" (Acts 7:57–60). The parallels with the first part of Luke-Acts are obvious (Luke 23:34, 36).
9. Alison, *The Joy of Being Wrong*, 80–81.
10. See also Matt. 21:42; Mark 12:10; Luke 20:17; 1 Pet. 2:7.
11. Heim, *Saved from Sacrifice*, xi.
12. Schwager, *Jesus in the Drama of Salvation*, 118.
13. Heim, *Saved from Sacrifice*, xi-xii.
14. Rahner, *Foundations of Christian Faith*, 93.
15. Ibid.
16. Ford, *Self and Salvation*, 202.
17. Ibid., 204.
18. Girard, *I See Satan Fall Like Lightning*, 143.
19. Alison, *Knowing Jesus*, 22.
20. Schillebeeckx, "Liberation from Panic (Easter Faith)," 122–27.
21. Acts 3:19–21; 3:38; 5:30–31; 10:43; 13:37–39; 17:30–31.
22. Compare the three narratives of Paul's conversion in Acts (9:1–19; 22:4–16; 26:9–18) with Galatians 1:13–17 and 1 Cor. 15:8.
23. Rahner, *Foundations of Christian Faith*, 107.
24. Ibid., 109.
25. Paul's anthropology represents anthropological monism, not dualism, as was explained in chapter 4.
26. Alison, *The Joy of Being Wrong*, 150.
27. Ibid., 151.
28. Paul's formulation "how much more" occurs four times in a short span (Rom. 5:9, 10, 15, 17), which Ricoeur argues extends the logic of excess expressed in Jesus' parables, proverbs, and exhortations to guide a more formally elaborated theology of sin and grace. Ricoeur suggests that our considerations of the theology of justification suffer if we do make this connection with the gospels explicit, particularly given our tendency to read the juridical language of justification in terms of retributive justice ("The Logic of Jesus, the Logic of God," 282).
29. Ibid., 100–101.
30. Alison, *Knowing Jesus*, 77.
31. Wright, *Jesus and the Victory of God*, 268–74. For the relevant scriptural passages, see Jer. 31:31–34; 33:4–11; Ezek. 36:24–6; Isa. 40:1–2; 43:25–44:3.
32. Volf, *Exclusion and Embrace*, 51.
33. Ibid. See also, Miroslav Volf, "Catholicity of 'Two or Three': Free Church Relations on the Catholicity of the Local Church," *The Jurist* 52.1 (1992): 525–46.
34. Moltmann, *The Coming of God*, 67.
35. Volf, *Exclusion and Embrace*, 116.

36. Ibid., 118.

37. Ibid. Italics original. Volf critiques Girard on this score too, saying that his intense emphasis on the innocence of the victim undermines the gospel's insistence on the need for repentance among both oppressed and oppressors (ibid.). From my point of view, Volf's critique, which is extremely brief, does not adequately take into account Girard's insistence upon Jesus as the *only* truly innocent victim. There is nothing in Girard's work to suggest that any particular group could lay claim to absolute innocence. As we saw in the previous chapter, Girard's work explicitly affirms that *all* of us — Jesus being the remarkable exception here — are involved in the production of victims, and that the scapegoating process identified and unmasked in the gospels is something for which we all must "be loosed," or "forgiven."

38. Williams, *Resurrection*, 17.

39. Aulén, *Christus Victor*, 4.

40. Irenaeus, *Against Heresies*, V.1.1, in von Balthasar, *The Scandal of the Incarnation*, 56.

41. Aulén, *Christus Victor*, 28, 54.

42. Ibid., 31. Jaroslav Pelikan writes that when a modern Western Christian looks back to the theologians of the second and third centuries, "it is neither their attention to the teachings and example of Christ (which he may, rather superficially, identify with that of Protestant liberalism) nor their preoccupation with the passion and death of Christ (which he may, with some justification, see as an ancestor of the orthodox doctrine of vicarious atonement), but their emphasis on the saving significance of the resurrection of Christ that he will find most unusual" (*The Emergence of the Catholic Tradition (100–600)*, vol. 1, *The Christian Tradition: A History of the Development of Doctrine* [Chicago: University of Chicago Press, 1971], 149).

43. Adv. Haer, IV., 39.3. (p. 24).

44. Gregory of Nyssa, "The Great Catechism," in *Nicene and Post-Nicene Fathers of the Christian Church*, vol. 5, *Gregory of Nyssa, Selected Works and Letters*, trans. William Moore and Henry Austin Wilson, ed. Philip Schaff & Henry Wace (Edinburgh: T. & T. Clark, 1994), XXIV, 494.

45. Ibid., XX, 492.

46. Ibid., XXIV, 494.

47. Girard, *I See Satan Fall Like Lightning*, 151–53.

48. Ibid., 189.

Chapter Nine

1. Karl Rahner, "On the Spirituality of the Easter Faith," *Theological Investigations* 17, 13.

2. Ibid., 14.

3. Lorenzen, *Resurrection and Discipleship*, 240–47.

4. Sandra M. Schneiders, *Written That You May Believe: Encountering Jesus in the Fourth Gospel*, 171.

5. Raymond E. Brown, *The Gospel According to John I–XII*, Anchor Bible (New York: Doubleday, 1964), 430.

6. Evans, *Resurrection and the New Testament*, 116.

7. Rudolf Bultmann, *Theology of the New Testament*, vol. 2 (New York: Scribners, 1955), 56.

8. Evans, *Resurrection and the New Testament*, 116, 124.

9. Dunn, *Christology in the Making*, 57. Italics original.
10. Brown, *The Gospel According to John I-XII*, CXIX.
11. John Ashton, *Understanding the Fourth Gospel* (Oxford: Clarendon Press, 1991), 383-406.
12. Robert Kysar, *John: The Maverick Gospel*, rev. ed. (Louisville: Westminster John Knox Press, 1994), 100-101. Kysar provides a helpful overview of the positions scholars take on Johannine eschatology while offering his own position that John emphasizes realized eschatology while preserving, and thus affirming, future eschatology (99-106).
13. Schneiders, "The Resurrection (of the Body) in the Fourth Gospel," 175.
14. John J. Collins, for example, maintains there is no suggestion of bodily resurrection in the Wisdom of Solomon (*Jewish Wisdom in the Hellenistic Age* [Louisville: Westminster John Knox Press, 1997], 183-87). Others, like N. T. Wright, argue that bodily resurrection is implied in it (*Resurrection of the Son of God*, 162-75). It is not vital to settle the matter here, though Collins seems to me to have the edge in the argument. The point for our purposes is that immortality and resurrection are not necessarily incompatible in late Jewish eschatology, as some suppose, and Wright makes this point clear enough.
15. Schneiders, "The Resurrection (of the Body) in the Fourth Gospel," 175.
16. Ibid., 175-76.
17. Ibid., 176.
18. Schneiders, *Written That You May Believe*, 57.
19. Ibid., 58.
20. C. H. Dodd, *The Interpretation of the Fourth Gospel* (Cambridge: Cambridge University Press, 1952), 442.
21. Responding to those who see only an accidental relationship between the narratives and the rest of the gospel, Schneiders states that John 20 is "not a concession to the constraints of early Christian tradition but a narrative-theological exploration of the Easter experience of the first disciples and its implications for the spirituality of the Johannine community" ("The Resurrection [of the Body] in the Fourth Gospel," 176). Schneiders suggests that even 21:1-25, which is regarded by many scholars as a post-Johannine addition, should be read as "an integral part of the Gospel" and "in fundamental theological continuity with chapters 1-20 and that its purpose is to bring the Gospel account to a close by transferring the reader's attention from the experience of the first disciples with the historical Jesus to the experience of the contemporary church with the glorified Jesus, that is, from the story of those who 'saw' to the story of those who 'believe without having seen' (see 20:29)" (*Written That You May Believe*, 224).
22. Hans Urs von Balthasar, *Theo-Drama: Theological Dramatic Theory*, vol. 5: *The Last Act*, trans. Graham Harrison (San Francisco: Ignatius Press, 1998), 25.
23. Barnabas Lindars, "The Fourth Gospel an Act of Contemplation," in *Studies in the Fourth Gospel*, ed. F. L. Cross (London: Mowbray, 1957), 25.
24. Tracy, *The Analogical Imagination*, 285.
25. Brown, *The Gospel According to John I-XXI*, cxvi.
26. Dodd, *The Interpretation of the Fourth Gospel*, 73.
27. For more on these parallels, see Brown, *The Gospel According to John I-XI*, lii-lxv; and Dodd, *The Interpretation of the Fourth Gospel*, 10-130.
28. Schneiders, *Written That You May Believe*, 51-53.

29. Dodd, *The Interpretation of the Fourth Gospel*, 366.
30. Schneiders, *Written That You May Believe*, 179.
31. Gerald O'Collins notes that the theme of love has been considerably underdeveloped in the theology of the resurrection. His own study provides helpful avenues for redressing this issue (see his *Jesus Risen*, 188–200).
32. Marion, *Prolegomena to Charity*, 141.
33. Ibid., 145.
34. Schneiders, "The Resurrection (of the Body) in the Fourth Gospel," 183–84, 188.
35. Ibid., 188–89.
36. Ward, *Cities of God*, 113.
37. For more on the emergence of christology in the context of prayer and liturgy, see Geoffrey Wainwright, *Doxology: The Praise of God in Worship, Doctrine, and Life* (New York: Oxford University Press, 1980), 45–86; Catherine LaCugna, *God for Us: The Trinity and Christian Life* (New York: HarperCollins, 1991), 111–42. In Jaroslav Pelikan's exhaustive doctrinal study the importance of liturgical prayers are duly noted (*The Christian Tradition*, vol. 1, 172–277). For how this is (or should be) true in contemporary christology, see William M. Thompson, *Christology and Spirituality* (New York: Crossroad, 1991), especially 1–44.
38. Maurice Wiles, *The Making of Christian Doctrine* (Cambridge: Cambridge University Press, 1967), 65.
39. Carnley, *The Structure of Resurrection Belief*, 6.
40. Ibid., 8.
41. Raymond E. Brown, *Introduction to New Testament Christology* (New York: Paulist Press, 1994), 107–8.
42. Schillebeeckx, *Jesus*, 514. See also Carnley, *The Structure of Resurrection Belief*, 7.
43. Another type of christology in which this contrast is a defining feature is the "Adam christology" in Paul (see Rom. 5:12–21; 1 Cor. 15:21–23, 45–49).
44. Brown, *An Introduction to New Testament Christology*, 108. Brown is careful not to characterize this historical development in an overly rigid way. For Brown's response to critics who charge that he has done so, see *The Birth of the Messiah: A Commentary on the Infancy Narratives in the Gospels of Matthew and Luke*, New Updated Version, The Anchor Bible Reference Library (New York: Doubleday, 1993), 709–12. For more on Brown's chronological assessment of New Testament Christology, see his "Christology," in *The New Jerome Biblical Commentary*, 81:1–24, 1254–59.
45. James Dunn, similar to Brown, writes that second generation christology evidences a historical development through "*the backward extension of the Son of God language* — from resurrection, death and resurrection, to the beginning of Jesus' ministry (Jordan) [which is what we find in Mark], to his conception and birth, to a timeless eternity" (*Christology in the Making*, 256). Many scholars maintain that the stories of Jesus' "transfiguration" (Mark 9:2–8; Matt. 17:1–8; Luke 9:28–36) are echoes of appearances stories similarly retrojected (see Perkins, *Resurrection*, 95–99).
46. For more on this retrojection of Son of God language in the infancy narratives, see Brown's exhaustive study narratives in his *The Birth of the Messiah*.
47. Dunn, *Christology in the Making*, 254.

48. For a seminal essay describing the different approaches in "ascending" and "descending" christologies, see Karl Rahner, "The Two Basic Types of Christology," *Theological Investigations,* 13, trans. David Bourke (New York: Crossroad, 1975), 213–23.
49. von Balthasar, *Mysterium Paschale,* 202.
50. Brown, *An Introduction to New Testament Christology,* 109. Italics mine.
51. Ibid., 105.
52. Following Dunn, I take "incarnation" to mean the following within New Testament theology: "'Incarnation' means initially that God's love and power had been experienced in fullest measure in, through and as this man Jesus, that Christ had to be experienced as God's self-expression, the Christ-event as the effect, re-creative power of God" (Dunn, *Christology in the Making,* 262).
53. Schillebeeckx, *Christ,* 402. See also *Jesus,* 543.
54. Hans Frei, *The Identity of Jesus Christ,* 159.
55. Ibid.
56. Schillebeeckx describes how this relationship becomes a form of "hermeneusis" in the gospel traditions: "Thus we end up in a remarkable hermeneutical circle: Jesus' living and dying on earth suggested to Christians, in virtue of their experiences after Jesus' death, the idea of the resurrection or of the coming Parousia of Jesus, while on the basis of their faith in the risen or coming crucified One they related the story of Jesus in the gospels; in other words, these gospel stories of Jesus are themselves a hermeneusis of Jesus' Parousia and resurrection, while belief in the Parousia or in the resurrection was engendered by things remembered of the historical Jesus. The 'matter to be interpreted' — Jesus of Nazareth — came eventually to be interpreted in and through the faith-inspired affirmation of his resurrection (Parousia), while that resurrection or Parousia is in its turn the 'object of interpretation' which is then interpreted through the gospel narratives as remembrances of Jesus' earthly life, as also in light of resurrection or coming Parousia" (*Jesus,* 401; see also 29).
57. Ibid., 171–72.
58. Ibid., 172.
59. Pannenberg, *Jesus — God and Man,* 69.
60. Ibid.
61. Ibid.
62. Karl Rahner, "The Mystery of the God-Man Jesus," *Theological Investigations* 13, 200.
63. Karl Rahner, "Christology Today?" *Theological Investigations* 17, trans. Margaret Kohl (London: Darton, Longman & Todd, 1981), 33–34.
64. Karl Rahner, "Dogmatic Questions on Easter," 128–29.
65. Karl Rahner, "Jesus Christ — The Meaning of Life," *Theological Investigations* 21, trans. Hugh M. Riley (New York: Crossroad, 1988), 217.
66. Rahner, "Christology Today?," 34.
67. Brian Hebblethwaite, "The Resurrection and the Incarnation," in *The Resurrection of Jesus Christ,* 160–63; Pannenberg, *Jesus — God and Man,* 152–54.
68. It is important to underscore that the gospel of John is not the only instance of preexistence christology in the New Testament. We find numerous intimations of preexistence and incarnation in several pre-Pauline hymns, in much of Paul's own thinking, and in the Letter to the Hebrews. Given this, the theology of preexistence was not a "Johannine aberration or creation from nothing but, at most, a

clarification within a Gospel framework of ideas that circulated elsewhere among early Christians." And yet, acknowledges Brown, the "implications of incarnation in John... seem to go beyond other NT works.... He retells the Jesus story from the viewpoint of the incarnation.... Almost every scene of the Gospel becomes a vehicle for manifesting the glory of Jesus, 'glory as of an only Son from the Father' (1:14)" (*An Introduction to New Testament Christology,* 140–41).

69. von Balthasar, *Mysterium Paschale,* 203.

70. Richard Bauckham, "God Who Raises the Dead: The Resurrection of Jesus and Early Christian Faith in God," in *The Resurrection of Jesus Christ,* ed. Paul Avis, 136.

71. Yves Congar, *I Believe in the Holy Spirit,* The Complete Three Volume Work in One Volume, trans. David Smith (New York: Crossroad, 1997), vol. 1, 32; vol. 2, 79–99.

72. von Balthasar, *Mysterium Paschale,* 214.

73. Ibid., 214–15.

74. Ibid., 213.

75. Ibid., 212, 222–24.

76. Karl Rahner, *The Trinity,* trans. Joseph Donceel (New York: Crossroad, 1997), 21–33.

Chapter Ten

1. Henri de Lubac, *The Discovery of God,* trans. Alexander Dru (Grand Rapids: Eerdmans, 1996), 66.

2. von Balthasar, *The Glory of the Lord,* vol. 1, *Seeing the Form,* 216.

3. Friedrich Nietzsche, *Beyond Good and Evil: Prelude to a Philosophy of the Future,* trans. R. J. Hollingdale (New York: Penguin, 1990), par. 259, 194.

4. Hart, *The Beauty of the Infinite,* 102.

5. "However one phrases the matter, this much is certain: insofar as the 'postmodern' is the completion of the deconstruction of metaphysics, it usually depends upon one immense and irreducible metaphysical assumption: that the unrepresentable *is*; more to the point, that the unrepresentable (call it *difference,* chaos, being, alterity, the infinite...) is somehow truer than the representable (which necessarily dissembles it), more original, and qualitatively *other*: that is, it does not differ from the representable by virtue of a greater fullness and unity of those transcendental moments that constitute the world of appearance, but by virtue of its absolute difference, its dialectical or negative indeterminacy, its no-thingness" (ibid., 52).

6. Ibid., 103.

7. Ibid., 93. Italics mine.

8. Ibid., 125. Similarly, John Milbank: "This preference for originality is purely (as Nietzsche admits) a matter of taste, and Nietzsche is not able to demonstrate that such a taste is more primordially lodged in human existence than the despised desires for security, consolation, mutuality, pleasure and contentment" (*Theology and Social Theory,* 282).

9. Heraclitus, "Fragments," in *The First Philosophers of Greece,* trans. and ed., Arthur Fairbanks (Scribner, 1898).

10. Girard, *I See Satan Fall Like Lightning,* 82. Girard notes that "the myths presenting the founding role of the primordial murder are so numerous that even

a comparative mythologies so little given to generalizations as Mircea Eliade considered it necessary to take into account. In his *Histoire des croyances et des idées religieuses* [in English, *A History of Religious Ideas*, trans. Willard R. Trask (Chicago: University of Chicago Press, 1978)], he speaks of a 'creative murder' (*meurtre créateur*) common to many stories of origin and founding myths throughout the world" (ibid., 83). Girard's most extensive study of these myths to date is still his *Violence and the Sacred*.

11. Quoted in Paul Ricoeur, *The Symbolism of Evil*, trans. Emerson Buchanan (Boston: Beacon Press, 1967), 180.

12. Ibid., 182.

13. Ibid., 194.

14. Ibid., 198.

15. Wink, *Engaging the Powers*, 14, 16–17.

16. Ricoeur, *The Symbolism of Evil*, 233.

17. Ibid., 239–40.

18. Alison, *The Joy of Being Wrong*, 97. See also his, *Raising Abel*, 34–56. See the illuminating remarks of James G. Williams in his *The Bible, Violence, and the Sacred*, 25–31.

19. This obviously need not mean that Israel only told stories about the origin of creation this late into its history, but that the writings represented in Genesis give evidence of redactional and compositional features that many scholars have come to identify with later periods of Israel's history.

20. Alison, *The Joy of Being Wrong*, 98.

21. While it is frequently stated that the doctrine of creation *ex nihilo* is not unambiguously affirmed in the Bible, but was only taught in the late second century among Christian theologians contending with neoplatonic and Gnostic teachings, there is considerable evidence to show that the affirmation is in fact much earlier. For more on this subject, see Paul Copan and William Lane Craig, *Creation Out of Nothing: A Biblical, Philosophical, and Scientific Exploration* (Grand Rapids: Baker Academic, 2004).

22. Alison, *The Joy of Being Wrong*, 99.

23. Ibid., 98.

24. Schneiders, *Written That You May Believe*, 217.

25. Alison, *The Joy of Being Wrong*, 190.

26. Karl Rahner, "Easter: A Faith that Loves the Earth," in *The Great Church Year: The Best of Karl Rahner's Homilies, Sermons, and Meditations,* ed. Albert Raffelt, translation edited by Harvey D. Egan, S.J. (New York: Crossroad), 195.

27. Quoted in Oliver Clément, *The Roots of Christian Mysticism*, trans. Theodore Berkeley, O.C.S.O. and Jeremy Hummerstone (Hyde Park, N.Y.: New City Press, 1995), 268.

28. Rahner, "Dogmatic Questions on Easter," 128–29.

29. Karl Rahner, "The Resurrection of the Body," 213.

30. Rahner, "Easter: A Faith that Loves the Earth," 194–95.

31. Rahner, "Dogmatic Questions on Easter," 123.

32. Aulén, *Christus Victor*, 18–21.

33. Rahner, "Dogmatic Questions on Easter," 126.

34. See, for example, Mark 8:35; Matt. 10:39; 16:25; Luke 9:24; 17:33; John 12:25.

35. In Scholastic theology, the "fittingness" of a theological truth refers to its symmetry or proportionality (*congruentia, proportion, harmonia*) with other theological truths. See Hans Urs von Balthasar's discussion of this in Thomas Aquinas (*The Glory of the Lord: A Theological Aesthetics,* vol. 4: *The Realm of Metaphysics in Antiquity* [San Francisco: Ignatius Press, 1989], 407ff).

36. Rahner, "Dogmatic Questions on Easter," 129.

37. Mark A. McIntosh, *Mystical Theology: The Integrity of Spirituality and Theology* (Oxford: Blackwell, 1998), 123–24.

38. Karl Rahner, "The Eternal Significance of the Humanity of Jesus for Our Relationship to God," trans. Karl H. and Boniface Kruger (London: Darton, Longman & Todd, 1967), 35–46.

39. See in the same volume the essay, "The Ignatian Mysticism of Joy in the World," 277–93.

40. Rahner, "The Eternal Significance of the Humanity of Jesus for Our Relationship to God," 42.

41. Ibid., 43.

42. Ibid.

43. Rahner, "Dogmatic Questions on Easter," 132.

44. Rahner, "The Eternal Significance of the Humanity of Jesus for Our Relationship to God," 44. Rahner notes that this dimension of the resurrection has not always been fully appreciated in Christian theology. Though it is not at all uncommon for theology to reflect on the mediating role of Jesus' humanity in terms of his earthly existence, the doctrine of the "physical instrumental causality exercised by the humanity of Christ for all grace" has not been sufficiently explored in theology. Rahner has on numerous occasions addressed this lacuna with a variety of specific purposes in mind: the theology of death and the intermediate state, Mariology, the theology of the body, the theology of the symbol, and Christian spirituality. "Every theologian should allow himself to be asked: have you a theology in which the Word — by the fact that he is man and in so far as he is this — is the necessary and permanent mediator of all salvation, not merely at some time in the past but now and for all eternity? Does your theology really see him in this way, so that by being this God-Man he also is so bound up by his humanity with the religious acts that this act goes (consciously or unconsciously) through his humanity to God, and so that this humanity is essentially and always the mediating object of the one act of *latria* which has God for its goal" (ibid., 45). For some examples of Rahner's discussion and application of this insight, see, "Current Problems in Christology," *Theological Investigations* 1, trans. Cornelius Ernst (Baltimore: Helicon Press, 1961), 199–200; "The Interpretation of the Dogma of the Assumption," *Theological Investigations* 1, 221–24; "The Resurrection of the Body," *Theological Investigations* 2, 203–16; "Dogmatic Questions on Easter," 124–27; "On the Spirituality of Easter Faith," 8–15; "What Does It Mean Today to Believe in Jesus Christ," *Theological Investigations* 18, trans. Edward Quinn (London: Darton, Longman & Todd, 1983), 154ff; "The Body in the Order of Salvation," *Theological Investigations* 17, 71–89.

45. Karl Rahner, "Easter: The Beginning of Glory," in *The Best of Karl Rahner's Homilies, Sermons, and Meditations,* 190.

46. Rahner, "Easter: A Faith that Loves the Earth," 195–96.

47. Rahner, "On the Spirituality of Easter Faith," 12.

48. Gerard Manley Hopkins, *Poems and Prose,* ed. W. H. Gardner (New York: Penguin, 1953), 65–66.
49. von Balthasar, *Seeing the Form,* vol. 1, *The Glory of the Lord,* 155.
50. Ibid., 216.
51. Hart, *The Beauty of the Infinite,* 252–53.
52. George Friedrich Hegel, *Lectures on the Philosophy of Religion,* trans. R. F. Brown, P. C. Hodgson, and J. M. Stewart (Berkeley: University of California Press, 1988), 469–70.
53. von Balthasar, *Seeing the Form,* vol. 1, *The Glory of the Lord,* 216. Hart writes similarly: "The resurrection vindicates the aesthetic particularity of truth over against the violences that seek to reduce particularity to nothingness, over against all economies of abstract wisdom, political, philosophical, social, or religious" (*The Beauty of the Infinite,* 333–34).

Scripture Index

OLD TESTAMENT

Genesis	253, 381
1:1	359
1:31	360
2:4	359
2:7	364
2:15–17	364
3:5	364
3:15	364
4:10	279
45:3–4	279
45:7	279

Exodus	189, 280
3:3	91
3:6	82–83, 200, 393n.40
3:17	200
3:81	199–200
6:6	200
13:3	199
13:15	200

Leviticus	253, 257

Deuteronomy	
30:19	238

Job	219, 280

Psalms	219, 253, 280
2:36	293
33:6	329
69:4	284
118:22	298

Proverbs	
8:27–30	329

Isaiah	241, 257, 309
2	199, 281
25:8	79
26	200
26:16–19	201
26:19	79
34:1–4	204–5
46:8	3
60:3–5	205, 308–9
60:17–19	205
66:22	172
66:22–23	205
66:25	205

Jeremiah	309
1:6–8	91

Lamentations	219

Ezekiel	200, 309
37	1–4, 201–2

Daniel	78, 197, 200, 204, 325
7	205–6
12	77, 203, 392n.30
12:1–3	78, 202
12:2	200

Amos	257
5:18–20	204

Zechariah	200

APOCRYPHA

Wisdom of Solomon	
2:21–25	392n.30
3:1–4	325–26
9:9	329

1 Maccabees	
1:54	203

2 Maccabees	325
7:9	203
7:10–11	392n.30
7:11	203
7:14	203
7:16–17	203
7:17	294
7:19	203
7:20–23	202–3
7:23	361
12:43–45	203

NEW TESTAMENT

Matthew	68, 322–23
5:38–44	295
5:44	249
10:34	288
18:20	5
18:22	295
22:23–33	80
24:36	85
25:31–46	320
25:34–46	307
25:40	232
27:64	35
28:7	99
28:9	94, 100
28:10	301
28:17	99
28:19	114
28:20	349

Mark	25, 68, 185, 200, 322–23
1:11	337
1:14	210
5:42	91
7:1	313
7:3	313
8:33	286
9:6	91
9:32	91
10:32	91

Mark (continued)	
12:18–27	80, 82
13	197, 313
13:32	173
13:33	85
14:25	84
14:28	90, 99
15:5	341
15:34	85
16:1–8	88, 90
16:2	90
16:5	90
16:6	3, 7, 68, 88, 90
16:7	89, 114
16:8	90
16:11	35
24:3–36	197

Luke	68, 322–23
1:29–30	91
1:35	338
1:46–55	276
2:30	183
6:20–23	230
12:51–53	288
14:26–27	288
15:20	295
18:7–9	84
19:12	183
20:23	302
20:27–40	80
21:7–36	197
23:6–12	422n.2
23:24	295
23:34	423n.8
23:36	423n.8
23:46	86
24:13–32	106–7
24:21	302
24:31	97
24:32	98
24:34	94, 106–7
24:36	301
24:36–53	106–7
24:37	98
24:39	98
24:47	302

Luke (continued)	
24:49	347
24:49–50	114
24:51	98
28:19–20	302

John	60, 68, 185, 186, 191, 320
1:1	285
1:1–5	363
1:3–4	329
1:4	326
1:5	326, 328
1:10–12	330
1:14	329–30
1:49	102
2:22	326
2:23	326
3:3	328
3:6	328
3:13	328
3:13–14	322
3:16	331
3:18	330
3:19	328
3:31	328
4:1	326
4:10–14	328
4:14	326
4:42	102
5:24	330
5:25	322
5:28–29	325
6:18–19	326
6:27	328
6:31	177
6:39–40	325
6:54	325
6:54–57	177
6:63	328
6:69	102
8:13	326
8:19	326
8:23	328
8:28	322
8:44	285
9:37	102
9:39	330

John (continued)	
10:16	326
10:17–18	326, 393n.45
11:25	325
11:25–27	321–22
11:27	102
11:47–53	281–82
11:49–52	322
11:50	189
11:52	322
12:1	326
12:25–26	330
12:31	330
12:32–33	322
12:48	325
13:31	348
14:2	370
14:2–3	325
14:6	283
14:12	348
14:18	349
14:18–20	328
14:21	364
14:28	327
14:30–32	284
15:3	326
15:8	326
15:15	348
15:22	284
15:25	284
15:26	348
16:2–3	284
16:10	327
16:16	327
16:20–23	348
16:30	102
17:20–24	348
17:22–23	332
17:24	325
17:26	348
18:37–38	283
19:10	283
19:12	283
19:15	294
19:21	284
19:30	322
20:1	363

John (continued)	
20:2	3
20:11–18	331
20:13	3, 89
20:15	3, 99
20:16	4, 100, 349
20:17	3, 100, 102, 114
20:18	100, 349
20:19	301–2, 363, 364
20:20–21	101
20:21	114, 301–2, 364
20:22	364
20:22–23	331, 348, 364
20:24–29	35, 331
20:25	101
20:26	301–2, 364
20:27	101, 301
20:28	102, 301
20:29	102, 113, 349
20:31	102
21:14	94
21:15	332
21:15–19	332
21:16	332
21:17	114, 332
21:19	114
21:25	108

Acts	230, 309
1:3	94, 106–7
1:10–11	98
2	188, 193, 228–29, 338
2:11	308
2:22–23	189, 292
2:23	230
2:24	190, 293
2:31	193
2:32	85–86, 336, 346
2:32–33	347
2:32–36	190
2:33	193
2:36	65, 293, 336
2:37	191, 241
2:38–40	191
2:38–39	294
3	194
3:14	229

Acts (continued)	
3:15	85–86, 295, 346
3:17–21	296
4:5–6	292
4:10	85–86, 229, 346
4:11	298, 308
4:11–12	191
4:12	183
4:25–26	293
4:27	189, 292
4:41–42	192
5:30	229
5:30–31	294
5:31	336
7:57–60	423n.8
9:5	302
9:8	302
9:9	302
9:17	94
10	337
10:36	229
10:40	27, 85–86, 94, 346
10:40–44	395n.72
13:28	229
13:31	94
13:32–33	336
26:16	94
26:18	302
28:19	347

Romans	
1:4	337, 346
2:19–20	305
3	209
4:17	346, 361
4:24	346
4:25	302
5:1	306
5:10	295
5:12	304
5:20–21	306
6	306
6:4	346
6:4–5	367
6:9–11	305
6:17	304
7:15–17	304
7:21–24	304

Romans (continued)	
7:24–25	305
8	210
8:9–11	338, 340
8:11	153, 243, 304, 346
8:15–17	347
8:17	346
8:18–24	211
8:19	347
8:19–21	364–65
8:21	347
8:22–23	153
8:23	172, 346
8:24	183
8:32	306
8:33–39	306
8:38–39	211
10:9	346
10:10	183
11:11	183
11:17	111
12:5	111
13:11	183

1 Corinthians	15
1:18	183
2:7–8	316
3:16	347
6:9–11	155
6:14	85, 346
6:14–15	156
6:15	177
7:31	210
10:16	177
10:16–17	176
11:20–22	176
12:12–13	174
13:12	169
15	62, 151, 156, 365
15:2	183
15:3–4	32
15:4	77
15:5–8	94
15:6	51
15:6–8	106–7
15:12–19	35
15:16	80
15:17	55, 80, 302

1 Corinthians (continued)	
15:20–23	183
15:22	80–81
15:24	172
15:26	172
15:28	172, 183
15:35	152
15:35–58	35
15:38–41	152
15:43	346
15:43–44	152
15:44	159
15:45	157
15:47	157
15:47–57	346
15:50	153, 154, 155
15:51	158–59
15:51–55	152
15:53	123, 157
15:54–56	157
15:54–58	183, 243
15:55	158
15:57	158
16:22	220

2 Corinthians	
1:9	346
2:15	183
3:17	347
4:14	346
5:1–5	346
5:19	19, 116
6:2	183

Galatians	
1:1	115, 346
1:16	94
2:20	347
3:26–28	175, 347
3:28	209
4:4–7	210

Ephesians	
1:20	346
2:8	183
2:14	209
6:12	234–35

Philippians _____ 60
1:21   347
2:5–8   297
2:6   370
2:8–9   337
2:9   108
2:9–11   297–98
2:12   183, 306
3:20   183
3:21   157, 346

Colossians _____
1:14   177
1:15   172
1:15–20   353
1:18   111, 210
2:12   346
2:20   85, 346
3:1–4   346

1 Thessalonians _____
4:15   35

1 Timothy _____
3:16   346

2 Timothy _____
1:9   183
2:18   35

Titus _____
3:5   183

Philemon _____
2:9–11   65

Hebrews _____ 60
1:3   349
2:8   183
5:9   183
11:3   361

1 Peter _____
1:5   183
1:9   183
1:21   346
3:15   22
3:18   346
3:21   183
4:18   183

Revelation _____ 197, 206
21   1, 172

General Index

Abel, 279
Adam, 359
absence, 34, 67–68, 71, 89, 332
aesthetics. *See* beauty
Alison, James, 104, 263–64, 272, 286–87, 291, 301, 334, 352–54, 359–61, 363
anthropology, 17, 20, 32, 52, 61, 119, 125–28, 177–78, 259–61, 325–26
Anselm of Canterbury, 9–10
Antiochus Epiphanes IV, 78, 203–4, 294
appearances, 18–19, 68, 98, 240, 332–33, 349, 395n.68
  alterity of, 93–95, 101
apocalypse, 53, 77–79, 196–97, 220, 237–38, 407n.8
  eschatology, 211–13, 324–25, 342–43, 407n.7, 409n.36
  language of, 195–209
  view of God, 218
apologetics, 17, 21–22, 34, 41, 106, 122–23
apologia, 24–25, 28–29
Apostles, 27
apostolic fraud, 44
Apostolic mission, 114–15
Apostolic witness, 27, 86
Arianism, 11, 13
Aristotle, 259
Athanasius, 14, 368
Athenagoras, 163
Ascension, 19, 35
Augustine, Saint, 3, 48, 125, 163
Aulén Gustav, 255, 314–15, 369
Avis, Paul, 19–20, 116–19, 155

baptism, 175
Ballie, Gil, 254, 266–68, 278, 281
Barth, Karl, 36, 183–84

beauty, 72–74, 96, 109, 378–82
Beker, Johan, 208
Bible, differences between Old and New Testaments, 250–51, 257–58
birth, 166–67
body, 21, 121–26, 130–34, 140
  dysfunction, 143–44
  as embodiment, 139
  fulfillment of, 160–61, 172–73
  as Other, 136–37, 142, 148–49, 160–66, 169–71
  phenomenological approach to, 134–37
  as self-identity, 148
  transformation of, 152–54
Borg, Marcus, 155, 288, 384n.22, 398n.3
Brown, Peter, 126–27
Brown, Raymond, 61, 117–18, 323–24, 336, 339
Brueggemann, Walter, 6, 9, 184, 186, 199–200, 280
Buechner, Frederick, 150
Bultmann, Rudolf, 41, 59–60, 244, 323, 421n.84
  on eschatology, 43, 53, 196
  on kerygma, 64, 92
  on modernity, 35–39, 50
Bynum, Carol Walker, 125, 128, 400n.37

Caiaphas, 188–89, 223, 255, 282–83, 285
Cain, 279
Caird, G. B., 84, 183
Carlson, Thomas A., 391n.24
Carnely, Peter, 336
Celsus, 23, 92, 121–24, 128, 385n.5
Certeau, Michael de, 109–10, 239
Chauvet, Louis-Marie, 27–28, 112, 165

Christ
  body of, 5, 22, 27, 103, 111–12, 113–14, 121, 168
  God in, 19
  in creation, 352–54
  ministry of, 12–13
  risen, 10, 112–13
  as Son of God, 10–11, 323–24, 336–38, 345
Christus Victor, 255, 314, 316–17
church, 21, 28, 174–76; see Christ: body
  early Christian, 61–63, 64–65, 87, 128–29
Collins, John J., 197
creation, 6, 8, 68, 359–62, 364, 371–72, 381
cross, 9–10, 12, 17–18, 59, 251–52, 300, 314, 317
Crossan, John Dominic, 50
community, 26–27
conversion, 307
cosmology, 35–36, 39, 61, 154, 214
Cullmann, Oscar, 40

Daley, Brian, 121
death, 126–30, 143, 152, 157–58, 190, 243–44, 295–96, 315
Derrida, Jacques, 148, 253
Descartes, 131–32, 146–47, 154
Dionysius, 274–76, 354–56
disciples, 12, 61, 64
divine justice, 78–79, 184
divine trickery, 316–17
docetism, 120
Dodd, C. H., 327
Dostoevsky, Fyodor, 217
doubt, 99
dualism, 134, 140, 145–46, 149, 154, 206, 401n.51
duality, 64, 70–72, 96
  of already/not yet, 40–41, 182, 238, 342–43
  of both/and, 104
  of body/soul, 23, 54, 130–32
  cosmic, temporal, and social, 207–9, 231–32

duality (*continued*)
  of phenomenal/noumenal, 37, 54
  of presence/absence, 25, 34, 66, 67–71, 86, 90, 106, 111
Dunn, James D. G., 15, 323, 427n.52

Easter faith, 38, 40
Edwards, Denis, 174
Egyptians, 9
Ellacuría, Ignacio, 241, 244
embodied relationality, 56–57
empty tomb, 17, 50, 64–65, 86–88, 91–93, 104, 398n.4
  as historical irrelevant, 50, 116–17, 398n.3
  narratives, 70, 398n.8
Enlightenment, 18, 235, 388n.59
Enuma Elish, 357, 359–60
Eucharist, 176–77
Evans, C. F., 8, 31, 70, 77, 87, 322–23
event-character, 15–16, 36, 38, 59
exodus, 6–9, 20, 77, 189, 198–99, 229, 279–80

faith experience, 59–60
  flexible, 19–20
festival, 151–52
Fiorenza, Francis Schüssler, 18
Ford, David, 299
forgiveness, 12, 23, 79, 192, 233, 249, 256, 279, 292–95, 299–302, 306
Frei, Hans, 139–41, 341, 392n.26
Freud, *see* psychology
Fuller, Reginald, 71, 389n.85
functionalist, 57–58, 62
fundamental theology, 18, 242
Funk, Robert, 49–51, 387n.44, 395n.68

Gadamer, Hans-Georg, 388n.59, 392n.26
Girard, René, 250, 268, 279–82, 291, 300, 312
  on desire, 261
  influence on others, 263, 352
  on myth, 275–77, 356–57, 359
  on scapegoating, 289, 358
  on violence, 253–55, 272, 317–18, 416n.15

General Index

God, 37
  acts, 341–42
  being with, 372–77
  differences in Bible, 250–52
  as healing, 230
  as human, 367–69
  love of, 162–63
  positive view of, 221
  as victim, 80, 224, 255, 285, 298, 308
  in violence, 12
Gospels, 5–7, 12, 15–16, 46–48, 54, 81, 97–103
  as biased, 47
  inconsistency in, 31–32, 35, 46, 106–8, 321–33, 338, 421n.82
  as narrative constructions, 48, 83–84
Gould, Stephen Jay, 45
grammar, 184–85
  of fulfillment, 196
  modes of, 186–87
Gregory of Nyssa, 125–30, 143, 156, 316–17, 333, 366, 368
Gundry, Robert, 89–90, 156
Gutiérrez, Gustavo, 217, 246–47

habit formation, 137–39
habitus, 26–28, 49, 103, 111, 226, 306
Hanson, Paul D., 407n.7, 409n.36
Hart, David Bentley, 73, 106, 355
Hauerwas, Stanley, 140
heaven, 35–37
Heidegger, Martin, 36, 143, 391n.13, 402n.65
Heim, S. Mark, 252–53, 257–58, 280, 298
hell, 35
Heraclitus, 121, 125, 140, 271, 356, 378–79
Hippolytus, 151
historical *aporia*, 34–36, 40, 48, 65–66, 88, 106
historical criticism, 32, 34, 43
history, 8, 13, 19, 21, 23–24, 28, 38–42, 61, 167, 213–24, 245–46
  first century, 61–63, 80–81, 87–88, 92, 117–18, 210, 235, 245, 287–88, 336–37

history (*continued*)
  second century, 17, 121–23, 155, 198, 251
  third century, 13, 17
  fourth century, 11, 126, 336–37, 349, 400n.37
  fifth century, 11, 13, 336–37, 349
  theological interpretations of, 45–47
Holocaust, 213–14, 217
hope, 215, 228, 237–38, 249
Hopkins, Gerard Manley, 366, 378–80
Horsley, Richard A., 208
hospitality, 21–23, 26, 37, 66, 80, 193
humanum, 23, 170, 172, 187, 236, 255, 283
Husserl, Edmund, 136

I-body, 162–64, 170
incarnation, 13–20, 341–45, 350, 427n.52
Irenaeus of Lyons, 17, 123, 177, 251, 256, 314–15, 317, 367, 368

Jeremiah, 287
Jerome, 163
Jesus
  appearances of, *see* appearances
  as God, 102, 340–41
  God's vindication of, 84–85, 189–92, 256
  historical, 43–44, 48, 50, 81, 387n.44
  killers of, 188–89
  lives, 62
  as obedient to God, 369–71
  as stranger, 93, 99–100
Job, 218, 220, 280–81
John, 11, 47, 321–33
John the Baptist, 63, 84, 210, 287
Johnson, Luke Timothy, 46
Joseph, 279
Jung, *see* psychology
Jüngel, Eberhard, 87–88
justice, 12, 23, 185–87, 192, 227–28, 245, 248

Kant, Immanuel, 36–39, 43–44, 50, 71–72, 216–17, 385n.14, 389n.82
Kasper, Walter, 16, 97

kerygma, 31–32, 36, 59–60, 64, 92, 247
knowledge, 22, 25, 33, 36–38, 54, 56, 72, 113, 146
Küng, Hans, 383n.6
Künneth, Walter, 9–10, 383n.6

Lampe, Peter, 157
Lazarus, 321–22, 331
learning, 259–63, 303
Leder, Drew, 134–36, 138, 141–42, 144–46, 166
Levinas, Emmanuel, 75, 215
Lindbeck, George, 389n.82, 392n.26
loss, 4, 89
love, 5, 97, 256, 317
Lubac, Henri de, 352
Luedemann, Gerd, 49–51

Macquarrie, John, 162
Marcion, 251, 257
Marion, Jean-Luc, 5, 67, 68, 71–77, 85, 88, 96–98, 108, 167, 217, 231, 391n.24
Markus, Robert, 129
Martelet, Gustave, 172
Martin, Dale, 153–55, 401n.51
Marxsen, Willi, 57–61, 63, 64, 92, 389n.81, 390n.88
Mary, mother of God, 3, 276
Mary, wife of Clopas, 3
Mary Magdalene, 3–4, 35, 68, 99–100, 102–3, 112, 114, 331–32, 349, 363–64
mass ecstasy, 51
materiality, 150, 154
McIntosh, Mark, 373
Meeks, Wayne, 198
Meier, John P., 44–50, 82–84, 387n.44
memoria, 6, 12–13, 222–25
Merchant, Carolyn, 132
Merleau-Ponty, Maurice, 134–35, 138, 170–71
Merton, Thomas, 67
metanoia, 306–7
metaphor, 365–66
metaphysics, 37–39, 110, 112, 140, 355
methodological agnosticism, 43–45, 49

Metz, Johann Baptist, 212–20, 222–25, 319, 411n.69
Milbank, John, 28
mimesis, 259–62, 265–71, 272–82, 286, 288, 297, 303–4, 307, 357–58
miracles, 18–19, 45, 388n.55
modernity, 21, 28, 52, 54, 214–15
Moltmann, Jürgen, 39, 42, 163–64, 171, 242–43, 309, 421n.84
Mozart, 72
mystery, 11, 65, 173
mythology, 6, 8, 38, 59–60, 276, 357–61

Newton, Sir Isaac, 52
Nietzsche, Friedrich, 232, 271–77, 283–84, 354–56, 359
non-foundational theology, 33, 48, 55, 86
novum ultimum, 42, 71, 77–78, 215

O'Collins, Gerald, 10, 167, 237, 384n.19, 389n.85, 398n.4
Old Testament, 6, 8, 77–78, 199–209, 231, 250–51, 278, 279–81, 359–64
Origen, 17
other, 75, 97, 100, 111–12, 176, 248–49, 260–67, 270–71, 297, 305
Oughourlian, Jean-Michel, 263

Pagels, Elaine, 386n.41
Pannenberg, Wolfhart, 15, 49, 51–53, 191, 228, 342–43, 388n.55
paradox, 7–8, 15, 26, 63–66, 108
Paul, 7, 10, 16, 31, 44, 49–51, 62, 103, 114, 150–59, 168–69, 197–98, 276
  on bodily resurrection, 398n.8
Perkins, Pheme, 7, 81, 389n.85, 339n.19
personal faith, 57–59
personalist, 57
Peter, 49–50, 67, 188–94, 276, 286, 386n.41
Phaedo, 131, 143
Philo of Alexandria, 80, 329
philosophy, 21, 37, 45, 126

General Index 443

Placher, William, 33
Plato, 131–32, 143, 147, 253, 259
Pontius Pilate, 283–84
Powell, Mark Allen, 51, 421n.84
prayer, 219, 335
primordial chaos, 9, 352
principalities and powers, 79, 234–36, 316
procreation, 125–27
Procrustean bed, 34
protology, 9, 11
Prusak, Bernard, 169
psychology, 94, 259–67
  Freudian analytical, 50
  Jungian depth, 50–51

Rahner, Karl, 10, 22, 65, 105, 125, 150–51, 159, 173, 233, 366
  on apocalyptic eschatology, 195–97, 211–12, 319
  on being with God, 375–77
  on Christ, 320, 374, 393n.44
  on the forgiveness of sin, 298–99, 303
  on incarnation, 343–45
  on the resurrection, 368–69, 371
  on suffering, 411n.69
  on the Trinity, 350–51
Ratzinger, Joseph, 168, 404n.25
reconciliation, 20, 24, 184–85
resurrection
  ambiguities of narrative, 33–34
  bodily, 17, 20, 23, 148–49, 150–59
  circularity of, 55
  contemporary states of, 31
  demythologization of, 36–37, 39, 71, 119, 206, 225, 363
  as event, 33, 49, 54, 59, 64, 87
  as God's vindication, 78, 199–204
  historical basis for, 43–44, 102, 322
  as historical event, 49–56, 421n.84
  historical irrelevance of, 38, 54, 287
  historicity of, 36, 39, 41, 88
  language of, 9, 39, 110, 220, 389n.81, 389n.82, 389n.85, 390n.88
  as legend, 19–20
  marginalization of, 12
  as miracle, 18
  as myth, 3, 36, 71, 165

resurrection (*continued*)
  as narratives, 114, 168, 226, 321–23
  as participation in God, 160
  phenomenological approach to, 66, 68–69, 75, 391n.24, 392n.26, 406n.71
  physical, 19
  as praxis for belief, 240–42, 245
  proof of, 18–19, 33, 83, 381–82
  removed from history, 36–39
  as salvation, 42, 68, 79, 105
  scapegoating of, 182
  as victory, 314
  without analogy, 87
reversal, as fulfillment, 13, 171–72, 190–91
Ricoeur, Paul, 76, 192, 295, 357, 359, 389n.84, 392n.26

sacrificial atonement theory, 9–10, 12, 18
Sadducees, 80–83, 200, 244
salvation, 10–13, 15, 20, 41–42, 63, 167, 183, 231
  already/not yet paradox of, 15–16, 183, 187
  history, 76–77
Sanders, E. P., 44–46
Satan, 255–56, 266
Saul, 67
scapegoating, 253–58, 262–63, 267–68, 272, 275–77, 279–89, 298, 308
Schillebeeckx, Edward, 43, 79, 161–62, 213, 216, 221–22, 242–43, 248, 319, 337
Schleiermacher, Friedrich, 39, 384n.21
Schneiders, Sandra, 100–101, 325–26, 333, 364
Schwager, Raymond, 250, 253, 280, 289, 298
Scott, Janny, 267
shalom, 23, 98, 101, 106, 301
sight, 147
silence, 67, 71, 91
Simon Peter, 3, 51, 331
sin, 234–36, 298–302, 316, 369–70
  original, 302–5, 419n.48

Sobrino, Jon, 227–44, 247, 310, 319–20
soma pneumatikon, 152–54, 156–57, 163
Spirit, 16, 48, 173, 176, 194, 346–51, 352, 364
soul, 37–38, 40, 125, 130, 148–49
Stephan, 103
suffering, 13, 213–17, 219–21, 222–24, 242, 275, 410n.51, 411n.63, 411n.69
sui generis, 21–22, 65, 71, 87, 106, 240
Suzuki, D. T., 251–52, 299–300

Taylor, Charles, 132, 146
Tertullian, 17, 105, 123, 163
Thiel, John E., 410n.51, 411n.63
Thiselton, Anthony, 156–57
Thomas, 35, 67, 101–3, 105, 112, 301, 331, 349
Tillich, Paul, 122
time, 14–15, 215, 245
Tolstoy, Leo, 74
Torah, 82–83, 209
transcendental analysis, 53, 56, 65
transfiguration, 40–42, 68, 87
transphysical reality, 158, 404n.25
transvaluation, 275–78, 298
travelers to Emmaus, 12, 67–68, 97–98
Trinity, 346–51

Vermes, Geza, 118–19
victims, 239, 269–70, 273–74, 277–82, 289–90, 359, 361
  God of, 12, 245–49

victims (*continued*)
  point of view of, 227–33, 256, 258, 292–93
  universal, 311
  vindication of, 79, 184–85, 187, 190–93, 209, 362
violence, 250–58, 266–72, 279–82, 356–58, 361, 416n.15, 419n.46
virginity, 19–20, 126–27, 143, 400n.41
Volf, Miraslov, 247–49, 264–65, 268–70, 284, 309, 311–13
von Balthasar, Hans Urs, 105–6, 109, 328, 339, 348–50, 354, 380–81

Ward, Graham, 111, 176, 239, 333
Watson, Francis, 90, 120
Wiles, Maurice, 335
Williams, James G., 279
Williams, Rowan, 34, 92, 189
Wink, Walter, 235–36, 266, 358
Witherington, Ben, 84
Wittgenstein, Ludwig, 145
World War I, 74
Wright, N. T., 117, 122–23, 225, 244–45, 309
  on empty tomb, 62, 87, 398n.8
  on history, 43, 388n.64
  knowledge, 52
  on objections to resurrection studies, 49, 51–54, 107, 386n.37
  on Paul, 398n.8
  on transphysicality, 158, 333, 404n.25

Yahweh, 9, 199–200, 206, 250, 279–80, 364

Of Related Interest

Michael E. Lee
Bearing the Weight of Salvation
The Soteriology of Ignacio Ellacuría

Basque-born Ignacio Ellacuría is best known as one of the group of six Jesuit priests assassinated in El Salvador in 1989. This book explores a central theme in the writings of this theologian-martyr: the nature of Christian salvation (soteriology) and its relation to Christian action (discipleship). The book argues that Ellacuría's soteriology, understood as having philosophical, Christological, and ecclesiological dimensions, not only makes a strong claim concerning the character of Christian discipleship, but provides a lens through which the enduring controversies over liberation theology might be understood.

Ellacuría's life and thought represent a new chapter in the ongoing attempt by Christians to articulate the good news of salvation and to witness to it with their very lives. He challenges critics of liberation theology, ranging from the Vatican to the thinkers of the Radical Orthodoxy, with a vision of Christian discipleship that entails a creative and mutually-transformative engagement with history.

"This book will richly reward anyone interested in what the next generation of liberation theologians, in Latin and North America, will look like." — Matthew Ashley

"An outstanding work — keen and mature analysis."
— Gustavo Gutiérrez

Michael E. Lee is an assistant professor of systematic theology at Fordham University. He lives in New York City.

978-0-8245-2421-0, paperback

Of Related Interest

Kevin Mongrain
THE SYSTEMATIC THOUGHT OF HANS URS VON BALTHASAR
An Irenaean Retrieval

Is there a single driving force unifying the diverse writings of Hans Urs von Balthasar? Kevin Mongrain points to von Balthasar's retrieval of Irenaeus of Lyons. In Irenaeus, von Balthasar found inspiration for a genuinely Christian theology that resists the recurring danger of gnosticism while honoring the Mystery of God.

"With astonishing rhetorical skill and an enviable command of Balthasar's vast corpus, Mongrain convincingly shows that Irenaeus is both the most crucial early Christian writer for Balthasar and a man whose basic mental outlook and theology of history closely parallel Balthasar's own."

—Edward T. Oakes in *Theological Studies*

978-0-8245-1927-2, paperback
A Herder & Herder Book

Support your local bookstore or order directly from the publisher at
www.CrossroadPublishing.com

To request a catalog or inquire about quantity orders, please e-mail
sales@CrossroadPublishing.com

www.ingramcontent.com/pod-product-compliance
Lightning Source LLC
Chambersburg PA
CBHW020632230426
43665CB00008B/138